THE CHEMISTRY OF BEHAVIOR

A Molecular Approach to
Neuronal Plasticity

THE CHEMISTRY OF BEHAVIOR

A Molecular Approach to Neuronal Plasticity

Stanislav Reinis
and
Jerome M. Goldman

University of Waterloo
Waterloo, Ontario, Canada

PLENUM PRESS • NEW YORK AND LONDON

Library of Congress Cataloging in Publication Data

Reinis, Stanislav.
    The chemistry of behavior.

    Includes bibliographies and index.
    1. Memory—Physiological aspects. 2. Neural circuitry—Adaptation. 3. Brain chemistry. I. Goldman, Jerome M. II. Title.
QP406.R44 1982   612′.825   82-13294
ISBN 0-306-41161-X

©1982 Plenum Press, New York
A Division of Plenum Publishing Corporation
233 Spring Street, New York, N.Y. 10013

To Milada, Barbara,
Renata, Michael, Stan, Teresa
and Rebecca Cheyenne

Our special people

Foreword

This book discusses a particular aspect of brain function, that of storage and retrieval of memory of past experience, in terms of neuronal plasticity. In discussing this aspect of brain functions, however, it discusses brain mechanisms in their wider sense as well. Clearly, the central nervous system is a highly interconnected system from all points of view, and it would not be possible to understand function in terms of only a single event or only a single neurotransmitter. This is true for any biochemical activity that accompanies neuronal functional activity and accompanies behavior. The authors have commendably recognized this complexity, and recognize still more the need to present information in a compact and uniform manner in spite of the tremendous expansion of our knowledge in recent years. It is a somewhat easier task to gather a set of authors and record their results for a multiauthor symposium, but it is a most admirable endeavor for two authors to summarize a field that encompasses subjects such as transmission barriers, lipids, proteins, energy, hormones, to name a few that this book covers so well in a compact manner, and in such depth as well. Metabolism and function cannot really be understood without understanding structural factors, changes in membrane properties, and changes in metabolism. Since so many areas need to be treated, it is not the right question to ask what is particular to the nervous system; rather one has to focus on the mechanisms that are involved in functions of the nervous system. We need to understand the basic processes, and to explain their alterations during function or pathology. There is a form of mental retardation now known for most metabolic errors, signifying that all aspects of brain metabolism have to function properly for the brain to function properly. This then explains the need to look at brain metabolism from several points of view. The present work, setting its sights on memory, learning, and connected brain plasticity, has very high aims and a novel approach; it eminently succeeds in discussing all functions of the brain that bear on these points. It not only documents our achievements in the very fine summaries after each of the sections, but in addition to presenting the picture in sufficient detail, each section goes beyond that and looks for attractive ideas for the future. This recognition that neurochemical mechanisms underlie both behavior and all aberrations of behavior is of tremendous importance for future understanding of the biology of the human brain in all its functional aspects. At the present time we see possibilities, we see pathways and approaches; the book shows us what possible and exciting avenues still lie ahead of us.

ABEL LAJTHA

Preface

Fifteen years have passed since 1967, when E. Roy John published his landmark *Mechanisms of Memory*. For neuroscientists tackling problems of this nature, those days were idyllic, in the sense that our understanding of brain mechanisms was much more simplistic. Concepts seemed clearer, and the overall approach to a problem was less cluttered by our knowledge of associate issues. We already knew that protein synthesis was somehow involved in the process of learning and memory. We had known, or at least suspected, that masses of neurons, rather than small closed circuits, were involved in even a simple behavioral act.

However, in the span of those fifteen years, our knowledge of brain functions has expanded tremendously. An abundance of electrophysiological, ultrastructural, behavioral, and neurochemical information has entered the literature, and the process continues at an ever-increasing rate. Areas, such as those concerned with a detailed analysis of the role of neurotransmitters and peptides in behavior, have even attracted the interest of those who possess only a limited working knowledge of biochemistry.

This book has been assembled in particular for those students and researchers who are less concerned with procedural and technical details or masses of descriptive data than with an appreciation of the functional and behavioral aspects of the chemical changes in the central nervous system. We felt that the time had come for an organization of the available research into a comprehensive presentation of the biochemical nature of neuronal plasticity. Therefore, we have attempted to describe those biochemical activities of the brain that have been found to accompany the modifications in neuronal function and, ultimately, behavior. At the outset, it should be understood that we find the idea of a "memory molecule", or any simple process to which the plasticity of neuronal function could be attributed, as untenable. On the contrary, it is becoming increasingly evident that such plasticity involves various parts of the neuron and different metabolic systems, each of which undergoes at least some degree of adjustment during the period of functional alteration.

Functional changes that take place over the life of the nerve cell depend primarily upon an increase or decrease in the traffic across its synapses. The activation of the synapses, i.e., their depolarization or hyperpolarization, induces various interrelated biochemical processes, including those involved with the energy supply, protein synthesis, lipid metabolism, the transport and release of materials, and neurotransmitter synthesis and degradation. Some of these processes last only milliseconds and involve movements of neurotransmitters and ions. Others, by modifying the structure and physicochemical characteristics of the neuronal membrane, are sustained for much longer periods. In such a complex, it would be difficult to say just where a unique, event-coded substance would fit and what would be its primary action.

These processes can be studied in simple systems, isolated cells or their components, and are important to our understanding of the basic mechanisms of neuronal plasticity. However, they attain their full significance only when they occur simultaneously in various neuronal systems within the brain structure. Whereas plasticity is a function of a single nerve cell, or even of a single synapse, the formation of a meaningful memory trace, its storage and retrieval, is a product of the activity of masses of ever-changing cellular units. Minor plastic changes of an individual neuron are undoubtedly indispensable building blocks of a "memory trace". But, such a trace is obviously more complex than a single synaptic change in one neuron, or even alterations within a small area of nervous tissue.

In the central nervous system, each of the component neurons and glial cells differs from all of the others by its shape, neuronal connections, inner structure, position, metabolic activity, function, and, in particular, previous history. While such divergence should be quite evident, it is often overlooked. Construction of models of the brain based upon a more or less homogeneous population of uniform units is, therefore, an undue simplification.

The large volume of impulses that impinge upon each neuron requires that it remain continuously responsive. As a result, the cell is constantly changing. Thousands of synapses which retain something of their own previous history and respond accordingly to new stimuli make each cell a permanently variable, continuously evolving unit. Nevertheless, the brain as a whole is able to maintain its stability and functional continuity.

External stimuli enter the brain as innumerable coded messages. Once having arrived, their fate is dependent upon the functional state and handling capacity of the nervous tissue. The informational content of many of the coded signals may be lost on or disregarded by the system, as in the central process of habituation. Other messages are transformed, stored, and eventually retrieved, possibly even to be used for the generation of new ideas that go beyond a mere restatement of deposited information.

Many components of this overall complex of events are still unknown. But, embedded within the ongoing functions of the central nervous system, small alterations occur in neuronal membranes and nuclei, cellular respiration, and the assembly of novel molecules. It is these changes that we have attempted to organize and integrate in a meaningful way in order to help understand those events associated with the storage and retrieval of past experience and the processes of behavioral regulation.

Since a plasticity of neuronal operations is a normal, ongoing activity of the brain, it would be impossible to explore the issues involved apart from a discussion of general brain chemistry. We have endeavored to touch as many pertinent issues as possible, but have necessarily had to balance scope with economy. Therefore, discussions of such things as brain development and cell-target interactions have not been included, inasmuch as we feel that these areas would be difficult to properly handle within a book of this size. For an expanded treatment of these areas, the interested reader is directed to Lund, *Development and Plasticity of the Brain: An Introduction*, Oxford University Press (1978) and Reinis and Goldman, *The Development of the Brain: Biological and Functional Perspectives*, Charles C. Thomas (1980).

While we have integrated much source material in support of information presented throughout the text, everything is not referenced. In view of the amount of information covered, we felt that we had to be somewhat selective, lest the text become hopelessly overburdened with references, seriously disrupting the flow of reading. Also, space considerations required that certain discussions within various chapters be kept to a reasonable length. Consequently, each section has been appended with a list of recommended readings. These books and articles are primarily review materials to help the reader further explore selected topics which may be of particular interest to him/her.

S. R.
J. M. G.

Acknowledgments

There are a number of individuals to whom we owe a debt of gratitude. Francis De Feudis, Antonio Giuditta and John Gaito provided valuable counsel concerning the content and direction of the manuscript. Also, both students and faculty of the Biopsychology Division within the Department of Psychology here at Waterloo shared relevant comments with us in both seminars and private conversation. We are grateful for their input. Dana Kral and Renata Krejcova worked many hours on the illustrations. They enrich the text, and we thank them for the contribution. Laurie Westlake, Bonnie Lee Bender, Paula Kovacs, Diane Hagan, Bev Dakins and Trenny Cook were able to cope admirably with the seemingly endless number of revisions in good humor. They must have done their grumbling in private. We genuinely appreciate their excellent assistance. Christine Ledbury thankfully took on the imposing task of typing the lists of references and recommended readings which accompany each section. She did a fine job under difficult circumstances. Iva Muellner assisted in checking the agreement between the references and their corresponding citations within the text. We are also extremely grateful to Cory Burgener and Vic Neglia of the University of Waterloo's Department of Computing Services, who helped prepare the manuscript for direct phototypesetting from computer disk stores. Cory put in many, often difficult hours organizing and then defining the necessary specifications for the computer-linked process. We also would like again to thank Dana Kral, this time for assembling the final, camera-ready copy. Finally, our appreciation is extended to those authors and publishers who kindly gave their consent to reproduce many of the illustrations found throughout the book.

Contents

SECTION VI

A MODEL OF NEURONAL PLASTICITY AND SOME
  SPECULATIONS ON ITS RELATIONSHIP TO LEARNING AND

I

THE MOLECULAR BASIS OF
NEURONAL ACTIVITY

Chapter 1

The Neuronal Membrane

All vertebrate behavior exists as a reflection of the functioning of the central nervous system, a consequence of the activity of two general classes of cells within the brain. These cells, the neurons and glia, while morphologically and functionally dissimilar, work in a coordinate and mutually supplemental fashion.

The neuron is a highly specialized excitable cell that is able to perform the elementary characteristic activities of the nervous system, namely the generation and conduction of nervous impulses that underlie the processing of sensory information and the appearance of particular behavioral events. It is a functional descendent of a form of primitive neuroeffector cell that responded to external stimuli by a process of contraction. With the evolution of larger and more complex organisms possessing an ever growing array of distinctive tissues and organs, there emerged receptor and effector cells that were able to rapidly transmit excitation over longer distances, permitting a degree of informational coordination that would be required for the growing response repertoire. The neuron exists as the refined unit of this system of rapid transmission.

The neurons and their processes, the axons and dendrites, are not uniform structures. They tend to vary in size, shape and their pattern of dendritic branching (Fig. 1.1, 1.2). And, different brain areas may possess a

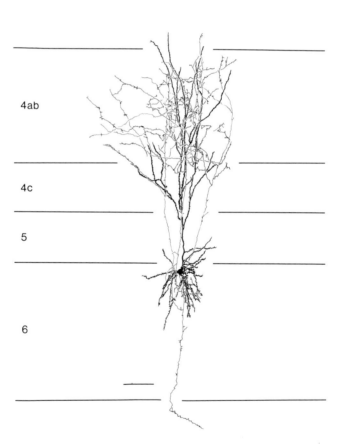

1

2·3

4ab

4c

5

6

Figure 1.1 A pyramidal cell in layer 6 of the cat cerebral cortex showing the complexity of the dendritic tree as well as the density of the dendritic spines [from C.D. Gilbert and T.N. Wiesel, *Nature* 280:120 (1979); © 1979 by Macmillan and Co.].

distinctive cytoarchitectonic pattern based upon a particular combination of these characteristics.

Although the activity underlying the brain functions is principally neuronal, these cells contribute only a portion of the total CNS biochemical activity. The second component of the nervous tissue, the glial cells, are also quite metabolically active. One of the fundamental difficulties in neurochemistry is to distinguish between the metabolism of these two types of functionally (and biochemically) distinct cells whose metabolic activity often responds to changes in function in opposite directions.

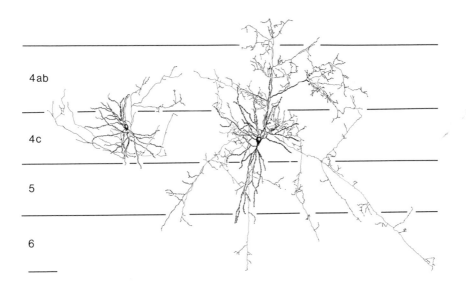

1

2+3

4ab

4c

5

6

Figure 1.2 A spiny stellate cell (left) and a smooth stellate cell (right) in layer 4c of the cat cerebral cortex [from C.D. Gilbert and T.N. Wiesel, *Nature* 280:120 (1979); © 1979 by Macmillan & Co.].

Neuroglia are smaller cells that are not directly involved in the generation and propagation of the nerve impulse. They were first described in 1846 by Virchow, who recognized the non-neuronal nature of the interstitial substance in the central nervous system. Noting that neuroglia separate nerve cells from one another and from the blood vessels, he assumed the glia to be merely structures filling the interstitial spaces within the brain. Until fairly recently this view prevailed in the neuroanatomical and neurophysiological literature.

On the basis of light and electron microscopic studies the non-neuronal cells of the central nervous system have been classified as follows:

(1) astroglia, also known as astrocytes (protoplasmic or fibrous),

(2) oligodendroglia or oligodendrocytes (perineuronal and interfascicular),

(3) subependymal cells (free or firmly bound to the subependymal layer), and

(4) microglia or microcytes.

Astrocytes, oligodendrocytes and subependymal cells are frequently lumped together as macroglia.

The membrane that surrounds the neurons and glia controls the manner in which the cell interacts with other cells and biochemicals in its environment. Its activity is able to reflect changes taking place within the neuron as well. The direction and nature of the ionic movements across the neuronal membrane determine whether the nerve cell becomes depolarized (excited) or hyperpolarized (inhibited). Biochemical events within the cell, such as the production and storage of high-energy compounds and the synthesis of proteins and lipids, serve one purpose, to sustain the normal activity of the neuronal membrane. All other components of the neuron only maintain and, if necessary, alter the membrane characteristics.

Numerous studies of the surface membranes of various plant and animal cells have demonstrated that the membrane possesses the properties of electrical resistance and capacitance, which indicate that it is able to behave as an insulator and resist the passage of polar molecules. But, unlike the plasma membranes of other types of cells, the neuronal surface additionally displays the characteristic excitability that leads to a propagated decrease of ohmic resistance across the axonal wall. Otherwise, the general features of the neuronal membrane do not differ substantially from membranes elsewhere in the body.

The membranes that cover the cell and various intracellular organelles have many things in common. They are all flexible, and properties such as their thickness, surface tension, buoyant density, permeability to water, and electrical resistance and capacitance are very similar. Functionally, the membranes are an effective barrier to the passage of solutes and water.

Their permeability to ions is usually low, but they will allow the passage of substances soluble in organic solvents. Most membranes also serve to form a structural base to which many enzymes are attached.

The membranes consist almost exclusively of proteins and lipids (primarily phospholipids), which in mammals constitute about 60% and 40% of the membrane dry weight, respectively. Their particular composition, however, does tend to vary. The less complex is the functional role of the membranes, the more lipids there are and the greater the lipid to protein ratio. For example, myelin membranes, which do not serve any significant transport or enzymatic function, have a high content of such lipids as cholesterol and sphingolipids. The excitable membrane of the neuron has, on the other hand, a high proportion of proteins.

The phospholipids in the membranes contain a strongly hydrophilic head that is polar and able to attract water molecules by its electronegative charge. Also present in the molecule are one or two hydrophobic, non-polar, fatty acid chains. Both the polar and non-polar ends of the phospholipid molecule are important in the maintenance of the cellular membrane structure. The optimal and energetically stable arrangement of the lipids is such that they form a bilayer, with polar ends in contact with the surrounding fluid and non-polar ends hidden in the interior of the membrane (Fig. 1.3).

This characteristic arrangement of lipids has been known for quite a while and was used by Danielli and Davson (1935) as a basis for their theory of membrane structure. Their model postulated a bimolecular lipid layer with continuous monomolecular layers of proteins on both sides. Electron microscopic pictures of cell membranes supported this theory, and for more than thirty years, it was predominant in membrane physiology.

However, misgivings about the Davson-Danielli model accumulated with time. The ratio of protein to lipid that has been found for most natural membranes is not high enough to conform to the model. This indicates that there is not enough protein, and continuous protein layers on both sides of the membrane could not be spontaneously formed. Also, careful fixation and preparation of tissue sections for electron microscopy and freeze-fracture electron microscopy, along with a number of biochemical methods, showed that the lipid bilayer was not continuous, and that protein particles were interspersed between the molecules of lipids.

Figure 1.3 Cross section through the lipid portion of a biological membrane. P: Polar heads of the lipids; N: nonpolar lipid tails.

The emerging information led Singer and Nicolson in 1972 to propose a fluid mosaic model. Their model is based upon considerations of the minimum free energy necessary for the optimal membrane lipid/protein arrangement and upon experiments with antigen markers. According to this model, the protein molecules are floating in a plastic, viscous, two-dimensional double layer of lipids (Fig. 1.4). This lipid bilayer is asymmetrical, with a higher proportion of phospholipids in the outer leaflet of the membrane, as opposed to the inner leaflet which contains a larger amount of unsaturated fatty acids.

The Singer-Nicolson model is able to explain several characteristics of the membrane with which older models could not adequately deal, notably the excitability and passive permeability to ions.

The protein and lipid components are attached to one another by both hydrophobic and hydrophilic interactions, giving stability to the membrane. There is intermolecular hydrogen bonding, which is dependent upon the presence of divalent cations, the ionic strength, lipid ionization and the local pH

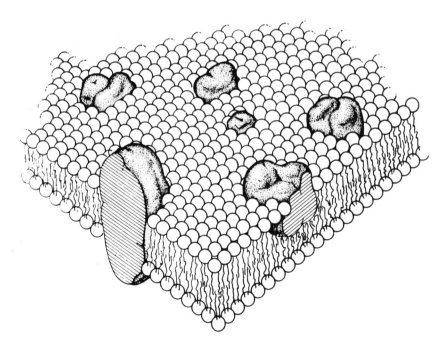

Figure 1.4 The lipid-globular protein mosaic model of the cell membrane with a lipid matrix. The solid bodies represent the integral proteins [from S.J. Singer and G.L. Nicholson, *Science* 197:720 (1972); © 1972 by The American Association for the Advancement of Science].

ECTOPROTEINS

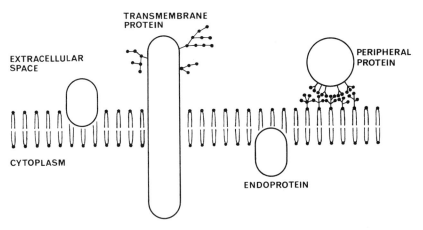

Figure 1.5 Arrangement of hypothetical peripheral and integral membrane proteins. Integral proteins are further subdivided into ectoproteins and endoproteins.

(Boggs, 1980). Additional factors, such as the saturation of membrane fatty acids and their degree of hydroxylation, are also involved.

There are two types of proteins associated with the membrane: peripheral and integral proteins. Peripheral proteins can be easily dissociated from the membranes and completely freed from lipids. They are also readily soluble in aqueous buffers. Two examples of such peripheral proteins are monoamine oxidase, an enzyme degrading catecholamines and a few related neurotransmitters, and cytochrome C, which is involved in energy transfer within the mitochondria.

Integral, or membrane-associated proteins, can be further categorized according to their position in the membrane, as either ecto- or endoproteins (Fig. 1.5). The integral proteins require a rather drastic treatment in order to be released from the membrane. They are firmly bound to membrane lipids, often remaining attached even after their isolation. Within the membrane, these proteins have frequently been found to form clusters and assemblies, whose localization appears to depend upon the function of the cell. Thus, in astrocytes they are localized on the membrane surface, in contact with the blood capillaries and CSF-filled spaces. Here they are involved in the exchange of ions and metabolities (Cullen and Gulley, 1980). In addition to acting as membrane transport proteins, they may also have some enzymatic role, or serve as drug and hormone receptors. The membrane-bound enzymes usually require the presence of lipids for their normal activity.

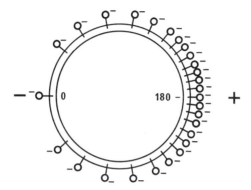

Figure 1.6 Distribution of mobile charged particles on the surface of a spheric cell at electrophoretic equilibrium [simplified from L.F. Jaffe, *Nature* 265:500 (1977); © 1977 by Macmillan and Co.].

The dependence of membrane enzymes upon lipids is crucial to the control of enzymatic activity in synapses and other excitable membranes. Modifications in the lipid content may actually alter the function of the synapse. The lipids may directly activate or inactivate the enzymes, serve as enzyme cofactors, or may activate the substrate of enzymatic activity. Membrane lipids are in a dynamic state of continuous change. Molecules or portions thereof undergo rapid turnover, and this process may also cause an alteration in enzymatic activity.

Most of the membrane enzymes require the presence of unsaturated fatty acids for their normal function. Changes in the fatty acid composition of the lipid - for example, from unsaturated to saturated - can alter the enzymatic activity of neighboring proteins. Farias *et al.* (1975) accordingly demonstrated that compositional shifts in the fatty acids could change the activity of Na^+, K^+-dependent adenosinetriphosphatase. In addition, the activity of acetylcholinesterase is similarly under lipid control. Such a controlled shift in the fatty acid composition of the synaptic membranes may therefore be one of the mechanisms increasing or decreasing synaptic efficiency.

The proteins that extend from the outer to the inner surface of the membrane, transmembrane proteins, have a relatively high molecular weight, about 100,000 daltons. It had been postulated that such proteins were involved in the transmembrane transport of materials by virtue of their supposed ability to rotate with a flip-flop movement within the membrane. However, this type of molecular movement, requiring the polar ends of the molecule to pass through a non-polar membrane interior, is for thermodynamic reasons rather difficult. And, although possible, it would be comparatively slow.

Protein and lipid molecules are able to move laterally within the membrane, and the ease with which they can do so depends upon the nature of the molecule. Bioelectric fields produced by the excitation/inhibition cycle may shift the charged components floating in the plasma membrane, e.g., head groups of the lipid molecules (Stulen, 1981), and segregate them (Fig. 1.6) (Jaffe, 1977). Movements of molecules along the membranes also depend upon the interactions of polar groups and upon cohesive forces between the apolar regions of the molecules.

The surface structures of the cell membrane are formed by a number of proteins that typically contain sugar residues, glycoproteins. Some are common to all cell types, while others are very specific and in certain instances can be used to characterize individual cell types. Some have been found to serve an important function in the process of intercellular communication, as for example, in cell-cell recognition and in the effect of hormones and other hormonal agents upon the cell. These functions are particularly important in the mutual recognition of axons and their target cells during the development of the central nervous system. Some of the proteins are the receptor components for particular neurotransmitters, and a number of them are responsible for the antigenic properties of the tissues.

The turnover of the membrane components is very fast. The life span of the surface proteins does not exceed 2-3 days (Hubbard and Cohn, 1975). They are probably shed into the extracellular space (Doljanski and Kapeller, 1976). But, it is uncertain how this process of elimination is directed, whether it is random and whether the shed molecules have some informational content.

EXCITABLE MEMBRANES

Excitable membranes are formed, as are other membrane types, by a mosaic of functionally diverse protein molecules embedded in a bimolecular lipid layer. The composition and configuration of these molecules and their positioning allow them to participate in such activities as the active transport of ions across the membrane and the utilization of energy provided in the form of ATP.

Excitability is a basic function of all parts of the neuronal membrane. The membranes will respond to adequate stimuli by changes in their ionic permeability which alter the membrane potential. The excitable membranes, then, first react by a local electrical change, a shift of the positively charged particles from the outer surface to the interior of the cell. This event may spread over the surface, either decrementally (non-regenerative form of electrogenesis) or non-decrementally (the regenerative form). The regenerative form of the electrical change is characterized by alterations in ionic permeability caused by a difference in the electrical potential which elicits further ionic currents that strengthen the original potential differences. Thus, the change spreads over the surface of the nerve cell. An example of this process is the generation and propagation of an action potential (Fig. 1.7) by a nerve cell or muscle fiber. The non-regenerative type of electrical change does not affect ionic permeability, and because it is not reinforced, it gradually fades without spreading far from its point of origin.

The acute change in ionic permeability is the predominant characteristic of excitable membranes. The passage of ions then depends upon an unequal distribution of ions on either side of the membrane. This concentration gradient is actively maintained, and its physico-chemical expression is the resting potential of the membrane. There is, nevertheless, some passive ionic diffusion along the concentration and electrical gradients enabled by membrane permeability to the major ions. A comparison among potassium, sodium and chloride ions shows the following ratio of permeabilities:

pK: pNa: pCl = 1: 0.04: 0.45.

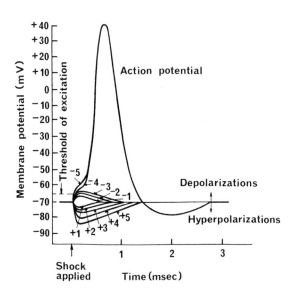

Figure 1.7 A schematic drawing of the effect of the nerve fiber stimulation by a subthreshold stimulus (non-regenerative form of electrogenesis) and a suprathreshold stimulus (the regenerative form). The numbers represent relative units of stimulation.

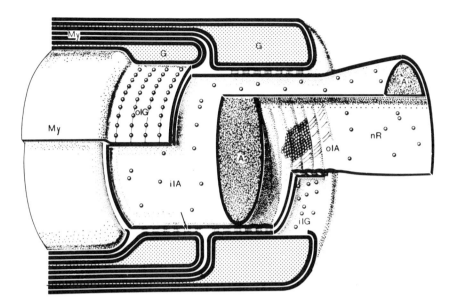

Figure 1.8 Representation of the paranodal region of the axon, showing all four membrane leaflet faces and their embedded particles. My, myelin; G, glial loops; olG, outer leaflet of glia membrane; ilG, inner leaflet of glia membrane; olA, outer leaflet of axonal membrane; ilA, inner leaflet of axonal membrane; A, axoplasm; nR, node of Ranvier [from R.B. Livingstone, K. Pfenninger, H. Moor and K. Akert, *Brain Res.* 58:1 (1973), © 1973 by Elsevier/North-Holland Biomedical Press].

In general, the molecular organization of the neuronal membrane does not substantially differ from other non-excitable membranes. There are patches of phospholipids interspersed with groups of protein molecules. The ratio of proteins to lipids has a rather broad range, even over portions of a single nerve cell. These regional differences within the neuron are quite distinct. A striking example of this is the postsynaptic membrane, receptive to a neurotransmitter, which markedly differs from the axonal membrane underneath the myelin sheath. There are also differences between the structure of axonal membrane underneath myelin and at the node of Ranvier. There is an increased density of particles under the nodal axolemma as compared with other areas of the neuron. The nodes of Ranvier and the initial axonal segment have membranes that are very similar, both having an increased density of intramembranous particles as well as a thick electron-dense layer that contains an extracellular carbohydrate network (Fig. 1.8).

Not all proteins in the neuronal membrane are freely mobile, and thus, they are unevenly distributed throughout the surface of the cell. Some anchoring mechanism is probably required, possibly one involving the microfilaments. The regulation of these mechanisms, as well as the control of the insertion of new components into the membrane, is largely unknown, although this knowledge could well contribute to our understanding of the plasticity of neuronal function. As a consequence of its functional importance, the structure of synaptic membranes is much more rigid than the structure of any other part of the nerve cell membrane. Using the photophysical quenching of native tryptophan fluorescence by chloroform, Hoss and Abood (1974) estimated that the fluidity of synaptic membranes is at least an order of magnitude lower than the values reported for the lipid bilayer portions of other neuronal membrane regions. The complexity of the events in synapses requires the imposition of stringent controls to ensure, for example, that the fluidity of the membrane is kept within the optimal range necessary to maintain its normal biological functions. The particular mechanisms involved in the control of membrane fluidity are not clear. Changes in environmental temperature, pH, or the presence of drugs alter this fluidity. But, after a period of time, the neuronal membranes can become adapted to them. This compensation of membrane fluidity appears to involve a differential uptake of fatty acids into the membrane (Chin and Goldstein, 1978).

A widely accepted view is that various neuronal membrane areas are either chemically excitable (and simultaneously electrically inexcitable), as are synaptic membranes, or they are electrically excitable. The tacit assumption has often been that electrically excitable membranes are chemically unresponsive. This is not the case. The electrically excitable axonal membranes also contain receptors for the various neurotransmitters – acetylcholine, norepinephrine, histamine, or serotonin. Iontophoretically administered neurotransmitters, even including minor biologically active substances, as tryptamine and 2-phenylethylamine, are able to trigger a firing or inhibit the ongoing nerve fiber activity (Sabelli and May, 1975). The existence of neurotransmitter receptors along the entire neuronal surface suggests that the neurotransmitters also play a role in local membrane functioning. Therefore, it is probable that the neurotransmitters diffusing from the synapses may influence the activity of neighboring axons and dendrites.

Nachmansohn, in a series of books and articles, relates the existence of acetylcholine receptors in the axonal membrane to the generation and spread of the nerve impulse. The release of acetylcholine, previously bound to a storage protein within the membrane, is hypothesized to occur when the electrical field of the membrane shifts. Acetylcholine is then attached to the receptor protein, which in turn releases calcium. Calcium   induces a conformational change in the ionic channels, allowing sodium to enter the cell. Acetylcholinesterase, by degrading the neurotransmitter, returns the membrane to its resting conformation (Nachmansohn and Neumann, 1975; Nachmansohn, 1977). Nachmansohn's hypothesis is an attempt to define a coherent mechanism for both synaptic transmission and axonal conduction.

Some degree of uncertainty still remains as to the exact nature of the entire sequence of events responsible for neuronal membrane excitability. The complete elaboration of these events rests not only on the study of individual membrane proteins and their changes during different functional states, but also on the role of lipids, ions, water and other cell components. Charged polar groups on protein, glycoprotein, and glycolipid molecules, as well as phospholipids containing isoelectric (neutral) polar groups (such as the lecithins and phosphatidylethanolamines), all exhibit ionic binding (Satomi, 1974). Consequently, they exert significant functional control over the state of the excitable membrane (Hauser et al., 1976).

MEMBRANE "PUMPS"

Most substances necessary for cellular metabolism are actively transported into the cell, while some metabolic products must be extruded. This two-way transport is another function of the cell membrane. Such an active transport requires energy, as well as the presence of carrier mechanisms extending across the cell membrane. However, only a few of these transport systems have been characterized and studied in detail. Thus far, all of those examined involve the use of glycoproteins which structurally span the membrane. The portion of these proteins that contains the sugar moieties is perhaps necessary for the fixation of the molecule within the membrane structure. The molecules or ions are then actively conveyed by small internal conformational changes within these transport molecules.

The transport mechanisms usually require energy for their activity. The most common donor of energy is ATP, which is then degraded into ADP and inorganic phosphate. In this way, these transport molecules also act as ATP-degrading enzymes, or adenosinetriphosphatases (ATPases). At least three types of ATPases are common in the membranes: magnesium-dependent ATPase, sodium-potassium dependent ATPase, and calcium-dependent ATPase. They are rather non-specific, and can also be found in non-excitable cells within the body. Due to their transport function, they are able to maintain stable levels of several ions within the cells.

The level of intracellular sodium is kept low, in spite of its continuous diffusion into the cell. On the other hand, potassium is accumulated by the cell and its internal levels are much higher than those in the extracellular fluid. In the nerve cells, internal sodium is continuously exchanged for external potassium. This is the primary function of Na^+, K^+ - dependent ATPase, also referred to as the "sodium pump". Since its action is asymmetrical, more sodium ions are pumped out than potassium ions are pumped in (Fig. 1.9). Also, the diffusion of sodium into the cell is much slower than is the diffusion of potassium out. These two factors contribute to the generation of the characteristic electrical potential difference on both sides of the surface membrane of the excitable (and some non-excitable) cells.

In the pump molecule, there are two sites of equal affinity for potassium binding and three sites of differing affinities for sodium binding. The movement of sodium through the axonal membrane is associated with a transfer of phosphate from ATP to the sodium pump molecule. The movement of potassium, a second step of the transport process, requires the release of inorganic phosphate from the enzyme into the cytoplasm.

The transport of sodium and potassium across the neuronal membrane is coupled, but the linkage is not fixed. It depends upon the concentration of the ions on both sides of the membrane. Generally, a single molecule of ATP yields enough energy for the extrusion of three sodium ions and the entry of two potassium ions. When the internal concentration of sodium decreases, the Na^+/K^+ ratio can fall to as low as 1:1. When the sodium and potassium

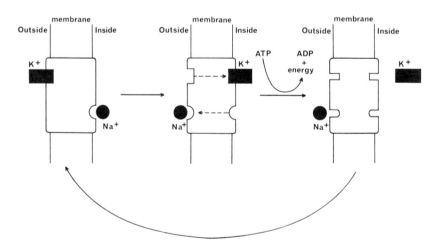

Figure 1.9 The functioning of the sodium pump. First step: the pump takes K^+ on the outer surface of the membrane, Na^+ on the inner surface. Second step: K^+ and Na^+ are translocated. Third step: the energy of ATP is consumed and K^+ and Na^+ are released.

gradients are very steep, the sodium pump may even function in reverse. Sodium ions are then transported into the cells; potassium is expelled; and ATP is synthesized at the expense of the downhill movement of the ions. Sodium may also be exchanged for sodium or potassium for potassium at a ratio of 1:1, and little or no ATP is then used.

Na^+, K^+-dependent adenosine triphosphatase has been biochemically extracted from the membranes and almost completely purified. It is composed of two polypeptide segments. The smaller is a glycoprotein and the larger contains the phosphorylation site. They link in a 1:1 fashion, but the complete molecule may be a dimer, since it contains two phosphorylation sites and two ATP binding sites. The structure of the ion-carrying component, the ionophore, would be of particular interest to those in the area of neuronal excitability. Unfortunately, little is known about its structure or its mechanism of function.

Several characteristics of this ATPase are altered when the enzyme is released from the membrane and solubilized, suggesting that its activity is modified by surrounding lipids. Accordingly, the removal of lipids from the membrane leads to a decrease of ATPase activity. Phospholipids and sphingolipids are involved in the control of ATPase, but the requirements for the optimal membrane composition differ in various cells and organelles. Certain ATPase types do not have any particular requirements in their lipid specificity, while others do (Roelofsen, 1981). Some, although perhaps not all, ATPases require the presence of gangliosides (see Chapter 2), particularly G_{M1} (Leon et al., 1981; Jeserich et al., 1981). Phospholipids may also be important in this respect, because there is a possibility that they might participate in the phosphate transfer to and from the enzyme (Stahl, 1973). The fatty acids components of the membrane lipids alter the performance of the sodium pump as well, with the long-chain fatty acids inhibiting its action. Also, the characteristics of the enzyme in different cell populations differ. Grisar et al. (1979), for example, found different kinetic properties of Na^+, K^+-ATPase in glial cells, neuronal perikarya and synaptosomes. This could be due to differences in the membrane lipids, or variations in the structure of the enzyme.

Neurotransmitters, such as norepinephrine, dopamine, serotonin and histamine, may also participate in the regulation of the pump. They have been found to enhance Na^+, K^+-ATPase activity in the cerebral synaptosomal fraction. This indicates that the depression of some neurons by these neurotransmitters may be caused by the increased activity of the sodium pump, which in turn induces hyperpolarization of the neuronal membrane (Lee and Phillis, 1977). The pump is, perhaps indirectly, also an important factor in the formation of the memory trace. Its inhibition by ouabain (Fig. 1.10), for instance, disrupts short term memory and the fixation of a perma-

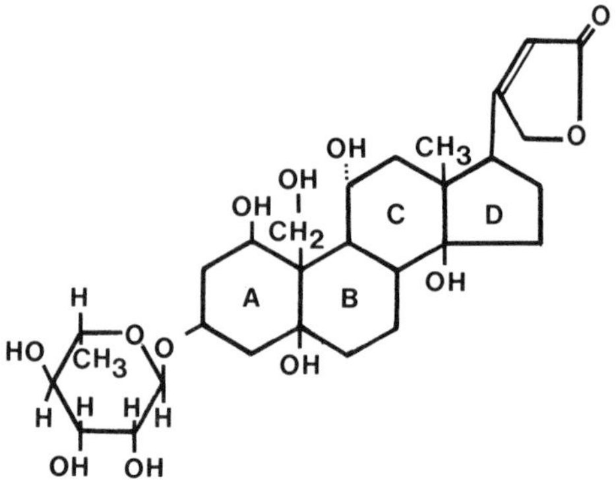

Figure 1.10 Ouabain, an inhibitor of the sodium pump.

nent memory trace (Watts and Mark, 1970; Gibbs and Ng, 1977). This may be caused by long-lasting depolarization of masses of neurons which renders them functionally unable to adjust.

IONIC CHANNELS

The passage of substances across the membrane and along the concentration or electrical gradients is a controlled, selective process. Only a few substances may cross the cell membrane freely, urea being an example. The diffusion of other molecules depends upon a number of factors, such as their lipid solubility, their binding to some carrier substance, or the existence of preformed membrane channels. Membrane permeability is a dynamic phenomenon and can be modified by many factors, including hormones (such as vasopressin) and drugs (such as harmaline). Sodium, potassium, and calcium, the three ions most important to the maintenance of membrane excitability, may enter or leave the cell when the appropriate ionic channels are open. The opening of the channels depends upon the state of the membrane and is related to the passage of electrical currents across it. A spontaneous opening is also possible, causing minor fluctuations in membrane polarization (Conti *et al.*, 1976).

The term "channel" is at present mostly operational. The actual inner structure of the channel molecule is not known. As a result of conformational changes in one or more macromolecules, or possibly due to the opening of a "pore" closed by a gating mechanism, the membrane proteins may temporarily allow the passage of ions. The ionic channels are functionally asymmetrical, and the movement of ions is usually possible in only one direction.

Some information about the structure of the channel has come from the study of the effect of hydrolytic enzymes on the membrane. The channel macromolecules are affected by phospholipases from both without and within, while proteolytic enzymes are only influential from within the cell. Both types of enzymes are able to interfere with the generation or conduction of the action potential, indicating that phospholipids and protein are both part of the channel organization. One particulary appealing approach, employing various behavioral mutants of *Paramecium tetraurelia*, has revealed the existence of several components involved in channel function, including sphingo- and phospholipids (Forte *et al.*, 1981).

The channels are highly specific, but not absolutely so. While the sodium and potassium channels are independent, the former (in this case, from the squid giant axons) are also permeable to lithium and other ions, in the following ratio:

pLi : pNa : pK : pCs = 1.1 : 1/12 : 1/40 : 1/61.

The ammonium ion may also pass through the sodium channel.

The potassium channel permeabilities are:

pK : pRb : pCs = 1 : 0.3 : 0.

Interestingly enough, the ammonium ion passes through the potassium channel more readily than does the potassium ion itself.

THE SODIUM CHANNEL

The number of sodium channels in the axonal membrane is relatively small; the lobster nerve has been found to contain about 13 per square micrometer (Moore *et al.*, 1967). In myelinated fibers, the numbers are higher in the area of the node of Ranvier than in the membrane underneath the myelin. Rabbit nerve fibers contain about 10,000 channels per sq. µm of nodal space, while in the frog the figure is about 2000 (Ritchie, 1980). Calculations of the ratio of the number of channels to the number of sodium ions entering the axon during one action potential indicate that several hundred sodium ions pass through a single channel within a millisecond (Lindemann and Van Driesche, 1977).

While there is a selectivity barrier, the inner diameter of the channel is rather wide. A model presented by Hille in 1976 contains four ion-binding sites, each with a different energy level. During its passage, the sodium ion loses a number of attached water molecules which had formed a "coating" around the ion. After passing through the narrowest point of the channel, the ion is re-coated before entering the cell.

Two types of sodium channels have been described; one is a neurotransmitter receptor-linked (primarily synaptic) channel, and the other is voltage-dependent. There are two forms of the voltage-dependent channel. The first is "early", opening shortly after the excitation of the membrane, while the second is "late", opening somewhat later during the period of depolarization and repolarization. The late channel is thought to be a funnel-shaped structure located near the inner surface of the membrane. The gating mechanism, serving to close the channel when it is not activated, is also near this inner surface. Recently, Culp and McKenzie (1981) have reported the successful extraction of the "gating component", which was bound to the neurotoxin complex from the scorpion *Leiurus quinquestriatus.*

There are probably two independent gating mechanisms within each channel, as had been predicted by the Hodgkin-Huxley equation (Hodgkin, 1958). Evidence has shown that the sodium channels, which open during the depolarization of the membrane, occasionally open spontaneously, causing fluctuations in the membrane potentials.

The opening of the channel permits the passage of ions across the membrane and may be recorded as a wave of electrical current. This "gating" current, lasting a few microseconds, precedes the sodium current, and it is actually due to a molecular rearrangement of the protein chains forming the channel (Hui, 1977).

The study of the structure and function of the sodium channel has been greatly facilitated by the discovery of several animal neurotoxins that specifically affect the channel. Some of the toxins keep the sodium channel permanently open, causing a lasting depolarization of the nerve fiber and a continuous sodium flux through the channel (Narahashi, 1974). They act at different sites on the channel molecule. For example, batrachotoxin (Fig. 1.11), a toxin from the skin secretions of the Colombian poison arrow frog, permanently activates one "regulatory site" of the channel. The venoms of

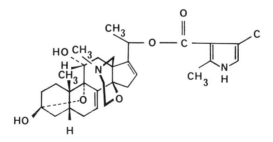

Figure 1.11 Structure of batrachotoxin.

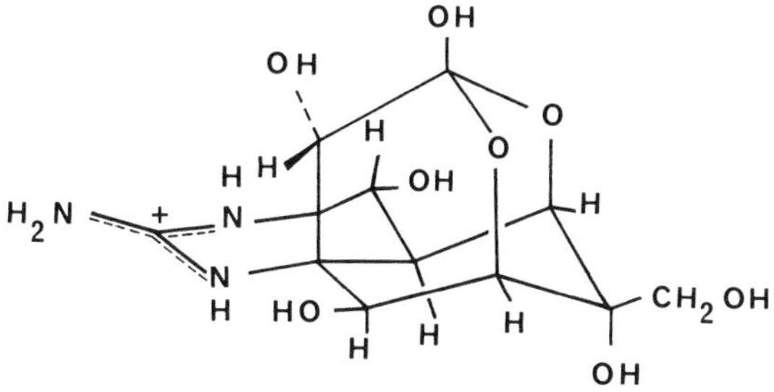

Figure 1.12 Structure of tetrodotoxin.

African scorpions bind to another "regulatory site", and their effect appears attributable to a blocking or a considerable slowdown of the flux through the channels.

Tetrodotoxin (Fig. 1.12), a venom extracted from the ovary and liver of several species of pufferfish and sunfish, blocks the increase in sodium conductance during the excitation of the nerve fiber. It acts on the "ion transport site" of the channel. The complex of tetrodotoxin bound to a membrane protein has been extracted and determined to have a molecular weight of about 500,000 daltons. The binding to this component is reversible, and it may be that this protein is the sodium channel.

Saxitoxin is a substance obtained from certain marine dinoflagellates. Although chemically different from tetrodotoxin, the actions of the two are similar. Saxitoxin binds to the sodium channel, probably to an acidic site within it, and blocks the inward sodium current.

In different parts of the nervous system, several types of sodium channels have been identified which differ in their sensitivity to toxins and in their dissociation constants. Some channels are even tetrodotoxin–resistant, such as those present in the Purkinje cell dendrites (Llinas and Hess, 1976).

THE POTASSIUM CHANNEL

By definition, the potassium channel permits the passage of potassium ions out of the cytoplasm. Both fast and slow types have been demonstrated in neurons. And, in the frog node of Ranvier, three types of membrane potassium channels have been reported (Dubois, 1981). The opening of the channel is voltage-dependent and occurs after the sodium channel opens. In addition to potassium, it will allow the passage of other ions, as rubidium, ammonium, lithium, guanidine, and hydroxylammonium. The maintenance of a closed channel configuration   probably requires energy, and in a metabolically exhausted membrane the channel remains permanently open (Fink and Wettwer, 1978). In such an exhausted fiber, the application of tetraethylammonium ion, a selective potassium channel blocker, is ineffective.

The potassium channel is probably activated by the entry of calcium through the cell surface during membrane depolarization. The potential-activated delayed current, which is responsible for repolarization and which is caused by the stream of potassium ions out of the cell, is preceded by a calcium-dependent current which likely represents the gating current for the channel. The slow channels are involved in the hyperpolarization of the neurons that follows the train of stimuli.

THE CALCIUM CHANNEL

Calcium is an ion with a large number of functions within the cell. It serves, for example, in the excitation-contraction coupling of the muscle fiber, the release of neurotransmitters and peptide hormones, and the regulation of catecholamine synthesis. Although calcium may be involved in the activities of both sodium and potassium channels, the existence of independent calcium channels, permitting the diffusion of calcium ions into the cell, has been confirmed. This channel is open during the excitation of the nerve or muscle fiber, and calcium ions can even replace sodium during the rising phase of the action potential.

In the presynaptic region, calcium enters the synaptic knob during depolarization in an amount that determines the quantity of neurotransmitter to be released, and consequently, the amplitude of the postsynaptic potential. Therefore, calcium is an important regulator of the efficiency of synaptic transmission and the excitability of the nerve cells. Thus, these channels may modulate the behavior of neuronal assemblies and, in so doing, participate in the processes underlying neuronal plasticity during learning (Ramos, 1975).

Using the freeze-fracture technique, where a frozen membrane is split preferentially through the middle of the lipid bilayer, Akert *et al.* (1972) identified a class of large particles which span the synaptic membrane. Heuser *et al.* (1974) believed that such particles were involved in neurotransmitter release, possibly serving as the calcium channel. Recent evidence (Pumplin *et al.*, 1981) supports this view and suggests that each large presynaptic particle corresponds to a single channel.

Chapter 2

Membrane Lipids

The various lipid species that have been detected in the neuronal membrane tend to be distributed there asymmetrically. Phosphatidylethanolamine, for example, can be found in the internal monolayer, whereas the glycolipids are built into the outer layer. The lipids are not generally synthesized in the membrane, but are produced elsewhere in at least partial form, before being transported towards the membrane for any necessary completion and incorporation. Since these lipids have been shown to have an important role in the control of neuronal excitability, vis-a-vis their association with membrane enzymes and ionic channels, it would be helpful to examine them in somewhat more detail, identifying a number of characteristics which may be involved in the plasticity of neuronal functions.

FATTY ACIDS IN THE BRAIN

The lipids are esters of fatty acids and various higher alcohols. Although fatty acids serve in other parts of the body as a source of energy, in the brain they are principally used for the synthesis of lipids. To this end, they are either produced *de novo* in the brain tissue or are transported from the circulation through the blood-brain barrier. Fatty acids can also be released from the brain. A few minutes of ischemia or convulsions will cause a prompt release into the circulation. The administration of several neurotransmitters may also initiate this process, which indicates that brain lipids are not very stable and may be readily hydrolyzed into free fatty acids and alcohols.

The synthesis of fatty acids in the brain involves a number of enzymatic steps. Using acetyl–CoA, malonyl-CoA and the reduced form of nicotinamide adenine dinucleotide phosphate (NADPH), *de novo* fatty acid synthesis proceeds under the control of a multienzyme system called fatty acid synthetase (Fig. 2.1). The process is one of elongation, involving the

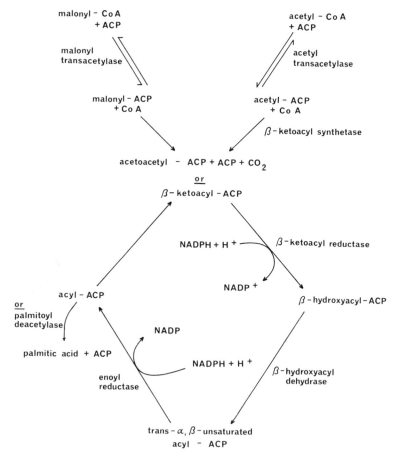

Figure 2.1 Steps in fatty acid synthesis.

formation of additional carbon-carbon bonds to a growing fatty acid molecule held in place by an "acyl carrier protein" (ACP). Acetyl coenzyme A donates an acetyl group to the acyl carrier protein. The acetyl group is incorporated into the newly begun fatty acid, and a molecule of carbon dioxide is released, a process which requires energy in the form of ATP. The reactions continue through the generation of early hydroxyacyl and α, β-unsaturated acyl intermediates before the elongating compound reaches the palmitoyl-ACP stage, at which time the process is either repeated or the product is released from the acyl carrier protein as palmitic acid, the primary product of fatty acid synthetase.

Fatty acids previously produced in the brain or those transported into it are also able to receive additional carbons. For these reactions, there are two distinct elongation systems in nervous tissue that have been detected in the mitochondrial and microsomal fractions. The resulting fatty acids are not released, but are directly used for lipid synthesis in the same cell (for review see Katiyar and Porter, 1977).

A unique feature of the mammalian brain is its high content of unsaturated fatty acids, some examples of which are shown in Figure 2.2. These levels are largely attributable to the activity of a desaturation pathway that uses saturated fatty acids (mostly contained within the phospholipid fraction) as substrates.

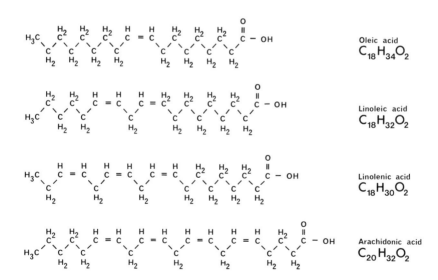

Figure 2.2 Unsaturated fatty acids.

Since the position of a double bond in an unsaturated fatty acid molecule may differ, there may exist several isomers of the same molecule. Accordingly, in the brain, up to 3-6 positional isomers of each single unsaturated fatty acid have been detected. Their proportion and positional specificity varies with age, nutritional status and disease, as well as with phospholipid type and position of the fatty acid within the lipid molecule (Spence, 1970).

The synthesis of fatty acids with several double bonds, the polyenoic acids, uses for starting material fatty acids that tend to be shorter in length. Linolenic acid is a common precursor. In the brain, these polyenoic acids are mostly incorporated into cholesterol esters and ethanolamine phosphoglycerides. Selective incorporation of unsaturated fatty acids with varying numbers and positions of double bonds into lipids depends upon a set of enzymes that are capable of discriminating between the isomers. These enzymes might be able to incorporate particular types of fatty acids according to the functional needs of the cell membrane. Consequently, these enzymes could, for instance, alter the excitability of a neuron or a particular synapse by modifying the structure of the lipids involved in particular enzymatic or channel activity.

TABLE 2.1

Representative α-Hydroxy Fatty Acids

General Formula	$CH_3(CH_2)_n\underset{OH}{CHCOOH}$	
No. of Carbons	Name of Acid	n
C_{12}	α-hydroxylauric	9
C_{14}	α-hydroxymyristic	11
C_{16}	α-hydroxypalmitic	13
C_{18}	α-hydroxystearic	15
C_{20}	α-hydroxyarachidic	17
C_{22}	α-hydroxybehenic	19
C_{24}	α-hydroxylignoceric	21

The hydroxylation of fatty acids is another common process in the brain. It involves the attachment of the hydroxyl (-OH) group to the α position of the carbon chain. For example, one hydroxy fatty acid, cerebronic acid (2-hydroxylignoceric acid), is synthesized from lignoceric acid. Several as yet incompletely characterized heat-labile and heat-stable factors are essential for this conversion (Singh and Kishimoto, 1981). And it is possible that they represent a functionally plastic metabolic system. This pathway is stimulated by the presence of sphingosine or psychosine, precursors of the brain sphingolipids, and inhibited by the reaction product, cerebronic acid itself. The preferential incorporation of α-hydroxy fatty acids into the basic sphingolipid, cerebroside, indicates their importance in the function of the cerebrosides. Of the total cerebroside fatty acid content, the α-hydroxy fatty acids (Table 2.1) comprise more than 50%.

GLYCEROPHOSPHATIDES IN THE BRAIN

Although the term phospholipid might initially be assumed to represent a relatively confined and closely related group of substances, it actually encompasses a broad range of compounds, whose similarity often ends with the presence of a phosphate group and a fatty acid chain. There are actually two very distinct phospholipid categories that are defined according to the kind of alcohol with which the fatty acids and phosphate are esterified. The glycerophosphatides, also known as glycerophospholipids or phosphoglycerides, contain glycerol as their alcohol. The phosphosphingolipids instead have sphingosine.

The glycerophosphatides are all formed from the precursor L-α-glycerophosphate, a product of glycolysis. They tend to be synthetized in the endoplasmic reticulum, although the enzyme initiating this process, glycerophosphate acyltransferase, has also been discovered in the outer mitochondrial membrane. The product of this reaction, phosphatidic acid (Fig. 2.3), serves as an intermediate in the formation of the major glycerophosphatides, namely phosphatidylserine, phosphatidylethanolamine,

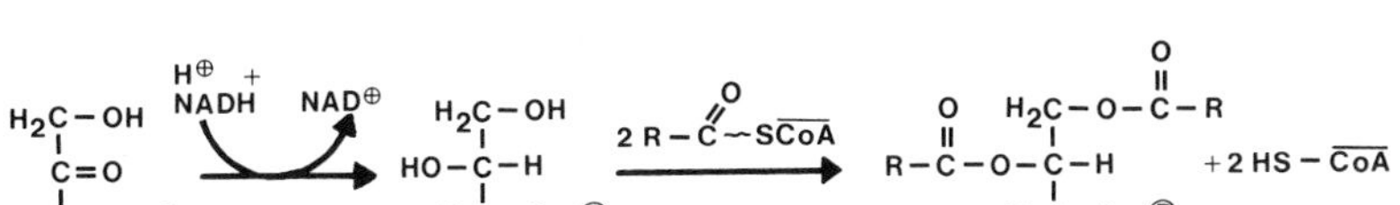

Figure 2.3 Synthesis of phosphatidic acid from α-glycerophosphate and two molecules of free fatty acids.

phosphatidylcholine, and phosphatidylinositol. Synthesis takes place in both the neurons and glia, and these two types of cells probably cooperate in this process (Marggraff *et al.*, 1979).

The basic structural arrangement of the glycerophosphatides can be found in Figure 2.4. The addition of fatty acids to phosphatidic acid takes place at the first and second carbons of the glycerol molecule. It is a process whose rate may be modified by several neurotransmitters. To the phosphate group on the third carbon, one of several types of alcohols is attached, whose name is typically used to define the compound (Fig. 2.5).

The glycerophosphatides are synthesized and modified in the brain by three metabolic pathways. One of them is the "net synthesis" pathway, whereby the molecule is completely assembled from its precursors. The second is the "base-exchange" pathway, in which one nitrogen-containing base, such as choline, is exchanged for another base, ethanolamine, for example. This pathway requires very little energy. The third is an *in situ* phospholipid methylation, whereby phosphatidylcholine is generated from

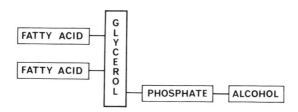

Figure 2.4 Basic structure of a glycerophosphatide.

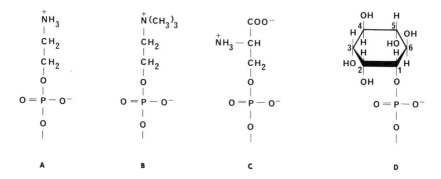

Figure 2.5 Polar head groups of the phosphoglycerides: A, phosphatidylethanolamine; B, phosphatidylcholine; C, phosphatidylserine; D, phosphatidylinositol.

phosphatidylethanolamine. These three systems probably play different physiological roles. The base exchange reaction modifies the polar portion of the phospholipids and while convincing evidence of its functional importance is not yet available, such an exchange could alter membrane function (Kanfer, 1980).

De novo "net" synthesis is present principally in synaptosomes. It is stimulated by calcium ions, and with the exception of the liver, its rate in the brain is higher than in any other part of the body. The bases required for *de novo* glycerophosphatide synthesis, ethanolamine, serine, choline, or inositol, are carried between individual phospholipids bound to phospholipid-exchange proteins. These base-exchange reactions are quickly able to supply specific glycerophosphatides whenever they are needed. Phospholipid methylation is likely also tied to the activity of the membrane. The process has been found to be regulated, at least in part, by a coupling of neurotransmitter receptors (β-adrenergic receptors, for example) with adenylate cyclase. Moreover, these methylated phospholipids are able to influence membrane receptor sensitivity (Hirata and Axelrod, 1980).

The methylating enzymes within the membrane are distributed there asymmetrically, and their topology makes possible the translocation of phospholipids from the cytoplasmic side to the outer surface of the membrane by a successive series of methylations. These events are initiated by the binding of a ligand to its receptors. According to Hirata and Axelrod (1980), each type of receptor appears to possess its own complement of phospholipid methylating enzymes. This process of methylation may then alter the membrane characteristics and so facilitate the lateral mobility of the receptor complex. It can also block calcium influx, the release of arachidonic acid for prostaglandin synthesis, or the formation of lysophosphatidylcholine. Thus, phospholipid methylation appears to be an initial common pathway for the transduction of receptor-mediated biological signals through the membrane. However appealing this mechanism may be, it must be cautioned that all receptor-mediated events need not involve phospholipid methylation. Furthermore, the bulk of experimentation in this area has been performed on erythrocyte membranes, so that the presence of the transmethylation pathway has not yet been demonstrated in the CNS.

The abundant nature of the phospholipids within the membrane suggests one role for these substances in the conduction of the nerve impulse. Excitation of rat and rabbit vagus nerves during their exposure to [^{32}P] orthophosphate causes a marked increase in the labeling of the phosphatidylinositides. The effect is inhibited by tetrodotoxin, which blocks sodium permeability (Salway and Hughes, 1972). The importance of the phospholipids in the transmission of the nerve impulse is still unclear. Some evidence suggests that these substances have no direct role in this process

(Rosenberg and Condrea, 1968; Rosenberg, 1970). The possibility does, nevertheless, exist that there are protein-bound phospholipids not affected by phospholipases which are important for neuronal excitation. Receptor-stimulated phosphatidylinositol metabolism may be one consequence of a mechanism serving to mobilize calcium ions within the cells (Michell *et al.*, 1981). The data, however, are inconsistent, since many cells in the body do not appear to require such mobilization for the metabolic response to occur.

In the synaptic area, stimulation of the muscarinic and α-adrenergic receptors activates the turnover of the polar head groups of phosphatidylinositol and phosphatidic acid. The breakdown of phosphatidylinositol to 1,2-diacylglycerol and its rapid regeneration through phosphatidic acid is probably a common consequence of an agonist-receptor interaction. Miller (1977) believes that this turnover probably plays a role in the response of the neuron to acetylcholine and catecholamine. The uptake of the neurotransmitter γ-aminobutyric acid into nerve endings does depend upon the membrane phospholipids, a process that can be modified by the base-exchange reaction (DeMedio *et al.*, 1980).

Phosphatidic acid has been suggested to participate in the fusion that takes place between synaptic vesicles and the plasma membrane during synaptic transmission (Pickard and Hawthorne, 1978). But, it is more probable that it regulates the calcium channel (Salmon and Honeyman, 1980). Accordingly, Harris *et al.* (1981) demonstrated that in striatal synaptosomes phosphatidic acid, but no other lipid, was capable of inducing the uptake of calcium ions.

Phosphatidylcholine, or lecithin, is the most common glycerophosphatide in the central nervous system. It is synthesized in large quantities during the period of nerve fiber myelination, but the synthesis drops off after that. The synthesis of lecithin requires the presence of the alcohol choline, setting up a competition for it with the acetylcholine synthetic system. The choline for these two reactions is transported into the central nervous system from the blood flow across the blood-brain barrier. The quantities that are available bias the direction in which it will go. At low concentrations of choline, the relative amounts of lecithin tend to be greater, while more acetylcholine is synthesized when high concentrations of choline are available. The choline entering these pathways must first be activated by phosphorylation, followed by a reaction with cytidine diphosphate (Arienti *et al.*, 1977). The activity of the corresponding enzyme, CTP-phosphocholine cytidylyltransferase, is the rate-limiting step in the synthesis of lecithin. A high level of potassium ions in the extracellular fluid, normally associated with neuronal firing, also is able to increase the synthesis of phospholipids, indicating a degree of synthetic control attributable to the functional state of the neuron.

The phosphoinositides have already been mentioned in reference to their association with the neuronal membrane. They are composed of glycerol, two residues of fatty acids, phosphate and inositol. Besides the monophosphoinositols, diphospho- and triphosphoinositols are also present in the brain where they are synthesized by the phosphorylation of the monophosphoinositol molecule. Although primarily found in myelin, they are also present in synapses.

The incorporation of phosphate into phosphoinositides is promoted by increased synaptic transmission and the actions of neurotransmitters, such as norepinephrine, dopamine or serotonin (Hawthorne, 1960; Larrabee and Leicht, 1965).

The synthesis of phospholipids in the brain is a heterogeneous process. Most are produced in the perikarya and transported toward the nerve endings (Toews *et al.*, 1980). However, the enzyme synthesizing the phosphatidylinositols is also carried along the axon to the nerve endings (Kumarasiri and Gould, 1980), indicating that some synthesis may also occur in the synaptic region. Degradation is by the phospholipases that exist in nervous tissue in several forms, each characterized by a different molecular site of action (Fig. 2.6) and, in general, a high degree of specificity. By convention, the phospholipases are termed A, B, C, and D. There are two types of phospholipase A in the brain, A_1 and A_2, with different physical properties (Gallai-Hatchard *et al.*, 1962) and distinct sites of hydrolysis (Woelk, 1974).

In a manner similar to their effect upon phosphoinositide synthesis, the neurotransmitters are also able to alter the rate of catabolism. Accordingly, acetylcholine will stimulate the enzymatic hydrolysis of synaptosomal phosphoinositides to diacylglycerols. This process is mediated by a phosphatidylinositol-specific phosphohydrolase (Irvine *et al.*, 1979). In synaptosomes, the degradation of diacylphosphoinositol is much more rapid than the degradation of other membrane diglycerides (Sun *et al.*, 1978).

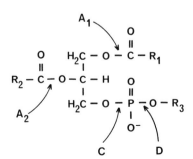

Figure 2.6 Sites of action of phospholipase A_1, A_2, C and D.

Phosphoinositide turnover increases rapidly when neurons are stimulated by electrical or pharmacological agents, and it appears that the effect is mostly attributable to the arrival of presynaptic impulses at the neuron (Lunt and Pickard, 1975). The receptors activating this "phosphatidylinositide effect" include cholinergic, muscarinic, and α-adrenergic types (Fisher *et al.*, 1981; Smith and Hauser, 1981). Moreover, it is not limited to neurons, but has also been detected in neutrophils, blood platelets, mast cells, the parotid gland, etc. (for review see Cockroft, 1981). The effect typically, but not always, requires the presence of calcium ions (Michell and Kirk, 1981; Smith and Hauser, 1981). In 1975, Michell first proposed that the activation of phosphatidylinositol turnover provided a direct link between the surface receptors and the membrane calcium channels. Putney (1981) suggests that in this association phosphatidic acid, newly generated by phosphatidylinositol breakdown, may function as an endogenous calcium ionophore. It may also serve as a source of arachidonic acid for prostaglandin and thromboxane synthesis (see Chapter 21) and may contribute to the desensitization of the receptor (Cockroft, 1981).

SPHINGOLIPIDS IN THE BRAIN

In mammals, at least four types of lipids are derived from the higher alcohol (aminodiol) sphingosine: sphingomyelins, cerebrosides, sulfatides and gangliosides. Sphingosine is synthesized in the body by the condensation of palmitoyl-CoA with serine followed by decarboxylation (Fig. 2.7). The product of this reaction, dihydrosphingosine, is then dehydrogenated into

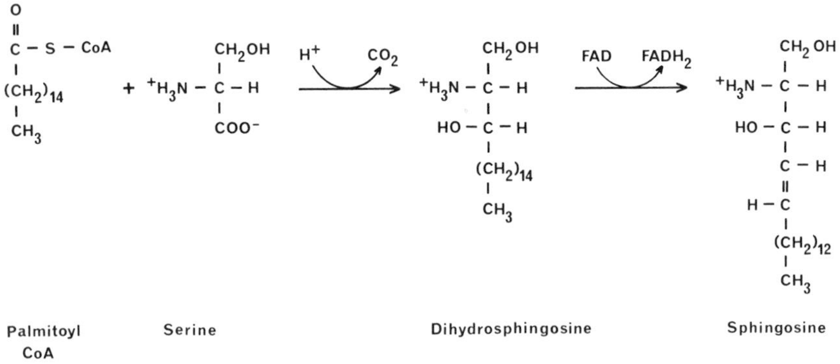

Figure 2.7 Synthesis of sphingosine.

sphingosine. Several isomers of sphingosine have been found in the nervous system that differ in the number of double bonds and the position of the hydroxyl groups.

The first step in the biosynthesis of the sphingolipids is the reaction of sphingosine with fatty acyl-CoA to form ceramide (Fig. 2.8), which then reacts with activated choline (cytidine diphosphate choline), galactose, glucose, or some other substance to form the sphingolipid molecule. Following the synthesis of this basic structure, sphingolipids may then undergo further transformation, such as the replacement of the fatty acid, or oxidation or reduction of the sphingosine moiety (Kishimoto and Kawamura, 1979). Additional alterations of this nature may affect the functional characteristics of the lipid.

Sphingomyelins

The sphingomyelins (Fig. 2.9) are the only membrane phospholipids that are not derived from glycerol. They instead contain sphingosine, along with a phosphate, choline and a fatty acid. Brain sphingomyelins with long-chain fatty acids over 20 carbons in length have been found primarily in myelin sheaths; whereas those with shorter-chain fatty acids are present mainly in non-myelin structures.

Figure 2.8 Ceramide.

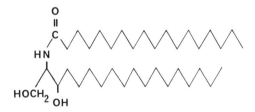

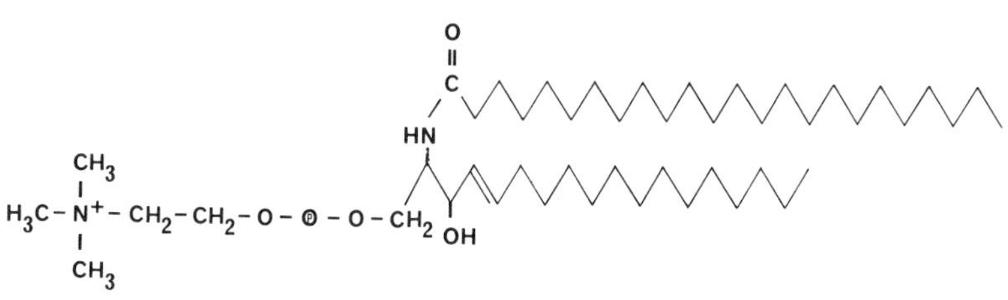

Figure 2.9 Sphingomyelin.

The entire synthetic pathway is present in brain tissue. And, there appear to be at least two independent mechanisms that synthesize sphingomyelins in the brain; one is stimulated by potassium ions, while the other is not. Sphingomyelinase, an enzyme that degrades sphingomyelin into ceramide and phosphorylcholine, has been found to increase in the brain during the period of myelination before undergoing a sharp decrease (Klein and Mandel, 1972).

Glycosphingolipids

As the term suggests, the glycosphingolipids are compounds that are characterized by the presence of one or more sugar groups attached to a sphingolipid backbone. The cerebrosides and gangliosides are the most prominent members of this category. The sulfatides belong to a broadly-defined class of sulfur-containing lipids known as the sulfolipids. While this latter term encompasses a large range of plant and animal substances, the sulfatides commonly refer to the cerebroside sulfates.

Cerebrosides.   In all sphingolipids, the amino group of sphingosine is acylated as the result of a reaction with a long-chain acyl CoA. This N-acyl sphingosine is also known as ceramide and is the precursor of sphingomyelin, the cerebrosides, and the gangliosides. The subsequent addition of either a glucose or galactose to ceramide through a glycosidic bond generates a cerebroside, the simplest of the glycosphingolipids (Fig. 2.10).

In the brain, the cerebrosides are synthesized predominantly in the microsomal fraction, although a significant amount of galactosyl transferase, the enzyme that catalyzes the addition of galactose to ceramide, has also been detected in purified myelin. Several research groups have reported a close correlation between the myelination of central and peripheral neurons

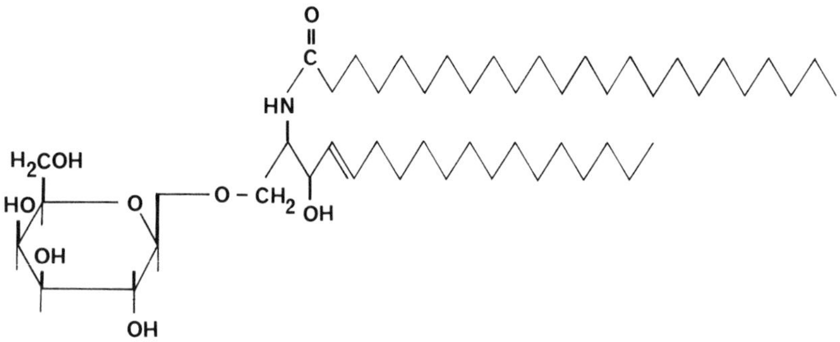

Figure 2.10 A cerebroside.

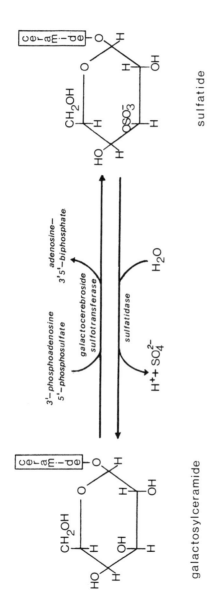

Figure 2.11 Synthesis of a sulfatide from a cerebroside.

and the accretion of cerebrosides. For this reason, the galactocerebrosides in myelin have been used as an indication of the rate of myelin formation (Foulkes and Patterson, 1974). Cerebrosides containing glucose (glucocerebrosides) are mostly produced in neurons, and are generally considered to be precursors of gangliosides.

The only known pathway for the breakdown of the glucosyl and galactosyl forms of cerebroside is via the β-glycosidases. One of them, β-galactosidase, removes galactose from its bond with ceramide, while the other, β-glucosidase, functions in a corresponding way on a glucosyl ceramide substrate.

Sulfatides.   As cerebroside sulfates, the sulfatides are, by composition, glycosphingolipids. They are generated in the brain by cerebroside sulfotransferase, which, as its name suggests, mediates the incorportion of a sulfate group into galactosyl ceramide (Fig. 2.11). The natural sulfate donor is 3'-phosphoadenosine 5'-phosphosulfate (PAPS), and a system for PAPS synthesis has been discovered in the 100,000 g supernatant fraction of rat brain.

The sulfatides are degraded by the sulfatide sulfatases, also known as the arylsulfatases. Isoelectric focusing has resolved three forms of the enzyme (Harzer *et al.*, 1973), which have been found to differ in their substrate specificity and their activity within various tissues.

Gangliosides.   The gangliosides are a group of phosphorus-free glycosphingolipids that are characterized by the presence of one or more residues of a nine-carbon acidic sugar. These particular sugars, in the brain predominantly N-acetylneuraminic acid (NANA), are also known as sialic acids, and it is their presence that defines the gangliosides as a distinct class of glycosphingolipids (Fig. 2.12).

The carbohydrate portion of the mammalian brain gangliosides is generally rather complex. All contain an oligosaccharide chain which can range

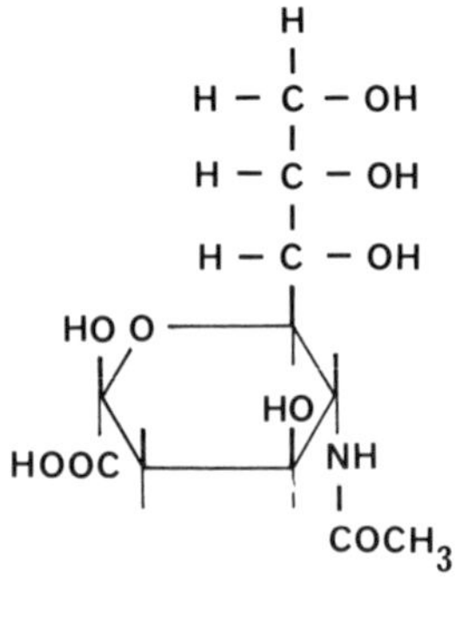

Figure 2.12 *N*-Acetylneuraminic acid.

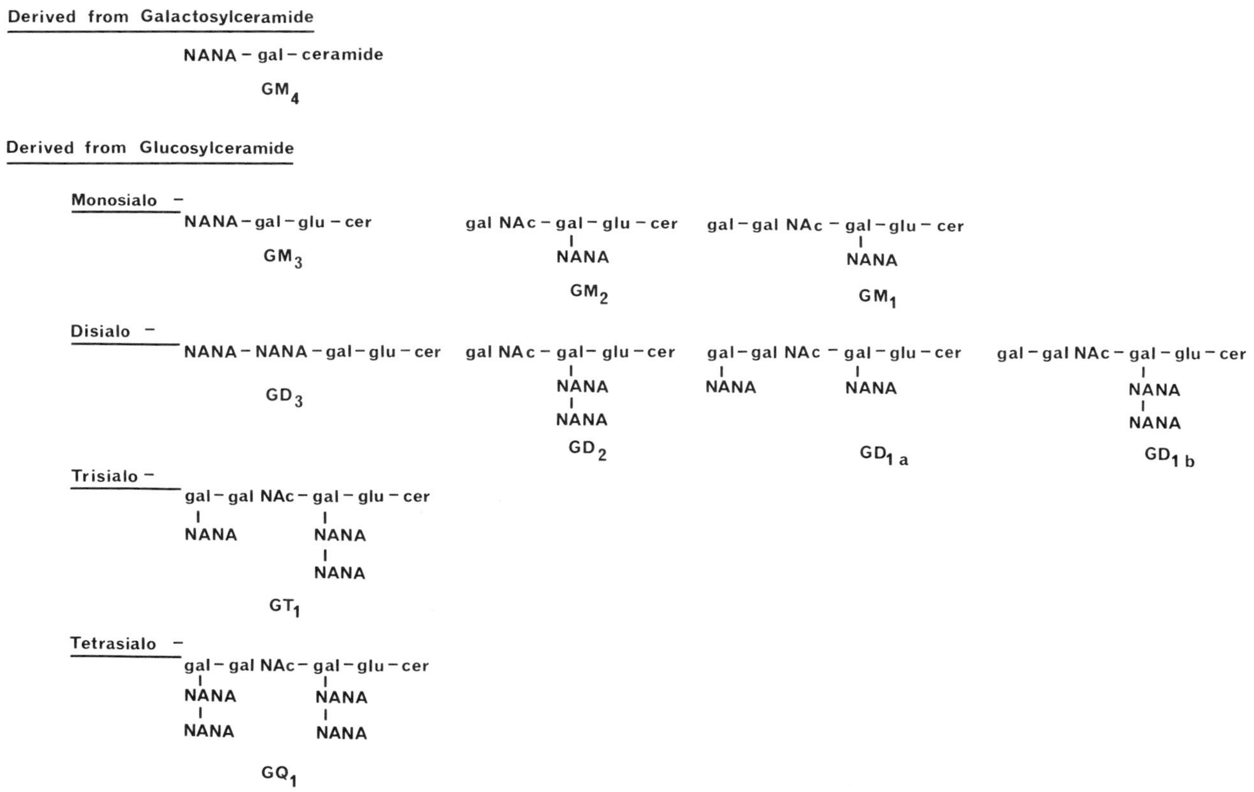

Figure 2.13 Structures of some important gangliosides.

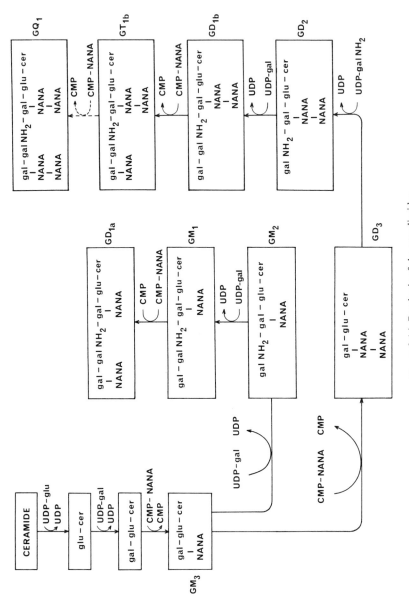

Figure 2.14 Synthesis of the gangliosides.

from two to four hexoses in length, although a tetrasaccharide is most common. Approximately 9 different gangliosides can be identified from brain tissue homogenates. They differ in the length of their carbohydrate chain and the number and position on the chain of the sialic acid groups (Fig. 2.13). These latter two variables, sialic acid number and position, provide a basis for grouping the individual ganglioside variants as monosialo-, disialo-, trisialo-, or tetrasialo- compounds.

The oligosaccharide chain is synthesized by a stepwise addition of single monosaccharides to ceramide (Fig. 2.14). The process requires a complex of membrane-bound enzymes, the glycosyltransferases, that activate different sugars and incorporate them into the growing chain. Glucosyltransferase, galactosyltransferase and CMP-NANA synthetase are all glycosyltransferases. CMP-NANA synthetase activates N-acetylneuraminic acid not only for incorporation into gangliosides, but also for its attachment to glycoproteins. The glycosyltransferases tend to be highly specific, and their sequence of action is closely ordered. Those that are involved in building a ganglioside form a complex that is bound to intracellular membranous systems, mostly the Golgi apparatus.

There are two pools of gangliosides in the brain - a small one, formed by intermediates of the glycosylation system, and a large one, composed of endproducts of the metabolism. The membranes of neuronal perikarya are enriched in the intermediate gangliosides and their related glycosyltranferases, while the nerve endings contain more of the end-product gangliosides (Landa et $al.$, 1979).

GM_3 is the basic unit from which all of the other glucosylceramide-derived gangliosides are formed. The synthetic pathway appears to be a divergent one, and its direction is controlled by the particular glycosyltransferase acting upon GM_3. Uridine diphosphate-N-acetylgalactosamine: GM_3 N-acetylgalactosaminyl transferase channels the synthesis through GM_2, GM_1, GD_{1a} and GT_{1b}. Cytidine monophosphate-N-acetylneuraminic acid: GM_3 sialyltransferase, on the other hand, adds a sialic acid to form a NANA-NANA linkage, generating GD_3, from which GD_2, GD_{1b}, and GT_{1b} are produced.

The synthesis of gangliosides is much higher in neuronal perikarya than in the whole brain homogenate. It is likely that they are produced in the cell body and then transported as a ganglioside-protein complex (Sonnino et $al.$, 1979) within the neuron for subsequent incorporation into the plasma membrane. A glycolipid-binding protein for mono- and dihexosylceramides which does not interact with phospholipids has already been isolated from pig brain (Abe et $al.$, 1982). It may function to relocate glycolipids from one membrane site to another.

Ganglioside synthesis may be completed at the time of transport, although it is possible that they receive some sialic acid residues at the site of incorporation.

From the estimates of Ledeen (1978), it appears that the large majority of gangliosides is located in the neuronal processes. The axon terminals, which have been reported to be enriched in gangliosides, account for only a small percentage of the total content. However, the importance of the synaptic area and the biophysical and biochemical characteristics of the gangliosides have given their presence in the region added attention. Their possible functional contribution here will be discussed somewhat later.

As is the case with most complex molecules, the gangliosides (and nonsialo glycosphingolipids) are probably broken down within the lysosomes. Under the control of a sequence of exoglycosidases, the degradation begins at the peripheral end of the oligosaccharide chain and continues as a stepwise cleavage of sugars.

The first catabolic step is the hydrolysis of the NANA-NANA bond to form G_{D1a}. Subsequent enzymatic cleavages generate, in turn, G_{M1}, G_{M2} and G_{M3}, before the molecule is shortened to lactosyl- and then glucosylceramide. A β-glucosidase displaces the final sugar, leaving a ceramide unit which may be further broken down into a fatty acid and sphingosine. Ganglioside neuraminidase, an enzyme which specifically cleaves sialic acid moieties, appears to exist in brain tissue in at least three forms:

(1) a soluble neuraminidase,
(2) a predominantly synaptosomal enzyme that will remove NANA from the polysialogangliosides and G_{M3}, and
(3) a lysosomal neuraminidase that is able to cleave NANA from G_{M1} and G_{M2}.

The synaptosomal enzyme is likely bound to the membrane (Schengrund et al., 1972), and its activity toward exogenous substrates, although not controlled by the presence of sodium, potassium, and calcium cations, is certainly influenced by their presence. The neuraminidase is activated by a low pH, releasing a strongly anionic sialic acid end-group from the synaptic membrane and, in doing so, possibly modifying synaptic efficacy. The presence of the enzyme in the membrane, along with the gangliosides and some sialyltransferase activity, has also prompted speculation that the alternate action of these two enzymes could function in some kind of ganglioside involvement in neurotransmitter binding and release.

The gangliosides are asymmetrically positioned in the membrane, so that the chained carbohydrate residues extend into the extracellular or the synaptic space, leaving the non-polar lipid portion anchored within the membrane. The principal ganglioside of the external surface of synaptosomes from the cerebral cortex is G_{M1} (Hungund and Mahadik, 1981), but their anatomical distribution tends to show some regional variation, involving shifts in the percentage contribution of each variant to the total. For example, the visual cortex has been reported to have higher proportionate amounts of G_{T1}, and a lower percentage of G_{D1a} as compared to other cortical areas (Suzuki, 1965).

The carbohydrate components are the primary determinants of the chemical and physical properties of the gangliosides. Their presence on the surface membrane of the neuron, extending as they do into the extracellular space, has made the gangliosides important candidates for various roles in intercellular communication, particularly synaptic transmission.

Hayashi and Katagiri (1974) noted that the gangliosides were able to interact with protein and Ca^{2+} to form a tight complex, which Rahmann *et al.* (1976) have hypothesized is involved in maintaining the ion-permeable resting state at the presynaptic membrane. The liberation of Ca^{2+} would then alter membrane permeability, permitting the calcium ion influx necessary for transmitter release (Fig. 2.15). The presence of acetylcholine was found to inhibit the ganglioside - Ca^{2+} complex formation (Probst *et al.*, 1979), and thus might delay the re-establishment of the resting state until the transmitter was metabolized by acetylcholinesterase. Therefore, a rapid conformational shift in the surface gangliosides as a consequence of calcium binding could be one of the characteristic changes during synaptic transmission. Simonneau *et al.* (1980) have also argued that gangliosides bind calcium after its entry into the nerve ending, and that this initiates the release of acetylcholine and other neurotransmitters. Neuraminidase administration would then block synaptic transmission (Tauc and Hinzen, 1974). Calcium also appears to have a regulatory role in the metabolism of some gangliosides (Bremer *et al.*, 1982).

McIlwain and Marks (Marks and McIlwain, 1959; McIlwain, 1961) noted that the application of electric pulses or potassium salts to incubated brain slices caused an increase in respiration which could be inhibited by cooling the tissue prior to incubation. This respiratory response to these types of manipulation can be restored by the addition of either gangliosides or sialoglycoproteins to the medium (Daurainville and Gayet, 1965; Prasal and Borkowski, 1968). The presence of added protamine or histones also inhibited the tissue respiratory response to the pulses (Wolfe and McIlwain, 1961).

The tissue slices reacted to the electrical stimulation by taking up sodium ions and losing potassium ions to the surrounding medium. Subsequently, depending upon the availability of glucose, a metabolic restoration of the normal Na^+ and K^+ levels took place. The basic proteins, however, blocked the movement of K^+ back into the tissue, an effect which did not occur in the presence of the gangliosides. But, only intact sialic acid

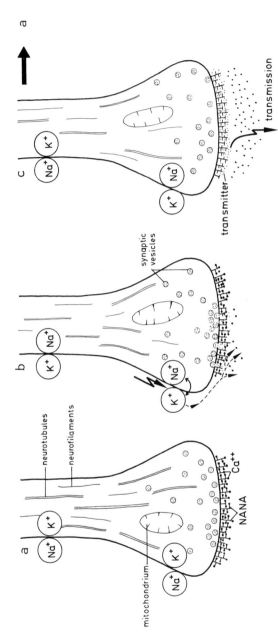

Figure 2.15 Functional states of the presynaptic membrane during synaptic transmission: (a) resting state presynaptic contact region "tightened" by calcium-ganglioside complexes; (b) arrival of the action potential, partial "opening" of the contact region following dissociation of the calcium-ganglioside complexes; (c) all calcium-ganglioside complexes dissociated and all available transmitter quanta released [from H. Rahmann, H. Rosner and H. Breer, *J. Theor. Biol.* 57:231 (1976); © 1976 by Academic Press Inc.].

containing glycosphingolipids were effective in this regard; neuraminidase-treated gangliosides were not. It is possible that the gangliosides, by virtue of their acidic sites, are involved in the transport of cations through the membrane pores. The basic proteins, by binding to the sites, would block cation movement and thus inhibit the increase in respiration.

A number of studies have demonstrated that individual gangliosides are capable of binding to certain viruses and bacterial toxins. Cholera toxin and tetanus toxin, for example, strongly interact with G_{M1} and G_{D1b}/G_{T1b}, respectively. Moreover, there is a peptide homology between the B chain of cholera toxin and the beta subunits of some glycoprotein hormones, notably thyrotropin, luteinizing hormone, human choriongonadotropin and follicle stimulating hormone. And, since there is an affinity of these hormones for particular ganglioside variants (Lee et al., 1976; Mullin et al., 1976; Chatelain et al., 1979), it is possible that the gangliosides may serve as their receptors, transporting them across the membrane (Olsnes et al., 1974). Interestingly, an increased binding of various hormones during different functional states is often accompanied by a rising level of gangliosides. For instance, in lactating rats, there is an elevation in the ganglioside levels throughout the brain (Berra et al., 1979).

The data do suggest that there is some role for the gangliosides in transmitting a hormonal message to the metabolic machinery of the cell. But, its involvement in this process might not always be as a particular molecule that itself binds the hormone, but as a component of a receptor complex on the membrane. Meldolesi et al. (1977) have data that suggest the thyrotropin receptor is composed of both ganglioside and glycoprotein portions and that it derives its properties from each.

An association between the gangliosides and neurotransmitters is not as apparent. There is evidence of a serotonin binding to gangliosides and, although they may function as receptors (Woolley and Gommi, 1964; van Heyningen, 1974), Gielen (1968) has suggested that gangliosides are more involved in mechanisms of serotonin storage. A few studies have reported the existance of a serotonin-binding protein whose activity was destroyed by neuraminidase treatment (Deul et al., 1968; Marchbanks, 1969). Correspondingly, its interaction with serotonin was enhanced by the addition of gangliosides (Tamir et al., 1980) which, in association with lecithin, probably regulate the serotonin-protein binding (Tamir et al., 1980a).

One could speculate that the primary mode of action of the hormone (or neurotransmitter) binding to the receptor complex is to alter the electrochemical ion gradients across the membrane. Work with an artificial lipid bilayer membrane containing ganglioside G_{T1} (Chatelain et al., 1979) has already demonstrated that the addition of luteinizing hormone (LH) results in a LH - G_{T1} interaction that leads to a four-fold increase in membrane conductance. The binding of thyrotropin to the thyroid cell membrane also causes a shift in membrane potential, in this case a hyperpolarization of the cells (Grollman *et al.*, 1977). The nature of these relationships may be crucial to an explanation of the effect of peptide hormones on neurons, synaptic transmission, and ultimately behavior. In this respect, gangliosides, peptides, and their interactions may be an important component of synaptic plasticity.

Alterations in ganglioside synthesis have been demonstrated between controls and experimental animals subjected to some form of behavioral stimulation [e.g., visual stimulation (DeMaccioni *et al.*, 1975) and escape (Irwin and Samson, 1971; Dunn and Hogan, 1974) and avoidance training (Savaki and Levis, 1977)]. Moreover, these studies have indicated that the changes are not evenly expressed for all the measured ganglioside variants. Subsequent discussions of these data have tended to suppose that the behavioral tasks employed resulted in some type of synaptic change, be it one involving the establishment of new contacts with novel surface membrane

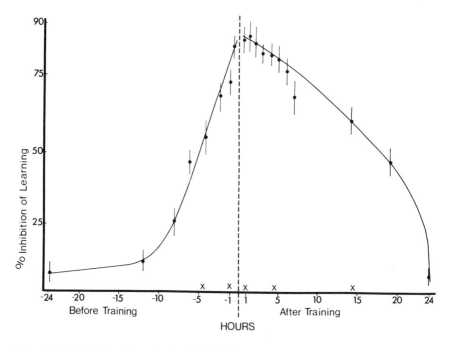

Figure 2.16 Inhibition of learning (± SEM) following intraventricular injection of antiserum to brain gangliosides at varying time intervals before and after training on a step-through passive avoidance task [from S.E. Karpiak and M.M. Rapport, *Behav. Neural Biol.* 27:146 (1979), © 1979 by Academic Press Inc.].

characteristics, or a shift in the ganglioside content of previously formed connections. The difficulty with such suggestions is that, for the most part, the analyses performed in these studies were on whole tissue extracts and not confined to material isolated from the nerve endings. And, since extra-synaptosomal structures could contribute up to 80% of the total ganglioside content (as argued by Ledeen, 1978), any inferences about synaptic change based upon whole tissue analysis would appear to be quite premature. Based upon the work of Hess *et al.* (1976) and Ledeen (1978), it appears that such changes in ganglioside concentration probably reflect changes in the relative mass of neuronal plasma membranes, since the synaptic concentrations have been estimated to account for only a small percentage of the total ganglio-side content.

While these changes may indicate an overall shift in membrane mass, other effects speak more directly to the involvement of the gangliosides in the process of learning. In a number of related studies, Karpiak and Rapport (Karpiak *et al.*, 1976, 1978; Rapport *et al.*, 1978) have found that antibodies raised against G_{M1} ganglioside, when injected into the brain, were able to disrupt a learned avoidance response, unlike corresponding preparations against 14-3-2 protein, myelin, or galactocerebroside (Fig. 2.16).

Also, there are some preliminary indications that the administration of mixed gangliosides is able to improve somewhat visual memory performance in patients displaying signs of mental deterioration (Miceli *et al.*, 1977). Their administration is able to reduce the behavioral and mental deterioration in cases of vascular and neoplastic brain lesions, senility, and arteriosclerotic dementia. Moreover, they appear to be effective in the treatment of traumatic, toxic, and degenerative lesions of the peripheral nervous system (Miceli *et al.*, 1977). This finding may be related to the fact that gangliosides act as survival factors for neurons *in vitro* (Morgan and Seifert, 1979).

Thus, the gangliosides, as a result of their structural variability, localization in the membranes, and possible receptor-type functions, may be one of the important components in the plasticity of synaptic activity and neuronal excitability.

ISOPRENOID LIPIDS

The isoprenoid lipids are all derivatives of a five-carbon isoprene unit that is itself formed from the acetate portion of acetyl-CoA. Some important members of this category are cholesterol and the five major types of steroid hormones that use cholesterol as a precursor: the progestagens (progesterone, pregnanediol), mineralocorticoids (aldosterone), glucocorticoids

$$CH_2$$
$$\parallel$$
$$C-CH_3$$
$$\vert$$
$$CH$$
$$\parallel$$
$$CH_2$$ **Figure 2.17** Structure of an isoprene unit.

(cortisol, corticosterone), androgens (testosterone, 4-androstene-3,17-dione) and estrogens (estrone, β-estradiol, estriol). Other isoprenoid lipids found in the brain include cholestanol, 24-hydroxycholesterol, and desmosterol.

Cholesterol is formed by a progressive attachment of activated isoprene units (Fig. 2.17) to a growing hydrocarbon chain. These reactions produce an intermediate molecule of squalene (Fig. 2.18), which then undergoes cyclization and a shifting of double bonds to yield lanosterol. The subsequent removal of three methyl groups, along with a reduction of one double bond and the migration of another, finally generates cholesterol (Fig. 2.19). The various reactions involved in this synthesis require the presence of at least three carrier proteins and a cell surface receptor, in addition to the various enzymes.

Cholesterol is a major constituent of both cell membranes and myelin sheaths, where it is relatively stable. Even prolonged starvation does not perceptibly alter its level in the adult brain. When labeled cholesterol is injected into recently hatched chicks, the radioactivity in liver and plasma virtually disappears in 3 to 8 weeks (Davison *et al.*, 1958). In the brain, however, a considerable amount persists for long periods of time, suggesting a difference in the enzyme system responsible for cholesterol breakdown.

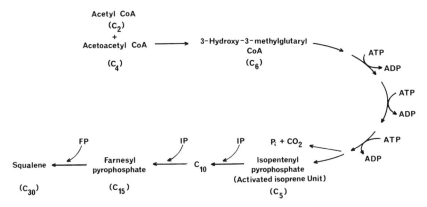

Figure 2.18 Synthesis of squalene, a precursor of the isoprenoid lipids. IP, isoprene unit; FP, farnesyl pyrophosphate.

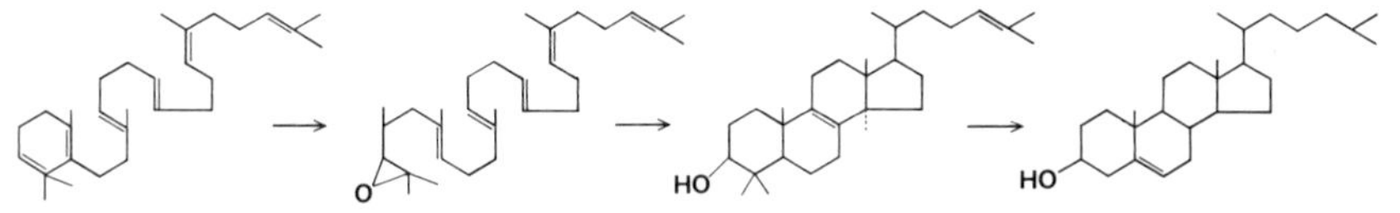

Squalene   Squalene epoxide   Lanosterol   Cholesterol

Figure 2.19 Synthesis of cholesterol from squalene.

One of the functions of isoprenoid lipids may be participation in the biosynthesis of some glycoproteins. Here they would possibly act as carriers of mono- or oligosaccharides which are then used for synthesis of the attached sugar chain (Kronquist and Lennarz, 1978). Using a sterol-specific probe, filipin, Garcia-Segura *et al.* (1982) detected variations in the distribution of sterol molecules in various parts of the neuron. The values for the dendritic membranes were found to be much lower than those for the perikaryal membrane. The data indicate that there exist differences in the organization of specific regions of the neuronal plasma membrane, which may relate to the functional activity in that area.

LIPOFUSCIN

Although initially observed in cells about 140 years ago, lipofuscin is still not a well-defined substance. In cells, it appears as round or oblong, yellowish-brown pigment granules that are believed to originate during the course of lysosomal degradation (Brunk and Ericsson, 1972).

Lipofuscin is a very compact substance (56% of its weight is solid material) that is found in all cells of the body. Until fairly recently, a chemical characterization has been impeded by an inability to isolate a suitably pure material for analysis. But, by using various column fractionation techniques, Taubold (1975) reported the isolation of a few related substances which were found to possess the general properties of lipofuscin. His analysis suggested that these pigments were primarily made up of polymeric lipid and phospholipid units to which amino acids were bound. The molecular weights of the molecules fall within the 6000-7000 dalton range.

The deposition of these substances is likely due to a lipid peroxidative process involving the production of reactive lipid hydroperoxides from membrane unsaturated fatty acids (Tappel, 1965; Chio *et al.*, 1969). In this context, it is a degenerative series of reactions that may eventually disrupt the integrity of the membrane.

The amount of lipofuscin in the central nervous system increases over time. Substantial amounts are already present in the brain by the end of the first decade of life, and the number of lipofuscin-containing cells continues to increase with age. In young individuals, the pigment tends to appear in the nerve cells as fine granules; later, it is clumped and concentrated as a localized mass. Large amounts of lipofuscin are found in brains of senile individuals and those with presenile dementias and heredodegenerative diseases. Although lipofuscin has often been called a "deterioration pigment", it is not always associated with structural and functional deterioration of the cells. For example, the amount of lipofuscin in heart muscle may be correlated with the degree of cardiac hypertrophy (Sandritter *et al.*, 1972).

MYELIN

During the prenatal and early postnatal periods of development, there occurs a gradual concentric ensheathment of many CNS nerve fibers with membranous processes of the oligodendroglial cell (Fig. 2.20). The covering, known as myelin, is responsible for the chemical distinctions between white and gray matter. Composed of proteins and lipids, it is a very stable substance and, consequently, is not able to participate in the rapid changes in brain activity that control behavior. Nevertheless, it is included in the present review of functional brain chemistry, since myelin is necessary for the swift transmission of nerve impulses along most axons. For more extensive discussions of myelin and the process of myelination, the reader is referred to Morrell (1977) and Davison and Peters (1970).

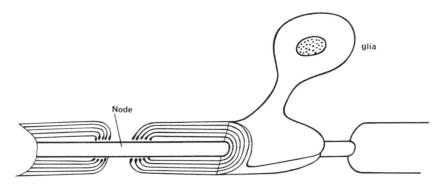

Figure 2.20 Structure of myelin.

Myelin is divided into short segments, or internodia, that are separated by unmyelinated gaps, the nodes of Ranvier. The size of this "node" is one of the factors that determines the velocity of nerve impulse conduction. The nodal length and diameter is related to the diameter of the nerve fiber, but the relationships are not linear (Dun, 1970).

X-ray diffraction, biochemical studies and other relevant methods have shown the internal structure of myelin to consist of concentric rings of material which may be impregnated by osmium tetroxide and thus visualized under the electron microscope. The distance between the rings is 170-180 A, and an electron density profile of the myelin shows that each ring is formed by two membranous layers.

Functionally, myelin allows the nerve impulse to propagate more rapidly down the axon by sequential membrane depolarizations at the nodes of Ranvier. And, since only these places along the fiber are excited (saltatory conduction), the propagation of the impulse requires less energy. Nervous transmission in fibers denuded of their myelin sheaths (e.g., due to toxic demyelination) is characterized by a decrement in conduction velocity, and even conduction failure. These axons are also more susceptible to exogenous influences, including the abnormal transmission of impulses from fiber to fiber (Waxman, 1977).

Chapter 3

The Nerve Impulse

The morphological and biochemical heterogeneity of CNS neurons means that these cells cannot be conceptualized simply as conductors that generate impulses according to some fixed percentage of activated synapses. Neurons differ from one another in a variety of ways. To a greater or lesser extent, each is biochemically unique and exhibits differences in cytoplasmic and membrane characteristics and the duration of sodium, potassium and calcium currents. Some cells have a low excitability, requiring a relatively intense stimulus to produce one or two spikes. Certain ones fire without apparent synaptic input, while others typically fire in bursts (Byrne, 1979). Moreover, the locus of generation of the impulse may vary. In pacemaker neurons, for example, the nerve spike is generally initiated in the cell body, while in nonpacemaker cells the locus may be the axon or axon hillock.

While these phenomena have been studied principally in defined neurons within the comparatively simple nervous systems of such animals as *Aplysia*, crayfish and leech, we can assume that a similar variability exists in the mammalian CNS. The action potential that is produced by a neuron is therefore an end-product of the interaction of incoming synaptic activity with the unique responsive nature of that particular cell.

Once generated, the action potentials that are conducted along the massive network of fibers within the nervous system represent a universal language of stereotyped signals. They are the means by which the brain receives, interprets, and responds to events in the external world. The signals are carried by the nerve fibers as electrical currents generated across their membranes.

In a resting state, the neuronal membrane itself is electrically negative (Segal, 1968). These negative fixed charges of about 1.9-4.2 x 10^{-8} Coulombs per sq. cm are balanced by the presence of neighboring electropositive ions. These positive ions are generally prevented from entering the membrane, but are present in the aqueous media which are in the contact with both surfaces (Fig. 3.1).

In the resting state, the surfaces of the neuronal membrane are polarized, with the outer cell surface being electropositive and the inner cell surface electronegative. This is the resting potential of the cell. The potential difference is about 70 millivolts (mV) and is attributable to an unequal distribution of ions, primarily sodium, potassium and chloride. In addition, there is a similar distribution of calcium which also contributes to the resting potential.

According to Hodgkin ond Huxley (1952), the nerve (and muscle) membrane is more permeable to potassium than it is to sodium, causing a relative loss of positively charged potassium ions from the cell. Together with the asymmetrical function of the Na^+, K^+-activated adenosine triphosphatase (as discussed in Chapter 1), the differences in sodium ond potassium ion permeability are able to maintain the resting potential.

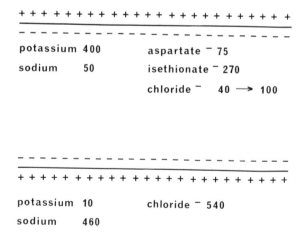

Figure 3.1 Distribution of ions on both sides of the neuronal membrane. Values in mmoles.

A number of responses may be generated from the polarized state: local responses, graded action potentials, "all-or-none" action potentials, and hyperpolarizing responses. The local response is an active electrotonic change caused by a subthreshold electrical stimulation of the neuronal membrane. A similar response also arises in the synaptic area, where it is due to specific chemical stimulation. The amplitude of the electrotonic response is proportional to the stimulus strength, but the relationship is not linear. The response has some characteristics similar to the action potential. It can develop as a consequence of an electrical current which may be much shorter than the local response itself. It is accompanied by a fall in the membrane impedance, and following the local response, there is a phase of decreased excitability, a "local relative refractory phase". It differs from the action potential, in that it has no precise threshold, no absolute refractory period, and is not an "all-or-none" change. Individual local responses may also be summed.

When local depolarization reaches a critical level, an action potential is generated. The excitability of the cell is a function of the difference between the initial (resting) potential and the critical value of the potential at which the membrane permeability to sodium suddenly increases and the action potential is generated. This critical value depends not only upon the functional characteristics of individual neurons, but also on the presence and concentration of ions on both sides of the excitable membrane. Accordingly, an increase in the calcium level in the extracellular fluid increases the threshold and the critical value. A decrease in calcium lowers the threshold and may even cause "spontaneous" firing of the neuron. Potassium ions in the extracellular fluid may alter the resting potential of the membrane and, with it, the excitability. An increasing level of extracellular potassium decreases membrane excitability, and at a potassium concentration of 27mM, no action potential is generated by the node of Ranvier.

Although the nerve impulse can be detected as a change in electrical potential, it is more than just a simple electrical shift. The longitudinal resistance of the axonal membrane is very high, 10^{10} ohms per cm of length, and this precludes any effective electrical conduction of the nerve impulse. Some reinforcing mechanism is therefore necessary which can sustain and propagate the action potential. When the impulse arrives at a given region of the membrane, the potential decreases until it reaches a threshold level where the permeability to sodium suddenly increases as the sodium channels open. This phenomenon is caused by an inner molecular reorganization of the channel, an "opening of the gates". The restructuring is accompanied by the generation of an electrical "gating charge", which had been postulated to exist as early as 1952 by Hodgkin and Huxley, but whose existence was not experimentally verified until somewhat later. A rapid phosphorylation and dephosphorylation of the proteins may be one of the factors involved in the molecular reorganization of the membrane (Schoffeniels and Margineanu, 1981).

The influx of sodium ions results in a rather uniform depolarization of the membrane and constitutes the so-called early sodium current (Fig. 3.2). The event has been directly observed by means of radioactively labeled sodium ions. The influx comes to a halt when the transmembrane difference in electrical potentials and the sodium concentration difference (the electrochemical gradient) are equalized.

The depolarization of the membrane is followed by a sudden increase in the permeabilities to potassium and chloride. As these two ions diffuse along their electrochemical gradients, potassium leaves the axon and chloride is carried inside. The potassium current depends upon a delayed (or "late") opening of the potassium channels which takes place at the end of depolarization, during the repolarization phase of the axonal membrane. Some sodium does enter the axoplasm during this repolarization (the descending phase of the action potential) and constitutes the "late" sodium current.

The net result of the action potential is an exchange of sodium ions for a comparable quantity of potassium ions. The shape and height of the action potential mostly depend upon the movements of these two ions. In myeli-

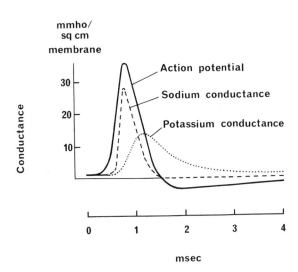

Figure 3.2 Changes in sodium and potassium conductance during the action potential of an axon. The unit of conductance is millimho, a reciprocal unit of milliohm.

nated axons, however, no potassium conductance has been demonstrated during the passage of the nerve impulse. Repolarization in these fibers has been explained in terms of a rapid sodium inactivation and a large leakage current (Chiu et al., 1979). This has been demonstrated both in peripheral (Horakova et al., 1968) and in central nerve fibers (Kocsis and Waxman, 1980).

From the standpoint of the relevant electrical phenomena (currents and the changes in permeability, resistance, and capacitance), our understanding of the nerve impulse is relatively complete. Unfortunately, the elaboration of the molecular mechanism responsible for changes in membrane permeability to different ions is still rudimentary. Most of the available data have been obtained from studies of the giant squid axon, an unmyelinated unbranched axon originating from the syncytium formed by the neurons of the hindmost stellar ganglion of the squid. This axon can be as large as one millimeter in diameter, and for experimental purposes, it is possible to remove its cytoplasm and replace it with a solution of known composition. The effects of changes in ionic composition, as well as the effects of drugs and enzymes applied internally or externally can be readily observed in this preparation.

Biochemical and structural alterations in the axonal membrane are also expressed as a change in the birefringence and fluorescence of the membrane that coincides with the time course of the action potential (Cohen et al., 1968). However, the functional implications of these changes are at present not clear. Also, modifications in the surface charges of the membrane may also be one of the factors regulating the activity of membrane-bound enzymes. Consequently, such changes may have a profound effect upon cell metabolism (Wojtczak and Nalecz, 1979).

The activity of the sodium and potassium channels during depolarization and repolarization is tied to the membrane lipids. Tasaki and Takenaka (1964) found that lipases and phospholipases, enzymes that hydrolyze the essential lipid components of the membrane, interfere with the generation and transmission of the nerve impulse. They are effective only when injected into the giant axon and not upon administration to the outer surface of the membrane.

Several substances that are able to bind to membrane structures also alter the nerve impulse. Local anesthetics of the procaine type, which are lipid soluble, are effective when applied to either side of the membrane. Although able to abolish the action potential, they have no effect upon the resting potential. Substances that block sodium and potassium channels, such as tetrodotoxin, saxitoxin, and the tetraethylammonium ion, will additionally interfere with the transmission of the impulse.

The upstroke of the action potential is accompanied by the production of heat and is therefore exergonic. The downturn on the other hand, is ender-

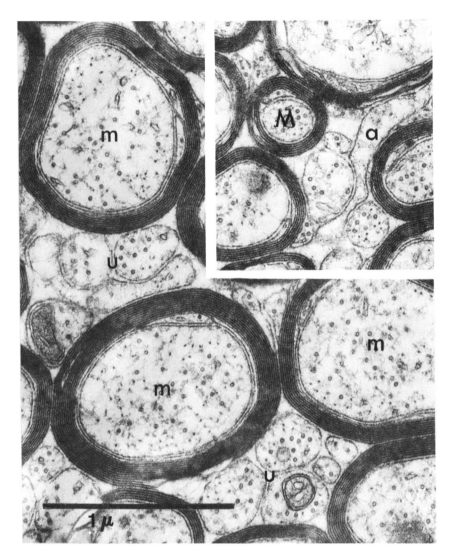

Figure 3.3 Electron micrograph of transverse sections of myelinated (m) and unmyelinated (u) axons in the splenium of rabbit corpus callosum; a,astrocytic process [from H.A. Waxman and H.A. Swadlow, *Progr. Neurobiol.* 8:297 (1977); © 1977 by Pergamon Press].

gonic. The production and consumption of heat probably depends on the movements of calcium, potassium and sodium ions. Keynes and Ritchie (1970) measured the heat released by the replacement of calcium for potassium in exchange resins and found their value of 2.7 kcal/mole to be similar to the heat evolved during the excitation.

The transmission of the nerve impulse activates the sodium pump to restore the hyperpolarized state. This mechanism requires energy. Thus, the activity of the pump is associated with a metabolic increment that involves glycolysis and respiration. The utilization of ATP associated with cation transport can be measured directly (Baker and Connelly, 1966). In nerve fibers, there is a quantitative relationship between sodium extrusion and oxygen consumption, as well as with high-energy phosphate utilization. It is postulated that ATP is also used to maintain a difference in specificity of the sodium-preferring site at the inner surface of the neuronal membrane and of the potassium-preferring site at the outer surface of the membrane.

The conduction velocity of the nerve impulse is partly dependent upon the presence or absence of myelin. A myelinated axon is depolarized only at the nodes of Ranvier, which contain a large number of sodium and potassium channels, making for a more rapid passage of ions and a faster potential shift at these points. The velocity also depends upon the fiber diameter. And, it has been found that the spike duration, the rise- and fall-times of the axon potential, the duration of the refractory period and the internodal conduction time all vary systematically with the diameter of the fiber (Swadlow and Waxman, 1976). While the thickest fibers show the greatest speed of conduction, this relationship is not linear, but has been calculated to have a logarithmic character. Keeping this in mind, it is interesting to note that in the central nervous system, most fibers are relatively thin. The majority in the major tracts are less than 3 μm thick. In the pyramidal tract, about 50% of the myelinated fibers are less than 1 μm thick, and only 6-9% have a diameter over 4 μm (Hildebrandt and Skoglund, 1971). The smallest myelinated fibers in the CNS are about 0.2 μm in diameter. These findings indicate that the overall conduction of impulses within the central nervous system tends to be at the slow end of the spectrum. Moreover, up to 50% of all fibers in central pathways are not myelinated. In the splenium of the corpus callosum, about 45% of the constituent fibers are nonmyelinated, and their diameter varies between 0.08 μm and 0.6 μm (Fig. 3.3). Also, most axons in the dorsal funiculus of the spinal cord are not myelinated (Langford and Coggeshall, 1981). Why these nonmyelinated, thin fibers are present is not known.

The passage of the action potential along a CNS axon is accompanied by a refractory period which can last up to 2msec. It is a time during which the nerve fiber is less excitable. But, the refractory stage is soon followed by a supernormal period that is characterized by an increased susceptibility to excitation and an increase in conduction velocity. In some nerve fibers, the supernormal period is, in turn, followed by a contrasting subnormal stage, having a lowered excitability and a slower conduction velocity (Waxman and Swadlow, 1977). These findings show that the conduction velocity is not invariant, but may depend upon the axon's immediate prior history of activity. Thus, the previous generation of nerve impulses may be important in the processing of subsequent neural information, because alterations in the conduction velocity of the fiber will modify the spatial distribution of impulses. And, this variation in velocity may even occur within the branches of a single axon.

The changes in conduction velocity may depend upon either a direct functional modification of membrane proteins or, more simply, upon the ionic composition of the extracellular fluid which would alter the behavior of proteins in the membrane. Early work by Hodgkin and Katz (1949) demonstrated that a decrease of the sodium level in the extracellular fluid lowered nerve fiber conduction velocity. This finding has since been confirmed for both nonmyelinated and myelinated fibers. And, this change in conduction velocity varies approximately with the logarithm of the extracellular sodium concentration (Colquhoun and Ritchie, 1972; Hardy, 1973).

Chapter 4

Synaptic Transmission

As discussed in the preceding chapters, the passage of the nerve impulse along the axon is influenced by the nature of the ionic environment and the previous history of the axon. This can also be true for several other parts of the nerve cell, such as the plasma and dendritic membranes and the axon hillock. But, it is the synapse that is probably the most plastic and variably responsive part of the neuron, so much so that the proposal by Tanzi in 1893 that learning is a synaptic event still remains an acceptable basis for hypotheses of neural plasticity.

Any examination of synaptic plasticity and those processes which contribute to the phenomenon first requires some familiarity with basic synaptic morphology and physiology.

ELECTROTONIC COMMUNICATION BETWEEN NEURONS

The passage of the nerve impulse from one cell to another may occur by either chemical or electrical means. Electrical transmission in the mammalian central nervous system involves a direct spread of currents to an adjoining neuron over a low resistance junction between the two cells. Between dendrites, this electrotonic form of transmission is an event that permits a rapid transfer of excitation through a group of neurons which are then able to act simultaneously. The activity of a command pacemaker cell may be rapidly transmitted to an effector organ by means of neighboring, electrotonically coupled cells. Thus, motoneurons controlling fin movement in some species of fish (hatchetfish, *Gastropelecus*) are coupled electrically (Auerbach and Bennet, 1969). Also, synchronously active effector organs, such as the electric organ of *Torpedo californica*, are controlled by neurons joined by electrotonic junctions.

It had first been believed that these junctions in a population of neurons had only an equalizing function and did not play an important role in the delicate functioning of the nervous system. This is not necessarily true. Kawato *et al.* (1979) have even described a neuronal model wherein the

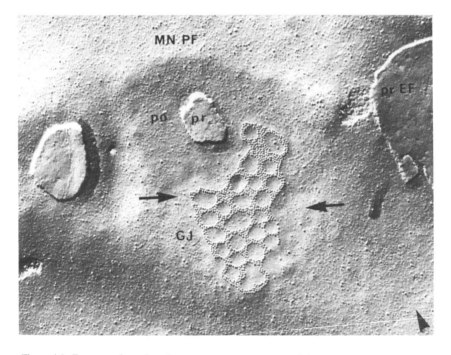

Figure 4.1 Fenestrated gap junction on a motorneuron soma of the membrane. MNPF, P-face of the membrane; GJ, gap junction; Po, Pr, membrane leaflets belonging to the postsynaptic and presynaptic membranes, respectively [from R. Taugner, U. Sonnhof, D.W. Richter and A. Schiller, *Cell Tiss. Res.* 193:61 (1978); © 1978 by Springer Verlag].

synchronous or alternating oscillation of two neurons could generate a rhythmic pattern of activity.

Ultrastructurally, the junctions between neurons which allow the passage of electrical current resemble the gap junctions previously described between epithelial cells (Farquhar and Palade, 1965). These gap junctions (Fig. 4.1) have been identified as the morphological substrate of low-resistance electrical pathways. According to Payton et al. (1969), there are channels in the tight junctions that connect the cytoplasm of the opposed cells (Fig. 4.2), allowing the passage of some ions and smaller molecules as sucrose. These junctions have been studied by an injection of a fluorescent dye, such as Lucifer Yellow CH, into single neurons. If a gap junction is present, it results in the staining of more than one cell. The presence of these junctions essentially means that the functional compartmental unit for some smaller cytoplasmic molecules is not a single cell, but the entire cell ensemble (for review see Loewenstein, 1981).

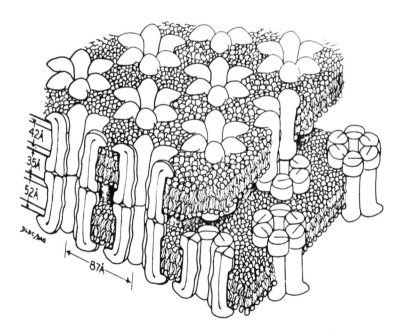

Figure 4.2 Schematic diagram of a gap junction (electrical synapse). Channel walls are composed of protein subunits which span the lipid bilayer of each plasma membrane [from L. Makowski, D.L.D. Caspar, W.C. Phillips, D.A. Goodenough, *J. Cell Biol.* 74:629 (1977); © 1977 by Rockefeller University Press].

Electrotonic synapses have been demonstrated in many areas of the mammalian central nervous system, but tend to be more frequently seen early in development (Pannese et al., 1977). About 10% of the neurons in the mesencephalic nucleus of the rat trigeminal nerve are coupled electrically. Other examples of this coupling have been found in the rat vestibular Deiters' nucleus (Korn et al., 1973) and in the inferior olive. Dye-coupled, vertically organized, neuronal aggregates have been detected in the superficial layers of guinea pig neocortex (Gutnick and Prince, 1981). Electrophysiological evidence has shown that these aggregates are able to interact electrotonically. MacVicar and Dudek (1980) found similarly coupled cells in the CA3 field of the hippocampus, while Andrew et al. (1981) were able to detect dye-coupling between neuroendocrine cells of the rat hypothalamus which terminate in the posterior pituitary.

Both depolarization and hyperpolarization may be transmitted, although somewhat attenuated, from one cell to another. If one cell is less depolarized than the other, it draws the current from the second cell and, in so doing, inhibits it.

Electrotonic junctions may be involved in the control of the transmission of chemical excitation from one neuron to another. An indication of this possibility was provided by Waziri in 1977. In the abdominal ganglion of Aplysia, the L1 neuron is electrotonically coupled with the L2 neuron. When L2 is depolarized, the amplitude of the excitatory postsynaptic potentials produced by different branches of L1 increases. A hyperpolarization of L2 has an opposite effect. The electrically coupled neuron may, therefore, serve an integrative role in the modulation of the efficacy of another neuron.

Electrotonic coupling may vary with time, and its efficacy probably depends on the concurrent activity of chemical synapses affecting the same neuron. Thus, neurons may fire simultaneously with others under certain circumstances and asynchronously under others (Bennet, 1970). The mutual effect of electrotonic and chemical synapses may be an important regulatory factor in the control of the activity of many areas of the central nervous system.

Most electrotonic junctions behave as fixed resistances, connecting coupled cells and transmitting current equally in both directions. However, in a few instances, they are able to rectify the current, and conduct in a single direction only. Furshpan and Potter (1959) described a one-way type of electrotonic transmission from the lateral giant fiber to the giant motor fiber of the crayfish. When the potential in the prejunctional lateral fiber is positive relative to the postjunctional fiber, the junctional resistance is high, but the electronegativity is transferred to the neighboring giant motor fiber. This situation favors orthodromic transmission over the antidromic direction.

These rectifying junctions appear morphologically similar to the more common bidirectional electrotonic junctions. However, Hanna *et al.* (1978) have observed some structural differences in them. They reported the presence of small vesicles in the prejunctional area, along with a mosaic of intramembranous particles distributed throughout the junction.

In addition to the existance of gap junctions between neurons, there does appear a corresponding interglial connection between astrocytes. In the superior cervical ganglion, these junctions are as plentiful as synapses (Tamarind and Quillam, 1971).

Some electrotonic junctions have heterogeneous characteristics. The gap junctions on the surface of the frog spinal motoneurons, for example, have areas resembling a chemical synapse, with synaptic vesicles and a thickening of the cell membrane. Such a structural heterology could suggest the existence of mixed synapses in the central nervous system (Sonnhof *et al.*, 1977).

THE STRUCTURE OF CHEMICAL SYNAPSES

A chemical synapse is characterized by the transfer of information in the form of a chemical transmitter substance from a nerve cell to a target cell. Morphologically, it is composed of a nerve ending (terminal bouton), containing a cluster of small vesicles and one or more mitochondria, that is attached to the outer membrane of an adjoining cell (Fig. 4.3). The 150-200 Angstrom gap between these structures is the synaptic cleft. There are membrane thickenings on both sides of the synaptic cleft that contain attached formations of electron microscopically dense material.

Most synapses are located on dendrites of the postsynaptic cell (axo-dendritic synapses) or on the cell body (axo-somatic synapses). Axo-axonal synapses, often found in sensory systems, are less frequently seen and consist of nerve terminals that are either attached to the terminal segment of the axon, or to its initial segment. The terminal is usually attached to the node of Ranvier. Somato-somatic, somato-dendritic, dendro-somatic and dendro-dendritic synapses have also been identified in brains of various vertebrates. Bjorklund and Lindvall (1975), among others, postulated a dendro-axonic form of transmission that has since been demonstrated by McGeer *et al.* (1979). This would mean that at times the functional connection between neurons could be in both directions.

The synaptic contacts of two dendrites may be reciprocal. The chemical transmission in these dendro-dendritic synapses may take place without the generation of a nerve impulse in the presynaptic area. The amount of transmitter released is then controlled by a graded polarization of the presynaptic site of the synapse (Raper, 1979).

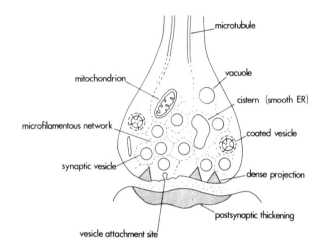

Figure 4.3 The presynaptic terminal of a central synapse with its major components [from D.G. Jones, *American Scientist* 69:200 (1981); © 1981 by Sigma Xi, The Scientific Research Society of North America].

The presynaptic area of the synapse is characterized by an electron dense network that includes synaptic vesicles. Jones *et al.* (1976) proposed a "vesicle network coincidence model" of synaptic structure based upon an interpretation of electron photomicrograms. The presynaptic grid appears to be attached to the inner surface of the presynaptic membrane by small pyramids on roughly hexagonal bases. These dense bases are arranged at the points of the triangular structure, with asymmetric hexagons in between. In the centers of the hexagons, the cell membrane is much thinner, and it is at these points, according to Akert *et al.* (1977), that synaptic vesicles are most likely positioned. However, the size of this space seems too restricted to permit direct vesicle-membrane contact to occur. The spiny tops of the pyramids are attached to a network of fine filaments, about 40-60A in diameter, forming a three-dimensional polygonal network with enmeshed synaptic vesicles and mitochondria that pervades the entire synaptic bag. This network is thought to be a derivation of the external coat of the vesicle (Jones, 1976).

The synaptic vesicles, containing the neurotransmitters and the various enzymes necessary for their synthesis, are universally present in synaptic bulbs. The vesicles are variable in size, shape and electron opacity. They are formed in the perikarya near the Golgi apparatus and are axonally transported to the terminal boutons.

Nerve endings also contain mitochondria, which serve as a source of energy for the synapse. Many synaptic boutons contain only one mitochondrion that has been described as being large, horseshoe-shaped, and flanked by an arc of several microtubules (Chan and Bunt, 1978).

The cleft region between the pre- and postsynaptic membranes is actually an electron dense area that contains numerous parallel intersynaptic filaments. These filaments, formed by glycoproteins and mucopolysaccharides, securely bind the synaptic membranes together, making the structure resistant to separation by homogenization and centrifugation. Such structural rigidity has permitted the separation of the nerve endings (often with attached postsynaptic membrane) from the rest of the brain homogenate. In these preparations, the nerve ending has become a discrete vesicle-filled body that is referred to as a synaptosome.

Under the electron microscope, the postsynaptic area of the neuronal membrane is thickened as a postsynaptic density (PSD) that is formed by a network of thin fibers, the postsynaptic web. The membrane also contains subjunctional bodies with a central core and lattice elements extending from it to neighboring subjunctional bodies and to the postsynaptic membrane thickening (Jones, 1976; Gulley et al., 1977). These PSDs exhibit such activity as γ-aminobutyric acid receptor-like binding (Matus et al., 1981) and protein kinase-catalyzed phosphorylation (Ng and Matus, 1979; Ueda et al., 1979), leading to some speculation that they may serve as a framework for the assembly and modification of transmitter receptor complexes.

FUNCTION OF THE SYNAPSE

The transmission of excitation from one nerve cell to another is divisible into several events. The arrival of the action potential into the terminal bouton causes a depolarization and, in doing so, induces the release of the chemical neurotransmitter into the synaptic gap. The mechanism by which this release occurs is not yet that well understood, but obviously requires a coupling of the electrical stimulus to the secretion of the transmitter. There are exceptions, however. Some neurons do not produce action potentials, and such non-spiking cells release neurotransmitters as a continuously graded function of the presynaptic voltage (Ripley et al., 1968). Graubard et al. (1980) have also reported that some spiking neurons (in lobster stomatogastric ganglia) are additionally capable of responding in this way.

The depolarization of the nerve ending upon the arrival of the action potential is initiated by the opening of the sodium channels and is rapidly followed by an increased permeability of the calcium channels. Although sodium ions are the first to enter the terminal, this event is probably not essential to transmitter release. A key role in the excitation-secretion coupling does belong to the movement of calcium ions. In this context, its function is actually a specialized case of a generally valid effect of the calcium ions upon the secretory or metabolic activity of many types of cells. For example, insulin secretion by the pancreatic islet cells, histamine release by the mast cells, human lymphocyte transformation or muscle contraction are all dependent upon extracellular calcium.

The movement of calcium into the nerve ending during synaptic transmission has been directly demonstrated by the use of the drug chlortetracycline, which in the presence of calcium ions exhibits a detectable fluorescence (Schaffer and Olson, 1976). In the terminal bouton, the ion

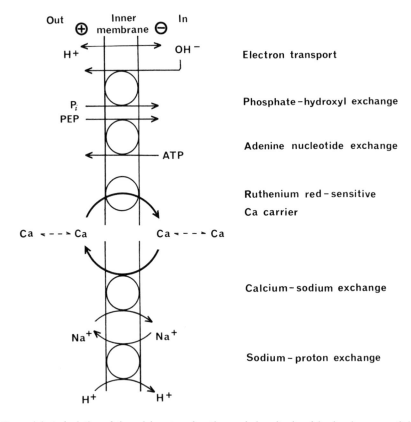

Figure 4.4 A depiction of the calcium translocation cycle in mitochondria showing some of the metabolite exchange systems located in the inner membrane which influence calcium ion dynamics [from F.L. Bygrave, *Biol. Rev.* 53:43 (1978); © 1978 by Cambridge University Press].

causes the release of the neurotransmitter into the synaptic gap by some yet poorly understood process. This relationship may have something to do with the stimulatory effect of calcium upon the phosphorylation of a number of endogenous proteins (see Chapter 15).

The level of intracellular calcium determines in a linear fashion both the amount of neurotransmitter that is released (and thus the magnitude of the postsynaptic potential) and the frequency of spontaneous miniature excitatory postsynaptic potentials (Llinas *et al.*, 1981). The ion is also able to bind to the synaptosomal membrane and, in the process, causes conformational changes in it. It appears that the ion is bound to several membrane components, including the sialic acid portions of the glycoprotein and ganglioside oligosaccharide chains (see Chapter 2).

Calcium is kept near the outer surface of the cell membranes by an external transport system which somehow channels the ions toward the cells, in a direction opposite to that of the membrane calcium pump. Such a system maintains a high concentration of these ions immediately external to the membrane (Hajdu and Leonard, 1976). The level of extracellular calcium therefore governs the amplitude and duration of the postsynaptic potentials (Parnas and Segel, 1981).

The termination of calcium action is a function of a number of different events. It has been found that during stimulation of the nerve endings, synaptic mitochondria accumulate increased amounts of calcium (Blaustein, 1971). Inhibitors of both oxidative phosphorylation and the electron transport chain block this accumulation and cause an increase in the frequency of the miniature excitatory postsynaptic potentials. This relationship suggests that the mitochondria may influence synaptic activity by participating in the regulation of intracellular free calcium (Fig. 4.4).

In the brain, as compared to other tissues such as the heart, the mitochondria have been reported to possess an increased capacity to accumulate calcium (Nicholls, 1978). The calcium-binding component is a glycoprotein that is present in both the inner and outer mitochondrial membranes. The binding capacity of this protein, then, represents a rate-limiting step in the efflux of calcium from the mitochondrion.

In addition to a mitochondrial uptake, calcium ions can be taken into other vesicular components of the synaptic region. The endoplasmic reticulum may also act as an intrasynaptosomal calcium regulator (Blaustein *et al.*, 1978, 1978a), although a major role for them in such regulation has been disputed (Nicholls and Akerman, 1981).

Calcium ions are also subject to extrusion from the cells. This membrane transport system is linked to Ca^{2+}, Mg^{2+} - activated adenosinetriphosphatase, whose activity in mammalian synaptic membranes is quite high. Here, ATP is required more as an enzymatic modulator than as an energy source. The transport requires the presence of external sodium or external calcium in association with another alkali metal ion. Calcium is then expelled from the cell by an exchange for sodium or for the alkali metal. It seems likely that three sodium ions are exchanged for every calcium ion (Blaustein, 1971). A reduction of extracellular sodium would consequently lead to a coordinate drop in the calcium efflux.

The contents of the synaptic vesicles are thought to be released from the nerve endings by a process called exocytosis. The vesicles approach the cell membrane and attach to it, then open to the outside to allow their contents (the neurotransmitter and enzymes, among other substances) to diffuse out. This "vesicular hypothesis" of Del Castillo and Katz (1957) had not been seriously challenged for a number of years. However, exocytosis of synaptic vesicles is actually too slow a process to be compatible with what is known about synaptic transmission (Llinas, 1977; Tauc, 1979). Moreover, synapses within the developing embryo are capable of transmitting nerve impulses at a stage when they still lack synaptic vesicles (Landmesser and Pilar, 1972). Thus, although exocytosis of synaptic vesicles has been observed, its function may not necessarily relate to synaptic transmission, but possibly to something like the excretion of catabolites and extraneous ions.

Some more recent observations suggest that vesicles are not the only source of released neurotransmitter, but that free neurotransmitter in the synaptosomal cytoplasm also may be released through a specific channel. For the amino acid neurotransmitters, which are primarily cytoplasmic, such a mechanism has been acknowledged for some time. It is the release of

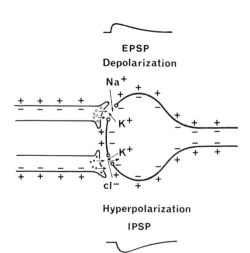

Figure 4.5 Generation of the excitatory and inhibitory postsynaptic potentials.

acetylcholine and the catecholamines which was considered to involve exclusively an exocytotic process. Using the neuromuscular junction, it has been found that acetylcholine is present in the cytoplasm of the nerve ending in a relatively high concentration. It is this cytoplasmic acetylcholine, and not that in the vesicles which is renewed during stimulation (Dunant *et al.*, 1980). Moreover, the enzymatic destruction of cytoplasmic acetylcholine will block synaptic transmission (Tauc, 1979). The finding that a potassium-induced release of neurotransmitter (mimicking the depolarization by an action potential) is only partially dependent upon calcium (Katz *et al.*, 1969; Redburn *et al.*, 1976) also indicates the presence of more than one neurotransmitter pool. While the calcium-dependent, vesicular pool would employ an exocytotic mechanism for its release, the liberation of transmitter from the cytoplasm may involve membrane transport processes (Haycock *et al.*, 1978) and be calcium- and voltage-independent (O'Fallon *et al.*, 1981).

After its release, the neurotransmitter diffuses across the cleft to the postsynaptic membrane and combines there with its receptor. The event triggers electrical changes in the postsynaptic membrane which are able to spread throughout the postsynaptic cell. These changes (see Fig. 4.5) are dependent upon movements of the ions across the postsynaptic membrane and are characterized by either depolarization (excitatory postsynaptic potential, EPSP) or hyperpolarization (inhibitory postsynaptic potential, IPSP).

In the meantime, the neurotransmitter is displaced either by enzymatic degradation or by a reabsorption back into the terminal bouton or into neighboring glial cells. The synapse is then prepared for the arrival of a new nerve impulse. The transport of the neurotransmitter back into the synaptic bouton is an active process that is dependent upon the energy supply. In most nerve endings, there are typically two such transport systems present in the presynaptic membrane, a high affinity and a low affinity system. It appears that the latter mechanism requires the presence of specific non-glycoprotein presynaptic receptors (Wang *et al.*, 1976) and is probably important in the feedback control of neurotransmitter synthesis.

Neurotransmitters may also be released from the neuron at non-synaptic points. Varicosities of nerve fibers, for example, contain large numbers of synaptic vesicles, as do the gemmules of internal granule cells of the olfactory bulb, where synapses are scarce. These neurotransmitters probably act at non-synaptic membranes (Ramon-Moliner, 1977).

The synthesis of the neurotransmitters, which is often a determining element in the activity of the central functional systems, is dependent upon a number of different factors that will be discussed in the succeeding chapters, including the activity of rate-limiting enzymes and the availability of precursor substances.

NEUROTRANSMITTERS

Of the two modes of intercellular passage taken by the nervous impulse in the central nervous system, chemical transmission appears to be the most prevalent. A host of known or strongly suspected neurotransmitter substances has been described. Along with acetylcholine, the catecholamines, and serotonin (5-hydroxytryptamine), the list includes histamine and the amino acids, glutamic acid, glycine, and γ-aminobutyric acid.

Substances that are normally not considered to be neurotransmitters can also, in certain cases, influence the rate of neuronal discharge. These substances have been termed neuromodulators, and the prostaglandins and hormones such as corticosterone are among the most notable examples. They are sometimes not synthesized within the presynaptic element, or even within nervous tissue, but they are able to affect the release of the neurotransmitters. These neuromodulators may interact with the postsynaptic neurotransmitter receptor or some other functional components of the postsynaptic membrane and modify their excitability.

The classification of a substance as either a transmitter or a modulator is not as clearcut a task as it may sound. For example, a growing number of neuronally active brain peptides have been labeled by some researchers as neurotransmitters, while others have considered them to be neuromodulators. Elliott and Barchas (1980) have offered for use the generic term neuroregulator, under which the two categories would fall. Neuromodulatory substances would then be further divided into synaptic or hormonal subclasses, depending upon whether their modes of action are local at the synapse or involve modulatory effects far from the site of release. But, the term "modulator" has been used rather loosely in the literature, and perhaps, as Dismukes (1979) suggests, there is presently little advantage in attempting to distinguish them from transmitters.

In 1966, Werman suggested the following criteria as a basis for determining whether a substance functions as a chemical neurotransmitter:

(1) It must be present in those neurons from which it is released.
(2) These neurons must contain the enzymes necessary for the production and release of the transmitter, as well as its precursors and metabolic intermediaries.
(3) The systems for the inactivation and reuptake of the transmitter must be present both in the target neuron and in the neuron that secretes the transmitter.
(4) During stimulation, the substance must be released from the nerve ending.
(5) When applied to the postsynaptic cell, it must produce the same effect as the natural transmitter.

(6) Pharmacological agents should interact with the neurotransmitter and with synaptic transmission in the same way.

For most neurotransmitters, it is impossible to satisfy all of these requirements. The term "putative neurotransmitter" is then applied to these substances. However, in light of the rapidly paced identification of large numbers of biologically active chemicals in the brain and our growing understanding of the nature of chemical transmission at the synapse, Werman's list of criteria may very well require some modification if it is to serve as a useful means of classification.

It had been a widely held belief (embodied as Dale's principle) that each neuron should only release a single chemical transmitter from any of its branches. For example, tissue cultures, each originating from individual neuroblastoma cells (a malignant tumor growth derived from immature neuroblast cells), were found to produce only a single type of neurotransmitter (Augusti-Tocco and Sato, 1969). Some strains were cholinergic; others were adrenergic. And, still others produced no transmitter whatsoever. None of the neuroblastoma cells was able to synthesize both acetylcholine and catecholamines, indicating that neurotransmitter synthesis is restricted in these cells. But, questions have arisen concerning validity of Dale's principle, since neurosecretory cells, for instance, are capable of secreting both a transmitter and a hormone (Burnstock, 1976). Moreover, there have been some examples of the presence of two neurotransmitters in a single neuron, although these have not yet been adequately confirmed (Hanley *et al.*, 1974). In fairness to Dale, the idea of the "chemical unity of the neuron" was presented in the mid 1930's as little more than an organization of material available at the time. The canonization is attributable to others, with his statements later being given a status unwarranted by the data.

In addition to their being discharged from the terminal region in response to the arrival of a nerve impulse, the neurotransmitters undergo a continuous spontaneous discharge. In between impulses, small amounts of a neurotransmitter enter the cleft, causing minute excitations of the postsynaptic membrane and minor fluctuations of the electrical potential. These latter changes, known as miniature postsynaptic potentials (m.p.p.), were first detected at the neuromuscular junction, but have also been found to exist in the CNS. While most researchers have described excitatory potentials, Alger and Nicoll (1980) reported the presence of miniature inhibitory potentials in the hippocampus.

It is believed that this potential shift is attributable to the release of a single "packet" of neurotransmitter, which in the neuromuscular junction has been calculated to be about 100,000 molecules of acetylcholine. In the central nervous system, the postsynaptic potentials responding to the release of the neurotransmitter also show statistical fluctuations in amplitude. These fluctuations are step-like in nature, indicating that the transmitters may be released in such packets or "quanta". The exact nature of the quantum is still not clear. It may be the content of a single synaptic vesicle, or a single shutter action of the membrane channel through which the cytoplasmic neurotransmitter is discharged.

A "quantum" of a neurotransmitter is not a uniform amount of the chemical, and it does have subunits. Katz and Miledi (1965) reported that much smaller elementary effects can be detected in the postsynaptic membranes. They are 1000 fold smaller than the m.p.p., only fractions of a microvolt in amplitude. These effects are probably caused by a transient opening of a single ionic channel in the postsynaptic membrane by one or more transmitter molecules.

NEUROTRANSMITTER RECEPTORS

After the neurotransmitter is released, it diffuses across the synaptic cleft to be bound by the postsynaptic membrane. The particular receptor components of the postsynaptic membrane that bind the neurotransmitter appear to vary rather widely in their chemical composition.

The isolation and characterization of a number of receptors have revealed that they are not identical with either ion channels or with the neurotransmitter degrading enzymes. All receptors that have been studied were sensitive to degradation by trypsin and chymotrypsin, as well as by phospholipase A. Therefore, they are protein in nature and either have a lipidic component, or are functionally dependent on the neighboring lipid. Their sensitivity to the neurotransmitter varies according to the previous history of the neuron. A number of them have been identified as glycoproteins, while others are possibly gangliosides that function in association with proteins.

These receptors likely change their molecular conformation upon attachment of the neurotransmitter, resulting in the opening of the specific ionic channels. The ions rush into the cell (or out of it), causing a rapid depolarization or hyperpolarization of the postsynaptic membrane. These sudden changes in polarity are quickly brought to a halt as the transmitter is either biochemically degraded (as with acetylcholine) or actively transported away from the synaptic cleft (as with the catecholamines). Immediately thereafter, the membrane undergoes rapid repolarization, as the system of membrane pumps regains control of the ionic flow.

Following the prolonged administration of the neurotransmitter or its agonist, the receptor may be desensitized and the ionic channels closed. This desensitization is a very fast process, developing in a matter of seconds. It seems likely, therefore, that it is caused by a rapid conformational change in the receptor. Conversely, receptor sensitization is also possible, usually due to an absence of the neurotransmitter.

The depolarization of the postsynaptic membrane is synonymous with an excitatory postsynaptic potential (EPSP), while an inhibitory postsynaptic potential (IPSP) represents a membrane hyperpolarization. Typically, the duration of these potentials is quite short-lived, on the order of a few milliseconds. However, in some synapses, such as those on mammalian sympathetic ganglion cells, the time period is prolonged up to several minutes.

While most synapses only respond either in an excitatory or an inhibitory direction, some are subject to both depolarization and hyperpolarization. Accordingly, Wachtel and Kandel (1971) described an *Aplysia* cell in which acetylcholine produced EPSPs at low firing rates that were converted to IPSPs as the firing rate increased. The phenomenon is probably due to the presence of two separate acetylcholine receptors. One type would be excitatory, with a low threshold to the neurotransmitter, and would be desensitized at high rates of stimulation. The other type of receptor would be inhibitory, with a higher threshold to acetylcholine.

Typically, those nerve cells subjected to a sufficient level of summated excitatory postsynaptic potentials are able to produce a nerve impulse. However, this rule is not inviolate. Some neurons, neural pacemakers for example, are able to generate nerve impulses spontaneously, without any EPSPs. These potentials are usually rhythmic in nature.

One of the best known of these pacemaker neurons is situated within the abdominal ganglion of *Aplysia californica*. Known as R15, this cell exhibits a bursting pattern of activity, in which groups of action potentials are separated by interburst hyperpolarizations. A number of reports (e.g., Smith *et al.*, 1975; Carnevale and Wachter, 1980) have indicated that the rhythmic depolarizations of R15 are attributable to a slowly inactivating inward sodium current which appears to be under the influence of cyclic nucleotides (see Chapter 15).

The excitability of the neurons can also be lowered if the interior is made increasingly negative with respect to the exterior. In other words, the voltage change is driven in a direction opposite to that required to generate an impulse. This IPSP hyperpolarization occurs at particular chemical synapses in response to the release of an inhibitory transmitter substance. The mechanism is believed to involve an increase in the membrane permeability to potassium and chloride ions, but not to sodium. This selective increase in permeability would probably not result in any significant movement of chloride, since these ions are already distributed in equilibrium according to their electrochemical gradient. Potassium, however, would move to the outside of the neuron, causing a relative increase in internal negativity and pushing the membrane potential toward a value of -80 mV.

Just as local EPSPs can be spatially or temporally summated over the postsynaptic membrane, so can these inhibitory potentials. However, the overall change in the excitability of the neuron is not a straightforward subtractive situation - summated IPSPs from summated EPSPs. Rather, the neuron is able to simultaneously evaluate many inputs and generate spikes according to its innate and previously acquired characteristics and the ionic state of the membrane at the time.

The traditional concept of synaptic transmission has recently been complicated by a number of intriguing findings. In addition to "fast" excitatory and inhibitory postsynaptic potentials, "slow" potentials have been described which do not involve the opening of ionic channels (Kobayashi and Libet, 1968). They may even be associated with an increase in membrane resistance (Weight, 1974). These slow potentials may serve in the modulation of fast synaptic activity and could perhaps even alter the threshold for spike generation. Also, neurons may communicate with one another through neurotransmitters released from non-synaptic parts of the membrane, axonal varicosities and dendrites.

Neurons may additionally produce more than one neuronal agent, communicating by means of peptides, neurohormones, or even macromolecules carried across the membrane. While often ignored, these factors must bear consideration when one attempts to clarify the influence of brain chemistry on neuronal activity and behavior.

SYNAPTOSOMAL METABOLISM

Although the nerve endings are physically a part of the neuron and are dependent upon it for many metabolic functions, several characteristics of synaptosomal metabolism deserve attention. For example, respiration in synaptosomal mitochondria is stimulated by a high level of sodium ions, whereas added potassium is without effect (Verity, 1972). Electrical stimulation also increases respiration in the same way. The glucose and oxygen consumption of the synaptosomes and indeed their rate of energy metabolism depend upon their functional activity. Correspondingly, the ionic gradients across the synaptic membranes depend upon oxidations and the supply of energy.

Protein synthesis in synaptosomes is particularly important, although most synaptic proteins are carried from the perikaryon by the fast and slow phases of axonal transport (to be discussed in Chapter 16) or, possibly, produced in the surrounding glia and transported into the neuron (Lasek et al.,

1976; Gainer *et al.*, 1977). The amount of protein transported in the slow phase is much greater than in the fast phase, and these proteins are incorporated into the axolemma and the synaptic membranes. Synaptosomal protein synthesis is partly dependent upon the mitochondria and partly upon the synthesis of proteins in the cytoplasm and surface membrane. It is sensitive to the antibiotic chloramphenicol, but not to cycloheximide, an inhibitor of ribosomal protein synthesis, suggesting the involvement of RNA bound to the synaptosomal membrane (Shashoua, 1973).

Several proteins are specific for synaptosomes. Some of them are soluble, while others are bound to membranous synaptosomal components. Studies have revealed the presence of several prominent glycoproteins and lipoproteins, an ATP-binding protein (Abood and Matsubara, 1968) and S-100 protein. Synaptic proteins such as these could be functionally important, since they may not only be responsible for the transfer of excitation from one neuron to another, but could potentially underlie plastic changes in neuronal transmission. Their localization, physical characteristics, and possible functional involvement in neuronal physiology will be examined in greater detail in Chapter 14.

Chapter 5

The Blood-Brain Barrier and Extracellular Fluid

Prior discussions of the importance of transmembrane ion movements and neurotransmitter release for the normal activity of the nerve cell have concerned themselves primarily with the neuron itself and its relationship to adjoining neurons by virtue of interposed synaptic associations. While not specifically mentioning it, such discussions at the same time stress the importance of the brain's extracellular fluid space and its compositional stability.

THE BLOOD-BRAIN BARRIER

A number of factors contribute to maintaining the composition of the extracellular fluid, including the cellular metabolic activity and the filtration of both water and solutes from the choroid plexus and circulation. While small foreign molecules introduced into the circulation rapidly distribute themselves throughout the body's extracellular fluids, they are generally unable to penetrate the tissues of the brain. This blood-brain barrier (BBB) has been found to function over all anatomical regions of the central nervous system, except for small areas around the pituitary stalk, the preoptic recess and the area postrema beneath the floor of the 4th ventricle. The basis for this barrier appears to be embodied in the endothelial cells of the blood capillaries in the brain. Whereas normal capillaries permit the passage of small molecules through intercellular clefts and poorly defined fenestral membranes, brain capillaries have tight junctions between their endothelia and have no fenestral openings (Fig. 5.1). Also, it is possible that larger molecules may pass across the walls of normal capillaries within the numerous pinocytotic vesicles that have been observed. In the brain, these capillary vesicles are rarely reported.

The blood-brain barrier appears to be established during the critical phase of brain growth that is present around the time of birth in most species. In a very immature brain, the tight endothelial junctions are already quite complex, and the brain is partly protected against the entry of some substances.

There are at least two protective barriers between the circulation and the brain tissue: the blood-brain barrier and the blood-cerebrospinal fluid barrier. They are not functionally identical, since some substances penetrate more easily through the choroid plexus than through the brain capillaries. Also, neither is a fixed barrier. They can be influenced by the metabolic

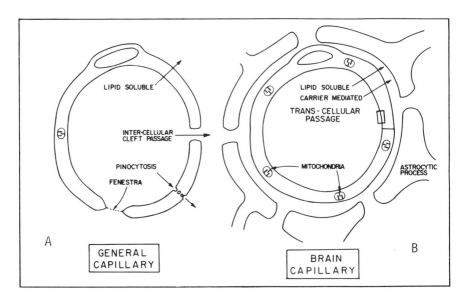

Figure 5.1 (A) The nonneural (general) capillary freely permeable to all small molecules and slightly permeable to large molecules. (B) In brain, there are no fenestrae, rare pinocytosis, and tight intercellular junctions [from W.H. Oldendorf, in: *The Nervous System,* D.B. Tower (Ed.), Vol. 1; © 1975 by Raven Press Publishers].

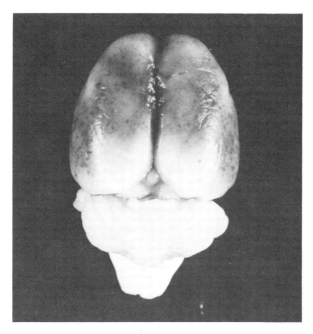

Figure 5.2 Disturbance of the blood-brain barrier following bicuculline-induced seizure activity. Dark areas: Protein extravasation into the cerebral tissue [from B. Johansson and B. Nilsson, *Acta Neuropath.* 38:153 (1977); © 1977 by Springer Verlag].

requirements of the brain, in addition to insults such as mechanical trauma, cerebral embolism, hypercapnia, hypoxia, extensive stress, radiation, electroconvulsive shock, explosive decompression, and various toxic substances. All of these conditions may alter the permeability of the barriers and, subsequently, the composition of the extracellular fluid. Marked shifts of this nature may lead to loss of consciousness and eventually to cerebral edema (Fig. 5.2).

Various substances are transported across the barriers either by passive diffusion or, more often, by a carrier-mediated or active form of transport. Even the movement of water across the capillary wall is limited.

Interposed between the blood and brain are several independent active transport systems for hexoses, monocarboxylic acids, nucleosides, purines, choline, and neutral, basic and acidic amino acids. These transport systems depend upon the activity of a limited number of carrier molecules, meaning that high levels of the transported substrate are able to saturate the system.

There is a non-saturable component in blood-brain transport systems, which probably reflects the activity of a low affinity, high capacity system, or simply the free diffusion of substances into the brain. One particular factor that relates to the rapidity with which a substance can penetrate the blood-brain barrier is its lipid solubility. More accurately, the penetration correlates with a partition coefficient derived from the relative solubility of substances in oil and water. A greater affinity for nonpolar solvents means a greater ability to cross the barrier. This lipid-mediated transport can occur at any place along the endothelial cell membrane.

The transport of substances to the brain is partly tied to function. Thus, during photic stimulation or following the administration of convulsive agents, the passage of substances into specific brain areas increases (Bondy and Purdy, 1974). This means that asymmetrical transport systems in the endothelia must adjust themselves to the functional requirements of that area.

Although they are difficult to demonstrate experimentally, active efflux systems also exist between the brain and circulatory system. They remove degraded substances or excess products of synthesis. These active systems impose a considerable energy demand on cerebral endothelia. This demand probably correlates with the high mitochondrial content of brain capillary endothelia.

BRAIN EXTRACELLULAR SPACE

In addition to its cellular and vascular components, brain tissue contains a certain amount of extracellular space, which is reported to be greater in gray matter than in white matter. For a time, the size and even the existence of this space had been a major point of contention within the neurosciences. Measurements using electrical impedence of the brain tissue and a number of marker substances thought to be unable to penetrate the cells to any significant extent have indicated that the extracellular space represents about 12-15% of the total brain volume. It also appears that in different species the size of the space varies as a function of the logarithm of the brain weight (Bourke *et al.*, 1965). However, in such marker studies none of these chemicals is without its drawbacks. Sodium, chloride, iodide, sulfate, thiocyanate and sucrose are either subject to rapid excretion from the tissue or do pass the cell membrane to an extent that would give high, inaccurate values. An exception appears to be inulin, which does provide a reliable measure, inasmuch as it does not return to the circulation following a subarachnoideal injection. Capillary endothelia have been found to be completely impermeable to it. It may, however, be taken up by neurons and glia. In rats, dogs, and cats, the inulin space varies between 17% and 23% of the total brain volume (Rall *et al.*, 1962). In the Rhesus monkey, extracellular space represents 18% of the gray matter volume and 15% of the white matter.

By simultaneously infusing various anions into the blood and the ventriculocisternal area, it is possible to define two compartments, one being the blood plus the brain and the second the cerebrospinal fluid plus the brain (Cheek and Holt, 1978). Because of the relatively narrow spaces and channels between the cells, which are about 100-150Å wide, the equilibration between these two compartments is relatively slow.

In addition, extracellular bulk flow has been demonstrated in the brain, but it is restricted by the tight junctions between cells which are ubiquitous within the central nervous system and by tortuous, narrow intercellular spaces. While some ions and substances simply just diffuse through the extracellular channels, the bulk flow is a common pathway for other ions, water, larger hormones, proteins and other nutrient molecules. Although the chemical composition of the brain's extracellular fluid is difficult to determine for obvious methodological reasons, it is likely closely related to the composition of the cerebrospinal fluid (CSF).

The sources of the brain's extracellular fluid are the intracerebral blood vessels, the choroid plexus and arachnoid membrane. From the choroid plexus, the fluid is filtered into the cerebral ventricles, where it slowly circulates. Part of it leaks into the brain tissue through ventricular walls and subarachnoid pial surfaces. Only about 30% comes from the blood capillaries within the nervous tissue.

THE CEREBROSPINAL FLUID

The production of the cerebrospinal fluid by cells of the choroid plexus is an active process, and therefore, its composition differs from that of the blood plasma ultrafiltrate. The CSF differs from the plasma mainly by its low concentration of proteins; the CSF normally contains only 0.5% of the plasma protein concentration. In addition to protein, the CSF contains lipids, glucose and several ions.

Mechanisms for active transport, facilitated diffusion and aqueous secretion are all present in the endothelia of the choroid plexus. CSF production takes place in the endothelia and depends primarily on the available energy supply, rather than on blood pressure or the pressure within the ventricles. The oxygen consumption of the choroid plexus is at least twice as high as that of the cerebral cortex (Thorn, 1973). This reflects a high consumption rate of energy-rich compounds necessary for the secretion.

The amount of CSF produced by the choroid plexus is controlled by sympathetic nerve fibers originating in the superior cervical ganglion. The stimulation of the sympathetic fibers reduces the production of the CSF (Lindvall et al., 1979), although it increases water permeability of intraparenchymal blood vessels, and, consequently, the amount of fluid filtered by them (Grubb *et al.*, 1978).

The majority of the cerebrospinal fluid (and the cerebral extracellular fluid that is slowly mixed with it) is removed via the arachnoid villi of the sagittal sinus into the venous blood. Some fluid additionally enters the lymphatic system. Although there is no true lymphatic system in the brain and retina, spaces around the blood vessels have lymphatic connections. These "prelymphatics" are also present in the adventitia of larger brain blood vessels and in the basement membrane region of the smaller ones. Therefore, lymphatic obstruction could conceivably be a cause of edema in the brain (lymphostatic encephalopathy). One of the major roles of this system is the removal of excess protein from the extracellular fluid of the brain. The question still remains (and this is true for other organs as well) as to the origin and function of this extracellular protein. Some protein is filtered from the blood vessels and some is actually transported between nerve cells, or between glia and neurons.

The brain extracellular fluid has several functions. It provides a stable internal milieu for the nerve cells, a necessary requirement for their proper functioning. This includes regulating the extracellular ionic concentrations of sodium, potassium, calcium, and magnesium, along with insuring a continuous supply of nutrients and the removal of metabolic products. This is so-called "sink action" of the cerebrospinal fluid.

The cerebrospinal fluid also maintains and protects, by its osmotic pressure, the cell volume of the neurons and glia, and the water content in them. One should not conclude, however, that these cells behave as passive bags filled with fluid. Cellular water retention does not depend only on an intact cell membrane, but also on a complex multilayer absorption of water and ions on proteins within the cells. The amount of water absorbed in this way is controlled in part by changes in the protein conformation (Ling and Walton, 1976). Therefore, although the brain is composed of approximately 80% water, much of it is osmotically unavailable (Nicholson, 1980). So, the brain cells would behave as imperfect osmometers, their cellular volumes being protected from changes in the osmolarity of the extracellular fluid by intracellular iso-osmotic regulation. For this reason, dramatic changes in brain function may occur in response to acute changes in plasma osmolarity. But, under chronic situations, brain function may be relatively spared, because intracellular osmotic pressure increases or decreases in parallel with osmotic changes in the plasma (Burton, 1973).

The regulation of the osmotic pressure of the extracellular fluid is related to the energy metabolism in the brain. Extracellular hypo-osmolarity, for example, depresses the oxidation of glucose to carbon dioxide, while hyper-osmolarity stimulates glucose oxidation (Fishman, *et al.*, 1977).

ACTIVITY OF NEUROGLIA

The stable ionic composition of the cerebral extracellular fluid is in part maintained by the active transport of ions to and from the neurons. Since the extracellular space in the gray matter of the brain is relatively small, a minor quantity of ions released from the neuron can substantially alter the ionic composition of the extracellular fluid and, consequently, the function of the neurons. In this regard, the quantity of potassium ions in the neighboring cleft could be doubled by the passage of one of two nerve impulses (Orkand, 1980).

Both the resting and action potentials are not actually very sensitive to the potassium level per se. Nerve impulse conduction is possible even up to an extracellular concentration of 20 μM, approximately twice as high as the upper limit of the physiologically normal range. However, the combination of changes in K^+ and Na^+ may block transmission in small unmyelinated axons (Orkand, 1980). The integrative activity of the neuron may also be affected. Hablitz and Lundervold (1981) reported that an increase in extracellular potassium which had little effect upon presynaptic potentials was capable of influencing excitatory postsynaptic potentials in the neurons of hippocampal area CA1. And Yarom and Spira (1982) found that action potentials generated in the giant interneurons within the cockroach nervous system were affected by alterations in the extracellular potassium concentration resulting from the firing a neighboring neuron.

While the functional importance of these changes is still not known and has been discounted (Somjen, 1975), it could be that the extracellular ion levels act as a form of communication channel between nearby cellular elements and that groups of neurons may consequently be able to influence one another (Nicholson, 1980). The data do, nevertheless, emphasize the necessity of a stable extracellular ionic environment.

Additional contributions to this homeostatic system are provided by a transport of ions, particularly potassium, into blood capillaries and into neuroglia. A quantity of ions is also removed by diffusion, but the decay time of the extracellular potassium level in the brain is about 100 times shorter than the time calculated for its diffusion (Vern et al., 1977; Cordingley and Somjen, 1978). Such diffusion is limited by the narrow spaces between cells and by the tight intercellular junctions.

Neuroglial cells are surrounded by a high resistance membrane. They contain a high level of potassium, about 100 mEq/liter, and their resting potential is greater than the neuronal resting potential, about 90mV (in *Necturus*) (Kuffler, 1967). Normally, the extracellular level of potassium ions in the brain is about 3 mEq/liter, but the impulse activity of the neurons and their axons (in particular, the non-myelinated axons) results in the release of potassium and its subsequent accumulation in the extracellular space. Thus, when the retina is illuminated, the level of potassium in the optic nerve, lateral geniculate body and visual cortex sharply increases (Singer and Lux, 1975). In the visual cortex, the level of extracellular potassium closely parallels the rate of firing of the neighboring cells. The increase lasts several seconds, before becoming normalized again (Singer and Lux, 1975). The local stimulation of various brain areas, along with spreading depression, arousal and epileptic seizures, also cause a large increase in extracellular potassium. And, evoked potentials and barbiturate spindles are associated with fluctuations of extracellular potassium. In these situations, the glial cells behave as precise potassium electrodes, altering their resting potential with changes in the level of extracellular potassium. An extracellular increase in this ion reduces their membrane potential. They are not excitable and cannot generate an action potential. But, the change in their membrane potential can be recorded and measured as a wave of gradual depolarization whose amplitude depends upon the decimal logarithm of the potassium concentration outside the cell. If potassium is manipulated between 3 and 40 mM, each ten-fold shift in the level of potassium induces a 38mV change in the membrane potential. Below 3 mM, glial hyperpolarization has been observed, but the slope is less steep than with high concentrations of potassium. In contrast, extracellular chloride and calcium are unable to alter the glial membrane potential.

The activity of the sodium pump within neuronal and glial membranes can lower the level of extracellular potassium below the normal level of 3 mM, causing a glial hyperpolarization.

The slow changes of the electrical potential in brain tissue recorded during neuronal activity therefore depend upon the levels of extracellular potassium and upon shifts in the polarization of the glial cell membrane. There are two distinctly different elevated levels of potassium. One, found *in vivo* during excitation and stimulus- and drug-induced seizures, has a maximum concentration of 10-12 mM and is associated with an increase in energy metabolism. This level is maintained by an active uptake mechanism which has been found to break down with an inadequate supply of oxygen in the tissue. As a result of this breakdown, another potassium level, above 20 mM, has been observed to occur during such conditions as spreading depression and hypoxia. In fact, levels of up to 90 mM can be reached during states of hypoxia. The levels of extracellular potassium are still adequately regulated even when the partial pressure of oxygen (pO_2) decreases to 20-23mm Hg.

The efflux of potassium from functioning cells is usually not accompanied by an increase in the ionic strength of the extracellular fluid, because calcium, sodium and chloride ions simultaneously enter the cells. On the contrary, the ionic strength of the extracellular fluid may even decrease (Kraig and Nicholson, 1978).

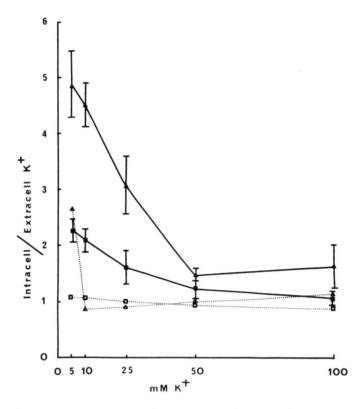

Figure 5.3 Effect of increasing external potassium concentration on the potassium accumulation of glial (triangles) and neuronal (squares) fractions; Ouabain 2 x 10^{-4} M - dotted lines; S.E.M. values indicated as vertical bars [from F.A. Henn, H. Haljamae and A. Hamberger, *Brain Res.* 43:437 (1972); © 1972 by Elsevier Publishing Company].

A high level of extracellular potassium also increases the oxygen consumption by cells, because the active transport of potassium into the cells requires energy (Fig. 5.3). This has been documented even in astrocytes cultivated *in vitro* (Schousboe *et al.*, 1970). Such a change in the energy consumption within brain cells has been demonstrated *in vivo* by a "nondestructive" optical method, involving a monitoring of the activity of mitochondrial oxidative enzymes in intact cerebral tissue. This spectrofluorometric method measures the fluorescence of intramitochondrial reduced nicotinamide-adenine-dinucleotide (NADH). When this substance is oxidized to NAD^+, the fluorescence of the tissue decreases. The oxidation of NADH to NAD^+ is induced by adenosine diphosphate, a product of the activity of membrane adenosinetriphosphatase. Thus, when the sodium-potassium exchange by the sodium pump requires more energy, the degradation of ATP to ADP is increased. ADP enters the mitochondria and activates the oxidation of NADH to NAD, a step which increases the oxygen consumption by the tissue (Lewis and Schuette, 1976). This process also corresponds to an elevation in glucose metabolism, which has been demonstrated to take place in leech and snail ganglia (Pentreath and Kai-Kai, 1982).

The extracellular concentration of calcium ions typically drops when neurons are active. From a baseline of 1.2 mM, the decrease is about 0.1-0.3 mM, a change that may also alter neuronal functioning (Llinas et al., 1979). Although there may additionally be effects that are attributable to shifts in extracellular chloride or sodium, the high levels of these ions in this space precludes, at least for the time being, any evaluation of the influence of minor fluctuations upon function.

The above relationship between neuronal activity and glial metabolism emphasizes the importance of normal glial functioning in brain activity. Long-lasting stimulation of brain tissue will activate the transport of potassium into glia. And, in 1974, Ransom showed that glial cells presumed to be present within an epileptic focus have an unusually high resting membrane potential, up to 105 mV, and a very intensive depolarization during seizures, on the average of 29 mV. These data indicate that during the intensive stimulation of nervous tissue, the removal of released potassium from the extracellular spaces undergoes a process of adaptation. The process could also be one of the mechanisms involved in long-lasting changes in the functional activity of the brain.

In addition to their role in the regulation of the extracellular ionic environment of neurons, the glia may be involved in the uptake from the extracellular space of certain amino acids having a possible neurotransmitter function. High-affinity glial transport systems have been reported for γ-aminobutyric acid (Henn and Hamberger, 1971), glutamate (Henn et al., 1972), and glycine (Henn, 1976). It is now beginning to appear that the astroglial membrane contains receptors for various drugs and neurotransmitters and that the binding of these substances may induce metabolic responses within the glial cell (Villegas, 1975; Henn and Henke, 1978; Henn and Henn, 1980).

The existence of these membrane receptors gives added importance to the relationship betwen glia and neurons. This is especially true since the great majority (possibly up to 90% or more) of the transmitter-containing axonal varicosities have been estimated to lack any synaptic contact with adjoining neurons (Tennyson et al., 1974; Descarries et al., 1977). The neurotransmitter liberated at these varicosities, then, might well bind to glial receptors and trigger various metabolic events within these cells. In short, the glia could be responsive to neuronal impulses and, through subsequent effects upon ionic and amino acid transport, might be capable of altering neuronal activity.

For a long time, it has been speculated that glia produced some sort of trophic factor (or factors) that was necessary for neuronal maintenance in the brain. But, it was not until 1980 that Banker was able to directly demonstrate the existence of such a factor. He found that astroglial cells in tissue culture released a substance into the culture medium which promoted the growth and prolonged the survival of the *in vitro* neurons. Thus, the glia have not only been found capable of altering neuronal functioning, but may serve to maintain the functional capacity of nerve cells as well.

Chapter 6

Synaptic Plasticity

The functional reorganization of neuronal networks likely involves two processes. One, a morphological restructuring of the neurons and their connections, will be explored in the succeeding chapter. The other process has been touched upon previously. It is an alteration in the efficacy of existing synaptic connections as the result of enduring changes in various synaptic events.

SYNAPTIC PLASTICITY AND LEARNING

A developing organism is initially endowed with a certain complement of genetically determined responses, from which it develops, through its own evolving experiential history, an immense spectrum of behaviors. But, as Hebb (1958) emphasized, the dichotomization of variables influencing development into hereditary and environmental is not a productive exercise. No response depends solely upon genetic factors. Attempts to calculate a proportional contribution of hereditary or environmental factors have been without success. In any case, behavioral changes obviously have an underlying physical basis.

The process of learning can be basically described as a behavioral adaptation that is related to previous experience. The question as to whether such a process involves some alteration in synaptic efficacy (a function of the EPSP amplitude and the responsiveness of the postsynaptic neuron) has often been posed in considerations of the nature of the biobehavioral linkage. The possibility has attracted considerable attention. Byrne (1979) has written:

"Indeed, a recurring problem with the cellular analysis of behaviour has been to determine quantitatively the causal contributions which individual neurons and their biophysical properties make to the behavioral response. Ultimately, one would like to know to what degree a specific neural circuit and its biophysical properties, proposed for a given behaviour, do actually account for that behaviour. Stated in a slightly different way, to what degree can the whole of a behaviour be fully described in terms of the sum of its neural components and their biophysical properties?"

At this point, for complex nervous systems, the problem posits little more than a rhetorical question. It is difficult to imagine that a behavior and its modification by experience are attributable primarily to changes within a single synapse or a single neuron. Large populations of cells are typically involved, with shifts in the efficacy of their numerous synapses likely occuring concurrently in both directions, toward their strengthening and attenuation. This would mean that during the process of learning, nervous transmission within many nerve cells and their connections would be inhibited (as a result of membrane hyperpolarizations), while the activity of many other cells would be promoted (by depolarizations).

The process of neuronal hyperpolarization that can follow a train of impulses has been often stressed as a important component of the learning process. This is a condition that has been observed to persist for several minutes after the original stimulation (Ritchie and Straub, 1956). It is generated by the activity of the electrogenic sodium pump and an increase in potassium conductance and is controlled by a calcium influx from the extracellular space. Gibbs and Ng (1979) believe that this process is somehow associated with the period of short-term memory and the successive labile phase of memory. The hyperpolarization has frequently been studied in hippocampus, where it may be associated with the process of long-term potentiation (Hotson and Prince, 1981).

The process of learning is not a uniform phenomenon. There is most likely more than one form of learning, and even the same behavior may be acquired through entirely different processes (Izquierdo and Elisabetsky, 1978). More than one system of storage and retrieval could exist, and individual components of a stored memory and the response it engenders may be acquired differently. Schneider (1975, 1977), for instance, demonstrated that a single avoidance trial leaves two separate memories, one for classically conditioned fear and another for instrumental inhibitory behavior. If our intent is to analyze the molecular mechanisms of behavior, learning and memory, this should be kept in mind.

Synaptic efficacy, which is probably closely related to the modification of behavior, is subject to large variations in different areas of the brain, in different neurons, and even in different synapses on the surface of a single neuron. The role of the synapse in the generation of the nerve impulse also varies according to its position on the neuronal surface. The synapses positioned near the axon hillock ("detonator synapses," according to Andersen and Lomo, 1966) are capable of more effectively eliciting a nerve impulse than synapses located on the tips of dendrites (intensifying synapses).

The handling of information is affected by the functional state of the brain, a term used to convey the existing conditions of excitation and inhibition of all brain neurons at any one point in time. These functional states represent a continuing series of adjustments in neuronal excitability and synaptic efficacy which are able to modify the strategies that the brain uses to process incoming information. They are determined by the interaction of a variety of factors that Koukkou and Lehmann (1980) have organized into 8 classes:

(1) The individual genetic composition.
(2) The particular stage of neural development, which provides age-specific variability.
(3) The functional plasticity of the brain during development, which contributes to the functional and structural shaping of the system.
(4) The motivational state, affected by the various biological drives, which channels behavior toward specific goals by setting priorities or prejudicing the context of particular types of incoming information.
(5) The availability of memory-stored information and related processing strategies, a factor which is closely associated with the motivational state.
(6) The environment, which can adjust the incoming information depending upon its momentary significance.
(7) Conditions of the metabolic/hormonal systems.
(8) Diseases or lesions of the brain which could possibly cause aberrant functional states.

The above factors, interacting with one another, act to continuously modify the functional state of the brain and shape the concurrent processes of learning and its associated purposeful behavior.

COMPLEX NATURE OF SYNAPTIC PLASTICITY

As described previously, synaptic activity is a complex physico-chemical process in which the components are precisely tuned to one another. If one postulates that experience alters synaptic effectiveness, then changes in all of these components must be taken into account. And, since different behavioral acts require the activity of pathways involving various neurotransmitters, functional changes in transmitter production, release and inactivation should be considered as well. Moreover, these changes depend upon a complex of biochemical mechanisms in both neurons and glia, including respiration, energy metabolism, protein and lipid synthesis and degradation. Thus, the study of synaptic plasticity necessarily requires an integration and interpretation of the many fragments of available information.

In the interest of fully exploring and characterizing a component of the learning process, research efforts have frequently been limited to the study of a single factor. There has appeared a tendency to focus, for example, upon the unique responsive nature of acetylcholine to observed behavioral change, or upon alterations in brain catecholamines, peptides, or protein synthesis. To a certain extent, such a restricted perspective has hindered to a proper understanding of the biochemical basis of behavior. While studies of this nature undoubtedly contribute valuable pieces to the assembly of the puzzle, the issue is not the choice of a single component upon which to focus, but a tendency of this component to be assigned a disproportionate importance in the overall process. All of the factors that are associated with brain plasticity must be taken under consideration for the phenomenon (or phenomena) to be understood. And, while a precise comprehensive theory of plasticity cannot yet be formulated, there can be at least a demonstration of the multiplicity of the factors involved and an attempt at some degree of integration. From this viewpoint, it is apparent that there does not have to exist a single change or process which is specific only to learning or memory storage. However, this does not mean to imply that a decision was made *a priori* to negate its existence completely. Instead, we found it preferable to conceptualize a chemistry of learning which is not predicated upon such an exclusive process, a concept which is still present in the literature (Rose, 1981).

A substantial body of evidence has shown that the activity of the synapse can increase or decrease, or the synaptic area may even become temporarily inactive. The synaptic activity within the central nervous system is electrophysiologically determined by the amplitude of the excitatory postsynaptic potential and the threshold firing level of the postsynaptic neuron.

On both a functional and structural level, alterations in synapses can be designated as either of short or long duration. The measure of such an alteration is the size and duration of the postsynaptic potential. Short-term functional changes involve the modification of synaptic excitability that occurs immediately following the passage of a single nerve impulse. Each impulse causes an immediate change in excitability that lasts about 2-6 msec and is primarily dependent upon movements of ions across the membrane of the synaptic knob. Repeated stimuli may alter the conductivity of the synapse for up to several minutes or even longer. While both a depression and a facilitation of synaptic transmission have been observed, the majority of cells are non-reactive in this regard. Boisacq-Schepens (1968), for example, found that only one cell in four reacts by a change in synaptic conductivity. Most subsequent studies have shown that there exist both modifiable and non-modifiable synapses.

Biochemical changes that are associated with an increase in synaptic activity have been extensively studied. Although they will also be discussed later in the book, an attempt has been made to present them here as they relate to the sequence of events at the synapse.

Each nerve impulse that reaches the synapse is able to leave a small amount of sodium or calcium ions inside the synaptic knob and, in so doing, can modify the resting membrane potentials and the response to subsequent nerve impulses. The efficacy of the synapse may therefore be altered by a repetition of nerve impulses, a phenomenon called posttetanic potentiation. The presence, extent and duration of this potentiation is itself affected by nerve fibers terminating presynaptically in an axo-axonal synapse.

An elevation in the levels of intracellular calcium tends to facilitate the process of synaptic transmission by causing an increase in the presynaptic release of the transmitter. Several authors, including Kuno (1973), feel that the efficacy of the synapse depends exclusively on the number of quanta of neurotransmitter or on the mean quantum content. The problem, however, appears to be more complex. Nevertheless, such an increase in neurotransmitter release undoubtedly does occur. For example, it has been documented in the case of the resting and evoked release of acetylcholine from hippocampus *in vitro,* where it is a factor in long-lasting synaptic potentiation (Skrede and Malthe-Sorensen, 1981).

An enhancement in the release of neurotransmitter in turn stimulates its own synthesis, so that a preferentially activated synapse produces and releases larger quantities of transmitter. An elevation in the amount of neurotransmitter that is released from the nerve ending first requires the presence of an adequate supply of precursor substances. In the case of acetylcholine, this would involve the active transport of choline, whereas the catecholamines and serotonin respectively require tyrosine and tryptophan.

An increase in synthesis also calls for a corresponding boost in the activity of the synthesizing enzymes. This activation is often due to the presence of "second messengers", such as calcium ions or cyclic adenosine monophosphate.

Cyclic AMP synthesis within the nerve endings is often triggered by neurotransmitters reacting with their presynaptic receptors. Thus, there exists specified feedback connection between neurotransmitter release and synthesis in the synaptic knob, one that will be explored in greater detail in Chapter 15.

The release of the neurotransmitter is followed by the activation of postsynaptic receptors. An elevation in the amount of neurotransmitter itself does not alter the synaptic activity for long. On the contrary, an increase in transmitter secretion causes a very rapid fall in the sensitivity of the receptor in the postsynaptic membrane. In contrast, the absence of the transmitter in the synapse results in receptor hypersensitivity. With this in mind, Gallego *et al.* (1979) speculated that a decrease in the neurotransmitter secretion, rather than an increase, is a process underlying synaptic plasticity and ultimately learning. Such a possibility would be difficult to support, since both a decrease and an increase in receptor sensitivity are reversible within fractions of a second. Also, if the synaptic efficacy (expressed as the amplitude, duration, and slope of increase of the postsynaptic potential) has to be continuously maintained at a higher level, it would require not only an increase in neurotransmitter synthesis and release, but an additional mechanism to protect the postsynaptic receptors against a change in sensitivity. The postsynaptic neuron may therefore respond to an increased amount of neurotransmitter in two ways: either by the presence or absence of a desensitization of its transmitter receptors. Desensitization is a rapid, active process which protects the postsynaptic cell against an overloading of synaptic input. The net effect of an elevation in the amount of transmitter would then be an unchanged or even lowered postsynaptic potential. The second situation, in which the sensitivity of the receptor does not fall (or may even show a rise), is followed by the generation of an augmented potential and/or by an increase in the probability of the cell firing. This is what occurs when the strength of the synapse increases.

Stabilization of the synaptic alteration is a complex process requiring several postsynaptic membrane components. It also involves a cooperation with other neurons and is directly or indirectly dependent upon many other events, such as alterations in membrane lipids, glycoproteins and phosphoproteins. One interesting possibility has been proposed by Baudry *et al.* (1980, 1981). They found that the binding of glutamate to hippocampal synaptic membranes is enhanced by calcium ions. This effect is partially irreversible and depends upon the stimulation of a membrane-associated thiol protease by calcium. Even in micromolar quantities the ions stimulated proteolysis. In this way, glutamate binding sites, previously inaccessible, become unmasked and able to bind the transmitter.

The fluidity of the postsynaptic membrane may also contribute to this phenomenon. Calcium ions, among their other functions, enhance the rigidity of the synaptic membranes. As a result of the changing ionic environment, each cell generates a small electrical field in its immediate space (for review see Adey, 1977), which may induce a segregation of the charged particles (Jaffe, 1977). These weak extracellular electric gradients could very possibly cause alterations in the binding of Ca^{2+} at the surface membrane (Kaczmarek and Adey, 1974), inducing short-lived shifts in membrane fluidity. Cuatrecasas (1974) has speculated that the fluidity of the membrane might allow a receptor-ligand complex to have a certain degree of lateral mobility. But, at least in mature neuromuscular synapses, acetylcholine receptors have been reported to be immobile (Axelrod et al., 1976; Heuser and Salpeter, 1979), possibly by virtue of an association with stable submembranous structures of the postsynaptic density. On the other hand, Blomberg et al. (1977) have suggested that movements of calcium ions could affect these relationships. Any such receptor effects may well involve the gangliosides. They have been implicated in membrane receptor activity and readily associate with divalent cations as calcium (see Chapter 2). Moreover, there has been some speculation (Tettamanti et al., 1980) that membrane gangliosides are able to form clusters, whose stability would depend upon the extracellular ionic environment. So, it could be that changes in the electric gradients that are associated with elevations in the impulse flow are followed by small redistributions in and/or conformational modifications of the surface receptors. The effects, if present, could contribute to any subsequent alterations in synaptic efficacy.

In emphasizing the potential importance of these ion/electrical gradients, Lazo et al. (1981) have suggested that they could function as an alternative to the second messenger activity of cyclic AMP (to be discussed in Chapter 15), or as a means by which the cAMP-synthesizing enzyme, adenylate cyclase, is regulated. These gradients, then, may exist as an additional mechanism for the transfer of information from one cell to another.

The concept of functional synaptic plasticity means that the excitability of the neuron can vary anywhere between zero [silent synapses (Aserinsky, 1961)] and a state wherein the cell generates a long series of spikes or fires completely spontaneously. The gradations within this range allow for an immense functional variability in networks of neurons.

Studies of simple systems have shown that the central nervous system contains neurons with intrinsically plastic properties, along with others that are not easily modified or perhaps are completely resistant to changes in their activity. It is quite possible that the normal functioning of the brain requires the presence both of neurons with plastic and non-plastic properties. Moreover, some neurons may even need protection from plastic changes, such as occur during habituation.

In *Aplysia* and other mollusks, so-called "command neurons" have recently come under scrutiny. These cells and their connections have been found to control specific behaviors and are well defined morphologically. They are hierarchically organized into a system which generates several classes of complex movement patterns. For example, the mollusk *Pleurobranchaea* has a rigidly hierarchical behavioral system in which feeding predominates over righting, withdrawal or copulation, but is subordinate to escape swimming (Fig. 6.1). However, there are times that this hierarchy is altered, as during the period of egg laying and immediately thereafter, when feeding is suppressed by a peptide hormone with a molecular weight of about 5000 daltons. But, the behavioral prepotence is not immutable; it also depends on the organisms's past experience and motivation and may be experimentally conditioned. Such conditioning involves a hyperpolarization of the command neurons, resulting in an inhibition of the particular behavior (Davis, 1979). This proces involves the participation of modulating nerve

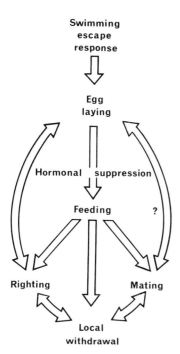

Figure 6.1 Behavioral hierarchy of the mollusk *Pleurobranchaea*. Unidirectional arrows signify the dominance of the behavior; bidirectional arrows signify mutual compatibility [redrawn from W.S. Davis, *Trends Neurosci.* 2:5 (1979); © 1979 by Elsevier/North-Holland Biomedical Press].

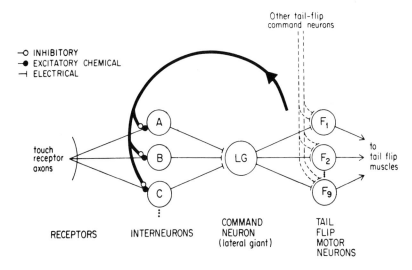

Figure 6.2 Crayfish lateral giant fiber escape circuit. The bold line indicates the pathway responsible for the protection phenomenon [from F.B. Krasne, *Brain Res.* 140:197 (1978); © 1978 by Elsevier/ North-Holland Biomedical Press].

cells, some of which have already been identified (Gillette *et al.*, 1978), that could participate along with the command neuron as components of feedback motor loops (Davis and Kovac, 1981).

The lateral giant neurons in the crayfish tail, which control tail flips (Fig. 6.2), can usually habituate. But, in constantly turbulent water, where tail flips are necessary for the maintenance of body position, the relevant command neurons must be shielded from habituation (Krasne, 1978). In this case, habituation is due to a depression of the initial synapses of the reflex arc, where the release of neurotransmitter from the presynaptic terminal is reduced. The process may be prevented presynaptically by the fibers from touch receptors.

Analogous command neurons are also present in mammals and even primates. There is evidence of their existence in the motor (Mountcastle *et al.*, 1975) and oculomotor systems (Mohler and Wurt, 1976). It is quite possible that an understanding of the mechanism of their selective adaptation may clarify some aspects of behavioral plasticity.

The adequacy of a response to a changing environment not only requires a plasticity of synaptic events, but also needs a system capable of "erasing" those plastic alterations. This would debias the synapses and nerve cells, freeing them for new input, and, ultimately, increase the storage capacity of the brain. Often, a brief period of hyperpolarization may return the neurons to their original, naive state.

It has also been postulated that a stabilization of synaptic changes takes place during sleep. It is possible that the synchronized EEG which is present during slow wave sleep serves this function, as there are waves of hyperpolarization passing through the nervous system. The generators of the slow rhythm are in the thalamus, and possibly the brain stem and orbital cortex. The slow EEG seen in sleep may be a response to a most acute need for a restoration of a brain carrying large amounts of new information (Glassman and Malamut, 1977).

Other plastic changes have to be retained. The stabilization of a synaptic alteration is also a complex process. In the brain, it could be associated with protein synthesis and its variations. Several authors have also related the stabilization to the activity of particular neuronal systems. Until the early seventies, there has been no direct evidence demonstrating that synapses in the brain could change their efficacy as a consequence of the passage of a train of impulses. But in 1973, Bliss and Lomo described long-lasting increases in synaptic efficacy within the rabbit hippocampus following repeated electrical stimulation of the perforant pathway. This pathway originates in the entorhinal cortex and terminates on the apical dendrites of the granule cells in the dentate area. Also, other pathways terminating in the hippocampus, such as the mossy fiber system or afferents from the septum have the same effect. A brief train causes a long-term potentiation (LTP) of hippocampal synapses without any accompanying change in overall excitability of the postsynaptic cells. It appears that only some synapses are affected. Thus, Levy and Steward (1979) found that while ipsilateral innervation from the entorhinal cortex induces LTP, contralateral innervation is without effect. It is possible that a critical number of synapses must be activated, otherwise, LTP cannot be sustained.

LTP is not a phenomenon that is exclusive to the hippocampus. It also has been detected in the rat superior cervical ganglion, implying that the process may exist as a more general feature of synaptic functioning (Brown and McAfee, 1982).

Long-term potentiation is a process which persists weeks, months, or might even be permanent, although it is initiated by a burst of impulses that may last only a few hundred milliseconds (Berger *et al.*, 1976). In this respect, it differs from post-tetanic potentiation which, in the past, had been considered a model of memory. But, post-tetanic potentiation usually continues for only minutes. A single nerve impulse can potentiate a response to a second stimulus, but this effect exponentially decreases within a period of 180 milliseconds. Pulse trains are able to induce a summation of this potentiation (Yamamoto *et al.*, 1980).

Further studies have shown that calcium ions are necessary for the initiation of LTP. The entry of calcium into nerve endings on the surface of the hippocampal neurons induces an after-hypopolarization and a long-lasting increase in potassium conductance of the surface membrane (Traub and Llinas, 1979). The ions enter the nerve terminals and activate phosphory-lase-β-kinase, which induces a phosphorylation of a single synaptic protein that resembles troponin T in its physico-chemical characteristics and molecular weight (40,000 daltons). LTP therefore appears to be associated with posttranslational alterations of proteins and with ionic movements. Protein synthesis is probably also involved, but only later.

It could be that this potentiation also modifies the number of synaptic receptors for neurotransmitters (Baudry and Lynch, 1981) and the dendritic spine morphology. Van Harreveld and Fifkova (1975) noted that stimulation of a perforant path results in a widening of the dendritic spines in the target area, and suggest that this morphological change is necessary for the long-lasting change in synaptic efficacy.

Additional factors which may affect neuronal plasticity include the possibility of extrasynaptic membrane changes, as a more rapid and less damped spreading of membrane depolarization and an increase in excitability of the area generating the action potentials. Such a membrane alteration, a reduction in an early voltage-dependent outward current of an identified neuron, has been documented in the central nervous system of the nudibranch mollusk *Hermissenda crassicornis* (Alkon *et al.*, 1982). Global membrane changes of this kind probably mediate mutual interactions of individual synapses, as well as the relationship between synaptic activity and the generation of the axon potential. Thus, Weight *et al.* (1979) found that long-lasting changes in the postsynaptic potential are capable of enhancing rapid EPSPs in another synapse of the same neuron. And, the generation of the action potential by the neuron can facilitate EPSPs triggered by its own synapses (Baranyi and Feher, 1981).

It can be said that each neuron has many unique biophysical properties. It may respond to stimulation with a single impulse or with a burst of impulses, or even with a long-lasting period of firing. These characteristics are not fixed, and in an examination of the origins of neuronal plasticity and its role in behavior, one must weigh factors such as these. This modulation of response to synaptic input is probably one of the important variables in neuronal function (Byrne, 1979).

The existence of widespread neuronal systems which control the plasticity of synaptic activity in the brain has to be taken into consideration when evaluating the functions of individual nerve cells. The brain is a highly organized and relatively stable structure wherein cells, assembled into systems, have specialized functions that depend upon the cooperation of other

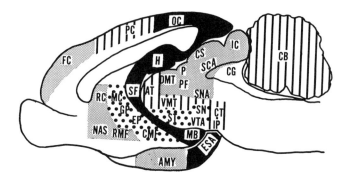

Figure 6.3 Schematic drawing of a parasagittal section of the rat brain showing the four functional blocks necessary for the performance of avoidance habits: the first block (areas occupied by black dots) is concerned with sensorimotor integration, the second block (stippled areas) plays a role in fear-initiated responses, the third block (areas occupied by vertical lines) has somatosensory functions, and fourth block (blackened areas) is involved in cognitive mapping. Abbreviations: AMY, amygdala; AT, anterior thalamus; CB, cerebellum; CG, central gray; CMF, caudal medial forebrain bundle; CS, superior colliculus; CT, central tegmentum; DMT, dorsomedial thalamus; EP, entopeduncular nucleus; ESA, entorhino-subicular area; FC, frontal cortex; GP, globus pallidus; H, hippocampus; IC, inferior colliculus; IP, interpeduncular nucleus; MB, mammillary bodies; MC, middle caudoputamen; NAS, nucleus accumbens septi; OC, occipital cortex; P, pretectal area; PC, parietal cortex; PF, parafascicular nucleus; RC, rostral medial forebrain bundle; SCA, subcollicular area; SF, septofornix area; SN, substantia nigra; SNA, supranigral area; ST, subthalamus; VMT, ventromedial thalamus; VTA, ventral tegmental area [from R. Thompson, *Physiol. Psychol.* 6:263 (1978); © 1978 by Psychonomic Society Inc.].

cells which may be widely dispersed throughout the brain. The basic cellular metabolic properties which have already been presented are necessarily related to the position of each individual cell within the system. It is now clear (see Thompson, 1978) that a number of different areas are involved in the expression of a particular physiological or behavioral response (Fig. 6.3). This is, perhaps, one of the reasons why the control of synaptic activity is so complex and why functions should not generally be conceptualized as involving global, uniform biochemical changes.

Morphological Changes
Associated with Brain Plasticity

The principal changes that have been demonstrated to occur in the brain during learning most likely involve some form of biochemical and ultrastructural modification of the synapses and possibly some other components of the nervous tissue. Some lines of evidence indicate that the functional adaptation of the brain also involves a morphological restructuring of neuronal connections as a result of the formation of new synapses, axonal sprouting and the growth of a more complex dendritic tree (for review see Tsukahara, 1981). While our knowledge of the mechanisms that control the restructuring of neural connections is scanty, it is postulated that there is an ongoing process involving the formation of transient synapses. Starting during the early developmental periods, a continuous reorganization of synaptic connections would take place in many areas of the brain (Knyihar et al., 1978).

Long term alterations in synaptic efficacy may involve an increase in the number of synapses as a consequence of axonal sprouting. However, this axonal growth response has only been demonstrated to occur following damage to nervous tissue. And, in such a situation, the overall number of synapses may actually decrease due to the degeneration of axonal collaterals.

A reorganization of this nature is probably also active following insults to the brain, such as the transection of nerve fibers or the destruction of those neurons innervated by these fibers. This reorganization could conceivably be a component of the functional compensation that has often been reported after brain damage.

This process of reorganization that has been frequently reported for the damaged and developing brain may have something in common with the restructuring that occurs during learning and functional adaptation. Several research groups [notably that of Greenough (e.g., Volkmar and Greenough, 1972; Greenough *et al.*, 1973)] have provided some support by demonstrating changes in the dendritic tree ramification of cortical neurons and in the number and size of synapses attached to them during different types of experience. For example, after training rats for 26 days in a Hebb-Williams maze, Greenough and his associates (1979) found that the apical dendrites of pyramidal neurons in cortical layers IV and V were more branched than those in the controls. Basal dendrites were unaffected, and no changes were seen in the branching of layer IV stellate neurons.

Using cichlid fish, Coss and Globus (1978) found that visual stimulation caused a shortening of the stems of dendritic spines. They believe that the process is correlated with an activation-induced swelling of the spines and that this was somehow involved in a change in synaptic effectiveness. Vrensen and Nunes Cardozo (1981) have reported alterations following visual training in the fine structural organization of rabbit synaptic junctional membranes. They observed increases in the thickness of the postsynaptic density and in the number of synapses exhibiting "perforations" in the PSD. The authors speculate that such changes are associated with an increase in the number of calcium channels, thereby, raising the probability of transmitter release. The net effect, they believe, is an enhancement in synaptic efficacy.

A morphological restructuring of neuronal systems may hypothetically involve the strengthening of existing connections by a sprouting of the afferent axon and a duplication of the synaptic connection between the same neurons. The new synapses may be localized nearer the axon hillock, the site at which the action potential is generated. Such a change could then increase the probability of the postsynaptic cell firing. In other words, the effect would involve a conversion of an "intensifying" synapse into more of a "detonator" synapse. Or, on the other hand, this additional connection might merely amplify the incoming signal by a process of summation. Alternatively, a sprouting axon may establish a connection with another neuron. However, it is difficult to satisfactorily explain how this latter event would be controlled and directed, not to mention how the connections would become selected and made functional.

The notion that mental activity is able to induce the growth in the brain is quite old, dating back to the proposals of Spurzheim in 1815. Acceptable experimental evidence for such a possibility has been available only since Hebb (1949) reared laboratory albino rats as pets in his home and found that, compared with the vivarium-bred rats, they behaved differently, even obtaining lower error scores in the Hebb-Williams rat mazes. Later studies by Bennett, Krech, Rosenzweig and Diamond at Berkeley (e.g., Bennett *et al.*, 1964; Diamond *et al.*, 1964; Rosenzweig *et al.*, 1971) improved the reproducibility of the experimental conditions and set the experimental standards for this type of work.

Rats or mice of different strains were weaned at 3 weeks of age and then reared for 30-80 days in one of three types of environments:

(1) Enriched conditions (ECT), usually associated with additional training. The animals were housed in large cages with different objects, wheels and toys. They were also trained once or twice daily in standardized mazes, wherein they could obtain food rewards.

(2) Impoverished conditions (IC). The animals were isolated in dimly lit and quiet cages, without being able to see or touch another animal. However, mutual auditory and olfactory contacts were still available.

(3) Standard conditions (SC), involving groups of 4-5 animals in toy-less cages illuminated for 12 hours daily.

Other groups of animals were also reared in a seminatural outdoor environment, where they were able to dig holes and build nests.

These studies were carried out on yoked groups of littermates to ensure that the initial morphological characteristics were comparable. Maternal competence, litter rearing and genetically determined growth potential may cause extensive variations in the state of the animals which preclude any meaningful comparison between them.

Bennett and his research colleagues discovered that the differential rearing yielded some very interesting results. The weight of the cerebral cortex in the enriched or seminatural environments was about 5% higher than in the animals living under impoverished conditions. The difference was very consistent and did not reflect the overall growth of the brain or the body size, nor variations in the fluid content of the brain tissue. In these experiments, other parts of the brain decreased in weight, and the overall body weight of the animals living in the enriched environment was even lower than those in the impoverished environment. The difference in body weight between the groups of animals was due to the fact that animals living in impoverished environments ate and drank more than the others (Fiala *et al.*, 1976). In the enriched group, the occipital cortex was thicker (6.2% increase) than the parietal cortex (2.7% increase), and there was an increase in the diameter of the blood capillaries. At the cellular level, the neuronal cell bodies were about 13% larger, and the glia/neuron ratio was found to be elevated.

The differences in brain morphology were most pronounced when animals housed under the two extreme environments (enriched and impoverished) were compared. Subsequent manipulations in the combination of environmental factors have afforded greater insight into their relative importance. Rats kept isolated in cages, but able to observe those animals in the enriched conditions, did not differ in cortical weight and cortical thickness from animals maintained in a standard colony. Similarly, pairing of the animals within a restricted environment had no effects upon the morphology of

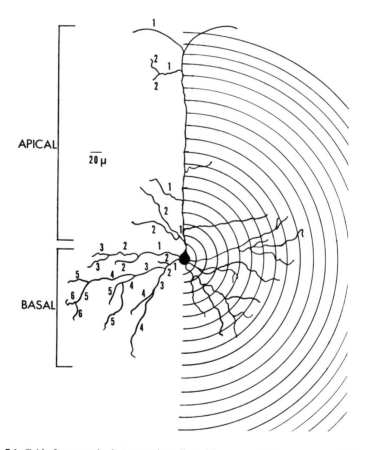

Figure 7.1 Grid of concentric rings over the cell used for a quantitative assessment of dendritic branching [from W.T. Greenough, *American Scientist* 63:37 (1975); © 1975 by Sigma Xi, The Scientific Research Society of North America].

the cerebral cortex. On the contrary, the animals that were placed alone in the enriched environment showed the increase in cortical growth. A similar change has been found in the brain weights of gerbils and mice of several inbred strains maintained in the enriched environment.

The thickness of the cortex, as measured in histological sections, was reported to be affected as well. Diamond *et al.* (1964), found that in the ECT animals, the cerebral cortex in the visual area was thicker. Similar, but less pronounced changes have been found in the somatosensory area, which again indicate that the morphological effects are selective and differ in individual brain areas. These changes were observed mainly in layers II and III; layer I was not involved. Although this increase in thickness was most distinct in the occipital area, blinding of the animals did not prevent the cortical growth, suggesting that these morphological changes do not depend upon visual experience.

Further observations by Walsh *et al.* (1972, 1973) revealed that animals housed in the enriched condition for 80 days also had a frontal cortex of diminished thickness. Moreover, the appearance of these effects is not limited to the period of growth. Similar changes were also found in animals kept in the enriched environment during the second year of life. Four days of stay in the enriched environment appeared sufficient for a significant change (Diamond *et al.*, 1979).

In the thicker cortex of ECT animals, the neurons and capillaries are less numerous when related to the volume of tissue. This indicates that the increase in thickness is not due to cortical cell division, but is caused by an increased volume of the neuropil, which is composed of dendrites, blood capillaries, and glial cells. By counting the branches of the Golgi-stained neurons (Fig. 7.1), Volkmar and Greenough (1972) demonstrated an increase in dendritic branching in animals bred within an enriched environment. The width of the dendrites remained unchanged, and the effects were limited to the basal dendrites; the apical branches were not affected.

The increase in the dendritic length was accompanied by an elevation in the number of detectable dendritic spines, which further implies a corresponding increase in the number of synapses. By counting the synaptic boutons in the dentate gyrus of rats that were handled daily, Chronister *et al.* (1973) were able to confirm this relationship. Changes in synaptic density, terminal size and postsynaptic membrane thickenings have been noted as well. Glial cells (oligodendrocytes and astrocytes) also multiply in the occipital cortex of animals living in the enriched environment, but in other areas of the brain, the change is much less obvious (Szeligo and Leblond, 1977).

More specific manipulations of the visual input have similarly been demonstrated to affect the dendritic trees. For example, rearing kittens in vertically or horizontally striped cylinders, which modifies the directional preference of visual cortical neurons, will alter the three-dimensional dendritic arrangement of these cells (Coleman et al., 1981).

Several biochemical alterations have also been noted within the cerebral cortices of ECT animals. An increase in protein synthesis, which is to be expected for such an effect, develops over a prolonged period and cannot be detected by the usual biochemical methods. The same is true for RNA. Essman (1971) did discover an elevation of glial RNA and a decrease in neuronal RNA in mice isolated for 28 days. Uphouse and Bonner (1975) extracted RNA from the brains of environmentally enriched rats and hybridized it to unique DNA sequences. They found that this RNA contained more unique sequences (probably mRNA) than RNA extracted from the brains of non-enriched controls. While it is necessary for these experiments to be replicated with updated research methods, the data do suggest that the increased activity due to environmental enrichment requires a larger variety of protein species. Some of them may be membrane proteins, or more specifically, glycoproteins, since the incorporation of the precursor glucosamine is greater in the cerebral cortex of ECT rats than in IC rats. The synaptosomal proteins in the "enriched" cortex also have a longer half-life (Levitan et al., 1972).

In both ECT and IC animals, brain glucose metabolism is altered. In the ECT group, more carbon from labelled glucose is incorporated into nucleic acids, proteins, and lipids of the brain and spinal cord (De Feudis and Black, 1972). In 1964, Bennett et al. found that cortical acetylcholinesterase was higher in rats from the enriched group. The increase was greatest in the visual cortex and lowest in the somesthetic area. In the IC rats, this value was even lower than in rats from the standard colony. Two hours of daily exposure to the enriched environment appears to be sufficient for this increase (Rosenzweig et al., 1971), a finding that has subsequently been confirmed in mice. These alternations are not permanent, and the induced cerebral effects may regress after animals are removed from the enriched conditions. The role of this increase is not clear, since this enzyme is always present in excess in the brain.

The details of the mechanism responsible for these changes are not known. Some authors postulate that the nonspecific activation of the cerebral cortex during arousal may underlie the morphological changes (Cummins et al., 1977). However, amphetamine-induced arousal does not lead to any known morphological changes in the cortex (Ferchmin and Eterovic, 1979). The activity of adrenal gland may also be involved (Devenport, 1979), since adrenalectomy causes an increase in brain weight, and isolation elevates adrenal weight (Brain and Benton, 1979).

Both isolation and crowding are stressful situations that cause endocrine and behavioral changes which could participate in the development of cortical thickening. Both factors also alter the metabolism of several neurotransmitters, particularly the biogenic amines. Social isolation causes a change in the number and responsiveness of α- and β-adrenergic receptors, along with alterations in the synaptosomal uptake of norepinephrine and the system generating cyclic adenosine monophosphate (Kraeuchi et al., 1981). Some neurotransmitter changes would seem to be due to stress-related hormonal effects (Brain and Benton, 1979). However, in a detailed examination of research in this area, Rosenzweig and Bennett (1978) argue that stress, although possibly involved, is not a primary contributing factor.

SUMMARY AND SPECULATIONS

All of the characteristic activity of the central nervous system relates to the concurrent functioning of two types of cells, the neurons and glia. The neurons are traditionally seen as the embodiment of the nervous system, carrying out its pre-eminent basic operations - the generation of electrical impulses and their transmission to other neurons or to various target tissues.

But, brain functioning is obviously more than merely a firing of millions of nerve cells. The brain is an organized complex of neurons, whose activities must be coordinated. In this sense, then, one may envision two levels of operations - one involving the neuron as a physiological unit and the other involving a functional integration of individual units.

A single CNS neuron does not store memory as such or on its own analyze a complex sensory stimulus. It is only able to respond to the flow of nerve impulses impinging upon its surface through its synapses and to chemical agents diffusing to it from more distant sources. The analysis of external stimuli and the processes of memory storage and retrieval are understandably coordinate, multi-neuronal processes.

On both a short- and long-term basis, single neurons organized into complex networks are able to alter their functional characteristics, a process which ultimately modifies the functioning of the entire system. As a result, there is actually a mutual relationship between functional alterations at a neuronal level and within the brain as a whole.

Throughout the evolution of experimental psychology and the neurosciences, there have been numerous attempts to define particular loci for memories in the brain. However, various experimental approaches to this problem have indicated that no such a thing as single locus for each bit of memory exists. There are only larger areas and interconnections of neurons that are more or less closely involved in the processes of learning, retention and recall. And, relatively minor plastic alterations in the masses of neurons likely determine the specificity or generality of behavioral events. During such a process, each neuron would behave differently, some being activated at a point in time, others being inhibited. These phenomena of activation (depolarization) and inhibition (hyperpolarization) are coordinate events that simultaneously occur over neuronal assemblies during each moment of activity. Nevertheless, some pathways and interneuronal connections are typically facilitated, while others are suppressed. Massive depolarizations (or hyperpolarizations) of neurons are pathological states contrary to the normal functioning of the brain.

The excitation and inhibition of the neurons ultimately depend upon intracellular biochemical processes. Consequently, a concern with the functional plasticity of nerve cells calls for an exploration of the biochemical changes that might underlie these plastic changes. Such changes are quite complex and cannot be reduced to shifts in a single component of a cell's biochemistry. Unfortunately, all too often in the past there has existed a tendency to elevate the importance of a plastic change in a single component of the cell (e.g., unique species of RNA or proteins or shifts in the level of individual neurotransmitters), which often served to effectively diminish the potential contributions of other components. The metabolic complexity of each neuron means that many systems and components cooperate in order to assure an adequate level of functioning. An acknowledgement that an increase in neuronal activity is followed by a corresponding increase in RNA and protein synthesis, still prompts a number of questions. How are the processes initiated and how are they controlled? From where do the necessary precursors and energy come? How are the new proteins used by the cell and how are they able to modify its function?

In considerations of neuronal plasticity one must also bear in mind the diverse nature of individual neurons. Unlike a man-made computer, the brain is not a highly organized assembly of identical units. It is a highly organized assembly of quite distinct units.

Each of the billions of CNS neurons is separated from the others by slight disparities in structure, metabolism and function. The overall variability of central nervous activity can be attributable to constant shifts in the neuronal firing pattern, which are continuous adjustments to a changing environment. In this respect, the functions of individual CNS components depend upon their structure and connections and upon their previous history. Each passing nerve impulse and each synaptic discharge leaves a trace in the neuron which can influence its ongoing activity, immediately thereafter or for extended periods of time.

One of the ways in which the plasticity of masses of individual neurons can be expressed is in the modification of behavior, such as that which is evident following learning. It is obvious that during the learning process, each neuron acts differently, some being activated, while others are inhibited. These processes of activation (depolarization) and inhibition (hyperpolarization) are coordinate events, and during learning, some pathways and interneuronal connections are enhanced at the same time others are suppressed. If all of the neurons are massively depolarized, such as by ouabain, a meaningful memory trace cannot be formed.

The alterations in neuronal functioning are mainly dependent upon the activity of the surrounding membrane, which is composed of various species of proteins and lipids. The activity is influenced by intracellular processes supplying energy and materials necessary for membrane maintenance and rebuilding. The membrane proteins include various enzymes, components of the ionic channels, transmembrane carrier mechanisms, particular transmitter- and hormone-sensitive receptors, and proteins (usually glycoproteins) that regulate the surface electrical charges and ionic composition and those that assure the selectivity of cell-to-cell contact.

The activity of the membrane-bound enzymes can be controlled by the surrounding lipids. In this regard, two types of lipids are important - phospholipids and glycolipids. Phospholipids, for example, have been found to control the activity of Na^+, K^+-ATPase. Membrane lipids may also regulate the activity of ionic channels, receptors and enzymes and as a result control the plasticity of the membranes.

The levels and characteristics of the membrane lipids therefore at least partly determine the function of the neuronal membrane. The nature of the fatty acids incorporated into the membrane can be altered by the activity of a set of enzymes which are able to discriminate between individual types and isomers of fatty acids in affecting their saturation, unsaturation, or hydroxylation. These enzymes are sensitive to membrane excitation caused by the presence of neurotransmitters or ions.

The neurotransmitters themselves can induce the release of free fatty acids from the nervous tissue and modify the synthesis of phosphatidic acid. Synaptic activity and the presence of dopamine and serotonin also promote the synthesis of phosphoinositol. There are additional augmentations of phospholipid base-exchange reactions and the de novo synthesis of glycerophosphatides. All of these effects demonstrate the importance of membrane lipids in the process of neuronal plasticity.

Long-lived changes in synaptic efficacy ultimately depend upon biochemical processes within the neuron. The local alterations in membrane lipids, which can accompany the action of the neurotransmitters, are supplemented by corresponding changes in lipid synthesis in the interior of the cell. Gangliosides, which are able to modify the functions of neuronal membranes, are synthesized in the perikaryon and transported, attached to a protein, toward the nerve endings, where they are bound to the cell membranes. These gangliosides are thought to be capable of modifying neuronal activity by serving as:

(1) activators of various enzymes,
(2) cell surface markers necessary for mutual cell recognition, and
(3) factors in the control of ionic movements (since calcium ions, for example, may be bound to the electrically negative sialic acid residues).

It is possible that gangliosidic structure is rapidly altered during synaptic transmission and that calcium ions are able to change the conformation of the G_D and G_T types. Also, hormonal binding to them causes a longlasting local depolarization or hyperpolarization of the neuronal membrane. The concentration of brain gangliosides increases with shifts in brain hormonal levels and during the process of learning, suggesting an involvement in the plasticity of neuronal functioning.

Proteins comprise the second major component of the neuronal membrane. They are unevenly distributed there, and their positions can be further modified by bioelectric fields which displace them along the membrane. In some places, such as in the synapses, the membrane is more rigid, with the proteins being anchored to some points along it. It is possible that restructuring of the membrane during the generation of the bioelectric fields participates in the alteration of neuronal activity during repeated excitation.

The passage of nerve impulses along the axons alters the conduction velocity. This increase or decrease in velocity depends upon membrane-bound proteins (myelin basic protein is probably one of them), as well as on the levels of ions in the extracellular and intracellular space. The conduction velocity of the axon is also related to extracellular sodium, along with extracellular calcium and potassium. These ions are able to modify membrane excitability, so that the composition of the extracellular fluid can alter, on a short- or long-term basis, membrane excitability and the generation and passage of nerve impulses.

The activity of the neurons induces continuous movements of ions across the membranes and thus variations in their levels within the extracellular fluid. The proper functioning of the nervous tissue therefore requires a prompt re-establishment of the cross-membrane ionic balance. This is a form of homeostasis which is at least partly attributable to the sodium pump within the neuronal and glial membranes. The activity of the pump is supported by intracellular oxidations and the production of ATP. In continuously stimulated areas, there may be an alteration in glial functions.

The function of the neuron is primarily related to the activity of its synapses, which implies that neuronal plasticity is associated with an increase or decrease in synaptic efficacy. These changes are either short-lived or fixed for extended periods of time. The maintenance of the altered synaptic efficacy is a complex process, wherein individual steps depend one upon the other. At a minimum, it involves a modification in the sensitivity of the neurotransmitter receptors and an alteration in the amount of released neurotransmitter. These shifts in neurotransmitter release are related to the supply of particular precursors (choline, tyrosine, tryptophan) in the nerve endings, a process that is activated by the impulse flow across the synapse. This impulse flow activates synthetic enzymes within the nerve endings, typically through second messengers, such as the cyclic nucleotides or calcium.

The release of an increased quantity of neurotransmitter is followed by the activation of the neurotransmitter receptors. But, these receptors are normally subject to short-term changes in which an increased amount of neurotransmitter causes a decrease in receptor sensitivity. A permanent change in synaptic efficacy would therefore seem to require some form of receptor protection against these short-term changes. This is probably a function of the membrane lipids, the glycoproteins and phosphoproteins surrounding the receptor. They could possible elevate the synaptic efficacy and maintain it on an indefinite basis.

The last of the synaptic events is the biochemical degradation of the neurotransmitter and/or its reuptake into the nerve endings. This process is regulated by a system of feedback relationships, involving presynaptic receptors and an activation or inactivation or enzymes by ions and second messengers. A permanent change in synaptic efficacy likely requires an adjustment in these feedback mechanisms. A special role in this process is probably played by calcium ions. They enter the nerve ending during depolarization and determine the amount of neurotransmitter to be released. The passage of calcium ions can therefore be an important step in the functional modification of the synapse. The binding of calcium further depends upon the presence of gangliosides and glycoproteins and on their conformations within the membrane. Calcium is also bound within the mitochondria and possibly the endoplasmic reticulum and is released during excitation, meaning that both types of organelles are, to a certain extent, able to affect the release of the neurotransmitter.

The long-term influences upon nervous tissue functioning probably include a sprouting of axons and the formation of new nerve endings, new dendritic spines and an enriched branching of the dendrites. This occurs along with a multiplication of glia and capillaries and an increase in the volume of the neuronal perikarya.

All of these changes might not affect all cells. There could be neurons in the central nervous system which are "plastic" and those which are not. But, since this dichotomy enters the realm of speculation, little has been offered on just how these two classes of cells might differ biochemically and functionally and on their relationship to one another.

This first section of the book has essentially been an introduction to the complex nature of the problems of neuronal plasticity. Many different tissue components interact in order to adjust the functional state of the neuron to the behavioral requirements. The following sections shall focus more specifically on these various interactions.

RECOMMENDED READINGS

Bradbury, M.: Why a blood-brain barrier? *Trends Neurosci.* 2:36-38 (1979).

Brain, P., Benton, D.: Interpretation of physiological correlates of differential housing in laboratory rats. *Life Sci.* 24:99-115 (1979).

Byrne, J.H.: Ionic currents and behavior. *Trends Neurosci.* 2:268-270 (1979).

Cheek, D.B., Holt, A.B.: Extracellular volume in the brain- The relevance of the chloride space. *Pediat. Res.* 12:635-645 (1978).

Cheung, W.Y.: *Calcium and Cell Function.* Vol.1. *Calmodulin.* Academic Press: New York (1980).

Davis, W.J.: Behavioral hierarchies. *Trends Neurosci.* 2:5-7 (1979).

Davison, A.N., Peters, A. (Eds.): *Myelination.* Charles C. Thomas: Springfield, Ill. (1970).

Dismukes, R.K.: New concepts of molecular communication among neurons. *Behav. Brain Sci.* 2:409-448 (1979).

Flood, J.F., Jarvik, M.E., Bennett, E.L., Orme, A.E., Rosenzweig, M.R.: Effect of stimulants, depressants, and protein synthesis inhibition on retention. *Behav. Biol.* 20:168-183 (1977).

Gibbs, M.E., Ng, K.T.: Psychobiology of memory- Towards a model of memory formation. *Biobehav. Rev.* 1:113-136 (1977).

Glees, P., Hasan, M.: Lipofuscin in neuronal aging and disease. *Normal and Pathological Anatomy,* W. Bargmann, W. Doerr (Eds.), Vol. 32. G. Thieme: Stuttgart (1976).

Glynn, I.M., Karlish, S.J.D.: The sodium pump. *Ann. Rev. Physiol.* 37:13-56 (1975).

Horcholle-Bossavit, G.: Electrotonic transmission in mammalian central nervous system (in French). *J. Physiol. (Paris)* 74:349-363 (1978).

Jones, D.G.: Morphological features of central synapses, with emphasis on the presynaptic terminal. *Life Sci.* 21:477-492 (1977).

Katiyar, S.S., Porter, J.W.: Mechanisms of fatty acid synthesis. *Life Sci.* 20:737-759 (1977).

Krasne, F.B.: Extrinsic control of intrinsic neuronal plasticity- Hypothesis from work on simple systems. *Brain Res.* 140:197-215 (1978).

Landowne, D., Potter, L.T., Terrar, D.A.: Structure-function relationships in excitable membranes. *Ann. Rev. Physiol.* 37:485-508 (1975).

Loewenstein, W.R.: Junctional intercellular communication: The cell-to-cell membrane channel. *Physiol. Rev.* 61:829-913 (1981).

Mark, R.: *Memory and Nerve Cell Connections.* Clarendon Press: Oxford (1974).

McIlwain, H.: Translocation of neural modulators- Second category of nerve signal. *Neurochem. Res.* 1:351-368 (1976).

Michell, R.H., Kirk, C.J., Jones, L.M., Downes, C.P., Creba, J.A.: The stimulation of inositol lipid metabolism that accompanies calcium mobilization in stimulated cells: Defined characteristics and unanswered questions. *Phil. Trans. Roy. Soc. Lond. B* 296:123-137 (1981).

Morrell, P. (Ed.): *Myelin.* Plenum Press: New York (1977).

Mpitsos, G.J., Collins, S.D., McClellan, A.D.: Learning: A model system for physiological studies. *Science* 199:497-506 (1978).

Nicholson, C.: Dynamics of the brain cell microenvironment. *Neurosci. Res. Progr. Bull.* 18:176-322 (1980).

Pardridge, W.M., Oldendorf, W.H.: Transport of metabolic substrates through the blood-brain barrier. *J. Neurochem.* 28:5-12 (1977).

Pfenninger, K.H.: Organization of neuronal membranes. *Ann. Rev. Neurosci.* 1:445-471 (1978).

Rapoport, S.I.: *Blood-Brain Barrier in Physiology and Medicine.* Raven Press: New York (1976).

Robertson, J.D.: Membrane structure. *J. Cell Biol.* 91:189s-204s (1981).

Roelofsen, B: The (non)specificity in the lipid-requirement of calcium and (sodium plus potassium) - transporting adenosine triphosphatases. *Life Sci.* 29:2235-2247 (1981).

Rose, S.P.R.: What should a biochemistry of learning and memory be about? *Neuroscience* 6:811-821 (1981).

Singer, S.J.: The molecular organization of membranes. *Ann. Rev. Biochem.* 43:805-833 (1974).

Somjen, G.G.: Electrophysiology of neuroglia. *Ann. Rev. Physiol.* 37:163-190 (1975).

Svennerholm, L.: Gangliosides and synaptic transmission. In: L. Svennerholm, P. Mandel, H. Dreyfus, P.-F. Urban (Eds.), *Structure and Function of Gangliosides.* Plenum Press: New York (1980). pp. 533-544.

Tsukahara, N.: Sprouting and the neuronal basis of learning. *Trends Neurosci.* 9:234-237 (1981).

Waxman, S.G., Swadlow, H.A.: Conduction properties of axons in central white matter. *Progr. Neurobiol.* 8:297-324 (1977).

Weight, F.F.: Modulation of synaptic excitability- Introduction. *Fed. Proc.* 38:2078-2079 (1979).

Yamagawa, T., Nagai, Y.: Glycolipids at the cell surface and their biological functions. *Trends Biochem. Sci.* 3:128-131 (1978).

REFERENCES

Abe, A., Yamada, K., Sasaki, T.: *Biochem. Biophys, Res. Commun.* 104:1386 (1982).

Abood, L., Matsubara, A.: *Biochim. Biophys. Acta* 163:531 (1968).

Adey, W.R: *BioSystems* 8:163 (1977).

Akert, K., Pfenninger, K., Sandri, C., Moor, H.: In: G.D. Pappas, D.P. Purpura (Eds.), *Structure and Function of Synapses.* Raven Press: New York (1972). p. 67.

Akert, K., Sandri, C., Cuenod, M., Moor, H.: *Neurosci. Lett.* 5:253 (1977).

Alger, B.E., Nicoll, R.A.: *Brain Res.* 200:195 (1980).

Alkon, D.L., Lederhendler, I., Shoukimas, J.J.: *Science* 215:693 (1982).

Anderson, P., Lomo, T.: *Exp. Brain Res.* 2:247 (1966).

Andrew, R.D., MacVicar, B.A., Dudek, F.E., Hatton, G.I.: *Science* 211:1187 (1981).
Arienti, G., Corazzi, L., Woelk, H., Porcellati, G.: *Brain Res.* 124:317 (1977).
Aserinsky, E.: *Exp. Neurol.* 3:467 (1961).
Auerbach, A.A., Bennett, M.V.L.: *J. Gen. Physiol.* 53:211 (1969).
Augusti-Tocco, G., Sato, G.: *Proc. Natl. Acad. Sci. USA* 64:311 (1969).
Axelrod, D., Ravdin, P., Koppel, D.E., Schlessinger, J., Webb, W.W., Elson, E.L., Podleski,
    T.R.: *Proc. Natl. Acad. Sci. USA* 73:4594 (1976).
Baker, P.F., Connelly, C.M.: *J. Physiol. (London)* 185:270 (1966).
Banker, G.A.: *Science* 209:809 (1980).
Baranyi, A., Feher, O.: *Neurosci. Lett.* 23:303 (1981).
Baudry, M., Lynch, G.: *Exp. Neurol.* 68:202 (1980).
Baudry, M., Lynch, G.: *Molec. Cell. Biochem.* 38:5 (1981).
Baudry, M., Bundman, M.C., Smith, E.K., Lynch, G.S.: *Science* 211:937 (1981).
Bennet, M.V.L.: *EEG Clin. Neurophysiol.* 29:409 (1970).
Bennett, E.L., Diamond, M.C., Krech, D., Rosenzweig, M.R.: *Science* 146:610 (1964).
Berger, T.W., Alger, B., Thompson, R.F.: *Science* 192:483 (1976).
Berra, B., Lindi, C., Omodeosa, F.: *Ital. J. Biochem.* 28:316 (1979).
Bjorklund, A., Lindvall, O.: *Brain Res.* 83:531 (1975).
Blaustein, M.P.: *Science* 172:391 (1971).
Blaustein, M.P., Ratzlaff, R.W., Kendrick, N.C., Schweitzer, E.S.: *J. Gen. Physiol.* 72:15
    (1978).
Blaustein, M.P., Ratzlaff, R.W., Schweitzer, E.S.: *J. Gen. Physiol.* 72:43 (1978a).
Bliss, T.V.P., Lomo, T.: *J. Physiol. (London)* 232:331 (1973).
Blomberg, F., Cohen, R.S., Siekevitz, P.: *J. Cell Biol.* 74:204 (1977).
Boggs, J.M.: *Can. J. Biochem.* 58:755 (1980).
Boisacg-Schepens, N.: *Arch. Int. Physiol.* 76:562 (1968).
Bondy, S.C., Purdy, J.L.: *Brain Res.* 76:542 (1974).
Bourke, R.S., Greenberg, E.S., Tower, D.B.: *Am. J. Physiol.* 208:682 (1965).
Bremer, E.G., Sapirstein, V.S., Savage, T., McCluer, R.H.: *J. Neurochem.* 38:333 (1982).
Brown, T.H., McAfee, D.A.: *Science* 215:1411 (1982).
Brunk, U., Ericsson, J.L.: *J. Ultrastruct. Res.* 38:192 (1972).
Burnstock, G.: *Neuroscience* 1:239 (1976).
Burton, R.F.: *Biol. Rev.* 48:195 (1973).
Byrne, J.H.: *Trends Neurosci.* 2:268 (1979).
Carnevale, N.T., Wachtel, H.: *Brain Res. Rev.* 2:45 (1980).
Chan, K.Y., Bunt, A.H.: *J. Neurocytol.* 7:137 (1978).
Chatelain, P., Deleer, M., Poss, A., Ruysschaert, J.M.: *Experientia* 35:334 (1979).
Cheek, D.B., Holt, A.B.: *Pediat. Res.* 12:635 (1978).
Chin, J.H., Goldstein, D.B.: *Biomedicine* 28:141 (1978).
Chio, K.S., Reiss, U., Fletcher, B., Tappel, A.L.: *Science* 166:1535 (1969).
Chiu, S.Y., Ritchie, J.M., Rogart, R.B., Stagg, D.: *J. Physiol. (London)* 292:149 (1979).
Chronister, R.B., Bernstein, J.J., Zornetzer, S.F., White, L.E.Jr.: *Experientia* 29:588 (1973).
Cockcroft, S.: *Trends Pharmacol. Sci.* 2:340 (1981).
Cohen, M.W., Gerschenfeld, H.M., Kuffler, S.W.: *J. Physiol. (London)* 197:363 (1968).
Coleman, P.D., Flood, D.G., Whitehead, M.C., Emerson, R.C.: *Brain Res.* 214:1 (1981).
Colquhoun, D., Ritchie, J.M.: *J. Physiol. (Lond.)* 221:533 (1972).
Conti, F., Hille, B., Neumcke, B., Nonner, W., Stampfli, R.: *J. Physiol. (London)* 262:699
    (1976).
Cordingley, G.E., Somjen, G.G.: *Brain Res.* 151:291 (1978).
Coss, R.G., Globus, A.: *Science* 200:787 (1978).

Cuatrecasas, P.: *Ann. Rev. Biochem.* 43:169 (1974).

Cullen, M.J., Gulley, R.J.: *Trends Neurosci.* 3:113 (1980).

Culp, W.J., McKenzie, D.T.: *Proc. Natl. Acad. Sci. USA* 78:7171 (1981).

Cummins, R.A., Livesey, P.J., Evans, J.G.M.: *Science* 197:692 (1977).

Dale, H.H.: *Proc. Roy. Soc. Med.* 28:319 (1935).

Danielli, J.F., Davson, H.: *J. Cell. Comp. Physiol.* 5:495 (1935).

Daurainville, J.-L., Gayet, J.: *J. Neurochem.* 12:771 (1965).

Davis, W.J.: *Trends Neurosci.* 2:5 (1979).

Davis, W.J., Kovac, M.P.: *Trends Neurosci.* 4:73 (1981).

Davison, A.N., Dobbing, J., Morgan, R.S., Payling Wright, G.: *J. Neurochem.* 3:89 (1958).

De Feudis, F.V., Black, W.C.: *Exp. Neurol.* 36:41 (1972).

Del Castillo, J., Katz, B.: *J. Physiol. (London)* 125:546 (1954).

DeMaccioni, A.H.R., Caputto, R.: *J. Neurochem.* 15:1257 (1968).

DeMedio, G.E., Trovarelli, G., Hamberger, A., Porcellati, G.: *Neurochem. Res.* 5:171 (1980).

Descarries, L., Watkins, K., Lapierre, Y.: *Brain Res.* 133:197 (1977).

Deul, D.H., Haisma, J.A., Van Breeman, J.F.L.: *Progr. Brain Res.* 29:125 (1968).

Devenport, L.D.: *Behav. Neural Biol.* 27:218 (1979).

Diamond, M.C., Krech, D., Rosenzweig, M.R.: *J. Comp. Neurol.* 123:111 (1964).

Diamond, M.C., Ingham, C.A., Johnson, R.E., Bennett, E.L., Rosenzweig, M.: *J. Neurobiol.* 7:75 (1979).

Dismukes, R.K.: *Behav. Brain Sci.* 2:409 (1979).

Doljanski, F., Kapeller, M.: *J. Theor. Biol.* 62:253 (1976).

Dubois, J.M.: *J. Physiol.* 318:297 (1981).

Dun, N.J.: *IEEE Transact., BME* 17:21 (1970).

Dunant, Y., Corthay, J., Loctin, F.: In: *Synaptic Constituents in Health and Disease,* M. Brzin, D. Sket, H. Bachelard (Eds.). Pergamon Press: Oxford (1980). p. 129.

Dunn, A.J., Hogan, E.L.: *Pharmacol. Biochem. Behav.* 3:605 (1975).

Elliott, G.R., Barchas, J.D.: In: D. De Wied, P.A. Van Keep (Eds.), *Hormones and the Brain.* University Park Press: Baltimore (1980). p. 43.

Essman, W.B.: *Biol. Psychiat.* 3:141 (1971).

Farias, R.N., Bloj, B., Morero, R.D., Sineriz, F., Trucco, R.E.: *Biochim. Biophys. Acta* 415:231 (1975).

Farquhar, M.G., Palade, G.E.: *J. Cell Biol.* 17:375 (1963).

Ferchmin, P.A., Eterovic, V.A.: *Science* 205:522 (1979).

Fiala, B., Snow, F.M., Greenough, W.T.: *Dev. Psychobiol.* 10:537 (1976).

Fink, R., Wettwer, E.: *Pflueger's Arch.* 374:289 (1978).

Fisher, S.H., Frey, K.A., Agranoff, B.W.: *J. Neurosci.* 1:1407 (1981).

Fishman, P.M., Reiner, M., Chan, P.H.: *J. Neurochem.* 28:1061 (1977).

Forte, M., Satow, Y., Nelson, D., Kung, C.: *Proc. Natl. Acad. Sci. USA* 78:7195 (1981).

Foulkes, J.A., Patterson, D.S.: *Brain Res.* 82:139 (1974).

Furshpan, K.J., Potter, D.D.: *J. Physiol. (London)* 145:289 (1959).

Gainer, H., Tasaki, I., Lasek, R.J.: *J. Cell Biol.* 74:524 (1977).

Gallai-Hatchard, J., Magee, W.L., Thompson, R.H.S., Webster, G.R.: *J. Neurochem.* 9:545 (1962).

Gallego, R., Kuno, M., Nunez, R., Snider, W.D.: *J. Physiol. (London)* 291:191 (1979).

Garcia-Segura, L.M., Baetens, D., Orci, L.: *Brain Res.* 234:494 (1982).

Gibbs, M.E., Ng, K.T.: *Biobehav. Rev.* 1:113 (1977).

Gibbs, M.E., Ng, K.T.: *Physiol. Behav.* 23:369 (1979).

Gielen, W.: *Z. Naturforsch. B.* 23b:117 (1968).

Gilette, R., Kovac, M.P., Davis, W.L.: *Science* 199:798 (1978).

Glassman, R.B., Malamut, B.L.: *Biosystems* 9:257 (1977).
Graubard, K., Raper, J.A., Hartline, D.K.: *Proc. Natl. Acad. Sci. USA* 77:3733 (1980).
Greenough, W.T., Volkmar, F.R., Juraska, J.M.: *Exp. Neurol.* 41:371 (1973).
Greenough, W.T., Juraska, J.M., Volkmar, F.R.: *Behav. Neural Biol.*, 26:287 (1979).
Grisar, T., Frere, J.M., Franck, G.: *Brain Res.* 165:87 (1979).
Grollman, E.F., Lee, G., Ambesi-Impiombato, F.S., Meldolesi, M.F., Aloj, S.M., Coon, H.G., Kaback, H.R., Kohn, L.D.: *Proc. Natl. Acad. Sci. USA* 74:2352 (1977).
Grubb, R.L., Jr., Raichle, M.E., Eichling, J.O.: *Brain Res.* 144:204 (1978).
Gulley, R.L., Wenthold, R.J., Neises, G.R.: *J. Cell Biol.* 75:837 (1977).
Gutnick, M.J., Prince, D.A.: *Science* 211:67 (1981).
Hablitz, J.J., Lundervold, A.: *Exp. Neurol.* 71:410 (1981).
Hajdu, S., Leonard, E.J.: *Life Sci.* 17:1527 (1976).
Hanley, M.R., Cotrell, G.A., Emson, P.C., Fonnum, F.: *Nature* 251:631 (1974).
Hanna, R.B., Keeter, J.S., Pappas, G.D.: *J. Cell Biol.* 79:764 (1978).
Hardy, W.L.: *Biophys. J.* 13:1051 (1973).
Harris, R.A., Schmidt, J., Hitzemann, B.A., Hitzemann, R.J.: *Science* 212:1290 (1981).
Harzer, K., Stinshoff, K., Mraz, W., Jatzkewitz, M.: *J. Neurochem.* 20:279 (1973).
Hauser, H., Levine, B.A., Williams, R.J.P.: *Trends Biochem. Sci.*, 1:278 (1976).
Hawthorne, J.N.: *J. Lipid Res.* 1:255 (1960)
Hayashi, K., Katagiri, A.: *Biochem. Biophys. Acta.*, 337:107 (1974).
Hebb, D.O.: *The Organization of Behaviour.* John Wiley & Sons: New York (1949). p.298.
Haycock, J.W., Levy, W.B., Denner, L.A., Cotman, C.W.: *J. Neurochem.* 30:1113 (1978).
Hebb, D.O.: *Textbook of Psychology* W.B. Saunders, Co.: Philadelphia (1958). p.120.
Henn, F.A.: *J. Neurosci. Res.*, 2:271 (1976).
Henn, F.A., Haljamae, H., Hamberger, A.: *Brain Res.*, 43:437 (1972).
Henn, F., Hamberger, A.: *Proc. Natl. Acad. Sci. USA* 68:2686 (1971).
Henn, F., Henke, D.: *Neuropharmacology* 17:985 (1978).
Henn, F., Henn, S.: *Progr. Neurobiol.* 15:1 (1980).
Hess, H.H., Bass, N.H., Thalheimer, C., Devarakonda, R.: *J. Neurochem.* 26:1115 (1976).
Heuser, J.E., Salpeter, S.R.: *J. Cell Biol.* 82:150 (1979).
Heuser, J.E., Reese, T.S., Landis, D.M.D.: *J. Neurocytol.* 3:109 (1974).
Hildebrandt, C., Skoglund, S.: *Acta. Physiol. Scand.* 197:5 (1971).
Hille, B.: *Ann. Rev. Physiol.* 38:139 (1976).
Hirata, F., Axelrod, J.: *Science* 209:1082 (1980).
Hodgkin, A.L.: *Proc. Roy. Soc. B.* 148:1 (1958).
Hodgkin, A.L., Huxley, A.F.: *J. Physiol. (London)* 117:500 (1952).
Hodgkin, A.L., Katz, B.: *J. Physiol (London)* 108:37 (1949).
Horakova, M., Nonner, W., Stampfli, R.: *Proc. Int. Un. Physiol. Sci.* 7:198 (1968).
Hoss, W., Abood, L.G.: *Eur. J. Biochem.* 50:177 (1974).
Hotson, J.R., Prince, D.A.: *J. Neurophysiol.* 43:409 (1981).
Hubbard, A.L., Cohn, Z.A.: *J. Cell Biol.* 64:461 (1975).
Hui, C.S.: *BioSystems* 8:207 (1977).
Hungund, B.L., Mahadik, S.P.: *Neurochem. Res.* 6:183 (1981).
Irvine, R.F., Hemington, N., Dawson, R.M.C.: *Eur. J. Biochem.* 99:525 (1979).
Irwin, L.N., Samson, F.E.: *J. Neurochem.* 18:203 (1971).
Izquierdo, I., Elisabetsky, E.: *Psychopharmacologia* 57:215 (1978).
Jaffe, L.F.: *Nature (London)* 265:600 (1977).
Joserieh, G , Breer, H., Duvel, M.: *Neurochem. Res.* 6:465 (1981).
Jones, D.G.: *J. Neurobiol.* 7:1 (1976).
Jones, D.G., Ellison, L.T., Reading, L.C., Dittmer, M.M.: *Cell Tissue Res.* 169:49 (1976)

Kaczmarek, L.K., Adey, W.R.: *Brain Res.* 66:537 (1974).
Kanfer, J.N.: *Can. J. Biochem.* 58:1370 (1980).
Karpiak, S.E., Graf, L., Rapport, M.M.: *Science* 194:735 (1976).
Karpiak, S.E., Graf, L., Rapport, M.M.: *Brain Res.* 151:637 (1978).
Katiyar, S.S., Porter, J.W.: *Life Sci.* 20:737 (1977).
Katz, B., Miledi, R.: *Proc. Roy. Soc. London Ser. B.* 161:483 (1965).
Katz, R.I., Chase, T.N., Kopin, I.J.: *J. Neurochem.* 16:961 (1969).
Kawato, M., Sokabe, M., Suzuki, R.: *Biol. Cybern.* 34:81 (1979).
Keynes, R.D., Ritchie, J.M.: *J. Physiol. (London)* 21:P29 (1970).
Kishimoto, Y., Kawamura, N.: *Mol. Cell Biochem.* 23:17 (1979).
Klein, F., Mandel, P.: *Biochimie* 54:371 (1972).
Knyihar, E., Csillik, B., Rakic, P.: *Science* 202:1207 (1978).
Kobayashi, H., Libet, B.: *Proc. Nat. Acad. Sci. USA* 69:1304 (1968).
Kocsis, J.D., Waxman, S.G.: *Nature (Lond.)* 287:348 (1980).
Korn, H., Sotelo, C., Crepel, F.: *Exp. Brain Res.* 16:255 (1973).
Koukkou, M., Lehmann, D.: In: *Functional States of the Brain: Their Determinants,* M. Koukkou, D. Lehmann, J. Angst (Eds.). Elsevier: Amsterdam (1980). p. 13.
Kraeuchi, K., Gentsch, C., Feer, H.: *J. Neural Transm.* 50:103 (1981).
Kraig, R.P., Nicholson, C.: *Neuroscience* 3:1045 (1978).
Krasne, F.: *Brain Res.* 140:197 (1978).
Kronquist, K.E., Lennarz, W.J.: *J. Supramol. Structure* 8:51 (1978).
Kuffler, S.W.: *Proc. Roy. Soc. B.* 168:1 (1967).
Kumarasiri, M.H., Gould, R.M.: *Brain Res.* 18:315 (1980).
Kuno, M.: *Physiol. Rev.* 51:647 (1971).
Landa, C.A., Maccioni, H.J.F., Caputto, B.: *J. Neurochem.* 33:825 (1979).
Landmesser, L., Pillar, G.: *J. Physiol. (London)* 222:691 (1972).
Langford, L.A., Coggeshall, R.E.: *Science* 211:176 (1981).
Larrabee, M.G., Leicht, W.S.: *J. Neurochem.* 12:1 (1965).
Lasek, R.J., Gainer, H., Barker, J.L.: *J. Cell Biol.* 74:501 (1976).
Lazo, P.S., Barros, F., de la Pena, P., Ramos, S.: *Trends Biochem. Sci.* 3:83 (1981).
Ledeen, R.W.: *J. Supramol. Struct.* 8:1 (1978).
Lee, G., Aloj, S.M., Brady, R.O., Kohn, L.D.: *Biochem. Biophys. Res. Commun.* 73:370 (1976).
Lee, S.L., Phillis, J.W.: *Can. J. Physiol. Pharmacol.* 55:961 (1977).
Leon, A., Facci, L., Toffano, G., Sonnino, S., Tettamanti, G.: *J. Neurochem.* 37:350 (1981).
Levitan, I.B., Mushynski, W.I., Ramirez, G.: *J. Neurochem.* 19:2621 (1972).
Levy, W.B., Steward, O.: *Brain Res.* 175:233 (1979).
Lewis, D.V., Schuette, W.H.: *Brain Res.* 110:523 (1976).
Lindemann, B., Van Driesche, W.: *Science* 195:292 (1977).
Lindvall, M., Edvinsson, L., Owman, C.: *Science* 201:176 (1979).
Ling, G.N., Walton, C.L.: *Science* 191:293 (1976).
Llinas, R.R.: *Soc. Neurosci. Symp.* 2:139 (1977).
Llinas, R., Hess, R.: *Proc. Natl. Acad. Sci. USA* 73:1520 (1976).
Llinas, R., Steinberg, I.Z., Walton, K.: *Brain Res. Bull.* 4:170 (1979).
Llinas, R., Steinberg, I.Z., Walton, K.: *Biophys. J.* 33:323 (1981).
Loewenstein, W.R.: *Physiol. Rev.* 61:829 (1981).
Lunt, G.G., Pickard, M.R.: *J. Neurochem.* 24:1203 (1975).
MacVicar, B.A., Dudek, F.E.: *Brain Res.* 196:494 (1980).
Marchbanks, R.M.: *J. Neurochem.* 13:1481 (1969).
Marggraf, W.D., Wang, H., Kanfer, J.N.: *J. Neurochem.* 32:353 (1979).

Marks, N., McIlwain, H.: *Biochem. J.* 73:401 (1959).

Matus, A.I., Pehling, G., Wilkinson, D.A.: *J. Neurobiol.* 12:67 (1981).

McGeer, P.L., McGeer, E.G., Innanen, V.T.: *Brain Res.* 169:433 (1979).

McIlwain, H.: *Biochem. J.* 78:24 (1961).

Meldolesi, M.F., Fishman, P.H., Aloj, S.N., Ledley, F.D., Lee, G., Bradley, R.M., Brady, R.O., Kohn, L.D.: *Biochem. Biophys. Res. Commun.* 75:581 (1977).

Miceli, G., Caltagirone, C., Gainotti, G.: *Acta. Psychiat. Scand.* 55:102 (1977).

Michell, R.H.: *Biochem. Biophys. Acta* 415:81 (1975).

Michell, R.H., Kirk, C.J.: *Trends Pharmacol. Sci.* 2:86 (1981).

Michell, R.H., Kirk, C.J., Jones, L.M., Downes, C.P., Creba, J.A.: *Phil Trans. Roy. Soc. Lond. B* 296:123 (1981).

Miller, J.C.: *Biochem. J.* 168:549 (1977).

Mohler, C.W., Wurt, R.H.: *J. Neurophysiol.* 39:722 (1976).

Moore, J.W., Narahashi, T., Shaw, T.I.: *J. Physiol. (London)* 188:99 (1967).

Morgan, J.I., Seifert, W.: *J. Supramol. Struct.* 10:111 (1979).

Mountcastle, V.B., Lynch, J.C., Georgopoulos, A., Sakata, H., Acuna, C.: *J. Neurophysiol.* 38:871 (1975).

Mullin, B.R., Fishman, P.H., Lee, G., Aloj, S.M., Ledley, F.D., Winand, R.J., Kohn, L.D., Brady, R.O.: *Proc. Natl. Acad. Sci. USA* 73:842 (1976).

Nachmansohn, D.: *Klin. Wschr.* 55:715 (1977).

Nachmansohn, D., Neumann, E.: *Chemical and Molecular Basis of Nerve Activity.* Academic Press: New York (1975).

Narahashi, T.: *Physiol. Rev.* 54:813 (1974).

Ng, M., Matus, A.I.: *Neuroscience* 4:169 (1979).

Nicholls, D.G.: *Biochem. J.* 170:511 (1978).

Nicholls, D.G., Akerman, K.E.O.: *Phil. Trans. Roy. Soc. Lond. B* 296:115 (1981).

Nicholson, C.: *Fed. Proc.* 39:1519 (1980).

Nicholson, C.: *Trends Neurosci.* 3:216 (1980a).

O'Fallon, J.V., Brosemer, R.W., Harding, J.W.: *J. Neurochem.* 36:369 (1981).

Olsnes, S., Saltvedt, E., Pihl, A.: *J. Biol. Chem.* 249:803 (1974).

Orkand, R.K., *Fed. Proc.* 39:1515 (1980).

Pannese, E., Luciano, L., Iurato, S., Reale, E.: *J. Ultrastruct. Res.* 60:169 (1977).

Parnas, H., Segel, L.A.: *J. Theor. Biol.* 91:125 (1981).

Payton, B.W., Bennet, M.V.I., Pappas, G.D.: *Science* 166:1641 (1969).

Pentreath, V.W., Kai-Kai, M.A.: *Nature* 295:59 (1982).

Peroutka, S.J., Snyder, S.H.: *Brain Res.* 208:339 (1981).

Pickard, M.R., Hawthorne, J.N.: *J. Neurochem.* 30:145 (1978).

Prasal, Z., Borkowski, T.: *Acta Physiol. Pol.* 19:857 (1968).

Probst, W., Rosner, H. Wiegandt, H., Rahmann, H.: *Hoppe-Seyler's Z. Physiol. Chem.* 360:979 (1979).

Pumplin, D.W., Reese, T.S., Llinas, R.: *Proc. Natl. Acad. Sci. USA* 78:7210 (1981).

Putney, J.W.Jr.: *Life Sci.* 29:1183 (1981).

Rahmann, H., Rosner, H., Breer, H.: *J. Theor. Biol.* 57:231 (1976).

Rall, D.P., Oppelt, W.W., Patlak, C.S.: *Life Sci.* 2:63 (1962).

Ramon-Moliner, E.: *Experientia* 33:1342 (1977).

Ramos, G.J.: *Acta Physiol. Latinoamer.* 25:288 (1975).

Ransom, B.R.: *Brain Res.* 69:83 (1974).

Raper, J.A.: *Science* 205:304 (1979).

Rapport, M.M., Karpiak, S.E., Mahodik, S.P.: *Fed. Proc.* 38:2391 (1978).

Redburn, D.A., Shelton, D., Cotman, C.W.: *J. Neurochem.* 26:297 (1976).

Ripley, S.H., Bush, B.M.H., Roberts, A.: *Nature* 218:1170 (1968).
Ritchie, J.M.: *Trends Pharmacol. Sci.* 1:275 (1980).
Ritchie, J.M., Straub, R.W.: *J. Physiol. (London)* 134:698 (1956).
Roelofsen, B.: *Life Sci.* 29:2235 (1981).
Rose, S.P.R.: *Neuroscience* 6:811 (1981).
Rosenberg, P.: *Toxicon* 8:147 (1970).
Rosenberg, P., Condrea, E.: *Biochem. Pharmacol.* 17:2033 (1968).
Rosenzweig, M.R., Bennett, E.L.: In: *Studies on the Development of Behavior and the Nervous System,* Vol. 4. *Early Influences,* G. Gottlieb (Ed.). Academic Press: New York (1978). p. 374.
Rosenzweig, M.R., Bennett, E.L., Diamond, M.C.: In: *Macromolecules and Behavior,* J. Gaito (Ed.). Appleton-Century-Crofts: New York (1971). p. 205.
Sabelli, H.C., May, J.: *Experientia* 31:1049 (1975).
Salmon, D.M., Honeyman, T.W.: *Nature* 284:364 (1980).
Salway, J.G., Hughes, I.E.: *J. Neurochem.* 19:1233 (1972).
Sandritter, W., Bierfreund, B., Pannen, F., Adler, C.P.: *Beitr. Path.* 174:280 (1972).
Satomi, D.: *J. Biochem.* 75:1313 (1974).
Savaki, H.E., Levis, G.M.: *Pharmacol. Biochem. Behav.* 7:7 (1977).
Schaffer, W.T., Olson, M.S.: *J. Neurochem.* 27:1319 (1976).
Schengrund, C.L., Jensen, D.S., Rosenberg, A.: *J. Biol. Chem.* 247:2742 (1972).
Schneider, A.M.: In: *Short-Term Memory,* D. Deutsch, J.A. Deutsch (Eds.). American Press: New York (1975). p. 340.
Schneider, A.M.: In: *Brain Mechanisms in Memory and Learning,* M.A.B. Brazier (Ed.), IBRO Monograph Series, vol. 4. Raven Press: New York (1979). p. 293.
Schoffeniels, E., Margineanu, D.G.: *J. Theor. Biol.* 92:1 (1981).
Schousboe, A., Booher, J., Hertz, L.: *J. Neurochem.* 17:1501 (1970).
Segal, J. R.: *Biophys. J.* 8:470 (1968).
Shashoua, V.E.: *Exp. Brain Res.* 17:139 (1973).
Simonneau, M. Baux, G., Tauc, L.: *J. Physiol. (Paris)* 76:427 (1980).
Singer, W., Lux, H.D.: *Brain Res.* 96:378 (1975).
Singer, S.J., Nicolson, G.L.: *Science* 175:720 (1972).
Singh, I., Kishimoto, Y.: *J. Neurochem.* 37:388 (1981).
Skrede, K.K., Malthe-Sorensen, D.: *Brain Res.* 208:436 (1981).
Smith, T.G., Barker, J.L., Gainer, H.: *Nature* 253:450 (1975).
Smith, T.L., Hauser, G.: *J. Neurochem.* 37:427 (1981).
Somjen, G.G.: *Ann. Rev. Physiol.* 37:163 (1975).
Sonnhof, U., Richter, D.W., Taugner, R.: *Brain Res.* 138:197 (1977).
Sonnino, S., Ghidoni, R., Marchesini, S., Tettamanti, G.: *J. Neurochem.* 33:117 (1979).
Spence, M.W.: *Biochim. Biophys. Acta* 218:347 (1970).
Spurzheim, J.G.: *The Physiognomical System of Drs. Gall and Spurzheim,* 2nd Ed. Baldwin, Cradock and Jody: London (1815). p. 554.
Stahl, W.L.: *Arch. Biochem. Biophys.* 154:56 (1973).
Stulen, G.: *Biochim. Biophys. Acta* 640:621 (1981).
Sun, G.Y., Su, K.L., Corbin, D.R.: In: *Proceedings of the International Conference on the Cyclitols and the Phosphoinositides,* W. Wells, F. Eisenberg (Eds.). Academic Press: New York (1978). p.549.
Suzuki, K.: *J. Neurochem.* 12:969 (1965).
Swadlow, H.A., Waxman, S.G.: *Exp. Neurol.* 53:128 (1976).
Szeligo, F., Leblond, C.P.: *J. Comp. Neurol.* 172:247 (1977).
Tamarind, D.M., Quillam, J.P.: *Med. Biol. Illustr.* 21:126 (1971).

Tamir, H., Bebirian, R., Muller, F., Casper, D.: *J. Neurochem.* 35:1033 (1980).

Tamir, H., Brunner, W., Casper, D., Rapport, M.M.: *J. Neurochem.* 34:1719 (1980a).

Tanzi, E.: *Rev. Sper. Freniat.* 19:419 (1893).

Tappel, A.L.: *Fed. Proc.* 24:73 (1965).

Tasaki, I., Takenaka, T.: *Proc. Natl. Acad. Sci. USA* 52:804 (1964).

Taubold, R.D.: *Lipids* 10:383 (1975).

Tauc, L.: *Biochemical. Pharm.* 27:3493 (1979).

Tauc, L., Hinzen, D.H.: *Brain Res.* 80:340 (1974).

Tennyson, U., Heikkila, R., Mytilineou, C., Cote, L., Cohen, G.: *Brain Res.* 82:341 (1974).

Tettamanti, G., Preti, A., Cestaro, B., Masserini, M., Sonnino, G., Ghidoni, R.: In: *Cell Surface Glycolipids,* C.C. Sweeley (Ed.). Am. Chem. Soc.: Washington (1980). p. 321.

Thompson, R.: *A Behavioral Atlas of the Rat Brain.* Oxford Univ. Press: New York (1978).

Thorn, L.: *Dtsche Med. Wschr.* 98:2253 (1973).

Toews, A.D., Padilla, S.S., Roger, L.J., Morell, P.: *Neurochem. Res.* 5:1175 (1980).

Traub, R.D., Llinas, R.: *J. Neurophysiol.* 42:476 (1979).

Tsukahara, N.: *Trends Neurosci.* 4:234 (1981).

Ueda, T., Greengard, P., Berzins, K., Cohen, R.S., Blomberg, F., Grab, D.J., Siekevitz, P.: *J. Cell. Biol.* 83:308 (1979).

Uphouse, L., Bonner, J.: *Dev. Psychobiol.* 8:171 (1975).

Van Harreveld, A., Fifkova, E.: *Exp. Neurol.* 49:736 (1975).

Van Heyningen, W.E.: *Nature* 249:415 (1974).

Verity, M.A.: *J. Neurochem.* 19:1305 (1972).

Vern, B.A., Schuette, W.H., Thibault, L.E.: *J. Neurophysiol.* 40:1015 (1977).

Villegas, J.: *J. Physiol.* 249:679 (1975).

Virchow, R.: *Allgem Z. Psychiat.* 3:424 (1846).

Volkmar, F.R., Greenough, W.T.: *Science* 176:1445 (1972).

Vrensen, G., Nunes Cardozo, J.: *Brain Res.* 218:79 (1981).

Wachtel, H., Kandel, E.R.: *J. Neurophysiol.* 34:56 (1971).

Walsh, R.N., Cummings, R.A., Budtz-Olsen, O.E.: *Dev. Psychobiol.* 6:3 (1973).

Walsh, R.N., Cummings, R.A., Budtz-Olsen, O.E., Torok, A.: *Int. J. Neurosci.* 4:239 (1972).

Wang, Y.J., Gurd, J.W., Mahler, H.R.: *Life Sci.* 17:725 (1976).

Watts, M.E., Mark, R.F.: *Proc. Aust. Phys. Pharm. Soc.* 1:27 (1970).

Waxman, S.G.: *Arch. Neurol.* 34:585 (1977).

Waxman, S.G., Swadlow, H.A.: *Progr. Neurobiol.* 8:297 (1977).

Waziri, R.: *Science* 195:790 (1977).

Weight, F.F.: In: *Synaptic Transmission and Neuronal Interaction,* M.V.L. Bennett (Ed.). Raven Press: New York (1974). p. 141.

Weight, F.F., Schulman, J.A., Smith, P.A., Busis, N.A.: *Fed. Proc.* 38:2084 (1979).

Werman, R.: *Comp. Biochem. Physiol.* 18:745 (1966).

Woelk, H., Goracci, G., Porcellati, G.: *Hoppe-Seyler's Z. Physiol. Chem.* 355:75 (1974).

Wojtczak, L., Nalecz, M.J.: *Eur. J. Biochem.* 94:99 (1979).

Wolfe, L.S., McIwain, H.: *Biochem. J.* 78:33 (1961).

Woolley, D.W., Gommi, B.W.: *Nature* 202:1074 (1964).

Yamamoto, C., Matsumoto, K., Takagi, M.: *Brain Res.* 38:469 (1980).

Yarom, Y., Spira, M.E.: *Science* 216:80 (1982).

II

THE ENERGY SUPPLY TO
THE NEURONS

Chapter 8

Glucose and Energy Metabolism in the Brain

Of all the nutrients used by the mammalian system, only glucose is able to satisfactorily maintain the metabolism of cerebral tissue. Although mannose and other sugars can also be metabolized, they must first be converted into glucose. On the other hand, fructose, another simple sugar, is capable of being utilized without conversion, but the process is a relatively slow one. And while the brain can additionally make use of ketone bodies, such as 2-hydroxybutyric acid, their low transport rate across the blood-brain barrier restricts their contribution to the production of energy (Hawkins and Biebuyck, 1979). Other substrates that support brain function are converted into glucose elsewhere in the body. Gluconeogenesis, the formation of new molecules of glucose from other components, is absent in the brain.

The brain, then, consumes glucose as an almost exclusive source of energy. Calculation of the ratio of generated carbon dioxide to consumed oxygen, referred to as the respiration quotient, approximates a value of 1. This would conform to the following formula for the oxidation of glucose:

$$C_6 H_{12} O_6 \rightarrow 6H_2O + 6 CO_2 + \text{energy (38 mol ATP)}$$

$$\text{Hence,} \quad \frac{6CO_2}{6O_2} = 1$$

There are only small reserves of brain glucose in the form of the polymer glycogen. These reserves are quickly consumed when there are interruptions in the glucose intake, as in ischemia or hypoglycemia. There is no evidence for the use of fats as an energy source in the adult central nervous system under normal conditions.

TRANSPORT AND CONSUMPTION OF GLUCOSE

Glucose is the only sugar which is actively transported into the brain in substantial quantities. Other sugars, such as fructose and galactose, are unable to pass the blood-brain barrier sufficiently. The glucose passes into the brain via molecular carrier mechanisms located in the endothelia of the brain capillaries. At least two transfer mechanisms have been described: a high-affinity, low capacity system and a low-affinity, high capacity system (Gjedde, 1981). They are strictly stereospecific; D-glucose is the only form transported. When hydrogen is substituted for a single hydroxyl group in the molecule, the entry of this substance (galactose, for example) is restricted. Such a "high-affinity" transport mechanism for glucose (Fig. 8.1) is independent of the presence of sodium ions (for review see Crone, 1978), although calcium ions may be involved (Elbrink and Bihler, 1975). Keller *et al.* (1981) reported the presence of an additional transport system in the neuronal membrane, which was apparently able to effectively regulate the use of glucose by the cell.

The clearance of glucose, that is the amount of sugar consumed by the brain per unit time, depends primarily upon its transport across the blood-brain barrier and the rate of blood flow through the brain, and not as much upon the plasma glucose level. Even after eight days of starvation, when the glucose level in the blood plasma is drastically decreased, the rate of glucose transport into the rat brain remains unchanged. Hyperglycemia may cause a substantial, but short-lived, increase in the cerebral gain of glucose. The excess amount of glucose is initially retained by the brain, but may later diffuse back into the blood.

The half-life of glucose in the brain is short, about 1.2 ± 0.2 minutes (Savaki *et al.*, 1980), and its level is actually rather small, approximately 1.5 micromoles per gram of wet tissue (about 27 milligrams per 100 grams). Of this amount, the intracellular content of the brain cells is probably extremely low.

Glucose is also transported into the cerebrospinal fluid via the choroid plexus, whose endothelia take it up and secrete it, at a lower concentration, into the CSF. The concentration of glucose here does not exceed 60% of its plasma level. The choroid plexus cannot concentrate glucose against the concentration gradient and is unable to actively transport it from the cerebrospinal fluid and the brain back into the blood plasma (Lorenzo, 1976).

Functionally active areas of the central nervous system require more energy and, consequently, more glucose. Such demands are reflected in an increase in the glucose transport rate, a process which is activated by the presence of calcium ions (Clausen, 1980). Probably the most important aspect of the glucose supply resides in the changes of local circulation that are attributable to the opening of brain capillaries.

Stressful situations and emotional arousal are quite often accompanied by transient hyperglycemia. Still, it seems improbable that a hyperglycemic condition is needed by the brain to assure an increase in neuronal activity.

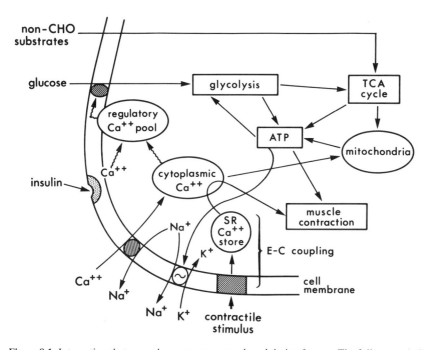

Figure 8.1 Interactions between glucose transport and modulating factors. The full arrows indicate metabolic pathways and ion fluxes; the wavy arrows show the effects of the regulatory calcium pool [from J. Elbrink and I. Bihler, *Science* 188:1177 (1975); © 1975 by the American Association for the Advancement of Science].

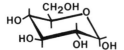

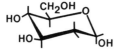

Figure 8.2 Structures of D-glucose (upper) and 2-deoxy-D-glucose (lower).

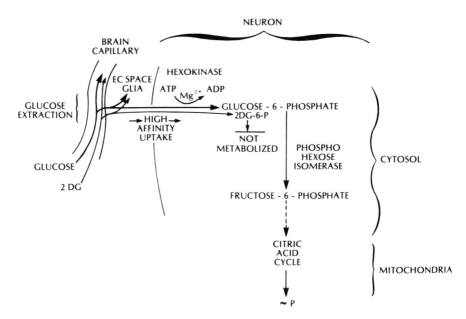

Figure 8.3 Pathways involved in the uptake and initial metabolism of glucose and 2-deoxyglucose (2DG) in nerve cells [from C.M. Shepherd, *The Synaptic Organization of the Brain,* 2nd Ed.; © 1979 by Oxford University Press, New York].

This emotional hyperglycemia is due to the release of adrenal epinephrine, and the excess glucose is primarily used by the skeletal muscles.

Once within the cells, glucose generally undergoes a rapid phosphorylation, leaving only small amount to exist in a free form (Crone, 1978). The rate of membrane transport into the brain cells normally exceeds the rate of glucose phosphorylation by at least one order of magnitude, an indication that it is not a rate-limiting step in the regulation of metabolism.

The overall consumption of glucose by the brain can be calculated by determining the arteriovenous glucose difference and the rate of blood flow (Kety, 1957). There are, in addition, several available methods for the measurement of regional glucose consumption. For example, 2-deoxy-D-glucose (Fig. 8.2) can be actively transported into the brain and neurons by the glucose-transporting carrier mechanism. But, in this form, the metabolic systems of the cell are unable to use it further, and the metabolic process is stopped at the first phosphorylation step (Fig. 8.3). Hexokinase, an enzyme which phosphorylates glucose, will produce the 2-deoxyglucose-6-phosphate, but this compound cannot be isomerized to fructose-6-phosphate and the metabolism ceases. By using a labeled 2-deoxy-D-glucose, the rate of glucose utilization can then be computed from the levels of radioactivity retained by the tissue. The mapping of neuronal activity by the 2-deoxyglucose method has enabled researchers to recognize, among other things, epileptogenic foci within the nervous tissue, alterations in the suprachiasmatic nucleus of the hypothalamus during circadian rhythms (Schwartz and Gainer, 1977), the metabolic response of the hippocampus to electrical stimulation, and the reaction of the brain to various drugs (such as apomorphine), or hormones and their fragments (Delanoy and Dunn, 1978).

Another method, employed by Shimada et al. (1977), involves a direct measurement of regional glucose consumption using postmortem microwave irradiation of the entire head, a treatment which inactivates all enzymes. Levels of [^{14}C]glucose or its metabolites may then be measured directly, and the glucose consumption estimated.

Using human volunteers, Phelps et al. (1979) measured glucose consumption in the brain by the intravenous injection of [^{18}F]-2-fluoro-2-deoxy-D-glucose. He then used computer-controlled tomography to detect the distribution of this radioactive material in the brain (Fig. 8.4). The method provides reproducible results which can be quantitatively evaluated. This isotope of fluorine emits a positron which collides with an electron present in the cell to produce a pair of high energy photons. Since this radiation has good tissue penetration, it may be detected externally by sensor. The data from the sensors may then be processed by computer to generate an image of the distribution of metabolic changes in the brain (Brownell et al.,

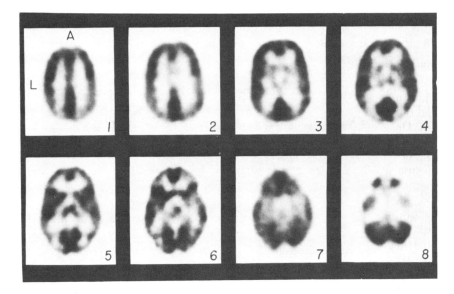

Figure 8.4   Local metabolic rate for glucose in a human brain determined by
[^{18}F]-2-fluoro-2-deoxyglucose administration in combination with tomography. Cross sections
through the brain from 8 cm above to 1 cm below the orbital meatus. L, left side; A, anterior.
Increasing tissue activity is shown as darker shades of gray [from M.E. Phelps, S.C. Huang,
E.J. Hoffman, C. Selin, L. Sokoloff, D.E. Kuhl, *Ann. Neurol.* 6:371 (1979); © 1978 by Michael
E. Phelps].

1982). This type of analysis is known as Positron Emission Tomography
(PET) and is presently able to provide a resolution of about 20 mm (Raichle,
1979). Technical improvements in the near future, however, should be able
to lower this figure to about 6 mm (i.e., a cube 6 mm on a side [Greenberg *et
al.*, 1981]).

   In addition to measuring local glucose consumption, PET techniques
can also detect oxygen utilization, blood flow and blood volume. It also
should eventually be possible to measure local protein or neurotransmitter
metabolism, neurotransmitter receptor binding and the penetration of various substances through the blood-brain barrier (Raichle, 1979). These
methods may eventually prove invaluable not only in clinical diagnosis, but
in delineating areas of the brain involved in various complex functions,
including information processing and storage.

   Gray matter consumes three times as much glucose as does white matter, at a rate varying from 50 to 200 μmol glucose/100g/min. The highest

local glucose metabolism in the brain has been found in the periventricular and preoptic nuclei of the hypothalamus. Also, the septum and amygdaloid nucleus have a higher rate than the neocortex, olfactory bulb, corpus striatum, cingulum, and fornix. The consumption in the substantia nigra and nucleus ruber is substantially lower than in other brain regions (Schwartz and Sharp, 1978). Stimulation of the sensory receptors causes an increase in the glucose consumption of the associated neuronal pathway. For example, noise increases the consumption in auditory pathway, whereas the rotation of the animal elevates glucose uptake in the vestibular nuclei and vestibulocerebellum (Sharp, 1976). Similarly, electrical stimulation of the sciatic nerve increases consumption in the lumbar segments of the spinal cord. This functionally related shift in glucose metabolism has proven quite useful methodologically for such things as the direct visualization of ocular dominance columns in the striate cortex of the monkey. Since the columns represent an alternating vertical pattern of inputs from each eye, a unilateral enucleation means that only the cortical columns receiving fibers from the intact eye will show predominant amounts of radioactive 2-deoxyglucose labeling (Fig. 8.5).

The consumption of glucose is also altered during the passage of a wave of cortical spreading depression, and is probably dependent upon high levels of extracellular potassium (Shinohara et al., 1979). At the same time, glucose consumption in many other brain areas is diminished. Although glucose consumption does not substantially change during epileptic convulsions, several other types of experimental seizures, including audiogenic seizures, may cause an increase in its utilization. Sometimes this increase is not sufficient to satisfy the demand and the energy reserves may be depleted.

Also strenuous exercise, such as swimming in rats, increases glucose consumption in many areas of the brain. The effect is greatest in the cerebellar vermis and least in the inferior colliculi (Sharp, 1976a).

The most important factor associated with glucose consumption by the brain is the extent of phosphorylation of the adenine nucleotides into adenosine triphosphoric acid, an event which is reflected by the ratio of oxidized and reduced forms of nicotinamide adenine dinucleotide (NAD/NADH ratio). The actual amount of ATP in the brain is very stable, and it is not substantially changed in different physiological states, even including mild hypoxia. What does shift, however, is the level of glucose utilization.

Several hormones are able to influence brain glucose metabolism. Progesterone, testosterone, deoxycorticosterone and other hormones have been found to inhibit oxygen consumption by brain cell suspensions. The metabolic effect of insulin upon brain glucose is debatable. Hypophysectomy has no effect on the overall glucose consumption, although it does produce a 25% increase in anaerobic glycolysis.

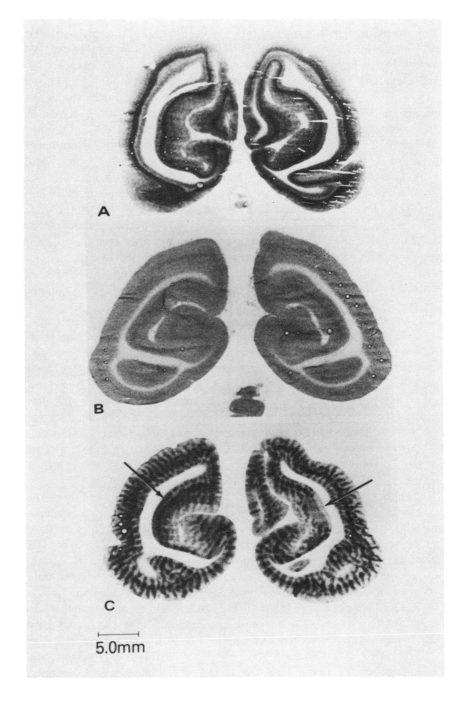

5.0mm

When slices of cerebral cortex are electrically stimulated *in vitro*, their glucose consumption and respiration increase. The addition of potassium ions to the incubation medium augments these effects even further. The brain appears singularly responsive to potassium in this way; other tissues are not so affected. Sodium ions are similar to potassium in this respect. Both electrical stimulation of the tissue slices and elevated levels of potassium in the incubation medium have the same mechanism of action, depolarizing both neuronal and glial membranes (McIlwain, 1966).

Glucose consumption is quite conspicuous in the nerve endings, where it is associated with synaptic transmission. Sodium ions have been found to stimulate synaptosomal glucose oxidation by 180%, while potassium ions are without effect (Diamond and Fishman, 1973). The association of this consumption with synaptic transmission is self-evident. Wieraszko (1982) found that the development of long-term potentiation in hippocampal slices leads to an increase in 2-deoxyglucose uptake when the potentiated synapses are pressed to become active. The data indicate that the biochemical components of LTP are energy-dependent and that this portion of cellular metabolic activity is adjusted to the functional demands of the synapse.

BRAIN GLYCOGEN

The level of glycogen in the brain, as compared with that in muscle, is low. In the human brain, it is only about 110 milligrams per 100 grams of the brain weight, and its turnover is very rapid. In the nerve cell, glycogen is usually localized in the cytoplasm and in mitochondria.

The level of glycogen in the brain is subject to the adequacy of the diet. Thus, twenty-four hours of food deprivation in the rat can lower the level of glycogen from 51 to 38 mg %. Convulsant drugs as well as methamphetamine and alcohol all decrease the level of glycogen in the brain. The administration of insulin depletes the CNS glycogen content, with some areas being affected more than others (Lust and Pasonneau, 1976). Epinephrine is without any sizeable effect, and hydrocortisone elevates the level, probably as a result of an increase in the transport of glucose.

←

Figure 8.5 Autoradiographs of coronal brain sections from the Rhesus monkey at the level of the striate cortex. A. Animal with normal bilateral vision. B. Animal with bilateral visual deprivation. C. Animal with right eye occluded [from C. Kennedy, M.H. DesRosiers, O. Sakurada, M. Shinohara, M. Reivich, J.W. Jehle, L. Sokoloff, *Proc. Natl. Acad. Sci. USA* 73:4230 (1976); © 1976 by C. Kennedy].

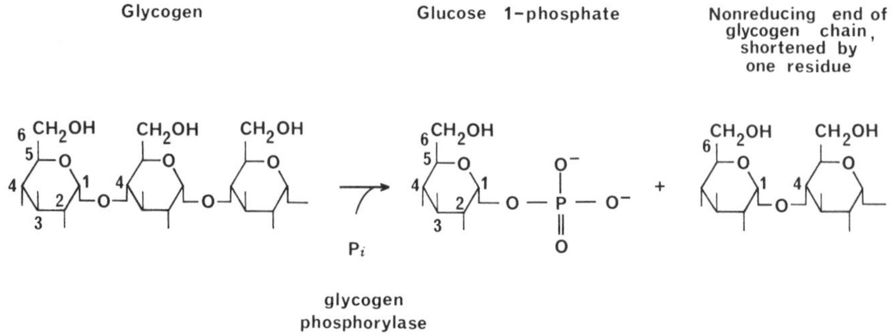

Glycogen   Glucose 1-phosphate   Nonreducing end of
                                                         glycogen chain,
                                                         shortened by
                                                         one residue

glycogen
phosphorylase

Figure 8.6 Removal of a glucose residue from the end of a glycogen molecule by phosphorylation.

The breakdown of glycogen into molecules of glucose-1-phosphate is catalyzed by the enzyme glycogen phosphorylase (Fig. 8.6). Of the three types of this enzyme, MM (muscle type), LL (liver type) and BB (brain type), the BB type is predominant in various fetal tissues, hepatomas, and the adult mammalian brain. It must first be activated by a phosphorylase kinase, an enzyme which in turn is activated by cyclic adenosine monophosphate, a mediator of neurotransmitter effects on neuronal metabolism (Lust and Pasonneau, 1976). For this reason, norepinephrine, dopamine, histamine and serotonin, all neurotransmitters stimulating the synthesis of cyclic adenosine monophosphate, also induce the degradation of glycogen in nervous tissue (Mrsulja, 1974). This mechanism represents an important connection between synaptic activity and metabolic activity of the neuron.

Of particular interest is the observation of Landowne and Ritchie (1971) that one of the ions controlling the breakdown of glycogen is calcium, which enters the nerve cell during depolarization. Such a chain of events would ensure an increased supply of energy at a time when the cell is active.

PATHWAYS OF GLUCOSE METABOLISM IN THE BRAIN

In principle, the glucose molecule is first activated by phosphorylation, and then split into two fragments containing three carbons, dihydroxyacetone phosphate and glyceraldehyde 3-phosphate. These fragments are interconvertible by isomerization and, as glyceraldehyde 3-phosphate, are phosphorylated and oxidized on their way to the production of pyruvate (Fig. 8.7). Pyruvate may then be reduced to lactate. The net energetic yield of this anaerobic process is two molecules of ATP per molecule of glucose.

A comparison of carbohydrate metabolism in the brain and another highly active organ, the liver, shows that its potential activity is apparently higher in the brain. Hexokinase and phosphofructokinase, enzymes which initiate glucose metabolism, determine how rapidly glucose is used within the central nervous system (Takagaki, 1968). They therefore represent a

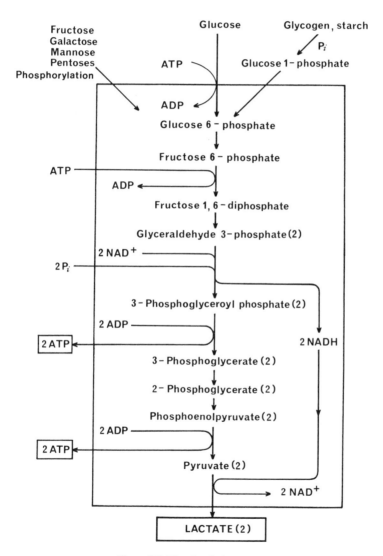

Figure 8.7 The glycolytic pathway.

rate-limiting step in glucose metabolism, since only glucose phosphorylated by them may enter other metabolic processes.

Most of the activity of hexokinase (ATP: D-hexose 6-phosphotransferase) in the brain is present in the outer mitochondrial membrane. This localization varies according to the neuronal activity (Knull *et al.*, 1974). The binding of brain hexokinase to the mitochondria is dependent upon its molecular structure and not on the mitochondria (Kurokawa *et al.*, 1979). Some hexokinase is also in the cytoplasm of nerve cell bodies and astrocytes. The concentration and localization differs in relation to the cell type. Thus, for example, in the cerebellum, the enzyme is high in the cytoplasm of the basket, stellate, granule, Golgi and Lugaro cells, and lower in Purkinje cells, where it is localized mainly in secondary and tertiary branches of the dendrites (Kao-Jen and Wilson, 1980). The enzyme utilizes glucose and adenosine triphosphate and produces glucose-6-phosphate. Adenosine diphosphate and glucose-6-phosphate, products of the reaction, are natural inhibitors of the reaction. This product inhibition is one of the control points in the process of brain glycolysis.

The phosphorylation of glucose in the brain is very rapid and efficient, and the only limiting factor is the rate of the reaction is the accessibility of glucose. The brain has been shown to have the highest hexokinase activity of any organ in the body, with about 40 to 50% of this activity being present in the synaptosomes (Wilson, 1973). The convulsions caused by electroshock, metrazol or intensive sound have been found to increase the V_{max} of brain hexokinase. On the other hand, several anaesthetics inhibit glucose phosphorylation in the brain (Bielicki and Krieglstein, 1977).

An enzyme with an opposing function is glucose-6-phosphatase. It removes the phosphate group from glucose-6-phosphate and has recently been discovered to be prominent in large neurons, Purkinje cells and the pyramidal cells of the cortex (Stephens and Sandborn, 1976). Its physiological function is unknown, although hepatic glucose-6-phosphatase is considered to be involved in the release of glucose into the blood. It has been found to be activated during sleep (Anchors *et al.*, 1977).

Glucose phosphate isomerase, the second enzyme of the glycolytic pathway, is involved in the conversion of glucose-6-phosphate into fructose-6-phosphate. In the brain, it is localized in the cellular cytoplasm, and, compared with other tissues, its activity there in all neural regions is very high.

Another glycolytic enzyme, phosphofructokinase, phosphorylates fructose-6-phosphate into fructose-1, 6-diphosphate. Its activity is controlled by the ratio of adenine nucleotides to inorganic phosphate and is thus functially dependent upon the rate of ATP hydrolysis by the neuron. This enzyme is probably the main control point in the glycolytic pathway. There is typically a high level of ATP in the brain, so that the activity of phosphofructokinase is somewhat suppressed. But, it is activated at times when the energy demands are greatly elevated, as during the convulsive activity or anoxia.

One possible explanation of the direct effect of glucose on neuronal activity and behavior can be found in the papers of Chaplain (1979). The author discovered that a recycling of components of the glycolytic pathway, fructose-6-phosphate   and   fructose-1,   6-diphosphate,   by   the membrane-bound   enzymes,   phosphofructokinase   and   fructose-1, 6-diphosphatase, causes a fluctuation of the neuronal membrane potential. The reversibility of this metabolic step is due to a redistribution of two kinetically distinct forms of phosphofructokinase, along with the presence of free hydrogen ions and ATP. Chaplain originally studied these metabolic changes in the pacemaker cells of *Aplysia* and concluded that this reversible step in the glycolytic pathway induced slow oscillations in the membrane potential and the rhythmic production of nerve impulses. He subsequently concluded that this reaction is also involved in the control of other non-rhythmic types of neuronal behavior, and possibly even in the consolidation of the memory trace. Accordingly, modifiers of phosphofructokinase activity are able to alter the retention of avoidance and discrimination learning in rats and honey bees. Thus, this reaction may, together with various other changes, such as the restructuring and degradation of sialic acid-containing substances, determine the actual membrane potential of the neuron, and consequently, its excitability.

The final products of anaerobic glycolysis are two acids, pyruvic and lactic. These acids are unable to cross the blood-brain barrier, so that, when present in the blood plasma, they are not taken up by the brain. Analogously, they are not generally released from the brain following their formation there. An exception has been found in the absence of oxygen, during which time there is some passage of pyruvic and lactic acids from brain tissue. Periods of activity, including stimulation by short electrical pulses, increase their levels.

Lactic dehydrogenase (L-lactate: NAD-oxidoreductase) catalyses the reduction of pyruvate to lactate. In the body, lactic dehydrogenase (LDH) exists in five molecular forms. All are formed by two types of subunits. The enzyme molecule is a tetramer, and its subunits are joined in random fashion, so that there are five possible combinations of this enzyme. In the adult brain, type 1 predominates, representing about 40% of the total activity. There its presence can be divided into three compartments, the cytoplasm, the fluid space of subcellular particles (including the synaptosomes) and the membranes (Berlet and Lehnert, 1978).

The aerobic breakdown of carbohydrates begins with the oxidative decarboxylation of pyruvic acid to acetic acid, which is then bound to coen-

zyme A. Coenzyme A is a trivial name for a complex molecule that contains
a nucleotide adenine, ribose, and several phosphate groups in addition to
some other components. The sulfhydryl group (SH) of the coenzyme is able
to form covalent bonds with other molecules It is the attachment of a molecule of an organic acid, acetate for example, to coenzyme A which
"activates" the molecule, enabling it to enter many different chemical reactions, including those within the citric acid cycle. Pyruvic acid may also be
carboxylated to produce oxaloacetate which then in combination with acetyl
coenzyme A initiates the tricarboxylic or citric acid cycle (Fig. 8.8).

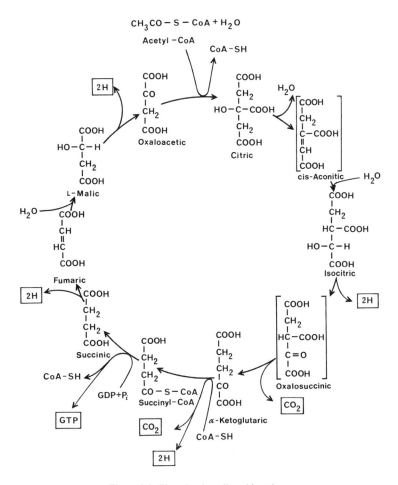

Figure 8.8 The tricarboxylic acid cycle.

The citric acid cycle which is also known as the Krebs cycle or tricarboxylic acid (TCA) cycle is the main metabolic pathway of glucose in the brain. Since the components of the TCA cycle may be used for the synthesis of amino acids and other compounds, the TCA cycle effectively unites the metabolic pathways of protein and carbohydrate metabolism. And, the amino acids that are derived from the intermediary metabolites of the cycle are believed to act in the CNS as putative neurotransmitters.

One of the final products of the TCA cycle is carbon dioxide. But, from the standpoint of energy release, this carbon dioxide production is of negligible importance. The main energetic yield of the metabolism of glucose comes from hydrogen atoms, and the synthesis of water molecules from hydrogen and oxygen provides energy for all the metabolic processes in the body.

Several of the enzymes of aerobic glycolysis have been examined in terms of how they relate to the functional state of the brain. As the neuronal activity increases, so does the activity of these enzymes. Succinic oxidase and pyruvate dehydrogenase are but two examples of enzymes that respond in this way. Pyruvate dehydrogenase is also crucial to other aspects of brain metabolism, and it may also influence the rate of synthesis of lipids, acetylcholine and several other molecules.

Uninterrupted neuronal activity is very much dependent upon both the integrity of the pathways involved in glucose metabolism and the adequacy of the energy supplies provided by them. These two factors are not necessarily synonymous. During hypoglycemia, stupor and the loss of consciousness appear long before there is a shortage of adenosine triphosphate and phosphocreatine. The level of these high-energy compounds may still be completely normal, even at the beginning of unconsciousness. When glucose metabolism returns to a seemingly normal level, it may take at least another ten minutes before the individual regains consciousness. A defect in the utilization of glucose by the neurons may therefore directly block neuronal activity without involving the high-energy compounds.

In 1968, Moore and Perez reported the isolation of a brain protein which was named 14-3-2 due to its chromatographic behavior. It is primarily a neuronal protein, and is a major component of the synaptosomal fraction (Packman et al., 1971). 14-3-2 (or nerve specific protein) has been found to be localized in the postsynaptic web near the postsynaptic membrane, in the presynaptic portion of the synapse and in the presynaptic densities (Ronnback et al., 1977). However, it does not appear to be present in synaptic vesicles. Several years later, it was discovered that this protein was identical with the neuronal form of a glycolytic enzyme, 2-phospho-D-glycerate hydrolase (Marangos and Zomzely-Neurath, 1976). This particular enzyme, also termed neuron-specific enolase (NSE), has not been found in glia, although these cells do contain another form of enolase, non-neuron-specific

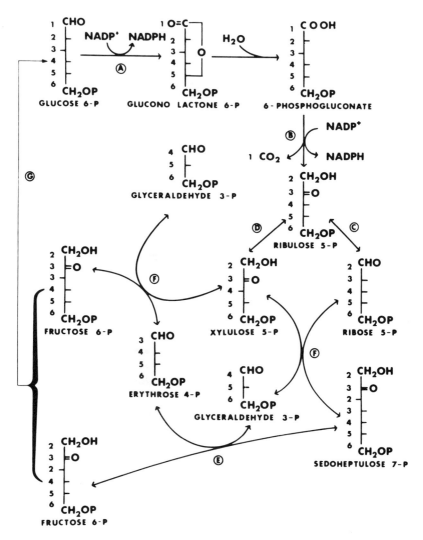

Figure 8.9 The classic phosphogluconate pathway. The associated enzymes are: A.. glu-cose-6-*P*-dehydrogenase; B. 6-phosphogluconate dehydrogenase; C. phosphate-5-*P*-isomerase; D. pentose-5-*P*-3′ epimerase; E. transaldolase; F. transketolase; G. phosphohexose isomerase [from J.F. Williams, *Trends Neurosci.* 3:315 (1980), © 1980 by Elsevier-North Holland Biomedical Press].

enolase (NNE). These two enzymes differ from one another in a number of ways, including their thermal stability and their sensitivity to such ions as potassium and sodium. In being highly active in synaptosomes, neuron-specific enolase is likely involved in neurotransmitter function and, possibly, in the longlasting adaptation of synaptic functions during the process of learning (Pickel *et al.*, 1975).

PENTOSE PHOSPHATE CYCLE

Prior discussions of glycolysis and the citric acid cycle concerned themselves with the use of glucose for the generation of energy in the form of ATP. However, various intermediates produced in the course of glycolysis may enter different pathways. One of these pathways, beginning with a dehydrogenation of glucose-6-phosphate, is the pentose phosphate cycle, also called the phosphogluconate pathway or the hexose monophosphate shunt (Fig. 8.9). Dehydrogenation reactions are biological oxidations. But, substances that are oxidized within the cell are seldom subjected to this type of reaction, as the term oxidation would imply, by having oxygen added to them. As a rule, biological oxidations take place by the removal of hydrogen atoms from the molecules undergoing the oxidation. These hydrogen atoms are typically displaced by the action of substrate-specific dehydrogenases in the presence of particular hydrogen acceptors acting as coenzymes. If molecular oxygen should serve as the hydrogen acceptor, then the enzymes are referred to as oxidases.

In the course of the metabolic breakdown of glucose, some displaced electrons and hydrogen atoms, instead of being transferred to oxygen to produce ATP, are used biosynthetically for other purposes, in this case for the eventual synthesis of the nucleic acids. The hydrogen acceptor involved in this initial channeling of hydrogen atoms into the pentose phosphate pathway is nicotinamide adenine dinucleotide phosphate. Although the energy yield of this pathway is negligible, it has several other functions. First, it generates reducing power in the form of NADPH. The hydrogen atoms displaced from glucose during its oxidation are usually tranferred to oxygen, but can also be used for the biosynthesis of NADPH. Second, in this cycle, hexoses are converted into pentoses, particularly into the D-ribose-5-phosphate required in the synthesis of nucleic acids. Third, it can also convert pentoses into hexoses which may be used as a source of energy.

The products of the pentose phosphate cycle are phosphorylated five-carbon sugars, or pentose phosphates. These sugars may then be split into two and three carbon fragments, which can be further degraded in the tricarboxylic acid cycle or recombined into several molecular forms as heptoses, hexoses, pentoses, tetroses and trioses. Of several enzymes of this cycle, two are important. These are transketolase and transaldolase (Fig. 8.10, 8.11). The basic difference between the reactions catalyzed by these enzymes is that transketolase transfers a two-carbon unit, while transaldolase does the same to a three-carbon unit. These enzymes provide a reversible association between glycolysis and the pentose phosphate pathway.

About 5-8% of brain glucose passes through the pentose phosphate cycle (in Rhesus monkey) (Hostetler *et al.*, 1970). Glucose-6-phosphate dehydrogenase activity is quite active, particularly in the white matter. The transketolase and transaldolase enzymes of the cycle also exhibit high levels of activity, and Kaufmann and Harkonen (1977) have suggested that alterations in this activity could represent an important component of the response of neural tissue to physiological and pharmacological stimuli. Neurotransmitters have, in this regard, been found to stimulate this activity in synaptosomes (Appel and Parrot, 1970). Moreover, the stimulation of cortical tissue slices by electrical pulses *in vitro* enhances the metabolism of glucose via the pentose phosphate pathway (Kimura *et al.*, 1974). The increased output of the products of this cycle during neuronal and synaptic activity is most likely necessary for the synthesis of several substances needed in the biochemical restructuring of the activated synapse.

While the pentose phosphate cycle is one of the channels through which the carbons from glucose can be directed, they may also be channeled via acetyl-coenzyme A into the tricarboxylic acid cycle, or into the production of amino acids, purine and pyrimidine bases, lipids, and glycoproteins.

About two-thirds of the glucose in the immature brain is used in this way, and the maximum rate of conversion occurs during the periods of rapid brain development, although the rate of the incorporation of carbon atoms into

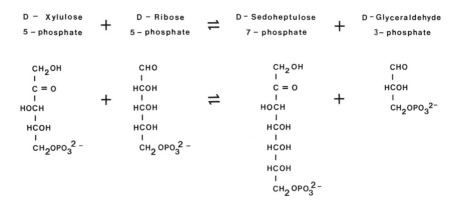

Figure 8.10 The transketolase reaction.

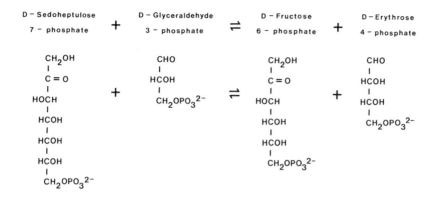

Figure 8.11 The transaldolase reaction.

various brain components is also dependent upon the functional state (De Feudis, 1971).

ENERGY METABOLISM IN BRAIN TISSUE

Back in 1929, Himwich and Nahum demonstrated that the energy supply of the brain differs from that of the other organs by being heavily dependent directly upon glucose. In addition, its energy consumption is higher than in other organs, and adult values are greater than those in the immature brain. Most changes in cellular energy metabolism that accompany neuronal activity are coupled to the maintenance and restoration of ionic gradients across the neuronal membranes. Some amount of energy is used for other aspects of neuronal and glial metabolism, although the proportioned channeling between these two components of brain metabolism remains to be clarified. Also, the metabolic rate reflects not only excitatory, but inhibitory processes as well. Both of them make demands upon the energy supply.

During development, the metabolism of glucose is differentiated into at least two compartments. One of them is used exclusively for the energy supply, and the intermediary products of the other are used for the synthesis of amino acid neurotransmitters. Accordingly, the mitochondria in the adult brain also form two populations - one with a high level of cytochrome C oxidase, which is predominantly involved in energy metabolism, and the second with a high level of monoamine oxidase that is primarily localized in nerve endings, but is also found in neuronal perikarya and glial cells. This monoamine oxidase is involved in the metabolism of neurotransmitters.

BRAIN OXYGEN CONSUMPTION

Although the brain represents only about 2% of the body weight, its oxygen consumption is about 20% of the total body oxygen requirements. During the prenatal and early postnatal periods, it can be as high as 50%. The products of the oxidations are water and carbon dioxide. But, not all carbon dioxide produced by the brain is derived directly from glucose. Some of it comes from various endogenous sources, such as amino acids, and this is largely attributable to the metabolically active pools of glutamate, GABA and succinic semialdehyde.

The activity of the brain is dependent upon a continuous supply of oxygen. The partial pressure of oxygen (pO_2) in the brain tissue is relatively high, at least 26-30mm Hg, and is associated with the degree of blood oxygenation in the carotid arteries. There is a linear relationship between arterial pO_2 and cerebral pO_2. When the partial pressure of oxygen in the venous blood decreases to 17-19mm Hg, the individual loses consciousness. This is known as the "critical threshold of oxygen" (Opitz and Schneider, 1950). At 12-14 mm Hg, life is threatened (the "deadly threshold").

The respiratory rate of phylogenetically young regions of the mammalian brain is higher than that of the older regions. This value, expressed as the amount of oxygen consumed per wet weight of the samples, decreases in a stepwise manner from cortex to medulla. If oxygen consumption is related to cell density, then the cortex has the highest metabolic rate, while the rest of the areas are approximately equal. This indicates that most regional differences in the rate of respiration reflect local differences in neuronal and glial cell density. The respiratory rate of neuronal and glial cells *in vitro* is almost the same, about $0.4 - 0.8 \times 10^{-5}$ µl O_2/hour/cell (Dittman *et al.*, 1973).

The concentration of ions in the extracellular fluid, and this is particularly true for potassium, is known to substantially influence the metabolic rate of nervous tissue. A potassium-induced increase in respiration, detected both *in vivo* and *in vitro*, depends primarily upon glial metabolism.

The stimulation of afferent sensory nerves boosts the metabolic rate in corresponding areas of the brain. Accordingly, olfactory stimulation with amyl acetate elevates the rate in the olfactory regions in the rat. On the other hand, a decrease in the excitation of the pathway lowers the respiratory rate of the entire pathway. Thus, auditory deprivation caused by a wax occlusion of both auditory canals causes a bilaterally symmetrical 35-60% depression in the auditory areas. Visual deprivation lowers the metabolic rate in the superior colliculi, lateral geniculate bodies and visual cortex (for review see Sokoloff, 1977).

Areas of the brain which are stimulated by the presence of hormones alter their metabolic rate in relation to the hormonal level. Oxygen consumption by the hypothalamus, for example, changes during the estrous cycle, during treatments with gonadal hormones or gonadotropins, and following hypophysectomy or castration (Mas and Solis, 1977).

Sleep has no effect on the respiratory rate, but still does cause a small increase in the cerebral blood flow. Anxiety and mental activity are both able to raise the cerebral metabolism and respiratory rate. During convulsions caused by electroconvulsive shock or flurothyl, the metabolic rate also increases substantially. Anaesthesia reduces the energy metabolism in all structures, although to a greater extent in gray matter. It also reduces the metabolic heterogeneity in different areas of the gray matter, although the supply of oxygen far exceeds the consumption (Buchweitz et al., 1980).

As expressed by its oxygen and glucose consumption, the conscious animal has a brain metabolism that is approximately twice as high as the in vitro rate. During convulsions, it increases even further. The glucose and oxygen consumption measured on tissue slices are almost equal to that of an animal in deep anesthesia, with extinguished reflexes (McIlwain, 1966).

A decrease in the oxygen supply can obviously interfere with brain functions. It may even destroy nerve cells. Because of the large demand for oxygen by brain tissue and the small store of high-energy compounds, the onset of the neurological symptoms of hypoxia appears earlier than in other tissues. According to Haldane (1919), hypoxia not only halts the machine, but wrecks the machinery. It causes a sharp decrease in the concentration of high energy compounds, which interferes with many functions of the nerve cells, including protein synthesis, amino acid transport, and nerve impulse conduction.

Changes in synaptic transmission are responsible for at least some of the neurological signs of hypoxia. Shortly after the onset, the presynaptic terminals appear enlarged. Later, they are seen to contain several multilamellar bodies, and the synaptic vesicles are clumped away from the synaptic cleft.

All of these hypoxic changes cause deficits in short-term memory (Sechzer, 1971). And, hypoxia induced immediately after operant conditioning in rats also interferes with long-term retention. Hypoxic conditions established 6-7 hours after training were without effect (Giurgea et al., 1971).

MITOCHONDRIA

The production of high-energy compounds in the brain, as in any other tissue, depends on the activity of mitochondria. The mitochondria are products of two genetic systems, a nucleo-cytoplastic system and a mitochondrial system. The nucleo-cytoplasmic system forms 90% of the mitochondrial proteins, which are transported into the mitochondria by an energy-dependent process (for a review see Schatz, 1979). The mitochondrial genome produces two ribosomal RNA species, about twenty different tRNA species, and a limited number of proteins which are part of the inner mitochondrial membrane. These organelles contain at least seventy different enzymes, most of which participate in converting the energy derived from oxidation into the "high-energy" chemical bonds of adenosinetriphosphoric acid (ATP).

Each nerve cell contains several hundred mitochondria. Morphologically, they are similar to those extracted from other organs. But, several populations of mitochondria in the brain reflect a biochemical compartmentation of metabolism in various brain structures and their involvement either in calcium transport in the metabolism of at least two putative nrurotransmitters, glutamic acid and γ-aminobutyric acid.

The surface of a mitochondrion is formed by two layers of membranes, with the inner one folded into several *cristae* (Fig. 8.12). The inner membrane contains all of the electron carriers, the ion transport mechanisms and all of the dehydrogenases, while the outer membrane contains monoamine oxidase, hexokinase and a number of other enzymes. The outer membrane is freely permeable to electrolytes, water, and sugars. The inner membrane is impermeable to hydrogen ions, sodium, chloride, potassium and magnesium.

The mitochondria contain those enzymes necessary for the metabolism of glucose, including succinic and lactic dehydrogenases, and glycerol kinase. The production of carbon dioxide from the oxidation of carbohydrates is not accompanied by any considerable yield of energy. In contrast, water produced from hydrogen ions carried by the reduced coenzymes of the respiratory chain and from atmospheric oxygen is a product of reactions that supply a considerable amount of energy for the synthesis of ATP. The most

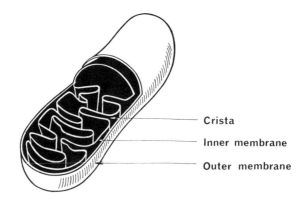

Crista

Inner membrane

Outer membrane

Figure 8.12 Drawing of a mitochondrion showing the inner arrangement of cristae.

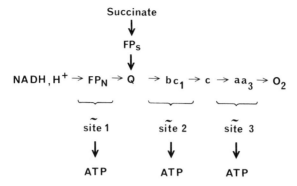

Figure 8.13 Electron transport chain in mitochondria. The three brackets designate the three "coupling sites" where energy from respiration is transferred to ATP. FP, flavoproteins; Q, ubiquinone; b, c_1, c, a, a_3, cytochromes.

common donor of hydrogen for this reaction is a system of flavoproteins (Fig. 8.13), the most important component of which, cytochrome oxidase, differs in various brain areas depending upon the function. In this regard, Wong-Riley (1976, 1979) found that visual and auditory deprivation causes a decrease in cytochrome oxidase in the visual and auditory systems, respectively.

The energy released by the gradual oxidation of hydrogen is trapped in a "high-energy" molecule of ATP (Fig. 8.14). This coupling of oxidation and phosphorylation is accomplished by several proteins attached to the mitochondrial membrane. One is easily detached from the membrane and

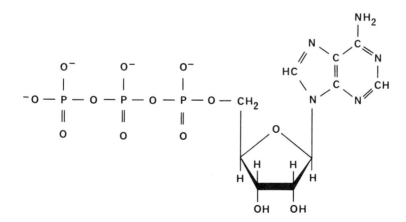

Figure 8.14 Structure of adenosine triphosphate.

contains a site where ATP synthesis takes place (F_1 peptide). The F fraction is an integral part of the membrane, and tranfers available energy to the ATP-synthesizing site. Once synthesized, the ATP is transported from the mitochondria into the cytoplasm. The oxidation-phosphorylation system also maintains the levels of intramitochondrial adenosine monophosphate, adenosine diphosphate and inorganic phosphate.

Our understanding of the transduction of energy from the oxidation of hydrogen to the formation of high-energy compounds is still incomplete. In spite of the uncertainties, three steps of the process have been delineated. First is the energy-yielding oxidation of NADH or other reduced metabolites at the inner mitochondrial membrane. Secondly it is known that there is a transfer and storage of energy in some form, where it is kept from being degraded to thermal energy. And lastly, the stored energy is used to drive the synthesis of ATP.

Chapter 9

Blood Flow and Temperature of the Brain

The brain is greatly dependent upon the permanent availability of oxygen and glucose, because its own energy stores are low. This means that there must be a steady, uninterrupted flow of blood through the brain and that an increase in the metabolic rate within an area requires a rapid adaptation of the regional blood flow.

The brain receives its supply of blood through a pair of internal carotid arteries and a pair of vertebral arteries (Fig. 9.1). Together, the vertebral arteries form a basilar artery, which is divided into two posterior cerebral arteries that are connected, through the posterior communicating branches, to middle cerebral arteries, forming the arterial circle of Willis.

The circle of Willis equilibrates the blood supply from the carotid and vertebral arteries. Several cerebral arteries originate from it. The anterior and middle cerebral arteries receive blood mainly from the internal carotid artery, while the posterior cerebral arteries branch off of the basilar artery. The veins returning blood from the brain are tributaries of the dural sinuses which empty into the internal jugular veins.

The cerebral blood flow (CBF) is remarkably stable over the range of systemic systolic blood pressures from 90 to 180 mm Hg (only 160 mm Hg

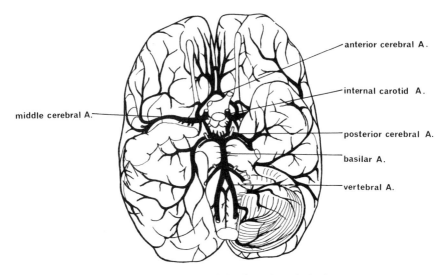

anterior cerebral A.

internal carotid A.

middle cerebral A.

posterior cerebral A.

basilar A.

vertebral A.

Figure 9.1 The arterial blood supply to the brain.

in the rat). Beyond these limits, the cerebral blood flow is pressure-dependent. The local chemical control of the CBF involves a direct combined effect on the blood vessels of the local levels of carbon dioxide, oxygen, potassium ions, adenine nucleotides, pH, and intermediate metabolites of the tricarboxylic acid cycle. These substances are probably able to influence directly the smooth muscles of the blood vessels and precapillary sphincters.

An increase in the rate of tissue metabolism may also lead to more permanent morphological changes in the vascular supply. The brain capillaries are the most important exchangers of oxygen and glucose, and their number and length reflect regional differences in metabolic activity. In guinea pigs trained daily on an activity wheel for two or three months, there was a 20% increase in the capillary length per unit volume in the motor cortex (Petren, 1938). Animals kept in darkness exhibited a decrease of vascularity in the visual cortex, but not in other areas of the brain (Gyllensten, 1959). High altitude adaptation also results in an increase in capillary diameter and length (Mercker and Schneider, 1949).

Compared with other tissues, the density of the capillary network in the brain is relatively sparse. The number of capillaries depends primarily on the presence of dendrites and synapses, and not on the number and density of the nerve cell bodies (Scharrer, 1945).

There are several non-invasive multi-regional techniques that have been used to measure the cerebral blood flow. Currently, two methods are most frequently employed. One involves measuring the local impedance which is

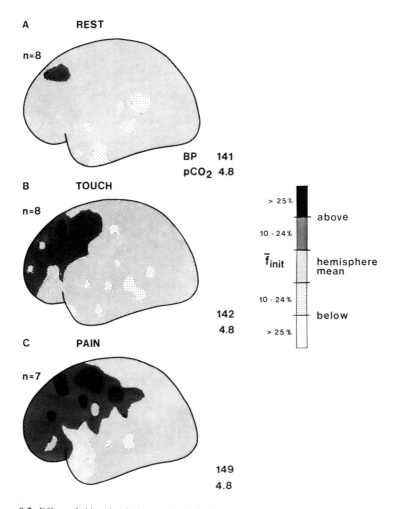

Figure 9.2 Effect of skin stimulation of the right hand upon the blood flow and its distribution in the left hemisphere. The relative distribution of the flow remained "hyperfrontal" in all situations [from D.H. Ingvar, I. Rosen, M. Eriksson, D. Elmquist, *Sensory Functions of the Skin, Wenner-Gren* Volume 27, Y. Zotterman (Ed.), p. 549; © 1976 by Pergamon Press].

dependent upon local blood flow (Jacquy *et al.*, 1975). The other, developed by Lassen and Ingvar (1972), uses the radioactive isotope Xenon 133. The radioactive gas is dissolved in a sterile saline solution and injected into the carotid artery. The arrival and subsequent clearance of the radioactivity is then detected by a battery of scintillation detectors attached to the scalp. However, a limitation of these methods, as compared with positron emission tomography, is an inability to measure specific metabolic changes. The spatial resolution in humans is about 1.5 cm, but computerized enhancement of the images may allow further refinement. Using baboons, Gur *et al.* (1982) have already achieved a resolution of about 4 mm.

Both methods are, nevertheless, able to detect local changes in CBF which accompany various sensory events, attention, or pathological processes affecting the brain. The refinement of such methods represents an important

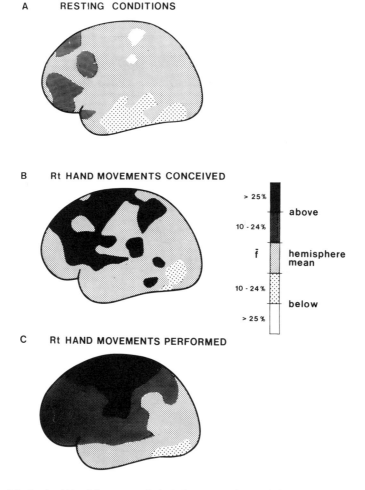

Figure 9.3 Cerebral blood flow at rest (A), during motor ideation (B), and during actual movements of the right hand (C) [from D.H. Ingvar and L. Philipson, *Ann. Neurol.* 2:230 (1977); © by the American Neurological Association].

development, inasmuch as they open the functioning brain to direct examination. Although subcortical changes in the blood flow have not as yet been directly observed in humans with these techniques, experimental animals have been used to demonstrate a selective vasodilatation in the hypothalamus during arousal (cat), or a decrease in the blood flow in the several parts of the visual pathway after monocular eyelid suture (Bondy, 1973).

In the undisturbed waking state, there is an elevation in the so-called hyperfrontal regional cerebral blood flow. The precentral-frontal area of the cortex has frequently been associated with a type of behavioral programming. The level of blood flow in this region increases during the waking state and may be twice as high as in other cortical areas, such as the temporal lobe.

Sensory/motor activities or mental activity affect blood flow in the corresponding cortical areas (Fig. 9.2, 9.3). A touch stimulus, noise or the spoken word all can alter the rate of flow. Interhemispheric differences pertaining to speech and listening are easily detectable, as is a change attributable to even such a relatively minor function as the control of eye movements by the frontal motor eye fields (Ingvar and Lassen, 1978). In addition, Roland (1977) has provided some interesting observations on the activation of left frontal and temporal areas in individuals listening to a Brahms' symphony. In children, cerebral blood flow has been observed to increase during reading in both hemispheres, whereas in the adults reading elevates the flow only in the dominant hemisphere. In blind individuals, the increased CBF during the reading of Braille materials has mostly been found in the left precentral and temporal areas and in the right parietal cortex (Leninger-Follert and Lubbers, 1976). These local changes correlate with the area of origin of primary evoked potentials (Leninger-Follert and Hossman, 1977) and with EEG changes (Menon *et al.*, 1980).

The response of the brain circulation to an external stimulus has two components. There first appears a nonspecific period in which there is a general increase in the blood flow that is related to the level of alertness. It is mediated by the sympathetic nervous system, which supplies all of the blood vessels of the brain via the superior cervical ganglion. Subsequently, there emerges a topically specific component that is associated with regional cortical activation. The selective expectation of a certain type of mental activity, such as mental alertness preceding a motor task, is accompanied by an increase in the CBF as well (Piraux *et al.*, 1976). During sleep, the cerebral blood flow also changes. In the REM phase, it increases, while in the non-REM sleep the changes are less consistent.

An interesting phenomenon, termed "cerebral deactivation", has been noted to accompany brain lesions. A substantial reduction in the cerebral blood flow takes place in the undamaged hemisphere of patients with a lesion in the contralateral hemisphere or the brain stem. A similar deactivation has been detected after spinal cord transection (Ingvar and Lassen, 1978). This drop in blood flow is probably a sign of a reduction in energy metabolism and a temporary decrease in neuronal function. Afterwards, during the period of functional compensation or recovery, CBF begins to rise, together with the metabolic activity and capillary network (Reinis, 1960, 1961).

Experimental studies have shown that both the general and local cerebral blood flow and the cerebrovascular tone are mainly controlled by the noradrenergic and cholinergic systems. Other, less global and more selective systems have been proposed that employ peptides, purines or dopamine. Local levels of carbon dioxide and oxygen also participate in the control. A

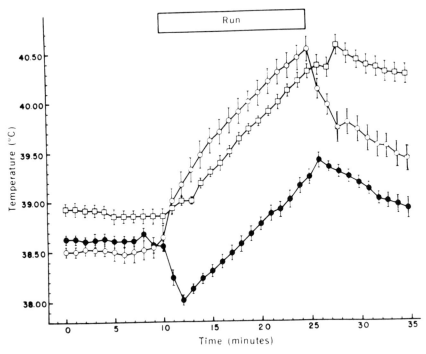

Figure 9.4 Brain (dots), carotid blood (circles), and rectal (squares) temperatures during exercise in dogs. Points are mean temperatures; vertical lines are standard errors. Between minutes 0 and 10, dogs were at rest on treadmill, usually lying down. During period marked *Run* (minutes 10 to 25), the dogs ran at a speed of 7.2 km/hr up a 14% slope. Treadmill stopped at minute 25, and animals sat for 10 min recovery period. Ambient temperature was 30^0C [from M.A. Baker, L.W. Chapman, *Science* 195:78 (1977); © 1977 by The American Association for the Advancement of Science].

decrease in the regional partial pressure of oxygen may precede local changes of cerebral blood flow. Following direct electrical stimulation of the cerebral cortex, the regional microflow increases within 1-2 seconds, indicating that the increased blood flow is not caused by local hypoxia.

BRAIN TEMPERATURE

Measurements of the temperature of the brain can serve as a useful method of directly tracing changes in the functional demands made on various CNS areas. Increases in the functional load and thus an elevation in regional metabolism is logically followed by a rise in local temperature. The clearance of heat due to convection and conduction and the temperature of the inflowing blood also contribute to the regional tissue temperature.

The core of the brain, the area between the thalamus and basal ganglia, is warmer than the cortex and the incoming blood (Serota and Gerard, 1938). Anesthesia and slow wave sleep cause a drop in brain temperature, while sensory stimulation and REM sleep raise it in the corresponding brain areas. Also, during spontaneous motor activity the temperature of the brain rises, particularly if it is associated with emotion.

In Carnivores, the blood reaching the brain is first cooled in the carotid rete, an area where the venous blood is able to exchange heat with the carotid blood. In a dog, the venous blood draining the nose and mouth is cooled there, so that the exchange of heat between arterial and venous blood in this area protects the brain against overheating during the severe thermal stress of exercise (Fig. 9.4).

Birds are also able to maintain the temperature of the brain below that of the body core, at least during heat stress (Richards, 1970). Their blood passes through a vascular network in the temporal region of the skull that is formed by branches of the ophthalmic artery which are in contact with the venous network originating in the orbit. The entire system functions as a heat exchanger. Moreover, Bernstein et al. (1979) discovered that evaporative cooling of the cornea plays a role in the cooling of the brain by this system.

SUMMARY AND SPECULATIONS

The adequate functioning of the central nervous system requires a continuous supply of glucose, oxygen and materials necessary for the building of new structures and the renewal of existing ones. The supply of glucose depends upon its active transport across the blood-brain barrier, a process which increases in functionally active areas of the brain. This effect is associated with a change in the barrier function and the blood flow through the region.

Glucose metabolism is activated by extracellular potassium, the level of which is increased during neuronal activity. Sodium ions are also able to stimulate glucose consumption, particularly in nerve endings.

Small amounts of glucose are stored in nervous tissue in the form of glycogen. Glycogen is degraded by glycogen phosphorylase, and the glucose that is released from it is activated by intracellular calcium, which enters the cells during depolarization. This mechanism ensures an adequate supply of energy at a time when the activity of the cell is elevated.

The glucose molecule within the cell is first activated by phosphorylation and degraded, anaerobically, into two fragments. This phase of glycolysis supplies a relatively small amount of energy. However, a reversible step in this process, the phosphorylation of fructose-1, 6-diphosphate, yields or consumes free hydrogen ions. It may participate in the direct control of the membrane potential, the excitability of the cell, and conceivably the alterations necessary for the formation of short-term memory.

The second phase of glucose metabolism, the aerobic breakdown of the three-carbon residues, supplies the major amount of energy for the cells and

157

also provides several products required for the synthesis of amino acids, fatty acids, and cholesterol. Some amino acids derived from the intermediary metabolites of the tricarboxylic acid cycle can act in the central nervous system as neurotransmitters. The rate of aerobic glycolysis is also related to the functional state of the brain and to an increase in neuronal activity. At least one enzyme associated with aerobic glycolysis, neuronal 2-phospho-D-glycerate enolase, has been linked to the process of learning, since its activity has been found to increase in neurons following acquisition.

Glucose metabolism is also associated with the functional plasticity of nervous tissue in terms of its involvement with the pentose phosphate cycle. The products of this cycle, several molecular forms of heptoses, hexoses, and pentoses, are necessary for the synthesis of functionally important compounds, especially nucleic acids. Therefore, enzymes of the pentose phosphate cycle, such as transketolase and transaldolase, are important components of the tissue response to a physiological stimulus, including the stimulation by several neurotransmitters.

The oxygen supply is closely associated with the regional activity and glucose consumption in the brain. The brain consumes about 20% of the body's total oxygen requirements, and its activity requires a continuous supply of oxygen. While the respiration of neurons depends upon their function, glial respiration is associated with the extracellular potassium released from the neurons during depolarization.

Glucose and oxygen are consumed by neuronal mitochondria, wherein the macroergic phosphate bonds of ATP are produced. The cell may then use ATP for various energy-dependent synthetic and transport functions. Both neuronal functioning and functional deprivation lead to a long-lasting modification in the activity of mitochondrial enzymes, such as cytochrome oxidase.

Oxygen, glucose, and other necessary materials are transported into the brain by the blood flow. Elevated tissue requirements are satisfied by local changes in the blood flow. When higher tissue requirements persist, there may be a shift to a more dense capillary network. Functionally triggered regional changes in the blood flow precede a local hypoxic condition and probably depend upon direct effects of the products of neuronal metabolism on blood vessels. Energy metabolism elevates the temperature of the central areas of the brain to a level greater than that of the incoming blood. Increased functional demands boost this temperature even further. The distribution of temperature changes within the brain also indicates the involvement of individual areas in global CNS activity.

One of the more valuable methods used in the study of local blood flow and metabolism is positron emission tomography. It holds considerable promise for future research into the importance of regional metabolic differences during various types of behavior.

RECOMMENDED READINGS

Brownell, G.L., Budinger, T.F., Lauterbur, P.C., McGeer, P.L.: Positron tomography and nuclear magnetic resonance imaging. *Science* 215:619-626 (1982).

Crone, C.: D-glucose - Fuel for brain. *Trends Neurosci.* 1:120-122 (1978).

Hall, E.R., Cottam, G.L.: Isozymes of pyruvate kinase in vertebrates: Their physical, chemical, kinetic and immunological properties. *Int. J. Biochem.* 9:785-793 (1978).

Kennedy, C., DesRosiers, M.H., Jehle, J.W., Reivich, M., Sharp, F.R., Sokoloff, L.: Mapping of functional neural pathways by autoradiographic survey of local metabolic rate with [^{14}C]deoxyglucose. *Science* 187:850-853 (1975).

Lacombe, P., Meric, A., Seylaz, J.: Validity of cerebral blood flow measurements obtained with quantitative tracer techniques. *Brain Res. Rev.* 2:105-169 (1980).

Purves, M.J.: *The Physiology of the Cerebral Circulation.* Cambridge Univ. Press: London (1972).

Raichle, M.E.: Quantitative in vivo autoradiography with positron emission tomography. *Brain Res. Rev.* 1:47-68 (1979).

Schatz, G.: How mitochondria import proteins from the cytoplasm. *FEBS Lett.* 103:201-211 (1979).

Sokoloff, L., Reivich, M., Kennedy, C., Des Rosiers, M.H., Patlak, C.S., Pettigrew, K.D., Sakurada, O., Shinohara, M.: [^{14}C]deoxyglucose method for the measurement of local cerebral glucose utilization: Theory, procedure, and normal values in the conscious and anesthetized albino rat. *J. Neurochem.* 28:897-916 (1977).

Yarowsky, P.J., Ingvar, D.H.: Neuronal activity and energy metabolism. *Fed. Proc.* 40:2353-2362 (1981).

REFERENCES

Anchors, J.M., Haggerty, D.F., Karnovsky, M.F.: *J. Biol. Chem.* 252:7035 (1977).

Appel, S.H., Parrot, B.L.: *J. Neurochem.* 17:1619 (1970).

Berlet, H.H., Lehnert, T.: *FEBS Lett.* 91:45 (1978).

Bernstein, M.H., Sandoval, I., Curtis, M.B., Hudson, D.M.: *J. Comp. Physiol.* 129:115 (1979).

Bielicki, L., Krieglstein, J.: *Naunyn-Schmiedeberg's Arch. Pharmacol.* 298:229 (1977).

Bondy, S.C.: *J. Neurol. Sci.* 19:425 (1973).

Brownell, G.L., Budinger, T.F., Lauterbur, P.C., McGeer, P.L.: *Science* 215:619 (1982).

Buchweitz, E., Sinha, A.K., Weiss, H.R.: *Science* 209:499 (1980).

Chaplain, R.A.: *J. Exp. Biol.* 81:113 (1979).

Clausen, T.: *Cell Calcium* 1:311 (1980).

Crone, C.: *Trends Neurosci.* 1:120 (1978).

De Feudis, F.V.: *Life Sci.* 10/11:1187 (1971).

Delanoy, R.L., Dunn, A.J.: *Pharmacol. Biochem. Behav.* 9:21 (1978).

Diamond, I., Fishman, R.A.: *J.Neurochem.* 21:1043 (1973).

Dittman, L., Sensenbrenner, M., Hertz, L., Mandel, P.: *J. Neurochem.* 21:191 (1973).

Elbrink, J., Bihler, I.: *Science* 188:1177 (1975).

Giurgea, C., Lefevre, D., Lescrenter, C., David-Remacle, M.: *Psychopharmacologia* 20:160 (1971).

Gjedde, A.: *J. Neurochem.* 36:1463 (1981).

Greenberg, J.H., Reivich, M., Alavi, A.,Hand, P., Rosenquist, A., Rintelmann, W., Stein, A., Tusa, R., Dann, R., Christman, D., Fowler, J., MacGregor, B., Wolf, A.: *Science* 212:678 (1981).

Gur, D., Good, W.F., Wolfson, S.K. Jr., Yonas, H., Shabason, L.: *Science* 215:1267 (1982).

Gyllensten, L.: *Acta Morphol. Neerl. Scand.* 2:331 (1959).

Haldane, J.S.: *Br. Med. J.* 2:65 (1919).

Hawkins, R.A., Biebuyck, J.F.: *Science* 205:325 (1979).

Himwich, H.E., Nahum, L.H.: *Am. J. Physiol.* 90:384 (1929).

Hostetler, K.Y., Landau, B.R., White, R.J., Albin, M.S., Yashon, D.: *J. Neurochem.* 17:33 (1970).

Ingvar, D.H., Lassen, N.A.:. *Acta Neurol. Scand.* 57:262 (1978).

Jacquy, J., Wilmotte, J., Piraux, A., Noel, G.: *Neuropsychobiology* 2:94 (1975).

Kao-Jen, J., Wilson, J.E.: *J. Neurochem.* 35:667 (1980).

Kaufmann, F.C., Harkonen, M.H.A.: *J. Neurochem.* 28:745 (1977).

Keller, K., Lange, K., Noske, W.: *J. Neurochem.* 36:1012 (1981).

Kety, S.S.: In: *Metabolism of the Nervous System.* D. Richter (Ed.), Pergamon Press, London (1957), p. 221.

Kimura, H., Naito, K., Nakagawa, K., Kuriyama, K.: *J. Neurochem.* 23:79 (1974).

Knull, H.R., Taylor, W.F., Wells, W.W.: *J. Biol. Chem.* 249:6930 (1974).

Kurokawa, M., Kimura, J., Tokuoka, S., Ishibashi, S.: *Brain Res.* 175:169 (1979).

Landowne, D., Ritchie, J.M.: *J. Physiol. (London)* 212:503 (1971).

Lassen, N.A., Ingvar, D.H.: *Progr. Nucl. Med.* 1:376 (1972).

Leninger-Follert, E., Hossmann, K.A.: *Brain Res.* 124:158 (1977).

Leninger-Follert, E., Lubbers, D.W.: *Pflueger's Arch.* 366:39 (1976).

Lorenzo, A.V.: *Brain Res.* 112:435 (1976).

Lust, W.D., Pasonneau, J.V.: *J. Neurochem.* 26:11 (1976).

Marangos, P.J., Zomzely-Neurath, C.: *Biochem. Biophys. Res. Commun.* 68:1309 (1976).

Mas, M., Solis, R.A.: *Experientia* 33:1390 (1977).

McIlwain, H.: *Biochemistry of the Central Nervous System.* 3rd ed., Churchill Ltd.:London (1966).

Menon, D., Koles, Z., Dobbs, A.: *Can. J. Neurol.* 7:195 (1980).

Mercker, H., Schneider, M.: *Pflueger's Arch.* 251:49 (1949).

Moore, B.W., Perez, V.J.: In: *Physiological and Biochemical Aspects of Nervous Integration.* F.D. Carlson (Ed.), Prentice-Hall, Englewood Cliffs, N.J. (1968), p. 343.

Mrsulja, B.B.: *Experientia* 30:66 (1974).

Opitz, E., Schneider, R.U.: *Ergebn. Physiol.* 46:126 (1950).

Packman, P.M., Blomstrand, C., Hamberger, A.: *J. Neurochem.* 18:479 (1971).

Petren, T.:. *Verhandl. Anat. Gesell.* 85:169 (1938).

Phelps, M.E., Huang, S.C., Hoffman, E.J., Selin, C., Sokoloff, L., Kuhl, D.E.: *Ann. Neurol.* 6:371 (1979).

Pickel, V.M., Reis, D.J., Marangos, P.J., Zomzely-Neurath, C.: *Brain Res.* 105:184 (1975).

Piraux, A., Jacquy, J., Lhoas, J.P., Wilmotte, J., Noel, G.: *Neuropsychobiology* 6:335 (1976).

Raichle, M.E.: *Brain Res. Rev.* 1:47 (1979).

Reinis, S.: *Pflueger's Arch.* 271:316 (1960).

Reinis, S.: *Acta Anat. (Basel)* 46:73 (1961).

Richards, S.A.: *Brain Res.* 23:265 (1970).

Roland, P.E.: *Acta Neurol. Scand.* 56:540 (1977).

Ronnback, L., Persson, L., Hansson, H.A., Haglid, K.G., Grasso, A.: *Experientia* 33:1094 (1977).

Savaki, H.E., Davidson, L., Smith, C., Sokoloff, L.: *J. Neurochem.* 35:495 (1980).

Scharrer, E.: *J. Comp. Neurol.* 83:237 (1945).

Schatz, G.: *FEBS Lett.* 103:201 (1979).

Schwartz, W.J., Gainer, H.: *Science* 197:1089 (1977).

Schwartz, W.J., Sharp, F.R.: *J. Comp. Neurol.* 177:335 (1978).

Sechzer, J.: *Science* 171:1173 (1971).

Serota, H.M., Gerard, R.W.: *J. Neurophysiol.* 1:115 (1938).

Sharp, F.R.: *Brain Res.* 107:663 (1976).

Sharp, F.R.: *Brain Res.* 110:127 (1976a).

Shimada, M., Kihara, T., Watanabe, M., Kurimoto, K.: *Neurochem. Res.* 2:595 (1977).

Shinohara, M., Dollinger, B., Brown, G., Rapoport, S., Sokoloff, L.: *Science* 203:188 (1979).

Sokoloff, L., Reivich, M., Kennedy, C., Des Rosiers, M.H., Patlak, C.S., Pettigrew, K.D., Sakurada, O., Shinohara, M.: *J. Neurochem.* 28:897 (1977).

Stephens, H.R., Sandborn, E.B.: *Brain Res.* 113:127 (1976).

Takagaki, G.: *J. Neurochem.* 15:903 (1968).

Wieraszko, A.: *Brain Res.* 237:449 (1982).

Wilson, J.E.: *Arch. Biochem. Biophys.* 154:332 (1973).

Wong-Riley, M.T.T.: *Brain Res.* 108:257 (1976).

Wong-Riley, M.T.T.: *Brain Res.* 171:11 (1979).

III

PROTEINS IN THE BRAIN: METABOLISM AND FUNCTION

Chapter 10

Purine and Pyrimidine Bases in the Brain

Any meaningful examination of brain cellular biochemistry and physiology must include a consideration of the metabolism and physicochemical properties of proteins. The synthesis and subsequent modification of proteins in nervous tissue are essential to the maintenance of continuous unimpaired CNS activity. All neuronal functions, the depolarization and repolarization of the membrane, ionic movements, neurotransmitter production, and functional plasticity, ultimately depend upon their continuous supply.

The machinery involved in the production of neuronal proteins is essentially the same as in those synthetic systems working to produce proteins in any other eukaryotic cell. But, neuronal function is able to markedly influence many of the components of the process, including the local synthesis of nucleotides, amino acids and various types of ribonucleic acids, the assembly of ribosomes, the construction of peptide chains and their modification by proteolysis, acetylation, methylation, and phosphorylation. It is this degree of responsiveness of protein synthesis to functional changes in neuronal activity which sets protein metabolism apart from comparable processes in other bodily tissues.

Adenine   Guanine

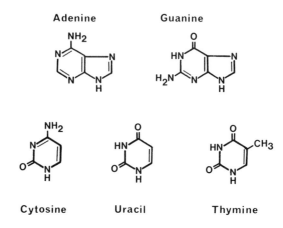

Cytosine   Uracil   Thymine

Figure 10.1 Purine and pyrimidine bases found in DNA and RNA.

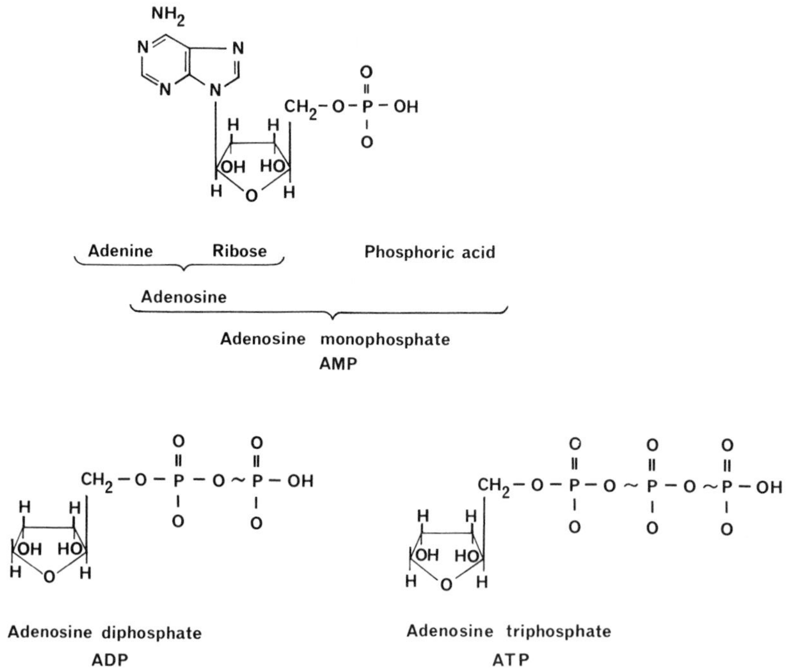

Adenine   Ribose   Phosphoric acid

Adenosine

Adenosine monophosphate
AMP

Adenosine diphosphate   Adenosine triphosphate
ADP   ATP

Figure 10.2 Adenine, adenosine, and adenosine phosphates.

Purine and pyrimidine bases are involved in a wide variety of cellular activities. They are used in nucleic acid synthesis and are essential for energy metabolism within the cell. They act as components of various cofactors that participate in a large number of enzymatic reactions. These bases also play some role in the transmission of nerve impulses and are involved in the direct regulation of local blood flow in brain arterioles and capillaries. Finally, cyclic forms of the nucleotides act as "second messengers" for the activation of various cellular enzymes (See Chapter 15). The chemical formulae of the most common purines and pyrimidines are shown in Figure 10.1.

Pyrimidine bases are chemically derived from pyrimidine, a compound with one six-membered ring containing two nitrogen atoms. The nucleotide pyrimidine bases bear oxygen in position 2 and an amino or hydroxy group in position 6. The most important of these bases are cytosine, uracil and thymine. Uracil is exclusively incorporated into the molecules of ribonucleic acids, while thymine has been found only in deoxyribonucleic acid. The purine bases are defined by a complex double ring which is assembled from five carbon and four nitrogen atoms that are furnished from a variety of different sources. The most common purines are adenine, guanine and xanthine.

When these purines and pyrimidines are linked with a pentose sugar (ribose or deoxyribose), the resultant complex is termed a nucleoside. More specifically, one may speak of cytidine, uridine, thymidine, adenosine, guanosine or xanthosine nucleosides. Another group of compounds, the nucleotides, additionally carry a phosphate residue in linkage with the pentose moiety. More complex compounds, such as adenosine triphosphate and uridine triphosphate, have three phosphate residues that are joined by a bond (a high-energy bond) that releases a considerable amount of energy upon dissociation (Fig. 10.2).

The purine nucleotides are synthesized in the brain by two routes: the *de novo* and the salvage pathways. In the *de novo* pathway, the sugar-phosphate component is synthesized first and is followed by the construction of the ring. This phosphorylated, active molecule is known as 5-phosphoribosyl-1-pyrophosphate (PRPP) and is synthesized from ATP and ribose-5-phosphate by the enzyme PRPP synthetase. The amount of available PRPP is a rate-limiting factor in the synthesis of these nucleotides. The purine ring is then attached to PRPP in a step-wise assembly from glutamine, glycine, formyl-coenzyme F, carbon dioxide and an aspartate amino group (Fig. 10.3). The final step in this synthesis, the closing of the purine ring by an activated formate (formyl-coenzyme F), generates inosinic acid, a parental substance for the further synthesis of adenosine monophosphate and guanosine monophosphate. The *de novo* pathway is more active in the brain than in any other tissue; radioactive glycine is incorporated into adenine within thirty minutes after its intracranial injection. The products of this purine biosynthesis are preferentially utilized by the cell, before those bases obtained from other sources (Held and Wells, 1969).

The yield of this pathway is insufficient to satisfy the biochemical requirements of a functioning nerve cell. Consequently, the brain also uses purine and pyrimidine bases and nucleosides made available by the degradation of nucleic acids and coenzymes. This is the so-called salvage pathway of nucleotide synthesis. There are several "salvage" reactions for the reutilization of purine and pyrimidine bases. In one, PRPP is attached to the base by enzymes called nucleotide pyrophosphorylases. One of the pyrophosphorylases, hypoxanthine-guanine phosphoribosyl transferase, binds PRPP to hypoxanthine or guanine, while adenine phosphoribosyl transferase binds PRPP to adenine. The second "salvage" reaction is a direct conversion of a base to a ribonucleotide, involving the attachment of PRPP to the base. The third reaction is a nucleoside to nucleotide conversion process, using ATP and catalyzed by nucleoside kinases. All of these associated regulatory

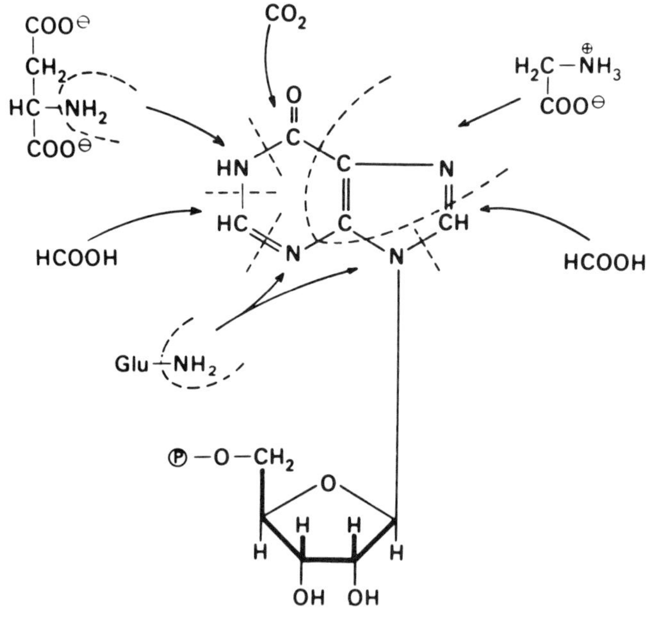

Figure 10.3 Components of the biosynthesis of purine nucleotides [from P. Karlson, *Kurzes Lebrbuch der Biochemie fuer Mediziner and Naturwissenschaftler*; © 1967 by Georg Thieme Verlag, Stuttgart].

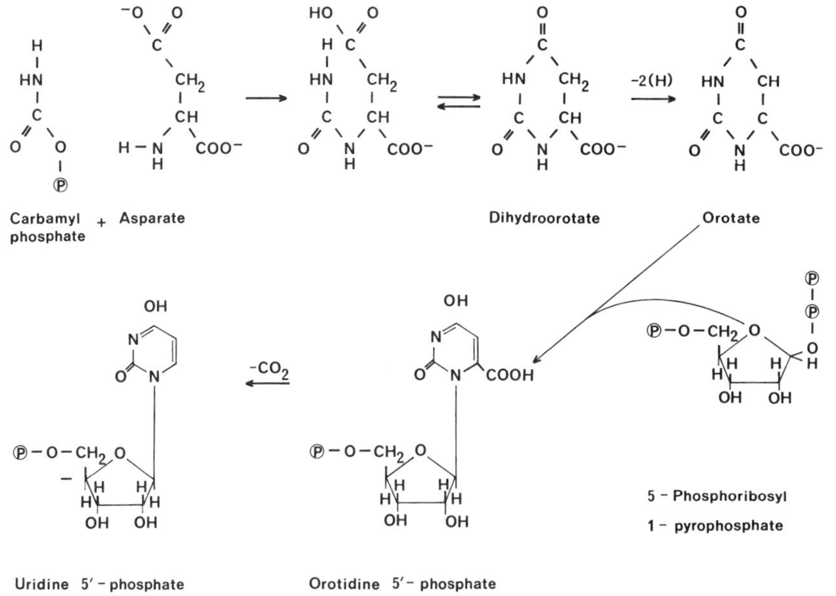

Figure 10.4 Synthesis of the pyrimidines.

mechanisms function to maintain constant levels of nucleotides in the cell during various functional states.

The brain is also quite active in the synthesis of pyrimidine rings (Tremblay et al., 1976). The precursors of this process are aspartate and carbamyl phosphate which are first condensed into carbamyl aspartate before being used to form the dihydroorotate ring. Dihydroorotate is further oxidized to orotate and attached to 5-phosphoribosyl-1-pyrophosphate (Fig. 10.4). The enzymes necessary for this synthesis, carbamoylphosphate synthetase, aspartate transcarbamylase, and dihydroorotase, are apparently products of the splitting of a single precursor protein having a molecular weight of 215 kilodaltons (Mally et al., 1981).

Orotic acid is the key precursor of all pyrimidine nucleotides, and its enzymatic decarboxylation yields uridine pyrophosphate. Other pyrimidines arise from uridine - cytidine by transamination and thymidine by methylation. The last enzymatic step of pyrimidine synthesis employs cytidine triphosphate synthetase [CTP synthetase, UTP: ammonia ligase (ADP)]. This enzyme represents the extreme end of the *de novo* pathway, and both its substrate, uridine triphosphate, and its product, cytidine triphosphate, are immediate precursors of RNA. The activity of CTP synthetase is, therefore, closely related to RNA metabolism, both in the brain and in other tissues

(Genchev and Mandel, 1976). These pathways are all subject to end-product inhibition by pyrimidine nucleotides, which act as regulators of the *de novo* synthesis (Smith, 1973).

Some purines and pyrimidines are also transported into the brain from the blood plasma. This mechanism is a second form of control that is able to stabilize the levels of purines and pyrimidines in the brain. Adenine, adenosine, guanine, guanosine, inosine and uridine are transported in measurable quantities (Cornford and Oldendorf, 1975). Some of this movement can take place against the concentration gradient. At least two independent transport systems have been found - one for adenine (inhibited by hypoxanthine) and another for which there is competition by adenosine, guanosine, inosine, and uridine. Thymidine is transported into the brain mainly through the choroid plexus and cerebrospinal fluid (Spector, 1980).

The synthesis of nucleic acids, neuronal energy metabolism, and the necessity for various coenzymes require the availability of a proper proportion of the various nucleotides. For this reason, the synthetic pathways of all purine and pyrimidine nucleotides are balanced and interconnected by various regulatory and feedback mechanisms. As a rule, the levels of purines are a controlling factor in pyrimidine synthesis, but not vice versa. These levels of purine and pyrimidine nucleotides in the brain are also regulated by a mutual influence upon degradation.

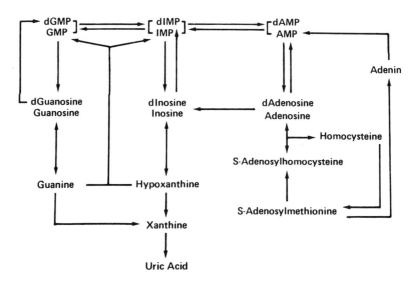

Figure 10.5 The interconversion and degradation of the purine nucleotides [from I.H. Fox, *Metabolism* 30:616 (1981); © 1981 by Grune and Stratton, Inc.] .

The catabolism of purines (Fig. 10.5) can be initiated by a deamination or a dephosphorylation of the nucleosides, involving either a specific 5-phosphomonoesterase or nonspecific alkaline and acid phosphatases. The activities of these enzymes are regulated by the nucleotide pools in the cells and the inorganic phosphate concentration. The deamination of AMP into inosine monophosphate is accompanied by the production of ammonia, as is the deamination of guanine. Actually, the turnover of purines is the largest source of ammonia in the brain (Schultz and Lowenstein, 1976).

One important mutually regulated process is the interconversion of adenine, inosine and guanine (see Fig. 10.5). The deamination of adenosine monophosphate generates inosine monophosphate which can then be used for the synthesis of guanyl compounds. The reactions are reversible, so that adenosine monophosphate may again be produced. These interconversion pathways constitute what is known as the purine nucleotide cycle.

Adenosine triphosphate plays an essential role in the regulation of purine metabolism. When the energy supply to the cell is blocked, such as by a 2-deoxyglucose interference with glucose metabolism, the level of ATP in the cell decreases. The effect leads to a temporary increase in AMP, an activation of AMP deaminase, and the production of IMP and GMP (Fox, 1974).

The degradation of guanine continues through a further deamination by guanine deaminase (Miyamoto et al., 1982) to xanthine. The product is then oxidized to uric acid. Similarly, inosine is metabolized to hypoxanthine, before being degraded to xanthine (by xanthine oxidase) and subsequently to uric acid. Uric acid is the final stage of purine metabolism in humans.

Several authors have attempted to correlate high blood plasma levels of uric acid with greater intelligence, drive and achievement, but the statistical data are not all that convincing. It has been postulated that uric acid may have a general excitatory effect on the nervous system similar to effects of the methylated xanthines, caffeine and theophylline. Uric acid is, nevertheless, also elevated in progressive cerebral atrophy and in Lesch-Nyhan syndrome. Both of these syndromes are associated with mental retardation and behavioral disorders.

There is less known about the degradation of pyrimidine bases. The principal end-product is β-alanine, and in the brain the rate of degradation of pyrimidine bases is tied to the rate of purine metabolism. Both pathways depend upon glycolysis and respiration, the availability of high-energy bonds, and the relationship between the activity of Na^+, K^+-dependent adenosine triphosphatase and the utilization of purines and pyrimidines as coenzymes and cyclic nucleotides in the synthesis of nucleic acids.

Taken together, the data on the metabolism of purine and pyrimidine bases underscore the interrelationships among various aspects of cellular activity. These different metabolic pathways represent just one of the linkages among many diverse processes within the brain. Any functional change in the activity of a nerve cell is dependent upon a complex of chemical and physico-chemical changes which cannot be considered in isolation from one another. Accordingly, plasticity, as a response to one or a series of environmental events, is really an encompassing consideration of the intertwining sequellae of these processes, whether they be viewed at a functional or strictly morphological level.

Chapter 11

Deoxyribonucleic Acid and Its Role in the Brain

Deoxyribonucleic acid (DNA) is a carrier of all of the cellular information contained within the genes. While some non-genetic cytoplasmic and membranous inheritance does exist, the nucleotide sequences present in DNA constitute the vast majority of information that is passed on from one cell generation to the next. As a result, DNA is one of the primary regulatory factors within the body's cells. Structurally, it is a linear polymer of nucleotides linked through their sugar (deoxyribose) components and phosphate groups (Fig. 11.1). The common bases in DNA are the pyrimidines - thymine and cytosine - and the purines - adenine and guanine. A molecule of DNA consists of two polynucleotide chains that are coiled together

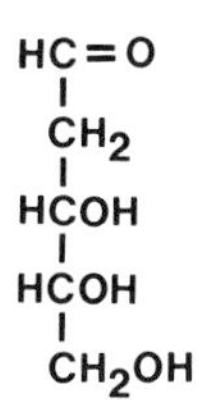

Figure 11.1 The structure of deoxyribose.

$$
\begin{array}{c}
HC = O \\
| \\
CH_2 \\
| \\
HCOH \\
| \\
HCOH \\
| \\
CH_2OH
\end{array}
$$

to form a double helix (Fig. 11.2). The helical structure is stabilized by hydrogen bonding between complementary base pairs, with an adenine of one chain attached to thymine of the other. A similar bonding occurs between guanine and cytosine (Fig. 11.3).

Each division of the cell is preceded by a replication of its DNA, yielding a duplicate set of strands. Replication begins in specific loci on the chromosome. Along particular portions of the molecule, the two strands are separated just enough to permit the replicative process to occur, before being reassociated again. At any one time, the two strands never separate completely down their length.

The genetic or informational content of DNA resides in its nucleotide sequence. The average gene consists of a linear arrangement of about 1000 base pairs. These genes, called structural genes, ultimately code for specific polypeptide chains. They usually exist in the genome in a small number of copies, or even in a single copy. They are interspersed between sequences that are repeated many times throughout the DNA strand. Thus, humans have about 50,000 genes in their genome, but the amount of DNA in their cell nuclei is sufficient for 50-100 times as many genes of an average length. Some of the repetitive sequences are inverted, or consist of long pyrimidine tracts (poly dC-dT). They may play some regulatory role or function to control the activity of the structural genes.

Some proteins are specified by several gene copies. These multiple copies arise by a selective amplification of genes which is quite often dependent upon function. Although this selective amplification was originally discovered in invertebrates and *Xenopus laevis* oocytes, it also exists in mammalian cells (Schimke *et al.*, 1978).

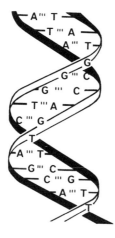

Figure 11.2 A typical DNA double helix.

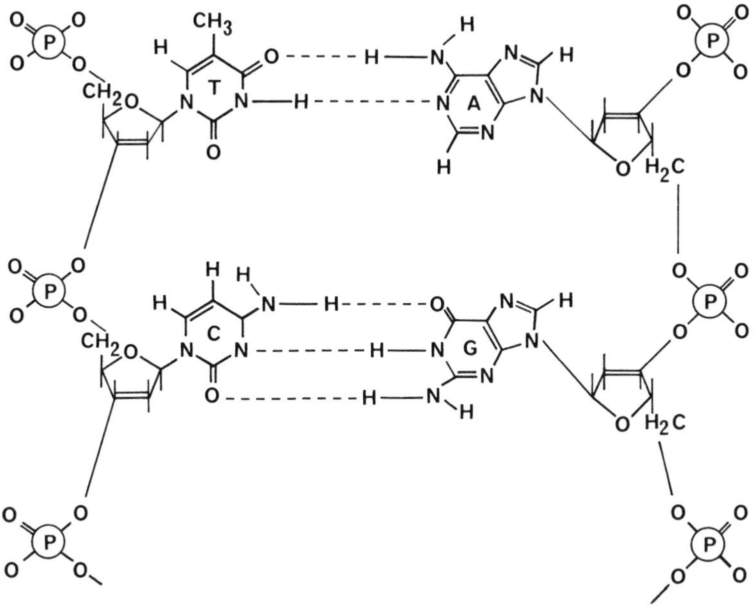

Figure 11.3 Hydrogen bridges between complementary bases in DNA.

Some parts of DNA are not arranged in the typical α-helix conformation, and may even exist as single strands. Such a discovery stood in sharp contrast to the commonly held idea that the genome was formed by individual genes attached one to another like beads on a string. Some segments of DNA are not even fixed to a particular site in the chromosome and can shift from place to place within the DNA molecule. Sequences of other genes were discovered to overlap, and in the structure of some genes are sequences that are not transcribed into messenger RNA. These unanticipated findings necessitated a reassessment of both structural and functional concepts in DNA research. The possibility exists that these unusual arrangements could actually serve as controlling mechanisms that determine which genes are activated within the cell at any particular time.

In the nucleus of the living non-dividing cell, DNA is a component of the chromatin, the loose interphase structuring of the chromosomes. About 50% of chromatin is formed by proteins, the majority of which are relatively small basic proteins known as histones. Other, non-histone proteins are rather complex, mostly acidic, and are often tissue- and cell-specific.

Chromatin can be cleaved by endogenous enzymes, the nucleases, into chromatin subunits called nucleosomes (nu bodies). These nu bodies are

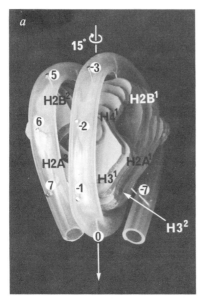 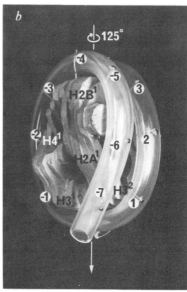

Figure 11.4 The nucleosome structure with the histone octamer (H2B^1, H2B^2, H2A^1, H2A^2, H3^1, H3^2, H4^1; H4^2 not visible). The DNA double helix is represented by a plastic tube. The numbers from -7 to +7 on the tube indicate the distances along the DNA molecule [from A. Klug, D. Rhodes, J. Smith and J.T. Finch, *Nature* 287:509 (1980); © 1970 by Macmillan and Co.].

convolutions of DNA strands with eight histone molecules attached (Fig. 11.4). In the intact chromatin, the nucleosomes are interconnected by a short DNA bridge. While the nucleosomes contain about 160 nucleotide pairs of DNA, these bridges tend to be about 40 pairs long. The bridges are susceptible to endonucleases, allowing the isolation of one nucleosome from another. The size of the nucleosomes depends upon the type of cell. The 160 base pairs mentioned above refers to a neuronal nucleosome, but in glia this number is about 200 (Thomas and Thompson, 1977).

    The nucleosomes contain eight molecules of four different types of histones, probably arranged as two tetramers. The overall structure is that of a short, wedge-shaped cylinder. The histone molecules are intertwined to define a coiled pathway for the DNA strand. The path of DNA is consistent with one and three-fourths turns supercoiled around the outside of a protein core (Bazett-Jones and Ottensmeyer, 1981).

    Neurons exhibit quantitative difference in their histone contents, particularly in the concentration of histone H$_1$ (Greenwood *et al.*, 1981). But, at present it is difficult to discern the meaning of these variations in the neuronal nucleosome structure.

NEURONAL DNA CONTENT

The diploid amount of DNA in a single cell nucleus is relatively stable, about 5.3 pg per cell (in cat or human cells). The amount of tissue DNA has therefore been frequently used as a measure of the number of cells. However, some cells may be polyploid, containing more than the diploid amount of DNA. The calculation of cell numbers in some tissues would then obviously be affected by this factor.

Since the neurons in the adult central nervous system are not known to divide, brain DNA had been considered to be very stable. Koenig (1968), however, reported that there is a slow turnover of brain DNA. Injections of radioactive thymidine, a precursor of newly synthesized DNA, into an adult brain is followed by an incorporation of the label into both neuronal and glial DNA. The DNA-bound labeled thymidine is then slowly eliminated over the course of the next several weeks. This is probably a sign of DNA turnover and not a consequence of radiation damage by the label and subsequent DNA repair. Besides demonstrating some synthesis of DNA in mature neurons, the data also show the presence of a slow process of DNA degradation (Kimberlin et al., 1974). Even Purkinje cells, which contain a very stable quantity of DNA, show some DNA turnover (Cameron et al., 1979).

The amount of DNA in individual neurons can vary from diploid values to almost complete tetraploidy (Sandritter et al., 1967; Herman and Lapham, 1969). In this situation, tetraploidy does not mean an increase in the number of complete sets of chromosomes, but only a corresponding increase in the amount of DNA.

While the possibility has often been discounted (e.g. Mann and Yates, 1973), in 1975 Bregnard et al., using both microfluorometry and UV-absorption by isolated neuronal nuclei, observed that almost all of the neuronal nuclei isolated from an adult cerebral cortex were hyperdiploid (Fig. 11.5). Only in the cortex of fetuses near term was there found to be a diploid amount of DNA. This amount began to rapidly rise after birth, and in rats reached an average value of three times the haploid amount (3c) in the seventh postnatal day, before climbing to about 3.5c at day 28, a value which remained reasonably constant for many adult cortical neurons. The increase in the amount of DNA is accompanied by a proportional jump in histone levels (Bregnard et al., 1979). Comparable results have been reported for mice, rabbits, cats and humans (McIlwain and Capps-Covey, 1976).

In some animal species, the neurons contain much more than a diploid or even tetraploid amount of DNA. Cells from the abdominal ganglion of Aplysia can contain up to 100,000 times the haploid level (Kleve et al., 1975). An extreme polyploidy has also been found in the subesophageal lobe of the octopus brain (De Marianis et al., 1979).

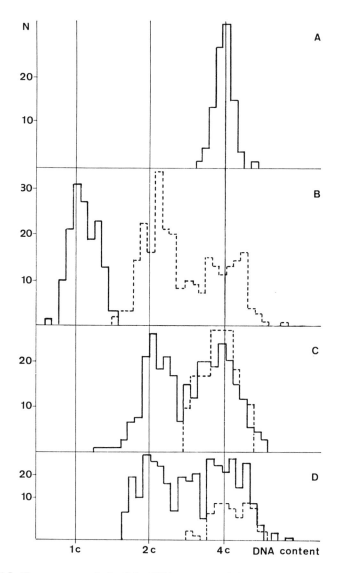

Figure 11.5 Fluorescence analysis of the DNA content in (A) Purkinje cells, (B) Bull sperm heads (full line) and rat liver nuclei (dashed line), (C) crude brain nuclei (full line) and neuronal nuclei (interrupted line); (D) UV-absorption (258 nm) of crude brain nuclei (full line) and neuronal nuclei (interrupted line); N, Number of measurements; C, relative DNA content [from A. Bregnard, A. Knuesel and C.C. Kuenzle, *Histochemistry* 43:59 (1975); © 1975 by Springer Verlag].

Figure 11.6 Camera lucida drawing of cells with tetraploid nuclei (represented by a dot) in layers I. to III. of the calcarine cortex of a normal person; x7 [from C.L. Scholtz and D.A. Mann, *Neuropath. Appl. Neurobiol.* 3:137 (1977); © 1977 by Blackwell Scientific Publ. Ltd.].

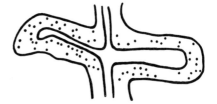

Although Mann and his associates disbelieve the existance of neuronal polyploidy within the brain, they did find a glial polyploidy that could be associated with brain function. They postulate that the appearance of tetraploid cells in the cerebellum is related to the development of coordinated movement. In addition, they reported (Scholtz and Mann, 1977) that an increase in tetraploid cells within the striate cortex was tied to the emergence of visual functioning. They estimated the existance of 2000-8000 tetraploid cells per square meter of the normal human visual cortex (Fig. 11.6). The number was significantly reduced in blind individuals. However,there was no indication whether the tetraploid cells were glia or neurons. This increase in DNA does not result in the production of any new sequences or novel genes (Tano *et al.*, 1970).

DNA REPLICATION

Since the possibility does exist that shifts in brain DNA may be related in some way to function, it would be helpful at this point to provide a brief description of those events that characterize DNA replication.

The replication of DNA is a precisely regulated process that takes place in a rigidly determined sequence. Not all chromosomes or their segments replicate at once. However, when they occur, the events proceed very rapidly, inasmuch as several small units of DNA (replicons) can be synthesized simultaneously, before being later attached one to another.

The replication (DNA-dependent DNA synthesis) is catalyzed by several types of DNA polymerases (DNA-nucleotidyltransferases). These enzymes require the presence of template DNA, divalent cations (magnesium or manganese) and all four types of deoxyribonucleotides in an activated triphosphate form. At least four DNA polymerases have been isolated and have been designated as α, β, γ and m (mitochondrial). α represents about 70-80% of the total DNA polymerase in a growing cell. Although it has been found mostly in the cytoplasm, it is probable that this observation is an artifact caused by the leakage of loosely bound enzyme from the cell nucleus during fractionation. DNA polymerase β is present primarily in the cell nuclei, and represents about 5-15% of the total DNA polymerase activity in growing cells and about 50% of the total in resting cells. It has been found to be capable of efficiently copying even a polymer containing ribose (ribohomopolymer). DNA polymerase γ and mitochondrial DNA polymerase appear to be minor components of the complete DNA synthesizing system.

The fidelity of replication is not as great as might be expected. The β and γ polymerases incorporate a non-complementary base with frequencies of 1 in 3000 and 1 in 8000, respectively. And, DNA polymerase α has an error rate of 1 in 30,000 (Kunkel and Loeb, 1981). Therefore, other factors must be involved ensuring the accuracy of replication and the preservation of genetic information. One group of these regulatory factors appears to be the polyamines. They are polyvalent cations which can be bound to the nucleic acids, affecting their conformation and perhaps increasing the fidelity of information transfer (Abraham and Pihl, 1981).

Three processes are necessary for DNA replication: Initiation, elongation of the DNA chains, and a termination with the release of DNA polymerase. The initiation phase involves the opening of one strand of the template by an endonuclease and the formation of the "priming" site. DNA polymerase is attached to this priming site and the synthesis of DNA begins, usually in the neighborhood of the nuclear membrane or on the periphery of the nucleolus.

The extent of DNA synthesis depends on the intensity of tissue growth. In regenerating tissues, the increase in DNA synthesis is due to a drastic elevation in the level of DNA polymerase α. The β and γ enzymes show little correlation with the rate of cell division. In the neurons, the activity of the α enzyme drops shortly after birth, following the cessation of neuroblastic division. But, DNA in the central nervous system still undergoes some turnover. Following an intracranial injection of radioactive thymidine, the specific activity of cerebral cortical DNA increases rapidly, reaching a maximum in approximately five hours. More than half of the labeled DNA then disappears over the next two hours. The decrement continues and after 41 hours, only small changes are observed. This turnover has also been noted in preparations of purified neuronal nuclei (Perrone-Capano et al., 1982).

DNA synthesis in adult neuronal nuclei is dependent upon the β enzyme, together with an enzyme (DNA ligase) that binds DNA fragments together (Inoue et al., 1979). Although these two enzymes are known to function in DNA repair instead of true replication (Inoue et al., 1976), in neurons they do appear to be involved in DNA synthesis. DNA ligase also is higher in neuronal nuclei than in glial and liver nuclei (Inoue and Kato, 1980).

Enzymes other than DNA polymerases may also play an important role in the control of DNA synthesis. For example, DNA unwinding proteins are required for the process of DNA replication. Also, the transcription of messenger RNA for thymidine kinase and thymidylate kinase from genes activated prior to DNA synthesis is necessary for the production of the DNA precursor thymidine triphosphate. Thymidine kinase will respond to the experimental stimulation of DNA synthesis, for instance, by estradiol benzoate in perinatal rats (Litteria, 1980). These two enzymes are reduced in the cell with the cessation of DNA synthesis, but small amounts remain present in the brains of mature animals (Yamada *et al.*, 1981; Suleiman and Spector, 1982).

DNA synthesis also depends upon various stimulating factors present in the cytoplasm at certain stages of cell development. The presence of hormones and various other agents (e.g., insulin, glucagon, epidermal growth factor, nerve growth factor) enhances this synthesis, as does the presence of electric fields and ions. Sodium and calcium fluxes into the cell have been noted to trigger DNA synthesis in several types of cells, including cartilage cells (chondrocytes) and neurons.

In neurons, sustained depolarization can be induced by ouabain, as a result of an inhibition of Na^+, K^+- dependent adenosine triphosphatase. Sodium ions then enter the neuron, but cannot be actively pumped out. In a tissue culture containing mature neurons from the chicken spinal cord, Cone and Cone (1976, 1978, 1978a; Cone *et al.*, 1977) were able to induce DNA synthesis by the addition of ouabain. They reported full replication of the neuronal genome, the formation of binucleate cells and a complete cell division. The mitogenesis of these mature neurons can be blocked by 5-fluoro-2'-deoxyuridine, a halogenated analog of thymidine. This substance is a powerful inhibitor of normal mitosis, because it prevents the synthesis of the thymidine triphosphate by thymidylate synthetase.

DNA synthesis may therefore be initiated by external stimuli, as in many other types of quiescent animal cells. Lymphocytes can circulate in the peripheral blood for a long time, without a replication of DNA. Yet, with an appropriate stimulus, the resting lymphocyte enlarges, replicates its DNA, and undergoes cell division. Even mature hen erythrocyte nuclei can be activated to resume DNA synthesis. Physiological stimuli, such as the cutting of the skin, partial hepatectomy, hypoxia or erythropoietin administration, can stimulate DNA synthesis and division in the epidermis, liver, and blood cells, respectively. Molecular phenomena triggering such DNA synthesis are poorly understood, but nucleo-cytoplasmic interactions are probably important in the induction of nuclear DNA synthesis (Kit, 1976).

FUNCTIONAL IMPORTANCE OF CHANGES IN DNA

The findings of Cone and his colleagues with cultures of mature CNS neurons, as well as the data from work with other tissues provide for some interesting possibilities concerning the role of changes in neuronal DNA during functional activation. Dropp and Sodetz (1971) discovered that after repeated electrical foot shocks in rats there was an elevation in the labeling of DNA in sympathetic ganglia neurons and glia. Neuroglial mitoses were increased, as was the number of binucleate neurons, and there was a hypertrophy of neuronal perikarya, cell nuclei and nucleoli.

Longlasting or repeated depolarization of some neurons, with a consequent induction of DNA synthesis, could also be predicted to occur during more complex processes, such as those involving acquisition of the memory trace. Reinis (1972; Reinis and Lamble, 1972; Reinis et al., 1972) examined the incorporation of tritiated thymidine during the training of mice in a passive avoidance situation and found that such training resulted in an increased incorporation of radioactivity into neuronal DNA, as compared with untrained animals or animals electrically stimulated without the opportunity for escape. In order to eliminate possible interfering factors, two independent sets of experiments were carried out, one involving the intraperitoneal injection of thymidine in order to avoid damage to the brain and the other employing an intracranial administration so as to not involve the blood-brain barrier.

Is such a change in the labeling of DNA during learning functionally important? The effect may relate to some completely irrelevant phenomenon which merely accompanies the process of learning, without having any direct significance for the retention of the memory trace. Such a possibility, for example, could be a multiplication of glia necessary for the metabolic support of the nerve cells. On the other hand, the change may reflect a process necessary for the a permanent storage of information, a failure of which would be accompanied by some deficit in retention.

In order to further explore these possibilities, an antimetabolite which interferes with the replication of the DNA molecule has been employed. 5-iodo-2'-deoxyuridine (IUdR) is a substance that is specifically incorporated quite readily into mouse tissue during DNA synthesis *in vivo* (Myers and Einendegen, 1975), where it is partly deiodinated and introduced into DNA in place of thymidine. However, it is transcribed as cytosine. Consequently, the IUdR-substituted DNA is unable to act as a proper template for the synthesis of enzymes normally required for cell functioning, although the enzyme molecules are generated (Aamodt and Goz, 1970). Thus, if there is any change in DNA which is part of the biochemical process necessary for the storage of memory, its alteration by an antimetabolite should cause a loss of memory. Such a loss has been demonstrated following the administration of iododeoxyuridine. This substance, if administered immediately before passive avoidance training, blocked the expression of the memory trace in testing up to one week after the initial training session. On the other hand, its injection five minutes after the acquisition trial is no longer effective (Reinis *et al.*, 1972a). It is also interesting that some blockers of DNA synthesis that have been used for the treatment of malignant tumors may cause intellectual impairments and interfere with learning. This has been true for methotrexate (after intrathecal injection) and decarbazine (Libiger and Ban, 1981).

The injection of increasing doses of thymidine in conjunction with IUdR suppressed the negative effect of IUdR on the retention of the passive avoidance task. This is the result of a competition by both substances for enzymes involved in DNA synthesis, with thymidine having the higher affinity. However, very high doses of thymidine have been found to inhibit DNA synthesis in tissue cultures and also interfere with the retention of the avoidance task. Radioactive thymidine is even more effective in this regard, probably due to radiochemical damage to the DNA into which it was incorporated. Other mutagens, such as 2, 6-diaminopurine, 6-mercaptopurine, 6-thioguanine, 5-iodouracil and 5-bromouracil also interfere with the memory for a passive avoidance task, if present in the brain during the acquisition trial or shortly thereafter. Moreover, electroconvulsive shock, which interferes with the performance of trained animals if administered shortly after the training (Fig. 11.7), has been found to inhibit thymidine incorporation into cortical DNA (Giuditta *et al.*, 1978).

The data suggest that changes in neuronal and glial DNA may be one component of the system necessary for the long-term storage of a memory trace and, accordingly, for the functional adaptation of the neurons. Although little is known concerning the mechanism of the changes, if we consider the distinct possibility that a replication of DNA takes place in mature neurons, then the entire process of neuronal plasticity might be divided into several steps. Initially, an increase in traffic through the synapse induces numerous intracellular and intrasynaptic events that include the activation of enzymes and the phosphorylation of proteins (to be discussed in Chapter 15). This induces, among other things, the production of new DNA, involving the replication of all genes in the duplicated part of the genome. Some of these genes may then be activated and used for new RNA synthesis. The final step in the process, the synthesis of new proteins and the assembly of new structures, would likely vary in different affected cells and brain areas according to their localization, neurotransmitter specificity and metabolic demands.

Another possibility is that changes in DNA induced by neuronal activity are caused by a mechanism using the enzymes of DNA repair. Following damage to the DNA molecule, such as by ultraviolet radiation, the damaged parts may be excised and replaced to restore the integrity of the molecule. This mechanism of repair requires a set of specialized enzymes, and although it is probably not very active in the brain, it is present there (Hubscher *et al.*, 1979). Still, this consideration does not rule out the possibility that the repair mechanisms and DNA polymerase β within the cell are also used for some other purposes.

The most promising explanation for these relationships may come from the findings of Brown (1981). Multigene families regulate the timing, diversity and extent of gene expression. This expression is accompanied by an amplification, rearrangement and loss of genes, events which involve, of course, thymidine incorporation into DNA. Such events make Carlson's (1977) statement that, "The suggestion that DNA changes must accompany

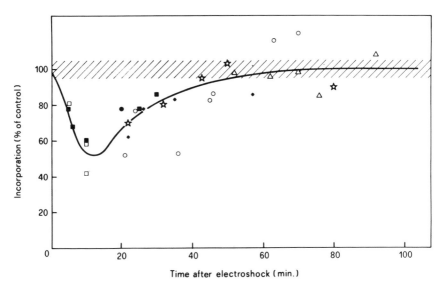

Figure 11.7 Time course of the effect of electroshock on thymidine incorporation into cortical DNA. Incorporation time was 15 min for all animals. On the horizontal axis time indicates the interval between a single electroshock and death. Intervals below 15 minutes were obtained by giving electroshock after the intracranial injection of thymidine. Different symbols refer to different experiments. For each experiment incorporation values were expressed as a percentage of the mean for controls. The shaded strip indicates the confidence limit of control values (p<.005). The curve relating to electroshocked rats was drawn by best visual fit [from A. Giuditta, P. Abrescia and B. Rutigliano, *J. Neurochem.* 31:983 (1978); © 1978 by International Society for Neurochemistry Ltd.].

learning argues for a novel mechanism in cellular machinery (p. 600)", at the very least, premature.

There is no doubt that an intact genome is necessary for the normal development and functioning of the brain. Mental retardation is a common trait in all autosomal unbalanced chromosomal aberrations, and frequently occurs in individuals with a greater than normal number of X or Y chromosomes. While these chromosomal aberrations are not associated with any major malformation of the brain, there sometimes are heterotopic nerve cells present in different areas of white or gray matter. The main functional defect could be a cellular biochemical change which leaves the cells unable to cope with the normal requirements of behavioral control. Mental retardation is common in trisomies which are characterized by the presence of an extra chromosome in the cell nucleus. Abberations of this kind, such as trisomy 21 (Down's syndrome), are accompanied by an altered cell generation time, probably due to a defect in DNA synthesis. These two functional disorders, mental retardation and a defect in DNA synthesis, also emphasize the importance of the proper control of DNA synthesis for the normal activity of the brain.

Ribonucleic Acids in the Brain

DNA transcribes its information into several different types of ribonucleic acid (RNA), which themselves share many common structural features. They are polymers of the four nucleotides (adenosine, guanosine, cytosine, and uridine) whose phosphoribose moieties form phosphodiester linkages identical to those in DNA. Three main types of RNA have been detected in the cell: ribosomal RNA (rRNA), transfer RNA (tRNA) and messenger RNA (mRNA). Other seemingly minor forms have been described, but their functions are less well understood.

Of the three, rRNA is by far the most abundant, constituting 50-80% of the total cellular RNA. But, the genes coding for it are highly redundant and represent only about .04% of the neuronal genome. The rRNA is typically found in the ribosomes attached to the endoplasmic reticulum, a complex characterized by early anatomists as Nissl substance.

Transfer RNA is the second most common type (10-20% of the total) and the smallest of the known RNAs. It contains approximately 70-80 nucleotides and is too small to be precipitated by conventional high-speed centrifugation techniques. Consequently, it is often included in the category of soluble RNA. As the name suggests, these nucleic acids function to carry the individual amino acids to the ribosome where the information in mRNA is translated into proteins. Arfin *et al.* (1977) have proposed that some

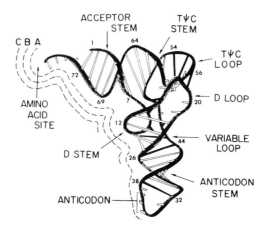

Figure 12.1 Folding of the polynucleotide chain in yeast phenylalanine tRNA. The ribose-phosphate backbone drawn as a continuous tube and cross bars indicate the bases. Nucleotide numbers are given [from A. Rich and P.R. Schimmel, *Nucleic Acid Res.* 4:1649 (1977); © 1977 by IRL Press, London, England].

aminoacyl-tRNA's may also be involved in the biosynthesis and transport of amino acids throughout the cell. In the brain it is possible that glutamic acid is transported in this manner (Vadeboncoeur and Lapointe, 1980).

In size, messenger RNA falls somewhere between the ribosomal and transfer forms. It operates as an informational intermediary between the coded DNA in the nucleus and the assembly of specific proteins in the cytoplasm. Unlike tRNA, which is known to have a number of unusual nucleotides, mRNA contains only sequences of adenine, guanine, cytosine, and uracil.

RNA polymers frequently assume specific confirmations. The reasons for these structural diversities are less well understood than those for the double helix conformation of DNA. Some RNA molecules appear to form double strands, with complementary base pairing. Some polymers of ribosomal RNA contain regions in which the polynucleotide strand doubles back on itself. Also, tRNA (Fig. 12.1) and mRNA (in at least one case) have been found to contain base-paired "hairpin" loops (White *et al.*, 1972).

RNA SYNTHESIS

DNA-dependent RNA polymerases (nucleotide triphosphate-RNA nucleotidyltransferases) are responsible for the synthesis of cellular RNA. They bind to DNA and polymerize ribonucleotides into an RNA molecule complementary to one strand of the DNA. A molecule of RNA is therefore a working copy of a gene. Both informational (messenger) RNA and noninformational (ribosomal and transfer) types of RNA are synthesized by these enzymes.

Multiple isoenzymes of RNA polymerase have been isolated and purified. They differ in structure, function, cellular localization, molecular size, order of chromatographic elution, and the extent of inhibition by various peptides. RNA polymerases differ from DNA polymerases in several ways. They need, for instance, no primer for the initiation of synthesis, and they can use duplex DNA as a template. RNA polymerases require divalent magnesium ions and all four ribonucleoside 5'-triphosphates for normal activity. The distinctions between the roles of these enzymes are not really clear. It is possible that different gene species may be transcribed by particular RNA polymerases with varying template specificities.

The potential and actual activity of RNA polymerases is higher in the brain than in the liver. They are activated by a number of divalent cations and several cAMP-activated protein kinases, as well as by protein kinases which are unresponsive to cAMP. They are also affected, directly or indirectly, by many hormones, such as estrogens, glucocorticoids, testosterone, triiodothyronine, ACTH, TSH, growth hormone and choriongonadotropin. These relationships will be individually discussed in later chapters.

The primary products of RNA polymerase activity are very large polymers, much larger than an average messenger RNA molecule (Fig. 12.2). They are present in the cell nucleus and are termed heterogeneous nuclear RNA (HnRNA). Although the evidence is still only indirect, it is believed that they are precursors of messenger RNA. Their turnover is very rapid, with only a very small portion of the nuclear HnRNA content ever reaching the cytoplasm.

Messenger RNA is likely formed from HnRNA by a partial degradation of the molecule. Parts of HnRNA are excised and transported into the cytoplasm as messenger RNA (mRNA). Messenger RNA often has, at its 5' terminus, a block of about 150 nucleotides, a "leader" that is attached to a "cap", an unusual methylated structure. Different mRNA molecules carry the same leader, with identical sequences at the capped end. In the CNS, as in any other eukaryotic mRNA, the cap structure has 7-methylguanosine as the 5'-terminal nucleotide. Its removal interferes with mRNA translation, and the effect may be partially overcome by the presence of homologous cytoplasmic brain initiation factors (Ven Murthy, 1982).

At the 3'-terminal, there appears a sequence of about 150-200 adenine nucleotides, which has also been found to be attached to HnRNA. In the brain, about 10-12% of RNA is associated with these polyadenine sequences. As reviewed by Brawerman (1981), the poly(A) sequence is believed to

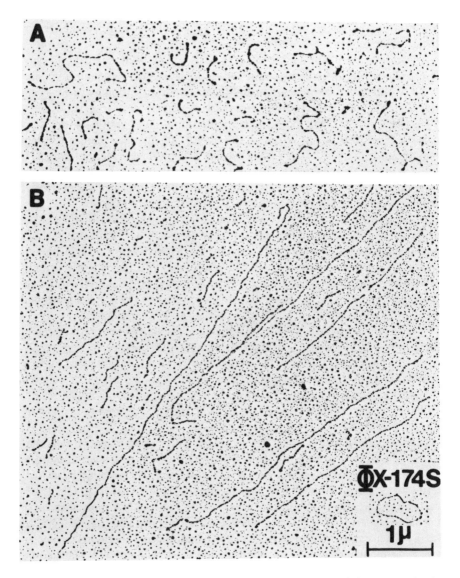

Figure 12.2 Electron photomicrographs of poly (A) mRNA and poly (A)hnRNA molecules [from J.A. Bantle and W.E. Hahn, *Cell* 8:130 (1976); © 1976 by Massachusetts Institute of Technology].

participate in the selection of the 3'-terminal regions of the mRNA chains during their genesis in the cell nucleus. It is also a component of the systems which control mRNA stability in the cytoplasm.

GENE EXPRESSION IN NEURONS

In terms of its diversity, brain messenger RNA is about four times as complex as that RNA in the liver. About 16-20% of unique DNA sequences is transcribed in the adult rodent brain (Bantle and Hahn, 1976). Chikaraishi *et al.* (1978) estimated this value at 31%, as compared with 10% in the kidney. This diversity probably depends upon the level of transcription specificity in individual types of neurons. Glial nuclei, on the other hand, do not show such high RNA diversity (Ozawa *et al.*, 1980). As an independent functioning unit, each neuron can play, at any one time, a different role in the brain. It might then require the activity of a slightly different set of enzymes and structural proteins. Accordingly, a pooled brain poly (A) mRNA population contains about 12,200 different sequences (Croizat *et al.*, 1979), an indication of the complexity of this tissue. Ryffel and McCarthy (1975) estimate this amount to be even higher, at 19,000 sequences.

Studies of gene expression in the neuron are still hampered by the gaps in our general understanding of gene controls in the eukaryotic cell. In these cells, the phenomena of gene expression include the loss, amplification and rearrangement of genetic material (Brown, 1981), changes in nucleosome structure (Johnson *et al.*, 1979), and DNA methylation (Razin and Riggs, 1980; Mohandas *et al.*, 1981). There is also an involvement of various nuclear proteins, both histones and nonhistones, some of which can serve in a repressor or activator capacity.

In the brain, nuclear proteins, which are brain- and even region-specific (Fujitani and Holoubek, 1974), have been found to be biochemically modified during various functional states. Histones can, for instance, be phosphorylated, acetylated or methylated. There is an acetylation of histones that has been specifically detected during learning in rats (Schmitt and Matthies, 1979). Once the animals are trained, the rate of acetylation decreases, as does the rate of phosphorylation (Glassman and Wilson, 1972).

Gene expression in neurons is also modifiable by such things as stimulation, drugs and stress. Once developed, the elaborate metabolic structure of the neuron and its specialized function has to be maintained over long periods of time. This requires either the presence of extremely long-lived macromolecules, or their continuous supply and turnover. The second mechanism is more probable, but it requires some type of long-lasting change that would sustain this continuous gene activation.

While it is possible that the various polymerases may have different roles in transcription, it is apparent that the regulation of transcription depends on those factors that control DNA availability and RNA chain initiation, termination, and release. Gene expression is linked to the activity of some DNA sequences, or "controlling elements", which are able to selectively activate a single gene. The controlling elements are not fixed at a particular site in the chromosome, but are capable of moving from one position to another. Thus, the activation of a particular gene can cause a rearrangement of adjacent DNA sequences (Nevers and Saedler, 1977).

The specificity of selective DNA template transcription in eukaryotic cells is partly controlled by nuclear proteins and possibly chromosomal RNA (Paul and Gilmour, 1968), although some specificity of transcription is apparently mediated by a variety of cytoplasmic "initiation factors" that have already been isolated from mammalian tissues.

One of the prominent characteristics of brain tissue is its morphological and biochemical heterogeneity. This heterogeneity is accompanied by differences in regional RNA content and turnover, so that neuronal and glial cell nuclei differ considerably in their DNA-dependent RNA polymerase activity. Moreover, this activity tends to be higher in neuronal than in glial or even liver cells. Interestingly, the number of initiation sites available for RNA polymerases is twice higher in neuronal nuclei as in oligodendroglial nuclei. In neuronal nuclei, the number of growing RNA chains is greater, and the average chain length longer than in liver or glial nuclei (Mizobe *et al.*, 1974). Also, the ratio of RNA to DNA is higher in neurons than in glia, meaning that regions rich in glial elements exhibit a lower RNA/DNA ratio than those rich in neurons.

In the brain, neuronal nuclei contain at least five times as much total protein as DNA, although there are regional differences in the relative amounts of several chromatin proteins. Overall differences also exist between the complements of neuronal and glial proteins. Certain proteins are specific for the central nervous system. DNA-110, for example, has been isolated from the brain and found to have a selective affinity for single-stranded DNA (Miani *et al.*, 1976). But, its function is not presently known.

The polyamines constitute a class of substances that are probably involved as regulatory agents in tissue differentiation and the activation and transcription fidelity of the genome. Putrescine, spermine and spermidine (Fig. 12.3) are three polyamines that strongly and specifically interact with nucleic acids and nucleic acid-containing structures, such as ribosomes. They stimulate the activity of DNA-dependent RNA polymerases and increase the synthesis of proteins at the ribosomes by influencing the conformation of the templates and/or products (for review see Abraham and Pihl, 1981). Accordingly, it has been noted that in many rapidly growing systems, includ-

SPERMINE $NH_3^+-(CH_2)_3-NH_2^+-(CH_2)_4-NH_2^+-(CH_2)_3-NH_3^+$

SPERMIDINE $NH_3^+-(CH_2)_4-NH_2^+-(CH_2)_3-NH_3^+$

PUTRESCINE $NH_3^+-CH_2-CH_2-CH_2-CH_2-NH_3^+$

Figure 12.3 Polyamines spermine, spermidine and putrescine.

ing the embryonic brain, the levels of RNA and spermidine increase together. On the other hand, spermine and especially spermidine have been reported to decrease the activity of the poly(A) polymerase responsible for catalyzing the addition of adenine nucleotide residues to the 3' end of newly synthesized RNA (Schumm and Richter, 1982).

Ornithine decarboxylase is the enzyme that generates putrescine from ornithine, while S-adenosyl-L-methionine decarboxylase and spermidine synthetase are involved in the production of spermine and spermidine, respectively (Fig. 12.4). All three exhibit high levels of activity in the brain. In the adult rat brain, S-adenosyl-L-methionine decarboxylase activity is higher than in most other tissues, although the levels of CNS polyamines are low, indicating that these substances undergo a rapid turnover.

The first, and probably the rate-limiting, step in polyamine biosynthesis is catalyzed by ornithine decarboxylase. The levels of this enzyme in the

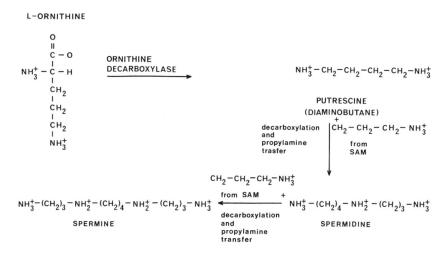

Figure 12.4 Synthesis of putrescine, spermidine and spermine. SAM, S-adenosyl-methionine.

brain vary with age, and its activity can be modified by such factors as the presence of some hormones (e.g. growth hormone and prolactin), reserpine administration, and maternal deprivation stress in the young (Butler and Schanberg, 1978). In addition, ACTH, glucocorticoids, estrogens, progesterone, and androgens are able to change the levels of ornithine decarboxylase levels in other organs as well. The polyamines are also carried into the brain. Spermine, according to Harman and Shaw (1981), is transported by two high-affinity, saturable components and a single unsaturable one.

Spermine and spermidine have been reported to modulate the phosphorylation and acetylation of histones in the rat cerebral cortex, an effect which has been found to decrease with age (Das and Kanungo, 1979). But, the particular mechanism by which the polyamines alter the production of RNA during different functional states is still uncertain. Additional research in this area could clarify whether the polyamines are directly involved in the control of neuronal RNA levels during changes in behavior.

BRAIN RNA

The synthesis and metabolism of RNA in adult nerve cells is known to be responsive to neuronal functioning. Thus, the stimulation of peripheral receptors and the consequent sensory activity increase the synthesis of ribonucleic acids throughout the entire sensory pathway. Conversely, a decrement in sensory stimulation diminishes RNA synthesis and the production of proteins. In the visual system, this drop in RNA and protein synthesis has been noted one hour after enucleation (Bondy and Margolis, 1969). The change is over the entire visual pathway, including the cerebral cortex (Dewar and Reading, 1970). The same response also follows light deprivation. In kittens that have had their eyelids sutured shut at birth, the complexity of RNA extracted from the visual cortex is substantially decreased (Grouse *et al.*, 1979).

Other types of sensory stimulation induce corresponding shifts. Rotational proprioceptive stimulation has been reported to increase the RNA level in Purkinje cells of the cerebellum and the neurons in the Deiters nucleus. Acoustic and olfactory stimulation have also been studied and have a comparable effect.

Work with individual neural components, such as the identified neurons of *Aplysia californica* or the neurons of the rat sympathetic ganglion, has revealed that neurotransmitter stimulation of the neuron triggers RNA synthesis there (Gisiger, 1971; Peterson and Erulkar, 1973). The onset of this increase is relatively late; new RNA enters the cytoplasm only about 90 minutes following the initial stimulation. In Gisiger's experiments with rat sympathetic ganglia, acetylcholine was a necessary inducing factor for RNA synthesis; direct depolarization of the cells with KCl was not effective. Therefore, the membrane neurotransmitter receptors had to be activated, causing not only a depolarization of the cell membrane, but an activation of the genome. It appears that this latter effect is, for the most part, indirect, using systems of second messengers which shall be discussed in Chapter 15.

The years when RNA was believed to be *the* substance responsible for the permanent fixation of the memory trace have comfortably passed. Although this position was enthusiastically embraced by a number of biologists and psychologists, none was able to satisfactorily explain how the sequence of nucleotides in RNA could directly influence the firing patterns of stimulated neurons. At present, there is still no evidence of any additional RNA function that does not involve protein synthesis.

Although there have been many different training paradigms employed to demonstrate an increase of RNA in the neurons, a detailed analysis of research in this area (Entingh *et al.*, 1974) revealed that the increase is actually rather small. These changes in RNA may last only a brief time following the learning of a task, or they may be gradual, protracted and extended over hours or days. In both situations, the increases in RNA metabolism detected by a single injection of a radioactive precursor could be nominal. Nonetheless, the realization that RNA is but one component of a system that functions to alter the activity of the neuron permits some insight into the experimental data from the 1960's and early 1970's which demonstrated a correlation between regional brain RNA synthesis and the acquisition and consolidation of memory.

The point has previously been stressed that repeated neuronal excitation modifies the characteristics of the neuronal membrane, and such a permanent, or at least long-lasting, change involves alterations in the demands placed upon the supply of proteins, phospholipids, glycerolipids and other membrane components. New structures are formed, including new synapses, axon collaterals, and dendritic branches. These processes all involve macromolecular synthesis and so logically require a change in the regulation of the genome. Shifts in the synthesis of RNA are therefore only a consequence of these nuclear regulatory changes and an intermediate step in the alterations of protein synthesis.

One of the main items of contention in research of this genre is the validity of the association between a specific biochemical process and learning, apart from contributions due to mere "stimulation" or the stressful nature of the task itself. Many studies have included elaborate controls in order to isolate effects that could then be attributed to the process of learning. However, concerns as to just what constitutes a learning situation, independent of stress and stimulation, do not make as much sense if one approaches the problem from a perspective of the functional complexity and diversity of individual neurons. On a conceptual level, there is a nebulous distinction between perception and learning (Hebb, 1949). The inclusion of various groups, each of which would just respond to a conditioning stimulus, an unconditioned stimulus, exercise, handling, frustration, fear, or whatever, can only tell us where metabolic changes are localized and consequently which areas are involved in that appropriate component of the complex behavioral process employed in the paradigm.

The overall complexity of the criterion behaviors used for an assessment of the learning situation, when viewed against the response diversity of the innumerable nerve cells involved in producing the behavior, emphasizes that such attempts to isolate the essence of the learning process as particular metabolic changes within a single neuron or a grouping of neurons is analogous to trying to understand the game of chess by focusing only on the activity of a single piece on the board.

RNA data are often difficult to interpret, since one must take into consideration a number of influential variables, including the rate of RNA degradation, the accessibility of precursors, and the available energy supply. Still, there are several interesting studies which have recently reported shifts in RNA synthesis in some areas of the brain that are associated with a learning situation. Cupello and Hyden (1976), for example, injected ^{14}C-labelled orotic acid into the hippocampus of rats trained to alter their response in a learned task. The incorporation of the precursor, pool-corrected, increased by 90% in comparison to control animals. Similar changes in RNA synthesis have been detected in area CA3 of the hippocampus, in the inferotemporal cortex and the principal gyrus of the frontal cortex of Rhesus monkeys trained to discriminate between two different shapes (Hyden et al., 1977). The largest change in the type of task was found in the inferotemporal cortex, while in a delayed alternation situation, the greatest increase was localized in the gyrus principalis.

In a study of brightness discrimination in rats, Wenzel et al. (1975) noted that during training there was an increase in the total number of ribosomes in the neurons within the hippocampal CA1 and CA3 fields. A similar change has also been observed in active controls exposed to randomly distributed footshocks. In addition, Smith (1975) found a shift in some fractions of rat brain cytoplasmic RNA following an operant task. The more complex was the task, the greater was the total uptake of ^{3}H-uridine into the brain. Smith concluded that the hippocampal changes in RNA synthesis were more related to the typical conditions present in a training situation than to specific learning.

A number of groups have reported a change in the base composition of newly formed RNA (e.g., Hyden, 1960; Shashoua, 1968). This may indicate either a formation of new RNA species, or a change in the quantitative proportions of existing species of RNA.

Increased RNA synthesis in the appropriate areas of the brain also depends upon an adequate supply of precursors. According to Matthies (1975), the supply of pyrimidine nucleotides is the rate-limiting step in the macromolecular synthesis involved in the consolidation of the long-term memory trace.

One of the most obvious questions raised by early researchers in this field has concerned the reason for these RNA changes. While learning per se was frequently suggested, there could reasonably be contributions by associated emotional and motivational components and visual, auditory, and/or olfactory stimulation. The increased firing of neurons and the consequent passage of a greater number of nerve impulses toward the postsynaptic cell could induce alterations in RNA and protein synthesis as well as changes in the neuronal membrane finally translated into the changes of behavior. Learning, then, could be a special case of functionally induced neuronal activation in a number of levels of the brain simultaneously.

There is presently no evidence showing that increased RNA synthesis in neurons is a specific response only to the "learning" process. Experiments with simple systems or with sensory stimulation indicate that sufficiently intensive postsynaptic excitation can itself elevate RNA synthesis. This effect involves the various forms of RNA (nuclear and cytoplasmic ribosomal RNA, messenger RNA and some transfer RNA) and RNA polymerase activity. Following intense stimulation, RNA associated changes will also appear in other organs. Popoli and Giuditta (1980), for example, found that while polysomes in the cerebral cortex responded to electroconvulsive shock by disaggregating, there were similar polysome effects in the kidney and liver.

The role of ribonucleic acids in learning and retention has also been studied by the administration of drugs which inhibit or stimulate RNA synthesis. Some of the stimulating substances, formerly hailed as memory improving drugs whose effects were attributable to a rise in RNA and protein synthesis, did not warrant the enthusiasm with which they had been welcomed.

Actinomycin D is a polypeptide antibiotic which can form complexes with DNA and, as a result, it is able to interfere with RNA synthesis. However, DNA segments devoid of the purine guanine do not form these complexes (Hamelin et al., 1973). Geller et al. (1969) found that even an 83% inhibition of RNA synthesis by actinomycin D did not substantially influence the retention rate, even if it was injected before the beginning of avoidance training. Several other groups also published negative results, and Batkin et al. (1966) even reported an enhancement of learning after an intracranial injection of actinomycin D. Further experimentation, however, did seem consistent with the position that actinomycin D could block the memory of a learned task in some animal species (e.g., rats, mice, salmon, goldfish, and chicks). But, because this drug has severe toxic effects on the central nervous system, no reliable conclusions can be drawn concerning a correlation between RNA synthesis and learning. Even low doses produce cellular damage that includes changes in the morphology of the nucleolus and a condensation of nuclear chromatin (Romen et al., 1977). Its injection into hippocampus impairs the performance of a maze task in the rat regardless of the time of the original training. However, at the same time, it causes epileptiform discharges that may influence behavior independently of any relationship to the actual mechanism of learning (Nakajima, 1969, 1972). Injections of actinomycin D into the cerebrospinal fluid or cerebral cortex can cause generalized tonic-clonic convulsions and death (Rowley and Yong, 1966). The nature of these effects make the results of such experiments with actinomycin D inconclusive at best.

A specific inhibitor of some types of DNA-dependent RNA polymerase, α-amanitin, has also been used in memory research. Alpha-amanitin is a bicyclic octapeptide with a molecular weight of 918 daltons. An intracranial injection six hours before the beginning of passive avoidance training was found to impair the performance of rats tested in the same situation one week later (Montanaro et al., 1971). The result has been confirmed in other situations and species. In 1977, Montanaro and his coworkers also reported that an increased activity of noradrenergic systems in the brain, caused by a simultaneous injection of D-amphetamine, had an anti-amnestic effect and interfered with the effect of α-amanitin. It appears, then, that increased synaptic activity was able to compensate for the antimetabolic actions of this drug. Campothecin, a plant alkaloid which blocks RNA synthesis in eukaryotic cells, also diminishes memory for a passive avoidance task when injected within 90 minutes after acquisition (Neale et al., 1973).

Another approach involves the use of purine and pyrimidine derivatives injected into the nervous tissue before or shortly after learning. Substances like 2,6-diaminopurine, 6-azaguanine, 5-iodouracil, 5-bromouracil, and 6-mercaptopurine may either block RNA synthesis, or be incorporated into RNA and disrupt the translation of mRNA on the ribosomes. Most of these drugs are able to impair the performance of the experimental animals in a passive avoidance situation (Reinis, 1971).

The various drug effects as well as the direct measurements of RNA levels in particular brain areas indicate that RNA synthesis, which is affected by increased synaptic activity, may be a component of the mechanism for storing memories within the brain. The antimetabolic actions may be overcome by an increase in synaptic activity. Also, non-associative influences have to be evaluated together with "learning per se". In spite of these limitations, RNA synthesis undoubtably must be a consideration in any efforts to construct a hypothesis of memory storage.

Chapter 13

Brain Amino Acids

Very simply, amino acids are the building blocks from which proteins are constructed. For this reason, the synthesis, metabolism, and degradation of amino acids contribute in a very essential way to protein functioning. The products of their breakdown may also be involved in the generation of energy-rich compounds in the body, and a number of amino acids have been identified as likely CNS neurotransmitters.

An amino acid is chemically defined by the presence of a carboxyl (-COOH) and an amino (-NH$_2$) group, with each typically being attached to an intervening carbon (Fig. 13.1). As a result, the molecule can behave either as an acid or as a base and thus functions as an amphoteric ion.

Amino acids may be classified as being neutral (containing one amino and one carboxyl group), acidic (one amino and two carboxyl groups), or basic (one carboxyl and two amino groups). Based upon the relative prevalence of members of these last two classes, proteins could have a predomi-

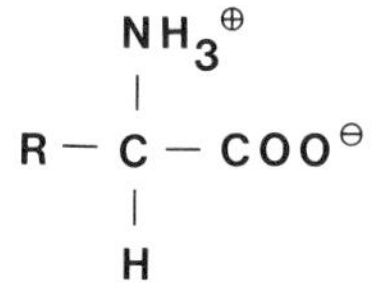

$$
\begin{array}{c}
\overset{\oplus}{NH_3} \\
| \\
R - C - COO^{\ominus} \\
| \\
H
\end{array}
$$

Figure 13.1 General formula of the amino acids.

201

nantly acidic or basic character. This assessment, in fact, is one of the principal means of protein classification. The distinction also is important because, as a rule, it groups amino acids which are carried into the brain by common transport systems.

The twenty different species of amino acids listed in Figures 13.2, 13.3, 13.4, and 13.5 are commonly incorporated into proteins. The brain also contains several additional amino acids which are infrequently detected and are not typical protein components. Some, such as β-alanine and γ-aminobutyric acid, have been implicated as neurotransmitters. The functions of others,

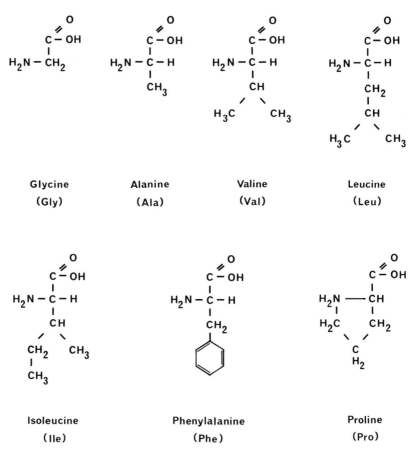

Figure 13.2 Neutral amino acids.

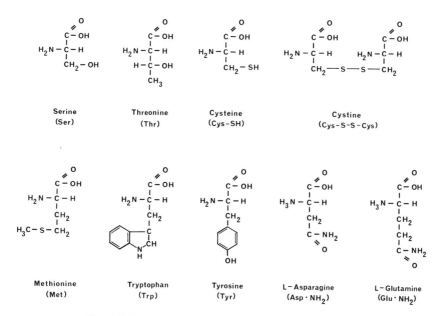

Figure 13.3 Amino acids with polar non-ionized substituents.

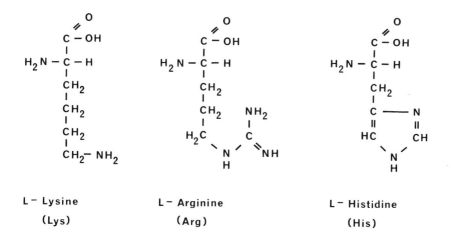

Figure 13.4 Basic amino acids.

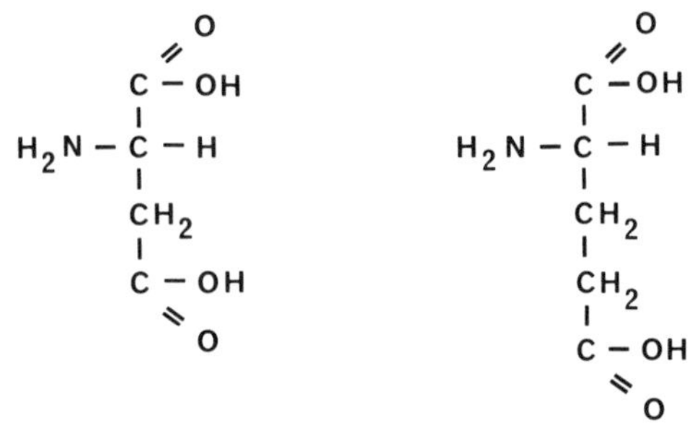

$$
\begin{array}{c}
\overset{\displaystyle O}{\underset{}{\text{C}}} \\
\text{C} - \text{OH} \\
\text{H}_2\text{N} - \text{C} - \text{H} \\
\text{CH}_2 \\
\text{C} - \text{OH} \\
\text{O}
\end{array}
\qquad
\begin{array}{c}
\overset{\displaystyle O}{\underset{}{\text{C}}} \\
\text{C} - \text{OH} \\
\text{H}_2\text{N} - \text{C} - \text{H} \\
\text{CH}_2 \\
\text{CH}_2 \\
\text{C} - \text{OH} \\
\text{O}
\end{array}
$$

L − Aspartate   L − Glutamate

(Asp)   (Glu)

Figure 13.5 Acidic amino acids.

including α-aminoisobutyrate, β-hydroxy-γ-aminobutyrate and γ-guanidinobutyrate, are unknown.

The composition of the amino acid pool within the central nervous system is different from that in any other tissue of the body and mirrors the amino acid requirements for different brain functions. For example, γ-aminobutyric acid and cystathionine are present in detectable quantities only in the brain and not in any other organ. There are also variations in the composition of the amino acid pool between animal species and between individual brain areas.

AMINO ACID TRANSPORT

Free amino acids, unbound to protein molecules, are partly transported into the brain from the blood plasma by active transport processes and partly synthesized *in situ*. Some amino acids, such as proline, are only carried across the capillary walls in small quantities and must enter the brain almost exclusively via the choroid plexus and cerebrospinal fluid.

The uptake of amino acids by the brain is a complex process that maintains tissue levels of these substances within the narrow limits necessary for various brain functions. The uptake depends upon specific energy-dependent transport mechanisms which have been experimentally demonstrated in the endothelia of brain capillaries. These mechanisms are stereospecific, saturable and work against the concentration gradient. At least three separate carrier-mediated transport systems are present in the portion of the capillary endothelial cell membrane that adjoins the brain tissue (Richter and

Wainer, 1971). One is for acidic amino acids; the other for basic; and the third for neutral amino acids. The luminal plasma membrane and the anti-luminal, or brain-side, endothelial membrane are therefore functionally distinct, and their polarity actively regulates the internal milieu of the brain (Betz and Goldstein, 1978).

The transport of the amino acids across the outer endothelial membrane is bidirectional, and some amino acids may actually be transported from the brain into the blood plasma. This is particularly true for the glutamine efflux, which is coupled to the influx of neutral amino acids (James and Fischer, 1981). There can also be a rapid exchange of amino acids across the blood-brain barrier without any net movement into the brain (Lajtha *et al.*, 1957).

The three systems of transport have somewhat overlapping transport specificities. And, a high concentration of one amino acid can interfere with the saturable transport of others, without itself being carried across the membrane. The mechanism of amino acid transport into the brain resembles similar transport systems which are present in other organs, such as the kidney (Meister, 1973). All of these systems depend on what is known as the γ-glutamyl cycle. Three membrane enzymes, γ-glutamyl transpeptidase, γ-glutamyl cyclotransferase and γ-cysteine synthetase, along with glutathione, a tripeptide formed by glycine, cysteine and γ-glutamate residues (Fig. 13.6), form the basis of the transport process.

Gamma-glutamyl transpeptidase removes the γ-glutamic acid of glutathione and temporarily binds to it. The free amino acids to be transported are then attached to the γ-glutamic acid residue (Fig. 13.7). The cysteinyl-glycine portion of glutathione is then released during this transpeptidation step, and the amino acid is transferred to the other surface of the membrane, before being released simultaneously with the γ-glutamic acid. This process

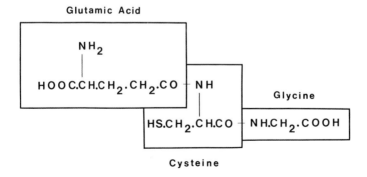

Figure 13.6 Glutathione.

operates in basically the same manner for the various amino acids, although some types require more than one transpeptidation step. It needs energy in the form of ATP, and its rate is influenced by several ions, primarily sodium and potassium, which serve as activators.

The enzymes of the γ-glutamyl cycle are present in the brain capillaries (Orlowski *et al.*, 1974), the choroid plexus, and, according to Reyes and Palmer (1976), also in glia and neurons, where they are responsible for the transport of amino acids into the cells. The activity of one of them, γ-glutamyl transpeptidase, is higher in glia than in neurons, at least in culture (Shine *et al.*, 1981). Gamma-glutamyl transpeptidase has been extracted and purified from the brain capillaries. It is a glycoprotein with a molecular weight of about 350,000 daltons. The molecule contains binding sites that are specific for each class of amino acids (Grandgeorge and Morelis, 1976). It has been found that the affinity of individual amino acids for this enzyme tends to vary. Thus, glutamine and cysteine have the highest affinity for the enzyme, while the acidic amino acids have the lowest (Karkowsky and Orlowski, 1978).

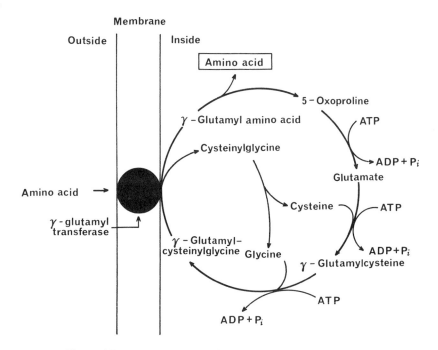

Figure 13.7 Membrane amino acid transport by the γ-glutamyl cycle.

The concentration of individual amino acids is not the sole factor that is able to influence the rate of transport. For some substances, such as tryptophan and tyrosine, the rate is also affected by glucose and insulin present in the circulating blood. Insulin is also able to govern the transport of other aromatic and large neutral amino acids into the brain (Fernando *et al.*, 1976).

Amino acids, particularly those which are believed to act as neurotransmitters, are released from the brain into the cerebrospinal fluid and from there into the circulation. So, for instance, glycine is released from the spinal cord into the subarachnoidal fluid, an efflux which is dependent upon the presence of calcium ions. Spreading depression or electrical stimulation of the cerebral cortex also causes a release of amino acids as the effect moves through the tissue. As a result, the amino acid content of the cerebrospinal fluid is not homogeneous and varies in different regions of the ventricular system and subarachnoidal space.

These two processes, the transport of amino acids into the brain and their metabolism and efflux from it, mean that the turnover of amino acids within the central nervous system is relatively rapid. For essential amino acids, the half-life in the brain is only 3-30 minutes. Non-essential amino acids, which can be synthesized in the brain, have a half-life of 2-24 hours (Toth and Lajtha, 1977).

Neurons and glia actively take up amino acids from the surrounding extracellular fluid. The glial cells, both *in vivo* and *in vitro,* have been found to absorb even more amino acids than the neurons (Logan, 1976). It appears, though, that the neuronal fraction, as compared to the glial fraction, displays (at least *in vitro)* a more intensive degree of incorporation of amino acids into protein and nucleotides into RNA. But, because of a smaller influx of these precursors, the neuronal production of proteins is less (Yanagihara, 1980).

The continuous transport of amino acids into neurons and glia also maintains the compositional stability of the extracellular fluid within the brain. Its disturbance by glial proliferation, for example, alters the microenvironment and can interfere with neuronal functioning.

Potassium ions in the extracellular fluid are known to affect the uptake of amino acids into the cells. Accordingly, a correlation exists between the ability of the cells to maintain the potassium concentration gradient across the cell membranes and the amino acid uptake. Increased neuronal activity, accompanied by release of potassium ions into the extracellular fluid, results in a larger quantity of amino acids that can be used for an increased protein synthesis, and thus, for a long-lasting functional adaptation of the cells. Both neurons and glia are involved in this process (Gainer *et al.*, 1977). Randt *et al.* (1976) have provided some evidence for such an adaptation. Inhibitors of the γ-glutamyl cycle, such as ICA (2-imidazoline-4-carboxylic acid) which

blocks amino acid transport into the brain, are also able to inhibit exploratory behavior, impair memory for foot shock and reduce operant responding
for food reinforcement. The appearance of all of these behavioral changes
corresponds to an interference with the uptake of large neutral amino acids.

Robertson *et al.* (1978) related the effect of impaired amino acid transport on retention to an interference with the labile phase of memory.
Between ten and thirty minutes after learning they injected rats with
α-aminoisobutyrate, a non-metabolizable amino acid which competes for
transport with amino acids necessary for protein synthesis. As a result, the
formation of the long-term memory trace was blocked. The authors surmised
that a supply of amino acids to the neurons during the labile phase of memory formation is necessary for "long-term memory" protein synthesis.

The transport of amino acids into the brain cells depends upon the
energy supply provided by glycolysis and on the activity of Na^+, K^+- dependent adenosine triphosphatase. Therefore, one might anticipate that the
effect of a non-metabolizable amino acid on memory could be overcome by a
drug that is able to stimulate the sodium pump. Such is the case with the
drug diphenylhydantoin. Inhibitors of the sodium pump, ouabain and etha-
crynic acid, also interfere with the labile phase of memory (Gibbs and Ng,
1976). The first ten minutes following acquisition are important in this
respect and determine the subsequent course of memory formation.

Genetic disorders of amino acid metabolism provide another line of evidence in support of a role for amino acid transport in memory. Inborn
defects of γ-glutamyl transpeptidase or erythrocyte γ-glutamyl cysteine
synthetase are both associated with mental retardation. And, elevated
plasma levels of some amino acids also diminish learning ability, probably
because a high level of a single amino acid interferes with the transport of
several other amino acids into the brain. The necessary amino acids are not
available then for the important metabolic processes that are involved in
plastic functional changes. The most common example of such a condition is
phenylketonuria, which is characterized by a deficiency in phenylalanine
hydroxylase, the enzyme that normally converts phenylalanine to tyrosine.

AMINO ACID SYNTHESIS

The brain levels of essential amino acids are controlled by the transport
mechanisms associated with the blood-brain barrier and by the rate of their
utilization. The levels of non-essential amino acids are also regulated by the
rates of glycolysis, transamination and oxidation. The synthesis of amino
acids depends upon the supply of carbon skeletons from glucose metabolism,
especially from the tricarboxylic acid cycle. Some amino acids are directly

synthesized by the transfer of an amino group to the acids of this cycle (Fig. 13.8). The conversion of glucose into amino acids is actually faster in the brain than in any other organ, and is even more intensive in the young, growing brain.

The transamination reactions, amination and deamination, are catalyzed by aminotransferases whose kinetics depend upon the nature of both the donor and the recipient acid. Glutamate, and aspartate for example, are the most important donors of amino groups to α-ketoglutarate and oxaloacetate. The activity, types and isoenzymes of the transaminases vary in different brain areas. Their activity is generally higher in gray matter than in white matter. The rate of transamination of some of the aromatic amino acids may also be significant in the metabolism of the catecholamine and indoleamine neurotransmitters.

There is evidence that the process of transamination is modified during various CNS functional states. Such changes have been observed during hypoxia, electrical stimulation, spreading depression, chilling, exercise, and the administration of neurotrophic drugs, CNS stimulants and CNS depressants.

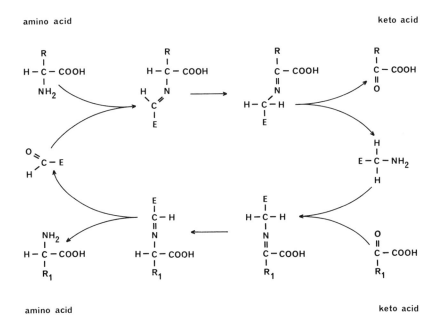

Figure 13.8 The formation of amino acids by the transamination reaction. Abbreviation: E, transaminase.

The deamination of amino acids is often followed by their oxidation. Mitochondrial glutamate and GABA are known to be metabolized in this way. And, glycine has been found to be oxidized up to carbon dioxide. It is possible, then, that these amino acids could serve as a source of cellular energy.

AMMONIA IN THE BRAIN

As early as 1922, Tashiro noticed that nervous activity is associated with the formation of ammonia. Two of the pathways that eventually generate this ammonia are the transamination and oxidative deamination of the amino acids. The preferential channeling of amino acids into one of these two processes is regulated by cellular levels of α-oxoglutarate and by the state of mitochondrial NADH. Neurons are believed to be the primary sites of ammonia production. And, according to Weil-Malherbe (1974), glutamate and GABA deamination account for almost 50% of the output.

Ammonia formation increases in such states as electrical stimulation of the brain, hypoxia, and convulsions (Torda, 1953), as well as following the injection of adrenocorticotrophic hormone and during the process of behavioral conditioning. The ammonia that is generated is then consumed in the citrulline cycle, and urea is formed. While this process is very intensive in the liver, the enzymes necessary for urea synthesis in the brain have a very low, marginally detectable activity. The brain, nevertheless, contains significant amounts of urea, of which it is probably able to synthesize at least a small portion, possibly from aspartic acid and citrulline.

Functional Aspects of Protein Synthesis in the Brain

In terms of their function, the proteins constitute a remarkable class of macromolecules. They are able to serve as structural materials which, by virtue of their properties of cross-linking, intertwining and interweaving, can be combined and built into almost any shape. As enzymes, they function to accelerate the vast number of chemical reactions within the body that would not otherwise be able to sustain life. As carrier proteins and channel components, they transport substances across cell membranes. Many hormones, as chemical agents coordinating the activities of diverse organs within the body, are protein in nature. And, it is becoming increasingly apparent that large numbers of smaller proteins or peptides are neurologically active, operating within the CNS either as transmitters or as modulators of neural activity.

SYNTHESIS OF PROTEINS

A protein is actually a linear polymer of amino acids linked together by peptide bonds (-CO:NH-). During protein synthesis, these bonds are formed from a carboxyl group (-COOH) of one amino acid and an amino group

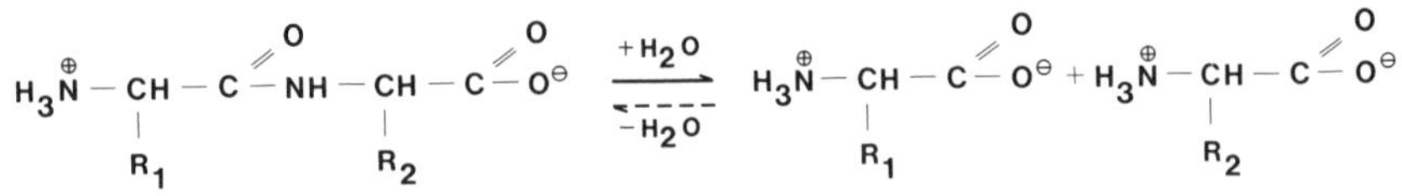

$$H_3\overset{\oplus}{N} - CH - \overset{O}{\overset{\parallel}{C}} - NH - CH - \overset{O}{\overset{\parallel}{C}} - O^{\ominus} \underset{-H_2O}{\overset{+H_2O}{\rightleftharpoons}} H_3\overset{\oplus}{N} - CH - \overset{O}{\overset{\parallel}{C}} - O^{\ominus} + H_3\overset{\oplus}{N} - CH - \overset{O}{\overset{\parallel}{C}} - O^{\ominus}$$

Figure 14.1 The cleavage and formation of the peptide bond.

($-NH_2$) of another, with the concurrent loss of a water molecule (Fig. 14.1). Variations in the sequence of amino acids ultimately determine the individual characteristics of proteins. This sequence is specified by the coding of DNA within the cell nucleus, and the basic mechanisms for converting this code into protein are the same throughout the body. DNA and DNA-dependent RNA polymerases direct the synthesis of the messenger, transfer, and ribosomal types of RNA. Molecules of specific transfer RNA each transport their own particular amino acids to the mRNA-ribosome complex, where messenger RNA directs the incorporation of individual amino acids into a growing polypeptide chain. Ribosomal RNA, in conjunction with ribosomal proteins, provides the matrix and modulation for this translation of RNA into protein (Fig. 14.2). In addition, several cytoplasmic initiation factors, activated in various systems by phosphorylation (Ochoa, 1981), are required for protein synthesis. But while they have already been demonstrated and characterized in the brain (Cosgrove and Brown, 1981; Gilbert and Mattick, 1981), little is known concerning their activation during the functional adaptation of the neuron.

Most of the protein synthesis is carried out in the neuronal perikaryon, predominantly in association with its endoplasmic reticulum. Since the synthesis of proteins in nerve cells is very extensive, the ribosome-studded endoplasmic reticulum is one of the most prominent features of the perikaryon and is often referred to as Nissl substance after its discoverer. The ribosomes can assume a proximate relationship. As a result, the structures are frequently termed polyribosomes or polysomes. Steward and Levy (1982) observed that within the neuron, most polysomes tend to be localized within close vicinity of the dendritic spines. This would seem to indicate a functional association between protein synthesis and the activity of the postsynaptic portion of the neuronal connection. Some synthetic activity also occurs in the cell nucleus, the mitochondria, dispersed polysomes, the axon hillock and perhaps in the nerve endings.

The production of a large number of copies of an enzyme-specific messenger RNA in the cell nucleus is one of the mechanisms regulating the quantity of newly synthesized proteins. While there is a great amount of speculation on this point, at least two such phenomena have been reported in nervous tissue. Sympathetic stimulation of the pineal gland induces the production of new molecules of hydroxyindole-*O*-methyltransferase (HIOMT), the enzyme that converts serotonin to melatonin. In addition, the prolonged neural stimulation of the adrenal medulla increase the level of tyrosine hydroxylase, the rate-limiting enzyme in the synthesis of norepinephrine and epinephrine. Both induction processes appear to occur as a result of the synthesis of a larger number of copies of enzyme-specific mRNA in response to the cellular stimulation.

The rate of protein synthesis in the ribosomes depends, among other things, on the available energy supply and the quantity of available free amino acids. The amino acids incorporated into protein are mostly derived from a precursor pool located in the extracellular space. This pool is in equilibrium with the intracellular free amino acids which originate from protein degradation and *de novo* biosynthesis. It has been determined that up to 40% of the amino acids made available in nervous tissue are provided by local degradative processes.

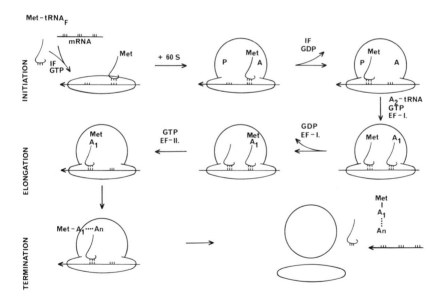

Figure 14.2 Schematic representation of the reactions involved in protein synthesis. IF, initiation factors; MET, formylmethionine; $A_1..A_n$, amino acid residue(s); P, peptidyl (donor) site of the ribosome; A, aminoacyl (acceptor) site of the ribosome; EF, elongation factor; GDP, guanosine diphosphate; GTP, guanosine triphosphate. 60s represents the larger of the two ribosomal subunits.. [redrawn from A.P. Grollman and M.T. Huang, *Fed. Proc.* 32:1673 (1972); © 1972 by Federation of American Societies for Experimental Biology].

Following its synthesis at the ribosome, the linear amino acid polymer undergoes one or more modifications. There are a number of things that can happen. Weak non-covalent interactions can cause a folding of the polypeptide chain. Individual chains can be associated with one another or with covalently bound ligands. Other substances may be attached to the protein, or the peptide bonds may be cleaved in certain places. The protein may also be subjected to phosphorylation, methylation, acetylation or hydroxylation. Although some of the changes take place when the nascent polypeptide chain is still attached to the polysomes, the majority of reactions occur following the completion of synthesis and after the protein has been released from the ribosome. The modification reactions are very specific and their sites within the peptide chain are identified by a particular amino acid sequence and selective enzyme actions. For example, protein kinases will phosphorylate serine or threonine only when they are bound within the sequence -Arg-X-Y-(Z)-Ser-(Thr)-.

The factors that regulate protein synthesis act at several levels, including the transcription of nuclear mRNA, its transport into the cytoplasm, and its binding to the ribosomes. There may also be a direct effect of regulatory factors on the translation of the genetic code into the sequence of amino acids within the ribosomes. Post-translational changes, such as the folding of the polypeptide chains, the attachment of different components, or the modification of individual amino acids, are also regulated processes and will be explored below in more detail.

PROTEIN SYNTHESIS IN THE BRAIN

The synthesis and degradation of proteins in the brain proceeds at a rate that is several times greater in neurons than in glia. And, during early postnatal development, this rate is even higher yet. There is a regional heterogeneity that shows a high rate of amino acid incorporation into proteins within the hippocampus and cerebral cortex. The lowest levels are generally found in the phylogenetically older regions.

As in other tissues, the initiation of protein synthesis requires ATP, GTP and energy-generating systems (Cosgrove and Brown, 1981). The ratio of GDP to GTP regulates the process of initiation, which is optimal at high potassium and low sodium levels (Dwyer and Wasterlain, 1980). The system synthesizing brain proteins is extremely sensitive to variations in the energy supply and the ionic composition of the extracellular fluid. It is also very responsive to agents such as the pituitary adrenocorticotrophic hormone (ACTH), which can intensively stimulate brain protein synthesis. In the absence of ACTH after hypophysectomy, this production decreases by 25% or more.

The protein synthetic process in mitochondria is relatively independent of corresponding activity in other cell components. Mitochondria have their own ribosomes, but require molecules of mRNA from the cell nucleus for about 80% of their proteins. The remaining 20% are coded by the genes in mitochondrial DNA. One of the main differences between the synthetic machinery for brain mitochondrial proteins and ribosomal proteins is a greater mitochondrial sensitivity to various antibiotics and inhibitors of oxidative phosphorylation. Protein synthesis in mitochondria can also be stimulated by the inhibitory amino acid neurotransmitter, γ-aminobutyric acid.

PROTEIN MODIFICATION

It is likely that the post-translational modification of proteins is one of the factors involved in the mechanisms of neuronal plasticity. The brain is rich in methylating enzymes which function to attach a methyl group to a number of amino acids, particularly to lysine, histidine, and arginine. During development, the peak activity of these enzymes appears in the fetal brain. And, although this activity decreases sharply after birth, the level remains rather high throughout life. The methyl group that is bound to the amino acid is derived from S-adenosylmethionine, an activated form of methionine. This substance is a major donor of methyl groups within the body. It is synthesized by the transfer of an adenosyl group from ATP to the sulfur of methionine. This process is all part of an activated methyl cycle (Fig. 14.3), in which the methyl groups are given up in some reactions and incorporated

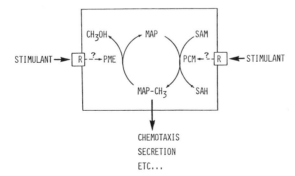

Figure 14.3 A model for the role of protein carboxyl-methylation in exocytotic secretion and chemotactic processes; PME, protein methylesterase; MAP, methyl-acceptor protein; SAM, S-adenosyl-methionine; SAH, S-adenosyl-homocysteine [from C. Gagnon and S. Heisler, *Life Sci.* 25:993 (1979); © 1979 by Pergamon Press Ltd.].

from other sources.   The labile methyl groups that are attached to homocysteine to produce methionine are formed from single-carbon units that can
be released during the metabolism of a variety of substances, including the
amino acids serine, glycine, histidine, and tryptophan. Activated homocysteine, *S*-adenosyl homocysteine, selectively and markedly inhibits the
methylation of brain proteins and phospholipids (Schatz *et al.*, 1981). This
would appear to be one of the ways by which methylation is controlled.

Several methylated amino acids have been identified in the brain. For
instance, trimethyllysine, mono- and dimethylarginine and mono- and
dimethylhistidine are components of a number of specific brain proteins,
including myelin basic protein and some histones. Overall, the highest levels
of methyllysine and dimethylhistidine have been found in brain gray matter
(Kakimoto *et al.*, 1975).

The activity of methylation in the synaptosomes increases during
depolarization, suggesting that the process may be important for the
modification of functionally induced synaptic activity (Eiden *et al.*, 1979).
In the endocrine organs, the methylation of membrane proteins is associated
with exocytosis from the secretary granules (Springer *et al.*, 1979). It is
possible that methyl groups in this situation bind to and neutralize
negatively charged carboxyl groups and, in so doing, alter the membrane
characteristics (Gagnon *et al.*, 1978). Although the mechanism of inactivation of carboxyl groups by methylation is not as yet known, the events are
very rapid and therefore capable of quickly altering the functional activity of
the synapse.

In perspective, methylation is but one of a number of modifying events
that employ proteins as substrates. Acetylation, hydroxylation, and
phosphorylation can also occur and are believed to be similarly capable of
inducing functional alterations in neurons. The process of phosphorylation
has been receiving an increasing amount of attention in recent years and will
be discussed in Chapter 15 as it relates to the activity of second messenger
systems.

TURNOVER OF BRAIN PROTEINS

Proteins within the brain are not only rapidly synthesized, but also rapidly degraded. And, while this process differs for individual protein species,
its rate is rather uniform throughout the various brain areas. Nevertheless,
an estimation of the turnover rate within a single region is rather difficult,
since some newly synthesized proteins are shortly thereafter transported into
other areas by the axoplasmic flow. Such transport contributes to the loss of
locally produced proteins and erroneously lowers estimates of their half-life.

In spite of this effect, the half-life is rather short, with about 0.65% of all proteins being replaced each hour. The range of turnover rates, however, is far from homogeneous and varies from a few hours up to 10 days (Lajtha, 1976).

Marks *et al.* (1970) have suggested that the breakdown of proteins is an orderly process in which different tissue peptide hydrolases liberate small peptides and amino acids. Lajtha and Dunlop (1981) have described a two-component system of protein turnover. A small, fast fraction (about 3.5% of all proteins) accounts for 50% of the rate, while the bulk of brain proteins turns over more slowly. These systems are subject to a modification by function, since electroconvulsive shock, hypophysectomy, hypothyroid states, as well as drugs and brain temperature are all able to alter the rate of turnover.

After the protein breakdown, a substantial portion of these released amino acids may then be reutilized in new protein synthesis. But, not all proteins are degraded at the same time. They are probably preselected for this process (Sobel and Bowman, 1971). The large number of degradative enzymes, their diverse intracellular distribution, and their apparently overlapping substrate specificities suggest a complex system for the controlled degradation and sequential splitting of proteins and polypeptides.

Some products of protein degradation in the brain may act specifically as neuromodulators and possibly neurotransmitters. These peptides, which will be discussed in more detail in Section V, are generated by specific proteases that cleave the peptide chain in particular places. The activities of these proteases appear to be controlled by endogenous inhibitory factors present in the neural tissue (Marks *et al.*, 1973).

SOME SPECIFIC BRAIN PROTEINS

In 1964, Bogoch and his colleagues separated extracts of brain proteins on DEAE cellulose and reported the presence of about 50 fractions. Many of these fractions were still heterogenous and required further separation. Eventually, however, Bogoch was able to detect about 200 different proteins in human gray matter. Weil and McIlwain (1981), using two-dimensional gel electrophoresis of the soluble proteins from bovine lumbar spinal motorneurons, isolated about 350 polypeptides with molecular weights ranging from 10,000 to 200,000 daltons.

The brain is the most membranous organ within the body, being highly structurally differentiated with a three-dimensional geometric membranous array. Most brain proteins are bound to the membrane, either as integral or peripheral proteins (see Chapter 1). Only about 10-20% of the total amount can be extracted by one or two homogenizations in aqueous buffers.

The widespread dichotomy between structural and enzymatic proteins is of limited usefulness. At present, there is no known "structural" protein which is common to all membranes. On the other hand, while the possibility does exist that a different unique structural protein may be present in each type of membrane, this has not yet been demonstrated. Also, many of the integral proteins which might be considered to have a structural role are themselves enzymes. And, in many membranes, they constitute the majority of the integral proteins.

Neurons and glial cells contain a sizable number of protein species that are not found in other parts of the body, which suggests that they participate in the function of the central nervous system. Some have already been isolated and purified, although, for the most part, their functions are still unknown. It seems that every year a number of new ones are identified, but since there is no unified terminology, some are probably just rediscovered species.

Immunological studies have shown that some brain proteins are common to all tissues, while others are brain-specific, glia- or neuron-specific, or characteristic for individual brain regions. The proteins that are unique to individual neurons or small groups of neurons have not yet been detected in the mammalian central nervous system, although they have been reported for such lower organisms as *Aplysia*. There, they are specific to single identified neurons, and their presence has been correlated with functions as neuroendocrine spontaneous pacemaker activity.

Schachner (1973; Chaffee and Schachner, 1978) has identified a series of brain cell membrane proteins, to which she has assigned the names NS-1 to NS-7. But, while NS-1 has been found to be exclusive to the glial membrane (and therefore is high in the white matter), others are not unique to the central nervous system. NS-3 and NS-5 cross-react with the kidney; NS-4 crossreacts with spermatozoa; and NS-6 is shared by brain, kidney and spermatozoa. Within the brain, these seven proteins, some of which may be glycoproteins, are not restricted to any particular brain region. Doyle *et al.* (1977) believe that most of them are antigens which originally belonged to a pluripotent neural progenitor cell. The roles of these antigenic surface proteins are unknown. However, Braun *et al.* (1981) found that the presence of at least three surface glycoproteins (out of 35 that were resolved from the membranes of cultured neurons) was dependent upon whether the cells were adrenergic or cholinergic. Also, Williams *et al.* (1980) found that antibodies to another surface glycoprotein, Thy-1, caused a selective inhibition of carbamylcholine-induced drinking when injected into the hypothalamus. Consequently, it appears that they may participate in the biochemical and functional characterization of individual cells, as well as in their mutual recognition during growth.

An interesting pair of proteins are actin and myosin. They have been generally associated with the process of muscle contraction, but are present in a variety of other cells, including those within the central nervous system. Actin and myosin in the brain represent about 1-3% of the total amount of protein (Fine and Bray, 1971). Synaptosomes contain relatively high concentrations of each, both in the presynaptic and postsynaptic portions (Blitz and Fine, 1974). Brain myosin has many properties in common with muscle myosin, including ATPase activity and the ability to interact with actin. However, the heavy chains of these two proteins do differ (Burridge and Bray, 1975).

The functional importance of actin and myosin in nonmuscle tissue is not clear, although several roles in the central nervous system have been postulated. They may be involved in cell motility during tissue morphogenesis, and in the adult CNS, they may be responsible for movements of some parts of the nerve cells, such as nerve endings (Santerre and Rich, 1976). Crick (1982) has proposed that contractile proteins in dendritic spines may quickly modify the shape of the spine and that this "twitching" may participate in rapid changes of synaptic activity.

The contractile proteins may also function in fast or slow axoplasmic transport, in the movements of growth cones during axonal regeneration, in secretory process and the release of neurotransmitters, and even in the modulation of cell surface receptors. With regard to this last possibility, clusters of membrane receptors may be capable of moving from one part of the cell surface to another (e.g., Craig and Cuatrecasas, 1975; Sedlacek et al., 1976), and their movement may be regulated at least in part by submembranous macromolecular assemblies. If so, actin and myosin may be one of the components of these assemblies. An actin-like protein, named protein C, is a component of vesicular, microsomal, and synaptosomal plasma membranes (Hofstein et al., 1982). And, interestingly, within the synaptosomes (but not in the other fractions) it undergoes an endogenous phosphorylation, which is dependent upon the presence of calcium ions (see Chapter 15).

An additional protein which may participate along with brain actin and myosin in movement-related activities within the neuron is clathrin. The CNS appears to contain considerable amounts of this protein (Pearse, 1976), which likely has a molecular weight of about 180,000. It is not unique to the brain, but does differ somewhat in composition from clathrin elsewhere in the body (see Puszkin et al., 1981). Clathrin shows a binding affinity for actin and is able to form cage- or basket-like submembranous assemblies in vitro (Puszkin et al., 1981). It is organized into a characteristic polyhedral network, which makes up the surface of the coated synaptic vesicles (Garber and Wu, 1981). As a result, it may prove important in the exocytotic mechanism of transmitter release. The extent of the polymerization and assembly of clathrin into its structural configuration seems to be influenced by the presence of several other proteins, which could function *in vivo* as modulatory substances (Lisanti *et al.*, 1982).

In 1971, Eng *et al.* isolated a specific glial protein from astrocytes that has been termed glial fibrillary acidic (GFA) protein. It has since been found in both normal and pathological glial tissue of many animal species and posesses a high degree of evolutionary stability, having very similar molecular weights, electrophoretic mobilities, extraction characteristics and immunological properties. GFA protein is present predominantly in the white matter and the periventricular glial layers. Antisera against it react with astrocytes (Bignami *et al.*, 1972), and this protein has been used as a specific astrocyte marker. In pathological conditions, it has been identified in leukotomy scars and in multiple sclerosis plaques.

The GFA protein molecule is composed of several peptides in the 40,500-59,000 dalton range. In situ, it is extremely susceptible to proteolysis, but the final products (polypeptides of about 40,000 daltons) are resistant to further tissue autolysis (Dahl and Bignami, 1976). The molecule closely resembles the neurofilament protein (see Chapter 16), but the two are not identical (Yen *et al.*, 1976). The function of GFA protein is not known. It forms filaments 8-10nm in diameter, and there is the possibility that it provides a degree of support for myelinated central nervous system axons which are highly susceptible to tearing. Fibers of GFA, along with actin and the fibroblast-type filament protein, vimentin (Chiu *et al.*, 1981), would create a firm skeleton to hold together bundles of nerve fibers.

In 1965, Moore reported the existance of a brain-specific acidic protein which was soluble in a saturated solution of ammonium sulfate at pH 7.0. It was termed S-100 protein and was characterized by a high acidity and a relatively large content of phenylalanine. Subsequent research has indicated, however, that what had originally been described as a single protein was likely a class of similar proteins, possibly as many as five of them, with molecular weights ranging from 19,500 to 24,000 daltons (Stewart, 1972).

Although found in extraneuronal tissues (Cocchia and Michetti, 1981; Cocchia *et al.*, 1981), S-100 proteins are many times more concentrated in the brain than in any other tissue, and close immunological cross-reactivity has been found for comparable forms in all vertebrate species. The proteins represent about 15% of the total protein synthesis in the brain. According to Pfeiffer *et al.* (1970), they are produced by glial cells. They have been found in fibrous and protoplasmic astrocytes and in ependymal cells (Cocchia, 1981). There is some evidence to argue that these glia represent the only true localization of S-100 and that all other reported places are attributable to nonspecific absorption, insufficiently specific antisera, or a damage-associated leakage of S-100 from its original site (Ghandour *et al.*, 1981). If this is so and can be corroborated by subsequent research, then it would be necessary to re-evaluate those data relating to S-100 function that are discussed below.

Nevertheless, at present S-100 proteins appear to be bound within the synaptic membrane to a specific receptor, primarily along the postsynaptic density. According to Donato (1980), the binding is specific, saturable, partly irreversible, and calcium- , time- , and temperature-dependent. And, antibodies against these proteins can affect the transmission of nerve impulses (De Robertis *et al.*, 1967).

Several functions of the S-100 class of proteins have been proposed. According to one hypothesis, calcium is bound specifically to two sites on a molecule of S-100, and this attachment is inhibited by sodium and potassium ions. The binding of calcium induces conformational changes in the molecule which then expose its hydrophobic parts, resulting in an increase in its binding to artificial membrane lipids. Bound to the membrane, it then might function to facilitate the transport of monovalent cations (Calissani *et al.*, 1974). S-100 has also been found to be one of the chromatin acidic proteins and has been implicated in the stimulation of nucleolar RNA polymerase activity, a necessary step in the synthesis of ribosomal RNA (Miani *et al.*, 1973).

Hyden and Lange (1970) have claimed that the level of S-100 increases in nervous tissue by about 10% during a behavioral task involving a reversal of handedness. The highest such increase was noted in the hippocampus. Moreover, anti-S-100 serum impaired the performance of experimental rats in several behavioral studies (Karpiak *et al.*, 1976). The exact nature of the functional involvement of S-100 in learning is still unknown, but the fact that this class of proteins is specific to the nervous system would seem to suggest some important role therein.

An acidic protein, detected both in central and peripheral nerves, for which a function has been determined is 14-3-2 or neuron-specific protein (NSP). In 1975, Bock and Dissing reported that NSP is one form of the enolase system that catalyzes the interconversion of 2-phospho-D-glycerate and 2-phosphoenolpyruvate in glycolysis (Chapter 8). It was also found that training in a performance task (as opposed to resting or random activity) significantly elevated the level of NSP in various areas of the rat brain (Zomzely-Neurath *et al.*, 1976).

An example of the specific expression of genetic information in a single functional system of the brain is the olfactory marker protein. It has been detected in several vertebrate species from fish to man within the primary olfactory pathway, including the olfactory epithelium, olfactory nerve, and olfactory bulb. It has not been found in any other part of the central nervous system, nor in any other tissue of the body. Olfactory marker protein is produced in the chemoreceptors of the olfactory epithelium, from which it is transported by the olfactory nerves into the brain. Its synthesis also requires the presence of the olfactory bulb, so that following the destruction of the olfactory epithelium, it disappears from the entire pathway. It may play an important role in the maintenance of function in this pathway, although at present such a possibility is still speculative (Margolis, 1972).

SYNAPTIC PROTEINS

The synaptic nerve endings with their adjacent postsynaptic membranes probably constitute the most important functional regions of the neuron. Studies of the variability and composition of their proteins have frequently been conducted in the hope that the knowledge could meaningfully contribute to an understanding of the mechanisms of neuronal plasticity.

While large numbers of proteins are produced in the nerve cell body and transported toward the synapses for use, some protein is synthesized in the nerve endings themselves. Such local synthesis is of special interest because of its potential relationship to the functional changes in synaptic activity. This synaptic process is partly dependent upon the mitochondria, which account for about 60% of synaptic protein synthesis (Austin and Morgan, 1967). The nerve endings do contain some RNA and ribosomes, most of which appear bound to the membranous structures (Shashoua, 1973). The use of these sites for protein synthesis is, however, uncertain.

Some protein species have been found exclusively in the nerve endings, and their alterations have been directly associated with changes in synaptic activity. One of them, termed synaptin, has been found in vesicle and synaptosomal plasma membranes (Bock et al., 1974). It possesses a carbohydrate moiety which reacts with a number of plant lectins. The presence of this carbohydrate component, together with the localization of synaptin in the vesicles, suggests that the protein may be involved in the exocytotic process by which the synaptic vesicles extrude their contents into the synaptic cleft.

Jorgensen and Bock (1974) isolated three proteins, termed D1, D2 and D3, from synaptosomal plasma membranes. They are also common to axons, but could not be detected in astrocytes or any other glial cells. Immunochemical techniques revealed that D1 and D2 were primarily, if not exclusively, present on the outer surface of the plasma membrane. D3, on the other hand, was found to be localized on the inner portion of the membrane (Jorgensen, 1977). The functions of the three proteins are unknown, but Jorgensen (1976) has noted that a drop in the concentration of D2 during early development (in correlation with the rate of synapse formation).

This, together with the effect of anti-D2 antibodies on neurite-neurite interaction, suggests a possible involvement of this protein in some form of intercellular recognition during the process of synaptogenesis (Jorgenson et al., 1980). Synaptin, D1 and D3 proteins have also been found in increased amounts in the occipital cortices of rats kept for four weeks in an "enriched" environment (Jorgensen and Bock, 1979).

Research in this area has profited from the recent introduction of techniques employing monoclonal antibodies. These antibodies are generated by hybrid cells which are typically formed by the fusion of a member of a lymphocyte population (generally an activated B-cell) and a myeloma (for review see Reichardt and Matthew, 1982). The hybridomas inherit from the parental cells both the capacity for unlimited growth in culture and the ability to produce significant quantities of a single species of antibody. Already, they have revealed the existence and localization of several synaptosomal types of synaptosomal proteins, along with the orientation, attachment, and movements of these proteins within the membrane (Smith and Loh, 1981). One set of antibodies has demonstrated the presence of forty classes of neurons in the leech nervous system. Some of these antibodies, moreover, are able to cause an inhibition of neurotransmitter binding in a particular brain area (Hofstein et al., 1981). Such an approach, then, appears quite likely to contribute in a substantial way to our understanding of the functional organization of the nerve ending.

SYNAPTIC GLYCOPROTEINS

Many proteins of the neuronal and glial membrane are glycoproteins, which means that in addition to the protein portion which anchors the molecule to the cell membrane, they also contain one or more chains of linked carbohydrate residues (Susz et al., 1973). Identified glycoprotein carbohydrates include galactose, mannose, fucose, glucosamine, galactosamine (Fig. 14.4), and N-acetylneuraminic acids (NANA) (see Fig. 2.12). The carbohydrate chain is bound to the protein component either by an N-glycosidic linkage of N-acetylglucosamine to the amide nitrogen of asparagine (Fig. 14.5), or by an O-glycosidic linkage of N-acetylgalactosamine to the hydroxyl group of serine or threonine (Fig. 14.6). The number of sugar residues in the carbohydrate chain is relatively low, and the chain is often branched. There is a large degree of glycoprotein heterogeneity, and individual species are typically present in small amounts (Zanetta et al., 1977).

Glycoproteins are synthesized in the endoplasmic reticulum and Golgi apparatus of the nerve cell body, and those that end up in the nerve ending region are transported there in the fast component of axoplasmic transport

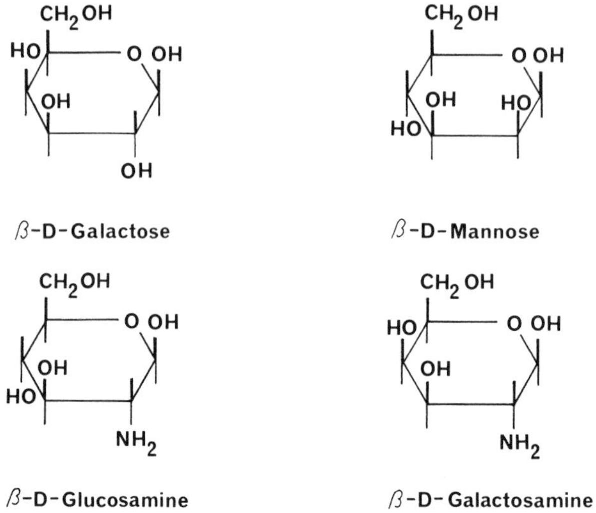

β-D-Galactose

β-D-Mannose

β-D-Glucosamine

β-D-Galactosamine

Figure 14.4 Structures of some important glycoprotein carbohydrates.

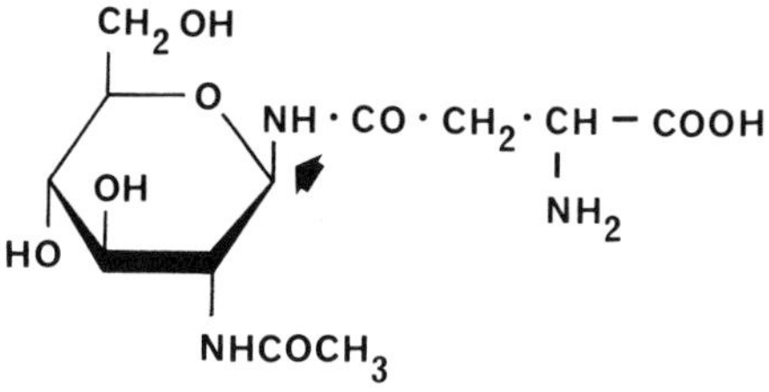

Figure 14.5 N-glycosidic bond of N-acetylglucosamine to asparagine.

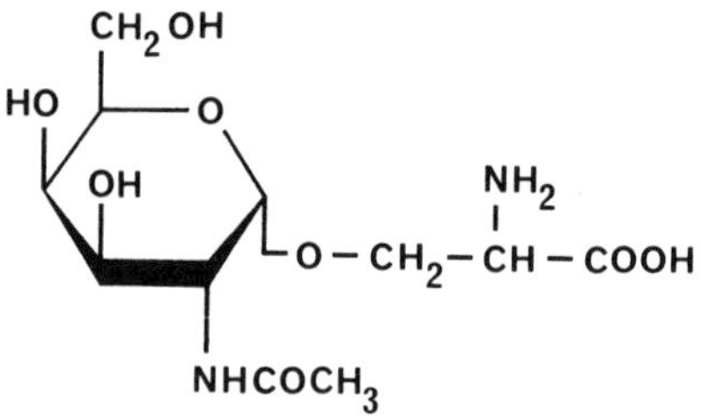

Figure 14.6 O-glycosidic bond of N-acetylgalactosamine to serine.

(see Chapter 16). There, they may undergo structural modification. The entire sugar moiety, for example, may be attached after their incorporation into the neuronal membranes (Barondes, 1968). The necessary enzymes, the glycosyl transferases, are present both in the particulate and soluble fractions of the nerve endings. These transferases are substrate-specific, and some have been purified. Fucosyltransferase, galactosyltransferase, N-acetyl-galactosaminyltransferase and several sialyltransferases have all been detected in synaptosomal membranes (Van den Eijnden and Van Dijk, 1974).

The glycoproteins can also be degraded in the nerve endings by several exoglycosidases, enzymes which remove single sugars from the carbohydrate chains. These two processes, glycoprotein synthesis and degradation, represent a flexible system which is able to continuously modify these molecules and could thus theoretically serve to alter the functional characteristics of the nerve endings.

The presence of sialic acid residues in glycoproteins makes them (and the surface of the membrane upon which they are localized) electrically negative. The number of these electronegative groups may influence the concentration of mobile positive ions, and therefore, the process of synaptic transmission. In this respect, the glycoproteins are analogous to the gangliosides.

A class of enzymes, the sialidases, functions to remove sialic acids from the glycoproteins and thus reduce the number of electrically   negative charges. The activity of these enzymes is enhanced by an acidic pH, a low sodium concentration, and high levels of potassium or calcium. Consequently, pH and ionic flux could, through these enzymes, indirectly control the density of fixed negative charges. In this manner, they may be capable of influencing synaptic transmission. One of these enzymes, a neuraminidase, has already been reported to decrease the amplitude of the excitatory postsynaptic potential (Tauc and Hinzen, 1974). In addition, a rapid modification of glycoprotein structure in the nerve ending, such as by the replacement of a neutral sugar (fucose) for a negatively charged sialic acid, could conceivably cause a fast functional change at the synapse (Barondes, 1974).

An additional series of events which may possibly be involved in the rapid alteration of synaptic activity has been proposed by Rahmann *et al.* (1975) and was briefly mentioned in Chapter 2. He suggested that in the resting state, synaptic membranes are not permeable ("closed") due to the presence of gangliosides and sialoglycoproteins complexed with calcium ions. During the depolarization of the presynaptic membrane, the efflux of potassium causes a dissociation of calcium ions from the gangliosides and glycoproteins, "opening" the membrane and allowing the calcium in and the neurotransmitters to flow out. The number of sialic acid residues in the membrane would therefore determine the amount of the neurotransmitter that is released. An additional accretion of sialyl groups would facilitate impulse transmission within the existing pathways. Rahmann *et al.* (1976) speculate that this could be a biochemical correlate of the engram.

Besides their ion-binding capacity, glycoproteins in the synaptic membrane also have some other functions. The acetylcholine receptor, for example, is a glycoprotein. Some of them are enzymes, such as ribonuclease or alkaline phosphatase, and others may control the activities of other enzymes. They are also believed to function in the process of recognition of one cell by another and the mutual adhesion between cells.

At least 28 major bands of glycoproteins have been separated in the synaptosomal plasma membranes, with at least eight classes of them within the postsynaptic membrane being capable of acting as receptors for lectins, substances with affinities for different sugars (Gurd, 1979). In addition, there are some glycoproteins in the intrasynaptosomal mitochondria and the synaptic vesicles. Those containing the sugar mannose represent about 25% of the total complement of glycoproteins.

Not all brain glycoproteins are localized in synapses. In fact, the first brain glycoprotein to be isolated, an α_2 protein, (Warecka and Bauer, 1967) was primarily found in white matter. It is water-soluble, relatively acidic, and contains neuraminic acid. Its appearance during brain development coincides with the appearance and differentiation of the neuroglia, particularly the myelination glia.

A major membrane glycoprotein specific to the brain and thymus is Thy-1. Its carbohydrate composition differs in the brain and thymus, but the protein portion is very similar in both. The molecules have MW of about 25,000, but they form large complexes of 270,000 (in brain) or 300,000 (in thymus) daltons.

A frequently studied brain glycoprotein is GP-350, electrophoretically a fast-moving species in a polyacrylamide gel. It is acidic, with a molecular weight of about $11,000 \pm 200$. GP-350 is a soluble protein, containing one sialic acid per molecule, although its membrane-bound form is immunologically detectable in the synaptosomal fraction (Van Nieuw Amerongen and Roukema, 1974). It is found exclusively in neurons and is especially high in the caudate nucleus, cerebellar gray matter and pons. Its function is unknown.

Soluble brain glycoproteins that have been referred to as "endogenous brain lectins" have been found in the developing brain (Simpson *et al.*, 1977). They are able to recognize a carbohydrate-containing receptor and in this way may mediate the intercellular recognition and adhesion of the nerve cells, before later disappearing from the brain. Their peak level coincides with the time course of maximum synapse formation in the brain cortex. Some of these soluble glycoproteins are bound by the plasma membranes of neurons, possibly stimulating the growth of axons during early development (Gombos *et al.*, 1971).

Of the synaptosomal proteins, the glycoproteins are likely candidates for an alteration by experience (Barondes, 1974). Injections of precursors of the glycoprotein sugar moieties - glucosamine, fucose, or other labeled monosaccharides - show a differential labeling of glycoproteins in areas such as the temporal cortex and caudo-putamen region following the acquisition of a simple step-up motor task (Routtenberg *et al.*, 1974). The placement of a mouse into an apparatus in which it normally would obtain footshock causes an increase in the incorporation of radioactive fucose into brain glycoproteins (Damstra *et al.*, 1975). The learning of a brightness discrimination is also accompanied by increased glycoprotein synthesis (Pohle *et al.*, 1979). For such a brightness discrimination in rats, Popov *et al.* (1976) found these changes in labeling in the hippocampus and visual cortex. Just where these effects occur morphologically is not, however, known, and Irwin *et al.* (1978) reported an inability to relate them to specific anatomical sites or subcellular components of the neurons. The products of glycoprotein synthesis that are involved in the processing of behavioral information are chemically specific, he claims, but broadly dispersed morphologically.

The available evidence shows that the observed changes are not very fast. Burgoyne and Rose (1980) examined the incorporation of radioactive lysine following the exposure of dark-reared rats to light and found an increase within one hour after the beginning of the exposure. Radioactive fucose was incorporated into the glycoprotein sugar moiety after about three hours, when the lysine incorporation was already depressed. In one-day-old chicks, passive avoidance training increased the incorporation of radioactive fucose into glycoproteins of the synaptic membranes, and all 9 observed peaks of glycoproteins were labeled (Burgoyne and Rose, 1980a).

GLYCOSAMINOGLYCANS

The glycosaminoglycans exist as complexes of polysaccharides that are bound in a chain-like fashion to a protein trunk. The linked sugar moities typically consist of a repeating disaccharide sequence that has been identified as a hexosamine (*N*-acetylglucosamine or *N*-acetylgalactosamine) and another sugar derivative, usually a uronic acid. Various glycosaminoglycans have also been determined to contain *N*-acetylated and *N*- and *O*-sulfated forms of glucosamine.

Until recently referred to as mucopolysaccharides, the glycosaminogly-cans can be found in most vertebrate tissues, including the brain. Structurally, these protein-polysaccharide complexes can be joined as subunits to create larger megacomplexes (Fig. 14.7), whose composition may vary according to the tissue.

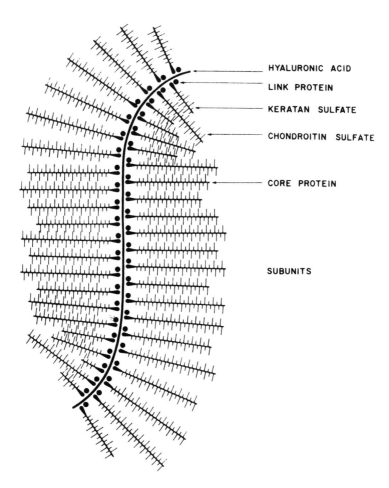

HYALURONIC ACID

LINK PROTEIN

KERATAN SULFATE

CHONDROITIN SULFATE

CORE PROTEIN

SUBUNITS

Figure 14.7 Model of the molecular structure of the proteoglycan aggregate [from L. Rosenberg, in: *Dynamics of Connective Tissue Macromolecules,* P.M.C. Burleigh and A.R. Poole (Eds.), p. 105; © 1973 by North Holland Publishing Co.].

The brain contains several types of glycosaminoglycans, notably hyaluronic acid, heparan sulfate, chondroitin-4-sulfate, chondroitin-6-sulfate, and possibly dermatan sulfate. Heparin and keratan sulfate, two other types found elsewhere in the body, do not appear to be present. They may form the interstitial ground substance of the brain (Feigin, 1980). In addition, relatively large concentrations of these substances have been detected in neuronal cell bodies and astrocytes (Margolis and Margolis, 1974). Subcellular fractionation techniques have indicated that the greatest percentage of these glycosaminoglycans that is not extracted with water is contained within the microsomal fraction (36-60%). The nuclei and tissue debris account for somewhat less (12-21%), while only about 1-5% of the total particulate glycosaminoglycan concentration is found within the crude mitochondrial fraction (Margolis *et al.*, 1975). Margolis and associates (1976) believe that the overall synaptosomal content is low, while White (1979) reported the extraction of at least three kinds of glycosaminoglycans from this purified fraction. But, it is the synaptic vesicles that have been reported to contain larger amounts of glycosaminoglycans, approximately twice the level of whole brain tissue when calculated per mg of protein. There is some question, however, as to the purity of the preparation, since gangliosides were found to be present, suggesting a plasma membrane contamination. Nonetheless, further studies have provided support for this association between the glycosaminoglycans and synaptic vesicles (Castejon and Castejon, 1975; Blaschka *et al.*, 1976).

The relatively high concentration of glycosaminoglycans in the synaptic vesicles suggests a role for these substances in neurotransmitter storage and release (Wang and Adey, 1969). A number of studies have tended to support this possibility (Blaschke, 1979). By supplementing a perfusing fluid with acetylcholine, Margolis *et al.* (1973) were able to demonstrate a coincidental increase in both sulfated glycosaminoglycans and catecholamines from the adrenal gland. Also, the denervation or stimulation of the gastrocnemius muscle caused opposing shifts in the levels of hyaluronate and chondroitin sulfate (Novikova and Glimenko, 1973). Bon *et al.* (1978) have further suggested that these complex carbohydrates may stabilize molecules of acetylcholinesterase bound to the membrane by their molecular "tail".

One of the properties of the glycosaminoglycans which could be seminal to their function(s) within the neural tissue is an ability to bind calcium ions. Such behavior would be consonant with their hypothesized involvement in neurotransmitter release and could contribute to the maintenance of the ionic environment within the synaptic area. An additional role could be in the mechanism of cellular adhesion that is associated with both the growth and differentiation of the brain and the binding of the nerve to the postsynaptic cell.

If the glycosaminoglycans do somehow participate in the process of neurotransmission, one might reasonably expect a manipulation of their concentration or activity to have some electrophysiological and behavioral consequences. There have been reports of the intraventricular administration of hyaluronidase causing lethargy, muscular rigidity, and even convulsions in cats (Custod and Young, 1968). Injections into the lateral geniculate body were also reported to cause seizure activity and an increase in the amplitude of the EEG (Marcovici *et al.*, 1964).

SYNAPTIC PHOSPHOPROTEINS

An interesting group of modified synaptic proteins is the phosphoproteins. These proteins may be phosphorylated *in situ,* and this event has been postulated as being one of the mechanisms involved in the mediation or modulation of synaptic transmission (Greengard, 1976). Phosphoproteins also activate the turnover of phosphatidylinositol and phosphatidic acid in the nerve endings, usually in response to neurotransmitter activity.

The posttranslational modification of synaptic proteins is probably an important process in altering the efficacy of synaptic transmission. Phosphorylation can actually occur within seconds, and there are indications that the newly formed phosphoproteins are capable of modifying synaptic efficacy for periods of time ranging from minutes to possibly months. Some of these proteins are phosphorylated by protein kinases, enzymes activated by cAMP or other intracellular messenger systems. These processes shall be explored in more detail in the following chapter.

PROTEIN SYNTHESIS AND BRAIN FUNCTION

Besides posttranslational protein modification, neuronal plasticity also requires the synthesis of new proteins. Considerations of the role of protein synthesis and modification in the fixation and retention of the memory trace are bolstered by a large body of experimental data demonstrating changes in brain protein during both sensory stimulation and learning.

Synaptic stimulation has been shown to increase not only RNA production, as described in Chapter 12, but also results in a synthesis of proteins. However, the demonstration of a clear-cut relationship between synaptic activity and protein synthesis is not that simple. Elevation in the rate of proteolysis quite often accompanies the increase in synthesis, and during maximal stimulation, proteolysis may predominate (McBride and Klingman, 1972). Long-lasting supramaximal stimulation will suppress protein synthesis, probably as a result of the channeling of high-energy compounds for use by the sodium pump. Mild stimulation, on the other hand, will augment the protein content of affected neurons. The change is selective and involves either an increase or decrease in the production of individual proteins. This is probably one of the reasons why the data on alterations in protein synthesis are often contradictory (Deutsch *et al.*, 1980). The change would also depend upon the area studied and experimental situation. Thus, long-term potentiation induced in hippocampal slices causes increased incorportion of a radioactive amino acid, but only in the potentiated area (Duffy *et al.*, 1981).

Experiments done with *Aplysia* have shown that each identifiable neuron within the ganglion has its own specific labelling pattern during stimulation (Gainer, 1971). However, an inhibition of this synthetic process for up to 30 hours in these identifiable *Aplysia* neurons does not interfere with the resting membrane potential, spike generation, firing pattern, or synaptic transmission (Schwartz *et al.*, 1971). It is probable that the added production of proteins is primarily necessary to supply building materials for the assembly of new structures and the modification of old ones. Nevertheless, the existing structures may function for some time without this supply.

At this point, it must be emphasized that the foregoing discussion of synaptic alterations in protein synthesis by no means implies that these effects are limited to this region. The entire metabolic apparatus of the neuron undergoes an adjustment as the changes in synaptic efficacy take place.

Researchers involved in the study of the role of proteins in behavior have often attempted to distinguish between "associative" and "non-associative" changes in protein synthesis. In other words, there is an effort to distinguish between the effects of learning and the effects of sensory stimulation per se. But as of yet, the evidence that has been published concerning qualitative differences between biochemical changes accompanying learning and simple sensory activity or even the response to simple electrical stimulation of sliced brain tissue is not all that compelling.

In the preface to this book, the point was made that there exists a relationship, but not a uniformity, between the cellular process of synaptic and neuronal plasticity and the general process of learning that affects large areas of the brain. The distinction may help one to understand the processes of learning, memory, and retrieval from a biochemical viewpoint. Each cell reacts to trains of stimuli, whether they originate from simple sensations or from the learning process. Learning would then depend upon the coordinated activity of various brain areas and the individual neurons residing therein. Each of the involved neurons is modified somewhat, with the result being a complex memory trace involving extensive brain areas. As a result, it would prove quite unprofitable to search for some exclusive metabolic changes specific for learning. From this perspective, the response of an individual neuron would be similar, if not identical in many diverse situations. The responses to sensory stimulation, drugs, brain damage, hormones, learning, or even to the continuing expression of the genome during development would be ultimately reflected by the same neuronal change. The specificity is in the localization, the degree of the changes, and in the neuronal interrelationships.

The process of plasticity is obviously not a simple one. The nerve cell is a unified metabolic system, wherein individual components are interconnected and interdependent. Events initiated by increased synaptic activity and depolarization of the neuronal membrane lead to changes in function and alterations in the cell's metabolism. The concept of neuronal plasticity essentially means that the homeostasis of the inner metabolic processes of the cell is disturbed and must be readjusted. Consequently, it would be difficult to distinguish between the functions of the "constitutive" neuronal proteins and of those which are altered by plastic changes of the neuron. The process of neuronal plasticity in its initial, as well as its later phases, depends upon these "constitutive" proteins which are continuously produced and keep the cell alive. Moreover, there is a dependence upon those "constitutive" proteins that are altered at the post-translational level and those whose synthesis is increased or decreased when the cell changes its function. Since these groupings are not necessarily exclusive, it would be difficult, if not impossible, to clearly classify such types of proteins. Consequently, we shall not attempt to distinguish between the shifts in protein synthesis caused by "stimulation" and those caused by "learning".

In the vertebrate brain, where these functionally related changes in protein synthesis have often been studied, the visual system is frequently the system of choice for this work. Experimental animals have been maintained in darkness for extended periods and then exposed to light. Their first exposure leads to an increased incorporation of different labeled amino acids into proteins throughout the entire visual pathway, including the retina (Richardson and Rose, 1973). In the retina, Rose (1973) found differences in the labeling pattern of several protein fractions, which Burgoyne *et al.* (1981) has determined to have molecular weights of 100K, 71K, 44K, and 38K. The 44 kilodalton protein has already been identified as actin. Similar changes have also been reported for the visual cortex (Jones-Lecointe *et al.*, 1975). This increased incorporation following the initial exposure to light is, however, only transient.

The increase in protein synthesis within the brain as a consequence of a learning experience follows a similar pattern. The early papers of Hyden's group (e.g., Hyden and McEwen, 1966), as well as those of many other researchers, noted a greater incorporation of radioactive amino acid precursors. A quantitative increase in protein synthesis during the process of learning has been detected in several brain areas, such as the hippocampus, visual cortex, and cingulate cortex. These changes have also been described for synaptosomal proteins during a required shift in "handedness" in the rat (Hyden *et al.*, 1977). In this study, there were elevations in the synthesis of several proteins whose molecular weights varied from 35,000 to 100,000 daltons.

Still, an overall increase in protein synthesis during acquisition has often been attributed more to a general response to stress than to learning. Rees *et al.* (1977) found that protein synthesis during one-way active avoidance training in mice is followed by an augmentations of protein synthesis

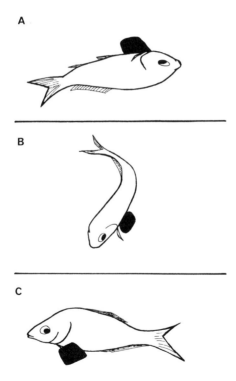

Figure 14.8 Stages in the ability of goldfish to swim in the normal position following the float (black) attachment; (A) 30-60 minutes after float attachment (fish upside-down); (B) 1-2 hours (intermittent diving); (C) 4 hr (swimming in the normal position) [redrawn from C.J. Woolf, G.H. Willies, H.R. Hepburn and C. Rosendorff, *Experientia* 30:761 (1974); © 1974 by Birkhaeuser Verlag, Switzerland].

both in the liver and the brain, leading the authors to conclude that the increase is more of a general response to stress in rodents than a specific response to learning.

An important question concerns the identity of the protein species that are increased during a functional adaptation of the CNS. Hyden and Lange (1976) reported an elevation in S-100. And, an antiserum against this protein prevented the further progress of a learned behavior. At least three proteins that are newly formed during the process of learning have been isolated by Shashoua (1976, 1977; Shashoua and Moore, 1978). In goldfish to which light plastic floats had been attached to the ventral midline (Fig. 14.8), the acquisition of a new swimming skill coincided with an increase in three protein bands, termed ependymin α, β and γ, which were present in the cytoplasmic fraction of the brain homogenate. Shashoua localized one of these proteins within a family of about 15,000 cells dispersed directly below the periventricular and external surfaces of the CNS from the spinal cord to the forebrain. But, these proteins did not represent new "task-specific" molecules, but rather products of an acceleration in the normal metabolic processes of the neurons (Benowitz and Shashoua, 1977). They were also found in the cerebrospinal fluid and even in blood serum (Schmidt and Shashoua, 1981). Antisera against these proteins, when injected 1-24 hours after the start of training, blocked the performance of the trained fish, who were unable to execute the learned task three days later.

While there are numerous learning studies examining the incorporation of radioactive precursors into proteins within specific brain areas, the results obtained by one laboratory are not easily related to those from another. There are often differences in the paradigms and labels employed that lead to regional variations in the appearance of labeled proteins that are difficult to explain. Moreover, some negative findings have been reported.

Autoradiographic studies have shown that proteins are labeled in different areas of the cortex and the brain in general. Thus, the reversal of handedness paradigm employed by Hyden's laboratory (e.g. Hyden and Lange, 1976) resulted in an increase in incorporation of labeled valine into the hippocampus, visual cortex, and anterior-dorsal hypothalamus. Brightness discrimination, used by Matthies and his group, induces changes in protein synthesis in the cingulate cortex, visual cortex, and dentate area. A fundamental point that these studies do make is that alterations of neuronal activity that occur during the acquisition of a simple task are widespread and involve large areas of nervous tissue.

ANTIBIOTICS AND PROTEIN SYNTHESIS

One method of assessing the functional importance of the increase in protein synthesis for the acquisition of a learned response is through the use of antibiotics which block the assembly of proteins at the ribosomes. The antibiotics puromycin, cycloheximide, acetoxycycloheximide and anisomycin have been most commonly used in this type of research.

Acetoxycycloheximide and cycloheximide (Fig. 14.9) belong to the glutarimide group. While they do not affect the formation of the complex between mRNA, tRNA and the ribosome, they do interfere with the movement of the ribosome along the mRNA strand and thus are able to prevent the translation of the genetic code into the amino acid sequence. They can also directly influence several other biochemical systems within the cell, such as the activity of tyrosine hydroxylase, dopamine-β-hydroxylase, acetylcholinesterase or tryptophan hydroxylase (Azmitia and McEwen, 1976; Brimijoin, 1976; Squire *et al.*, 1974).

If these antibiotics are injected before or immediately after the acquisition session, memory is retained for a few hours (in most learning situations for about 1-3 hours), and then the animals behave as if the learning had never taken place. But, overtraining (Barondes and Cohen, 1966) and substances stimulating adrenergic systems (Serota *et al.*, 1972) have been found to protect against the drug-induced amnesia suggesting that glutarimide antibiotics actually interfere only with the activity of adrenergic neurons (Jeffrey and Gibbs, 1976). Most evidence indicates that the lost memory is later re-accessible. The recovery of memory may either be spontaneous, or be induced by "reminders" such as foot shocks (Quartermain, 1970).

Anisomycin (Fig. 14.10), another protein synthesis inhibitor, affects the translocation of the peptide chain on the ribosome. It probably causes a defect in the joining of the 60S ribosomal subunit to the smaller subunit to form the 80S ribosome necessary for the translation to begin (van Venrooij

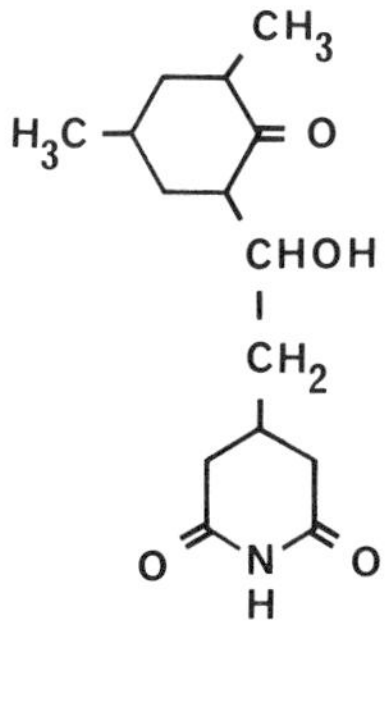

Figure 14.9 Cycloheximide.

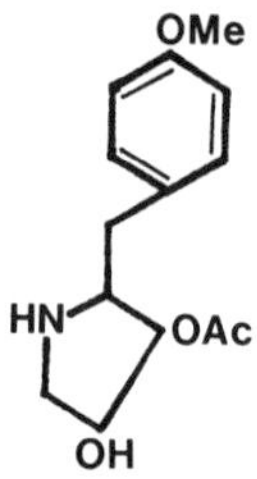

Figure 14.10 Anisomycin.

et al., 1977). The inhibition of protein synthesis in the brain lasts at least two hours, and its duration can be controlled by the administration of successive doses of the drug. The mortality of animals given anisomycin is low, and it does not affect the electroencephalogram. This makes anisomycin a useful and sensitive tool for studying the role of protein synthesis in memory (Bull *et al.*, 1976).

This drug was observed to cause amnesia for a passive avoidance habit in mice (Flood *et al.*, 1973). The greater duration of inhibition, the more likely amnesia was to occur. For example, an inhibition for two hours did not block a pole jump as an active avoidance response, but a longer period of 6-8 hours did. Also, stimulants such as caffeine, nicotine, amphetamine, strychnine and picrotoxin did not interfere with the development of amnesia (Flood *et al.*, 1977; 1978).

Anisomycin can also cause a prolongation of the short-term memory period. After a passive avoidance trial, electroconvulsive shock may typically block memory for the task for up to thirty minutes. But, in anisomycin-treated mice, this period can last up to eight hours (Flood *et al.*, 1977a). This relationship is difficult to explain. It definitely casts a shadow over the reverberation hypothesis of short term memory. Perhaps, the decay in short-term memory also depends upon active protein synthesis, so that if this process is inhibited, short-term memory may persist for longer periods of time.

An experimental manipulation following training may modify the period during which the animals are sensitive to anisomycin. Judge and Quartermain (1982) found that in an approach-avoidance behavioral paradigm mice would exhibit amnesia even when injected up to two hours after training. If the animal is instead exposed again briefly to the experimental apparatus three hours following training before receiving anisomycin, a robust amnesia develops, which persists for about four days.

A third antibiotic that is able to block the performance of trained animals is puromycin (Fig. 14.11). It interferes with the translation of mRNA at the ribosome, probably by acting as an analog of aminoacyl-tRNA. It would then be bound to a growing peptide chain instead of tRNA, tightly linked to the carboxyl end of the peptide. This would then halt further translation, and the incomplete peptide with its attached puromycin would be released. The events would also dissociate the polyribosomes to monoribosomes.

Puromycin has several other biochemical actions. It induces mitochondrial swelling, with a dilatation of cisterns of rough endoplasmic reticulum. It can even inhibit DNA synthesis (Hori and Lark, 1973) by preventing the initiation of replication. Puromycin also decreases the activity of the proteolytic enzymes, inhibits cyclic adenosine monophosphate phosphodiesterase (independent of its effect upon protein synthesis), and binds to acetylcholinesterase. And, it has a direct, prompt, and reversible depressant action upon synaptic transmission.

The study of the effects of puromycin on learning began with the Flexners' work in 1962. They and their associates found that an intracranial injection of puromycin in mice before training in an electrified Y maze interfered with their performance when tested four days after training. These experiments were later repeated by Agranoff's group, using goldfish. It was determined that the injections cause about an 80-90% inhibition of protein synthesis. But, puromycin injected 24 hours prior to the training did not interfere with acquisition (Springer *et al.*, 1975).

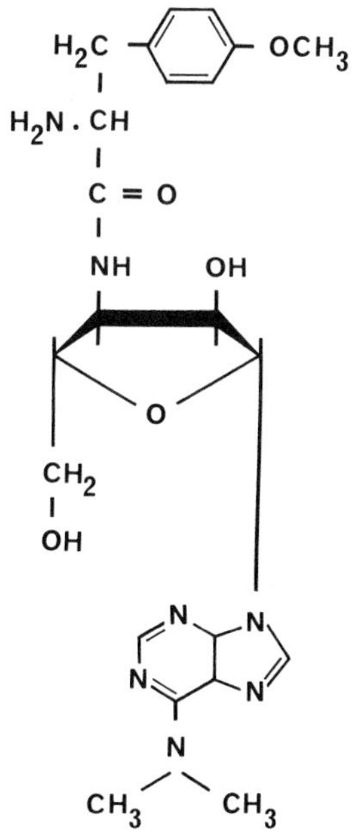

Figure 14.11 Puromycin.

In the puromycin experiments, there is little evidence for a temporal gradient of memory consolidation that is so characteristic for glutarimides and anisomycin. A puromycin injection 24 hours or even weeks following training impairs the memory of a previously learned task (at least in mice), and no spontaneous recovery has been reported. The inhibition of protein synthesis is therefore not the principal action by which the drug interferes with the memory mechanisms. It is believed that puromycin with its attached incomplete peptide (peptidyl-puromycin fragments) may displace some normal peptides from neuronal structures and, as a result, alter the activity of neurons necessary for the fixation or recall of the memory trace (Flexner et al., 1967).

An intracranial injection of saline, however, does restore the memory, even days after the puromycin administration (Flexner and Flexner, 1968). A reasonable explanation would be that saline produces a conformational change in the membrane proteins, causing a release of the puromycin-peptidyl fragments. Potassium chloride, lithium chloride, calcium chloride and magnesium chloride all have the same effect.

The action of puromycin may also be prevented by overtraining and the administration of amphetamine, strychnine, pentylenetetrazole and caffeine. Drugs affecting the adrenergic neurons can restore the memory. Barraco and Stettner (1978) claim that puromycin fragments primarily interfere with adrenergic neuronal activity and possibly with the activity of task-specific cholinergic neurons. The state of arousal, which is increased by these drugs, is probably an important factor in the conversion of short-term memory to long-term memory (Flood et al., 1978). Stimulants, however, prolong the labile phase of memory, while CNS depressants enhance the antibiotic-induced amnesia (Flood et al., 1977). The amnesia may also be attentuated by injections of arginine vasopressin, oxytocin and synthetic peptides, such as C-terminal tripeptides, derived from these two hormones. These peptides have been found to be capable of displacing puromycin-peptides from the membranes. Bilateral adrenalectomy can protect against these amnesic effects, as can high levels of ACTH (as a cortrophin gel injected subcutaneously for three days before training).

The use of antibiotics in studies of the relationship between protein synthesis and memory indicates that the production of new proteins may play some role in the fixation and retrieval of the memory trace. But, since one is dealing with a massive suppression of protein synthesis, it is difficult to assess whether the effects upon the performance of a previously learned task (which lead us to infer disturbances in memory formation and recall) are caused by a disruption of some specific memory mechanism or by a general depression of cellular biochemical systems. One must take into consideration that these drugs could cause changes in motility and motivation of the experimental animal and could otherwise influence peripheral functions and general health in some nonspecific way which may contribute to the observed effects on performance.

It is difficult to construct a generally acceptable hypothesis of the mechanisms of memory based upon these types of experiments. Learning studies have shown that there is a time span of about 3 hours following the initial training situation, during which an induced impairment of memory is still possible. This has been taken to be a period when memory and recall are dependent upon "short-term" mechanisms. It is possible that these short-term memory mechanisms trigger a protein synthesis necessary for retention and that antibiotics may, to a certain extent, interfere with this process. Such proteins may still be present during the first hours following the antibiotic injection, but having a short half-life, they eventually may be consumed or degraded (Barondes, 1974). Memory would then fail. But, at the same time, the synthesis of all neuronal proteins is inhibited, disrupting the general functioning of the neuron as well. The main action of these antibiotics on learning may be completely different. All four of them, puromycin, cycloheximide, acetoxycycloheximide and anisomycin, inhibit tyrosine hydroxylase, and consequently, catecholamine synthesis (Flood et al., 1980). And, as shown by Rainbow et al. (1980), at certain time periods after the injection, there is a large inhibition of protein synthesis, up to 95%, but no amnesia. Hambley and Rogers (1979) have even drawn on association between retardations in learning and an accumulation of brain glutamate and asparatate induced by cycloheximide.

Since memories can be formed and recovered even while protein synthesis is effectively inhibited, it may be that while the production of proteins is generally necessary, or at least useful, for the formation of a memory trace, this process is only one component of a more complex series of events. The process of memory consolidation is actually based upon a number of simultaneous interconnected metabolic processes which are mutually reinforcing. A disturbance in one of them, protein synthesis, for instance, may be compensated for by a shift in another, such as a post-translational change of synaptic proteins. In this way, the neuron actively responds to the metabolic inhibition.

The nerve cell, as a homeostatically balanced system, is capable of adjusting its numerous metabolic activities when disturbed. Such an adjustment may take place in response to the central effects of antibiotics, eventually allowing normal neuronal function to recover. The events which do not directly depend on protein synthesis, notably ionic movements and RNA synthesis, are still active and may eventually be able to induce functional changes in the neuron in spite of the antibiotic effects.

Second Messenger Systems in the Brain

About 25 years ago, Sutherland and his colleagues made an important discovery. Epinephrine and glucagon, acting as hormones, were both known to be able to profoundly affect the activity of the liver phosphorylase that catalyzes the conversion of glycogen to glucose 1-phosphate. Sutherland and Rall (1958), however, noted that the hormonal stimulation of phosphorylase activity did not take place in a medium that was devoid of the enzyme adenylate cyclase. Continuing studies demonstrated that the action of epinephrine and glucagon was directly on this enzyme rather than on the kinase that was responsible for the generation of liver phosphorylase (Fig. 15.1). What was happening was that the hormones were stimulating adenylate cyclase to convert ATP into cyclic adenosine 3',5' monophosphate (cyclic AMP or cAMP). This cyclic AMP then triggered a phosphorylase kinase to activate the liver phosphorylase by attaching to it a phosphate group from a donor ATP.

By elucidating this mechanism, Sutherland and his associates provided a basis for the concept of a "second messenger" system. In the hormonally-stimulated breakdown of glycogen, cyclic AMP was acting as a "messenger" of the hormonal action. Since that time, a number of second messenger sys-

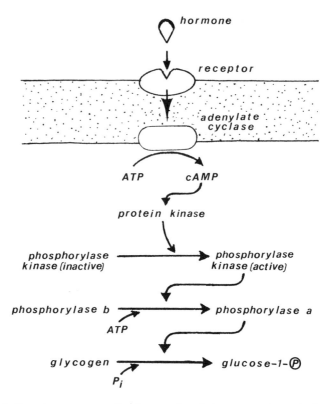

Figure 15.1 Second messenger-mediated conversion of glycogen to glucose-1-phosphate by a hormone.

tems have been uncovered that involve not only cAMP, but certain ions and other cyclic nucleotides as well (Fig. 15.2). They interact with one another, so that each is capable of modifying the metabolism and physiological actions of the others. Together, these systems comprise one of the most important factors concerned with the control of protein synthesis and the further modification of protein structure (Fig. 15.3).

CYCLIC ADENOSINE MONOPHOSPHATE

The second messenger systems in the central nervous system are intimately involved in many aspects of cellular metabolism, converting extracellular messages to intracellular activity. The best known is the system of adenylate cyclase - cyclic 3′5′ adenosine monophosphate - cAMP phosphodiesterase.

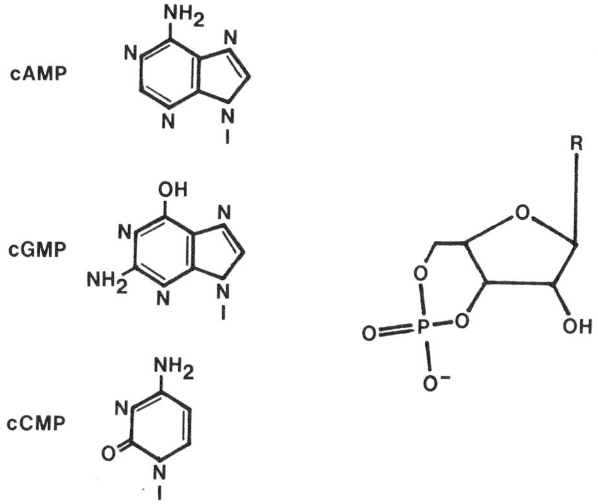

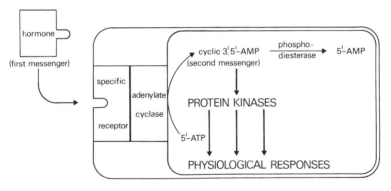

Figure 15.2 Cyclic nucleotide structures.

Figure 15.3 Schematic representation of the second messenger concept [from V.M. Wiegant, *Brain Res. Bull.* 3:611 (1978); © 1978 by ANKHO International Inc.].

The synthesis and degradation of cAMP are straightforward. In the cell membrane, ATP is used for the synthesis of cAMP by adenylate cyclase. Since cAMP still retains a high-energy bond, it is able to activate several enzymes and other proteins. It is then degraded by 3′,5′-phosphodiesterase to a linear 5′-adenosine monophosphate.

Adenylate cyclase is a ubiquitous membrane-bound enzyme, whose activity in the brain is among the highest anywhere in the body. It can be found in a variety of places within the cell: in the surface membrane, along with the membranes of the nucleus, endoplasmic reticulum, mitochondrial cristae, and within the postsynaptic densities of most synapses (French *et al.*, 1978). Some adenylate cyclase activity has also been found in the presynaptic region of the synapse (Weller, 1977).

The enzyme complex contains three parts: a hormone- or ligand-binding portion, a catalytic unit, and an associated guanine nucleotide-sensitive regulatory component which complexes the first two parts (Ross and Gilman, 1980). This regulatory component has been variously termed N (Johnson, 1978; Johnson *et al.*, 1980), G (Pfeuffer, 1979), and G/F (Ross *et al.*, 1978). Interposed in this way, it might conceivably serve to modify the duration of a stimulatory effect upon adenylate cyclase in response to a brief exposure to a hormone. Moreover, its modification could function to regulate the sensitivity of the cAMP response to the hormone (or neurotransmitter) without entailing a change in the number of receptors or their binding capacity. And, it could conceivably be involved in the inhibition of adenylate cyclase activity which has been observed in response to the presence of some hormones and neurotransmitters (Jakobs *et al.*, 1981). Accordingly, Cooper (1982) has proposed the existence of at least two forms of the regulatory component, one of which would be stimulatory and the other inhibitory. However, the opposing effects could simply reflect multiple states of a single substance.

In a number of tissues, guanosine triphosphate (GTP) does modify the sensitivity of adenylate cyclase to hormones. And, in the brain, it boosts the activating effect of dopamine on this enzyme. Rodbell (1980) has hypothesized that receptor complexes for peptide hormones normally exist as multimeric structures and that the binding of the particular hormone renders the complex sensitive to GTP. The attachment of GTP then induces a dissociation of the multimers into monomers and an association with the adenylate cyclase-cAMP system.

In addition to their association with the enzymes of the second messenger system, membrane receptors for neurotransmitters and hormones have also been linked to an ionophore, a molecule that allows the passage of ions across the cell membrane. McGeer, Eccles and McGeer (1979) distinguish two types of synapses - ionotropic, whose effects are based upon the movement of ions across the postsynaptic membrane, and metabotropic, through which metabolic changes are induced within the cell. Both actions may, however, be functions of a single synapse or, at least, these two effects of neurotransmitters and hormones (their action on depolarization and the second messenger system) are probably closely connected. The work of Ahnert and his group indicates that toxins, such as sea anemone toxin II (ATX II) which keeps activated sodium channels open, are also able to raise the levels of cAMP and cGMP (Ahnert *et al.*, 1979). This effect can be prevented by tetrodotoxin, another toxin affecting sodium channels, suggesting that the ionophores may be related, both functionally and structurally, to adenylate and guanylate cyclases.

There is also a growing body of evidence which demonstrates an association between the bursting pacemaker activity of *Aplysia* cell R15 (Chapter 4) and the cyclic nucleotides. For example, cyclic nucleotides, their degradative enzymes (the phosphodiesterases), phosphodiesterase inhibitors, and activators of adenylate cyclase are all able to alter the bursting activity (Treisman and Levitan, 1976, 1976a). In fact, the phosphodiesterase inhibitor IBMX, by boosting cAMP levels, has been shown to induce such pacemaker activity in the normally silent *Aplysia* metacerebral giant cell (Drake and Treistman, 1980). The effect appears to be associated with changes in both the sodium and potassium fluxes (Drake and Treistman, 1981).

Along with the GTP-binding component, a number of additional factors contribute to the regulation of adenylate cyclase activity. One of them, the presence of adenosine, will be discussed in Chapter 21. The divalent cations Mg^{2+}, Mn^{2+} and Ca^{2+} constitute another form of regulation, since they may associate with separate sites on the enzyme and so modulate its activity (Rodbell *et al.*, 1981). On a more long-term basis, the activity of adenylate cyclase is probably controlled by the lipid components of the membrane. High levels of phospholipids can inhibit its stimulation by dopamine (Leon *et al.*, 1978). And, mixed brain gangliosides have been found to initially augment the activity of this enzyme in cerebral cortex membrane preparations (Partington and Daly, 1979). The data are consistent with reports that cholera toxin, which binds to ganglioside G_{M1}, is similarly able to trigger a substantial rise in the adenylate cyclase activity (Minneman and Iverson, 1976). And, on the other hand, ganglioside synthesis can be stimulated by cAMP, which is able to regulate the glycosyltransferases (McLawhon *et al.*, 1981).

Although the response to gangliosides was apparently unaffected by calcium, the ion has been found to influence adenylate cyclase activity. Lower calcium concentrations have a stimulatory effect, while high concentrations are inhibitory (Bradham *et al.*, 1970). Partington and Daly (1979) have attempted to explain this inhibitory effect by postulating the existence of a calcium-dependent membrane-bound protease which is able to degrade and thus inactivate adenylate cyclase.

In cultures of hybrid neuroblastoma X glioma cells, both morphine and norepinephrine will depress adenylate cyclase activity, but then cause a more gradual long-lived increase in the enzyme (Wilkening and Nirenberg, 1980). The nature of the increase required the presence of lipids in the growth medium. For norepinephrine, the absence of these lipids significantly suppressed the enzyme, but did not eliminate a later comparable percentage rise in its activity. There was also some specificity in the lipid effect, since the increase in activity could be restored by the addition of linoleic acid (a prostaglandin precursor - see Chapter 21), but not with supplements of oleic or stearic acids.

The phosphodiesterases (PDE) that inactivate cyclic AMP open the cyclic phosphate bond to produce a molecule of adenosine monophosphate. They have been detected in the brain in high concentrations, higher than in any other tissue. They can be found predominantly in the postsynaptic area of the nerve endings, immediately adjacent to the synaptic membrane (Florendo *et al.*, 1971). Various forms of this enzyme have been described that differ in their substrate specificity, ion dependence, and sensitivity to activation by protein factors. Little is known concerning a possible role for these forms in brain cell function.

PDE activity in the cell is controlled by calcium, lipids such as lecithin and phosphatidylinositol, and possibly by the inhibitory actions of one or more endogenous proteins (Wang and Desai, 1976) and oligopeptides (Collier *et al.*, 1982). Several protein activators of this enzyme have also been detected (Cheung, 1970; Kakiuchi *et al.*, 1970, 1972), including a factor, later termed calmodulin (see below), that renders phosphodiesterases sensitive to the stimulating effect of calcium ions. But, only some forms of phosphodiesterase are activated by this factor (Pledger *et al.*, 1975; Grab *et al.*, 1981). At least a part of the enzyme exists in nervous tissue in a latent form that is influenced by neurotransmitters or microenvironmental changes within the membrane (Baba *et al.*, 1978).

Phosphodiesterase activity is also blocked by several drugs. The best known are the methylxanthines, a group that includes such substances as caffeine and theophylline. Drugs that alleviate anxiety, for example diazepam, meprobamate and pentobarbital, also block phosphodiesterase. Moreover, Samir Amer and Kreighbaum (1975) have gone so far as to claim that all useful drugs act through an inhibition of phosphodiesterase activity.

The principal, and possibly the only function of neuronal cyclic AMP is the activation of protein kinases. The protein kinases transfer the γ-phosphate group of ATP to a protein substrate in a reaction that does not consume cAMP. Before entering these reactions, cAMP is bound to a specific cAMP-binding protein (Walter *et al.*, 1980), which renders it inaccessible to degradation by phosphodiesterase. The complex, along with ATP, then serves to activate the protein kinase by phosphorylation. There do exist, however, other protein kinases which may either be actually inhibited by cAMP or not affected at all (for review, see Rodnight, 1980).

The activation is often a result of a cAMP-mediated dissociation of two functional subunits of the kinase, a regulatory and catalytic portion. When joined together, regulatory subunit inhibits the activity of the catalytic part.

The activated kinase catalyzes the phosphorylation of several cell proteins, among them those present in the synaptic membranes. This process affects the tertiary and quaternary structure of the proteins and in so doing can change the functional properties of the membrane by altering the permeability or the sensitivity to neurotransmitters. It means that a relatively simple molecule of cyclic AMP is capable of promoting a variety of biological responses whose specificity resides in the recognition between neurotransmitter (or hormone) and receptor and in the nature of the kinases and substrate proteins.

The phosphate group can be bound covalently to the brain proteins in one of two ways. It may be attached by a relatively stable ester linkage to the hydroxyl groups of serine or threonine, with phosphorylserine being the more prominent type. Or, there can be a labile acyl linkage involving γ-carboxyl groups of acidic amino acids. The removal of this phosphate moiety by the action of a protein phosphatase returns the protein to its prior state.

The activation of protein kinases by cAMP is associated with the oxidation and reduction of the protein SH groups. Thus, substances involved in the alteration of SH groups, such as glutathione, may at this level interact with the effects of cyclic AMP.

Protein phosphorylation has been implicated in such widespread cellular processes as membrane permeability, synaptic transmission, secretion, transport pheonomena, the mobilization of carbohydrate reserves, mRNA translation, enzyme activation, cell division, cell adhesion, and growth and differentiation. Cellular proteins are phosphorylated by cAMP in the cytosol, synaptosomes, myelin and other formed components. Since each cellular fraction has a characteristic pattern of phosphorylation that is related to the diversity of cellular functions, cAMP is able to simultaneously activate several metabolic systems necessary for the continuity and plasticity of neuronal functioning.

PHOSPHORYLATION OF NUCLEAR PROTEINS

The phosphorylation of proteins is one of the homeostatic mechanisms which serve to regulate and coordinate the metabolic activity of multicellular organisms. One of basic processes with which it is involved is the control of the activity of the genome. Gene transcription in the cell nucleus is activated, among other mechanisms, by a phosphorylation of nonhistone chromosomal proteins. They determine the availability of DNA sequences, modulate the activity of RNA polymerases and influence the interaction of DNA with these polymerases (Pastan and Perlman, 1970). The phosphorylation of chromosomal proteins is catalyzed by nuclear protein kinases that are activated by cAMP. The process may be indirect, mediated by a nuclear cAMP receptor protein (CRP) (O'Neill *et al.*, 1981). Some of the protein kinases are first activated in the cytoplasm before being transferred into the cell nucleus.

The reassociation of the two nuclear protein kinase subunits requires the presence of intact chromatin (Jungmann *et al.*, 1975). In addition, nuclear histones are phosphorylated by a histone kinase that is present in the cell nuclei (Pierre and Loeb, 1971). This entire process is a critical step in the regulation of gene expression, and consequently, cAMP is involved in genome activation. Such a cAMP-mediated activation is very possibly a critical component of the biochemical processes that are necessary for longlasting changes in neuronal activity. Figure 15.4 presents a temporal sequence of one possibility, in which a transmitter-induced production of cAMP in the adrenal medulla is able to stimulate the phosphorylation of nuclear histones, causing mRNA synthesis and a consequent de novo production of tyrosine hydroxylase and catecholamines.

Nuclear phosphoproteins in the hippocampus and caudate nucleus were reported to be synthesized at an increased rate during various forms of shut-

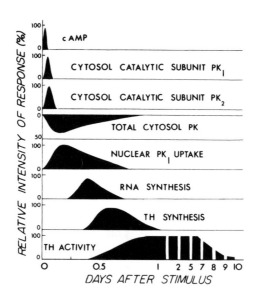

Figure 15.4 Temporal sequence of molecular events taking place in chromaffin cells of the adrenal medulla during transsynaptic induction of tyrosine hydroxylase. Abbreviations: PK, protein kinase; TH, tyrosine hydroxylase. [from A. Guidotti and E. Costa, *Biochem. Pharmacol.* 26:817 (1977); © 1977 by Pergamon Press].

tle box training (Souza *et al.*, 1980). This increase lasted for 5-25 minutes and was also present after administration of a buzzer as the conditioning stimulus, or after a simple administration of footshock.

PHOSPHORYLATION OF SYNAPTIC PROTEINS

In the brain, the highest activity of protein kinases has been detected in the synaptic membranes. Accordingly, many of them are dependent upon cAMP. The enzymes dephosphorylating these protein kinases, thereby inactivating them, are also primarily associated with membranes of the synapse. This would suggest that the phosphorylation of synaptic proteins is related to synaptic transmission. Greengard and his associates (Greengard, 1976; Ueda and Greengard, 1977; Ueda *et al.*, 1973) have isolated three synaptic proteins which they have labeled proteins Ia, Ib and II. Protein II was further resolved into two subunits and has been identified as a protein kinase. Types Ia and Ib appear to be only present in nervous tissue, being particularly high in synaptic vesicles and postsynaptic densities (Dolphin and Greengard, 1981). They are now known to be substrates of a membrane-bound cAMP-dependent protein kinase and a membrane-bound phosphoprotein phosphatase. The phosphorylation of these proteins is associated with various functional events. For example, CNS depressants (pentobarbital, urethane and chloralhydrate) can decrease their phosphorylation, while pentylenetetrazole and picrotoxin or synaptic stimulation are able to increase it. Also hormones, such as corticosterone within the rat hippocampus (Nestler *et al.*, 1981) and ACTH$_{1-24}$ (Oestreicher *et al.*, 1981) have been found to activate it. The phosphorylation of synaptic proteins is generally a rather slow process, and it takes several minutes to saturate all of the phosphate acceptor sites (Weller, 1979). However, *in vitro* the above three proteins are phosphorylated within fifteen seconds following their incubation with the magnesium salt of ATP (Breithaupt and Babitch, 1979). Fifteen additional proteins were also found to be phosphorylated during a 15 minute incubation period. And, Boehme *et al.* (1978) reported the presence of at least thirty phosphorylated protein bands in electrophoretic preparations of synaptosomal fractions. There is some evidence that the phosphorylation of a number of these synaptic proteins may even be irreversible (Ng and Matus, 1979).

Hershkowitz (1978) found that the phosphorylated synaptosomal proteins in his fractions all had molecular weights above 35,000 daltons. Phosphorylation was enhanced in the presence of Mg^{2+}, cAMP and cGMP and blocked by the application of theophylline, a possible adenylate cyclase inhibitor. However, the phosphorylation of one additional band (termed protein C, M.W. 41,000-43,000) was not affected by the cyclic nucleotides or theophylline, but was stimulated by substances that trigger a liberation of the neurotransmitter (Ca^{2+} and the ionophores X537A and A23187) and blocked by Mg^{2+}, an inhibitor of this release. These effects upon this band suggest that protein C might be somehow associated with the mechanism of neurotransmitter release.

The binding of a neurotransmitter to its receptor causes a turnover of the membrane phospholipid, phosphatidylinositol (Chapter 2). It is possible that this effect serves to regulate the membrane permeability during synaptic transmission (Michell, 1975; Hawthorne and Pickard, 1979). Phosphatidylinositol also undergoes a phosphorylation to phosphatidylinositol-4-phosphate (DPI) and phosphatidylinositol-4,5-diphosphate (TPI). The generation of TPI is under the control of DPI kinase, an enzyme whose activity has been reported to be associated with the phosphorylation of a 48,000 dalton synaptic membrane protein termed B-50 (Jolles *et al.*, 1980). An inverse relationship between B-50 phosphorylation and TPI synthesis suggests that the phosphorylated state of B-50 may control DPI-kinase activity and consequently the phospholipid characteristics of the membrane.

Routtenberg and his group (for review see Routtenberg, 1979) noted that some synaptic proteins were phosphorylated during the initial phases of memory formation. Of the proteins which they have been able to electrophoretically fractionate from the synaptic membrane, one band, termed F, was found to be responsive to behavioral change. Its turnover is very fast, the most rapid among all of the phosphoprotein bands. The band is actually comprised of two proteins, F_1 and F_2, that are differentially affected by pentobarbital (Conway and Routtenberg, 1979). Protein F_1 was reported to be phosphorylated during a passive avoidance task, while F_2 was phosphorylated in animals receiving an aversive foot shock. These are rapid changes that appear mainly in the hippocampus and are not thought to involve cAMP. As was true for Hershkowitz's protein C, the F_2 band was found to have a molecular weight of around 41,000 daltons (Routtenberg and Benson, 1980). Considering their seeming responsiveness to transmitter-related events, it is possible that these proteins are the same. The findings have led Routtenberg and his co-workers to suggest that the proteins of the F group participate in the state-related functioning of the brain, possibly serving a role in the early phases of learning. Still, the F proteins remain in an altered state for some time after learning has occurred, suggesting that they could be concerned with a more persistent change in synaptic efficacy.

There are several postulated functions of phosphorylated synaptic proteins. Beside serving in neurotransmitter release (Amy and Kirshner, 1981), they may also be involved in an activation and inactivation of receptors (Chuang and Costa, 1979; Burgoyne, 1980). The biochemical studies of

Famulski *et al.* (1979) and Wojtczak and Nalecz (1979) have suggested that the phosphorylation of membrane proteins alters the activity of some membrane enzymes, tyrosine hydroxylase being a notable example (Vrana *et al.*, 1981).

Protein kinases and protein phosphatases may therefore influence the passage of information across the synapse. Browning *et al.* (1979) found that electrical stimulation of isolated slices of hippocampus caused a long-term potentiation of synaptic activity. The process was dependent upon the concentration of calcium ions in the medium and was accompanied by the phosphorylation of a 40,000 dalton synaptic protein, which was later tentatively identified as a subunit of pyruvate dehydrogenase (Browning *et al.*, 1981).

OTHER FUNCTIONS OF CYCLIC AMP

An important aspect of cyclic AMP action concerns its duration. Following the binding of the neurotransmitter to its receptor, cAMP is present in the cells for prolonged periods of time, and may even diffuse from one cell to be actively taken up into another. The persistence of cAMP within the nerve cell extends its range of action by allowing it to migrate to various cellular components. And, McIlwain (1977) has argued that this persistence may contribute to iconic or even short-term memory.

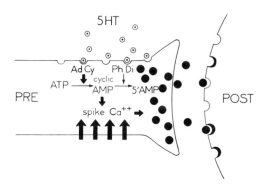

Figure 15.5 Schematic diagram of a possible role of cAMP in heterosynaptic facilitation. The 5-HT released from a heterosynaptic neuron activates adenylate cyclase at the terminal which in turn stimulates the synthesis of cAMP. The accumulation of cAMP at the terminal increases active Ca^{2+} permeability and transmitter release. Abbreviations: Ad Cy, Adenylate cyclase; Ph Di, Phosphodiesterase. [from T. Shimahara and L. Tauc, *J. Physiol. (Paris)* 74:515 (1978); © 1978 by Masson, Paris].

Cyclic AMP is probably not directly involved in synaptic transmission. Its synthesis, activity and degradation would seem to be too slow for the high-speed communication between neurons. But, while cAMP does not initiate neuronal activity, it may modulate the ongoing activity of the synapses through changes in the membrane characteristics, the activation of neurotransmitter synthesis, or the microtubule-controlled intracellular movements. Cyclic AMP could, for instance, be bound to the neurotubular subunit protein and so activate the intracellular transport systems.

The cyclic nucleotides themselves produce little or no change in membrane potentials (Busis et al., 1978). However, the activity of one synapse may actually, through a cyclic AMP-induced process, activate another synapse belonging to the same nerve cell (Kandel and Tauc, 1965). This heterosynaptic facilitation can be mimicked by cAMP (Shimahara and Tauc, 1978), in that this substance increases the voltage-dependent calcium conductance (Fig. 15.5). These findings could suggest that the super- or subsensitivity of a neuronal pathway may be at least partly dependent upon the intracellular activity of cAMP.

FUNCTIONAL ASPECTS OF cAMP METABOLISM

The nature of these effects of cyclic AMP implies that it also may influence behavior. There have, in fact, been frequent studies of the behavioral effects of injections of cyclic AMP and its synthetic derivatives, such as dibutyryl cyclic AMP. Their introduction into various areas of the central nervous system has had a rather non-specific influence. There are reports of agitation, increased spontaneous locomotor activity (with injections into the lateral ventricles), catatonia, decreased locomotor activity, and sleep (if injected intraperitoneally or into the mesencephalic reticular formation). In addition, the introduction of cAMP into the rat hypothalamus has been observed to induce ingestive behavior.

The release of cAMP from the brain during various functional states has also been examined. It has been shown that in a freely moving, conscious animal there are daily circadian fluctuations in the level of cAMP within the cerebrospinal fluid. There is an increase in the release of cAMP during seizures, either spontaneously appearing ones or those induced by an electroconvulsive shock. A similar increase has also been noted to follow various stressful stimuli (Biggio and Giudotti, 1976). And, inhibitors of phosphodiesterase enhance the rate of passive avoidance training in mice (Villinger and Dunn, 1981).

CYCLIC GUANOSINE MONOPHOSPHATE

Another cyclic nucleotide that has often been mentioned as a possible second messenger is cyclic guanosine monophosphate (cGMP) (see Fig. 15.2). But, in comparison it has received much less attention than cyclic AMP, and there are reservations as to whether it does serve similar functions (Wiegant, 1978). It may activate some protein kinases, but appears to be much less influential in this respect than cAMP. At least one protein kinase with a relative specificity for cGMP has been isolated, but its function and natural substrate are unclear (Hardman et al., 1971). In some systems, such as the mammalian superior cervical ganglion, cGMP has been found to have actions opposite to those of cAMP.

The level of brain cGMP is the highest of any tissue and is independent of the level of cAMP. It is synthesized from guanosine triphosphate by the action of guanylate cyclase. In nervous tissue, this enzyme is found in the synaptosomal soluble fraction (Schultz et al., 1969; White and Auerbach, 1969), but it also seems likely that glial cells are a major site of cGMP production (Chan-Palay and Palay, 1979; Tjornhammer et al., 1979). It can additionally be identified in the choroid plexus, pial and arachnoidal membranes, and in brain capillaries (Palmer, 1981).

Subsequent studies have shown that two distinct forms of guanylate cyclase exist, one soluble and the other membrane-bound (Nakazawa et al., 1976; Troyer and Ferrendelli, 1976). The activity of guanylate cyclase is dependent upon the availability of manganese (Goldberg and Haddox, 1977) and seems unaffected by the presence of magnesium or calcium. The regulation of guanylate cyclase activity appears to involve a number of factors, including a direct phosphorylation of the enzyme by a cAMP-dependent protein kinase (Zwiller et al., 1981a) and the action of phospholipase A_2 (Zwiller et al., 1982).

In different regions of the brain, the synthesis of cGMP can be stimulated by acetylcholine (through the muscarinic receptors), norepinephrine (α-receptors), histamine (H_1 receptor), γ-aminobutyric acid, and glutamic acid. There is, however, some question as to the activation of guanylate cyclase by catecholamine binding to the α-receptors, since α-adrenergic blockers did not inhibit the increase in cGMP synthesis (Liang and Sacktor, 1978). Also, Frey et al. (1980) have reported that the activity of soluble guanylate cyclase from caudate nucleus was inhibited by catecholamines, particularly dopamine. Lipids also appear to play a role, since Zwiller et al. (1981) found that guanylate cyclase was activated in vitro by lysophosphatidylcholine and oleic acid, while being inhibited by arachidonic acid.

Cyclic GMP is degraded by several phosphodiesterases, with none having a complete specificity for it. It is likely, then, that both cAMP and cGMP compete for these same enzymes. The activity of the phosphodiesterases in the brain is generally high, especially in the hippocampus (Davies and Taylor, 1979). In contrast, the cerebellum contains very low levels of these enzymes, while the activity of guanylate cyclase is but moderately low. Cerebellar concentrations of cGMP are about one order of magnitude higher than in other areas of the brain. Depolarizing agents, such as potassium ions, can increase values in this area up to 50-fold, 6 to 7 times the enhancement seen in other regions. These findings emphasize the pre-eminent role of phosphodiesterase activity in controlling the level of cGMP in the cerebellum.

Synaptic activity may alter the intracellular ratio of cAMP and cGMP, because as a general rule, most behavioral agents shift the levels of these substances in opposite directions. Consequently, the phosphorylation and dephosphorylation of different proteins may vary, affecting the impedance and excitability of the neuronal membrane. In the cerebellum, cGMP is involved in the regulation of Purkinje cell activity. As the cellular activity increases, so does the level of cGMP. One particular protein band with a molecular weight of 23,000 is phosphorylated by this cyclic nucleotide (Schlichter et al., 1978). The effect is specific to cGMP; cAMP is ineffective.

In the retina, there are indications that cyclic GMP may function somewhere between the capture of photons by the rods and changes in membrane permeability. Light, for example, reduces its level in the retinal photoreceptors, probably by activating phosphodiesterase. This substance also appears to modulate an inhibitory pathway for pain, but without observably depressing the CNS.

A third candidate for a role as an intracellular second messenger is cyclic cytidine monophosphate (cCMP) (see Fig. 15.2). It is formed mainly in rapidly proliferating tissues and thus may have some involvement in cell division and growth. A defect in retinal cCMP phosphodiesterase causes a rod-cone dysplasia in Irish setters, and there may exist an analogous condition in humans (Freinkel et al., 1978). In spite of these observations, little information is presently available on cyclic CMP and its functional importance.

CALCIUM AS A SECOND MESSENGER

Functionally interposed among these cyclic nucleotide-related postsynaptic events is another second messenger system that is comprised of calcium and a number of associated binding proteins, the most prominent of which is a calcium - dependent regulator known as calmodulin (Cheung, 1967; Watterson et al., 1976). As mentioned previously, these systems typically serve to regulate various cellular metabolic processes in response to particular types of external stimulation. For calcium to be effective in this manner, calmodulin (CaM) is frequently used as a mediator of the calcium signal. An additional binding protein, dependent upon vitamin D, has recently been identified in the brain (Jande et al., 1981). However, its function at present is not clear.

Neuronal activity is accompanied by a reduction in the extracellular calcium level, because significant quantities of the ion enter the neuron during depolarization. Once inside the cell, they influence a number of metabolic events, before being extruded or actively transported into the mitochondria or endoplasmic reticulum. Both of these organelles therefore participate in the regulation of intracellular calcium. In the nerve endings, they can release Ca^{2+} when needed, increasing the liberation of the transmitter as a result (Sandoval, 1980).

The binding of calcium to calmodulin triggers the protein to associate with and then modulate the activity of various Ca^{2+}-dependent enzymes. Such a dependency has been demonstrated for certain types of adenylate cyclase (Brostrom et al., 1975; Cheung et al., 1975), phosphodiesterase (Kakiuchi et al., 1971), and adenosine triphosphatase (Trotta and DeMeis, 1975) in the brain, along with phospholipase A_2 (Frei and Zahler, 1979) and a phosphorylase kinase (Cohen et al., 1978). It also can act upon chromatin-associated proteins, such as the histones (Iwasa et al., 1981). The existence of these interactions shows a direct linkage among the second messenger systems and suggests that there may exist mutual forms of regulation between them (Krueger et al., 1977).

Calmodulin has a molecular weight of about 16,700 and contains within its chain of 148 amino acids a single unusual trimethyl-lysine, while being completely devoid of both cysteine and tryptophan. A large portion of this protein has been found to be membrane-bound, and most of this is associated with the postsynaptic densities (Watterson et al., 1976; Costa et al., 1977).

The nature of the relationship between calcium and the receptor coupling to adenylate cyclase is the subject of some disagreement. The brain contains both Ca^{2+} - dependent and Ca^{2+} - independent types of adenylate cyclase (Brostrom et al., 1977), and there is evidence to suggest that both are linked to the receptors for norepinephrine, dopamine and histamine (Brostrom et al., 1976; Gnegy et al., 1976; Roufogalis, 1980). Calmodulin-activated adenylate cyclase may be unique to the brain. Other tissues containing calmodulin do not appear to possess a CaM-responsive adenylate cyclase, possibly as a result of structural dissimilarities in the enzyme (Salter et al., 1981).

By incubating particulate fractions of rat caudate nucleus with cyclic AMP, ATP, and cAMP-dependent protein kinase, Costa *et al.* (1977) noted that there occurred a movement of calmodulin from the membrane to the cytosol that was correlated with a drop in the sensitivity of adenylate cyclase to dopamine. These results suggested to them that this sensitivity requires the presence of membrane calmodulin, but that the increase in the level of cAMP generated by the binding of the neurotransmitter to its receptor triggered a release of calmodulin from the membrane, thereby lowering the adenylate cyclase sensitivity.

Calmodulin has also been found to stimulate the activity of Ca^{2+}-dependent phosphodiesterase by binding to the enzyme and converting it from a less active to a more active form (Wang and Waisman, 1979). The mechanism likely involves a CaM-induced conformational change in the enzyme, which either creates or exposes catalytic sites (Tucker *et al.*, 1981). The translocation of calmodulin from the membrane to the cytoplasm then would be associated with a breakdown of cAMP as a result of the augmentation in PDE activity (Fig. 15.6). Costa and his colleagues (1977) speculate that this decrease in cAMP would permit a reassociation of the calmodulin with the membrane to complete the cycle.

It appears that this CaM-mediated activation of brain phosphodiesterase and adenylate cyclase is regulated by an attachment to calmodulin of a

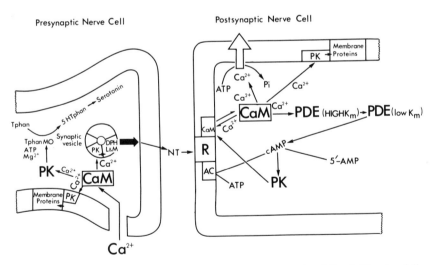

Figure 15.6 Possible events in synaptic transmission affected by calmodulin. CaM, calmodulin; AC, adenylate cyclase; R, receptor; NT, neurotransmitter; PDE, phosphodiesterase; PK, protein kinase; DPML and M, diphenylhydantoin-sensitive proteins L and M [from B.D. Roufogalis, *Trends Neurosci.* 3:240 (1980); © 1980 by Elsevier/ North-Holland Biomedical Press].

specific modulator binding protein. A number of CaM-binding proteins have been identified, some of which are already well known [myelin basic protein, for example (Grand and Perry, 1979)]. One, with a molecular weight of 80K, has been termed calcineurin on the basis of its apparent localization within the nervous system (Wang and Desai, 1977; Wallace *et al.*, 1978). Its association with calmodulin is Ca^{2+}-dependent and reversible (Klee and Krinks, 1978) and could represent an additional regulatory process in this second messenger system (Sano and Drummond, 1981).

Partington *et al.* (1980) reported that the desensitization of adenylate cyclase to various activators was both calcium - and temperature - dependent, suggesting to them the involvement of a Ca^{2+}-dependent enzyme, possibly a protease. Inoue *et al.* (1976) have already characterized a calcium-dependent protease in the rat brain that transforms a cAMP-independent protein kinase proenzyme into an active form. However, without a purification and characterization of the enzyme(s) in question, it would be difficult to assess whether the calcium was acting on a protease or a calcium-dependent regulator protein.

Various naturally-occurring lipids have been observed to modify the activities of different phosphodiesterases in the brain (Bublitz, 1973; Baba *et al.*, 1978). Such findings, together with the lipid effects mentioned previously, suggest that changes in the lipid microenvironment may contribute to lasting alterations in cAMP-related enzyme activity and changes in synaptic efficacy. In this regard, it is interesting to note that the enzymes of the base exchange system that serves to incorporate choline, ethanolamine and L-serine into various membrane phospholipids are differentially influenced by Ca^{2+} (Gaiti *et al.*, 1974). And, Buchanan and Kanfer (1980) have shown that the effect may be mediated by calmodulin. Such a differential activation may present pertinent possibilities for changes in membrane phospholipids.

Synaptic vesicles have been shown to display phospholipase A_2 activity, which was activated by the presence of calcium ions (Moskowitz *et al.*, 1982). Moreover, substances that stimulated vesicular phospholipase A_2 were associated with an aggregation of the vesicles, intimating that these events may be components of calcium-mediated stimulus-secretion coupling in axon terminals, as well as serve as a final common pathway for the action of various neuromodulators.

Calmodulin contains four binding sites for calcium, and the binding induces significant conformational changes in the protein molecules. Klee (1977) has found that calcium is attached to these four sites in a specific ordered sequence and that each addition to calmodulin results in a particular shift in conformation. If the sites are designated A, B, C, and D, starting from the NH_2 terminus, the order of binding is believed to be B, A, C, and

D (Haiech *et al.*, 1981). Klee has speculated that, depending upon the number of these ions that are bound, there may be a differential recognition by an enzyme for the calmodulin. Consequently, differences in calcium concentrations within membrane microenvironments could, for example, cause diverse effects upon the enzymes of the base exchange system and corresponding changes in phospholipid synthesis and the subsequent ionotropic and metabotropic responsiveness to neurotransmitters. In general terms, then, calmodulin may be able to translate quantitative differences in the calcium presence into one of a number of qualitative cellular responses. In this way, it may also modulate the calcium pump activity of Ca^{2+}-dependent ATPase (Michell, 1982).

Over the past few years, what has become increasingly clear is that in a variety of tissues second messenger systems provide a link between the activation of membrane receptors and the ensuing cellular metabolic responses. The very nature of the involvement suggests that these systems could contribute in an essential way to a neuronal adaptation to alterations in synaptic activity - the core concept of functional brain plasticity.

Chapter 16

Transport of Substances Throughout the Neuron

The substances that are synthesized in the nerve cell body either remain in the perikaryon, or are transported toward the periphery along the dendrites or axon. For the most part, the axonal and dendritic processes are metabolically dependent upon the synthetic capacity of the perikaryon. They require regular provisions of macromolecules and organelles, the great percentage of which is supplied by this active movement from the sites of synthesis.

The concept of axoplasmic transport was first proposed by Gerard in 1932, although experimental evidence for this phenomenon was not available until much later (Weiss and Hiscoe, 1948). In their study, Weiss and Hiscoe placed a ligature on a peripheral nerve and noticed a turgid, enlarged area proximal to the ligature. Their findings led them to conclude that some materials were actively passed along the nerve fibers in a distal direction.

BASIC CHARACTERISTICS OF AXOPLASMIC FLOW

Axoplasmic transport has several general characteristics. Although they are heterogeneous in nature, the transported materials do not represent just a bulk portion of cell contents; the process is a selective one. Also, once the passage of substances along the axon has begun, it is not directly dependent upon the metabolism of the perikaryon. It is capable of continuing even in an isolated segment of the axon. However, local hypoxic conditions in the nerve may slow down the transport or block it completely. Therefore, the essential driving energy of the process is not a diffusion, but involves local oxidative metabolic activity.

All of the materials that are carried as part of the axoplasmic flow do not travel at the same rate. A number of distinct waves of transport have been described, ranging from one having a rate of more than 200 mm/day through waves of 34-68 mm/day, 4-8 mm/day and 2-4 mm/day down to a rate of 0.7 - 1.1 mm/day. Consequently, one may talk about groupings of "fast" and "slow" transport (Fig. 16.1). These processes are probably independent, and according to the "Central Theory of Axonal Transport" (Lasek, 1980), each rate component is equivalent to a different structure moving in the axon.

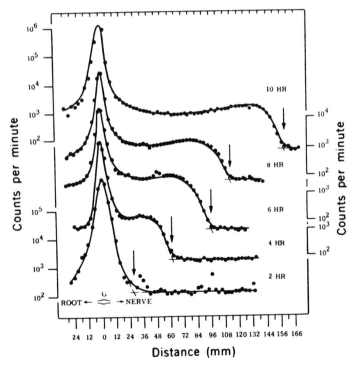

Figure 16.1 Distribution of radioactivity in the dorsal root ganglia and sciatic nerves of cats taken between 2 to 10 hours after injecting [³H]-leucine into the L7 ganglia. [from S. Ochs, *Science* 176:252 (1972); © 1972 by the American Association for the Advancement of Science].

As much as 80% of all proteins entering the axoplasmic flow is carried by the slow transport system. These are predominantly soluble proteins. It appears that five protein species account for more than 75% of the total of transported polypeptides. The rate of the slow flow can differ in different neurons, and even in two branches of a single bifurcating axon. Lasek and Hoffman (1976) found two particular subcomponents of this slow transport, SCa and SCb, which were dissimilar in their rates of migration, the molecular species transported, and their role in axonal regeneration.

Fast transport has been considered to range anywhere from 40 mm/day (Miani, 1962) to 700 mm/day (Kerkut *et al.*, 1967), although a rate of about 400 mm/day is usually considered the maximum velocity (Ochs, 1981). The rate is constant and does not vary with size of the nerve or the fiber diameter. The proteins that are carried by the fast system typically have a shorter half-life than those transported by the slow system. In addition to norepinephrine storage granules and enzymes, such as dopamine-β-hydroxylase, fast transport probably moves proteins (many of which are glycoproteins) responsible for the renewal of various membrane components. All of the particulate substances, the lipids, peptides and even the free amino acids that are carried down the nerve as part of the fast transport, move at the same rate, suggesting that a common carrier may exist for all of them. Two subcomponents of this transport have been reported, with the velocity of one being 3-4 times that of the other.

MECHANISM OF TRANSPORT

The mechanism(s) of transport is still not well understood. It does depend upon a steady local supply of Ca^{2+} and oxygen (Fig. 16.2). The anterograde flow is likely associated with membrane-confined compartments which are morphologically similar to smooth endoplasmic reticulum. Imaging of the axon by high-voltage electron microscopy has revealed the presence of three-dimensional structures ("microtrabecular lattice") composed of endoplasmic reticulum, microtubules, neurofilaments, mitochondria, and a variety of vesicles. Within this structure, the microtubules presumably serve a skeletal function (Ellisman, 1981; Thoenen, 1981). But, it is possible that the microtubules move along the axon, carrying transported material with them. Such movement may be via a continuous addition of the protein tubulin at one end and a tubulin loss at the opposite end, in a kind of microtubular "treadmilling" (Margolis and Wilson, 1981). However, an open question still persists as to whether all types of transport are dependent upon a single mechanism.

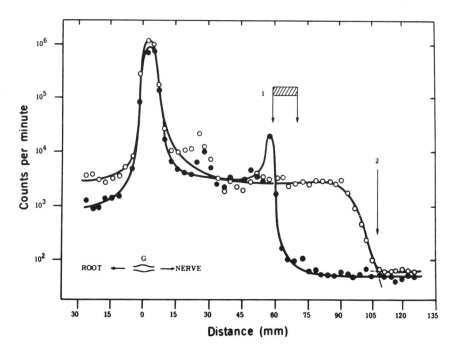

Figure 16.2 Distribution of radioactivity in the dorsal root ganglion and sciatic nerve of a cat injected with [^{3}H] leucine. The control nerve was flushed with 95% O_2 -5% CO_2 (empty circles); the opposite nerve (full circles) was covered with petroleum jelly over a length of 15 mm between arrows and the hatched bar [from S. Ochs, *Proc. Natl. Acad. Sci. USA* 68:1279 (1971); © 1971 by S. Ochs].

Microtubules are tubular structures of varying lengths (Fig. 16.3) that are composed of subunits of the protein tubulin. They are contained within the cytoplasm of most mammalian cells, particularly those which are secretory in nature and those which undergo changes in shape during development or migration. Along with other filamentous structures, the microtubules are considered to be involved with the various forms of eukaryotic cell movement that includes both changes in individual cell shape and position and the active migration of many intracellular organelles and materials.

A unit molecule of tubulin is globular in shape and is composed of two distinct subunits, termed α and β, both of which have a molecular weight of about 52,000 daltons. In the microtubules, tubulin molecules form aggregates, along with several minor components which are probably necessary for the process of assembly. One such component, tau protein (Cleveland *et al.*, 1977), is closely bound to tubulin even through several successive cycles of polymerization and depolymerization. Another, a dynein-like protein, has ATPase characteristics and perhaps is involved in the formation of side-arms and bridges between microtubules. Its subunits have a high molecular weight, ranging between 355,000 and 370,000 daltons. A cAMP-stimulated protein kinase with a MW of about 280,000 is also strongly attached to tubulin and remains so even through 2-4 polymerizations and depolymerizations. Colchicine, an alkaloid present in the seeds of the autumn crocus, will bind to tubulin, probably by attaching to sites which act as receptors of endogenous cellular molecules (Lockwood, 1979). Consequently, it has frequently been used as a blocking agent in studies of axoplasmic transport.

The axonal neurofilaments are fibrous structures that are thinner than microtubules and have many "arms" or projections along their length. Their diameter is only about 10 nm, and they are irregularly distributed within the axon in poorly defined tangles which often end on the axolemma. The neurofilament proteins are composed of a "triad" - one protein with a MW of 200,000 daltons, another of 140,000 daltons and a third of 70,000 daltons (Hoffman and Lasek, 1975). Several other minor proteins are attached to them as well. Their relationship to axoplasmic transport is not clear, and, as mentioned above, they may only provide a supporting lattice that gives the axon its shape.

Calcium ions are likely involved in the mechanism of transport. The absence of this ion in an incubating medium causes a depression in the quantity of particles carried, but not their rate of transport. This effect was reported by Hammerschlag (1980; Hammerschlag *et al.*, 1975), who studied changes in fast axoplasmic flow in cultures maintained in media of varying composition. Calcium is also required in the perikarya, as it is involved in the initiation of transport, including the coupling of proteins to the transport system. Moreover, the assembly of the microtubules is extremely sensitive to the absence of these ions. Calcium itself has been reported to be carried

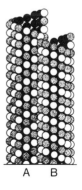

Figure 16.3 Diagram of a doublet microtubule. A complete tubule (A) shares a small portion of its wall with an interlocking partial tubule (B) both together forming a doublet microtubule [from L.A. Amos and A. Klug, *J. Cell Sci.* 14: 523: (1974); modified by R.E. Stephens and K.T. Edds, *Physiol. Rev.* 56:709 (1976); © 1974 by Company of Biologists Ltd., Cambridge, England].

A   B

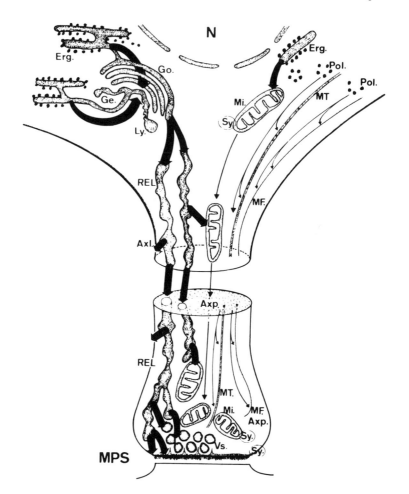

Figure 16.4 Diagrammatic representation of the contribution of the axonal migration of macromolecules to the maintenance of nerve cell processes and synapses. On the left side, the thick arrows indicate the part taken by the fast transport. Polypeptide chains synthesized in the endoplasmic reticulum (Erg) are transferred to the Golgi apparatus (Go) and give rise to protein and glycoprotein sequestered in the smooth endoplasmic reticulum (REL). Passing into the axon with the axonal endoplasmic reticulum, they are transported at a high speed and yield new membrane components to the axolemma (Axl) and mitochondria (Mi). They accumulate in the terminal part of the axon and ensure the renewal of constituents of synaptic vesicles (Vs) a presynaptic plasma membranes (MPS). Thus, the fast transport provides new membrane components and the logistical support for the conduction and (mainly) transmission of nerve impulse. On the right side, the thin arrows point to the elements transported with the slow axonal flow. Polypeptide chains are released from free polyribosomes (Pol) into the neuronal cytoplasm a migrate slowly into the axoplasm (Axp). They may assemble as protein subunits, giving rise to microfilaments (MF) and microtubules (MT). Mitochondria receive by transfer the great majority of their own proteins; these organelles are displaced along the axon and continue to

along the axon mostly bound to the calcium-binding protein, calmodulin, at a rate comparable to that of rapidly transported labeled proteins (Iqbal and Ochs, 1978). However, there are some conflicting data (Brady *et al.*, 1981) that suggest the association of calmodulin with the components of fast transport may be transient and that the bulk of this protein moves as part of the SCb complex.

THE ROLE OF AXOPLASMIC TRANSPORT

The material carried by both the fast and slow components of axoplasmic transport has several functions. The most important is the replenishment of enzymes and other proteins in the axoplasm and the maintenance of the membrane and other subcellular axonal structures (Fig. 16.4). It has also been frequently suggested that trophic factors responsible for intercellular regulatory phenomena are transported. This trophic function is presumably associated with the release of proteins from the nerve endings. One such protein may be sciatin, a glycoprotein isolated from sciatic nerve, which has a trophic effect upon maturation and the maintenance of skeletal muscle cells in culture (Markelonis and Oh, 1981). In this regard, it is known that during stimulation of the nerve, there is an increase in the protein efflux from the nerve endings (Musick and Hubbard, 1972). Axoplasmic flow may additionally supply the macromolecules which may be involved in the modification of synaptic transmission during functional adaptation. There is, however, very little hard evidence for this role.

The major portion of the transported substances is comprised of proteins, a large number of which contribute to the synaptic complement. The ratio of synaptic proteins synthesized within the synapse to those arriving along the axon is approximately 50:50. Water-soluble proteins tend to be produced more in the synapse than are the insoluble proteins. And, they typically have a smaller molecular weight than proteins carried by the fast portion of the axoplasmic flow.

On polyacrylamide gels, rapidly transported proteins can be divided into at least 60-100 polypeptide bands, with molecular weights ranging from 18,000 to 150,000 daltons (Siegel and McClure, 1975). Most of them are released into the axon immediately following their synthesis in the perikaryon, although some are released gradually, over a period of time. The major-

exhibit slight synthesis of hydrophobic polypeptides (Sy). The retrograde axonal transport has not been represented in this figure [from B. Droz, in: *The Nervous System,* D.B. Tower, R.O. Brady (Eds.), Vol. 1, p.111 (1975); © 1975 by Raven Press Inc., New York].

ity of these proteins is left behind by the first wave of transport and deposited in the axon, possibly contributing to what is interpreted as the intermediate rate of flow.

Some proteins may be modified or degraded during their passage down the axon, and some products of this intra-axonal degradation may be biologically important (Livett, 1981). The fast moving proteins are mainly assigned to the structural renewal of the axonal membrane and endoplasmic reticulum and are found mostly in the external portions of the synaptosomal membranes (Hammerschlag and Stone, 1982). One of them, termed fodrin, is a protein associated with the outer cytoplasm of the axon. The slowly moving proteins are mostly involved in replacing the axoplasmic components and the mitochondria. Certain ones, known a GAPS or growth-associated proteins, are axonally transported at elevated levels during times of axon elongation (for review see Levine *et al.*, 1981).

Of the transported proteins, several have an enzymatic function. Dopamine-β-hydroxylase, aromatic L-amino acid decarboxylase, choline acetyltransferase, acetylcholinesterase, and glutamic dehydrogenase are carried from the perikarya to the nerve endings. Some of them, moreover, may be transported back again by retrograde transport. Low-molecular weight substances, as lipids, nucleotides, nucleosides, thiamine, and perhaps amino acids, move along the axon as well.

Theoretically, the rate of transport can serve as a factor which influences the quantity of released neurotransmitter and the synaptic activity and excitability. Accordingly, during the process of behavioral modification or synaptic stimulation, one might anticipate an increase in the rate of protein movement and a possible shift in the composition of the proteins arriving at the nerve ending. Evidence for these changes, however, is scanty, and light deprivation and physiological or electrical stimulation of the nerve have not been found to alter the rate of axoplasmic transport.

According to Grafstein *et al.* (1972), the rate of fast transport is not dependent upon function, although there does appear to be a functionally related shift in the slow component. But, the amount of transported proteins may vary. Clingbine (1977) has shown that the transport inhibitors colchicine and vinblastine can interfere with the formation of a long-term memory trace in goldfish in a dose-dependent fashion. This effect is evident when colchicine is combined with anisomycin, an inhibitor of protein synthesis (Flood *et al.*, 1981). Also, rats reared in an enriched environment, as compared with those brought up in an impoverished environment, have more microtubular protein in their occipital cortices. This is, however, mainly associated with an increase in the amount of neuropil and the number of dendritic projections (Jorgensen and Meier, 1979).

RETROGRADE TRANSPORT

Most proteins carried from the perikaryon toward the nerve endings can then be transported back. One example of such a protein is dopamine-β-hydroxylase. Other proteins enter the nerve endings from the extracellular space by endocytosis (Hendry and Hill, 1980). All of these proteins can subsequently be moved in a direction back toward the nerve cell body. Overall, this retrograde form of transport is neither as fast as the previously discussed anterograde transport, nor does it carry a comparable amount of material. With an average rate of 24 mm/day, retrograde transport is highly selective, and even a small change in the molecular structure of the transported component is enough to halt its movement completely.

Horseradish peroxidase (HRP) is a protein which, following its topical administration, is selectively carried from the nerve endings toward the nerve cell bodies. It is taken up into the presynaptic terminals from the extracellular fluid. During stimulation of the nerve endings, the uptake of HRP increases (Theodosis, 1979). A similar increase also occurs during an elevation in the secretion of the hormones of the posterior pituitary, when HRP is taken up into the endings of the hypothalamo-hypophysial tract.

The presence of HRP may be accurately detected by histochemical methods, and for this reason, it has often been employed in experimental studies of retrograde axonal transport. It has also been used for the tracing of neural connections within the central nervous system. And, since it is taken up into the dendrites, it can serve to visualize dendritic details.

Tetanus toxin is another substance that moves in a retrograde direction. It is taken up by motor nerve endings in the muscles and transported toward the motoneurons (Price et al., 1975). It is also transported along the optic nerve. Nerve growth factor, a substance naturally produced in the body and necessary for the growth and maintenance of catecholaminergic neurons, is also transported as part of the retrograde flow.

Calcium ions can be transported bidirectionally, as can some low-molecular substances, such as adenosine and glutamine. Retrograde transport therefore might be one of the processes for removing proteins from the nerve endings. Bisby (1977), however, has reported a difference in endogenous protein transport between motor and sensory nerves that is likely attributable to the absence of a retrograde mechanism in the latter.

Retrograde transport may also be a way in which the nerve endings can metabolically communicate with the perikarya. The tissue-derived macromolecules, such as nerve growth factor and other trophic factors, may influence the pre-synaptic units in this way. Thus, this transport may be an important element in the alteration of synaptic activity following periods of shifts in the functional demands. Experimental evidence for this possibility has not, however, been presented.

TRANSNEURONAL TRANSPORT

There exists a well documented uptake and release of proteins from the nerve terminals. An elevation in their efflux from the nerve endings is associated with an increase in synaptic traffic, so that during induced cortical epileptiform episodes in the cat, for example, there is a release of larger quantities of several protein species, including glycoproteins, from the cortical surface (Kaczmarek and Adey, 1975).

The influx of macromolecules into the neurons has also been studied, and some examples have already been mentioned previously with regard to retrograde transport. Proteins may penetrate into the nerve cells both pre- and postsynaptically (Fig. 16.5). Greenough *et al.* (1978) have described what they have termed subsynaptic plate perforations (SSPP), irregularly distributed in the rat postsynaptic membranes, which are seemingly wide enough to permit the passage of proteins. Although the number of these perforations is not dependent upon the size of the synapse, it was increased when the animals were maintained in a stimulating, enriched environment. It is interesting to speculate that the transneuronal transport of various substances, including proteins, may play an important role in the functional adaptation of neuronal connections. However, the indications for such a relationship are still indirect, and there is no evidence presently available to clearly demonstrate that proteins having a functional importance are passed from one neuron to another.

Ryser (1968) has already claimed that such a transfer is possible, and that it is selective, requires little energy, and has a preference for cationic macromolecules. He postulated that the transported proteins act as carriers, precursors of active agents or regulators of metabolic functions in the target cells. This type of transport may be bidirectional, allowing the cells to communicate back and forth between the presynaptic and postsynaptic regions. This would permit dendritic secretion of the materials. Procion yel-

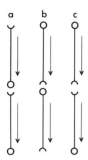

Figure 16.5 Types of the transneuronal transport in the CNS (a) retrograde, (b) anterograde, (c) combined.

low, a substance with a rather high molecular weight, is transported in both directions across the synapses within the guinea pig lateral geniculate body, but only when the synapses are activated (Kuhnt et al., 1979).

The intraocular injection of radioactive proline or fucose in the mouse is shortly followed by their incorporation into proteins and/or glycoproteins of the ganglion cells. These materials are then transported along the axons of the optic nerve and optic tract toward the lateral geniculate nucleus (LGN). Some radioactivity, about 2% of the originally injected amount, is carried up to the cerebral cortex (Grafstein, 1971) and is principally found in layer four of the visual cortex. It is not clear how this material is transported across the geniculate synapses. It may be carried bound to macromolecules, but at least a part of it is likely degraded in the nerve endings and the radioactive precursors reutilized postsynaptically.

The radioactivity may then travel to the cortex in either an anterograde or retrograde direction. The great part of labeled proline arrives in the cortex bound to a single protein (very possibly a glycoprotein) that has a molecular weight of about 68,000 daltons (Reinis et al., 1976). This protein is either a carrier of radioactive proline which specifically binds and moves the label from laternal geniculate to cortex, or a single protein transported trans-synaptically in the LGN. Interestingly, Fink and Gainer (1980) found a sciatic nerve protein of a similar molecular weight that traveled by retrograde transport and carried almost all of a label moving in this direction. This would suggest that in the above situation, a retrograde movement is more likely.

The function(s) of these transneuronally transported proteins have yet to be determined. One of the more intriguing possibilities is that some of them may act as neuronotropic factors. Such factors, which would serve to maintain the functional capacity of the neuron and ensure neuronal survival, have already been reported in the mammalian ciliary body and dorsal root ganglionic neurons (Manthorpe et al., 1982).

From what is now known about neuronal physiology, axoplasmic transport is a necessary condition for the proper functioning of the nerve cell, supplementing the peripheral portions of the neuron with needed materials and removing substances from the nerve terminals for transport to the perikaryon. And, although the transport of intact macromolecules across the synapse has not been unequivocally demonstrated, it may exist as just a special case of the transcellular passage of proteins which has been found between neurons and adjacent glia.

SUMMARY AND SPECULATIONS

By virtue of their morphological and functional ubiquity within the brain, any examination of the phenomenon of neuronal plasticity must include the proteins and their synthetic and degradative systems. Both the neurons and glia require continual and regulated provisions of proteins during times of both relative quiescence and increased activity. This of course places certain demands upon the precursor pools, energy supply and all of those enzymes and cofactors that are involved throughout the entire pathway from nucleic acids to the assembly of proteins at the ribosome.

Purines and pyrimidines are synthesized *de novo* in the brain or are reutilized by salvage pathways which conserve them following the degradation of old molecules of nucleic acids. Speculations aside, thus far there has been no evidence that either of these pathways is altered in response to changes in neuronal functioning.

DNA, as the repository for the genetic information that is passed from one cell generation to the next, has traditionally been assumed to be a rather inert substance within the mature, post-mitotic nerve cell. However, several recent studies have indicated that there is a continuous turnover of DNA in the neurons, a gradual degradation and resynthesis of portions of the molecules. In most neuronal nuclei, it appears that this DNA exists in amounts greater than the diploid levels found elsewhere and may even exceed tetraploid quantities in some cells. It is possible that the additional DNA is related to neuronal functioning, since experiments with pyrimidine derivatives have suggested that neuronal plasticity correlates with these changes.

Three major species of RNA are transcribed from DNA - rRNA, tRNA, and mRNA - and each is a necessary component of the protein synthetic system. Synaptic activity, sensory stimulation, or direct electrical stimulation of the neuron are all capable of stimulating increased RNA production. Although it is difficult to interpret and evaluate the great quantity of data on the association between RNA synthesis and learning, it is highly probable that the production of new RNA accompanies learning and possible that it may be a component of the lasting fixation of the memory trace. But, it must be stressed again that this RNA does not serve in any way to encode memory per se, but probably functions to generate the proteins necessary for the various events involved in neuronal adaptation.

The amino acids necessary for protein synthesis need to be continuously supplied. The essential amino acids must be provided in the diet and transported into the brain across the blood-brain barrier. The non-essential forms can be produced in nervous tissue, mainly from components of the tricarboxylic acid cycle. The rate of amino acid transport into the neurons and glia depends upon neuronal activity. Transient, elevated levels of extracellular potassium, an indicator of such activity, increases the cellular amino acid uptake in both nerve and glial cells. There is also evidence that interference with this process impairs subsequent plastic metabolic changes in the neurons. This is true for inhibitors of transport, including high levels of nonmetabolizable amino acids, which are most effective during the labile phase of memory, shortly after acquisition.

The synthesis of proteins by the neurons and glia is no different than in any other tissues, although the process is substantially influenced by the functional state of the tissue and the ionic composition of the extracellular fluid. A portion of the perikaryal proteins, once assembled, is carried to the dendrites and axon terminals by the axoplasmic flow. This is also true for a variety of other substances, since the periphery is significantly dependent upon the synthetic capacity of the cell body. The transport is metabolically tied to the local energy supply and functions as a rather fixed system that is probably not substantially altered as the changes in neuronal activity occur.

The details of the role protein synthesis plays in neuronal functioning and adaptability is partly a matter of speculation. Newly assembled proteins are probably necessary for the building of new structures and the physiological modification of various aspects of cellular metabolism. Consequently, they may be able to alter the functional characteristics of the neuronal membrane and the excitability of the cell.

These functional changes may also be related to the modification of already existing proteins. The methylation, glycosylation and phosphorylation of membrane (and possibly intracellular) proteins have all been suggested to contribute to the shifts in excitability.

Many cellular events, including RNA and protein synthesis, protein activation, and membrane depolarization, have been attributed to the operation of systems of second messengers, notably calcium, cyclic AMP, cyclic GMP, and cyclic CMP. In the neuron, the binding of the neurotransmitter to its receptor activates one (or more) second messenger(s), which in turn will influence the subsequent metabolism of the cell. Therefore, these messenger systems represent a link between synaptic functioning and intracellular metabolic activity, and it is very likely that the process of neuronal plasticity is dependent upon them.

RECOMMENDED READINGS

Allaudeen, H.S.: DNA and RNA polymerases of mammalian cells and tumor viruses. *Pharmac. Ther. A* 2:447-476 (1978).

Barondes, S.H.: Synaptic macromolecules: Identification and metabolism. *Ann. Rev. Biochem.* 43:147-168 (1974).

Barraco, R.A., Stettner, L.J.: Antibiotics and memory. *Psychol. Bull.* 83:242-302 (1976).

Baldessarini, R.J., Karobath, M.: Biochemical physiology of central synapses. *Ann. Rev. Physiol.* 35:273-304 (1973).

Bock, E.: Nervous system specific proteins. *J. Neurochem.* 30:7-14 (1978).

Brawerman, G.: The role of the poly(A) sequence in mammalian messenger RNA. *Crit. Rev. Biochem.* 10:1-38 (1981).

Cheung, W.Y.: Calmodulin plays a pivotal role in cellular regulation. *Science* 207:19-27 (1980).

Fox, I.H.: Purine ribonucleotide catabolism: Clinical and biochemical significance. *Nutr. Metabol.* 16:65-78 (1974).

Gagnon, C., Heisler, S.: Protein carboxyl-methylation - Role in exocytosis and chemotaxis. *Life Sci.* 25:993-1000 (1979).

Grafstein, B., Forman, D.S.: Intracellular transport in neurons. *Physiol. Rev.* 60:1168-1282 (1980).

Greengard, P.: *Cyclic Nucleotides, Phosphorylated Proteins, and Neuronal Function.* Raven Press: New York (1978).

Grollman, A.P., Huang, M.T.: Inhibitors of protein synthesis in eukaryotes: Tools in cell research. *Fed. Proc.* 32:1673-1678 (1973).

Hebb, D.O.: *The Organization of Behavior.* Wiley: New York (1949).

Jungmann, R.A., Kranias, E.G.: Nuclear phosphoprotein kinases and the regulation of gene transcription. *Int. J. Biochem.* 8:819-830 (1977).

Levine, J., Skene, P., Willard, M.: GAPS and fodrin. Novel axonally transported proteins. *Trends Neurosci.* 4:273-277 (1981).

Lincoln, T.M., Corbin, J.D.: Hypothesis - Role of cAMP and cGMP - dependent protein kinases in cell-function. *J. Cycl. Nucleotide Res.* 4:3-14 (1978).

Margolis, R.U., Margolis, R.K.: Metabolism and function of glycoproteins and glycosaminoglycans in nervous tissue. *Int. J. Biochem.* 8:85-91 (1977).

Marks, N.: Exopeptidases of the nervous system. *Int. Rev. Neurobiol.* 11:57-97 (1968).

McIlwain, H.: Extended roles in the brain for second - messenger systems. *Neuroscience* 2:357-372 (1977).

Nathanson, J.A.: Cyclic nucleotides and nervous system function. *Physiol. Rev.* 57:157-256 (1979).

Nicholls, D.G., Crompton, M.: Mitochondrial calcium transport. *FEBS Lett.* 111:261-268 (1980).

Routtenberg, A.: Anatomical localization of phosphoprotein and glycoprotein substrates of memory. *Progr. Neurobiol.* 12:85-113 (1979).

Samir Amer, M., Kreighbaum, W.E.: Cyclic nucleotide phosphodiesterases - Properties, activators, inhibitors, structure-activity-relationships, and possible role in drug development. *J. Pharmaceut. Sci.* 64:1-37 (1975).

Schwab, M.E., Thoenen, N.: Retrograde axonal and transsynaptic transport of macromolecules - physiological and pathophysiological importance. *Agents Actions* 7:361-368 (1977).

Wang, J.H., Waisman, D.M.: Calmodulin and its role in the second messenger system. In: *Current Topics in Cellular Regulation,* Vol. 15, B.L. Horecker, E.R. Stadtman (Eds.), Academic Press: New York (1979), pp.47-107.

Wiegant, V.M.: Cyclic nucleotides in nervous tissue. *Brain Res. Bull.* 3:611-622 (1978).

Zomzely-Neurath, C., Keller, A.: Nervous system - specific proteins of vertebrates. *Neurochem. Res.* 2:353-377 (1977).

REFERENCES

Aamodt, L., Goz, B.: *Biochem. Pharmacol.* 19:2400 (1970).

Abraham, A., Pihl, A.: *Trends Biochem. Sci.* 6:106 (1981).

Ahnert, G., Glossmann, H., Habermann, E.: *Naunyn-Schmiedeberg's Arch. Pharmacol.* 307:159 (1979).

Arfin, S.M., Simpson, D.R., Chiang, C.S., Andrulis, I.L., Hatfield, G.W.: *Proc. Natl. Acad. Sci. USA* 74:2367 (1977).

Amy, C.M., Kirshner, N.: *J. Neurochem.* 36:847 (1981).

Austin, L., Morgan, I.G.: *J. Neurochem.* 14:377 (1967).

Azmitia, E.C., McEwen, B.S.: *J. Neurochem.* 27:773 (1976).

Baba, A., Tsukamoto, T., Matsuda, T., Iwata, H.: *Experientia* 34:1139 (1978).

Bantle, J.A., Hahn, W.E.: *Cell* 8:139 (1976).

Barondes, S.H.: *J. Neurochem.* 15:699 (1968).

Barondes, S.H.: *Ann. Rev. Biochem.* 43:147 (1974).

Barondes, S.H., Cohen, H.D.: *Science* 151:594 (1966).

Barraco, R.A., Stettner, L.J.: *Psychol. Bull.* 83:242 (1976).

Batkin, S., Woodward, W.T., Cole, R.E., Hall, J.B.: *Psychon. Sci.* 5:345 (1966).

Bazett-Jones, D.P., Ottensmeyer, F.P.: *Science* 211:169 (1981).

Benowitz, L., Shashoua, V.E.: *Brain Res.* 136:227 (1977).

Betz, A.L., Goldstein, G.W.: *Science* 202:225 (1978).

Biggio, G., Giudotti, A.: *Brain Res.* 107:365 (1976).

Bignami, A., Eng, L.F., Dahl, D., Uyeda, C.T.: *Brain Res.* 43:429 (1972).

Bisby, M.A.: *J. Neurochem.* 28:249 (1977).

Blaschka, E., Bergqvist, U., Uvnas, B.: *Acta Physiol. Scand.* 97:110 (1976).

Blaschke, E.: *Acta Physiol. Scand.* Suppl. 466 (1979).

Blitz, A.L., Fine, R.E: *Proc. Natl. Acad. Sci. USA* 71:4472 (1974).

Bock, E., Dissing, J.: *Scand. J. Immunol.* 4(Suppl. 2):31 (1975).

Bock, E., Jorgensen, O.S., Morris, S.J.: *J. Neurochem.* 22:1013 (1974).

Boehme, D.H., Kosecki, R., Marks, N.: *Brain Res. Bull.* 3:697 (1978).

Bogoch, S., Ramjam, P.C., Belval, P.C.: *Nature* 204:73 (1964).
Bon, S.: *Eur. J. Biochem.* 85:1 (1978).
Bondy, S.C., Margolis, F.L.: *Exp. Neurol.* 25:447 (1969).
Bradham, L.S., Holt, D.A., Sims, M.: *Biochim. Biophys. Acta* 201:250 (1970).
Brady, S.T., Tytell, M., Heriot, K., Lasek, R.J.: *J. Cell Biol.* 89:607 (1981).
Braun, S.J., Sweadner, K.J., Patterson, P.H.: *J. Neurosci.* 1:1397 (1981).
Brawerman, G.: *Crit. Rev. Biochem.* 10:1 (1981)
Bregnard, A., Knusel, A., Kuenzle, C.C.: *Histochemistry* 43:59 (1975).
Bregnard, A., Ruch, F., Lutz, H., Kuenzle, C.C.: *Histochemistry* 61:271 (1979).
Breithaupt, T.B., Babitch, J.A.: *J. Neurobiol.* 10:169 (1979).
Brimijoin, S.: *J. Neurochem.* 26:35 (1976).
Brostrom, C.O., Huang, Y.C., Breckenridge, B. M., Wolff, D.J.: *Proc. Natl. Acad. Sci. USA* 72:64 (1975).
Brostrom, C.O., Wolff, D.J.: *Arch. Biochem. Biophys.* 172:301 (1976).
Brostrom, C.O., Brostrom, M.A., Wolff, D.J.: *J. Biol. Chem.* 252:5677 (1977).
Brostrom, M.A., Brostrom, C.O., Breckenridge, B.M.L., Wolff, D.J.: *J. Biol. Chem.* 251:4744 (1976).
Brown, D.D.: *Science* 211:667 (1981).
Browning, M., Bennett, W.F., Kelly, P., Lynch, G.: *Brain Res.* 218:255 (1981).
Browning, M., Dunwiddie, T., Bennet, W., Gispen, W., Lynch, G.: *Science* 203:60 (1979).
Bublitz, C.: *Biochem. Biophys. Res. Commun.* 52:173 (1973).
Buchanan, A.G., Kanfer, J.N.: *J. Neurochem.* 35:814 (1980).
Bull, R., Ferrera, E., Orrego, F.: *J. Neurobiol.* 7:37 (1976).
Burgoyne, R.D.: *FEBS Lett.* 122:288 (1980).
Burgoyne, R.D., Rose, S.P.R.: *J Neurochem.* 34:510 (1980).
Burgoyne, R.D., Rose, S.P.R.: *Neurosci. Lett.* 19:343 (1980a).
Burgoyne, R.D., Rose, S.P.R., Harding, S.: *J. Neurochem.* 26:2089 (1981).
Burridge, K., Bray, D.: *J. Mol. Biol.* 99:1 (1975).
Busis, N.A., Weight, F.F., Smith, P.A.: *Science* 200:1079 (1978).
Butler, S.R., Schanberg, S.M.: *Life Sci.* 21:877 (1978).
Calissani, P., Alema, S., Fasella, P.: *Biochemistry* 13:4553 (1974).
Cameron, I.L., Pool, M.R.H., Hoage, T.R.: *Cell Tissue Kinet.* 12:445 (1979).
Carlson, N.R.: *Physiology of Behavior.* Allyn and Bacon: Boston (1977). p.600.
Castejon, H.V., Castejon, O.J.: *Acta Histochem.* 55:300 (1975).
Chaffee, J.K., Schachner, M.: *Dev. Biol.* 62:173 (1978).
Chan-Palay, V., Palay S.L.: *Proc. Natl. Acad. Sci. USA* 76:1485 (1979).
Cheung, W.Y.: *J. Biol. Chem.* 246:2859 (1967).
Cheung, W.Y.: *Biochem. Biophys. Res. Commun.* 38:533 (1970).
Cheung, W.Y., Bradham, L.S., Lynch, T.J., Lin, Y.M., Tallant, E.A.: *Biochem. Biophys. Res. Commun.* 66:1055 (1975).
Chikaraishi, D.M., Deeb, S.S., Sueoka, N.: *Cell* 13:111 (1978).
Chiu, F.C., Norton, W.T., Fields, K.L.: *J. Neurochem.* 37:147 (1981).
Chuang, D.M., Costa, E.: *Proc. Natl. Acad. Sci. USA* 76:3024 (1979).
Cleveland, D.W., Hwo, S.Y., Kirschner, M.W.: *J. Mol. Biol.* 116:207 (1977).
Clingbine, G.: *Br. J. Pharmacol.* 59;449P (1977).
Cocchia, D.: *Cell Tissue Res.* 214:529 (1981).
Cocchia, D., Michetti, F.: *Cell Tissue Res.* 215:103 (1981).
Cocchia, D., Michetti, F., Donato, R.: *Nature* 294:85 (1981).
Cohen, P., Burchell, A., Foulkes, J.G., Cohen, P.T.W., Vanaman, T.C., Nairn, A.C.: *FEBS Lett.* 91:287 (1978).

Collier, H.O.J., Butt, N.M., Saeed, S.A.: *J. Neurochem.* 38:275 (1982).
Cone, C.D. Jr., Cone, C.M.: *Science* 192:155 (1976).
Cone, C.D., Jr., Cone, C.M.: *Exp. Neurol.* 60:41 (1978).
Cone, C.D., Jr., Cone, C.M.: *Brain Res.* 151:545 (1978a).
Cone, C.D., Jr., Tongier, N., Jr., Cone, C.M.: *Exp. Neurol.* 57:396 (1977).
Conway, R.G., Routtenberg, A.: *Brain Res.* 170:313 (1979).
Cooper, D.M.F.: *FEBS Lett.* 138:157 (1982).
Cornford, E.M., Oldendorf, W.H.: *Biochim. Biophys. Acta* 394:211 (1975).
Cosgrove, J.W., Brown, I.R.: *J. Neurochem.* 36:1026 (1981).
Cosgrove, J.W., Brown, I.R.: *J. Neurochem.* 36:1026 (1981).
Costa, E., Gnegy, M., Revuelta, A., Uzunov, P.: *Adv. Biochem. Psychopharmacol.* 16:403 (1977).
Craig, S.W., Cuatrecasas, P.: *Proc. Natl. Acad. Sci. USA* 72:3844 (1975).
Crick, F.: *Trends Neurosci.* 5/2:44 (1982).
Croizat, B., Berthelot, F., Felsani, A., Gros, F.: *FEBS Lett.* 103:138 (1979).
Cupello, A., Hyden, H.: *Brain Res.* 114:453 (1976).
Custod, J.T., Young, I.J.: *J. Neurochem.* 15:809 (1968).
Dahl, D., Bignami, A.: *Brain Res.* 116:150 (1976).
Damstra, T., Entingh, D., Wilson, J.E., Glassman, E.: *Behav. Biol.* 13:121 (1975).
Das, R., Kanungo, M.S.: *Biochem. Biophys. Res. Commun.* 70:708 (1979).
Davies, L.P., Taylor, K.M.: *J. Neurochem.* 33:951 (1979).
De Marianis, B., Olmo, E., Giuditta, A.: *J. Comp. Neurol.* 186:293 (1979).
De Robertis, E., Rodriguez De Lores Arnaiz, G., Alberici, M.: *J. Biol. Chem.* 242:3487 (1967).
Deutsch, D.G., Schechter, N., Brecha, N., Quitschke, W., Schulman, P., Cane, M., Gazzaniga, M.S., Simpson, M.V.: *Brain Res.* 198:135 (1980).
Dewar, A.J., Reading, H.W.: *Nature* 225:869 (1970).
Dolphin, A.C., Greengard, P.: *J. Neurosci.* 1:192 (1981).
Donato, R.: *J. Neurochem.* 36:532 (1980).
Doyle, J.M., Schachner, M., Davidson, R.L.: *J. Cell Physiol.* 93:197 (1977).
Drake, P.F., Treistman, S.N.: *J. Neurobiol.* 11:476 (1980).
Drake, P.F., Treistman, S.N.: *Brain Res.* 218:243 (1981).
Dropp, J.J., Sodetz, F.: *Brain Res.* 33:419 (1971).
Duffy, C., Teyler, T.J., Shashoua, V.E.: *Science* 212:1148 (1981).
Dunn, A.: *Ann. Rev. Psychol.* 31:343 (1980).
Dwyer, B., Wasterlain, C.G.: *J. Neurochem.* 34:1639 (1980).
Eiden, L.E., Borchardt, R.T., Rutledge, C.O.: *Dev. Neurosci.* 5:539 (1979).
Ellisman, M.H.: *Neurosci. Res. Progr. Bull.* 20:79 (1981).
Eng, L.F., Vanderhaeghen, J.J., Bignami, A., Gerstl, B.: *Brain Res.* 28:351 (1971).
Entingh, D., Damstra-Entingh, T., Dunn, A., Wilson, J.E., Glassman, E.: *Brain Res.* 70:131 (1974).
Famulski, K.S., Nalecz, M.J., Wojtczak, L.: *FEBS Lett.* 103:260 (1979).
Feigin, I.: *J. Neuropath. Exp. Neurol.* 39:1 (1980).
Fernando, J.C., Knott, P.J., Curzon, D.: *J. Neurochem.* 27:343 (1976).
Fine, R.E., Bray, D.: *Nature New Biol.* 234:115 (1971).
Fink, D.J., Gainer, H.: *Science* 208:303 (1980).
Flexner, J.B., Flexner, L.B., Stellar, E., de La Haba, G., Roberts, R., *J. Neurochem.* 9:595 (1962).
Flexner, J.B., Flexner, L.B., Hoffman, P.L., Walter, R.: *Brain Res.* 134:139 (1977).
Flexner, L.B., Flexner, J.B.: *Science* 159:330 (1968).

Flexner, L.B., Flexner, J.B., Stellar, E.: *Exp. Neurol.* 13:264 (1965).

Flexner, L.B., Flexner, J.B., Roberts, R.B.: *Science* 155:1377 (1967).

Flood, J.F., Bennett, E.L., Rosenzweig, M.R., Orme, A.E.: *Physiol. Behav.* 10:555 (1973).

Flood, J.F., Bennett, E.L., Orme, A.E., Rosenzweig, M.R., Jarvik, M.E.: *Pharmacol. Biochem. Behav.* 7:71 (1977).

Flood, J.F., Jarvik, M.E., Bennett, E.L., Orme, A.E., Rosenzweig, M.R.: *Behav. Biol.* 20:168 (1977a).

Flood, J.F., Bennett, E.L., Orme, A.E., Rosenzweig, M.R., Jarvik, M.E.: *Science* 199:324 (1978).

Flood, J.F., Smith, G.E., Jarvik, M.E.: *Brain Res.* 197:153 (1980).

Flood, J.F., Landry, D.W., Bennett, E.L., Jarvik, M.E.: *Pharm. Biochem. Behav.* 15:289 (1981).

Florendo, N.I., Barrnett, R.J., Greengard, P.: *Science* 173:745 (1971).

Fox, I.H.: *Nutr. Metabol.* 16:65 (1974).

Frei, E., Zahler, P.: *Biochim. Biophys. Acta* 550:450 (1979).

Freinkel, N., Pedley, K.C., Wooding, P., Dawson, R.M.C.: *Science* 201:1133 (1978).

French, S.W., Palmer, D.S., Caldwell, M.: *Can. J. Neurol. Sci.* 5:33 (1978).

Frey, W.H., Senogles, S.E., Heston, L.L., Tuason, V.B., Nicol, S.E.: *J. Neurochem.* 35:1418 (1980).

Fujitani, H., Holoubek, V.: *J. Neurochem.* 23:1215 (1974).

Gagnon, C., Viveros, O.H., Diliberto, E.J. Jr., Axelrod, J.: *J. Biol. Chem.* 253:3778 (1978).

Gainer, H.: *Anal. Biochem.* 44:589 (1971).

Gainer, H., Tasaki, I., Lasek, R.J.: *J. Cell Biol.* 74:524 (1977).

Gaiti, A., De Medio, G.E., Brunetti, M., Amaducci, L., Porcellati, G.: *J. Neurochem.* 23:1153 (1974).

Garber, N.J.Y., Wu, J.Y.: *J. Neurochem.* 36:602 (1981).

Geller, A., Robustelli, F., Barondes, S.H., Cohen, H.D., Jarvik, M.E.: *Psychopharmacologia* 14:371 (1969).

Genchev, D.D., Mandel, P.: *J. Neurosci. Res.* 2:413 (1976).

Gerard, R.W.: *Physiol. Rev.* 12:469 (1932).

Ghandour, M.S., Langley, O.K., Labourdette, G., Vincendon, G., Gombos, G.: *Develop. Neurosci.* 4:66 (1981).

Gibbs, M.E., Ng, K.T.: *Neurosci. Lett.* 2:165 (1976).

Gilbert, B.E., Mattick, J.S.: *J. Neurochem.* 37:325 (1981).

Gisiger, V.: *Brain Res.* 33:139 (1971).

Giuditta, A., Abrescia, P., Rutigliano, B.: *J. Neurochem.* 31:983 (1978).

Glassman, E., Wilson, J.E.: *Ergebn. Exp. Med.* 10:19 (1972).

Gnegy, M.E., Nathanson, J.A., Uzunov, P.: *Biochim. Biophys. Acta* 497:75 (1976).

Goldberg, N.D., Haddox, M.K.: *Ann. Rev. Biochem.* 46:823 (1977).

Gombos, G., Filipowicz, W., VIncendon, G.: *Brain Res.* 26:475 (1971).

Grab, D.J., Carlin, R.K., Siekevitz, P.: *J. Cell Biol.* 89:433 (1981).

Grafstein, B.: *Science* 172:177 (1971).

Grafstein, B., Forman, D.S., McEwen, B.S.: *Exp. Neurol.* 34:158 (1972).

Grand, R.J.A., Perry, S.V.: *Biochem. J.* 183:285 (1979).

Grandgeorge, M., Morelis, P.: *Biochimie* 58:275 (1976).

Greengard, P.: *Nature* 260:101 (1976).

Greenough, W.T., West, R.W., Devoogt, T.J.: *Science* 202:1096 (1978).

Greenwood, P.D., Silver, J.C., Brown, I.R.: *J. Neurochem.* 37:498 (1981).

Grouse, L.D., Schrier, B.K., Nelson, P.G.: *Exp. Neurol.* 64:354 (1979).

Gurd, J.W.: *Biochim. Biophys. Acta* 555:221 (1979).

Haiech, J., Klee, C.B., Demaille, J.G.: *Biochemistry* 20:3890 (1981).
Hambley, J.W., Rogers, L.J.: *Neuroscience* 4:677 (1979).
Hamelin, R., Larsen, C.J., Tavitian, A.: *Eur. J. Biochem.* 35:350 (1973).
Hammerschlag, R.: *Fed. Proc.* 39:2809 (1980).
Hammerschlag, R., Stone, G.C.: *Trends Neurosci.* 5:12 (1982).
Hammerschlag, R., Dravid, A.R., Chiu, A.Y.: *Science* 188:273 (1975).
Hardman, J.G., Beavo, J.A., Gray, J.P., Chrisman, T.D., Patterson, W.D., Sutherland, E.W.: *Ann. N.Y. Acad. Sci.* 185:27 (1971).
Harman, R.J., Shaw, G.G.: *J. Neurochem.* 26:1609 (1981).
Hawthorne, J.N., Pickard, M.R.: *J. Neurochem.* 32:5 (1979).
Hebb, D.O.: *The Organization of Behavior.* Wiley: New York (1949).
Held, I., Wells, W.: *J. Neurochem.* 16:529 (1969).
Hendry, I.A., Hill, C.E.: *Nature* 287:647 (1980).
Herman, C.J., Lapham, L.W.: *Brain Res.* 15:35 (1969).
Hershkowitz, M.: *Biochim. Biophys. Acta* 542:274 (1978).
Hoffman, P.N., Lasek, R.J.: *J. Cell Biol.* 66:351 (1975).
Hofstein, R., Barnett, B., Samuel, D.: *J. Neurochem.* 37:14 (1981).
Hofstein, R., Hershkowitz, M., Gozes, I., Samuel, D.: *Biochem. Biophys. Acta* 624:153 (1982).
Hori, T., Lark, K.G.: *J. Mol. Biol.* 77:391 (1973).
Hubscher, V., Kuenzle, C.C., Spadari, S.: *Proc. Natl. Acad. Sci. USA* 76:2316 (1979).
Hyden, H.: In: *The Cell,* Vol. 4, J. Brachet, A. Mirsky (Eds.). Academic Press: New York (1960).
Hyden, H., Lange, P.W.: *Proc. Natl. Acad. Sci. USA* 65:898 (1970).
Hyden, H., Lange, P.W.: *J. Neurosci. Res.* 2:439 (1976).
Hyden, H., McEwen, B.: *Proc. Natl. Acad. Sci. USA* 55:354 (1966).
Hyden, H., Lange, P.W., Perrin, C.H.L.: *Brain Res.* 119:427 (1977).
Inoue, N., Kato, T.: *J. Neurochem.* 34:1574 (1980).
Inoue, N., Ono, T., Kato, T.: *Biochem. J.* 180;471 (1979).
Inoue, N., Suzuki, O., Kato, T.: *J. Neurochem.* 27:113 (1976).
Iqbal, Z., Ochs, S.: *J. Neurochem.* 31:409 (1978).
Irwin, L.N., Barraco, R.A., Terrian, D.M.: *Neuroscience* 3:457 (1978).
Iwasa, Y., Iwasa, T., Matsui, K., Higashi, K., Miyamoto, E.: *Life Sci.* 29:1369 (1981).
Jakobs, K.H., Aktories, K., Schultz, G.: *Adv. Cycl. Nucl. Res.* 14:173 (1981).
James, J.H., Fischer, J.E.: *Pharmacology* 22:1 (1981).
Jande, S.S., Maler, L., Lawson, D.E.M.: *Nature* 294:765 (1981).
Jeffrey, P.L., Gibbs, M.E.: *Pharmacol. Biochem. Behav.* 5:571 (1976).
Johnson, E.M., Campbell, G.R., Allfrey, V.G.: *Science* 206:1192 (1979).
Johnson, G.L.: *Proc. Natl. Acad. Sci. USA* 75:3113 (1978).
Johnson, G.L., Kaslow, H.R., Farkel, Z., Bourne, H.R.: *Adv. Cycl. Nucl. Res.* 13:1 (1980).
Johnston, C.A., Demarest, K.T., Moore, K.E.: *Brain Res.* 195:236 (1980).
Jolles, J., Zwiers, H., Schotman, P., Gispen, W.H.: *Synaptic Constituents in Health and Disease.* M. Brzin, D. Sket, H. Bachelard (Eds.). Pergamon Press: Oxford (1980). p.269.
Jones-Lecointe, A., Rose, S.P.R., Sinha, H.: *J. Neurochem.* 26:929 (1975).
Jorgensen, O.S.: *J. Neurochem.* 27:1223 (1976).
Jorgensen, O.S.: *FEBS Lett.* 79:42 (1977).
Jorgensen, O.S., Bock, E.: *J. Neurochem.* 23:879 (1974).
Jorgensen, O.S., Bock, E.: *Neurochem. Res.* 4:175 (1979).
Jorgensen, O.S., Meier, E.: *J. Neurochem.* 33:381 (1979).
Jorgensen, O.S., Delouvee, A., Thiery, J.P., Edelman, G.M.: *FEBS Lett.* 111:39 (1980).
Judge, M.E., Quartermain, D.: *Neurosci. Lett.* 24:313 (1981).

Judge, M.E., Quartermain, D.: *Physiol. Behav.* 28:585 (1982).

Jungmann, R.A., Lee, S.G., DeAngelo, A.B.: *Adv. Cycl. Nucl. Res.* 5:281 (1975).

Kaczmarek, L.K., Adey, W.R.: *Epilepsia* 16:19 (1975).

Kakimoto, Y., Matsuoka, Y., Miyake, M., Konishi, H.: *J. Neurochem.* 24:893 (1975).

Kakiuchi, S., Yamazaki, R., Nakajima, H.: *Proc. Jap. Acad.* 46:589 (1970).

Kakiuchi, S., Yamazaki, R., Teshima, Y.: *Biochem. Biophys. Res. Commun.* 42:968 (1971).

Kakiuchi, S., Yamazaki, R., Teshima, Y.: *Adv. Cycl. Nucl. Res.* 1:455 (1972).

Kandel, E.R., Tauc, L.: *J. Physiol. (London)* 181:1 (1965).

Karkowsky, A.M., Orlowski, M.: *J. Biol. Chem.* 253:1574 (1978).

Karpiak, S.E., Serokosz, M., Rapport, M.M.: *Brain Res.* 102:313 (1976).

Kerkut, G.A., Shapira, A., Walker, R.J.: *Comp. Biochem. Physiol.* 23:729 (1967).

Kimberlin, R.H., Shirt, D.B., Collis, S.C.: *J. Neurochem.* 23:241 (1974).

Kit, S.: *Mol. Cell. Biochem.* 11:161 (1976).

Klee, C.B.: *Biochemistry* 16:1017 (1977).

Klee, C.B., Krinks, M.H.: *Biochemistry* 17:120 (1978).

Kleve, L.J., Suddith, R.L., Hutchison, H.T.: *J. Cell Biol.* 67:217A (1975).

Koenig, E.: *J. Cell Biol.* 38:562 (1968).

Krueger, B.K., Forn, J., Greengard, P.: *J. Biol. Chem.* 252:2764 (1977).

Kuhnt, U., Kelly, K.J., Schaumberg, G.: *Exp. Brain Res.* 35:371 (1979).

Kunkel, T.A., Loeb, L.A.: *Science* 213:765 (1981).

Lajtha, A.: *Biochim. Biophys. Acta* 425:511 (1976).

Lajtha, A., Dunlop, D.: *Life Sci.* 29:755 (1981).

Lajtha, A., Furst, S., Gerstein, A.: *J. Neurochem.* 1:289 (1957).

Lasek, R.J.: *Trends Neurosci.* 3:87 (1980).

Lasek, R.J., Hoffman, P.N.: In: *Cell Mobility. Cold Spring Harbor Conference on Cell Proliferation,* Vol. 3, R. Goldman, T. Pollard, J. Rosenbaum (Eds.). Cold Spring Harbor Lab.: Cold Spring Harbor, N.Y. (1976). p.1021.

Leon, A., Benvegnu, D., Toffano, G., Orlando, P., Massari, P.: *J. Neurochem.* 30:23 (1978).

Levine, J., Skene, P., Willard, M.: *Trends Neurosci.* 4:273 (1981).

Liang, C.T., Sacktor, B.: *J. Cycl. Nucleotide Res.* 4:97 (1978).

Libiger J., Ban, T.A.: *Progr. Neuropsychopharmacology* 4:561 (1981).

Lisanti, M.P., Schook, W., Moskowitz, N., Beckenstein, W., Bloom, S., Ores, C., Puszkin, S.: *Eur. J. Biochem.* 121:617 (1982).

Litteria, M.: *Dev. Neurosci.* 3:209 (1980).

Livett, B.G.: *Neurosci. Res. Prog. Bull.* 20:39 (1981).

Lockwood, A.H.: *Proc. Natl. Acad. Sci. USA* 76:1184 (1979).

Logan, W.J.: *Exp. Neurol.* 53:431 (1976).

Mally, M.I., Grayson, D.R., Evans, D.R.: *Proc. Natl. Acad. Sci. USA* 78:6647 (1981).

Mann, D.M.A., Yates, P.O.: *J. Neurol. Sci.* 18:183 (1973).

Manthorpe, M., Skaper, S.D., Barbin, G., Varon, S.: *J. Neurochem.* 38:415 (1982).

Marcovici, N., Stoica, I., Petrescu, A.R.. Marcovici, G.: *Rev. Rouman. Neurol.* 1:37 (1964).

Margolis, F.L.: *Proc. Natl. Acad. Sci. USA* 69:1221 (1972).

Margolis, R.L., Wilson, L.: *Nature* 293:705 (1981).

Margolis, R.K., Crockett, C.P., Kiang, W.L., Margolis, R.U.: *Biochim. Biophys. Acta* 452:465 (1976).

Margolis, R.K., Jaanus, S.D., Margolis, R.U.: *Mol. Pharmacol.* 9:590 (1973).

Margolis, R.K., Margolis, R.U., Preti, C., Lai, D.: *Biochemistry* 14:4797 (1975).

Margolis, R.V., Margolis, R.K.: *Biochemistry* 13:2848 (1974).

Markelonis, G.J., Oh, T.H.: *J. Neurochem.* 37:95 (1981).

Marks, N., D'Monte, N., Bellman, C., Lajtha, A.: *Brain Res.* 18:309 (1970).

Marks, N., D'Monte, B., Lajtha, A.: *Texas Rep. Biol. Med.* 31:345 (1973).
Matthies, H.: *Life Sci.* 15:2017 (1975).
McBride, W.J., Klingman, J.D.: *J. Neurochem.* 19:865 (1972).
McGeer, P.L., Eccles, J.C., McGeer, E.G.: *Molecular Neurobiology of the Mammalian Brain.*
    Plenum Press: New York (1979). p. 141.
McIlwain, D.L., Capps-Covey, P.: *J. Neurochem.* 27:109 (1976).
McIlwain, H.: *Neuroscience* 2:357 (1977).
McLawhon, R.W., Schoon, G.S., Dawson, G.: *J. Neurochem.* 37:132 (1981).
Meister, A.: *Science* 180:33 (1973).
Mertz, D.P.: *Dtsche Med. Wschr.* 1:24 (1974).
Miani, N.: *Nature* 193:887 (1962).
Miani, N., Caniglia, A., Panetta, V.: *J. Neurochem.* 27:145 (1976).
Miani, N., Michetti, F., Renzis, G.D., Caniglia, A.: *Experientia* 29:1499 (1973).
Michell, R.H.: *Biochim. Biophys. Acta* 415:81 (1975).
Michell, B.: *Trends Biochem. Sci.* 7:123 (1982).
Minneman, K.P., Iverson, L.L.: *Science* 192:803 (1976).
Miyamoto, S., Ogawa, H., Shiraki, H., Nakagawa, H.: *J. Biochem.* 91:167 (1982).
Mizobe, F., Tashiro, T., Kurokawa, M.: *Eur. J. Biochem.* 48:25 (1974).
Mohandaas, T., Sparkes, R.S., Shapiro, L.J.: *Science* 211:393 (1981).
Montanaro, N., Novello, F., Stirpe, F.: *Biochem. J.* 125:1087 (1971).
Montanaro, N., Strocchi, P., Dallolio, R., Gandolfi, O.: *Neuropsychobiology* 3:1 (1977).
Moore, B.W.: *Biochem. Biophys. Res. Commun.* 19:739 (1965).
Moskowitz, N., Schook, W., Puszkin, S.: *Science* 216:305 (1982).
Musick, J., Hubbard, J.I.: *Nature* 237:279 (1972).
Myers, D.K., Einendegen, L.E.: *Can. J. Physiol. Pharmacol.* 53:1014 (1975).
Nakajima, S.: *J. Comp. Physiol. Psychol.* 67:457 (1969).
Nakajima, S.: *Physiol. Behav.* 8:1063 (1972).
Nakazawa, K., Sano, M., Saito, T.: *Biochim. Biophys. Acta* 444:563 (1976).
Neale, J.H., Klinger, P.D., Agranoff, B.W.: *Science* 179:1243 (1973).
Nestler, E.J., Rainbow, T.C., McEwen, B.S., Greengard, P.: *Science* 212:1162 (1981).
Nevers, P., Saedler, H.: *Nature* 268:109 (1977).
Ng, M., Matus, A.I.: *Neuroscience* 4:1265 (1979).
Novikova, A.N., Glimenko, L.G.: *Ukr. Biokhim. Zh.* 45:398 (1973).
Ochoa, S.: *Eur. J. Cell Biol.* 26:212 (1981).
Ochs, S.: *Neurosci. Res. Progr. Bull.* 20:19 (1981).
Oestreicher, A.B., Zwiers, H., Schotman, P., Gispen, W.H.: *Brain Res. Bull.* 6:145 (1981).
O'Neill, M.C., Amass, K., DeCrombrugghe, B.: *Proc. Natl. Acad. Sci. USA* 78:2213 (1981).
Orlowski, M., Sessa, G., Green Jack, P.: *Science* 184.66 (1974).
Ozawa, H., Kushiya, E., Takahashi, Y.: *Neurosci. Lett.* 18:191 (1980).
Palmer, G.C.: *Neuroscience* 6:2547 (1981).
Partington, C.R., Daly, J.W.: *Mol. Pharmacol.* 15:484 (1979).
Partington, C.R., Edwards, M.W., Daly, J.W.: *J. Neurochem.* 34:76 (1980).
Pastan, I., Perlman, R.: *Science* 169:339 (1970).
Paul, J., Gilmour, R.S.: *J. Mol. Biol.* 34:305 (1968).
Pearse, B.M.F.: *Proc. Natl. Acad. Sci. USA* 73:1255 (1976).
Perrone-Capano, C., D'Onofrio, G., Giuditta, A.: *J. Neurochem.* 38:52 (1982).
Peterson, R.P., Erulkar, S.D.: *Brain Res.* 60:177 (1973).
Pfeiffer, S.E., Herschman, H.R., Lightbody, J., Sato, G.: *J. Cell Physiol.* 75:329 (1970).
Pfeuffer, T.: *FEBS Lett.* 101:85 (1979).
Pierre, M., Loeb, J.E.: *Biochimie* 53:727 (1971).

Pledger, W.J., Thompson, W.J., Strada, S.J.: *Biochim. Biophys. Acta* 391:334 (1975).
Pohle, W., Ruthrich, H.L., Popov, N., Matthies, H.: *Acta Biol. Med. Germ.* 38:53 (1979).
Popoli, M., Giuditta, A.: *J. Neurochem.* 35:1319 (1980).
Popov, N., Ruthrich, H.L., Pohle, W., Schulzeck, S., Matthies, H.: *Brain Res.* 101:295 (1976).
Price, D.L., Griffin, J., Young, A., Peck, K., Stocks, A.: *Science* 188;945 (1975).
Puszkin, S., Haver, K., Schook, W.: In: *Regulatory Mechanisms of Synaptic Transmission,* R. Tapia, C.W. Cotman (Eds.). Plenum Press: New York (1981). p. 241.
Quartermain, D., McEwen, B.S., Azmitia, E.C.: *Science* 169:683 (1970).
Rahmann, H., Rosner, H., Breer, H.: *J. Med. Sci.* 3:110 (1975).
Rahmann, H., Rosner, H., Breer, H.: *J. Theor. Biol.* 57:231 (1976).
Rainbow, A.J., Hoffman, P.L., Flexner, L.B.: *Pharmacol. Biochem. Behav.* 12:79 (1980).
Randt, C.T., Samuels, S., Fish, I.: *Pharmacol. Biochem. Behav.* 4:689 (1976).
Razin, S., Riggs, A.D.: *Science* 210:604 (1980).
Rees, H.D., Brogan, L.L., Entingh, D.J., Dunn, A.J., Shinkman, P.G., Damstra-Entingh, T., Wilson, J.E., Glassman, G.: *Brain Res.* 68:143 (1974).
Rees, H.D., Entingh, D.J., Dunn, A.J.: *Brain Res. Bull.* 2:243 (1977).
Reichardt, L.F., Matthew, W.D.: *Trends Neurosci.* 5:24 (1982).
Reinis, S.: *Psychopharmacologia* 19:34 (1971).
Reinis, S.: *Physiol. Chem. Phys.* 4:391 (1972).
Reinis, S., Lamble, R.W.: *Physiol. Chem. Phys.* 4:338 (1972).
Reinis, S., Abbott, J., Clarke, J.J.: *Physiol. Chem. Phys.* 4:440 (1972).
Reinis, S., Goldman, J.M., Klieb, J., Black, P.: *Neurosci. Abstr.* 2:48 (1976).
Reyes, E., Palmer, G.C.: *Res. Com. Chem. Path. Pharm.* 14:759 (1976).
Richardson, K., Rose, S.P.R.: *J. Neurochem.* 21:521 (1973).
Richter, J.J., Wainer, A.: *J. Neurochem.* 18:613 (1971).
Robertson, S., Gibbs, M.E., Ng, K.T.: *Brain Res. Bull.* 3:53 (1978).
Rodbell, M.: *Nature* 284:17 (1980).
Rodbell, M., Lad, P.M., Nielsen, T.B., Cooper, D.M.F., Schlegel, W., Preston, M.S., Londos, C., Kempner, E.S.: *Adv. Cycl. Nucl. Res.* 14:3 (1981).
Rodnight, R.: In: *Synaptic Constituents in Health and Disease.* M. Brzin, D. Sket, H. Bachelard (Eds.). Pergamon Press: Oxford (1980). p. 81.
Romen, W., Knobloch, V., Altman, H.W.: *Virchow's Arch. (Zellpathol.)* 23:93 (1977).
Rose, S.P.R.: *J. Neurochem.* 21:539 (1973).
Ross, E.M., Gilman, A.G.: *Ann. Rev. Biochem.* 49:533 (1980).
Ross, E.M., Howlett, A.C., Ferguson, K.M., Gilman, A.G.: *J. Biol. Chem.* 253:6401 (1978).
Roufogalis, B.D.: *Trends Neurosci.* 3:238 (1980).
Routtenberg, A.: *Progr. Neurobiol.* 12:85 (1979).
Routtenberg, A., Benson, G.E.: *Behav. Neural Biol.* 29:168 (1980).
Routtenberg, A., George, D., Davis, L., Brunngraber, E.: *Behav. Biol.* 12:461 (1974).
Rowley, W.F., Young, I.J.: *Recent Adv. Biol. Psychiat.* 9:251 (1966).
Ryffel, G.U., McCarthy, B.J.: *Biochemistry* 14:1379 (1975).
Ryser, U.: *Science* 161:321 (1968).
Salter, R.S., Krinks, M.H., Klee, C.B., Neer, E.J.: *J. Biol. Chem.* 256:9830 (1981).
Samir Amer, M., Kreighbaum, W.E.: *J. Pharmaceut. Sci.* 64:1 (1975).
Sandoval, M.E.: *Brain Res.* 181:357 (1980).
Sandritter, W., Novakova, V., Pilny, J., Kiefer, G.: *Z. Zell Mikr.* 80:145 (1967).
Sano, M., Drummond, G.I.: *J. Neurochem.* 37:558 (1981).
Santerre, R.F., Rich, A.: *Dev. Biol.* 54:1 (1976).
Schachner, M.: *Nature New Biol.* 243:117 (1973).
Schatz, R.A., Wilens, T.E., Sellinger, O.Z.: *Biochem. Biophys. Res. Commun.* 98:1097 (1981).

Schimke, R.T., Kaufman, R.J., Alt, F.W., Kellems, R.F.: *Science* 20:1051 (1978).

Schlichter, D.J., Casnellie, J.E., Greengard, P.: *Nature* 273:61 (1978).

Schmidt, R., Shashoua, V.E.: *J. Neurochem.* 36:1368 (1981).

Schmitt, M., Matthies, H.: *Acta Biol. Med. Germ.* 38:673 (1979).

Scholtz, C.L., Mann, D.M.A.: *Neuropath. Appl. Neurobiol.* 3:137 (1977).

Schultz, G., Bohme, E., Munske, K.: *Life Sci.* 8:1323 (1969).

Schultz, V., Lowenstein, J.M.: *J. Biol. Chem.* 251:485 (1976).

Schumm, D.E., Richter, R.: *J. Neurochem.* 38:925 (1982).

Schwartz, J.H., Castelluci, V.F., Kandel, E.R.: *J. Neurophysiol.* 24:939 (1971).

Sedlacek, H.H., Stark, J., Seiler, F.R., Ziegler, W., Wiegandt, H.: *FEBS Lett.* 61:272 (1976).

Serota, R.G., Roberts, R.B., Flexner, L.B.: *Proc. Natl. Acad. Sci. USA* 69:340 (1972).

Shashoua, V.E.; *Nature* 217:238 (1968).

Shashoua, V.E.: *Exp. Brain Res.* 17:139 (1973).

Shashoua, V.E.: *Brain Res.* 111:347 (1976).

Shashoua, V.E.: *Brain Res.* 122:113 (1977).

Shashoua, V.E., Moore, M.E.: *Brain Res.* 148:441 (1978).

Shimahara, T., Tauc, L.: *J. Physiol. (Paris)* 74:515 (1978).

Shine, H.D., Hertz, L., DeVellis, J., Haber, B.: *Neurochem. Res.* 6:453 (1981).

Siegel, L.G., McClure, W.O.: *Neurobiology* 5:167 (1975).

Simpson, D.L., Thorne, D.R., Loh, H.H.: *Nature* 266:367 (1977).

Smith, A.P., Loh, H.H.: *J. Neurochem.* 36:1749 (1981).

Smith, J.E.: *Pharmacol. Biochem. Behav.* 3:455 (1975).

Smith, J.H., Jr.: *N. Engl. J. Med.* 288:764 (1973).

Sobel, H., Bowman. R.: *Experientia* 27:1163 (1971).

Souza, D.O., Elisabetsky, E., Izquierdo, I.: *Pharmacol. Biochem. Behav.* 12:481 (1980).

Spector, R.: *J. Neurochem.* 35:1092 (1980).

Springer, A.D., Schoel, W.M., Klinger, P.D., Agranoff, B.W.: *Behav. Biol.* 13:467 (1975).

Springer, M.S., Goy, M.F., Adler, J.: *Nature* 280:279 (1979).

Squire, L.R., Kuczenski, R., Barondes, S.H.: *Brain Res.* 82:241 (1974).

Steward, O., Levy, W.B.: *J. Neurosci.* 2:284 (1982).

Stewart, J.A.: *Biochem. Biophys. Res. Com.* 46:1405 (1972).

Suleiman, S.A., Spector, R.: *J. Neurochem.* 38:392 (1982).

Susz, J.P., Hof, H.I., Brunngraber, E.G.: *FEBS Lett.* 32:289 (1973).

Sutherland, E.W., Rall, T.W.: *J. Biol. Chem.* 232:1077 (1958).

Tano, S., Mizuno, S., Shirahata, S.: *Biochim. Biophys. Acta* 213:45 (1970).

Tashiro, S.: *Am. J. Physiol.* 60:519 (1922).

Tauc, L., Hinzen, D.H.: *Brain Res.* 80:340 (1974).

Theodosis, D.T.: *Neuroscience* 4:417 (1979).

Thoenen, H.: *Neurosci. Res. Progr. Bull.* 20:7 (1981).

Thomas, J.O., Thompson, R.J.: *Cell* 10:633 (1977).

Tjornhammer, M.-L., Schwarcz, R., Bartfai, T., Fuxe, K.: *Brain Res.* 171:567 (1979).

Torda, C.: *J. Pharmacol. Exp. Ther.* 107:197 (1953).

Toth, J., Lajtha, A.: *Neurochem. Res.* 2:149 (1977).

Treistman, S.N., Levitan, I.B.: *Nature* 261:62 (1976).

Treistman, S.N., Levitan, I.B.: *Proc. Natl. Acad. Sci. USA* 73:4689 (1976a).

Tremblay, G.C., Jimenez, V., Crandall, D.E.: *J. Neurochem.* 26:57 (1976).

Trotta, E.E., DeMeis, L.: *Biochim. Biophys. Acta* 394:239 (1975).

Troyer, E.W., Ferrendelli, J.A.: *Fed. Proc.* 35:456 (1976).

Tucker, M.M., Robinson, J.B.Jr., Stellwagen, E.: *J. Biol. Chem.* 256:9051 (1981).

Ueda, T., Greengard, P.: *J. Biol. Chem.* 252:5155 (1977).

Ueda, T., Maeno, H., Greengard, P.: *J. Biol. Chem.* 248:8295 (1973).

Vadeboncoeur, C., Lapointe, J.: *Brain Res.* 129:138 (1980).

Van den Eijnden, D.H., Van Dijk, W.: *Biochim. Biophys. Acta* 312:136 (1974).

Van Nieuw Amerongen, A., Roukema, P.A.: *J. Neurochem.* 23:85 (1974).

Van Venrooij, W.J., Vaneenben, J., Janssen, A.P.M.: *Biochemistry* 16:2343 (1977).

Ven Murthy, M.R.: *J. Neurochem.* 38:41 (1982).

Villiger, J.W., Dunn, A.J.: *Behav. Neural Biol.* 31:354 (1981).

Vrana, K.E., Allhiser, C.L., Roskoski, R., Jr.: *J. Neurochem.* 36:92 (1981).

Wallace, R.W., Lynch, T.J., Tallant, E.A., Cheung, W.Y.: *Arch. Biochem. Biophys.* 87:328 (1978).

Walter, R., Hoffman, P.L., Flexner, J.B., Flexner, L.B.: *Int. J. Peptide Protein Res.* 16:482 (1980).

Wang, H.H., Adey, S.R.: *Exp. Neurol.* 25:70 (1969).

Wang, J.H., Desai, R.: *Biochem. Biophys. Res. Commun.* 72:926 (1976).

Wang, J.H., Desai, R.: *J. Biol. Chem.* 252:4175 (1977).

Wang, J.H., Waisman, D.M.: *Curr. Top. Cell Reg.* 15:47 (1979).

Warecka, K., Bauer, H.: *J. Neurochem.* 19:2195 (1967).

Watterson, D.M., Harrelson, W.G., Keller, P.M., Sharief, F., Vanaman, T.C.: *J. Biol. Chem.* 251:4501 (1976).

Weil, D.E., McIlwain, D.L.: *J. Neurochem.* 36:242 (1981).

Weil-Malherbe, H.: *Mol. Cell. Biochem.* 4:31 (1974).

Weiss, P., Hiscoe, H.B.: *J. Exp. Zool.* 107:315 (1948).

Weller, M.: *Biochim. Biophys. Acta* 469:350 (1977).

Weller, M.: *Mol. Cell Biochem.* 27:71 (1979).

Wenzel, J., David, H., Pohle, W., Marx, I., Matthies, H.: *Brain Res.* 84:99 (1975).

White, A.A., Auerbach, G.D.: *Biochim. Biophys. Acta* 191:686 (1969).

White, C.J.B.: *J. Neurol. Sci.* 41:261 (1979).

White, H.B. III, Laux, B.E., Dennis, D.: *Science* 175:1264 (1972).

Wiegant, V.M.: *Brain Res. Bull.* 3:611 (1978).

Wilkening, D., Nirenberg, M.: *J. Neurochem.* 34:321 (1980).

Williams, C.A., Barna, J., Schupf, N.: *Nature* 283:82 (1980).

Wojtczak, L., Nalecz, M.J.: *Eur. J. Biochem.* 94:99 (1979).

Wolff, D.J., Brostrom, C.O.: *Adv. Cyclic. Nucl. Res.* 11:27 (1979).

Yamada, N., Sawasaki, Y., Nakajima, H.: *Brain Res.* 195:484 (1981).

Yanagihara, T.: *J. Neurochem.* 35:1209 (1980).

Yen, S.-H., Dahl, D., Schachner, M., Shelanski, M.L.: *Proc. Natl. Acad. Sci. USA* 73:529 (1976).

Zanetta, J.P., Reeber, A., Vincendon, G., Gombos, G.: *Brain Res.* 138;317 (1977).

Zomzely-Neurath, C., Marangos, P.J., York, C., Hymowitz, N., Perl, W., Zayas, V., Cua, W.: *Trans. Am. Soc. Neurochem.* 7:242 (1976).

Zwiller, J., Basset, P., Mandel, P.: *Biochim. Biophys. Acta* 658:64 (1981).

Zwiller, J., Revel, M.-O., Basset, P.: *Biochem. Biophys. Res. Commun.* 101:1381 (1981a).

Zwiller, J., Ciesielski-Treska, J., Ulrich, G., Revel, M.O., Mandel, P.: *J. Neurochem.* 38:856 (1982).

IV

FUNCTIONAL ASPECTS OF NEUROTRANSMITTER ACTIVITY

Chapter 17

Cholinergic Systems

Within certain limits, the activity of the synapse is relatively well stabilized. Individual components of a synapse together are able to maintain a functional balance that relates to a dependence both upon one another and upon other metabolic systems of the neuron. Consequently, a change in the synaptic efficacy is not a simple process involving an increase in the amount of neurotransmitter produced, nor is it a function exclusively involving the receptor. Alterations in the activity of the synapse probably involve many simultaneous processes, including those concerned with the supply of neurotransmitter precursors, enzymatic synthesis, the release of the neurotransmitter, enzymatic systems necessary for the neurotransmitter degradation, and the maintenance of a stabilized receptor sensitivity. All of these processes are responsive to a change in the functional requirements of the synapse. These interrelationships will be stressed throughout this section in the course of discussions of the activity of the various neurotransmitters.

The first convincing evidence for the existence of chemical transmission was reported in 1921 by Otto Loewi. By stimulating the cardiac branch of the frog vagus nerve, he found that an inhibitory substance was released into a perfusing fluid. Transfer of the fluid into a second heart caused a slowing in the contraction of the heart muscle. Loewi termed this substance "Vagusstoff" and found it to be extremely potent, but rapidly broken down

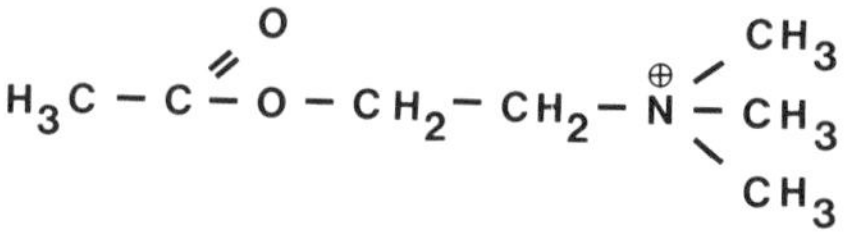

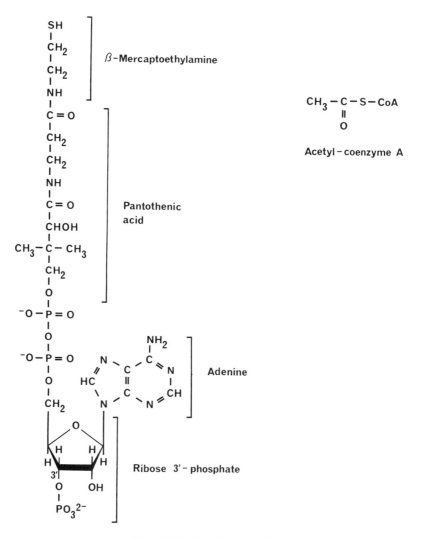

Figure 17.1 Acetylcholine.

Figure 17.2 Acetyl coenzyme A.

once released. The inhibitory material was subsequently identified as acetylcholine. Its discovery opened the door to an understanding of the way in which nerve cells communicate with one another and to an eventual appreciation of the complexity of synaptic functions.

BIOCHEMISTRY OF ACETYLCHOLINE

The localization and function of acetylcholine (ACh) (Fig. 17.1) in the peripheral nervous system are well known. It is used as the neurotransmitter of all preganglionic vegetative nerve fibers, postganglionic parasympathetic fibers, the neuromuscular junctions innervating skeletal muscles and the postganglionic sympathetic fibers innervating the salivary and sweat glands. In the central nervous system, there are also several areas where acetylcholine may have either a known excitatory or inhibitory action. These will be discussed somewhat later in the chapter.

Role of Acetyl-Coenzyme A

One of the precursors of acetylcholine is activated acetate, acetyl-coenzyme A (Fig. 17.2). The source of the acetate residue in the brain can ultimately be traced back to glucose, and in very young individuals perhaps also to the ketone bodies. Its immediate precursor is pyruvate, which is converted to acetate by a multi-enzyme complex, pyruvate dehydrogenase, localized in mitochondria. This pathway represents a direct linkage between carbohydrate metabolism and acetylcholine synthesis (Fig. 17.3) (Jope and Jenden, 1980).

There is some evidence that the availability of acetyl-coenzyme A is a rate-limiting step in acetylcholine synthesis (Jope and Jenden, 1977). If this is true, it would stress the importance of the control of pyruvate dehydrogenase in the function of the cholinergic synapse. This control is based on a cycle of phosphorylation and dephosphorylation of the enzyme. Pyruvate dehydrogenase (PDH) is activated by dephosphorylation by PDH phosphorylase and inactivated by a PDH kinase-catalyzed phosphorylation. The phosphorylation is stimulated by ATP, and dephosphorylation by pyruvate, ADP, and calcium and magnesium ions. These latter factors therefore activate acetylcholine synthesis.

Role of Choline

Choline, the second precursor of the neurotransmitter, is provided mostly by the circulating blood. Some portion is also made available by acetylcholine hydrolysis and the *de novo* synthesis of choline by a stepwise methylation of phosphatidylethanolamine (Kewitz and Pleul, 1976). An additional quantity is released from choline-containing lipids of the cell membranes (Fig. 17.4). There is a net efflux of choline from the brain, which indicates that choline is synthesized there principally in synaptosomes (Blusztajn and Wurtman, 1981).

Most choline in the body is synthesized in the liver and is transported from the circulation into the brain in lipid-bound form as phosphatidylcholine, lysophosphatidylcholine or sphingomyelin. Free choline is then

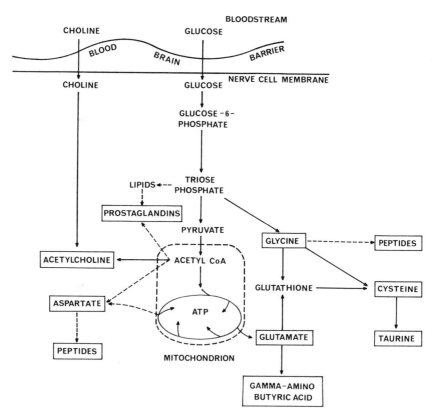

Figure 17.3 Summary of the role of glucose in the synthesis of acetylcholine and other neurotransmitters.

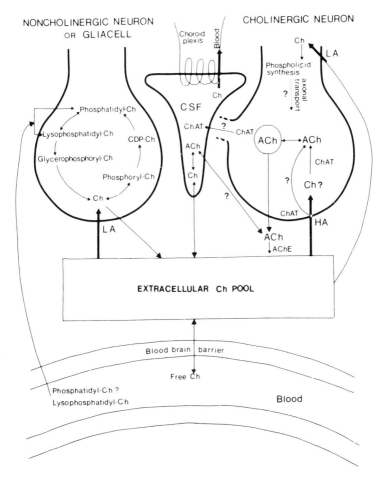

Figure 17.4 Uptake compartmentation and metabolism of choline in the brain [from S.A. Eckernas, *Acta Physiol. Scand.* Suppl. 449 (1977); © 1977 by Acta Physiologica Scandinavica].

liberated from these substances by the activity of the enzymes, phospholipase A and sphingomyelinase (Ansell and Spanner, 1971).

The uptake of choline into the cholinergic nerve cell is an active, saturable process. A low-affinity transport system is spread throughout the cell membrane and supplies the choline that is primarily used for the synthesis of lipids. There is also a high-affinity system that is sodium-dependent and provides the choline for acetylcholine synthesis. Potassium is also involved, because when it is present in physiological concentrations, the transport reaches peak values. If the extracellular potassium level is above or below normal, the transport is depressed (for review see Murrin, 1980). The dependence of acetylcholine production upon this high-affinity uptake mechanism is, however, open to some question (Wong *et al.*, 1980).

The production of acetylcholine is coupled to the transport process. But, only about 50% of the choline taken into the nerve endings is converted to acetylcholine. Work with radioactive labels has shown that while a portion of labeled choline entering the brain is initially used for acetylcholine synthesis, a growing ratio becomes part of a phosphocholine pool which can be drawn upon for the production of lipids, such as choline plasmalogen and lysophosphatidylcholine. This conversion of water-soluble choline into membrane-localized derivatives is relatively prompt, but can be at least 70% blocked by the administration of phenobarbital (Diamond, 1971).

The level of acetylcholine in the synapse regulates the high affinity uptake of choline (Jenden *et al.*, 1976) and, in doing so, maintains the concentration of acetylcholine within a relatively confined range, in spite of an increase in its release and catabolism during periods of greater functional activity over the pathway. The transport is also chloride- and calcium-dependent and is generally coupled with the impulse flow, which increases the V_{max} of the transport without changing the activity of choline acetyltransferase (Barker, 1976). The reason for the change in the transport during synaptic depolarization is not clear. The affinity of the carrier for choline is not altered; only the maximal velocity of transport is increased (Simon and Kuhar, 1975). However, these data conflict with those of Carroll and Goldberg (1975), casting some doubt on the nature of the response.

Under physiological conditions, the membrane carrier system that transports choline into cholinergic neurons is not saturated. Actually the concentration of free choline in the brain is insufficient to saturate acetylcholine synthesis at its maximal rate. This means that the availability of choline in nervous tissue regulates the rate of synthesis in the brain (Eisenstadt and Schwartz, 1975). Even the level of dietary choline may have an effect upon this rate (Cohen and Wurtman, 1976). Accordingly, the ingestion of larger quantities of choline compounds, such as lecithin, is able to elevate concentration of choline and acetylcholine in the brain, demonstrating that the level of these substances is under short-term nutritional control (Hirsch and Wurtman, 1979).

Some problems of memory in the aged have been linked to a deficiency of hippocampal acetylcholine synthesis. Consequently, attempts have been made to manipulate the cholinergic system by altering the dietary intake of choline. In senescent mice, a choline-enriched diet does appear to improve retention (Bartus *et al.*, 1980). And, scopolamine-induced amnesia can be partly reversed by choline (Mohs *et al.*, 1981). A depletion of acetylcholine in the hippocampus by atropine administration is also alleviated by choline administration (Schmidt and Wecker, 1981). However, clinical trials have thus far been unsuccessful (Ferris *et al.*, 1979).

Biosynthesis of Acetylcholine

Compared with the other putative neurotransmitters, the concentration of acetylcholine in the mammalian brain is maintained within rather confined limits, while at the same time undergoing a rapid turnover. The initial step in the synthesis of acetylcholine is the activation of choline by choline kinase (ATP: choline phosphotransferase). This is actually a phosphorylation that is stimulated by the presence of acetylcholine. Thus, acetylcholine is capable of controlling the availability of the precursor for its own synthesis. Its synthesis depends mainly on the activity of the enzyme choline acetyltransferase (acetyl-CoA: choline-*O*-acetyltransferase) which generates acetylcholine from acetyl-coenzyme A and choline. The enzyme is present in the neuronal perikaryon, either loosely bound to the membranes or within the cytoplasm. It has also been reported in nerve endings. Its activity is highest in the putamen and lowest in the cerebellum. Chemically, choline acetyltransferase is a stable, relatively basic protein that is composed of six identical subunits with 133 amino acid residues each (Chao, 1975). There are several molecular species in different animal brains. Thus, the mouse and monkey brain contain three species, while the rabbit brain contains only two. However, Jope (1979) is of the opinion that the isoenzymes described in the literature may be an artifact of the isolation procedures.

Typically, the activity of choline acetyltransferase *in vitro* is inhibited by acetylcholine as the reaction product. According to Malthe-Sorenssen and Fonnum (1972), this is an inhibition of only one of the molecular forms; the others do not appear to be markedly inhibited by physiological concentrations of acetylcholine.

The synthesis of acetylcholine by membrane-bound choline acetyltransferase is more efficient than its synthesis by the free enzyme and is prevalent in adult brains. The enzymatic activity is enhanced by various depolarizing agents, such as ouabain, protoveratrin, or a high level of extracellular potassium (Grewaal and Quastel, 1973). The long-term activation of choline acetyltransferase depends upon the traffic of nerve impulses in the cell. Although this hypothesis had been formulated by Nordenfelt in 1964, the experimental evidence in support of it was not provided until much later (Ekstrom, 1978). Still, choline acetyltransferase is not a rate-limiting enzyme for acetylcholine synthesis, since its reaction velocity far exceeds the production of acetylcholine *in vivo*. This means that those models contending that the control of acetylcholine synthesis occurs via a feedback inhibition by the reaction product are not entirely justified.

RELEASE OF ACETYLCHOLINE

In nerve endings, the ACh that is synthesized may remain free in the cytoplasm or, after a time, be transported into synaptic vesicles. This latter process occurs via a simple diffusional equilibrium; ATP or some other macroergic compound is not involved.

The origin of acetylcholine that is released from nerve endings during depolarization is at present uncertain. It is doubtful that the majority comes from the synaptic vesicles. At least 50% of the acetylcholine is found in the cytoplasm, and the enzyme synthesizing it, choline acetyltransferase, is not present in the synaptic vesicles. It may be that the cytoplasmic fraction is released by some hitherto unknown gating mechanism. As a matter of fact, newly formed cytoplasmic acetylcholine remains in the nerve ending cytoplasm for at least 60 minutes, and is then released preferentially over vesicular acetylcholine (Molenaar and Polak, 1976). This mechanism of release is associated with the inhibition of Na^+, K^+-dependent ATPase (Meyer and Cooper, 1981). Calcium and potassium ions and the presynaptic acetylcholine receptors (particularly those of the muscarinic type) are also involved. By loading minced mouse forebrain with the "false" neurotransmitter acetylhomocholine, Carrol and Aspry (1980) were able to calculate the ratio of acetylcholine to this transmitter in the cytoplasm of nerve endings and in the synaptic vesicles. They found that an evoked release, requiring the presence of calcium ions, had the same ratio of false to true neurotransmitter as in the cytoplasm. This would indicate that it is the cytoplasmic acetylcholine that is released during synaptic transmission.

ACETYLCHOLINESTERASES

The action of acetylcholine is terminated by its hydrolysis into acetate and choline. While choline itself is also able to excite some neurons, e.g. in the cortex, its action is eight times weaker than the action of acetylcholine (Krnjevic and Reinhardt, 1979). All tissues are able to hydrolyze acetylcholine quickly and efficiently, employing enzymes classified as choline esterases. International nomenclature recognizes the existence of both a specific enzyme, acetylcholinesterase (acetylcholine hydrolase) and an enzyme with slightly broader range of substrate specificity, cholinesterase (acylcholine acylhydrolase).

Acetylcholinesterase (AChE) is specifically responsible for the inactivation of acetylcholine in the synapses (Fig. 17.5). It is membrane-bound and has been obtained in purified form from the electric organs of different species of fish, including *Electrophorus electricus* and *Torpedo californica*. Acetylcholinesterase is widely distributed throughout the brain, being present even in some neurons which are not cholinergic, and has an activity that is two orders of magnitude greater than choline acetyltransferase. It can be found both in presynaptic and postsynaptic membranes and in the cytoplasm, but not in synaptic vesicles. The enzyme is produced in the perikarya and transported toward the nerve endings by axoplasmic transport. In addition to its release into the synaptic cleft in response to the arrival of a nerve impulse, some AChE can enter the cerebrospinal fluid (Inestrosa *et al.*, 1977).

Several forms of acetylcholinesterase have been described, and they probably arise from differences in the aggregation of subunits. For example, in the porcine brain a form having a molecular weight of about 270,000 daltons prevails in purified synaptosomes, while the motor endplates contain a

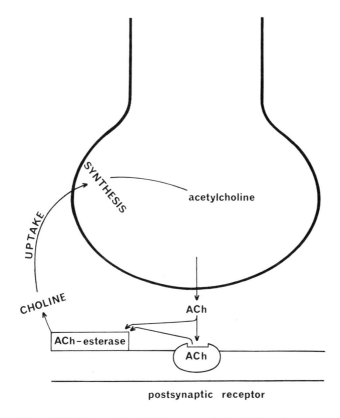

Figure 17.5 Scheme of metabolic processes in the cholinergic synapse.

unique type that is absent in other cells and tissues (McIntosh and Plummer, 1976). These acetylcholinesterases differ in the extent of their ability to bind to the membrane and in their appearance during brain development. Using chickens, Marchand *et al.* (1977) have reported that the appearance of a heavy form with a sedimentation constant of 11S correlated with a sensitivity to imprinting.

The native form of the enzyme has an elongated structure that contains a multisubunit head attached to a tail portion. The tail is anchored in the membrane and its structured peptide resembles collagen. The head contains the catalytic subunits (Bon *et al.*, 1973). The active site of acetylcholinesterase has two subsites. One of them is comprised of a group of negatively charged anionic sites, while the other, the esteratic site, contains both acidic (electrophilic) and basic (nucleophilic) groups (Fig. 17.6). The quaternary nitrogen of acetylcholine is bound to the anionic site, presenting the carbonyl group of the molecule to the esteratic site. Electron shifts at the esteratic site are responsible for the liberation of choline (Roufogalis and Wickson, 1975). The acetyl group remains briefly bound to the enzyme. Hydrolysis is very rapid, and free acetic acid is quickly released. An objection to this model is that 3,3-dimethylbutylacetate, in which the quaternary nitrogen is replaced by an uncharged carbon atom, and even phenylacetate or naphthylacetate, which do not resemble acetylcholine at all, are also split by the enzyme. It appears, then, that only the presence of an acetyl group, and not the quaternary nitrogen, is critical for the activity.

Different forms of the enzyme contain two, four, or six active sites per molecule (Gordon *et al.*, 1976). Acetylcholinesterase also contains several control sites which react with the corresponding ligand, resulting in a change

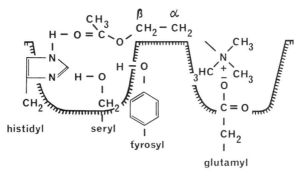

Figure 17.6 Model of the active site of acetylcholinesterase.

in the conformation of the enzyme (allosteric sites). These sites are therefore capable of modulating the activity of the catalytic surfaces. This is one of the mechanisms involved in the functional control of the enzyme. Long-lasting regulation depends, in some tissues, on a neurotrophic protein that is transported from the cell body toward the nerve endings. Such a protein has already been isolated from peripheral nerve by Oh and Markelonis (1978). And, it is possible that polyamines may also play a somewhat similar role in AChE activity.

AChE degrades only a portion of the acetylcholine that is released at the synapse. The rest is taken up against the concentration gradient into the postsynaptic neuron, possibly by a transport carrier mechanism. This transport has also been demonstrated *in vivo* (Levinger and Edery, 1971), where there are high- and low-affinity uptake systems. The sites on the membrane responsible for the transport are not identical with the acetylcholine receptor sites. The mechanism requires energy in the form of ATP and probably depends on the activity of the sodium pump.

ACETYLCHOLINE RECEPTORS

Following its release from the presynaptic knob, acetylcholine diffuses across the synaptic cleft and combines with the specific acetylcholine receptor in the postsynaptic membrane. Based upon their pharmacological characteristics, two types of acetylcholine receptors have been identified - nicotinic and muscarinic. The nicotinic receptors are pharmacologically stimulated by nicotine and blocked by curare. They are found mainly in neuromuscular junctions and autonomic ganglia, but have been identified in the mammalian brain (for review see Morley and Kemp, 1981). Muscarinic receptors are stimulated by muscarine and blocked by atropine. In both cases the effector part of the molecule is a positively charged nitrogen.

The receptors have already been successfully isolated and purified (Schmidt and Raftery, 1973). The electroplax of *Torpedo marmorata* or *Torpedo californica* contains large quantities of the nicotinic receptor that can be labeled by a specific radioactive antagonist, α-bungarotoxin. The receptor from *Torpedo californica* is composed of subunits formed by four polypeptide chains (α, β, γ, and δ) and contains about 5% carbohydrate (Weill *et al.*, 1974). After their translation, these subunits undergo a modification, e.g. by carboxymethylation (Kloog *et al.*, 1979) and are transported from the perikaryon by the axonal flow (Laduron, 1980a). It is the alpha chain that contains two binding sites for cholinergic effectors, although all of the subunits are structurally related and play a functional role. Computer image-averaging (Zingsheim *et al.*, 1980) of electron micrographs of stained receptor membranes has indicated that the receptor is a horseshoe-shaped structure. The purified complex is 80A in width. In its center, there is an electron dense pit of 20A, which protrudes about 50A from the lipid matrix of the membrane (for review see Hucho, 1981). The turnover of these receptors is rather slow and in the synapses is greater than 100 hours (Cohen and Changeux, 1975).

After the receptor interacts with the neurotransmitter, it somehow translocates cations across the postsynaptic membrane. A purified receptor from *Torpedo* contains both a neurotransmitter recognition site (with a second neurotransmitter binding subsite) and a site complexing with the inorganic cations, sodium, potassium and calcium (Michaelson *et al.*, 1975). Acetylcholine that binds to the receptor causes a fall in the electrical resistance of the subsynaptic membrane, generating an electrical current. Upon complexing with acetylcholine, the receptor presumably undergoes a change in its conformation, resulting in the shift in the ionic permeability of the membrane.

The acetylcholine receptor has a high binding capacity for calcium ions; up to 60 ions can be bound to one receptor molecule. These ions actually compete with acetylcholine for the binding site, and when acetylcholine is bound to the receptor, about 4-6 bound calcium ions are released (Chang and Neumann, 1976). Intracellular calcium is also able to stimulate receptor synthesis (McManaman *et al.*, 1981).

Both muscarinic and nicotinic cholinergic receptors have been detected in the brain and subsequently purified from synaptosomal fractions (Moore and Brady, 1976; Blas and Mahler, 1976). According to Seto *et al.* (1977), the nicotinic receptor in the brain is a complex glycoprotein with a molecular weight of about 700,000 daltons and resembles nicotinic receptors in the skeletal muscles and electric organs. The prevalence of one type of receptor over the other tends to vary in different areas of the brain. Generally, the muscarinic receptors are high in the telencephalic areas, while the nicotinic receptors tend to be higher in the brain stem nuclei.

The binding capacity of the receptors for acetylcholine and the passage of ions through the membrane are under the control of rapid regulatory mechanisms. One regulatory component in the postsynaptic membrane may be the status of receptor phosphorylation. Both phosphorylation by a membrane-bound protein kinase and dephosphorylation by a phosphatase have been reported *in situ* (Gordon and Diamond, 1979). And, since protein phosphorylation has been implicated as a regulatory mechanism influencing the responsiveness of the cell to various biochemical signals (e.g., Robison *et al.*, 1968; Fox *et al.*, 1980), its association with the acetylcholine receptor intimates a functional role in receptor-mediated events.

It had been mentioned previously that the continuous presence of an elevated concentration of acetylcholine causes a progressive desensitization of the receptor. A diminished quantity of neurotransmitter, on the other hand, sensitizes the receptor. These two processes are the result of a quick transformation of the receptor from an active to an inactive state and back that is probably due to a change in its molecular conformation (Gibson *et al.*, 1977). The presence of sodium ions is required for this shift. These changes mean that the number of the receptors is altered, or that the binding capacity of the receptor to the transmitter or ionophore is somehow modified. The mechanisms responsible for the change in receptor excitability are not completely known. It is even possible that the higher doses of agonists and antagonists that are used in many pharmacological studies create an entirely different situation from that present with the neurotransmitter.

An important factor in the control of the receptor binding capacity is its lipid and protein membrane environment. The removal of phospholipids from the membrane decreases the affinity of the receptor for acetylcholine

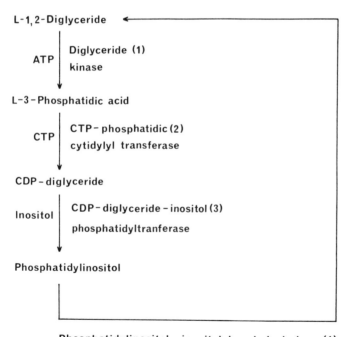

Phosphatidylinositol - inositolphosphohydrolase (4)

Figure 17.7 Breakdown and resynthesis of phosphatidylinositol in response to acetylcholine. Numbers 1 - 4 depict individual steps of the reaction. [from E.G. Lapetina, J.N. Hawthorne, *Biochem. J.* 122:171 (1971); © 1971 by Biochemical Society, London].

by an order of two. The administration of lipids, such as phosphatidylinositol or phosphatidylcholine, is able to restore the high affinity state (Chang and Bock, 1979). Unsaturated fatty acids, but not saturated ones, are also able to influence the binding of acetylcholine to its receptors (Aronstam *et al.*, 1977). The neutral fats are without effect. Lipids probably protect the free sulfhydryl groups of the receptor from oxidation. Changes in receptor excitability due to alterations of membrane phospholipids are, in turn, induced by a phospholipid base exchange system present in the synaptosomal plasma membrane. This process is activated by acetylcholine (Fig. 17.7) (Wirtz *et al.*, 1976; Lapetina and Michell, 1972).

Another factor controlling the sensitization and desensitization of cholinergic receptors is the difference in electrical potentials across the membrane. This has been demonstrated in skeletal muscle (Kordas, 1969) and the central nervous system (Van der Kloot and Cohen, 1979). The excitability of the receptor and the coupling between the receptor and ionic channel also depends upon enzymes, such as membrane bound phospholipid methylase, calcium-dependent protein kinases, adenylate cyclase and calcium-dependent cysteine proteinase (Costa *et al.*, 1981). Costa *et al.* proposed that nerve endings not only release a classical neurotransmitter, acetylcholine for example, but also a "cotransmitter" peptide. This peptide then would modulate the sensitivity of the acetylcholine receptors. The effect may be an allosteric action, but the mechanism is not known. Moreover, other factors, such as glutamate (Brookes and Burt, 1980), guanine nucleotides, SH regents and ions (Ehlert *et al.*, 1981) may be involved.

All of these findings support the contention that the acetylcholine receptors in the postsynaptic membrane can exist in physiologically heterogeneous states which may differ in such characteristics as saturability and the binding capacity for drugs. This heterogeneity may prove to be an important consideration in various types of long-term alterations in synaptic excitability.

The distribution of the acetylcholine receptors in the postsynaptic membrane is under the influence of the presynaptic fibers. Such is the case in skeletal muscles where the activity in the motor nerves has been found to control the number of receptors. When botulinum toxin is used to block the release of acetylcholine from the nerve ending, the number of receptors increases. The effect is a relatively slow one and occurs even outside of the synaptic region. It may be at least partly attributable to the presence of hypothetical trophic regulatory substances carried by axonal transport, and to the presence of acetylcholine itself in the postsynaptic membrane.

A blockage of acetylcholine receptors by neurotoxins may temporarily halt transmission across the synapse. At the same time it causes the sprouting of nerve terminals and the formation of new synapses. In the brain, these new junctions retain the orderliness of normal synaptic connections, a phenomenon that has been observed by Freeman (1977). By establishing a neurotoxic blockade, he noted that there occurred a detectable sprouting of optic nerve terminals in the lateral geniculate body which appeared to retain the typical retinotopic organization. This experiment suggests that the postsynaptic cell helps to maintain normal synaptic connections and a flow of impulses toward it. Work with motor nerve terminals (Pestronk and Drachman, 1978) has revealed that the sprouting is a response to functional denervation that can be caused by a presynaptic blockade with botulinum toxin. A postsynaptic blockade by α-bungarotoxin, another agent interfering with nicotinic cholinergic transmission, had no such effect. However, α-bungarotoxin is not bound to all receptors (Oswald and Freeman, 1981). It appears that the extra-junctional acetylcholine receptors are involved in this growth response (Brown and Ironton, 1977; Brown et al., 1977). The extent of sprouting seems closely tied to the number of these acetylcholine receptors.

CHOLINERGIC SYSTEMS

The proportion of cholinergic neurons in the central nervous system is probably relatively small. However, at some non-cholinergic synapses, acetylcholine may play a modulatory rather than neurotransmitter role. Through its transmitter and neuromodulator functions, acetylcholine participates in appetitive control, thermoregulation, conditioning and learning, aggression, and in certain phases of sleep.

Attempts have been made to classify the central cholinergic pathways (Shute and Lewis, 1967; Pepeu et al., 1973; Silver, 1974) and, although the authors may differ in some respects, there is common agreement on the major systems, which tend to be grouped biochemically and functionally, rather than anatomically. The following pathways have been identified:

(1) A diffuse system ascending from the mesencephalic reticular formation to the cerebral cortex, tectum, metathalamus, and thalamus, which is probably associated with the arousal reaction.

(2) A diffuse system from the septum to the cerebral cortex and fibers in the septo-hippocampal pathway as well as synapses in other parts of the limbic system, medial septum, olfactory tubercle, and nucleus of the diagonal band. Here, it has a presynaptic inhibitory effect (Valentino and Dingledine, 1981), as well as a disinhibitory one (Krnjevic et al., 1981).

(3) A diffuse intracortical system, which may be responsible for acetylcholine release from the cortex during paradoxical sleep.

(4) Fibers from the midbrain reticular formation to the medial and lateral geniculate bodies.

(5) Cholinergic synapses in the caudate nucleus, putamen and amygdala, some fibers of which are believed to originate in the thalamus. Otherwise, striatal cholinergic neurons are mostly interneurons.

(6) Cholinergic synapses in the hypothalamus, which appear to be involved in the control of water diuresis and body temperature and the regulation of the cyclic changes of sexual activity.

(7) Cholinergic synapses in the red nucleus, cerebellum, and some areas of the medulla and pons.

(8) Well-documented cholinergic neurons in the spinal cord are ventral horn motoneurons innervating the voluntary muscles. All other cholinergic synapses in the spinal cord require more verification.

Along with the use of an immunohistochemical method for the detection of choline acetyltransferase (Sternberg *et al.*, 1970), cholinergic mechanisms have been studied by the microiontophoresis of acetylcholine and the subsequent recording of unit electrical activity. With this method, it has been found that the muscarinic excitatory action of acetylcholine in the cerebral cortex is responsible for the stimulation of pyramidal tract cells. There is also muscarinic inhibition in the cortex that is associated with other types of cells. The ascending cholinergic reticular system, whose activity affects the cortex, originates from different areas of the brain stem, including the anterior thalamus. These fibers are responsible for arousal and for cortical epileptiform discharges. And, during the arousal, acetylcholine is released from the surface of the cortex.

Another important system is in the striatum. The simultaneous activity of dopaminergic, GABA-ergic, serotonergic, and cholinergic systems in this area controls general motility. The caudate nucleus has the highest level of acetylcholine in the brain, and a lesion of the substantia nigra causes a decrease in the acetylcholine concentration in the caudate (Butcher and Butcher, 1974).

ACETYLCHOLINE AND BEHAVIOR

Studies on the relationship of the different cholinergic systems to various types of behavior are hampered by the fact that the experiments have generally been designed to record the effects of parenterally administered drugs. The drugs would then act upon the entire cholinergic system with all of its components. And, these components may well have contrasting effects upon behavior. For this reason, it is necessary to distinguish pharmacological neurotransmitter systems from functional behavioral systems.

Many neurologists, neurophysiologists, and psychologists frequently think in terms of "cholinergic", "adrenergic", "dopaminergic" or other systems which have exclusive priority over processes such as learning and memory, mental illness, and various emotional states. Most of the time, this is a rather pointless exercise. Complex physiological functions are typically controlled by systems involving several neurotransmitters, and any alteration in the production of one transmitter is often followed by a rapid shift in the activity of nerve cells generating others. This change may often be compensatory. The various types of behavioral changes are typically a response to a complex interplay of different systems, and any attempted classification of these systems based upon behavior is usually only schematic. For this reason, any hypothesis concerning the role of a single neurotransmitter in a particular aspect of behavior requires a parallel consideration of the possible indirect effects on the other transmitters.

The interactions of different neurotransmitters have already been mentioned in reference to the control of motility by the basal ganglia. Disorders of motility can be elicited by the local administration of muscimol (an antagonist of dopamine), amino-oxyacetic acid (an antagonist of γ-aminobutyric acid) and nicotine (an acetylcholine antagonist). Anticholinergic drugs induce hypermotility in the mouse or rat, although this is not necessarily due to a direct effect upon the systems controlling movement. Some types of movements, such as yawning and headshaking, also appear cholinergically mediated (Holmgren and Urba-Holmgren, 1978). And, tonic immobility, also referred to as animal hypnosis, is believed to involve cholinergic systems in the septum and hippocampus (Thompson, 1977).

Cholinergic systems are also involved in more complex types of behavior. Aggression is one of them. Mouse-killing behavior in rats is suppressed by atropine and scopolamine. Killer rats have been found to have an elevated level of diencephalic acetylcholine. And, the repeated application of pilocarpine (an acetylcholinesterase inhibitor) may even convert nonkillers to killers (McCarthy, 1966). A direct cholinergic stimulation of the lateral hypothalamus can also trigger this activity. Cholinergic agonists will generally facilitate or induce predatory biting attacks or threat behavior. Central muscarinic receptors seem to be involved in the control of this behavior. Muscarinic agonists, such as arecoline, pilocarpine and oxotremorine, reduce the attacks, while antagonists like nicotine suppress them completely. All of these data again indicate the existence of a complex control mechanism which cannot be simply reduced to a single transmitter system or an antagonism between two different systems.

Cholinergic mechanisms have also been reported to be involved in exploratory behavior. Anticholinergic drugs tend to prolong and intensify exploratory activity in mice, results which has been taken to mean that cholinergic mechanisms inhibit nonreinforced orientational responses. These effects are genotype- and species-dependent (for review see Van Abeelen, 1974).

Cholinergic drugs influence sexual behavior as well. In the male rat, an increase in cholinergic activity by eserine (an acetylcholinesterase inhibitor) blocks sexual activity (Soulairac, 1963). The same effect can be elicited with the anticholinergic drug atropine. In the female rat, a stimulation of central muscarinic receptors by pilocarpine, oxotremorine or arecoline has been observed to lower sexual activity (Lindstrom, 1972).

Pharmacological research into the appetitive behaviors has shown that scopolamine, an anticholinergic drug, reduces the amount of food eaten, while also inhibiting spontaneous motor activity (Adams, 1973).

The role of the cholinergic fiber tracts in thermoregulation (Feldberg and Myers, 1963) is under dispute. Although it is believed that the biogenic amines, norepinephrine and serotonin, control the activity of thermoregulatory centers, separate cholinergic pathways may also be involved (Myers and Yaksh, 1969). Acetylcholine is released from the hypothalamus during experimental hyperthermia, and acetylcholine injected into the third ventricle causes hyperthermia in pigeons (Chawla et al., 1975)..Laudenslager and Carlisle (1976) have suggested that the main action of acetylcholine in thermoregulation is the control of a heat-dissipating system in the hypothalamus, and that its hyperthermic effect is nonspecific.

In 1967, Jouvet presented data implicating acetylcholine in paradoxical sleep. Hemicholinium, a competitive inhibitor of acetylcholine synthesis, increases slow wave sleep and drastically reduces paradoxical sleep (Hazra, 1970). This effect upon paradoxical sleep is true for atropine administration as well. On the other hand, physostigmine, an antiacetylcholinesterase agent, induces it. All of these actions are probably centralized in the pontine brain stem (Amatruda et al., 1975). The acetylcholine-containing neurons in some brain stem pontine loci overlap monoamine-containing neurons. For this reason, one system cannot be ablated without damaging the other. Consequently, acetylcholine injected into various brainstem loci sometimes causes slow-wave sleep and sometimes REM sleep. These effects can be prevented by a blockade of the medial forebrain bundle. Acetylcholine therefore acts at different levels of the brainstem and is involved in all three stages of vigilance (waking, slow wave sleep and REM sleep).

Acetylcholine and Learning

The various behavioral effects that can be at least partly attributable to cholinergic system activity serve to emphasize the care that must be taken in evaluating the role of cholinergic mechanisms in learning and memory. These "nonassociative" factors may not only determine the response rate under normal conditions, but also the modified responding in animals under the influence of drugs.

One of the approaches used to analyze the role of cholinergic systems in learning and memory is a performance comparison of different strains of animals with varying levels of brain acetylcholine. Accordingly in mice, the DBA strain has a higher level of acetylcholinesterase activity than does the C57BL/6 strain, and they also score better on an avoidance learning task (Ebel *et al.*, 1973). These results are supported by the older findings of Krech *et al.* (1963), among others. However, interpretations based upon such genetic comparisons would require a more thorough series of selective cross-breeding experiments to satisfactorily substantiate the relationship between performance and AChE. Moreover, this higher level of acetylcholinesterase has also been correlated with higher brain levels of glutamic acid decarboxylase and GABA (Geller *et al.*, 1965) in the same strain of mice, indicating that AChE may be just one of the components of a system concerned with recall and performance on a particular type of learning task.

In a sequence of studies, Deutsch explored the effects of several anticholinesterases (diisopropylfluorophosphate, physostigmine), anticholinergic drugs (scopolamine, atropine), and cholinomimetic agents (carbachol, oxotremorine). For his conditioning paradigm, rats were trained to escape into the safe area of a Y maze. They were then injected with one of the drugs at a period of 30 minutes, 3, 5, or 14 days after learning. Administration of the anticholinergic drugs caused a temporary amnesia, the extent of which was dependent upon the time interval between the training and the injection. Deutsch concluded from these experiments that after conditioning the "conductance" of the involved synapses gradually increased, peaking at about 7-14 days after training. The process then underwent a reversal, during which time the animal began forgetting. These experiments, however, did not take into consideration the multiple and overlapping side effects of the drugs, the relationship of acetylcholine to other transmitters, and the development of tolerance to cholinesterase inhibitors. The studies were on a nonmonotonic function, examining the effect of a single dose of each drug upon the base response, instead of constructing more thorough dose-response curves.

The influence of anticholinergic drugs upon learning generally depends upon a number of factors: the level of training, the experimental procedure, the animal species employed, and the type of behavior used for conditioning. Also, the novelty of the initial experience with the drug during the first injection could be interpreted as an impairment of training. It is possible, for example, to demonstrate facilitating or impairing effects of various drugs, depending upon the learning task required of the animal. Atropine and scopolamine both increase the rate of responding in rats in an avoidance situation, but have a disruptive effect on pole climbing and one-trial passive avoidance (Oliverio, 1967).

In studies of this nature, it is useful to introduce the drugs into a specific area of the brain rather than administer them intraperitoneally. These regional injections have shown the hippocampus to be an important area for acquisition and consolidation. This has also been confirmed by analytical studies measuring the hippocampal level of acetylcholine. Following the learning of a brightness discrimination task, for example, the acetylcholine content of the rat hippocampus is elevated (Matthies *et al.*, 1974). Increases in other areas, such as the visual cortex, auditory cortex, and corpus striatum are marginal. But, an injection of scopolamine into the caudate nucleus can also cause a learning deficit (Prado-Alcala *et al.*, 1981). According to Jaffard *et al.* (1974), the cholinergic hippocampal mechanisms are concerned with behavioral inhibition. Strains of mice with low levels of choline acetyltransferase in the dorsal hippocampus were faster to associate a barpress with reinforcement. The argument, then, is that acetylcholine availability at the hippocampal synapses retarded the acquisition of learned responses. In a similar experiment, Jaffard *et al.* (1980) found that a relatively brief exposure of mice to a bar-press operant situation with food reward led to a decrease of hippocampal choline acetyltransferase. This might be a reason why physostigmine, an inhibitor of acetylcholinesterase, impairs retention in good learners, while improving retention in poor learners (Stratton and Petrinovich, 1963). In addition, oxotremorine, a cholinomimetic drug, improves retention, but the effect is restricted to rats performing well during the acquisition phase. According to Grecksch *et al.* (1978), a septo-hippocampal cholinergic system is involved in these effects.

The localized administration of anticholinergic drugs has shown that it is unwarranted to talk about a single system operating in some general process of learning. Fear conditioning, for example, is believed to be mediated by at least two separate cholinergic pathways (Pert and Avis, 1974). And, the central cholinergic muscarinic mechanism for habituation is involved with still different pathways.

It is evident from the available data that the activity of the cholinergic system can be modified by increases in synaptic activity. In particular, the transport of choline into the nerve endings and the sensitivity of the acetylcholine receptors may be quickly adjusted to the needs of the shifts in synaptic transmission. The cholinergic systems of the brain are involved in the learning process, but the degree of the involvement depends upon the learned task, the extent of conditioning, the types of behavior required for the learned response, and the choice of the experimental subject.

Chapter 18

Catecholaminergic Systems

Catecholamines are putative neurotransmitters which are present both in the central and peripheral nervous systems. The term "catecholamine" indicates that these substances are derived chemically from an aromatic compound, catechol. The term "biogenic amine", very often used, is broader, referring to substances with a transmitter function which contain an amino ($-NH_2$) group. Amino acid transmitters, however, are not considered to be biogenic amines.

The most important catecholamines are norepinephrine, epinephrine, and dopamine. Some other members of this category present in the central nervous system are tyramine, octopamine, and phenylethylamine. Catecholamines are also released by the adrenal medulla and nerve endings of the peripheral sympathetic nervous system. As a rule, the catecholamines circulating in the blood do not cross the blood-brain barrier.

SYNTHESIS AND METABOLISM OF CATECHOLAMINES

All of the catecholamines are synthesized from two precursors, the amino acids phenylalanine and tyrosine. Tyrosine may be synthesized from phenylalanine by hydroxylation, a process that is very active in the liver.

Both amino acids are actively transported from the blood through blood-brain barrier into the brain. But, the process is not a rate-limiting step in the synthesis of catecholamines. Their synthesis from tyrosine is only one, relatively minor, pathway of tyrosine metabolism. As an amino acid, much of it is incorporated into proteins.

The decarboxylation of phenylalanine produces phenylethylamine, a process that has also been detected in synaptosomes (Bagchi and Smith, 1979). This substance may readily cross the blood-brain barrier and could be a precursor of tyramine, although it supposedly has an effect on the neurons. It is one of the "trace amines" detected in the mammalian brain in low quantities. While probably not a true neurotransmitter, phenylethylamine may modulate tha actions of some other neurotransmitters (Sabelli *et al.*, 1978) and thus be responsible for some functions generally attributed to brain catecholamines. In pharmacological doses, it has amphetamine-like effects, desynchronizing the electroencephalogram and causing increased exploration and motor activity. Receptors for phenylethylamine have not been demonstrated, and it may actually exist only as a byproduct of brain catecholamine synthesis.

The direct decarboxylation of tyrosine yields tyramine (Fig. 18.1), a substance with a postulated neurotransmitter or synaptic modulatory action. Tyramine has been detected in the synaptosomal fraction of brain tissue (Philips *et al.*, 1978), and cocaine has been found to interfere with its metabolism and transport.

Octopamine (Fig. 18.2), a major catecholamine derived from tyramine, was first identified in the invertebrate *Aplysia*. It is widely distributed in the nervous systems of invertebrates and is a normal constituent of the mammalian brain. It has also been found in the rabbit retina, particularly in dopaminergic cells (Ehinger, 1976). Octopamine is synthesized from tyramine by tyramine-β-hydroxylase, but its function in the mammalian CNS is unknown.

The precursor of the major catecholamines, L-3,4-dihydroxyphenylalanine (L-DOPA), is synthesized from tyrosine (Fig.

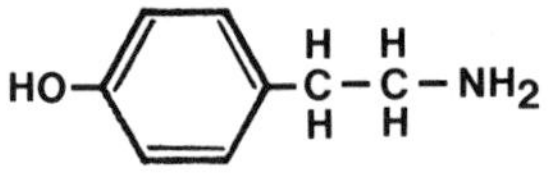

Figure 18.1 Tyramine.

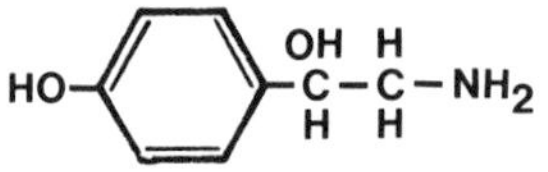

Figure 18.2 Octopamine.

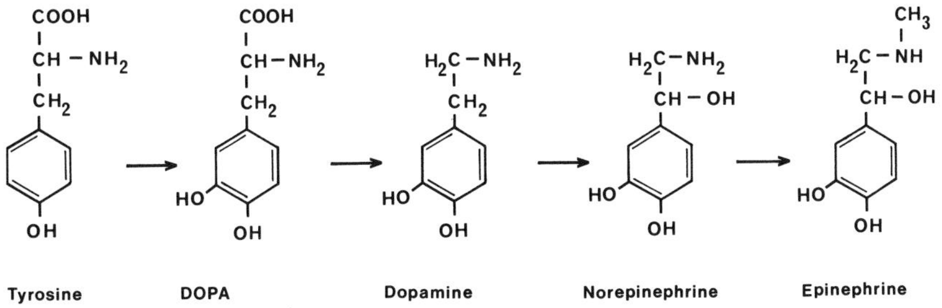

Figure 18.3 Synthesis of catecholamines.

18.3) by the action of tyrosine hydroxylase (TH). In the brain, this enzyme exists in two distinct forms, one soluble and one membrane-bound. The soluble enzyme is probably relatively inactive, while some authors consider the membrane-bound form to be an artifact (Wurtzburger and Musacchio, 1971).

In the nerve endings, TH can be found in both the cytoplasm and in the dense granular and clear synaptic vesicles. It is a rate-limiting enzyme that controls the level of catecholamines present in nervous tissue. Therefore, the regulation of its activity is an important part of the adaptation of catecholaminergic neurons to shifts in functional requirements.

The activity of tyrosine hydroxylase is under the influence of a number of factors. One of them, the presence of a pteridine cofactor, is required by the enzyme. Its production is initiated by the action of guanosine triphosphate cyclohydrolase, which has been identified in dopaminergic nerve endings. The activity of dihydropteridine reductase then generates the tetrahydrobiopteridine that serves as the TH cofactor. This is itself a rate-limiting step in the activity of TH (Musacchio, 1969). The enzyme is activated by phosphorylation, and this activation is followed by an increase in the affinity of TH for both its substrate and possibly its pteridine cofactor. The affinity for the end-product inhibitor, norepinephrine, decreases (Roth et al., 1974; Levine et al., 1981).

The control of TH activity is linked to the phosphorylation of the enzyme by a cAMP-dependent protein kinase and to the firing rate of the monoaminergic neurons (Drummond et al., 1978). The impulse flow and the depletion of norepinephrine or dopamine increases its activity. The impulse-induced activation of TH is a receptor-mediated event which could be due to an increase in the affinity of the enzyme for its cofactor and/or an effect upon the cyclic nucleotides (Ikeno et al., 1981).

Tyrosine hydroxylase is susceptible to a competitive feedback inhibition by DOPA, dopamine and norepinephrine (Bacopoulos and Bhatnagar,

1977). The membrane-bound form has a higher affinity for its competitive feedback inhibitors, norepinephrine and dopamine. Since the affinity for dopamine is the greatest, it is the most important catecholamine in TH regulation. Short-term regulation therefore depends upon the actual levels of the end-products of TH activity in the nerve endings. There are, however, exceptions to this rule. In the cortex, it appears that this regulation tends to be more dependent upon end-product inhibition than upon dopamine autoreceptors (Bannon *et al.*, 1981).

A long-term increase in TH due to the functional activity of catecholaminergic neurons is more dependent upon an increase in protein synthesis, generating new molecules of the enzyme, than on an activation of existing molecules by phosphorylation (Guidotti and Costa, 1977). This increase in enzyme synthesis requires long-lasting forms of stimulation and depends upon nicotinic receptors and an enhanced sodium influx to adrenergic neurons (Bonisch *et al.*, 1980). In the brain, the activity of TH is known to be increased by electroconvulsive and foot shocks, isolation of the animal, glucocorticoids, cold exposure, and the depolarization of nerve endings by potassium ions. There is, however, no direct correlation between the level of TH activity and behavior, although Masserano *et al.* (1981) believe that this increase may contribute to the long-lasting antidepressant effects of the electroconvulsive treatment.

As was mentioned above, tyrosine hydroxylase mediates the formation of L-DOPA. While L-DOPA is a precursor of most catecholamines, this substance by itself probably does not have any neurotransmitter action. Unlike other catecholamines, L-DOPA can easily cross the blood-brain barrier. This means that high plasma levels of DOPA can influence the rate of dopamine synthesis in the brain. The production of norepinephrine is, however, not substantially affected. The DOPA that is present in the brain is rapidly consumed for dopamine synthesis. This keeps DOPA levels in individual brain areas relatively low. In the nerve endings, newly transported L-DOPA, tyrosine and phenylalanine are preferentially used for the production of neurotransmitters.

The next enzyme in the pathway, DOPA-decarboxylase, forms dopamine from DOPA. It can be found in both neurons and glia and is most active in the brain in those areas containing relatively high levels of catecholamines, such as the substantia nigra and striatum. DOPA-decarboxylase is not a very specific enzyme, since it also will decarboxylate histidine, phenylalanine, tryptophan and 5-hydroxytryptophan. The product, dopamine, is a direct precursor of norepinephrine.

In the peripheral nervous system, dopamine has a weak sympathomimetic effect. Although it was first discovered in the extracts of suprarenal glands, it has been detected in much higher amounts in several brain areas, particularly the corpus striatum. Its concentration in different brain regions does not follow the levels of norepinephrine, which also indicates that dopamine does not only serve as a precursor of norepinephrine, but also acts as an independent neurotransmitter. Some aspects of the regulation of dopamine synthesis are summarized in Figure 18.4.

The rate of dopamine synthesis in the nerve endings depends upon the flow of nerve impulses through the synapse. This effect is mediated by dopamine receptors which are present in the membranes of the presynaptic nerve endings. However, the relationship of these presynaptic receptors to dopamine synthesis has not been unequivocally demonstrated. Anden and Wachtel (1977) claim that it is actually the muscarinic receptor that regulates the synthesis and release of dopamine. These muscarinic receptors are also localized on the surface of the dopaminergic nerve terminals.

The enzyme dopamine-β-hydroxylase (DBH; 3,4-dihydroxyphenylethylamine, ascorbate: oxygen oxido-reductase) is responsible for the conversion of dopamine to norepinephrine. It may also catalyze the β-hydroxylation of several other phenylethylamine derivatives, such as tyramine. The molecule of DBH contains two copper ions, and its activity is dependent upon the presence of molecular oxygen and ascorbic

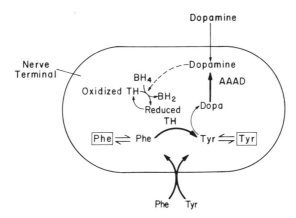

Figure 18.4 A schematic conceptualization of dopamine biosynthesis from L-tyrosine and L-phenylalanine by synaptosomes. Newly transported Phe is preferentially converted to Tyr prior to mixing with the endogenous intracellular Phe pool (indicated by a box). Likewise, Tyr, whether transported from the medium or formed from Phe, is assumed to be preferentially converted to DOPA prior to mixing with intracellular Tyr (box). This conversion of Tyr to DOPA (light arrow) is believed to be the rate-limiting step in the entire sequence of steps (others indicated by heavy arrows) by which extracellular Phe and Tyr are ultimately converted to dopamine. Dopamine (DA) can regulate this step through feedback inhibition (dotted arrows) [from G. Kapatos and M. Zigmond, *J. Neurochem.* 28:1109 (1977); © 1977 by Pergamon Press].

acid as a cofactor. The conversion of dopamine to norepinephrine is stimulated by ATP and the presence of acetylcholine (Laduron, 1975; Karahasanoglu *et al.*, 1976). *In vivo,* DBH activity is controlled by heat-labile endogenous inhibitors, which have been detected in most tissues.

DBH is synthesized in the nerve cell bodies and transported along the axons by rapid axoplasmic flow (Wooten, 1973). It is also transported back, by a retrograde process, in an inactive form (Fillenz *et al.*, 1976). Still, it is the nerve endings that possess the highest concentration of the enzyme. DBH is not present in dopaminergic neurons, and its activity and localization in the CNS parallel the local concentration of norepinephrine.

Norepinephrine was first isolated and identified by von Euler (1946) in the peripheral sympathetic nervous system. But, it was not until 1954 that Vogt was able to convincingly demonstrate its presence in the brain.

An increase in nervous activity stimulates the synthesis of norepinephrine, although a previously high level of norepinephrine can prevent this increase. Also, potassium ions, at least *in vitro,* are known to similarly activate its synthesis (Harris and Roth, 1971). The post-stimulatory increase in norepinephrine production can be blocked by puromycin and cycloheximide, antibiotics that inhibit protein synthesis. This may indicate that such an increase depends upon an induced synthesis of the relevant enzymes. Actinomycin D, which blocks the production of new ribonucleic acids, has the same effect.

Newly synthesized norepinephrine appears to be released preferentially from the nerve endings. It is in a constant state of flux, with a turnover that

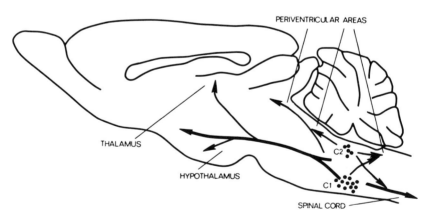

Figure 18.5 Sagittal section of rat brain showing PNMT-containing cell groups (C_1 and C_2) and hypothetical adrenergic connections [from T. Hokfelt, K. Fuxe, M. Goldstein, Ö. Johansson, *Brain Res.* 66:235 (1974); © 1974 by Elseier/North-Holland Biomedical Press].

is highest in the cerebellum and lowest in the hypothalamus. The turnover can be altered by sleep and a variety of stressful factors.

The third major monoaminergic neurotransmitter, epinephrine (adrenaline), is generated by the methylation of norepinephrine by phenylethanolamine-*N*-methyl transferase (*S*-adenosylmethionine: phenylethanolamine-*N*-methyl transferase (PNMT) (for review see Beart, 1979). Contrary to previously held beliefs, enzymatic epinephrine synthesis is present in the brain (Pohorecky *et al.*, 1969), albeit at a concentration that is less than 5% of the norepinephrine level. Neurons containing PNMT and epinephrine have been localized in the ventrolateral reticular formation of the rostral medulla oblongata and in a group of cells in close proximity to the fourth ventricle (Fig. 18.5). The axon terminals of these neuronal groups are in various nuclei of the brain stem and the spinal cord (Reid *et al.*, 1975).

There appears to be an overall association between the firing rate of the neurons and catecholamine synthesis. Underlying this effect are shifts in the production and activity of the catecholamine-synthesizing enzymes. But, catecholamine synthesis is also under the control of general trophic substances, including nerve growth factor, hypothalamic releasing factors [such as thyrotropin releasing hormone (TRH) and melanocyte inhibitory factor (MIF)], pituitary hormones [such as ACTH], sex hormones and adrenocortical hormones.

Genetic or strain differences in catecholamine synthesis have been noted. Different inbred strains of mice possess various inherited patterns of tyrosine hydroxylase and phenylethanolamine-*N*-methyltransferase, both in the brain and in the peripheral sympathetic system. The genetic differences in the level of TH can be high, up to four-fold. This could be important for various forms of behavioral control.

CATECHOLAMINE STORAGE, RELEASE AND INACTIVATION

Catecholamine synthesis can take place either in the nerve ending region or in the nerve cell body. Catecholamines that are produced in the cell body are transported inside granular synaptic vesicles along the axon to the terminals. The life span of these vesicles is about 25 days (in the rat brain), but can range up to 70 days (in the cat). The turnover rate of the catecholamines is much faster, less than 24 hours, and indicates that after synaptic vesicles discharge the neurotransmitter, they remain in the nerve ending and possibly function further. *In vitro*, the amount of neurotransmitter release has been calculated to be an exponential function of the actual concentration of catecholamines in the synaptic cleft (Baumann and Koella, 1980). And, the presence of the synaptic membrane is necessary for the release of catecholamines from synaptic vesicles (Takeda and Tanaka, 1979).

The regulation of the amount of neurotransmitter that is released probably also depends upon presynaptic receptors. And, in some areas this control may be rather complex. Accordingly, Ennis *et al.* (1981) have described a serotonergic presynaptic control of dopamine release in the striatum.

In the central nervous system, catecholamines are not only liberated from the nerve endings, but also from cell-soma membranes (Suetake *et al.*, 1981) and from dendrites. It now appears that this dendritic release is

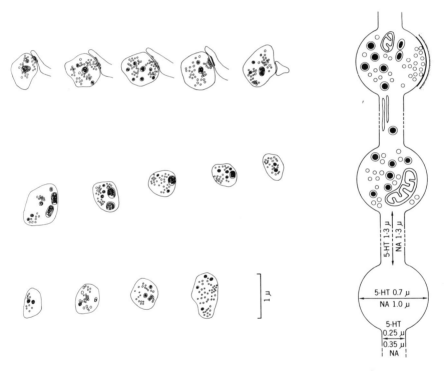

Figure 18.6 Schematized representation of noradrenergic and serotonergic axons in rat cerebral cortex. On the left, three 5-HT-containing varicosities, probably belonging to to the same fiber, have been outlined as observed in five adjacent thin sections. The drawing on the right is based on the examination of more than 2000 labeled varicosities and depicts the general configuration and ultrastructural content of both noradrenaline (NA)- and 5-HT-containing axon terminals. The varicosities invariably contain several large granular vesicles (mean number estimated at seven) associated with clear, agranular 'synaptic' vesicles. Only a small proportion appears to be engaged in morphologically defined synaptic relationships [from A. Beaudet, L. Descarries, *Neuroscience* 3:851 (1978); © 1978 by Pergamon Press Ltd.].

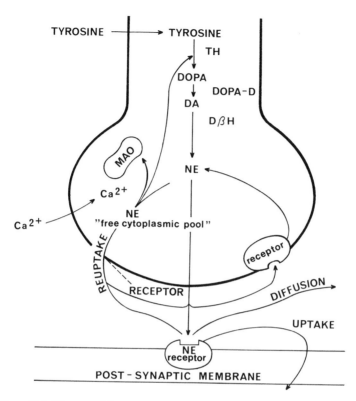

Figure 18.7 Diagram of the metabolic processes in the catecholaminergic nerve endings.

involved in the self-regulation of dopaminergic cells in substantia nigra (for review see Cheramy *et al.*, 1981). The catecholamines are also stored in varicosities along the nerve fibers (Fig. 18.6), some of which probably have restricted synaptic contacts with adjoining neurons (Olschowka *et al.*, 1981). During the stimulation of these fibers, the varicosities release their neurotransmitter in amounts that appear to be governed by the presence of free calcium ions, probably in relation to the gangliosides (Cumar *et al.*, 1978). The transmitter may then bind to glial or neuronal membrane receptors, thereby inducing a variety of associated extrasynaptic metabolic events, beginning with the activation of adenylate cyclase.

After the catecholamines are released from the nerve endings and varicosities and react with the postsynaptic receptors (Fig. 18.7), they are inactivated by transport back into the nerve endings (Bogdanski and Brodie, 1969). This re-uptake is critical to their inactivation and occurs via the activity of specific, sodium dependent transport systems. At least two independent transport systems are present here: one localized in the neuronal membrane and the other present in the synaptic vesicles ("amine pump"). The process of re-uptake into the nerve endings requires the activity of Na^+, K^+ - dependent ATPase and may be inhibited by the presence of ouabain, as well as by tricyclic antidepressants. The second step, a reentry into the synaptic vesicles, can be inhibited by reserpine. The affinity of this system for catecholamines depends upon the functional state of the nervous tissue. During conditions of intense nervous stimulation, including fighting or electroconvulsive shock, it decreases (Welch *et al.*, 1974). The decrement

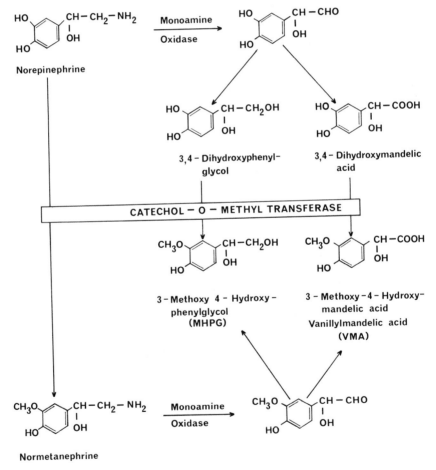

Figure 18.8 Catabolism of norepinephrine.

means that catecholamines remain free for longer periods of time. Consequently, they could facilitate alerting during active stress and emergencies. The non-neuronal cells in the brain are also able to take up catecholamines, but their system lacks stereospecificity, so that all catecholamines are equally good substrates.

The process of reuptake is followed by intracellular degradation. This process can proceed by one of two interlocking pathways (Fig. 18.8). The oxidative deamination of norepinephrine by monoamine oxidase (MAO) generates the compound 3,4–dihydroxyphenylglycolaldehyde. This is further broken down to either 3,4–dihydroxyphenylglycol (DOPEG) under the control of alcohol dehydrogenase, or to 3,4-dihydroxy-D-mandelic acid (DOMA) by aldehyde dehydrogenase. DOMA may then be methylated by the action of catechol-O-methyltransferase (COMT) to the end-product 3-methoxy-4-hydroxymandelic acid (vanillylmandelic acid or VMA). In addition to catalyzing the oxidative deamination of norepinephrine, monoamine oxidase (monoamine: oxidoreductase) is also able to mediate similar reactions using dopamine, tyramine, tryptamine and serotonin as substrates.

The second pathway involves the direct methylation of NE by COMT to form 4-hydroxy-3–methoxyphenylethanolamine (normetanephrine) which can then be deaminated and metabolized to either VMA or to 4-hydroxy-3–methoxyphenylglycol (MOPEG). Comparatively little is known about the fate of DOPEG and MOPEG.

The catabolism of dopamine is also rather complex (for review see Zumstein *et al.*, 1981). The major metabolites are homovanillic acid (3-methoxy-4–hydroxyphenylacetic acid) and 3-methoxy-4–hydroxyphenyllactic acid, in addition to 3,4–dihydroxyphenylacetic acid (DOPAC).

Monoamine oxidase is localized in the outer mitochondrial membrane, nuclear envelope, and endoplasmic reticulum. Two main forms have been reported, MAO-A and MAO-B. There is an MAO-C form, but it does not appear to be present in the brain (Toyoshima *et al.*, 1979). The A and B forms differ in their substrate specificity. MAO-A inactivates norepinephrine and, in many tissues, serotonin; MAO-B specifically uses phenylethylamine as its substrate. Dopamine, together with tyramine and octopamine, is inactivated by both A and B forms. These two types also differ in their sensitivity to various pharmacological inhibitors. The A form, for instance, is more affected by clorgyline and harmaline (for review see Murphy, 1978).

There is a direct association between MAO activity and the presence of membrane phospholipids. In lipid-depleted brain mitochondrial preparations, phosphatidylinositol was able to stimulate MAO-A activity 80% over that in the originally intact mitochondria (Huang and Faulkner, 1981). Although they did not have as dramatic an influence upon the A form, other negatively charged phospholipids were at least partially able to re-establish

MAO-A or B activity. However, Buckman *et al.* (1982) report the presence of a specific inhibition of MAO-B, which was associated with an incorporation of phosphatidylserine into the mitochondrial membranes.

This classification of MAO into distinct species based upon disparities in their substrate specificities and responsiveness to pharmacological agents should be tempered with a cautionary note. It may just be that the observed differences are attributable to multiple binding sites on the same molecular entity (Schurr, 1982).

In the brain, MAO can be principally found in the presynaptic portion of the synaptosomes. It not only degrades catecholamines entering the cytoplasm by reuptake, but also metabolizes any that leak from the synaptic vesicles. Some MAO activity is localized in non-neuronal cells of the CNS, which suggests that these cells are also involved in inactivation of catecholamines (Muller and DaLage, 1977).

In addition to an influence upon catecholamine synthesis, functional requirements are able to alter the activity of the degradative pathways. Environmental stress in newborn rats, for example, increases MAO activity in the midbrain, cerebral cortex, cerebellum, hypothalamus and hippocampus (Maura *et al.*, 1978). The pharmacological inhibition of monoamine oxidase increases the level of catecholamines. Since this has an antidepressant effect, inhibitors of monoamine oxidase, such as pargyline, tranylcypromine and isocarboxazid, have been used in psychiatry for the treatment of severe depression.

As mentioned above, the products of MAO activity are further metabolized by methoxylation. The reaction is catalyzed by catechol-*O*-methyltransferase (COMT) and requires *S*-adenosylmethionine as a methyl donor. The metabolism of catecholamines by COMT appears to principally take place outside the nerve terminals, methylating that norepinephrine which is released from the nerve ending and not inactivated by reuptake (Axelrod, 1966).

Without first being subjected to oxidation and methylation, most catecholamines are unable to leave the central nervous system. When they are metabolized in this way, they are transported from the brain by a relatively specific, saturable, transport system. Some catabolites enter the cerebrospinal fluid, where a fluctuation in their level accompanies different CNS functional states.

One additional catabolic process is dehydroxylation, the removal of one of the hydroxyl groups bound to the benzene ring. The products of this type of reaction are either meta- or para-tyramine. Also, small quantities dopamine may leave the brain in an unmetabolized form or be transformed via as yet unknown metabolic pathways (Westerink, 1979).

α- AND β-ADRENERGIC RECEPTORS

In 1948, Ahlquist distinguished two types of catecholamine receptors. These receptors, simply termed α and β, exhibit a differential responsiveness to the catecholamine neurotransmitters. Norepinephrine typically excites only the α receptors, whereas epinephrine is able to excite both α and β types. Activation of the α receptors causes a depolarization of the cellular membrane, generating a fast excitatory postsynaptic potential. In contrast, β receptors cause a hyperpolarization of the cells, because the increase in metabolism provides the cell with more energy which is used for the active extrusion of sodium ions from the interior. Two types of α receptors (α_1 and α_2) have been pharmacologically differentiated. And, recent evidence suggests that multiple forms of the β receptor may also exist, although this issue is still unresolved (Leclerc et al., 1981).

The membrane receptors for catecholamines typically display the characteristics of high molecular weight glycoproteins. There is a finite, but not fixed, number of receptors in the cellular membrane. They are continuously formed and degraded. The number of β-adrenergic receptors also fluctuates during different functional states. This is probably one of the contributing mechanisms which serves to adjust the excitability of the postsynaptic cell. It is likely that this process involves both α and β receptors. Thus, the regulatory influence of thyroid hormones upon α_1-receptors in the cerebral cortex includes a elevation in receptor number (Gross et al., 1981; Reisine, 1981). Similarly, an injection of 6-hydroxydopamine (6-OHDA), which selectively destroys catecholaminergic neurons, causes an increase in the density of β-adrenergic receptors in the rat cerebral cortex. This increase may be involved in the 6-OHDA-induced supersensitivity of central noradrenergic synapses. McNamara (1978) also drew an association between the consequences of regular, daily electrical amygdaloid stimulation, known as "kindling", and a selective reduction of β-adrenergic receptor activity in both the stimulated and contralateral amygdaloid regions. Age has also been found to decrease the number of receptors in the brain (Misra, 1980).

In addition to changes in the number of receptors, the affinity of adrenergic receptors to their ligands can be altered. Several affinity states have been described for both α and β receptors. Sodium ions and guanine nucleotides, as well as several divalent cations, are able to influence this binding (Michel et al., 1980; Glossman et al., 1980). One regulatory factor may be the methylation of membrane phospholipids. Stimulation of the β-adrenergic receptors has been reported to augment methylation and induce the synthesis of phosphatidyl-N-monomethylethanolamine by methyltransferase I. This enhances the ability of the β-adrenergic receptor to couple with adenylate cyclase (Strittmatter *et al.*, 1981).

The existence of a relationship between catecholamine synthesis and the activity of monoaminergic neurons has already been mentioned. For some time, the application of adrenergic receptor blockers has been known to affect the production and turnover of catecholamines. The data suggest the operation of one or more feedback mechanisms that respond to the receptor blockade. Chlorpromazine and other like α-adrenergic blockers enhance both the synthesis and the release of norepinephrine (Anden *et al.*, 1964; Da Prada and Pletscher, 1966). And, the reduction of both processes by the α-adrenergic stimulating agent, clonidine, corroborated the idea of a receptor-mediated regulation of catecholamine metabolism.

One of the interesting contributions to this issue of feedback regulation has been the discovery that there exist catecholaminergic receptors on presynaptic nerve terminals that have been termed autoreceptors. Alpha-adrenergic receptors are present on all norepinephrinergic nerve endings, and they have been found to inhibit the release of the neurotransmitter (Dismukes *et al.*, 1977). This presynaptic transmitter action has been unequivocally demonstrated only for norepinephrine, although the existence of dopamine autoreceptors has often been accepted as well. The nature of the release inhibition is not known, but it is possible that the α and β receptors block a calcium-dependent exocytotic release mechanism (Starke and Endo, 1976).

The modulation of neurotransmitter synthesis and release by a specific presynaptic receptor system appears to be one of the components which regulate the efficacy of the synapse. The system is likely complex and could involve not only an autoregulation by the transmitter in question, but also contributions from other neurotransmitters, hormones or peptides such as acetylcholine, the prostaglandins, and angiotensin (Starke, 1980).

Extended treatments with drugs as chlorpromazine, imipramine (Schultz, 1976), desimipramine, and iprindole (Vetulani *et al.*, 1976) diminish the sensitivity of the β-adrenergic receptors, as measured by a change in the ability to stimulate cAMP synthesis. In addition, such treatments cause a decrement in the number of receptors (Molinoff *et al.*, 1978). But, the actual mechanisms responsible for this loss in sensitivity are still not clearly understood.

By using cultures of a mutant mouse cell line deficient in cAMP production, Shear *et al.* (1976) determined that a stimulation-induced subsensitive state did correlate with a loss in β-adrenergic receptors and alterations in the β-receptor-adenylate cyclase complex. There was no involvement of cAMP-dependent protein kinases. Cells that contained β-receptors, but were deficient in adenylate cyclase, did not undergo a drop in receptor number following the application of isoproterenol, a β-adrenergic agonist which is not subject to presynaptic reuptake mechanisms.

The overall situation, however, appears to be more complex, since the results of experimentation with different cell lines have been contradictory (Browning *et al.*, 1976; Terasaki *et al.*, 1978). Various types of β-receptor-associated subsensitivity could exist (Remold-O'Donnell, 1974; Terasaki *et al.*, 1978) with each dependent upon a different mechanism.

DOPAMINERGIC RECEPTORS

Dopaminergic receptors in the central nervous system are independent entities, distinct from α- and β-adrenergic receptors. Struyker Boudier et al. (1974) have recognized two types of dopaminergic receptors, the excitation-mediating (DE) and the inhibition-mediating (DI) forms. DE receptors are selectively activated by neuroleptics, such as haloperidol, while DI receptors are selectively inhibited by the α-adrenergic blocker, ergometrine, an ergot alkaloid.

The receptors binding dopamine are most concentrated in the caudate nucleus, putamen, and olfactory tubercle, but they have been detected in the cerebral cortex, thalamus, hippocampus, hypothalamus and cerebellum. In addition, some dopamine binding has been found in the amygdala and midbrain (Snyder *et al.*, 1975).

The ability of many neurotransmitter- and hormone-stimulated receptors to activate adenylate cyclase has already been discussed in Chapter 15. Kebabian (1979) recognized two types of dopaminergic receptors based upon their relationship to adenylate cyclase. Type D_1 is linked to the enzyme, while D_2 is either independent of it, or functions to suppress adenylate cyclase activity directly or indirectly, thereby lowering cAMP formation (Stoof and Kebabian, 1981). Kebabian and Calne (1979) believe that further subcategories of the D_1 and D_2 receptors can be identified which differ in their sensitivities to dopamine and its various antagonists. As in any emerging area of research, where a number of laboratories are engaged in similar work, the terminology has not yet become unified. Cools (1981), for example, has reported finding three dopamine receptors and has labeled them DAi, DAe, and DAi/e. Perhaps at this time, it would be useful to adopt Creese's (1982) proposal that there are three classes of dopamine-binding sites, termed D1, D2 and D3. The D3 designation would be used to identify those sites which are involved in the autoregulation of dopaminergic neurons.

ATP and guanine nucleotides are involved in the regulation of adenylate cyclase sensitivity to dopamine. This effect is mediated by a guanine nucleotide-binding regulatory factor (Chapter 15). When the receptor is stimulated, it likely becomes coupled to this factor. The event is associated with a loss of bound GDP and a binding of GTP (Anand-Srivastava and Johnson, 1980). This binding frees the receptor, and N-protein charged with GTP then activates the catalytic moiety of adenylate cyclase (for review see Lefkowitz and Hoffmann, 1980). In fact, the added presence of GTP is able to restore the ability of β-adrenergic agonists to stimulate adenylate cyclase in a system previously rendered "subsensitive" by an extended exposure of the β-receptors to the agonists (Rodbell *et al.*, 1975; Williams and Lefkowitz, 1978). Similar effects of GTP have been observed following induced dopamine receptor subsensitivity (Creese and Snyder, 1978).

This guanine nucleotide regulatory mechanism, by altering the receptor binding capacity, could adjust the sensitivity of the cell to the transmitter. And, the system may be subject to modification by such things as denervation, electroconvulsive treatment, hormones, and the process of aging.

The functioning of this system depends upon alterations in receptor density (Fuxe *et al.*, 1981) and the presence of membrane phospholipids (Calderini *et al.*, 1981). It is adversely affected by treatment with phospholipases A_2 and C, and this loss in activity can be partially restored by subsequent provisions of membrane lipids or purified phospholipids (Levey, 1971; Anand-Srivastava and Johnson, 1981). It may be that these phospholipids serve as the intermediary between the receptor and the transducing regulatory protein elements of the cyclase system.

EFFECTS OF CATECHOLAMINES ON NEURONS

The principal action of norepinephrine on neurons is its depression of the neuronal firing rate, by which it is able to modify the response of the cell to other neurotransmitters (for review see Woodward *et al.*, 1979). The effect is a consequence of a hyperpolarization of the neuronal membrane without a corresponding change in the membrane resistance. The hyperpolarization results from a decrease in the resting membrane conductances to sodium and potassium ions (Marshall and Engberg, 1979, in spinal motoneurons). The voltage-sensitive calcium current is also antagonized (Horn and McAfee, 1979). These responses are relatively slow, lasting up to 120 seconds (Reader *et al.*, 1979). Such a depression of the firing rate has been found in many areas of the brain, including the cerebral cortex, hippocampus, cerebellum, and spinal cord.

Thus, norepinephrine in the central nervous system quite often acts more as a neuromodulator than as a neurotransmitter. The term neuromodulation is at present purely descriptive, and in many systems the mechanisms by which it operates are unknown. However, it adequately describes the effects of various chemicals on neurons which cannot be clearly and unequivocally attributed to synaptic transmitter actions. Reader *et al.* (1979) explain this modulatory action by an effect upon intracellular cyclic nucleotides. The balance between the level of cyclic AMP and cyclic GMP is altered by slow-acting biogenic amines, and this is believed to affect the excitability of the neurons.

The norephinephrine effects on receptors are further modified by intrinsic modulators. These modulators are glycoproteins that possess a high binding capacity for norepinephrine and may cause a hypersensitivity of the neural structures (Lee, 1974). Some modulators have also been noted to have an inhibitory action (Hollett, 1974).

Catecholamines, acetylcholine, and serotonin can additionally be found in the dendrites of the neurons. The enzymes synthesizing these neurotransmitters are present near the postsynaptic area of the synapse. Therefore, the neurotransmitters are probably also released from the dendrites toward the synaptic endings, and function to reverse the communication between postsynaptic and presynaptic areas of the synapses (Hattori *et al.*, 1979). This mechanism further complicates the already complex issue of interneuronal communication within the central nervous system.

CATECHOLAMINERGIC NEUROANATOMY

Nerve cell bodies themselves contain only small amounts of catecholamines. The major portion of the catecholamines is located in synapses and presynaptic structures, in addition to quantities in varicosities and arborizations of the axons. They are stored mostly in synaptic vesicles, although in the striatum, dopamine is free in the synaptosomal cytoplasm.

The brain appears to contain only a small number of catecholaminergic neurons which are concentrated in a few discrete neuronal groups. The cell groups give rise to ascending and descending catecholaminergic pathways and are predominately found in the medulla, pons and mesencephalon (for review see Ungerstedt, 1973).

The dopaminergic system is more discrete and more highly localized than the other monoamine nerve fiber systems. Long dopaminergic fibers arise from cell bodies in the vicinity of the substantia nigra and from its zona compacta, eventually terminating in areas as the striatum, hippocampus, subthalamic nucleus, and olfactory tubercule (Fig. 18.9). In the terminology of Dahlstrom and Fuxe (1965), this is the A8, A9 and A10 group of neurons. Stimulation of this pathway will alter, for example, the firing rates of striatal neurons.

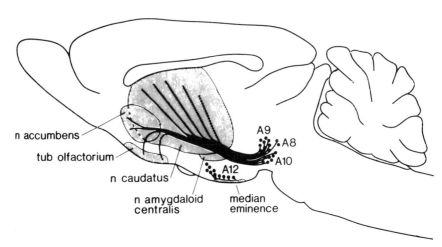

Figure 18.9 The distribution of dopamine-containing neurons in the rat brain [from U. Ungerstedt, *Acta Physiol. Scand.* Suppl. 367:1 (1971); © 1971 by Acta Physiologica Scandinavica].

Large groups of dopamine-producing cell bodies are also found in other parts of the substantia nigra and in the tegmental areas adjacent to it. Two pathways originate in this region: the mesolimbic fibers (to nucleus accumbens and olfactory tubercle) and the nigrostriatal tract (through the lateral hypothalamus into the internal capsule and striatum) (Fig. 18.10). Some other parts of the brain contain dopaminergic nerve endings as well, namely the central amygdaloid nucleus, cerebral cortex, stria terminalis, and limbic cortex.

The short dopaminergic fibers that both originate and terminate in the zona compacta of the substantia nigra may influence the activity of the nigrostriatal pathways. They are likely a part of a nigrostriatal feedback loop. Dopamine here probably modulates the release of GABA or substance P from terminals afferent to the substantia nigra (Phillipson *et al.*, 1977). Other dopaminergic fibers originate from globus pallidus and the tail of the caudate.

The systems containing norepinephrine are more complex. There are at least five groups of neurons in the medulla and pons that send ascending fibers to various areas of the brain and descending fibers to the spinal cord. These groups of noradrenergic medullar nuclei supply several nuclei of the cranial nerves, pontine reticular formation and spinal cord. Ascending fibers join the medial forebrain bundle and reach the mesencephalon and lateral and preoptic areas of the hypothalamus (Fig. 18.11). This is the ventral pathway. The dorsal noradrenergic pathway originates from the locus coeruleus and extends to the cerebral and cerebellar cortex and to various structures from the motor nucleus of the vagus to the thalamus and hippocampus. Thus, each neuron of the locus coeruleus has extensive ramifications within the central nervous system, suggesting that this system may be involved in some form of global regulation. In the cerebral cortex, these fibers are distributed throughout all six layers. About 10% of nerve endings appear to be associated with the presence of a synapse. A further 10% include some synaptic features. However, 80% of the endings exhibit no such relationships (Itakura *et al.*, 1981). The axons take a tangential course and, consequently, may be involved in the innervation of wide areas of neocortex (Morrison *et al.*, 1981).

In the thalamus, where some norepinephrine-containing fibers also terminate, norepinephrine is high in the pulvinar of the left side and in the somatosensory input areas of the right side. These differences could reflect hemispheric specialization of the brain (Oke *et al.*, 1978).

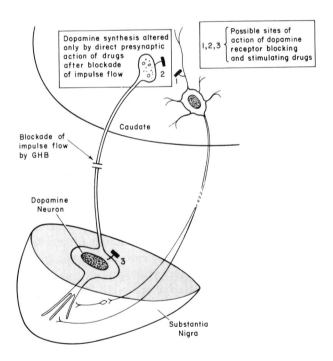

Figure 18.10 Diagrammatic representation of the nigro-neostriatal dopaminergic pathway and the hypothesized striato-nigral feedback loop. Numbers indicate sites of proposed dopamine receptors on the (1) post- and (2) pre-synaptic side of the dopamine synapse and on the (3) cell body [from J. Walter and R.H. Roth, *Naunyn-Schmiedeberg's Arch. Pharmacol.* 296:5 (1976); © 1976 by Springer Verlag].

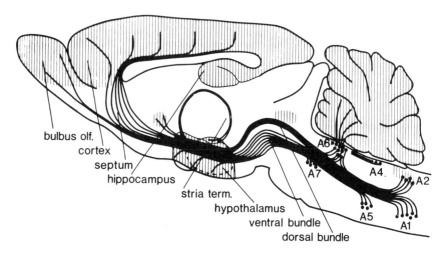

Figure 18.11 Sagittal projection of the ascending norepinephrinergic pathways [from U. Ungerstedt, *Acta Physiol. Scand.* 62, suppl. 232: 1 (1971); © 1971 by Acta Physiologica Scandinavica].

Some norepinephrinergic fibers also reach the raphe nuclei, especially the raphe dorsalis, where the serotonergic nerve fibers originate. And, in turn, fibers from the raphe nuclei pass back toward the locus coeruleus (Jouvet, 1972). The dorsal raphe nucleus may, therefore, also play an important role in the brainstem modulation of neural function.

In the cerebral cortex, the fibers containing norepinephrine, dopamine, and serotonin form widespread networks. Dopamine - containing nerve terminals originate from rostral mesencephalic nerve cell groups and distribute themselves in deep layers of some restricted cortical areas. Norepinephrinergic fibers originate from the locus coeruleus and are associated with all areas of the cortex. Serotonin-containing fibers arrive from the mesencephalic raphe nuclei, dorsalis and centralis superior and can be found in the superficial layers of the cortex.

The varicosities within the catecholaminergic fibers have several large granular vesicles that contain the neurotransmitter. These fibers are nonmyelinated, and the varicosities are distributed along them at distances of 1-3 micrometers between them. In the presence of calcium ions, the varicosities may release their biogenic amines, either through synaptic connections with adjacent neurons, or perhaps into the cortical extracellular space (Orrego and Miranda, 1977). These neurotransmitters, particularly norepinephrine and serotonin, could then diffuse into larger areas of the cortex where they would be able to influence neuronal (and glial) activity for relatively long periods of time, seconds or even minutes. They might then depress the excitatory action of other neurotransmitters, such as acetylcholine. In such case, norepinephrine and serotonin would act as neuromodulators. However, it must be stressed that this neuromodulatory action is just a possibility. As of yet, there is no compelling evidence that the release of neurotransmitter from the varicosities is into the extracellular space and not at synaptic regions, as suggested by Olschowka *et al.* (1981).

ACTIONS OF CATECHOLAMINERGIC SYSTEMS

Most attempts to explain the functions of the catecholaminergic systems (particularly those associated with the locus coeruleus) have ascribed to them a general arousal function. Accordingly, the firing of neurons in the locus coeruleus varies with the phases of sleep, being highest during periods of wakefulness (Aston-Jones and Bloom, 1981). This cannot be directly related to the known hyperpolarizing and inhibitory actions of norepinephrine. Perhaps the main role of these systems is the inhibition of inhibitory neurons. Accordingly, Phillis and Kostopoulos (1977) reported that locus coeruleus stimulation causes an inhibition of many neurons in the cerebral cortex, hippocampus and cerebellar cortex. Most of the evidence for such an interpretation comes from the study of various drugs used for the treatment of depression. Other theories have postulated that the locus coeruleus fibers are responsible for the reinforcement and reward functions originally studied by the local stimulation and self-stimulation of various brain areas. Monoaminergic fibers may, therefore, be involved in the pleasure-reward system spread through several areas of the brain stem. The dorsal noradrenergic bundle and the dopaminergic neurons (but not the ventral noradrenergic bundle) might facilitate an organism's response toward biologically significant features of the environment, such as food, and ensure the reinforcement of previously successful behavioral responses (Crow, 1973). Activation of the dopamine system, on the other hand, causes an increase in motor activity, possibly also in connection with the incentive aspects of the environment.

Norepinephrine and dopamine are critical in self-stimulation behavior (for review see Wise, 1978). The reinforcing stimulation activates catecholaminergic pathways, while drugs that interfere with catecholamine synthesis, storage, and receptor function attenuate it. Also, dopamine agonists increase the rate of responding for reward, as opposed to dopamine antagonists, which cause a decrement (Wauquier and Niemegeers, 1972). It seems that both DE and DI receptors are involved in the mediation of this reinforcing effect (Katz, 1979).

However, the involvement of these neurotransmitters in the reward system is not all that clear-cut. Corbett *et al.* (1977) found that the dorsal noradrenergic bundle is not crucial to intracranial self-stimulation. The locus coeruleus also lacks the multiple sensory input necessary for a selective process of reward. In the rat, the locus coeruleus contains only about 1500 neurons, a number which would seem anatomically insufficient for such a function (Margules and Margules, 1973).

The hypothalamus is quite rich in catecholaminergic innervation, and varicosities along the nerve fibers are present in large numbers (Cheung and Sladek, 1975). This is especially true for the anterior periventricular nucleus. Here, the catecholamines play an important role in regulating the secretion of follicle stimulating hormone, luteinizing hormone and prolactin. This suggests, then, that they are associated with the control of maternal behavior. Lesions of the dorsal noradrenergic fiber system, for example, disrupt the onset of maternal behavior in primiparous rats (Steele *et al.*, 1979).

The catecholamines have also been found to have some connection with the stress response, which is at least partly mediated by the hypothalamus. When this area is stimulated, its norepinephrine level drops. The effect has been reported for stress attributed to various factors, including injury, fighting, and running. This may later lead to an increased synthesis of norepinephrine in the hypothalamus, but not necessarily in other brain areas (Stone, 1973).

During certain aggressive behaviors, there are shifts in catecholamine levels. In rodents, fighting between males is accompanied by such a change that is very much dependent upon the species involved. The norepinephrine level in mice, for example, decreases, whereas in rats it increases. Other types of aggression, such as that which is fear or shock-induced, territorial, or maternal, may also be linked to the metabolism of the catecholamines, although their involvement is less clear. There are additionally changes in the turnover of serotonin and acetylcholine, but again these are also dependent upon the type of aggression and the animal species (see review by Daruna, 1978).

In the hypothalamus, norepinephrine is involved in feeding behavior. As an experimental rat consumes food pellets, there occurs a release of norepinephrine and its *O*-methylated metabolites (McCaleb *et al.*, 1975). Even the observation of another animal eating or the odor of food elicits a similar response (Myers *et al.*, 1979). Dopamine in the ascending dopaminergic fibers is also an important factor in the control of eating. Lesioning these fibers with 6-hydroxydopamine interferes with the appearance of the hyperphagia syndrome following damage to the ventromedial hypothalamic area. Neurons involved in feeding motivation are localized in substantia nigra. Their firing is dependent upon the nutritional demands of the organism and can be suppressed by glucose in a concentration similar to that produced by an ingested meal (Saller and Chiodo, 1980).

One of the most important actions of catecholamines is their association with motor activity. Increased motor activity may be elicited by L-DOPA or amphetamines, and a chronic deprivation of dopaminergic receptors by a continuous stimulation with dopamine results in a supersensitivity of these receptors, particularly in response to the dopaminergic agonists. A supersensitivity of dopamine-sensitive adenylate cyclase has also been observed. The motor effect involves the activity of the nigrostriatal tract.

While dopamine is of basic importance to locomotor activity, norepinephrine facilitates and modifies it. In other words, norepinephrine receptor stimulation enhances the locomotor responses that are attributable to dopamine. The dopaminergic involvement in this control of motility is mediated by at least two areas of the brain, the basal ganglia and periaqueductal gray. Here, it is involved in the control of rotational behavior, turning around and circus movements. Exploratory activity can also be altered by lesions of the dorsal noradrenergic bundle. The application of 6-hydroxydopamine to it decreases general activity and the response to novelty (Mason and Fibiger, 1979a).

According to several theories, catecholamines play an important role in the sleep-wakefulness cycle. However, the exact nature of that role is difficult to assess. Both phases of the circadian cycle are influenced by catecholamines and serotonin, as well as by other neurotransmitters. Moreover, there is no simple schematic explanation able to presently account for the appearance and disappearance of the two phases of sleep, slow-wave and rapid eye movement (REM). A widely accepted hypothesis (Dement et al., 1976) postulates that serotonergic neurons, whose cell bodies lie in the midbrain raphe nuclei, induce and maintain the non-REM state. These same circuits are able to trigger REM sleep, which itself is regulated by norepinephrine. But, the tonic and phasic events that occur during the REM phase, such as rapid eye movements, changes in muscle tonus, and heart rate fluctuations, may be mediated by serotoninergic and cholinergic systems. Waking and arousal are also mediated by noradrenergic, serotonergic and cholinergic circuits.

Lesions of serotonergic neurons in the brainstem raphe nuclei in cats and rats cause EEG arousal and discrete damage in rostral and caudal groups of raphe cells, probably through the reduction of forebrain serotonin. On the other hand, lesions in the dorsal noradrenergic bundle increase both REM and non-REM sleep and diminish waking time through reduced forebrain norepinephrine. A general reduction in brain amines by reserpine leads to the loss of both REM and non-REM sleep, although it would be difficult to draw any conclusions from this finding.

An interesting hypothesis by Stern and Morgane (1974) states that REM sleep is responsible for the maintenance of the catecholaminergic system in the brain. Some evidence does exist for this possibility, including the fact that following REM deprivation the responsiveness of the catecholaminergic systems is depressed. Any drugs which enhance catecholaminergic activity can reverse some behavioral deficits that occur after REM deprivation. It could be that the deprivation of REM sleep induces a supersensitivity of dopaminergic receptors (Tufik *et al.*, 1978).

After a careful consideration of the available evidence, Ramm (1979) concluded that the locus coeruleus and the entire catecholaminergic system are not directly involved in the control of REM sleep, and that any influence upon sleep reflects more a general neuromodulatory function of the locus coeruleus neurons. An interesting supplementary piece of evidence on the effect of the locus coeruleus on sleep, wakefulness and alertness has been provided by the morphological examination of its neurons. According to

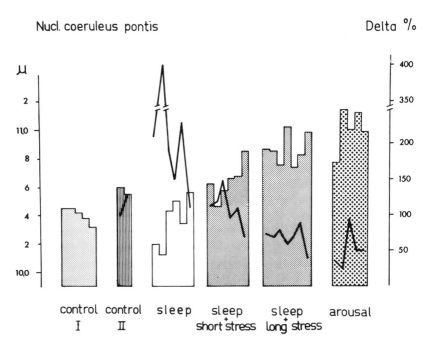

Figure 18.12 A. Histogram of the nucleus diameter of NC cells (in micrometers) in the various animals used for control, sleep, stress-induced sleep resistance, or arousal. The corresponding average delta value for the last 10-min period of the stimulation experiment is indicated in percent by the curve and the corresponding scale on the right [from G. Bubenik and M. Monnier, *Exp. Neurol.* 35:1 (1972); © 1972 by Academic Press, Inc.].

Bubenik and Monnier (1972), the size of the neuronal nucleus can be taken as an index of the state of cellular activity. And, the size of the cell nucleus of these neurons is sensitive to variations in the state of wakefulness. More properly, the nuclear diameter is smaller during sleep, and increases in size during periods of stress (Fig. 18.12).

The general modulatory effect of biogenic amines on the central nervous system has been suggested to influence the mood and the feeling of well-being. Accordingly, the excessive activity or a hypoactivity of the noradrenergic, serotonergic and cholinergic systems is believed by some to contribute to the onset of affective disorders, such as depression. The principal evidence for this position comes from determinations of the physiological and biochemical actions of the mood-altering drugs. These drugs are able to alter the release of biogenic amines from the nerve endings, to delay the inactivation of neurotransmitters, or to modify the sensitivity of the postsynaptic receptors. Reserpine, for example, can cause a depletion of biogenic amines from the nerve endings and induce a psychomotor retardation or even sedation. At the same time, it may also trigger a state of depression. The tricyclic antidepressants react with the presynaptic receptors to inhibit the reuptake of neurotransmitters and consequently prolong transmitter action in the synapse. However, tryptophan and 5-hydroxytryptophan, which accelerate serotonin synthesis, also have an antidepressant action. Electroconvulsive treatments, which can bring improvements in the mood of depressed patients, have been found to increase the sensitivity of monoamine receptors in the mouse brain (Modigh, 1973). This increased sensitivity may depend upon a state of hypocalcemia that is observed after a few (3-5) electroconvulsive treatments (Carman et al., 1977).

The sensitivity of the β-adrenergic receptors decreases in the brain following electroconvulsive treatment (Pandey et al., 1979), and the density of these receptors also drops (Bergstrom and Kellar, 1979). This probably augments the postsynaptic availability of catecholamines for binding to the receptors and eventually, due to feedback inhibition of catecholamine synthesis, the general activation of the norepinphrinergic cerebral cortical system (Gillespie et al., 1979).

The available data on the relationship between neurotransmitters and the affective disorders have generated various hypotheses that attribute these conditions to disruptions in catecholaminergic (Schildkraut, 1965), serotoninergic (Coppen, 1967), or dualistic (Bueno and Himwich, 1967) mechanisms, or to the production of abnormal metabolites (Roberts and Broadley, 1965). While a detailed discussion of the evidence for and against these theories is beyond the scope of this book, a few important points should be mentioned. Any meaningful theory concerning these affective disorders must take into consideration not only the catecholamines or the biogenic amines, but other neurotransmitters and distinct anatomically defined systems as well. When one pharmacosystem is functionally modified, other systems are obviously affected as well and can in turn influence the originally altered system. These changes can particularly hold true for the pharmacological effects of antidepressant, mood-improving or mood-depressing drugs.

There are a few additional effects that are associated with the noradrenergic systems. The locus coeruleus is known to be able to inhibit the cerebellar Purkinje cells and hippocampal pyramidal cells. It can also enhance cardiovascular responsiveness, maintain the orthostatic vascular reflex systems, and suppress the cardiovascular depressor system of central nervous origin. And finally, the bulbo-spinal noradrenergic fibers appear to be involved in a feedback system of pain control (Takagi *et al.*, 1979) which is partly activated by pain and partly by the brain stem antinociceptive opioid systems (Chapter 28).

CATECHOLAMINES AND LEARNING

It has been shown that the parenteral administration of catecholaminergic agonists and antagonists is able to modify the process of learning. Typically, the antagonists interfere with it, while the agonists are facilitating (Dunn, 1980). Thus, a depletion of catecholamines caused by α-methyl-*p*-tyrosine induces an amnesia (Chute *et al.*, 1981) which may be antagonized by increased levels of cAMP. Also, the effects of inhibitors of protein synthesis on learning can be attenuated by catecholaminergic agonists. But, the literature in this area is inconsistent, and the data do not fit any cohesive picture. Thus, according to Gold and van Buskirk (1978), a subcutaneous injection of epinephrine can produce retrograde amnesia. Following training, norepinephrine in the brain temporarily decreases, and Sternberg and Gold (1980) postulate that the drop has an "optimal" value, and any deviation from this optimal decrease would mean poor retention.

Many investigations of the association between catecholamines and the process of learning have suffered, among other things, from the treatment of the catecholaminergic systems as a unit. Expectations were often that the catecholamines and the neurons containing them would all function together, in one direction, during the acquisition and retention of all learned tasks. Realistically, from what is known about these systems, it would be unreasonable to expect this type of action. A better approach would be to study the role of selected parts of the neurotransmitter systems and their functional state during behavioral acquisition.

Probably the most discussed area of the catecholaminergic system, as it relates to learning, has been the locus coeruleus together with the dorsal and ventral noradrenergic bundles (for review see Amaral and Sinnamon, 1977). It has been suggested to play an important role in retaining the memory of events that have survival value. According to Kety (1970), this system is able to identify situations and memories necessary for survival and, in doing so, gives the cerebral cortex a "now print" instruction.

Pettigrew (1978) believes that the noradrenergic system is able to act in opposition to the serotonergic raphe system. Cortical plasticity would then be maintained by a widespread system of monoaminergic fibers that could be activated during the acquisition of new behaviors. The dorsal noradrenergic bundle would be a critical pathway in this schema. A coeruleo-cortical theory of learning has been formulated by Crow (1973), who believes that norepinephrine is released in the cortex as a result of changes in reinforcement and, through the activation of certain synapses, is able to encode experience. According to this theory, the destruction of the locus coeruleus should prevent the acquisition. But, this does not hold true in all learning situations, and rats with depleted levels of brain norepinephrine were even capable of learning a two-way avoidance task more quickly (Mason and Fibiger, 1979).

If there are any effects of the dorsal noradrenergic bundle on learning and memory, they are rather discrete. Mason and Fibiger (1979) and Mason et al. (1979) found that a depletion of brain catecholamines induced a resistance to the extinction of various behavioral tasks. The depletion, however, must be present during acquisition, and the effect can be prevented by adrenalectomy. Mason et al. postulate that a lesion of the dorsal noradrenergic bundle affects fear motivation more than learning itself. And accordingly, the locus coeruleus may influence learning through a change in the reactivity to external stimuli (Segal and Edelson, 1978). Animals with a lesion of the dorsal noradrenergic bundle are presumably unable to ignore redundant information (Lorden et al., 1980) and consequently have deficits in attention.

While the idea that the locus coeruleus and noradrenergic bundles are responsible for learning may have limited support, this system may still participate in some aspects of learning. But, the anatomy of the locus coeruleus and dorsal noradrenergic bundle indicates that this system is not well suited to the mediation of some specific responses. Its role could be modulatory, and, through the augmentation of excitation or inhibition, it could participate in acquisition and retention. Some corroborative evidence on the role of the locus coeruleus has been presented by Pettigrew and Kasamatsu (1978), who studied visual plasticity in young kittens. Monocular deprivation in these animals alters the firing of cells in the lateral geniculate body and visual cortex. When the noradrenergic input is destroyed by 6-hydroxydopamine, the changes in the unit activity of binocular neurons do not take place. Perfusion of the corresponding area of the cortex with norepinephrine restores the plasticity of the cortex. These effects indicate that the noradrenergic fibers facilitate the process, whatever it is, by which changes occur in the patterns of connectivity following visual deprivation. A corresponding influence of noradrenergic fibers upon local functional changes in the cortex has also been detected in adult cats. Here, the occlusion of the eye causes a loss in the response of binocular neurons, but only in the presence of norepinephrine.

There also appears to be a dopaminergic component in learning, particularly for the dopamine-containing nigro-neostriatal bundle. According to Fibiger and Phillips (1966), stimulation of the zona compacta of the substantia nigra impairs the long-term retention of a step-down passive avoidance task. Also, the administration of apomorphine, a direct stimulant of brain dopaminergic receptors, can impair the retention of a passive avoidance task, if administered prior to the acquisition trial (Fernandez-Tome et al., 1979). Nevertheless, it is likely that the substantia nigra is not critical to the process of learning and that dopamine in this area only indirectly modifies the process. Using rhesus monkeys, Brozoski et al. (1979) reported a role in learning for dopaminergic innervation in the dorsolateral frontal cortex. A lesion of this area causes an impairment of spatial delayed alternation performance. The local depletion of dopamine here has the same effect, which can be reversed by the administration of L-DOPA. The results imply that dopamine is involved in the functioning of the cortical field necessary for this particular type of learning.

The involvement of the catecholamines in the learning, retention and recall of a memory trace is probably only one of the components which may vary according to the type of learning. In addition, there may be a role for peripheral catecholamines, since the drug syrosingopine, an analog of reserpine with an almost exclusive peripheral action, causes amnesia for a passive avoidance task, if injected before training (Walsh and Palfai, 1979).

Chapter 19

Serotonergic and Histaminergic Systems

Apart from the catecholamines, the most important of the biogenic amines presumed to have a neurotransmitter function are serotonin and histamine. Although the powerful vasoconstrictive action of serotonin (5-hydroxytryptamine or 5-HT) has been known for many years, it was not until 1964 that serotonergic neurons were first demonstrated in histochemical studies by Dahlstrom and Fuxe. The substance actually occurs widely in nature in both plants and animals. The greatest concentrations in mammals can be found in the enterochromaffin cells of the intestine and in the pineal gland. And, in relation to other organs of the body, the levels of 5-HT in the central nervous system are very low, comprising in man only about 1 to 2% of the whole body content.

SYNTHESIS AND METABOLISM OF SEROTONIN

Since the solubility characteristics of serotonin only permit the passage of small quantities into the brain, most of it must be produced by the CNS itself. The initial substrate for serotonin synthesis is the amino acid trypto-

337

phan, which is actively transported across the blood-brain barrier from the circulation. While the synthetic process actually consumes only about 1% of the total tryptophan in the brain, it is still strongly influenced by tryptophan levels in the blood plasma.

The transport of tryptophan across the blood-brain barrier is the most important initial control step in serotonin synthesis. The mechanism appears to involve the glial cells and is responsive to elevations in the plasma levels of insulin (and consequently carbohydrate intake), which increase tryptophan uptake from the blood. This transport process is also independent of feedback inhibition by serotonin, so that the amount of tryptophan in the diet is capable of influencing serotonin metabolism in the brain. As a result, marked shifts in the dietary content of tryptophan can alter the effectiveness of some psychoactive drugs acting through serotonergic synapses. There is also some evidence that the behavioral state can affect tryptophan uptake (Messing *et al.*, 1956). Restraint stress in rats, for instance, has been observed to increase its level in the brain (Kennett and Joseph, 1981).

There is a regulatory barrier between extracellular brain tryptophan and the intraneuronal serotonin synthetic systems. In the surface membranes of synaptosomes from serotonin - rich areas, there are two tryptophan uptake systems, one with a high and the other with a low affinity. The accumulation of tryptophan in synapses is a process that requires energy and depends on the ratio of potassium to sodium ions in the extracellular fluid. The process has been detected in all brain areas containing serotonergic nerve endings, although its rate characteristics differ in various parts of the brain (Martinet *et al.*, 1979).

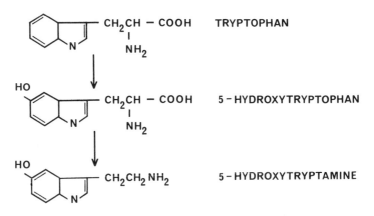

Figure 19.1 Synthesis of serotonin.

The synthesis of serotonin in the brain begins with the hydroxylation of tryptophan to a 5-hydroxy derivative by the action of the enzyme tryptophan hydroxylase (Fig. 19.1). Although this is considered to be the rate-limiting step in serotonin production, the Michaelis constant (Km) for the enzyme is much greater than the normal tryptophan content. This means that the rate of serotonin synthesis is directly tied to the availability of tryptophan.

Tryptophan hydroxylase is present in the nerve cell bodies and nerve endings (Meek and Neckers, 1975). Reports of its subcellular distribution are conflicting, although most assert that it is soluble and present in the nerve ending cytoplasm. While it has been purified, its molecular weight is still uncertain, mainly due to a lack of agreement over whether a molecule of the isolated material is an artificial aggregate created during the purification process, or is actually a single enzyme composed of multiple subunits.

Tryptophan hydroxylase is activated by the passage of nerve impulses through the synapse (Herr et al., 1975). Acute changes in the rate of serotonin synthesis do not depend upon shifts of tryptophan uptake and availability, but rather upon the activation of tryptophan hydroxylase in central serotonergic neurons. Allosteric changes in the shape of the enzyme modify its activity, possibly with the help of a small-molecule regulator. And, a number of substances have been reported to stimulate its activity. Hamon et al. (1978) have, for example, suggested that membrane phospholipids could normally serve as an activator. Tryptophan hydroxylase is activated by phosphorylation (Kuhn et al., 1978), which appears to be independent of the cyclic nucleotides, but requires calcium ions and calmodulin (Yamauchi and Fujisawa, 1979). An increase in serotonin biosynthesis and release that is induced by neural activation is therefore associated with the influx of calcium ions that occurs during the passage of the impulse (Boadle-Biber, 1975).

One of the mechanisms regulating tryptophan hydroxylase activity may involve adrenal corticosteroids (Azmitia and McEwen, 1969). After adrenalectomy, for example, there is a drop in the synthesis of serotonin that can subsequently be restored by injections of corticosterone. Sze et al. (1976) believe that these changes are not due to a direct effect of corticosteroids on tryptophan hydroxylase, but to an effect on tryptophan transport. Glucocorticoids stimulate the uptake of tryptophan by the nerve terminals and, as a consequence, are able to accelerate serotonin synthesis. Glucocorticoids are also necessary as an inductive signal for the synthesis of tryptophan hydroxylase during prenatal and neonatal development.

The product of tryptophan hydroxylase activity is 5-hydroxytryptophan. Its level in the brain is very low, about 5-25 ng/g, indicating that virtually all of it is rapidly metabolized to serotonin soon after it is formed. When administered in high doses to experimental animals, it causes some behavioral changes, such as head-twitching in mice. But, because of the high level of 5-hydroxytryptophan decarboxylase, its effect depends more on an increase in the production of serotonin than on a direct action upon the neurons. Its administration has also been observed to elevate mood in nondepressed human subjects and to stimulate growth hormone and prolactin release.

There are two enzymes able to mediate the decarboxylation of 5-hydroxytryptophan to 5-hydroxytryptamine. One is a highly specific enzyme, 5-hydroxytryptophan decarboxylase, that is present in large quantities in nervous tissue, with an activity that has been reported to be 50 to 100 times greater than that of tryptophan hydroxylase. The other is a nonspecific L-amino acid decarboxylase which is also able to decarboxylate L-DOPA and a variety of other substrates, including tryptophan (Lovenberg *et al.*, 1962).

The product of the decarboxylation of a tryptophan, tryptamine, has been postulated to have a neurotransmitter action. Its concentration parallels the levels of tryptophan in the brain, with the highest levels typically being present in the spinal cord (Fig. 19.2). When transected, tryptaminergic endings in the spinal cord do not disappear, indicating that the source of tryptamine is the nerve cell bodies within the spinal cord. It also suggests

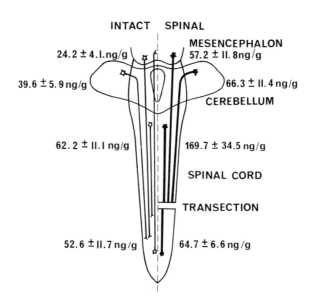

Figure 19.2 A schematic diagram illustrating hypothetical tryptaminergic pathways in the intact (left side) and the chronic spinal (right side) dog [redrawn from W.R. Martin, J.W. Sloan, W.F. Buchwald and T.H. Clements, *Psychopharmacologia* 43:131 (1975); © 1975 by Springer Verlag].

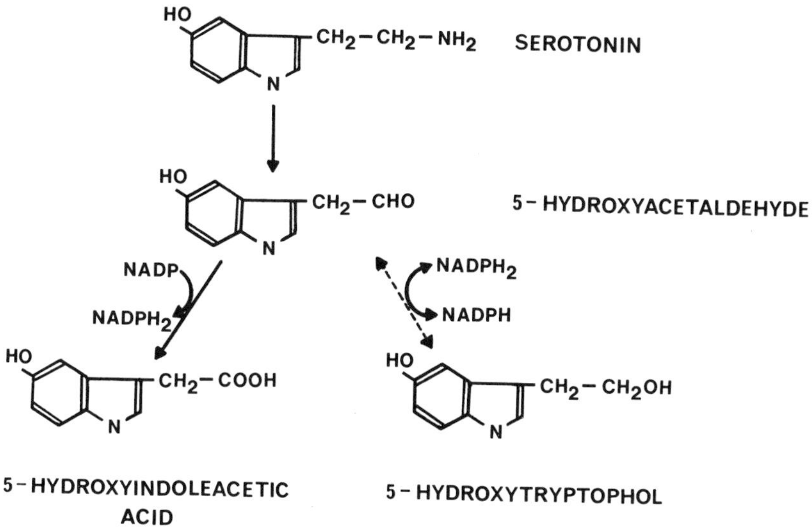

Figure 19.3 Breakdown of serotonin.

that tryptamine may act as a neurotransmitter in short spinal neurons. There have also been reports of the existence of long ascending and descending tryptaminergic pathways (Martin *et al.*, 1975).

Tryptamine is known to facilitate spinal reflexes. It has also been proposed that it may be involved in schizophrenia and affective disorders and could possibly mediate some drug-induced hallucinations (Coppen, 1972). Nevertheless, the effects of tryptamine upon cerebral neurons and overall brain function are mostly unknown.

The degradation of serotonin is a two-step process, catalyzed by monoamine oxidase, that begins with a deamination to 5-hydroxyindoleacetaldehyde (Fig. 19.3). The subsequent reaction can be channeled in one of two directions, typically dependent upon the tissue ratio of $NAD^+/NADH$. The oxidation of 5-hydroxyindoleacetaldehyde to 5-hydroxyindoleacetic acid (5-HIAA) is far more common than its reduction to 5-hydroxytryptophol. And, in the brain there is a question as to whether this latter pathway exists at all. Once produced, 5-HIAA is transported across the blood-brain barrier by a specific carrier mechanism to be eliminated from the body in the urine.

In the pineal gland, the formation of 5-hydroxyindoleacetaldehyde is followed by a number of different chemical reactions, such as the reduction of the aldehyde into alcohol, the acetylation of serotonin into

N-acetylserotonin, or the *O*-methylation to 5-methoxy-*N*-acetyltryptamine (melatonin) and 5-methoxyindoleacetic acid (Fig. 19.4).

There is an equilibrium between 5-HIAA in the brain tissue and in the cerebrospinal fluid, and 5-HIAA that is injected into one part of the ventricular system quickly diffuses throughout (Burns *et al.*, 1976). The 5-HIAA that is present in the fluid surrounding the spinal cord originates mainly from the cord and is for the most part a reflection of serotonin metabolism there. In addition, the CSF levels of 5-HIAA to a certain extent can provide information vis-a-vis the functional state of the brain. Accordingly, Asberg *et al.* (1976) found that depressed patients that have contemplated suicide had high levels of CSF 5-HIAA.

Some amount of serotonin is not degraded after its release from the presynaptic region, but taken back up into the nerve endings. There are two different uptake systems in the nerve ending membrane. One involves a high-affinity, saturable mechanism; the other is a more low-affinity system that is also able to accumulate serotonin in catecholaminergic neurons. Both nerve endings and axons can take up the transmitter by an energy- and

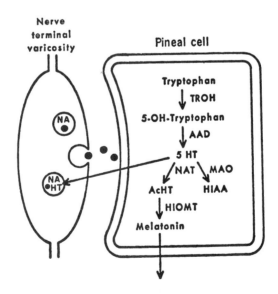

Figure 19.4   The pineal cell, sympathetic nerve, and melatonin synthesis.   Abbreviations: TROH, tryptophan hydroxylase; AAD, aromatic amino acid decarboxylase; 5 HT, serotonin; NAT, serotonin N-acetyltransferase; MAO, monoamine oxidase; AcHT, N-acetylserotonin; HIAA, 5-hydroxyindoleacetic acid; HIOMT, hydroxyindole-*O*-methyltransferase; and NA, noradrenaline [from J. Axelrod, *Science* 184:1341 (1974); © 1974 by American Association for the Advancement of Science].

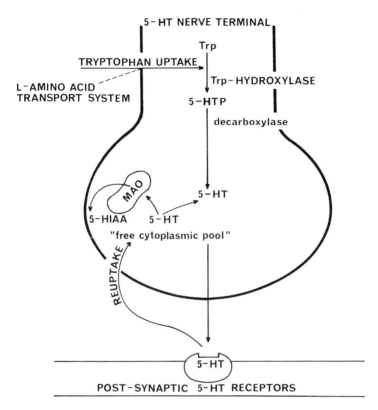

Figure 19.5 Diagram of the metabolic activities at a serotonergic synapse. Abbreviations: 5-HT, serotonin; Trp, Tryptophan; 5-HTP, 5-hydroxytryptophan; 5-HIAA, 5-hydroxyindoleacetic acid.

sodium-dependent process. Small quantities of potassium and chloride ions are also required (for review see Ross, 1980). But, whether the serotonin enters the storage vesicles in the terminals has not been experimentally verified.

The synaptosomes have been found to contain a soluble serotonin-binding protein that is associated with the synaptic vesicles (Tamir and Gershon, 1979). In addition to the brain serotonergic neurons, it is present in the gut, thyroid, and the blood platelets in forms that may differ in composition. Neuronal serotonin-binding protein itself is synthesized in the perikaryon and carried along the axon to the nerve endings, where it could be involved with the transport of the neurotransmitter to the synaptic vesicles and with its intracellular storage. Sodium, potassium, and calcium ions have been suggested to control the dissociation of the complex, freeing the amine (Tamir and Liu, 1982).

The binding of serotonin to this protein is inhibited by the non-cyclic adenosine phosphates and GTP. Ferrous ions and gangliosides, in contrast, enhance the binding, although by themselves, the gangliosides are ineffective (Tamir *et al.*, 1980). The response requires the presence of phosphatidylcholine. The mechanism of this lecithin effect is presently unclear, but it is known that membrane lipids are able to affect the actions of proteins and other lipids (see Chapter 2). The relationship among the ferrous ions, lecithin and the serotonin-binding protein does suggest the existance of a protein-Fe^{2+} complex, whose interaction with the gangliosides enhances its binding to serotonin. Functionally, the gangliosides could participate in the passage of serotonin across the synaptic membrane.

Serotonin released from the nerve endings and varicosities of the serotonergic nerve fibers reacts with membrane receptors (Fig. 19.5), some of which are associated with a serotonin-sensitive adenylate cyclase (Von Hungen *et al.*, 1975). Therefore, two types of serotonin receptors can be distinguished, each having a distinctive regional distribution (Peroutka and Snyder, 1981). Receptor 1 interacts with adenylate cyclase, while receptor 2 does not (Peroutka *et al.*, 1981). For this effect upon adenylate cyclase, these serotonin 1 receptors must first act upon the guanyl nucleotides (Nelson *et al.*, 1980). This means that the neurotransmitter is able to induce the synthesis of cyclic AMP (Fillion *et al.*, 1979). The removal of N-acetylneuraminic acid from the cell membrane inactivates the receptor (Dalton, 1979), indicating that the receptor may be a glycolipid or glycoprotein or a complex with components of each.

Ennis and Cox (1982) also distinguished two types of receptors, but their classification is based upon pharmacological differences. They identified one class as serotonin autoreceptors on cell bodies and dendrites. These were reported to be present in the raphe nuclei. The second class was categorized as postsynaptic serotonin receptors. Baumann and Waldmeier (1981) also postulate the existence of presynaptic autoreceptors which could control serotonin release. These have been already demonstrated in the central nervous system of *Helix pomatia* (Juel, 1981).

ANATOMY OF SEROTONERGIC NEURONS

All forebrain serotonergic fibers are associated with two phylogenetically older brain stem nuclei, the dorsal and medial raphe nuclei (Fig. 19.6). Descending pathways originating in these nuclei carry serotonin into the spinal cord, while ascending pathways comprise a well-circumscribed structure, the medial forebrain bundle, from which tracts of fibers separate to enter a number of diencephalic and telencephalic regions, including the hippocampus, septum, hypothalamus, subcommissural organ and cerebral cortex (Kuhar *et al.*, 1972). An additional ascending tract from the raphe system runs somewhat lateral to the medial forebrain bundle and innervates the corpus striatum (Fig. 19.7). The fibers containing serotonin are either thin with varicosities, or thick and myelinated, having numerous terminal branches (Kohler *et al.*, 1981).

The presence of serotonin in the hypothalamus is well established, and in concert with norepinephrine, the neurotransmitter is able to modify several hypothalamic endocrine functions. In the pituitary stalk, the number of serotonergic nerve endings exceeds that in the hypothalamus. It seems likely that serotonin participates in the regulation of anterior pituitary activity through its release into the hypothalamo-pituitary portal system.

Serotonergic endings in the cerebral cortex are primarily present in the upper three cortical layers, but axonal varicosities and boutons can be found in all layers except VI. Small numbers of serotonergic neurons have also been identified in the locus coeruleus, but their functional significance is unknown (Sladek and Walker, 1977).

The pineal gland, actually a part of the epithalamus, contains the highest concentrations of serotonin and its metabolites (particularly melatonin)

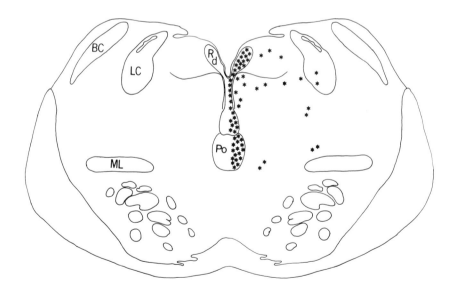

Figure 19.6 Localization of serotonergic neurons in the raphe nuclei of *Macaca arctoides*. BC, brachium conjunctivum; LC, locus coeruleus; ML, medial lemniscus; Rd, nucleus raphe dorsalis; PO, nucleus raphe pontis [from J.R. Sladek Jr. and P. Walker, *Brain Res.* 134:359 (1977); © 1977 by Elsevier/North-Holland Biomedical Press].

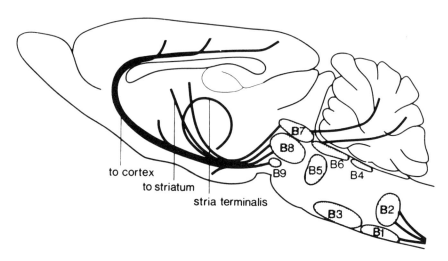

Figure 19.7 Schematic diagram of the central serotonergic cell groups and projections in a sagittal section from rat brain [from K. Fuxe and O. Johansson, in: *Advances in Biochemical Pharmacology*, Vol. 10, E. Costa, G.L. Gessa, M. Sandler (Eds.), p. 1 (1974); © 1974 by Raven Press Inc.].

in the brain. These levels are controlled at least in part by noradrenergic nerve fibers from the superior cervical ganglion. The levels vary over the course of the day and represent a circadian metabolic rhythm. The daily rhythm of the metabolites depends upon fluctuations in enzymatic activity, particularly serotonin-*N*-acetyltransferase (NAT). The serotonin rhythm is an endogenous one, which persists even in blinded animals, but can be suppressed by continuous illumination.

The only serotonin derivative strongly suspected of having a physiological role in mammals is pineal melatonin. It appears to have an antigonadal effect upon the mammalian reproductive system, although the reported effects have been inconsistent. Since the pineal gland is an organ involved in the control of circadian metabolic rhythms, melatonin may have a neurotransmitter or neuromodulatory function in the brain associated with these rhythms. In animals, it has been found capable, for example, of inducing sleep and prolonging pentobarbital-induced sleep, in addition to decreasing motor activity. It also has been observed to facilitate the extinction of the learned avoidance responses (for review see Datta and King, 1978).

In 1957, Brodie and Shore proposed the existence of two functionally opposing central systems, one containing serotonin and the other norepinephrine. Of these two, the noradrenergic system was considered to be dominant, controlling the synthesis and metabolism of serotonin. Accordingly, destruction of the locus coeruleus or transection of the ascending dorsal noradrenergic pathway that originates in this nucleus causes an increase in serotonin turnover in the telencephalon. An understanding of this relationship, along with the knowledge that there exists a functional balance between dopamine and serotonin in the striatum, is important to any interpretation of neuropharmacological data that concern changes in one or both systems.

CELLULAR ACTIONS OF SEROTONIN

At a cellular level, serotonin can cause both depolarization and hyperpolarization of the neurons. The two responses can be the result of several different ionic mechanisms. For example, in some snail neurons, there may be a selective increase in the membrane permeability to chloride, allowing a net influx of chloride. In other snail neurons, there may be a selective increase in potassium permeability with net efflux of potassium. In *Aplysia*, there are at least three different excitatory and three different inhibitory neuronal responses, fast or slow (sustained), each with a different ionic mechanism involving an activation of different voltage-sensitive channels.

Serotonin also has a direct stimulating effect upon presynaptic nerve endings and a sensitizing effect upon sensory afferents. Accordingly, nerve fibers can be depolarized in Locke solution when serotonin is added, even in very low concentrations. The depolarization is caused by an increase in the resting sodium permeability and is followed by a subsequent fall in the height of the action potentials (Riccioppo Neto, 1978).

In various identified neurons of *Aplysia*, serotonin has a neuromodulatory function. Here, a serotonergic neuron, termed a metacerebral cell, modifies the actions of motoneurons in the buccal ganglion, as well as the contractile strength of the buccal muscles. The metacerebral cell itself becomes activated by the exposure of the animal to food stimuli. This form of arousal is characterized by an enhanced strength and an increased frequency of biting. Consequently, the serotoninergic neuron in this system modulates behavior depending upon the food supply (Kupfermann *et al.*, 1979).

Serotonin is also able to alter the amplitude and rate of decay of the posttetanic potentiation in identified synapses in the abdominal ganglion of *Aplysia californica*. And, it may change the amplitude of an individual excitatory postsynaptic potential (EPSP). Such a neuromodulatory action is probably attributable to a modification of neurotransmitter release (Newlin *et al.*, 1980).

ACTIONS OF SEROTONERGIC SYSTEMS

The anatomy of the serotonergic system in the brain and the distribution of its fibers over extensive brain areas imply that serotonin is involved in the control, or perhaps the modulation, of several brain functions.

Following injection, it elicits a "serotonin behavioral syndrome" with displays of hyperactivity, head shakes, resting tremor and hypertonicity (Grahame-Smith, 1971). But, the effect of infused serotonin depends upon the area of the brain involved. Thus, Davis *et al.* (1980) showed that serotonin injected into the lateral ventricle depressed the acoustic startle reflex, whereas after its injection into the spinal cord there was an increase in this response. The results again suggest that the same transmitter is able to regulate a particular behavior in various ways, depending upon the part of the CNS affected.

When administered into the cerebral ventricles or into the carotid artery, the neurotransmitter elicits electroencephalographic signs of slow wave sleep (Hingtgen and Aprison, 1975). Following its injection, serotonin has a "tranquilizing" effect that is evident, for instance, in the induction of hibernation in the ground squirrel (Spafford and Pengelley, 1971). During this winter sleep, the brain contains more serotonin than during the summer months. And, in this regard, a lesion of the medial raphe nuclei causes the disruption of this state. Serotonin is also able to potentiate the effect of barbiturates (for review see Samanin and Garattini, 1975).

These findings indicate that serotonin may be involved in the control of sleep (Jouvet, 1969). However, its direct association with slow wave sleep, as claimed during the 1960's, has recently been disputed. As a matter of fact, in different animal species, the effect of serotonin is to reduce REM sleep. Methysergide, a serotonin receptor blocker, decreases REM sleep in man, suggesting a close relationship of the neurotransmitter to REM sleep (Jacobs and Trulson, 1979).

A serotonergic system may also be involved in the control of the brain reward system. However, numerous reviews have mentioned both an inhibitory and excitatory role for serotonin in intracranial self-stimulation. Most probably the system functions in an inhibitory manner, which has been suggested by a decrease in the rate of self-stimulation in response to depletion of serotonin by parachlorophenylalanine (PCPA) (Miliaressis, 1977).

Serotonin appears to also be involved in several forms of aggression. In male mice, aggressive behavior elicited by prolonged isolation is accompanied by a decrease in the turnover of brain serotonin. Also, the inhibition of serotonin synthesis by parachlorophenylalanine alters aggressiveness in rats, cats and mice (Dominguez and Longo, 1969; Welch and Welch, 1968). A depletion of serotonin in the amygdala by 5,7-dihydroxytryptamine induces more submissive forms of behavior in male rats, along with reductions in motor behavior and social interactions (File *et al.*, 1981). But, here again, there seem to be differences in the role of serotonin in various animal species and types of aggression.

The fibers descending from pontine and medullary raphe nuclei reach the cells of the ventral and dorsal horns through the anterior and lateral columns of the spinal cord. These pathways, together with the ascending serotonergic fibers, may be connected with the perception of pain (for review see Messing and Lytle, 1977). A local injection of serotonin into the lumbar spinal subarachnoidal space causes an elevation of the pain threshold (Yaksh and Wilson, 1979), suggesting that serotonin has an antinociceptive action. In several animal species, including humans, parachlorophenylalanine induces a hyperalgesia that lasts several days. And, there are reports that electrolytic lesions in the medial forebrain bundle which reduce forebrain serotonin also increase pain sensitivity. The effect can be reversed by serotonin administration. Experimental animals with such a lesion are also hyperactive and have deficits in the regulation of food and water intake. Even a tryptophan-poor corn diet in rats lowers the pain threshold, together with a decrease in brain serotonin (Harvey and Lints, 1971). The result is a facilitated acquisition of an avoidance reponse (Tenen, 1967) which shows a negative correlation with the serotonin level in the frontal pole of the cerebral hemispheres. Together, the data indicate that a serotonergic system interferes with the effect of painful stimuli on the organism.

Serotonin, in conjunction with the catecholamines, has been suggested to modulate motility. A drop in the level of brain serotonin, induced by, for example, a lesion of the medial raphe nucleus, causes a marked, long-lasting increase in locomotor activity. In contrast, a lesion of the dorsal raphe nucleus is without effect (Jacobs *et al.*, 1974). Moreover, a unilateral depletion of serotonin in the rat results in persistent turning in a contralateral direction (Jacobs *et al.*, 1977). Other motor responses to a surgical or pharmacological disruption of the serotonergic system have been reported. An increase in the stimulation of the postsynaptic serotonin receptors causes hyperactivity and hyperreactivity together with a resting tremor, rigidity and hypertonus, reciprocal forepaw treading, hindlimb abduction and lateral head weaving. With the exception of hyperreactivity, all of these signs are specific to an effect upon the serotonergic system.

There appears to be some connection between serotonin and the tonic immobility that is produced by a brief period of physical restraint. An injection of tryptophan causes a dose-dependent increase in the duration of the immobility, while a tryptophan-free diet abolishes the reaction (Gallup *et al.*, 1977). A decrease in brain serotonin also causes overeating. After the administration of PCPA, this excessive eating lasts for at least 1-2 weeks, demonstrating a serotonin involvement in the control of food intake.

Another important function in which serotonin has been implicated is temperature regulation. The injection of serotonin into the ventricles of unanesthetized cats produces hyperthermia (Feldberg and Myers, 1964). This type of research has led to speculation that serotonin is a neurotransmitter of the hypothalamic thermoreceptors (Cremer and Bligh, 1969), and its injection alters the process of thermoregulation (Gorynia and Bartsch, 1975). It might be that the effect of serotonin is antagonistic to that of norepinephrine.

SEROTONIN AND LEARNING

While the aforementioned physiological actions of the serotonergic pathways may be associated with the process of learning and its modification of behavior, the data supporting this relationship are not that clear. Wooley and Van der Hoeven (1965) have claimed that learning ability tends to vary inversely with the concentration of brain serotonin. When the level of brain serotonin increases, mice show a deficit in T-maze learning. A decrease in serotonin that is induced by electrolytic lesions of midbrain nuclei enhances the acquisition of active avoidance in a Y maze. But, according to Steranka and Barrett (1974), these findings are not due to a direct effect upon the learning process, but can be explained by a lesion-induced attenuation of the behavioral suppression or freezing that follows a foot shock. Fibers from the raphe nuclei to the hippocampus that inhibit behavioral arousal may be responsible for this action (Mabry and Campbell, 1973).

Data presented by Leonard and Rigter (1975) show that after the mastery of a passive avoidance task, serotonin in the hippocampus and brain stem is elevated. Genetic differences between individual strains of mice and rats also indicate some relationship of the overall level of serotonin to various types of learning. Thus, DBA mice, as compared with the C57BL/6 strain, have higher levels of serotonin in the hippocampus and also a better retention of a passive avoidance learning (Church and Sprott, 1979).

Open-field behavior has also been correlated with serotonin levels in the brain stem and limbic system. But, while some correlation is evident in inbred rats (Sudak and Maas, 1964), it does not tend to be consistent (Blizard and Liang, 1979). Overall, the relationship between the serotonergic systems and learning and behavior is not a straightforward one, but does suggest that these systems act in cooperation with several other neurotransmitter systems (Kovacs et al., 1976).

HISTAMINE AS A NEUROTRANSMITTER

Attempts to demonstrate that histamine plays a role in synaptic transmission have been less successful than comparable efforts with the other biogenic amines. Consequently, at the present time the evidence to support the transmitter candidacy of histamine at any mammalian synapse is limited. In 1977, Weinreich did find two identified neurons in *Aplysia californica* that contained a specific histidine decarboxylating enzyme and were able to synthesize and store histamine. It was suggested that histamine could possibly function here as a neurotransmitter to elicit excitatory and inhibitory postsynaptic potentials in different follower neurons. This has been demonstrated in tissue cultures of hypothalamus by Geller (1981), who detected both excitation and depression of unit activity.

The major store of histamine in the brain, larger than the neuronal histaminergic level, is contained within the mast cells. These cells, similar to mast cells throughout the body, can be found in the meninges and around the cerebral blood vessels. In animals, there is a large degree of species and individual variability in the numbers of these cells that depends upon such things as age and postnatal-preweaning handling, in addition to other factors which are presently unspecifiable (Persinger, 1977).

SYNTHESIS AND METABOLISM OF HISTAMINE

The precursor of histamine is histidine, but its decarboxylation to histamine by histidine decarboxylase is only a minor metabolic pathway (Fig. 19.8). There are two types of histamine-forming enzymes in mammalian tissues: a relatively non-specific one that is probably identical with DOPA decarboxylase and a substrate-specific L-histidine decarboxylase (for review see Maslinski, 1975). In the brain, the activity of the specific enzyme is highest in the hypothalamus and is influenced by the tissue level of histidine. In other areas of the brain, its activity is low. In the hippocampus, histamine-containing fibers arrive via the fimbriae and fornix superior (dorsal route), as well as by a ventral route via the amygdaloid area. Histidine decarboxylase in the nerve endings of this area disappears after deafferentation (Barbin *et al.*, 1976).

The inactivation of histamine in the brain is rapid, and the resulting aldehydes, alcohols and acids are quickly removed. Although unaltered histamine has been detected in the urine following its intracranial injection, the major means of histamine disposal in the brain is by methylation. Accordingly, the main catabolic enzyme is histamine-N-methyltransferase.

The highest levels of this enzyme have been found within the nuclei of some nerve cells of hypothalamus, thalamus, pituitary, and pineal gland. This methylhistamine can then be deaminated in the rat brain by monoamine oxidase B (Waldmeier *et al.*, 1977; Sperk *et al.*, 1981). Another pathway of histamine degradation is an oxidation by diamine oxidase. The relative activity of these two pathways varies according to the organ and the species.

Histamine derivatives that are present in various tissues may account for a number of different biological actions. Histamine can be methylated either on its ring nitrogen or on its lateral chain (Roseghini, 1976). But, while the ring-methylated derivatives have no physiological effects, the histamines methylated on the lateral chain nitrogen (*N'*-methylated) are poten-

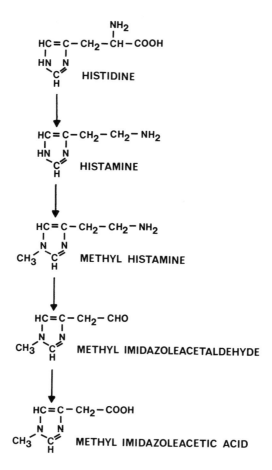

Figure 19.8 Synthesis and metabolism of histamine.

tially active. N'-acetylhistamine has been detected in several tissues, including the mammalian brain. And, histamine-adenine dinucleotide, a substance analogous to nicotinamide–adenine dinucleotide (NAD), could have some as yet undetermined physiological role.

After its release from the cells, histamine reacts with the membrane receptors. Pharmacological studies have revealed the existance of two types of histamine receptors, labeled H_1 and H_2. Both classes are found distributed throughout most areas of the brain. The majority of neurons which are selectively excited by histamine contain both types of receptors (Haas and Bucher, 1975). The H_1 receptor, isolated and purified by Uchida in 1978, is blocked by the classical antihistaminics and may be responsible for their sedative effects. It appears that these H_1 receptors have excitatory effects upon the neurons, while the H_2 types are inhibitory (Geller, 1981). Both receptors in the brain are coupled to adenylate cyclase, so that histamine is able to induce the synthesis of cyclic AMP. In this respect, the H_1 receptors are the more effective (Psychoyos, 1978). When activated in the presence of extracellular calcium, adenylate cyclase is able to depress the firing rate of some nerve cells (Hegstrand et al., 1976). One other interesting effect is an H_1-mediated stimulation of phospholipid turnover, which may be involved in cell surface regulatory interactions (Subramanian et al., 1980).

PHYSIOLOGICAL ACTIONS OF HISTAMINE

Electrophysiological studies of neurons responsive to histamine have demonstrated several types of reactions, including fast and slow excitatory responses and fast and slow inhibitory responses. It is the latter inhibitory activity that was found to be much more frequent (Schwartz, 1979).

In addition to catecholaminergic and serotonergic fibers, the medial forebrain bundle is comprised of histamine-containing axons. Moreover, upon stimulation, the ascending catecholaminergic systems will release histamine. These fibers terminate diffusely in many brain regions, including the cerebral cortex and hippocampus (Garbarg et al., 1974). And, when the cerebral cortex is undercut, the content and release of histamine from it decreases.

The content of histamine is relatively high in the hypothalamus and striatum, while it tends to be lower in the hippocampus and cerebral cortex. Its release is enhanced by both calcium and potassium, although the latter ion seems to be the more effective in this regard (Subramanian and Mulder, 1976).

In the hypothalamus, histamine is thought to participate in prolactin secretion (Arakelian and Libertun, 1977), thermoregulation (Green et al.,

1976), the control of central autonomic responses, and the release of antidiuretic hormone. Its introduction into the rat lateral hypothalamus inhibits electrical self-stimulation at the injection site. Finally, serotonin appears to mediate some of the actions of histamine, including thermoregulation (Pilc and Nowak, 1979).

Little is known about the effect of histaminergic neurotransmission on learning, although intraventricular injections of this substance will depress continuous avoidance (Gerald and Maickel, 1972).

Amino Acids as Neurotransmitters

It has been estimated that norepinephrine serves as the neurotransmitter for only about 1% of all synapses in the CNS. Dopamine constitutes about the same percentage, while an even smaller number of brain neurons contain serotonin. Cholinergic nerve endings involve only about 10% of brain synapses. These figures emphasize that many prominent neurotransmitters have yet to be identified.

A number of amino acids and their derivatives have frequently been mentioned as likely transmitter candidates. Certainly, some of them, namely γ-aminobutyric acid (GABA) and glycine, are now commonly acknowledged to perform such a role. And, in terms of their concentrations, several other types are readily available. Fairly large amounts of free amino acids are present in nervous tissue. The most prominent, glycine, taurine, β-alanine and glutamic, aspartic, acetylaspartic, cysteic and γ-aminobutyric acids, have pronounced excitatory and inhibitory actions on neurons. Back in 1959, Purpura and his associates had first observed that amino acids were able to alter the firing of cortical neurons, leading Krnjevic *et al.* (1964) to suggest that at least two of them, glutamate and aspartate, were possible neurotransmitters.

Based upon their effects on neurons, the amino acids can be classified as either excitatory or inhibitory. The excitatory ones, glutamic, aspartic, cysteic and homocysteic acids act to depolarize the postsynaptic membrane, whereas the inhibitory amino acids, GABA, glycine, β-alanine, and possibly taurine and proline have been found to be hyperpolarizing.

Some of these amino acids comprise structurally similar pairs, one being excitatory and the other inhibitory (Fig. 20.1). Examples of such pairs are: L-aspartic acid and β-alanine, L-cysteic acid and taurine, and L-glutamic and γ-aminobutyric acid. The excitatory amino acids typically contain two carboxyl groups. The removal of the carboxyl group in the alpha position

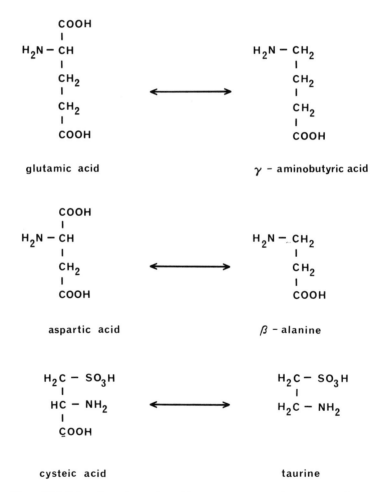

Figure 20.1 Pairs of putative amino acid neurotransmitters with opposing effects.

(α-decarboxylation) is usually the modification that transforms an excitatory amino acid into an inhibitory one (Bun *et al.*, 1976). This relationship is also reflected in the structure of amino-acidergic receptors. Both excitatory and inhibitory receptors have two active centers in common, one for the amino group, the other for the ω-acidic group. A single protein should then theoretically be capable of binding both classes of amino acids (Van Gelder, 1971). But, the evidence for this possiblity is still incomplete, and it could well be that the excitatory and inhibitory receptors are different proteins.

Receptors for various amino acids have been recognized in many neurons of the central nervous system. Also well-known are the reuptake systems for these amino acids, many of which are dependent upon both the energy supply and the presence of sodium. Sodium-independent reuptake systems, such as the glycine system, have also been described. As a rule, amino acids are partly taken up into the synaptosomes and partly into the astroglia (Fig. 20.2). The high-affinity glial uptake system for amino acid neurotransmitters is probably one of the principal ways of inactivating them. After they are taken up, these amino acids may be either metabolically altered, or released intact from the glia back into the extracellular space, an

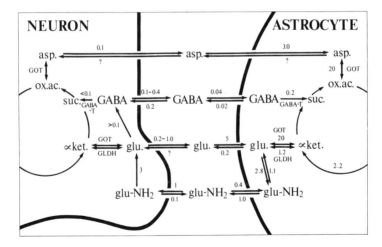

Figure 20.2 Diagrammatic representation of rates of uptake and release for glutamate, GABA, glutamine, and aspartate into neurons (nerve endings) and astrocytes, together with rates of metabolic interconversion between these amino acids or between individual amino acids and corresponding tricarboxylic acid cycle intermediates. Abbreviations: asp, aspartate; GABA-T, GABA-Transaminase; GOT, glutamic oxalic transaminase; glu-NH$_2$, glutamine; GLDH, glutamate dehydrogenase; α ket, α-ketoglutarate; ox. ac, oxaloacetate; suc., succinate. [from L. Hertz, *Progr. Neurobiol.* 13:277 (1979); © 1979 by Pergamon Press, Ltd].

efflux that is stimulated by potassium ions. Details of the processes involving the various individual amino acids will be discussed in corresponding parts of this chapter.

GLUTAMIC ACID

The brain contains larger amounts of free glutamic acid than are found in any other tissue. Throughout the brain, however, differences exist in the relevant metabolic machinery and rate of glutamic acid synthesis, as well as in the source of precursor material. As a result, glutamic acid is often spoken of as belonging to one of two "compartments" or pools. Metabolically, glucose and pyruvate enter both of these pools, the "large" and "small", whereas acetate, acetaldehyde, propionate, butyrate, citrate, GABA, glutamate, aspartate, leucine, bicarbonate and succinate predominatly enter the "small" pool. From a morphological standpoint, nerve endings and neuronal perikarya are probably found in the large compartment, releasing glutamate, while the glial cells belong in a small, glutamate accumulating and metabolizing pool (Martinez-Hernandez *et al.*, 1977). Adding to the several models of this system that have already been proposed (Benjamin and Quastel, 1972; Cremer *et al.*, 1971; Hertz, 1978), Dennis *et al.* (1977) demonstrated that synaptic and non-synaptic mitochondria differ in their glutamic acid pathways. Such heterogeneity could provide a further justification for compartmentalizing glutamate metabolism.

Glutamic acid is synthesized in the brain from α-ketoglutaric acid by transamination reactions (Fig. 20.3). Possible donors of amino groups for this reaction include glutamate, aspartate, γ-aminobutyrate, alanine, valine, leucine, isoleucine, tryptophan, 5-hydroxytryptophan, phenylalanine, tyrosine, cystine, cysteic acid, methionine, and ornithine. The most active are glutamate and aspartate. Several transaminating enzymes, or transaminases, are involved in these reactions.

The level of glutamic acid in the brain is also regulated by glutamate dehydrogenase (L-glutamate: NAD oxidoreductase). The level of activity of this enzyme, which catalyses the formation of glutamate from α-ketoglutarate and ammonia, therefore can affect neuronal functioning. This activity, in addition, is affected by several humoral agents, steroid hormones, serotonin, acetylcholine, norepinephrine and epinephrine. The precursor, α-ketoglutarate, is either a product of the tricarboxylic acid cycle, or a product of carboxylation by the attachment of CO_2 to pyruvate. This latter process is active in the brain. The existance of a high-affinity sodium-dependent uptake system in the nerve endings has been reported for α-ketoglutarate (Kanner and Sharon, 1978; Shank and Campbell, 1981).

Glutamine, the amide of glutamic acid. is synthesized from glutamic acid by the enzyme glutamine synthetase. In contrast to glutamic acid, glutamine has been considered to be physiologically inactive. However, it was recently reported to be capable of producting seizures and retrograde amnesia in the chick (Davis and Cherkin, 1981). Glutamine synthetase has not been detected in neurons, synaptic endings, oligodendrocytes, microglial cells, or endothelial cells, meaning that glutamine synthesis does not occur in any of these structures. It is present in astrocytes (Norenberg and Martinez-Hernandez, 1979), although trace amounts can be found in the ependymal cells. The level of enzymatic activity varies according to the brain area and is highest in the hippocampus (Norenberg, 1979). The enzyme also catalyzes a key step in the detoxification of ammonia in the brain and is

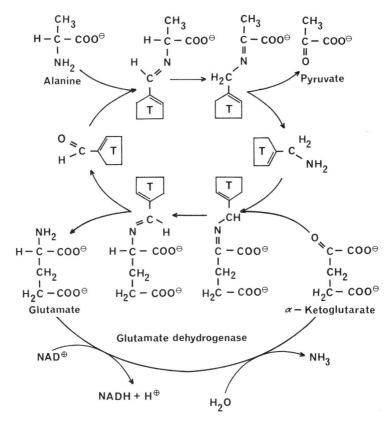

Figure 20.3 Transamination reaction in the synthesis of glutamate and pyruvate from α-ketoglutarate and alanine. T, transaminase.

involved in the synthesis of glycosaminoglycans and nucleic acids. Moreover, it functions to inactivate glutamic acid that is released from the synapse. Thus, the content of glutamine synthetase in various brain areas may be correlated with the local glutamatergic activity.

Glutamine itself may be metabolized by a transfer of the amide group to some recipient molecule by a glutamine transaminase-ω-amidase system, or by a reconversion to glutamic acid by means of the enzyme glutaminase (Fig. 20.4). The latter enzyme is activated by phosphorylation and inhibited by its glutamic acid product (Kvamme and Olsen, 1981). Following its liberation from the nerve endings, glutamate is taken up by the neighboring astrocytes and converted to glutamine before being released into the extracellular space and then actively transported into the nerve terminals. Once in the terminals, the molecules would be deaminated and used again for neurotransmission (Shank and Aprison, 1981). The process is a major source of glutamate and GABA for synaptic transmission.

The release of glutamate from the nerve endings is followed shortly thereafter by a corresponding increase in glutamate synthesis. This means

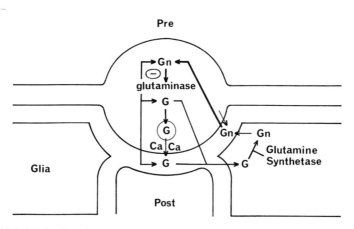

Figure 20.4 Mechanisms in the regulation of glutamate (G) synthesis from glutamine (Gn). Upon release of glutamate, glutamine uptake is stimulated and glutaminase activity is stimulated due to a decrease in end product inhibition. Released glutamate can be recaptured by the bouton or enter glial cells where it is converted to glutamine, released and becomes available to refuel the releasable glutamate pools. Since glutamine is synthesized in glial cells, glutamatergic boutons and glial cells form an interdependent cycle [redrawn from A. Hamberger, G.H. Chiang, E. Sandoval and C.W. Cotman, *Brain Res.* 168:531 (1979); © 1979 by Elsevier/North Holland Biomedical Press].

that the depolarization of the nerve ending and the component shifts of potassium and calcium ions are able to stimulate this synthesis (Hamberger *et al.*, 1979).

After its release from the nerve ending, glutamic acid diffuses toward the postsynaptic membrane and there reacts with the glutamate receptor. It then uncouples from the receptor and is reabsorbed into the astrocytes, either by a high- or a low-affinity system. This transport into the astrocytes is very rapid and is sufficient to remove the glutamate that is released during synaptic activation (Hertz *et al.*, 1978). The process requires sodium and is little affected by the external glutamate concentration. The high-affinity system, however, is not very specific and other amino acids may compete with glutamate for the transport mechanism (White and Neal, 1976). A high-affinity reuptake into synaptosomes also has often been reported. About 15% of synaptosomes appear to take up glutamate (Hertz, 1979) in the presence of external sodium and internal potassium. The transport carrier is specific, and its energy is obtained from the passage of ions.

Glutamic acid transported electrophoretically to the neuron produces a fast, reversible depolarization of the cell membrane (Krnjevic *et al.*, 1964) by increasing the permeability of the membrane to sodium. About 50% or more of all neurons in the cerebral cortex are excited in this manner. Because of this widespread action of glutamate, it has been suggested that this amino acid is not a genuine neurotransmitter (Curtis *et al.*, 1960). But neurons which lack synapses, such as the dorsal root ganglion cells, are insensitive to glutamate (De Groat *et al.*, 1972). Also, quantitative differences in the neuronal sensitivity to glutamate have been noted, leading McLennan (1968) to propose the presence of two types of glutamate receptors. One is considered to be a nonspecific form that is located on most neurons and can react with several different amino acids. The other is a specific receptor that is found on certain neurons and is only activated by glutamate.

After identifying specific binding sites for glutamate in the rat brain, Michaelis *et al.* (1974) solubilized the synaptic membranes and observed the effects of various enzymes and the glycoside-binding lectin, concanavalin A, upon glutamate attachment. Their results suggested that the receptor is a glycoprotein that interacts closely with membrane phospholipids. Aspartic acid, homocysteic acid and cysteine sulfinic acid all compete with glutamate for the binding site, while inhibition by glycine, β-alanine and GABA is negligible (Biziere *et al.*, 1980).

In the cerebral cortex, the principal action of glutamic acid is an excitatory one, but some neurons have been observed to be inhibited by it. Hess and Murata (1974), however, believe that the inhibition is due to an indirect effect upon nearby inhibitory interneurons. McLennan and Liu (1981) claim that the excitation of some neurons by L-glutamate and L-aspartate is succeeded by a period of reduced excitability. They postulate that this period may be caused by a decarboxylation of the excitatory amino acids which gives rise to the inhibitory amino acids, GABA or β-alanine.

An accurate measurement of the level of glutamic acid in the brain is possible only after a rapid inactivation of the brain enzymes, such as by microwave irradiation. Methods of this nature have shown that the highest level of glutamic acid is in the cerebral cortex, followed by the cerebellum, pons and medulla, striatum, and hippocampus. Very low levels have been detected in substantia nigra and septal nuclei (Balcom *et al.*, 1976). In the spinal cord, glutamate is rather evenly distributed, with the dorsal gray matter having slightly higher values than the ventral gray. Similarly, the dorsal roots are somewhat higher in glutamate than the ventral roots.

In the cerebellum, acidic amino acids, including glutamic acid, excite the Purkinje cells both *in vivo* and *in vitro* (Crawford *et al.*, 1966). Glutamate also affects a large number of cells in the granular layer. Of these responsive cells, approximately one-half are excited and the other half are inhibited by this amino acid (Yamamoto *et al.*, 1976). Here, glutamate is considered as a putative transmitter (Levi and Gallo, 1981).

At the present time, there is no unequivocally accepted glutamatergic pathway. Circumstantial evidence suggests that glutamic acid serves as the transmitter for the cerebellar granule cells (Young *et al.*, 1974), cortical pyramidal cells (Divac *et al.*, 1977; Lund-Karlsen and Fonnum, 1978) and the primary sensory afferents (Johnson, 1972). And, it is possible that the perforant pathway in the hippocampal dentate gyrus of the rat may use it (Storm-Mathisen, 1977). Similar suggestions have been made for the entorhinal and commissural hippocampal projections, as well as for some dorsal tracts at the spinal level (Stone, 1979). It may also be the neurotransmitter in the intermediate nucleus tractus solitarii where it might mediate the action of afferent fibers from arterial baroreceptors (Talman *et al.*, 1980).

Changes in the concentration of glutamic acid in the brain have been observed to accompany different functional states. For instance, long-lasting photic stimulation significantly decreases the level of glutamate, as compared with controls kept in darkness for a comparable period of time (Simhadri and Devi, 1970). Convulsions lower the level of glutamic acid. Here, there is a drop in the incorporation of glucose carbons into glutamic acid because glutamic dehydrogenase [L-glutamate: NADP oxidoreductase (deaminating)], which converts 2-oxoglutaric acid into glutamic acid and vice versa, decreases in the epileptogenic focus. Other enzymes, such as aspartic-glutamic transaminase or glutamine synthetase, are not affected.

Some authors have tied the actions of glutamic acid to the process of learning. Van Harreveld and Fifkova (1974) proposed a mechanism for the synaptic plasticity that was based upon the neurotransmitter activity of glutamic acid. Glutamate released during the passage of the nerve impulse across the synapse increased the permeability of the postsynaptic membrane to sodium, which then entered the dendritic spine together with water. This was hypothesized to increase the volume of the dendritic spine, while decreasing its length. The effect was to shorten the distance between the pre- and postsynaptic portions of the synapse, enhancing the likelihood of a discharge. Van Harreveld (1978) also proposed that glutamate, together with potassium ions, was involved in the mechanism of spreading depression.

Baudry and Lynch (1981) have proposed that a calcium stimulation of glutamate binding in the hippocampus may be associated with a shift in the number of synaptic glutamate receptors. Such a change, they believe, could govern long-lasting effects upon hippocampal synaptic transmission (long-term potentiation).

In rodents, the intraperitoneal injection of large quantities of glutamic acid, or its monosodium salt, has a toxic effect upon the retina and some areas of the brain, particularly the arcuate nucleus of the hypothalamus, laminae terminalis of the organum vasculosum, subcommissural organ and subfornical organ (Olney, 1971). The cellular damage involves neuronal and glial edema, neuronal death, and the migration of phagocytes, followed by the proliferation of astrocytes. In the neurons, there is cytoplasmic ballooning, chromatin dumping, pyknosis (Takasaki, 1978) and a profound long-lasting depolarization of the cells which is caused by alterations in sodium and potassium conductances. The lesion is followed by several endocrinopathies, such as hypogonadism, hypothyroidism, and pituitary atrophy, and by certain behavioral deficits, that include diminished locomotor and exploratory activity, tail automutilation, and obesity. The plasma levels of growth and thyroid hormones are diminished and prolactin is elevated. Luteinizing hormone, thyroid stimulating hormone, and glucagon are, however, unchanged (Nemeroff et al., 1978). This endocrine deficiency results, at least in part, from the destruction of cholinergic and dopaminergic tubero-infundibular tracts and systems. Some damage has also been found in the preoptic region, the dorsolateral thalamus, hippocampal dentate gyrus, and the cerebral cortex.

Several other excitatory amino acids, aspartic acid, cysteine, cysteic and homocysteic acids, have similar effects that are most pronounced in newborn and young rodents. The destruction of neurons by MSG has also been used as an experimental method of lesioning the hypothalamus. The cell bodies are selectively destroyed, while the axons passing through the region are spared.

ASPARTIC ACID

An amino acid that is closely allied with glutamic acid and often suspected along with it of having a role as a neurotransmitter is aspartic acid. When iontophoretically applied to the vicinity of some neurons, it usually increases their firing rate, an effect which appears to be the result of a direct postsynaptic action. This response to aspartic acid has been detected in the retina, spinal cord, cerebral cortex, and several other areas of the brain. It can be synthesized in synaptosomes from glutamine, among other sources, and then released both *in vivo* (and then taken up by astrocytes) and from isolated synaptosomes by electrical pulses or by high concentrations of potassium in a calcium-dependent fashion (Clark and Collins, 1976).

Inasmuch as glutamate and aspartate excite just about all CNS neurons and aspartate binds competitively to solubilized glutamate receptors, there is a question as to whether their effects are mediated through the same receptors. Recent evidence has indicated that aspartate could well be a genuine neurotransmitter that affects specific receptor molecules (De Robertis and De Plazas, 1976; Yarowsky and Carpenter, 1976) on separate aspartatergic, non-glutamatergic neurons. These cells presumably exist in the cerebral cortex, particularly in the sixth layer (Baughman and Gilbert, 1980; 1981), and perhaps in other parts of the CNS. The cortico-pontine nerve endings release aspartate, and the release is potassium-evoked and calcium-dependent (Thagnipon and Storm-Mathisen, 1981). DiLauro *et al.* (1981) argue that aspartic acid (and not glutamic acid) is the transmitter in the perforant pathway extending from the entorhinal cortex to the fascia dentata.

There are differences in the relative potencies of glutamic and aspartic acids on diverse groups of neurons. Interneurons of the dorsal horns that receive direct primary afferent input are more responsive to glutamate, while the Renshaw cells that receive impulses from the excitatory interneurons (but not the primary afferents) are more sensitive to aspartate. These findings intimate, as Davidoff *et al.* (1967) have suggested, that aspartate could serve as the excitatory transmitter for spinal interneurons, while glutamate may be involved with the primary afferents.

Glutamate and aspartate have synergistic actions at some synapses. The postsynaptic response to the simultaneous application of both of them tends to be higher than when each is applied alone (McBurney and Crawford, 1979). According to McBurney and Crawford, aspartate enhances the binding of glutamate to the receptor. It also stimulates cAMP synthesis in the brain and may be involved in the pathogenesis of seizures and various other functional brain states. However, there is still a paucity of knowledge in this area, so much so that aspartate, as compared with some of the other amino acids, is still not considered to be strong candidate for a neurotransmitter function.

A derivative of aspartate, N-acetylaspartic acid, may also influence neuronal excitability, but it appears to be metabolically inert with a very slow rate of turnover. Therefore, a neurotransmitter role is improbable. Its concentration in the brain far exceeds its levels in other tissues, but its primary function could be the induction of some metabolic process, such as the initiation of protein synthesis.

GLYCINE

Structurally, the simplest of the amino acids is glycine (Fig. 20.5). It is present in all tissues and is an important part of the metabolism of a large number of other biologically important end products that contain nitrogen. Until about 15 years ago, glycine was not suspected of having any other functional significance in the central nervous system. Then in 1965, Aprison and Werman reported differences in its distribution within the central nervous system, and a marked rostro-caudal gradient became apparent (Fig. 20.6). The concentration of glycine in the cord tissue is almost four-fold greater than in the cerebral cortex. Subsequent research on the distribution, metabolism, uptake, and pharmacology of glycine has provided an impressive array of evidence in support of a role for the amino acid as a major inhibitory transmitter in the spinal cord.

Glycine is a non-essential amino acid and can be synthesized in the body from other materials. In the rat and mouse brain, virtually all of it appears to be derived from serine, which in turn uses glucose as an original source of carbons. Moreover, most of the synthetic process has been found to occur in the brain itself, since the blood-brain barrier imposes limitations on the quantities of serine and glycine that may pass into the CNS from the circulation. The serine to glycine conversion is catalyzed by serine hydroxymethyltransferase, and the regulation of glycine levels in nervous tissue is probably dependent upon this reaction (Davies and Johnston, 1973). On the other hand, glycine is catabolized by incorporation into proteins or glutathione (Douglas and Martensen, 1956; Globus et al., 1968), or it can be transformed back into serine by the action of serine hydroxymethyltransferase (Roberts and Hammerschlag, 1976).

Electrical stimulation and elevations in the level of external potassium both significantly enhance the release of glycine from nervous tissue.

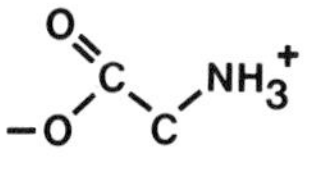

Figure 20.5 Glycine.

Electrical depolarization, however, is not a very discriminating stimulus and can effect the release of almost all amino acids (Katz *et al.*, 1969). Potassium depolarization, on the other hand, is specific and, in the case of glycine, demonstrates a difference between an efflux from slices of spinal cord tissue and the cerebral cortex. Values for the spinal cord are almost six times as large as those for the cortex. This release could be calcium dependent, although the issue has not yet been satisfactorily resolved.

In the brain, glycine that is released is bound postsynaptically to its receptor (for review see De Feudis, 1977). This binding is independent of the

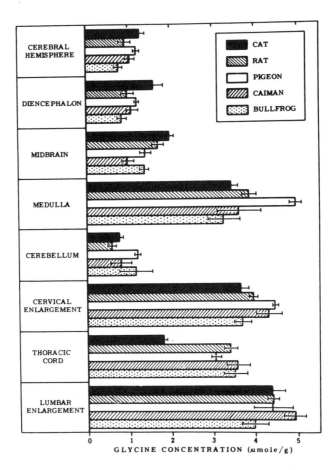

Figure 20.6 Comparison of the glycine concentration at various levels of the neuraxis in five different vertebrates. The mean concentration and the standard error of the mean are shown [from M.H. Aprison, R.P. Shank, R.A. Davidoff and R. Werman, *Life Sci.* 7:583 (1968); © 1968 by Pergamon Press, Inc.].

energy supply, but requires the presence of sodium ions. Strychnine blocks it by attaching itself to the receptor. Strychnine actually has a higher affinity for glycine receptors than does glycine and, if radioactively labeled, can be a means of identifying these receptors. Using radioactive glycine, about 25% of all synapses in the spinal cord can be labeled. The binding of glycine in the telencephalon is considerably lower than in the cord, unlike in the medulla and pons, where it is almost as high. This is also true for strychnine binding and is an indication that the potency of glycine as a neurotransmitter decreases as the neuraxis is ascended.

After the attachment of glycine to the receptor, there is an increase in the chloride permeability of the postsynaptic membrane, which increases the polarization of the membrane and generates an inhibitory postsynaptic potential. The glycine is then taken up into synaptosomes and, perhaps, into the glia. The uptake can be via a high- or low-affinity transport system and is sodium dependent and inhibited by ouabain. According to Logan and Snyder (1971, 1972), only the low-affinity system is present in the cerebral cortex; the high-affinity sodium-dependent system predominates in the spinal cord and distal parts of the brainstem.

Purpura and his colleagues (1959) noted that the inhibitory effect of glycine on the electrical activity of the cerebral cortex was not very strong. GABA is a much more potent depressant for cortical neurons. There is some physiological and neurochemical evidence for a glycinergic cortico-hypothalamic tract (Kita, 1968; McGeer and Singh, 1980) which may be involved with the release of growth hormone (Kasai et al., 1980). Glycine has also been mentioned as a possible neurotransmitter in the substantia nigra, optic tectum, retina, and neostriatum (for review see Pycock and Kerwin, 1981). It has a very strong inhibitory action when administered to spinal motoneurons and interneurons, as demonstrated by iontophoretic application (Curtis and Watkins, 1960). The mechanism of action appears to involve an increase in the conductance to chloride ions.

In the spinal cord, the glycine concentration is highest in the ventral gray matter and lowest in the dorsal and ventral roots, which do not contain any interneurons (Fig. 20.7). The levels in the medulla oblongata and cervical and lumbar enlargements of the spinal cord are greater than in all other brain areas rostral to the medulla. Nevertheless, it has been found in relatively high concentrations in the cochlear nuclei (Godfrey et al., 1977), the optic tectum, the reticulospinal neurons, and in the retina. In the retina, it consistently depresses the spontaneous and evoked activity in all cell types, and its effects are indistinguishable from those of GABA. The release of glycine from the retina increases during photic stimulation, although the effect has only been noted for light flashes and not continuous illumination.

When the interneurons in the spinal cord are destroyed, such as follows

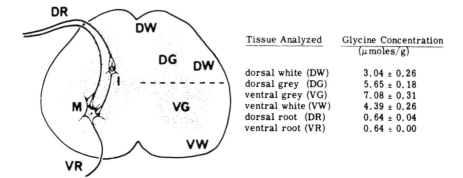

Tissue Analyzed	Glycine Concentration (μmoles/g)
dorsal white (DW)	3.04 ± 0.26
dorsal grey (DG)	5.65 ± 0.18
ventral grey (VG)	7.08 ± 0.31
ventral white (VW)	4.39 ± 0.26
dorsal root (DR)	0.64 ± 0.04
ventral root (VR)	0.64 ± 0.00

Figure 20.7 Glycine distribution in cross sections of cat lumbar spinal cord. Synapses between dorsal root fibers and an interneuron and a motoneuron are illustrated [from M.H. Aprison, R.A. Davidoff, R. Werman, in: *Handbook of Neurochemistry*, A. Lajtha (Ed.), vol. 3, p. 381 (1970); © 1970 by Plenum Press, New York].

hypoxia due to aortic occlusion, there is also a decrease in the concentration of glycine in this area. The disappearance of glycine is accompanied by a loss of inhibitory reflexes. And, there seems to be a direct correlation between the number of remaining interneurons and the glycine concentration.

The iontophoretic administration of glycine to motoneurons hyperpolarizes the neuronal membrane, blocks the production of spikes, and decreases the amplitude of excitatory and inhibitory postsynaptic potentials (Curtis *et al.*, 1968). On this population of cells, it is more powerful than GABA. However, this does not mean to suggest that GABA does not participate in the inhibitory activity within the spinal cord. It likely does and is probably released by the Renshaw cells.

Changes in the metabolism of glycine during various functional states have not been examined with any consistency. The binding of glycine in the brain does decrease during long-lasting isolation in mice, and this might be due to structural changes in the glycine receptor (De Feudis *et al.*, 1976).

β-ALANINE

The amino acid β-alanine is found in relatively high concentrations in the brain, as compared with other tissues. Its values approximately equal those of acetylcholine or norepinephrine, and its regional distribution parallels that of GABA, with its highest value being reported for the mesencephalon. The levels then decrease along the rostro-caudal gradient. In the central nervous system, it is synthesized from aspartate and degraded by a transamination with α-oxoglutarate in the mitochondria (for review see De Feudis and Martin Del Rio, 1977).

β-alanine has a potent depressant action on central neurons, causing a hyperpolarization of the neuronal membrane. Neither the receptor, nor the mechanism of action appear to be the same as those of either GABA or glycine, although its inhibitory effect is antagonized by strychnine (but not by bicuculline, an antagonist of GABA).

After its depressant action, β-alanine is taken up by some neurons and glial cells. This system of transport has been reported for the retina, cerebral cortex and a number of other CNS areas. It is competitively inhibited by GABA, but has not been found to be affected by glycine.

The available data in support of a neurotransmitter role for β-alanine are relatively scanty; very little is actually known about the functional aspects of its action or its contribution to the plasticity of brain function.

TAURINE

With the exception of the dicarboxylic amino acids, taurine (Fig. 20.8) is the most abundant amino acid in the central nervous system, with a concentration about twice that of glycine. Because of the growing consensus as to the role of some amino acids in the process of synaptic transmission, these relatively high levels of taurine have attracted considerable attention. The potent inhibitory effects of taurine on neuronal excitability in retina and spinal cord are certainly suggestive of such a role (for review see Sturman and Hayes, 1980).

While a small amount of dietary taurine is able to reach the brain from the circulation, the great majority is probably synthesized from the amino acid cysteine, which is transported into the nerve endings by a high-affinity system (Misra, 1980). The first enzyme of this pathway, cysteine oxidase, catalyzes the oxidation of cysteine to cysteine sulfinic and cysteine sulfonic acids. It is high in some parts of the brain, notably the pons and medulla, and lowest in the cerebral cortex (Misra and Olney, 1975). Cysteine sulfinic

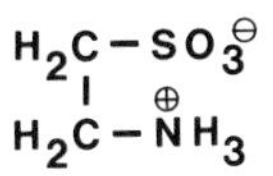

$$H_2C - SO_3^{\ominus}$$
$$|$$
Figure 20.8 Taurine. $$H_2C - \overset{\oplus}{N}H_3$$

acid decarboxylase (L-cysteine sulfinate carboxylase) synthesizes taurine via hypotaurine. This enzyme is present primarily in nerve cell bodies and appears to be absent in axons (Sturman, 1981).

Taurine is released from the nerve endings during stimulation, a response that can be demonstrated *in vitro* following electrical stimulation or in a medium rich in potassium (Jasper and Koyama, 1969). The presence of calcium ions potentiates this effect (Collins and Topiwala, 1974). Taurine is also released from the brain during arousal and seizure activity, and its administration increases the amplitude of all EEG frequencies (Kaczmarek and Adey, 1974).

Taurine causes a marked depression of neurons in the spinal cord, medulla and retina. Inhibitory effects are also present in the thalamus, cerebellum and cerebral cortex, but are much less striking. These responses can be blocked by the administration of strychnine. As with glycine, the mechanism of taurine action seems to involve a change in chloride conductance.

The rat cerebral cortex has a rather low uptake rate of taurine (Honegger *et al.*, 1973), seemingly insufficient for a neurotransmitter. But, a sodium-dependent, saturable, high-affinity uptake system, suitable for the removal of extracellular neurotransmitter, has been found in astrocytes (Schousboe *et al.*, 1976). And recently, Kontro and Oja (1979) did report the presence of a saturable, high-affinity, sodium-dependent system in rat brain synaptosomes. The system required three sodium ions for the transport of one taurine molecule.

The possibility exists that taurine functions more as a modulator of membrane excitability than as a neurotransmitter. In a sense, it could act to "stabilize" the excitable membranes (Gruener and Bryant, 1975). Izumi *et al.* (1977) and Pasantes-Morales and Gamboa (1980) suggest that taurine may regulate the level of free calcium in the nervous tissue and, in the process, modulate the ionic fluxes across the neuronal membrane.

The injection of taurine into the ventricles causes a depression of psychomotor activity, loss of body balance, ataxic gait and a complete loss of thermoregulation (Sgaragli and Paran, 1972). In high doses, it may even cause analgesia. An intraperitonal injection also lowers the body temperature and induces hypophagia and a decreased water drive. Taurine also has an antiepileptic action, delaying the onset and development of focal epileptic activity. Accordingly, it has been effective in the control of seizures in various experimental models of epilepsy. It may also be able to control naturally occuring seizures (e.g., in the babboon [Barbeau *et al.*, 1975] and in the cat [Van Gelder *et al.*, 1977]). But, up until now there has only been a marginal effect in the control of seizure activity in epileptic patients.

PROLINE

Proline (see Fig. 13.2) has been found to have a relatively weak depressant action on spinal and Purkinje neurons. It is transported into synaptosomes by a high-affinity, sodium-dependent system (Peterson and Ragupathy, 1972) that appears to be more active in some regions (e.g., lateral reticular nucleus) than others. Proline is released from synaptosomes in an atypical manner. One peak of release occurs upon exposure to an increase in potassium concentration and another appears in response to a restoration of the normal potassium level (Nickolson, 1982).

The concentrations of proline in the mammalian central nervous system are rather low, and at the present time there is little evidence in support of a neurotransmitter role. From the viewpoint of functional brain biochemistry, one of the most interesting aspects of proline activity is its effect upon learning. In 1976, Cherkin *et al.* found that an intracerebral injection of proline in chickens trained in a one-trial avoidance task impairs their memory for the task when tested 24 hours later. This amnesia was not accompanied by occult seizures, and there was only a brief depression of the electrophysiological activities that was followed by a transient rebound hyperexcitability (Gerbrandt *et al.*, 1977). L-proline was found to be more potent than D-proline, so that the L-configuration is somehow essential for the amnestic effect. It is difficult to explain these findings, but the effect does not appear to depend upon the inhibition of protein synthesis (Cherkin *et al.*, 1981). Van Harreveld (1979) believes that proline counteracts the effect of glutamic acid on memory and that it and glutamate compete for the glutamate receptor. In small concentrations, it has been found to behave as a glutamate agonist, while in higher concentrations it acts as an antagonist (Van Harreveld and Strumwasser, 1981). This possibility is at least consonant with their opposing effects on spreading cortical depression.

γ-AMINOBUTYRIC ACID

Discovered in 1883 by Schotten, GABA was the first amino acid demonstrated to have strong potential as a neurotransmitter (Florey, 1954; Bazemore *et al.*, 1957). It has been calculated to be the putative inhibitory transmitter of about 20% of the synapses in the mammalian brain and is widely distributed in concentrations that range from 200 to 1000 times greater than those of the other major neurotransmitters.

The immediate precursor of GABA is glutamate, and the synthetic pathway, off of the tricarboxylic acid (TCA) cycle, constitutes a circular system that is known as the "GABA shunt" (Fig. 20.9). It processes about 8-10% of

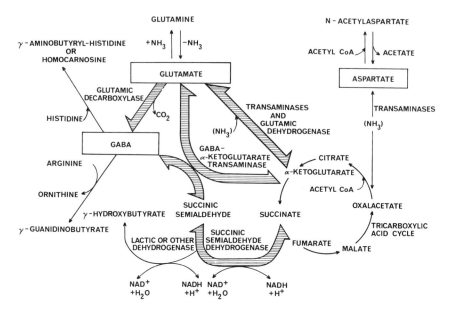

Figure 20.9 Outline of principal reactions of GABA, glutamate and aspartate in the nervous system. The reactions pertinent to GABA metabolism are emphasized by the large arrows [redrawn from E. Roberts, *Biochem. Pharmacol.* 23:2637 (1974); © 1974 by Pergamon Press, Inc.].

the TCA cycle residues. This pathway is active even after death and is responsible for the postmortem accumulation of GABA in the brain. A secondary biosynthetic pathway does exist, using putrescine as a precursor (Seiler *et al.*, 1971).

The enzyme responsible for the production of GABA from glutamic acid, glutamic acid decarboxylase (GAD), is localized only in neurons that synthesize GABA. Two isoenzymes of GAD were isolated in 1970 by Haber *et al.* GAD I is mostly found in synaptosomes and is inhibited by anions, while GAD II is primarily in the mitochondria and, in contrast, is stimulated by anions. Other potent inhibitors of GAD activity are norepinephrine and serotonin. The glutamic acid that is decarboxylated by this enzyme originates exclusively from a pool that is heavily labeled when glucose is oxidized in the tissue (Patel *et al.*, 1974).

The level of GABA in the brain depends primarily on the activity of GAD, more so than on the activity of enzymes responsible for GABA degradation (Fahn and Cote, 1968). The concentration of endogenous GABA regulates the activity of both GAD isoenzymes, probably by a product repression of the synthesis. The GABA system, and GAD in particular, is responsive to various brain functional needs. GAD activity, for example, is lower in isolated mice than in mice kept in groups (Blindermann et al., 1979).

Pyridoxal-5'-phosphate is a necessary cofactor of this enzyme, but in vivo GAD is generally only partially saturated by it. Pyridoxal-5'-phosphate may therefore be one of the components of the system controlling GAD. In addition, some factors endogenous to the brain probably suppress the binding of the cofactor to the enzyme, and so contribute to the control of the GABA level. One of these factors is glutamate, which inactivates GAD by promoting the dissociation of pyridoxal-5'-phosphate from the enzyme. The inactive apoenzyme that is produced may then be reactivated by combining with available pyridoxal-5'-phosphate. Adenine nucleotides are also involved in the control of GABA synthesis. The enzyme has been found to inhibited by ATP, ADP, cAMP and cGMP (Seligman et al., 1978).

The major enzyme responsible for the degradation of GABA is γ-aminobutyric acid - α-ketoglutaric transaminase (4-aminobutyrate: 1-oxoglutarate aminotransferase or GABA-T). GABA-T is a mitochondrial enzyme that is found in neurons that receive inhibitory inputs mediated by GABA. It is localized almost exclusively in the gray matter of the brain. While it is probably present in small quantities in the white matter, its activity there is extremely low.

GABA-T requires sodium ions and the cofactor pyridoxal-5'-phosphate for its activity. This cofactor also acts upon a number of ω-amino acids, such as β-alanine and α, γ-diaminoglutaric acid. Ho et al. (1975) distinguished two forms of GABA-T, cytoplasmic and synaptosomal. Both are inhibited by glutamate and aspartate, while they differ in their sensitivity to the pharmacological inhibitors, 2,4-diaminobutyric acid and aminooxyacetic acid.

The third GABA shunt enzyme, succinic semialdehyde dehydrogenase, oxidizes succinic semialdehyde, the product of GABA-T activity, to succinic acid. It is a mitochondrial enzyme, whose activity in the brain is very high. The metabolism of succinic semialdehyde is therefore very rapid and its level is kept quite low.

The release of GABA from nerve endings depends upon the presence of potassium and calcium ions. With the continued application of calcium, there is a progressive decrease in this efflux. It is probable that this release takes place preferentially from the cytoplasmic pool (De Belleroche and Bradford, 1973). The release in enhanced by antibodies to gangliosides, an effect which again underscores the active participation of membrane lipids in transmitter events (Frieder and Rapport, 1981).

The action of GABA in the synapse is terminated by its reuptake into nerve endings and glia (Fig. 20.10). The cell membrane contains two uptake systems, a high affinity and a low affinity one. Labeled GABA can also be exchanged with GABA from the endogenous pool, and this exchange may simulate the high affinity uptake. A net transport has, however, been well documented. The uptake into the synaptosomes is sodium-dependent and resembles the transport systems of several other amino acids, but is specific for GABA. Two activating sites are probably present on the transport molecule which bind sodium (Wheeler, 1980).

Phosphatidylserine has been discovered to enhance the uptake of labeled GABA into synaptosomes by 48% (Chweh and Leslie, 1982). Phosphatidylethanolamine, phosphatidylinositol, phosphatidic acid, gangliosides, and sulfatides had no such effect. The results argue for a contribution by phosphatidylserine to the process of presynaptic GABA uptake.

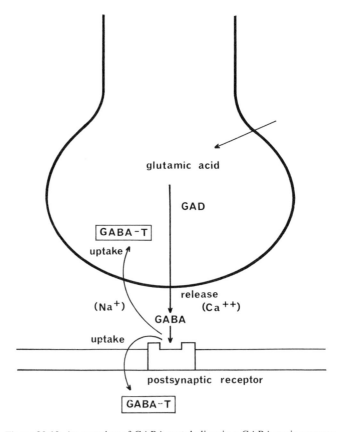

Figure 20.10 An overview of GABA metabolism in a GABA-ergic synapse.

The intensity of GABA uptake into the synaptosomes differs in various brain regions. For example, more is taken up by synaptosomes from the diencephalon than from any other area of the brain (Levi *et al.*, 1974). The uptake is additionally altered by adrenal steroids, and pipecolic acid, a product of L-lysine metabolism (Nomura *et al.*, 1981). After adrenalectomy, the uptake into isolated hippocampal synaptosomes increases. A similar transport into synaptosomes from frontal cortex or cerebellum was not changed. These findings indicate that synapses in the hippocampus which employ GABA as a neurotransmitter are functionally responsive to their hormonal environment.

Glial cells are also involved in the uptake of GABA (Henn and Hamberger, 1971). This process has been demonstrated *in vitro* with cloned astrocytoma cell lines. The uptake is coupled to the intracellular GABA metabolism and can be reduced by lowering the external sodium. The glia are also involved in the control of GABA efflux from the nerve endings, since the glial cells regulate the extracellular calcium concentration (Henn, 1976).

GABA is almost exclusively an inhibitory neurotransmitter. Its presence at the postsynaptic membrane causes a hyperpolarization by increasing the membrane permeability to chloride ions. Negative charges entering the cell increase the difference between the electrical potential on the inside and the outside of the cell, thus preventing the normal depolarizing response to excitatory inputs. Alger and Nicoll (1979) have described a biphasic effect of GABA on the membrane potential of central neurons, and both its negative and positive components block the firing of the cell. And, some GABA-mediated inhibitory postsynaptic potentials may even be depolarizing (Misgeld *et al.*, 1982).

In the spinal cord, GABA may depolarize primary afferent fibers and increase their excitability. Dorsal root depolarization is also mediated by GABA. The effect is presynaptic, and a similar depolarization due to a presynaptic effect of GABA has also been observed in the olfactory and prepyriform cortices.

In the postsynaptic membrane, GABA binds to receptors which Chude (1979) has solubilized and partially purified from the mouse brain. The GABA receptor is a complex structure composed of a variety of independent, but interrelated, sites (for review see Enna, 1981). One of them is a recognition site, which binds GABA and a GABA agonist, muscimol. The second site is closely associated with the chloride channel. Some depressant barbiturates may react with this ionophore portion as agonists, unlike the action of picrotoxin, which functions as an antagonist.

Coupled to these two components appears to be a binding site which has tentatively been termed the benzodiazepine receptor (Valdes *et al.*, 1981).

The endogenous ligand for this receptor is not presently known, but peptides (Davis *et al.*, 1981), inosine, hypoxanthine, nicotinamide, and thromboxane A_2 (Mohler, 1981) have all been suggested. The coupling of the GABA receptor to the benzodiazepine receptor could be a modulatory association and may be absent in some neurons or parts of the brain. While Brennan (1982) confirmed the existence of GABA autoreceptors on GABA-ergic terminals in the rat cerebral cortex, his pharmacological analysis showed that these receptors were not functionally coupled to the benzodiazepine receptors. Consequently, it seems that only the postsynaptic response to GABA is modulated by the benzodiazepines (Olsen, 1981).

GABA receptors are also under the influence of an endogenous factor, referred to as GABA modulin (Massotti *et al.*, 1981). This research group has detected two apparent populations of binding sites for GABA in synaptic membranes: one with a low affinity constant and the other with a high constant. Treatment with the detergent Triton X-100 caused an increase in the number of high-affinity sites, while the number of low-affinity ones remained unchanged. GABA modulin added to the synaptic membrane fraction reduced the number of binding sites to their original level.

GABA receptors also have been divided into at least two subclasses according to various criteria, such as the presence or absence of bicuculline binding (Browner *et al.*, 1981), different types of receptor-effector coupling (Olsen *et al.*, 1981), and a dependence of GABA binding upon sodium. However, the use of a ^{3}H-GABA ligand has indicated that the sodium-dependent binding may be an attachment to the GABA transport system, whereas the sodium-independent binding is more characteristic of the receptor site (Lester and Peck, 1979; Winkler *et al.*, 1979).

The attachment to the receptor is specific. Even amino acids with a similar chemical structure, such as β-alanine, have a reduced affinity for it. The binding is decreased by proteolytic enzymes (trypsin, pronase) and increased by phospholipase C (Enna and Snyder, 1977). Recent work with phospholipase C and Triton X-100 to deplete membrane phospholipids and proteins has led Toffano and his associates (1981) to speculate that phospholipids, although not directly involved in the regulation of transmitter binding, may actually be the GABA-binding component of the receptor site. Phospholipids (phosphatidylethanolamine and phosphatidylcholine) compete for the receptor with GABA, suggesting that they regulate the accessibility of the binding site (Lloyd and Davidson, 1979). Other studies (Johnston and Kennedy, 1978; Toffano *et al.*, 1978) are consistent with such an interpretation and imply that these modulator phospholipids can allosterically alter the conformation of the recognition site on the receptor and so modify the affinity for the transmitter.

The synapses of GABA-containing cells can be identified by morphological and biochemical methods. Iverson and Snyder (1968) fractionated synaptosomes by centrifugation and found one fraction that selectively accumulated labelled GABA. GABA-containing synaptosomes were discovered to be lighter than those containing catecholamines. They also contain fewer mitochondria and display greater variations in size.

Studies of the regional distribution of GABA in the mammalian CNS have revealed the presence of relatively high levels in the substantia nigra and globus pallidus (Bertilsson *et al.*, 1977). Here, GABA may be a transmitter substance for caudate-nigral and caudate-pallidal inhibitory transmission (Fig. 20.11). Significant concentrations were also found in the hypothalamus (Knieriem *et al.*, 1977), the median eminence and the globus pallidus (Van der Heyden *et al.*, 1979). An exceptionally large concentration has been reported in the zona reticulata of the substantia nigra. Using histochemical and biochemical methods, a number of papers have described high levels of GABA in the corpora quadrigemina, cerebellar cortex, and in hippocampus. However, without a microwave inactivation of the enzymes, the validity of such values is questionable.

GABA-ergic pathways have been detected in a number of brain regions. For example, in the auditory system, short-axon GABA-ergic interneurons

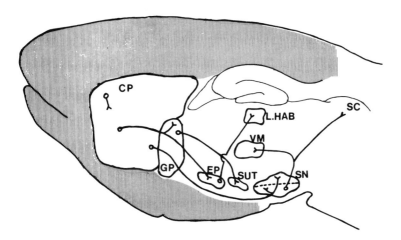

Figure 20.11 Organization of some GABAergic projections in the extrapyramidal system. SN, substantia nigra; GP, globus pallidus; EP, endopeduncular nucleus; VT, subthalamic nucleus; L. HAB, lateral habenular nucleus; VM, ventromedial nucleus of the thalamus; SN, substantia nigra; SC, superior colliculus [redrawn from H.C. Fibiger, *Can. J. Neurol. Sci.* 7:251 (1980); © 1980 by Canadian Journal of Neurological Sciences].

are present in the inferior colliculus and dorsal cochlear nucleus. In the basal ganglia, the striato-nigral pathway contains GABA, and its fibers terminate on the dopaminergic neurons of the substantia nigra. This pathway has an inhibitory effect on the nigral cells. After its destruction, these neurons show a GABA supersensitivity (Waddington and Cross, 1978). Here, GABA-ergic neurons are part of a complex system of dopaminergic, cholinergic, and other fibers controlling motility (Schwarcz and Coyle, 1977). The activity of this system also appears to be regulated by neurons containing endorphins (Glass et al., 1980).

Destruction of GABA-ergic neurons in the substantia nigra by a structural analog of glutamate, kainic acid, causes disorders of motility, such as a continuous turning toward the side contralateral to the lesion. GABA is abundant in those thalamic nuclei which control motility. The GABA-ergic mechanisms in the thalamus play an important role in postural regulation and in the mediation of certain motor responses arising in the striatum (Di Chiara et al., 1979).

Another area concerned with the control of motility is the nucleus accumbens. The injection of GABA into it causes a short-lasting hypomotility and general hypoactivity that is probably due to a stimulation of postsynaptic GABA receptors in this area. There is a descending GABA-ergic pathway from the nucleus accumbens which terminates in the ventral tegmental nucleus (McGeer et al., 1978). The accumbens-pallidal projection is GABA-ergic and contributes to the initiation of locomotor responses (Mogenson et al., 1980). The cerebellum is also involved in the control of movement. Here, GABA is the neurotransmitter of Purkinje cells.

GABA is high in the hippocampus and is concentrated in basket cells which inhibit the hippocampal pyramidal cells. In the hypothalamus, most GABA-ergic neurons are interneurons that originate and terminate there (Tappaz and Brownstein, 1977).

The inhibition of the granule cells in the olfactory bulb is mediated by GABA. Also, the periglomerular cells are affected by it. Electron microscopy (Ribak et al., 1977) has demonstrated the presence of GABA-containing synaptic junctions between granule and mitral cells of the glomerule.

The release of GABA from brain tissue depends upon the function of a particular area. GABA is normally released spontaneously from the cerebral cortex. But, the amount released is very small, and in order to obtain reliable results, the tissue has to be loaded first with radioactive GABA. Simultaneously, GABA metabolism has to be blocked by amino-oxyacetic acid. By this method, it was found that lesions of the reticular formation increase the GABA efflux, as does slow-wave sleep and the direct electrical stimulation of the cortex.

GABA has an inhibitory effect upon animal behavior, decreasing spontaneous and conditioned activity. The intracranial injection of GABA in cats decreases their defensive reactions and improves their sociability. An antimetabolite, *n*-dipropylacetate, elevates the level of GABA in the brain and inhibits spontaneous behavior and active avoidance (Misslin *et al.*, 1976). In low doses, however, this drug was reported to improve learning.

An increase in GABA levels induced by aminooxyacetic acid, an inhibitor of GABA-T, does not affect the process of learning within a single session. But, the consolidation of learning from one session to another is absent (Katz and Liebler, 1978). In addition, picrotoxin, a GABA receptor blocker, reportedly facilitates the acquisition of maze learning (Essman, 1971).

Most of these effects are probably primarily related to the level of general behavioral arousal and to the control of the behavioral output. Command neurons, which are thought to initiate behavior and activate the behavioral sequences, are normally depressed by an inhibitory neurotransmitter. An increase in the level of GABA would therefore lower behavioral output (Freed and Michaelis, 1976).

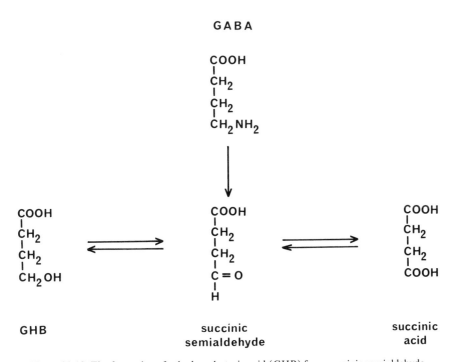

Figure 20.12 The formation of γ-hydroxybutyric acid (GHB) from succinic semialdehyde.

γ-HYDROXYBUTYRIC ACID

Instead of being oxidized to succinic acid, the succinic semialdehyde of the GABA shunt may undergo a reduction to γ-hydroxybutyric acid (GHB) (Fig. 20.12). This reaction has been established to occur in the brain (Fishbein and Bessman, 1964), and an enzyme apparently specific for GHB synthesis has been identified in both human and rat (Cash *et al.*, 1979; Rumigny *et al.*, 1980). Benavides *et al.* (1982) also have reported that GHB in rat brain is bound to high affinity neuronal sites which are likely specific and sodium-independent.

The administration of GHB to animals and humans induces an anesthesia with an electroencephalographic pattern similar to that recorded during an episode of petit mal epilepsy (Godschalk *et al.*, 1977). Anti-petit mal drugs interfere with this pattern (Godschalk *et al.*, 1976), leading to some speculation that GHB may be of significance in the pathology of epilepsy (Snead, 1978). But, the actual role of GHB is not known. Its binding specificity and generation within the neurons are suggestive of a neuromodulatory or neurotransmitter function, although the available evidence for such a possibility is still too sparse.

Chapter 21

Other Putative Neurotransmitters and Neuromodulators

There are a number of substances present in the brain in relatively large concentrations that are able to influence the firing rate of many neurons. While their functions in neural transmission have yet to be determined, the indications are that they operate either as genuine neurotransmitters or as modulators of the activity of other transmitters. The present chapter will focus on two classes of these agents - the purines and the prostaglandins.

PURINES

At least two purines, adenosine and inosine, have been suspected to function as messengers between individual cells in the brain. For several years, evidence has been accumulating that adenosine is capable of acting as either a transmitter or a modulator of many central and peripheral synapses. Furthermore, Trams (1981) has postulated that the purine derivatives may have served as the primordial transmitter substances.

Simple adenosine derivatives (adenosine and its mono-, di-, and triphosphates) are present in the mammalian brain in a relatively high concentration. Adenosine is released both from perfused cerebral cortex *in vivo* and from isolated cortical slabs *in vitro* (Sulakhe and Phillis, 1975). Excitation has been observed to increase this output, especially in the more anterior portions of the neocortex. This extracellular adenosine has a potent depressant action on neurons of the cerebral cortex (particularly the cortico-spinal cells) and on cerebellar Purkinje cells (for review see Stone, 1980).

Adenosine released from the neurons during excitation probably originates from the adenosine triphosphate efflux into the synaptic area. This ATP can actually be released from both neurons and from various secreting cells, along with their secretory products - hormones or neurotransmitters. It is possible that with each nerve impulse, a neurotransmitter, such as acetylcholine, is released together with ATP from the nerve ending. A presynaptic release of adenosine phosphates has already been documented in the hippocampus (Lee *et al.*, 1982). ATP is then degraded by enzymes located on the outer surface of the postsynaptic membrane, the ectoenzymes. At least three enzymes are involved in this degradation, ATPase (probably a magnesium-dependent form), adenylate kinase and 5′-nucleotidase. By the sequential removal of phosphate residues, adenosine is finally produced which then reacts with a specific adenosine receptor. The release of adenosine is also induced by ouabain, an inhibitor of the sodium pump. A similar effect of potassium is believed to be limited, or the response may even follow the removal of potassium (Hollins and Stone, 1980).

The presence of extracellular ATP has been found to block the release of acetylcholine (Israel and Meunier, 1978). The work carried out with cortical synaptosomes and *in vitro* preparations from *Torpedo* electroplax has demonstrated similar effects with the other adenine nucleotides (Ginsborg and Hirst, 1972).

Adenosine triphosphate and the triphosphates of other purines and pyrimidines (ITP, GTP, UTP and CTP) have either an excitatory postsynaptic action upon neurons, or are able to enhance the neuronal response to other transmitters (Phillis and Wu, 1981). Nevertheless, the current evidence for adenosine as a classical neurotransmitter in a "purinergic" pathway is not all that convincing (Stone, 1981). It appears then that ATP serves in a modulatory capacity.

The depressant actions of adenosine upon central neurons can most readily be explained by postulating a presynaptic action which is characterized by a decrement in the quantity of neurotransmitter that is released (Krnjevic and Lekic, 1977). Moreover, adenosine administered by iontophoresis is effective in physiological concentrations (Schubert and Mitzdorf, 1979). It has also been reported to reduce the release of acetylcholine, norepinephrine (Hedquist and Fredholm, 1976; Harms *et al.*, 1978), dopamine (Michaelis *et al.*, 1979), and serotonin (Harms *et al.*, 1979). In this way, it would exert an important influence over the efficacy of synaptic transmission.

The modulatory effect and the receptor involved seem to be specific for adenosine, so that adenine nucleotides must be converted to adenosine in order to exert an effect. The presynaptic actions of adenosine probably result from a reduction in the calcium permeability of the nerve terminal membrane. This drop would then cause a corresponding decrease in transmitter release. But, adenosine also modulates the activity of adenylate cyclase. On a molecule of the enzyme two binding sites for adenosine have been identified (Trost and Stock, 1977). One, a high-affinity R-site, appears to have subclasses which either stimulate or inhibit the activity of adenylate cyclase (Van Calker *et al.*, 1978; Schwabe *et al.*, 1979; Wolff *et al.*, 1981). The other, a low affinity P-site, appears to mediate an inhibition of the same enzyme (Londos and Wolff, 1977). The binding of adenosine to the high affinity site on the presynaptic neuron has been suggested to lead to an increase in neurotransmitter synthesis (Kuroda, 1978).

Work with turkey erythrocytes has indicated that the adenosine receptor is permanently coupled to the cyclase system (Braun and Levitzki, 1979), and its activity apparently depends upon the presence of phospholipids (Anand-Srivastava and Johnson, 1981). However, it may be, as Newman and Levitzki (1982) caution, that the increase in cAMP which has been observed following the application of adenosine to isolated brain slices is not a direct response, but one that represents a process secondary to the presynaptic mediating effect of adenosine upon transmitter release.

Schultz (1975) claims that the increased level of cAMP is caused by a reversal of the activation of phosphodiesterase. Several drugs, such as the CNS stimulants theophyllin and caffeine, can inhibit this effect. Although it was originally believed that they acted to lower the activity of phosphodiesterase, their action as stimulants may involve a blockage of the depressant effect of adenosine upon cortical neurons (Snyder, 1981).

The inactivation and reuptake of adenosine is a slow process, such that adenosine released from axon terminals and dendrites is able to mediate long-lasting effects of active neurons on their target cells. The action of adenosine is terminated by a reuptake into both neurons and astrocytes by at least two high-affinity transport systems (Bender *et al.*, 1980). And, when taken up by the nerve endings, it can be transported in a retrograde direction to the nerve cell bodies (Schubert and Kreutzberg, 1974; Schubert *et al.*, 1977).

In addition to its release from the brain during excitation, there is also an efflux of adenosine during hypoxia and hypoglycemia (Kleihues *et al.*, 1974). Also, spreading cortical depression causes an adenosine-mediated augmentation in the level of cAMP in the cerebral cortex (Krivanek, 1976).

And, the injection of adenosine into the brain ventricles has a sedative effect (Haulica *et al.*, 1973).

Recent studies of benzodiazepine receptors in the brain, summarized in a review by Marangos *et al.* (1979), indicate that some purines may act as endogenous ligands for these receptors. This work has primarily focused upon inosine and hypoxanthine. Inosine competes with benzodiazepines for the receptor site, causing a rapidly desensitizing excitatory response and non-desensitizing inhibitory response (MacDonald *et al.*, 1979). These findings suggest that inosine could act as a neuromodulator of certain synapses. Inosine and hypoxanthine are actually relatively weak competitive inhibitors of benzodiazepine binding, but they are found in the brain in comparatively large quantities and may therefore act at effective concentrations. Also, their levels in the brain tissue increase several-fold when it is subjected to depolarizing stimuli (Sun *et al.*, 1977).

EICOSANOIDS IN THE BRAIN

Introduced in 1980 by Corey *et al.*, the term eicosanoids encompasses a family of biologically active derivatives of 20-carbon unsaturated fatty acids. They are ubiquitous humoral agents that are generated in nearly all cells and are among the most potent naturally produced substances, being effective at extremely low concentrations. They are able to elicit a large number of biological responses both *in vivo* and *in vitro*. However, other than their potency, few generalizations concerning their activity can be made, since one eicosanoid may have a specific effect which is not typical of others with a similar structure. There is little evidence that they act as neurotransmitters, but they may function as modulators of the actions of several transmitters, hormones and other biologically active agents (for review see Vapaatalo and Parantainen, 1978; Wolfe, 1982).

The oldest known members of this class of substances are the prostaglandins. Their existence was first noted by Kurzrok and Lieb (1930), who found that human semen influenced the contractility of uterine muscle strips. In subsequent research, it has been demonstrated that they are involved in the activities of the male and female reproductive systems, in the motility and secretion of the gastrointestinal tract, in blood clotting and platelet aggregation, in immunological reactions and in the cardiovascular and renal systems. They also affect the release of fat from adipose tissue, and they may be involved in the hemopoietic system, the transmembrane movement of water and electrolytes, and the pathogenesis of asthma.

In 1960, Bergstrom and Sjoval isolated two fractions of prostaglandins, one soluble in ether (PGE) and the other soluble in phosphate buffers

(PGF). Over the course of the next several years, other prostaglandins were identified. All are chemical derivatives of prostanoic acid, a twenty-carbon fatty acid with a five-member ring and a hairpin configuration (Fig. 21.1). There are presently about twenty natural forms, which are grouped according to the structure of their cyclopentane ring (Fig. 21.2). The main groups, E, F, A, B, C, and D, are further divided into subgroups 1, 2 and 3 on the basis of the number of double bonds in the molecule.

In the body, prostaglandins are synthesized from arachidonic acid (all-cis-5,8,11,14-eicosatetraenoic acid) and dihomo-γ-linolenic acid, which are themselves derived from membrane lipids such as the phospholipids, cholesterol esters, and triglycerides. The pathway first involves the splitting of arachidonic acid from the membrane lipid by phospholipase A. This is the rate-limiting step in prostaglandin synthesis. The conversion of arachidonic acid to the prostaglandins is catalyzed by prostaglandin synthetase (Fig. 21.3). There is, however, some question as to whether this process takes place in the brain (Pace-Asciak and Nashat, 1976).

Prostaglandin synthetase can be identified in many tissues, including the brain, associated with the microsomal fraction. It is actually a group of enzymes necessary for a number of sequential steps in the pathway. The initial step in this conversion is catalyzed by the action of prostaglandin cyclooxygenase. Two atoms of oxygen are added to the fatty acid precursor to generate the endoperoxides PGG_2 and PGH_2. The synthesis of the endoperoxides by this enzyme is very fast, but the yield is low; only a small percentage of substrate molecules are converted.

The endoperoxides are subsequently used for the synthesis of the prostaglandins by peroxidase or endoperoxide isomerase. The same peroxides may also be converted to thromboxane A_2, its hydrolysis product - thromboxane B_2, and the prostacyclins (PGX_2, PGI_2). As A_2 thrombox-

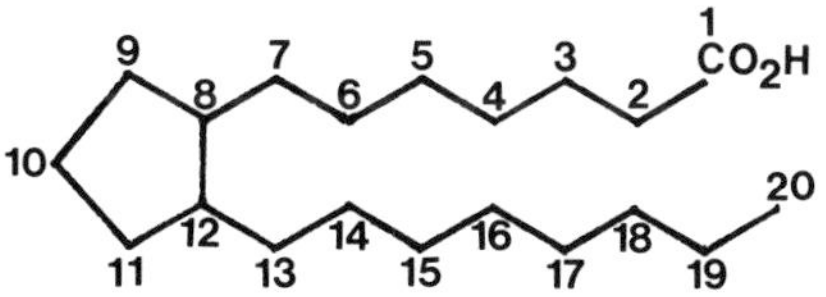

Figure 21.1 Prostanoic acid.

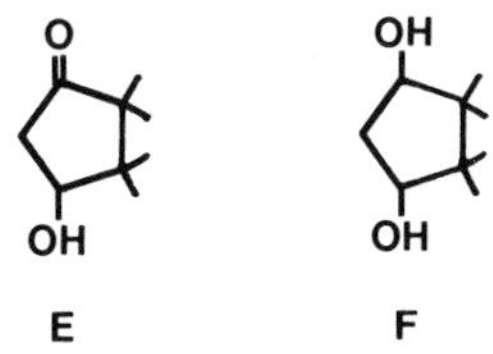

Figure 21.2 Structure of the cyclopentane ring of the prostaglandins of the PGE and PGF group.

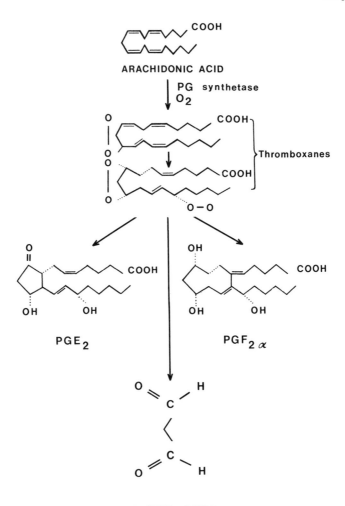

Figure 21.3 Synthesis of some thromboxanes and prostaglandins.

anes, the molecules are many times more biologically potent than the prostaglandins. However, the thromboxanes and prostacyclins have very short half-lives in aqueous solution, and thromboxane A_2 is quickly trans-formed in the body to the less active B_2 form. Work by Wolfe *et al.* (1976) indicates that this B_2 form is produced in the brain in significant quantities.

While the effects of prostaglandins upon a variety of cells and tissues are already reasonably detailed, the functional importance of both prostaglandins and thromboxanes in the CNS in uncertain. Their typical physiological levels in the brain are quite low and increase only during various traumatic conditions, electroconvulsive shock, hypoxia, hypoglycemia and pyrogen fever. The main CNS prostaglandins, PGD_2, PGE_2 and PGF_2, are synthesized in the brain from the endoperoxides PGG_2 and PGH_2. PGF_2 is generated in much larger quantities than PGE_2, and this difference is further augmented by serotonin, norepinephrine, epinephrine and DOPA (Leslie, 1976; Wolfe et al., 1976a). Catecholamines and indoleamines may also function as natural cofactors of prostaglandin synthetase, stimulating prostaglandin synthesis. Glucocorticoids, in contrast, inhibit this process. Much of the work on mammalian CNS prostaglandins, however, has been on the rodent brain and may not be generalizable to other mammalian species. The cat and human brains, for example, appear to synthesize little, if any, PGD_2 (Abdel-Halim et al., 1980; Bishai and Coceani, 1980).

According to Gross et al. (1977), prostaglandins are synthesized in the postsynaptic area of the neuron by a process coupled with the binding of a neurotransmitter to its postsynaptic receptor. The onset of this synthesis is very fast. The process is inhibited by several divalent cations, including copper, zinc and cadmium, as well as by the analogs of essential fatty acids, such as linoleic and linolenic acid. Endogenous inhibitors of prostaglandin synthetases are in blood plasma and serum, and glucocorticoids increase the extent of this inhibition. This system, therefore, represents a natural mechanism for controlling prostaglandin synthesis (Saeed et al., 1977).

The degradation of prostaglandins E_2 and F_2 in the brain is quite slow, although it is rapid in the circulating blood. Prostaglandin half-life in the plasma is about one minute, which would indicate that they probably do not function as circulating hormones. The degradative enzymes are prostaglandin-15-dehydrogenase, prostaglandin reductase, prostaglandin isomerase, and a number of other enzymes catalyzing the β-oxidation and ω-oxidation of the fatty acids.

Keuhl and Humes (1972) proposed that prostaglandins react with their own, specific receptors. This binding is calcium-dependent, unlike the non-specific, calcium-independent binding of prostaglandins to other tissue components. After the binding, prostaglandins of the E group stimulate adenylate cyclase, while F prostaglandins activate guanylate cyclase. The E group prostaglandins stimulate the in vivo and in vitro accumulation of cAMP in the brain. The increase is highest in the cerebral cortex and lowest in the brain stem. The administration of pharmacological doses of prostaglandins, however, leads to a progressive loss of responsiveness of the cAMP-synthesizing system (Su et al., 1976), which suggests that these substances may play a role in the development of neuronal subsensitivity during

periods of increased stimulation. Since cAMP and cGMP supposedly promote opposing metabolic processes, their relative concentrations (and the
relative amounts of prostaglandins E and F) could determine the cell
responsiveness and firing rate.

The most potent activators of guanylate cyclase may actually be the
peroxides, particularly the PGG endoperoxides (Goldberg and Haddox,
1977; Hidaka and Asano, 1977). If this is the case in the brain, then the
possibility exists (Horrobin, 1978) that the PGG endoperoxides might stimulate cGMP synthesis, but upon conversion to the prostaglandins, the effect
could shift to adenylate cyclase, thereby augmenting cAMP levels. This
might mean that the ratio of cGMP/cAMP could, at least in part, be governed by the regulation of this endoperoxide-to-prostaglandin conversion.

Prostaglandins have been noted to influence adenylate cyclase and
guanylate cyclase activity not only in the neurons, but also in the adipocytes,
blood platelets and ovaries. This has been suggested to be the principal
mechanism by which prostaglandins are able to modify tissue metabolism
(Coceani and Pace-Asciak, 1976). There may also be a direct effect.
Microiontophoresis of prostaglandins increases the firing rate of some neurons in the medulla and spinal cord. In the spinal cord, the depolarized neurons are both interneurons and motoneurons, and the excitatory action has
both a rapid onset and termination (Coceani and Viti, 1975). Some cells
may also be inhibited. The administration of prostaglandins into the gray
matter of the spinal cord can potentiate or inhibit monosynaptic or crossed
spinal reflexes.

As many as 50% of CNS neurons are unresponsive to prostaglandins,
and those in the cerebral cortex do not appear to be responsive at all. Still,
these substances are produced in the brain spontaneously, and this synthesis
is higher in the cortex than in the cerebral white matter. In addition, the
glial cells have also been found to synthesize them (Carlson, 1977).

During transcallosal stimulation, the direct electrical stimulation of the
cortex, or the peripheral sensory nerves, prostaglandins are released from the
cortex into the cerebrospinal fluid. PGE_2, in turn, has been demonstrated to
decrease the catecholamines released from the stimulated cortex and striatal
tissue and to decrease the turnover of these amines. The PGE_2 release by the
postsynaptic effector membrane inhibits the presynaptic release of
norepinephrine (Hedqvist, 1973). This PGE action may be related to a
blockade of calcium influx, and can be reversed by PGF_2. Pharmacological
inhibition of PGE synthesis is associated with a greater transmitter release
for a given impulse.

In individual brain areas, prostaglandins are involved in a number of diverse activities. In the hypothalamus, they participate in the control of water
metabolism, food intake, and thermoregulation. Pyrogen-induced fever is

mediated by PGE_1 and PGE_2, although not by prostaglandins of the A or F series. The injection of these prostaglandins into the third ventricle increases the body temperature. PGE_1 is the most potent pyrogenic substance known, and its synthesis in hypothalamus is enhanced by various pyrogenic drugs. Possibly, the prostaglandins are the ultimate mediators of fever in the anterior hypothalamic preoptic region (Williams *et al.*, 1977). They mobilize cold defense mechanisms and, as a consequence, induce hyperthermia.

In the hypothalamus, prostaglandin E_2 activates the secretion of releasing hormones such as LHRH. Accordingly, the intraventricular injection of PGE_2 can induce ovulation (Lippert, 1977). Hypothalamic prostaglandins are probably a component of a positive and negative estrogen feedback mechanism, whose amplitude is subject to modification by them (Shearer and Cudkowicz, 1975). PGF_2 is likely the main modulating agent in this area. In addition, prostaglandins activate the secretion of ACTH, growth hormone, TSH and prolactin. They are also involved in the synthesis and release of the antidiuretic hormone. Accordingly, an intraventricular injection of PGE_1 or PGE_2 enhances the release of ADH and elicits drinking.

Several prostaglandins (PGE_1, PGE_2, PGF_2, PGF_1, and PGA) have been noted to reduce feeding behavior in fasting rats. An injection of PGE_1 into rats two hours before meals was able to lower the food intake (Baile *et al.*, 1973). Microinjections of PGE_1 into the lateral and medial hypothalamus have the same effect. There is undoubtedly a relationship between the state of energy depots and feeding behavior. The metabolizable energy stored in fat deposits is controlled by an adjustment of the food intake. Prostaglandins synthesized in adipose tissue may be a mediator of this linkage, with signals relating the state of fat deposits and the energy balance.

Prostaglandins injected intravenously into the brain ventricles can induce a general sedation, often with stupor, catatonia, uncoordination, paradoxical sleep, and an overall reduction of spontaneous motor activity. Prostaglandins of the E group (PGE_1, PGE_2, and PGE_3) are especially effective in this manner. PGE_1 also has an anticonvulsive action, protecting an experimental animal against convulsions induced by pentylenetetrazol or strychnine. It is additionally able to potentiate barbiturate sleeping time. These sedative and tranquilizing actions are probably associated with the accumulation of cAMP in the neurons, and consequently with a neuronal hyperpolarization. Thus, for example, PGE_1 interacts with dibutyryl-cAMP, causing a decrease in locomotor and exploratory behaviors.

The effect of prostaglandins on behavior depends upon the type, route of administration, and the animal species to which they are administered. Associated with the general sedation and reduced locomotor activity is an effect upon the process of learning. Thus, an intraperitoneal injection of PGE_2 is able to block a conditioned avoidance response.

SUMMARY AND SPECULATIONS

Throughout the various chapters in Section IV, we have continued to examine the concept of synaptic efficacy, particularly as it relates to pre- and postsynaptic neurotransmitter activity and to the functioning of neurotransmitter systems. Because of the complexity of the neuronal pathways in which multiple neurotransmitters interact, it is difficult to assign a particular neurophysiological function to any transmitter system. Consequently, studies that have attempted to subordinate any global brain function, such as mood, feeding, motility, sleep, and learning and memory, to the action of an individual neurotransmitter in most cases have provided results that are ambiguous and controversial. There is little reason to suspect that a single transmitter substance is exclusively responsible for the process of learning and memory, or for its underlying neuronal plasticity.

An evaluation of such factors as neurotransmitter synthesis, release, membrane receptor binding, and inactivation/degradation indicates that all types of synapses are theoretically capable of altering their activity. These changes, possibly activated by the impulse flow and/or by the presence of hormones or neuromodulators, may be either immediate, involving a rapid, local modification of functional proteins (such as by phosphorylation or conformational shifts), or they may have a slower onset and be longer-lasting, entailing new RNA and protein synthesis. But, logic aside, it is not clear whether all synapses are modifiable. If not, a major question would concern how their stability could be maintained during variations in the impulse flow.

An increase in synaptic activity will involve a number of metabolic adjustments, such as:

(1) a boost in the availability of precursors in the nerve ending,
(2) an activation of neurotransmitter synthesis,
(3) a change in the ionic binding to the cell membrane,
(4) a stabilization of receptor sensitivity, and
(5) the inactivation and removal of the neurotransmitter from the synapse.

In the case of a cholinergic synapse, supplies of acetyl-coenzyme A must first be augmented to satisfy the demand for an increase in the release of synaptic acetylcholine. The availability of acetyl-CoA is dependent upon glucose metabolism within the nerve ending. A critical enzyme, in this respect, is pyruvate dehydrogenase. Its activity is altered by phosphorylation, a process which itself requires an appropriate kinase. For its activity, the kinase depends upon the presence of calcium and magnesium ions and ATP. The passage of Ca^{2+} into the nerve terminals during synaptic transmission is already a well-known phenomenon.

The second component of the synthetic system is the supply of choline. The active, saturable transport system for it is coupled to the level of synaptic acetylcholine, the nerve impulse flow across the synapse, and the presence of calcium and chloride ions. The available choline is activated by a phosphorylation that is probably induced by the acetylcholine at hand. The reaction involving the final enzyme in the pathway, choline acetyltransferase, is typically not completely saturated by the available precursors and therefore functions below its capacity. Nevertheless, it still responds to an increase in the flow of impulses across the synapse.

An augmentation in the supplies of acetylcholine in response to this increase in impulse flow is not, by itself, sufficient for a shift in the efficacy of the synapse. The acetylcholine receptors likely require some form of protection against a drop in responsivity due to an elevated level of acetylcholine in the synapse. This type of regulation could depend upon shifts in both electrical potentials and membrane phospholipids, particularly upon changes in phosphatidylcholine, phosphatidylinositol, and their unsaturated fatty acids. Alterations in these substances involve base exchange reactions and the participation of a phospholipid exchange protein which is activated by acetylcholine. There may also be a change in the number of receptors in the postsynaptic membrane. And, the presynaptic cell may contribute to this effect by virtue of an additional release of neuromodulators and transmitters.

The enzyme degrading acetylcholine, acetylcholinesterase, is under the control of several humoral factors that act at numerous allosteric control sites. Therefore, changes in the availability of these factors also contribute to shifts in synaptic efficacy.

As in cholinergic transmission, catecholaminergic synapses are influenced by the impulse flow. The rate-limiting enzyme controlling catecholamine synthesis is tyrosine hydroxylase. It is activated by phosphorylation, a reaction subject to the activity of cAMP-dependent kinase. Elevations in the impulse flow, along with the depletion of norepinephrine, increase tyrosine hydroxylase activity, while excess DOPA, dopamine, and norepinephrine inhibit it.

An additional factor, dihydropteridine reductase, is required for this elevation in tyrosine hydroxylase activity, and it is similarly responsive to the impulse flow. An extended effect on tyrosine hydroxylase requires the induction of protein synthesis and the generation of a larger number of enzyme molecules.

Other enzymes involved in catecholamine synthesis that are also affected by the rate of impulses reaching the synapse are DOPA decarboxylase and dopamine-β-hydroxylase. Their production and activity, moreover, are additionally under the influence of presynaptic receptors. The postsynaptic receptors depend on the activity within the catecholaminergic system, and their number is regulated by the level of catecholamines in the tissue. The reuptake of the catecholamines is also variable and can shift in response to the functional state of the brain. During periods of intense stimulation, for example, the uptake decreases, sustaining the postsynaptic transmitter effects.

One of the more intriguing modifications of synaptic activity involves the release of neurotransmitters from areas other than the presynaptic terminal region. A transmitter secretion from the postsynaptic element can take place, meaning that there can be a reversal in the normal direction of informational flow, permitting two-way intersynaptic communication. Also, the release of norepinephrine and serotonin from synaptic and non-synaptic varicosities on the neuron may serve to modulate the synaptic activity of other neurons. Documentation of this latter possibility, however, is still incomplete.

The regulation of serotonin secretion depends upon both the active transport of the precursor tryptophan into the nerve endings and the activity of the enzyme tryptophan hydroxylase. The flow of impulses across the synapse, the entrance of Ca^{2+} into the cell, and changes in the membrane phospholipids all contribute to the ensuing serotonin release.

The relationship of amino acid synthesis and the functioning of amino acid neurotransmitters to neuronal plasticity is less well-known and largely unexplored. There is some evidence, though, that they may have a role in learning and memory.

A number of low molecular weight substances that are capable of influencing neuronal activity appear to act more like neuromodulators than neurotransmitters. Two of the more prominent ones, adenosine and the prostaglandins, were explored more fully in Chapter 21. Adenosine is released from the postsynaptic neuron in the form of ATP, which after a sequence of dephosphorylations, may interfere with the presynaptic neurotransmitter release. It likely reacts with its own presynaptic receptors and could affect synaptic efficacy through its involvement in cyclic AMP production. A presynaptic liberation of adenosine has also been described, and the adenosine receptors are associated with the adenylate cyclase complex.

Prostaglandins are synthesized from arachidonic acid that is released from the membrane lipids. The synthesis is dependent upon the binding of neurotransmitters (catecholamines and indoleamines) to their postsynaptic receptors. The prostaglandins then, in turn, may affect the secretion of catecholamines by blocking calcium entry into the cells. Prostaglandins PGE and PGF are also able to activate adenylate cyclase and guanylate cyclase, respectively. Consequently, they are capable of modifying the responsiveness of the neurons.

Each of the discussions of the various neurotransmitters that comprise Section IV is intended to further add to an understanding of the nature of those processes that contribute to the control of synaptic activity and to an awareness of the relationships that exist between particular transmitter systems and behavior. The following section will examine the activity of naturally-occurring CNS modulator substances and how they relate to alterations in the functioning of the brain.

RECOMMENDED READINGS

Amaral, D.G., Sinnamon, H.M.: The locus coeruleus: Neurobiology of a central noradrenergic nucleus. *Progr. Neurobiol.* 9:147-196 (1977).

Anisman, H.: Time-dependent variations in aversively motivated behaviors: Nonassociative effects of cholinergic and catecholaminergic activity. *Psychol. Rev.* 82:359-385 (1975).

Beart, P.M.: Adrenaline - The cryptic central catecholamine. *Trends Neurosci.* 2:295-297 (1979).

Beaudet, A., Descarries, L.: The monoamine innervation of rat cerebral cortex: Synaptic and nonsynaptic axon terminals. *Neuroscience* 3:851-862 (1978).

Buu, N.T., Buil, E., Van Gelder, N.M.: Receptors for amino acids in excitable tissues. *Gen. Pharmacol.* 7:574-580 (1976).

Cheramy, A., Leviel, V., Glowinski, J.: Dendritic release of dopamine in the substantia nigra. *Nature* 299:537-542 (1981).

Cohen, J.B., Changeux, J.P.: The cholinergic receptor protein in its membrane environment. *Ann. Rev. Pharmacol.* 15:83-103 (1975).

Crow, T.J.: The chemistry of reward. *Trends Biochem. Sci.* 1:287-291 (1976).

Daruna, S.H.: Patterns of brain monoamine activity and aggressive behaviour. *Neurosci. Biobehav. Rev.* 2:101-113 (1978).

Daly, J.W.: Nature of receptors regulating formation of cyclic AMP in brain tissue. *Life Sci.* 18:1349-1361 (1976).

De Feudis, F.V., Martin DelRio, R.: Is β-alanine an inhibitory neurotransmitter? *Gen. Pharmacol.* 8:177-180 (1977).

Dement, W., Holman, R.B., Guilleminault, C.: Neurochemical and neuropharmacological foundations of the sleep disorders. *Psychopharmacol. Commun.* 2:77-90 (1976).

Dunn, A.: Neurochemistry of learning and memory - Evaluation of recent data. *Ann. Rev. Psychol.* 31:343-390 (1980).

Enna, S.J.: GABA receptors. *Trends Pharmacol. Sci.* 2:62-64 (1981).

Gross, H.A., Dunner, D.L., Lafleur, D., Meltzer, H.L., Muhlbauer, H.L., Fieve, R.R.: Prostaglandins - Review of neurophysiology and psychiatric implications. *Arch. Gen. Psychiat.* 34:1189-1196 (1977).

Haubrich, D.R., Chippendale, T.J.: Regulation of acetylcholine synthesis in nervous tissue. *Life Sci.* 20:1465-1478 (1977).

Hertz, L.: Functional interactions between neurons and astrocytes. I. Turnover and metabolism of putative amino-acid transmitters. *Progr. Neurobiol.* 13:277-323 (1979).

Hucho, F.: The nicotinic acetylcholine receptor. *Trends Biochem. Sci.* 6/9:242-244 (1981).

Jope, R.S.: High affinity choline transport and acetyl CoA production in brain and their roles in the regulation of acetylcholine synthesis. *Brain Res. Rev.* 1:313-344 (1979).

Juan, H.: Prostaglandins as modulators of pain. *Gen. Pharmacol.* 9:403-409 (1978).

Kebabian, J.W., Cote, T.E.: Dopamine receptors and cyclic AMP: A decade of progress. *Trends Pharmacol. Sci.* 2:69-71 (1981).

Kety, S.S.: The biogenic amines in the central nervous system. Their possible roles in arousal, emotion and learning. In: *The Neurosciences: The Second Study Program,* F.O. Schmitt (Ed.), Rockefeller University Press: New York (1970). pp.324-336.

Lefkowitz, R.J., Hoffman, B.B.: New directions in adrenergic-receptor research. *Trends Pharmacol. Sci.* 1:314-318 (1980).

Lehmann, J., Fibiger, H.C.: Acetylcholinesterase and the cholinergic neuron. *Life Sci.* 25:1939-1947 (1979).

Libet, B.: Which postsynaptic action of dopamine is mediated by cyclic AMP? *Life Sci.* 24:1043-1058 (1979).

Marangos, P.J., Paul, S.M., Goodwin, F.K., Skolnick, P.: Putative endogenous ligands for the benzodiazepine receptor. *Life Sci.* 25:1093-1102 (1979).

Maslinski, C.: Histamine and its metabolism in mammals. I. *Agents Actions* 5:87-107 (1975).

Messing, R.B., Lytle, L.D.: Serotonin-containing neurons: Their possible role in pain and analgesia. *Pain* 4:1-21 (1977).

Moore, R.Y., Bloom, F.E.: Gentral catecholamine neuron systems: Anatomy and physiology of the dopamine systems. *Ann. Rev. Neurosci.* 1:129-129 (1978).

Murphy, D.L.: Substrate-selective monoamine oxidases - inhibitor, tissue, species and functional differences. *Biochem. Pharmacol.* 27:1889-1893 (1978).

Murrin, L.C.: High-affinity transport of choline in neuronal tissue. *Pharmacology* 21:132-140 (1980).

Pettigrew, J.D.: Locus coeruleus cortical plasticity. *Trends Neurosci.* 1:73-74 (1978).

Phillis, J.W., Wu, P.H.: The role of adenosine and its nucleotides in central synaptic transmission. *Progr. Neurobiol.* 16:187-239 (1981).

Ramm, P.: Locus coeruleus, catecholamines, and REM sleep - Critical review. *Behav. Neural Biol.* 25:415-448 (1979).

Ross, S.B.: Neuronal transport of 5-hydroxytryptamine. *Pharmacology* 21:123-131 (1980).

Sabelli, H.C., Borison, R.L., Diamond, B.I., Havdala, H.S., Narashimhan, N.: Phenylethylamine and brain function. *Biochem. Pharmacol.* 27:1729-1730 (1978).

Samanin, R., Garattini, S.: Serotonergic system in brain and its possible functional connections with other aminergic systems. *Life Sci.* 17:1201-1210 (1975).

Schwartz, J.C.: Histamine receptors in brain. *Life Sci.* 25:895-912 (1979).

Starke, K.: Presynaptic receptors and the control of noradrenaline release. *Trends Pharmacol. Sci.* 1:268-271 (1980).

Stone, T.W.: Purinergic transmission in the CNS? *Trends Pharmacol. Sci.* 1:273-275 (1980).

Uchida, M.K.: Purification of histamine H_1 receptor. *Gen. Pharmacol.* 9:145-150 (1978).

Ungerstedt, U.: Selective lesions of central catecholamine pathways: Application in functional studies. In: *Neurosciences Research.* Vol. 5. S. Ehrenpreis, I.J. Kopin, (Eds.), Academic Press:New York (1973). pp. 73-96.

Van Abeelen, J.H.F.: Genotype and the cholinergic control of exploratory behaviour in mice. In: *The Genetics of Behaviour.* J.H.F. Van Abeelen (Ed.). Elsevier: New York (1974). pp.347-374.

Vapaatalo, H., Parantainen, J.: Prostaglandins: Their biological and pharmacological role. *Med. Biol.* 56:163-183 (1978).

Wise, R.A.: Neuroleptic attenuation of intracranial self-stimulation: Reward or performance deficits? *Life Sci.* 22:535-544 (1978).

Wolfe, L.S.: Eicosanoids: Prostaglandins, thromboxanes, leukotrienes, and other derivatives of carbon-20 unsaturated fatty acids. *J. Neurochem.* 38:1-14 (1982).

Woodward, D.J., Moises, H.C., Waterhouse, B.D., Hoffer, B.J., Freedman, R.: Modulatory actions of norepinephrine in the central nervous system. *Fed. Proc.* 38:2109-2113 (1979).

Zumstein, A., Karduck, W., Starke, K.: Pathways of dopamine metabolism in the rabbit caudate nucleus *in vitro. Naunyn-Schmiedeberg's Arch. Pharmacol.* 316:205-217 (1981).

REFERENCES

Abdel-Halim, M.S., Von Holst, H., Meyerson, B., Sachs, C., Anggard, E.: *J. Neurochem.* 34:1331 (1980).

Adams, P.M.: *Neuropharmacology* 12:825 (1973).

Ahlquist, R.P.: *Amer. J. Physiol.* 153:586 (1948).

Alger, B.E., Nicoll, R.A.: *Nature* 281:315 (1979).

Amaral, D.G., Sinnamon, H.M.: *Progr. Neurobiol.* 9:147 (1977).

Amatruda, T.T., Black, D.A., McKenna, T.M., McCarley, R.W., Hobson, J.A.: *Brain Res.* 98:501 (1975).

Anand-Srivastava, M.B., Johnson, R.A.: *J. Neurochem.* 36:1819 (1981).

Anden, N.E., Carlsson, A., Dahlstrom, A., Fuxe, K., Hillarp, N.A., Larsson, K.: *Life Sci.* 3:523 (1964).

Anden, N.E., Wachtel, H.: *J. Pharm. Pharmacol.* 29:435 (1977).

Ansell, G.B., Spanner, S.: *Biochem. J.* 122:741 (1971).

Aprison, M.R., Werman, R.: *Life Sci.* 4:2075 (1965).

Arakelian, M.C., Libertun, C.: *Endocrinology* 100:890 (1977).

Aronstam, R.S., Abood, L.G., Baumgold, J.: *Biochem. Pharmacol.* 26:1689 (1977).

Asberg, M., Traksman, L., Thoren, P.: *Arch. Gen. Psychiat.* 33:1193 (1976).

Aston-Jones, G., Bloom, F.E.: *J. Neurosci.* 1:876 (1981).

Axelrod, J.: *Pharmacol. Rev.* 18:95 (1966).

Azmitia, E.R., McEwen, B.S.: *Science* 166:1274 (1969).

Bacopoulos, N.G., Bhatnagar, R.K.: *J. Neurochem.* 29:639 (1977).
Bagchi, S.P., Smith, T.M.: *Biochem. Pharmacol.* 26:900 (1979).
Baile, C.A., Simpson, C.W., Bean, S.M., McLaughin, C.L., Jacobs, H.L.: *Physiol. Behav.* 10:1077 (1973).
Balcom, G.J., Lenox, R.H., Meyerhof, J.L.: *J. Neurochem.* 26:423 (1976).
Bannon, M.J., Michaud, R.L., Roth, R.H.: *Mol. Pharmacol.* 19:270 (1981).
Barbeau, A., Inoue, N., Tsukada, Y., Butterworth, R.F.: *Life Sci.* 17:669 (1975).
Barbin, G., Garbarg, M., Schwartz, J.C., Storm-Mathisen, J.: *J. Neurochem.* 26:259 (1976).
Barker, L.A.: *Life Sci.* 18:725 (1976).
Bartus, R.T., Dean, R.L., Goas, J.A., Lippa, A.S.: *Science* 209:301 (1980).
Baudry, M., Lynch, G.: *Molec. Cell. Biochem.* 38:5 (1981).
Baughman, R.W., Gilbert, C.D.: *Nature* 287:848 (1980).
Baughman, R.W., Gilbert, C.D.: *J. Neurosci.* 1:427 (1981).
Baumann, P.A., Koella, W.P.: *Brain Res.* 189:437 (1980).
Baumann, P.A., Waldmeier, P.C.: *Naunyn-Schmiedeberg's Arch. Pharmacol.* 317:36 (1981).
Bazemore, A.W., Elliott, K.A.C., Florey, E.: *J. Neurochem.* 1:334 (1957).
Beart, P.M.: *Trends Neurosci.* 2:295 (1979).
Benavides, J., Rumigny, J.F., Bourguignon, J.J., Cash, C., Wermuth, C.G., Mandel, P., Vincendon, G., Maitre, M.: *Life Sci.* 30:953 (1982).
Bender, A.S., Wu, P.H., Phillis, J.W.: *J.Neurochem.* 35:629 (1980).
Benjamin, A.M., Quastel, J.H.: *Biochem. J.* 128:631 (1972).
Bergstrom, D.A., Kellar, K.J.: *Nature* 278:464 (1979).
Bergstrom, S., Sjoval, J.: *Acta Chem. Scand.* 16:1693 (1960).
Bertilsson, L., Mao, C.C., Costa, E.: *J. Pharm. Exp. Ther.* 200:277 (1977).
Bishai, I., Coceani, F.: In: B. Samuelson, P.W. Ramwell, R. Paoletti (Eds.), *Advances in Prostaglandin and Thromboxane Research,* Vol. 8. Raven Press: New York (1980). p.1221.
Biziere, K., Thompson, H., Coyle, J.T.: *Brain Res.* 183:421 (1980).
Blas, A.L.D., Mahler, H.R.: *Fed. Proc.* 35:1576 (1976).
Blindermann, J.M., De Feudis, F.V., Maitre, M., Misslin, R., Wolff, P., Mandel, P.: *J. Neurochem.* 32:1357 (1979).
Blizard, D.A., Liang, B.: *Behav. Genet.* 9:413 (1979).
Blusztajn, J.K., Wurtman, R.J.: *Nature* 290:417 (1981).
Boadle-Biber, M.C.: *Biochem. Pharmacol.* 24:1455 (1975).
Bogdanski, D.F., Brodie, B.B.: *J. Pharmacol. Exp. Ther.* 165:181 (1969).
Bon, S., Rieger, F., Massouile, J.: *Eur. J. Biochem.* 35:372 (1973).
Bonisch, H., Otten, U., Thoenen, H.: *Arch. Pharmacol.* 313:199 (1980).
Braun, S., Levitzki, A.: *Molec. Pharmacol.* 16:737 (1979).
Brennan, M.J.W.: *J. Neurochem.* 38:264 (1982).
Brodie, B.B., Shore, P.A.: *Ann. N.Y. Acad. Sci.* 66:631 (1957).
Brookes, N., Burt, D.R.: *Dev. Neurosci.* 3:118 (1980).
Brown, M.C., Ironton, R.: *Nature* 265:459 (1977).
Brown, M.C., Goodwin, G.M., Ironton, R.: *J. Physiol. (Lond.)* 267:P42 (1977).
Browner, M., Ferkany, J.W., Enna, S.J.: *J. Neurosci.* 1:514 (1981).
Browning, E.T., Brostrom, C.O., Groppi, V.E.: *Mol. Pharmacol.* 12:32 (1976).
Brozoski, T.J., Brown, R.M., Rosvold, H.E., Goldman, P.S.: *Science* 205:929 (1979).
Bubenik, G., Monnier, M.: *Exp. Neurol.* 35:1 (1972).
Buckman, T., Chang, R., Boscia, R., Eiduson, S.: *Trans. Am. Soc. Neurochem.* 13:118 (1982).
Bueno, J.R., Himwich, H.E.: *Psychosomatics* 8:82 (1967).
Burns, D., London, J., Brunswick, D.J., Pring, M., Garfinkel, D., Rabinowitz, J.L., Mendels, J.: *Biol. Psychiat.* 11:125 (1976).

Butcher, S.G., Butcher, L.L.: *Brain Res.* 71:167 (1974).

Calderini, G., Teolato, S., Bonetti, A.C., Battistella, A., Toffano, G.: *Life Sci.* 28:2367 (1981).

Carlson, J.: *Lakartidningen* 74:2629 (1977).

Carman, J.S., Post, R.M., Goodwin, F.K., Bunney, W.E.: *Biol. Psychiat.* 12:5 (1977).

Carroll, P.T., Aspry, J.A.M.: *Science* 210:641 (1980).

Carroll, P.T., Goldberg, A.M.: *Neurosci. Abstr.* 2:991 (1976).

Cash, C.D., Maitre, M., Mandel, P.: *J. Neurochem.* 33:1169 (1979).

Chang, H.W., Bock, E.: *Biochemistry* 18:172 (1979).

Chang, H.W., Neumann, E.: *Proc. Natl. Acad. Sci. USA* 73:3364 (1976).

Chao, L.P.: *J.Neurochem.* 25:261 (1975).

Chawla, N., Johri, M.B.L., Saxena, P.N., Singhal, K.C.: *Br. J. Pharmacol.* 53:317 (1975).

Cheramy, A., Leviel, V., Glowinski, J.: *Nature* 299:537 (1981).

Cherkin, A., Eckardt, M.J., Gerbrandt, L.K.: *Science* 193:242 (1976).

Cherkin, A., Bennett, E.L., Davis, J.L.: *Brain Res.* 223:455 (1981).

Cheung, Y., Sladek, J.R.Jr.: *J. Comp. Neurol.* 164:339 (1975).

Chude, O.: *J. Neurochem.* 33:621 (1979).

Church, A.C., Sprott, R.L.: *Physiol. Psychol.* 7:84 (1979).

Chute, D.L., Villiger, J.W., Kirton, N.F.: *Psychopharmacology* 74:129 (1981).

Chweh, A.Y., Leslie, S.W.: *J. Neurochem.* 38:691 (1982).

Clark, R.M., Collins, G.G.S.: *J.Physiol. (London)* 262:383 (1976).

Coceani, F., Pace-Asciak, C.R.: In: *Prostaglandins: Physiological, Pharmacological and Pathological Aspects,* S.M.M. Karim (Ed.). MTP Press: Lancaster (1976). p.20.

Coceani, F., Viti, A.: *Can. J. Physiol. Pharmacol.* 53:273 (1975).

Cohen, E.L., Wurtman, R.J.: *Science* 191:561 (1976).

Cohen, J.B., Changeux, J.P.: *Ann. Rev. Pharmacol.* 15:83 (1975).

Collins, G.C.S., Topiwala, S.H.: *Br. J. Pharmacol.* 50:451P (1974).

Cools, A.R.: *Trends Pharmacol. Sci.* 2:178 (1981).

Coppen, A.: *Br. J. Psychiat.* 113:1237 (1967).

Coppen, A.: *J. Psychiat. Res.* 9:163 (1972).

Corbett, D., Skelton, R.W., Wise, R.A.: *Brain Res.* 133:37 (1977).

Corey, E.J., Niwa, H., Falck, J.R., Mioskowski, C., Arai, Y., Marfat, A.: In: B. Samuelsson, P.W. Ramwell, R. Paoletti (Eds.), *Advances in Prostaglandin and Thromboxane Research,* Vol. 6. Raven Press: New York (1980). p. 19.

Costa, E., Giudotti, A., Hanbauer, I., Hexum, T., Saiani, L., Stine, S., Yang, H.Y.T.: *Fed. Proc.* 40:160 (1981).

Crawford, J.M., Curtis, D.R., Voorhoeven, P.E., Wilson, V.J.: *J. Physiol. (London)* 186:139 (1966).

Creese, I.: *Trends Neurosci.* 5/2:40 (1982).

Creese, I., Snyder, S.H.: *Eur. J. Pharmacol.* 50:459 (1978).

Cremer, J.E.: *Biochem. J.* 122:135 (1971).

Cremer, J.E., Bligh, J.: *Br. Med. Bull.* 25:299 (1969).

Crow, T.J.: *Psychol. Med.* 3:66 (1973).

Cumar, F.A., Maggio, B., Caputto, R.: *Biochem. Biophys. Res. Commun.* 84:65 (1978).

Curtis, D.R., Hosli, L., Johnston, G.A.R., Johnston, I.H.: *Exp. Brain Res.* 5:235 (1968).

Curtis, D.R., Perrin, D.D., Watkins, J.C.: *J. Neurochem.* 6:1 (1960).

Curtis, D.R., Watkins, J.C.: *J. Neurochem.* 6:117 (1960).

Dahlstrom, A., Fuxe, K.: *Acta Physiol. Scand.* 62 (Suppl. 232):1 (1964).

Dahlstrom, A., Fuxe, K.: *Acta Physiol. Scand.* 64 (Suppl. 247):1 (1965).

Dalton, T.: *Biochim. Biophys. Acta* 555:362 (1979).

Da   Prada, M., Pletscher, A.: *Experientia* 22:465 (1966).

Daruna, S.H.: *Neurosci. Biobehav. Rev.* 2:101 (1978).

Datta, P.C., King, M.G.: *Neurosci. Biobehav. Rev.* 4:451 (1978).

Davidoff, R.A., Graham, L.T., Shank, R.P., Werman, R., Aprison, M.H.: *J. Neurochem.* 14:1025 (1967).

Davies, I.P., Johnston, G.A.R.: *Brain Res.* 54:149 (1973).

Davis, J.L., Cherkin, A.: *Pharmacol. Biochem. Behav.* 15:367 (1981).

Davis, L.G., McIntosh, H., Reker, D.: *Pharmacol. Biochem. Behav.* 14:839 (1981).

Davis, M., Astrachan, D.L., Kass, E.: *Science* 209:521 (1980).

De Belleroche, J.S., Bradford, H.F.: *J. Neurochem.* 21:441 (1973).

De Feudis, F.V.: *Acta Physiol. Latinoamer.* 27:131 (1977).

De Feudis, F.V., Madtes, P., Gervasca, J.: *Exp. Neurol.* 50:207 (1976).

De Groat, W.C., Lalley, P.M., Saum, W.R.: *Brain Res.* 44:213 (1972).

Dement, W., Holman, R.B., Guilleminault, C.: *Psychopharmacol. Commun.* 2:77 (1976).

Dennis, S.C., Lai, J.C.K., Clark, J.B.: *Biochem. J.* 164:727 (1977).

De Robertis, E., De Plazas, S.F.: *J. Neurochem.* 26:1237 (1976).

Deutsch, J.A.: *Science* 174:778 (1971).

Deutsch, J.A., Lutzky, H.: *Nature* 213:742 (1967).

Diamond, I.: *Arch. Neurol.* 24:333 (1971).

Di Chiara, G., Morelli, M., Porcedou, M.L., Gessa, G.L.: *Neuroscience* 4:1453 (1979).

Di Lauro, A., Schmid, R.W., Meek, J.L.: *Brain Res.* 207:476 (1981).

Dismukes, K., DeBoer, A.A., Mulder, A.H.: *Naunyn-Schmiedeberg's Arch. Pharmacol.* 299:115 (1977).

Divac, I., Fonnum, F., Storm-Mathisen, J.: *Nature* 266:377 (1977).

Dominguez, M., Longo, V.G.: *Physiol. Behav.* 4:1031 (1969).

Douglas, G.W., Martensen, R.A.: *J. Biol. Chem.* 222:581 (1956).

Drummond, G.S., Symchowicz, E., Goldstein, M., Shenkman, L.: *J. Neural Transm.* 42:139 (1978).

Dunn, A.: *Ann. Rev. Psychol.* 31:343 (1980).

Ebel, A., Mack, G., Stefanovic, V., Mandel, P.: *Brain Res.* 57:248 (1973).

Ehinger, B.: *Experientia* 32:890 (1976).

Ehlert, F.J., Roeske, W.R., Yamamura, H.I.: *Fed. Proc.* 40:153 (1981).

Eisenstadt, M.L., Schwartz, J.H.: *J. Gen. Physiol.* 65:293 (1975).

Ekstrom, J.: *Experientia* 34:1247 (1978).

Enna, S.J.: *Trends Pharmacol. Sci.* 2:62 (1981).

Enna, S.J., Snyder, S.H.: *Mol. Pharmacol.* 13:442 (1977).

Ennis, C., Cox, B.: *Neuropharmacology* 21:41 (1982).

Ennis, C., Kemp, J.D., Cox, B.: *J. Neurochem.* 36:1515 (1981).

Essman, W.B.: *Adv. Pharmacol. Chemother.* 9:241 (1971).

Fahn, S., Cote, L.J.: *J. Neurochem.* 15:209 (1968).

Feldberg, W., Myers, R.D.: *Nature* 200:1325 (1963).

Feldberg, W., Myers, R.D.: *J. Physiol. (London)* 173:25 (1964).

Fernandez-Tome, M.P., Sanchez-Blazquez, P., Del Rio, J.: *Psychopharmacologia* 61:43 (1979).

Ferris, S.H., Sathananthan, G., Reisberg, B., Gershon, S.: *Science* 205:1039 (1979).

Fibiger, H.C., Phillips, A.G.: *Brain Res.* 116:23 (1966).

File, S.E., James, T.A., Macleod, N.K.: *J. Neural Transm.* 50:1 (1981).

Fillenz, M., Gagnon, C., Stoeckel, K., Thoenen, H.: *Brain Res.* 114:292 (1976).

Fillion, G.M.B., Rousselle, J.C., Beaudoin, D., Pradelles, P., Goiny, M., Dray, F., Jacob, J.: *Life Sci.* 24:1813 (1979).

Fishbein, W.N., Bessman, S.P.: *J. Biol. Chem.* 239:357 (1964).

Florey, E.: *Arch. Intern. Physiol.* 62:33 (1954).
Fox, F., Linsley, P., Iwata, K., Landen, C.F.: *J. Supramolec. Struct.* 13:100 (1980).
Freed, W.J., Michaelis, E.K.: *Pharmacol. Biochem. Behav.* 5:11 (1976).
Freeman, J.A.: *Nature* 269:218 (1977).
Frieder, B., Rapport, M.M.: *J. Neurochem.* 37:634 (1981).
Fuxe, K., Agnati, L.F., Kohler, C., Kuonen, D., Ogren, S.-O., Andersson, K., Hokfelt, T.: *J. Neural Transm.* 51:3 (1981).
Gallup, G.G. Jr., Wallnau, L.B., Boren, J.L., Gagliardi, G.J., Maser, J.D., Edson, P.H.: *J. Comp. Physiol. Psychiol.* 91:642 (1977).
Garbarg, M., Barbin, G., Figer, J., Schwartz, J.C.: *Science* 186:833 (1974).
Geller, E., Yuwiler, A., Zolman, J.F.: *J. Neurochem.* 12:949 (1965).
Geller, H.M.: *Neurosci. Lett.* 14:49 (1981).
Gerald, M.C., Maickel, R.P.: *Br. J. Pharmacol.* 44:462 (1972).
Gerbrandt, L.K., Eckardt, M.J., Davis, J.L., Cherkin, A.: *Physiol. Behav.* 19:723 (1977).
Gibson, R.E., Juni, S., O'Brien, R.D.: *Arch. Biochem. Biophys.* 179:183 (1977).
Gillespie, D.D., Manier, D.H., Sulser, F.: *Comm. Psychopharmacologia* 3:191 (1979).
Ginsborg, B.L., Hirst, G.D.S.: *J. Physiol. (London)* 224:629 (1972).
Glass, J.D., Fromm, G.H., Chattha, A.S.: *EEG Clin. Neurophysiol.* 48:16 (1980).
Globus, A., Lux, H.D., Schubert, P.: *Brain Res.* 11:440 (1968).
Glossman, H., Hornung, R., Schlusche, R.: *Naunyn-Schmiedeberg's Arch. Pharmacol.* 314:101 (1980).
Godfrey, D.A., Carter, J.A., Berger, S.J., Lowrey, O.H., Matschinski, F.M.: *J. Histochem. Cytochem.* 25:417 (1977).
Godschalk, M., Dzolzic, M.R., Bonta, I.L.: *Neurosci. Lett.* 3:145 (1976).
Godschalk, M., Dzolzic, M.R., Bonta, I.L.: *Eur. J. Pharmacol.* 44:105 (1977).
Gold, P.E., Van Buskirk, R.B.: *Behav. Biol.* 24:168 (1978).
Goldberg, N.D., Haddox, M.K.: *Ann. Rev. Biochem.* 46:823 (1977).
Gordon, A., Diamond, I.: *Adv. Exptl. Med. Biol.* 116:175 (1979).
Gordon, M.A., Chan, S.L., Trevor, A.J.: *Biochem. J.* 157:69 (1976).
Gorynia, I., Bartsch, P.: *Acta Biol. Med. Germ.* 34:53 (1975).
Grahame-Smith, D.G.: *J. Neurochem.* 18:1053 (1971).
Grecksch, G., Ott, T., Matthies, H.: *Pharmacol. Biochem. Behav.* 8:215 (1978).
Green, M.D., Cox, B., Lomax, P.: *Neuropharmacology* 15:321 (1976).
Grewaal, D.S., Quastel, J.H.: *Biochem. J.* 132:1 (1973).
Gross, G., Brodde, O.E., Schumann, H.J.: *Naunyn-Schmiedeberg's Arch. Pharmacol.* 316:45 (1981).
Gruener, R., Bryant, H.J.: *J. Pharm. Exp. Ther.* 194:514 (1975).
Guidotti, A., Costa, E.: *Biochem. Pharmacol.* 26:817 (1977).
Haas, H.L., Bucher, U.M.: *Nature* 255:634 (1975).
Haber, B., Kuriyama, K., Roberts, E.: *Brain Res.* 22:105 (1970).
Hamberger, A.C., Chiang, G.H., Nylen, E.S., Scheff, S.W., Cotman, C.W.: *Brain Res.* 168:513 (1979).
Hamon, M., Bourgoin, S., Hery, F., Simmonet, G.: *Biochem. Pharmacol.* 27:915 (1978).
Harms, H.H., Warden, G., Mulder, A.H.: *Eur. J. Pharmacol.* 49:305 (1978).
Harms, H.H., Warden, G., Mulder, A.H.: *Neuropharmacology* 18:577 (1979).
Harris, J.E., Roth, R.H.: *Mol. Pharmacol.* 7:593 (1971).
Harvey J.A., Lints, C.E.: *J. Comp. Physiol. Psychol.* 74:28 (1971).
Hattori, T., McGeer, P.L., McGeer, E.G.: *Brain Res.* 170:71 (1979).
Haulica, I., Ababei, L., Branisteanu, D., Topoliceanu, F.: *J. Neurochem.* 21:1019 (1973).
Hazra, J.: *Eur. J. Pharmacol.* 11:395 (1970).

Hedqvist, P.: *Acta Physiol. Scand.* 79(Suppl.345):1 (1970).

Hedqvist, P.: In: *The Prostaglandins,* Vol. 1, P.W. Ramwell (Ed.), Plenum Press: New York (1973). p.101.

Hedqvist, P., Fredholm, B.B.: *Naunyn-Schmiedeberg's Arch. Pharmacol.* 293:217 (1976).

Hegstrand, L.R., Kanof, P.D., Greengard, P.: *Nature* 260:163 (1976).

Henn, F.A.: *J. Neurosci. Res.* 2:271 (1976).

Henn, F.A., Hamberger, A.: *Proc. Natl. Acad. Sci. USA* 68:2686 (1971).

Herr, B.E., Gallager, D.W., Roth, R.H.: *Biochem. Pharmacol.* 24:2019 (1975).

Hertz, L., Schousboe, A., Boechler, N., Mukerji, S., Fedoroff, S.: *Neurochem. Res.* 3:1 (1978).

Hess, R., Murata, K.: *Exp. Brain Res.* 21:285 (1974).

Hidaka, H., Asano, T.: *Proc. Natl. Acad. Sci. USA* 74:3657 (1977).

Hingtgen, J.N., Aprison, M.H.: *Life Sci.* 16:1471 (1975).

Hirsch, M.J., Wurtman, R.J.: *Science* 202:223 (1979).

Ho, P.P.K., Young, A.L., Walters, P.C.: *Enzyme* 19:244 (1975).

Hollett, C.R.: *Biochem. Pharmacol.* 23:989 (1974).

Hollins, C., Stone, T.W.: *J. Physiol. (London)* 303:73 (1980).

Holmgren, B., Urba-Holmgren, R.: *Acta Neurobiol. Exp.* 38:11 (1978).

Honegger, C.G., Krepelka, L.M., Steiner, M., Hahn, H.P.V.: *Experientia* 29:1235 (1973).

Horn, J.P., McAfee, D.A.: *Science* 204:1233 (1979).

Horrobin, D.F.: *Prostaglandins: Physiology, Pharmacology and Clinical Significance.* Eden Press: Montreal (1978). p.155.

Huang, R.H., Faulkner, R.: *J. Biol. Chem.* 256:9211 (1981).

Hucho, F.: *Trends Biochem. Sci.* 6/9:242 (1981).

Huppert, F.A., Deutsch, J.A.: *Quart. J. Exp. Psychol.* 21:267 (1969).

Ikeno, T., Dickens, G., Lloyd, T., Guroff, G.: *J. Neurochem.* 36:1632 (1981).

Inestrosa, N.C., Ramirez, B.U., Fernandez, H.L.: *J. Neurochem.* 28:941 (1977).

Israel, M., Meunier, F.M.: *J. Physiol. (Paris)* 74:485 (1978).

Itakura, T., Kasamatsu, T., Pettigrew, J.D.: *Neuroscience* 6:159 (1981).

Iverson, L.L., Snyder, S.H.: *Nature* 220:796 (1968).

Izumi, K., Butterworth, R.F., Barbeau, A.: *Life Sci.* 20:943 (1977).

Jacobs, B.L., Trulson, M.E.: *Trends Neurosci.* 2:276 (1979).

Jacobs, B.L., Wise, W.D., Taylor, K.M.: *Brain Res.* 79:353 (1974).

Jacobs, B.L., Simon, S.M., Ruimy, D.D., Trulson, M.E.: *Brain Res.* 124:271 (1977).

Jaffard, R., Destrade, C., Soumireu-Mourat, B., Cardo, B.: *Behav. Biol.* 10:89 (1974).

Jaffard, R., Destrade, C., Soumireu-Mourat, B., Durkin, T., Ebel, A.: *Neurosci. Lett.* 19:349 (1980)

Jasper, H.H., Koyama, L.K.: *Can. J. Physiol. Pharmacol.* 47:889 (1969).

Jenden, D.J., Jope, R.S., Weiler, M.H.: *Science* 194:635 (1976).

Johnson, J.L.: *Brain Res.* 37:1 (1972).

Johnston, G.A.R., Kennedy, S.M.E.: In: *Amino Acids as Chemical Transmitters,* F. Fonnum (Ed.). Plenum Press: New York (1978). p.507.

Jope, R.S.: *Brain Res. Rev.* 1:313 (1979).

Jope, R.S., Jenden, D.J.: *Life Sci.* 20:1389 (1977).

Jope, R.S., Jenden, D.J.: *J. Neurochem.* 35:318 (1980).

Jouvet, M.: *EEG Clin. Neurophysiol.* 23:284 (1967).

Jouvet, M.: *Science* 196:32 (1969).

Jouvet, M.: *Ergebn. Physiol. Biol. Chem.* 64:166 (1972).

Juel, C.: *Neuropharmacology* 20:323 (1981).

Kaczmarek, L.K., Adey, W.R.: *Brain Res.* 76:83 (1974).

Kanner, B.I., Sharon, I.: *Biochemistry* 17:3949 (1978).

Karahasanoglu, A.M., Edwards, E.H., Tildon, J.T., Ozand, P.T.: *J. Neurosci. Res.* 2:401 (1976).
Kasai, K., Suzuki, H., Nakamura, T., Shiina, H., Shimoda, S.I.: *Acta Endocrinol.* 93:283 (1980).
Katz, R.J.: *Psychopharmacologia* 61:39 (1979).
Katz, R.J., Liebler, L.: *Psychopharmacologia* 56:191 (1978).
Katz, R.J., Chase, T.N., Kopin, J.J.: *J. Neurochem.* 16:961 (1969).
Kebabian, J.W.: *Nature* 277:93 (1979).
Kebabian, J.W., Calne, D.B.: *Nature* 277:93 (1979).
Kebabian, J.W., Cote, T.E.: *Trends Pharmacol. Sci.* 2:69 (1981).
Kennett, G.A., Joseph, M.H.: *Neuropharmacology* 20:39 (1981).
Kety, S.S.: In: *The Neurosciences: The Second Study Program,* F.O. Schmitt (Ed). Rockefeller Univ. Press: New York (1970). p. 324.
Kewitz, H., Pleul, O.: *Proc. Natl. Acad. Sci. USA* 73:2181 (1976).
Kita, H., Oomura, Y.: *Brain Res.* 235:131 (1982).
Kleihues, P., Kobayashi, H., Hossmann, K.A.: *J. Neurochem.* 23:417 (1974).
Kloog, Y., Egozi, Y., Sokolovskij, M.: *Mol. Pharmacol.* 15:545 (1979).
Knieriem, K.M., Medina, M.A., Stavinoha, W.B.: *J. Neurochem.* 28:885 (1977).
Kohler, C., Chan-Palay, V., Steinbusch, H.: *Anat. Embryol.* 161:237 (1981).
Kontro, P., Oja, S.S.: *Neuroscience* 3:761 (1978).
Kordas, M.: *J. Physiol. (London)* 204:493 (1969).
Kovacs, G.L., Telegdy, G., Lissak, K.: *Psychoneuroendocrinology* 1:219 (1976).
Krech, D., Rosenzweig, M.R., Bennett, E.L.: *Arch. Neurol.* 8:403 (1963).
Krivanek, J.: *J. Neurochem.* 26:413 (1976).
Krnjevic, K., Lekic, D.: *Can. J. Physiol. Pharmacol.* 55:1391 (1977).
Krnjevic, K., Reinhardt, W.: *Science* 206:1321 (1979).
Krnjevic, K., Randic, M., Straughan, D.W.: *J. Physiol. (London)* 170:70 (1964).
Krnjevic, K., Reiffenstein, R.J., Ropert, N.: *Neuroscience* 6:2465 (1981).
Kuehl, F.A., Humes, J.L.: *Proc. Natl. Acad. Sci. USA* 19:480 (1972).
Kuhar, M.J., Aghajanian, G.K., Roth, R.H.: *Brain Res.* 44:165 (1972).
Kuhn, D.M., Vogel, R.L., Lovenberg, W.: *Biochem. Biophys. Res. Commun.* 82:759 (1978).
Kupfermann, I., Cohen, J.L., Mandelbaum, D.E., Schonberg, M., Susswein, A.J., Weiss, K.R.: *Fed. Proc.* 38:2095 (1979).
Kuroda, Y.: *J. Physiol. (Paris)* 74:463 (1978).
Kurzrok, R., Lieb, H.: *Proc. Soc. Exp. Biol. Med.* 28:268 (1930).
Kvamme, E., Olsen, B.E.: *J. Neurochem.* 36:1916 (1981).
Laduron, P.: *Biochem. Pharmacol.* 24:1547 (1975).
Laduron, P.: *Trends Pharmacol. Sci.* 1:471 (1980).
Laduron, P.: *Arch. Int. Pharmacodyn. Ther.* 244:338 (1980a).
Lapetina, E.G., Michell, R.H.: *Biochem. J.* 126:1141 (1972).
Laudenslager, M.L., Carlisle, H.J.: *Pharmacol. Biochem. Behav.* 4:369 (1976).
Leclerc, G., Rouot, B., Velly, J., Schwartz, J.: *Trend Pharmacol. Sci.* 2:18 (1981).
Lee, C.J.: *Brain Res.* 81:497 (1974).
Lee, K., Schubert, P., Gribkoff, V., Sherman, B., Lynch, G.: *J. Neurochem.* 38:80 (1982).
Lefkowitz, R.J., Hoffman, B.B.: *Trends Pharmacol. Sci.* 1:314 (1980).
Leonard, B.E., Rigter, H.: *Pharmacol. Biochem. Behav.* 3:775 (1975).
Leslie, C.A.: *Res. Commun. Chem. Path. Pharm.* 14:455 (1976).
Lester, B.R., Peck, E.J. Jr.: *Brain Res.* 161:79 (1979).
Levey, G.S.: *J. Biol. Chem.* 246:7405 (1971).
Levi, G., Gallo, V.: *J. Neurochem.* 37:22 (1981).

Levi, G., Bertollini, A., Chen, J., Raiter, M.: *J. Pharm. Exp. Ther.* 188:429 (1974).
Levine, R.A., Miller, L.P., Lovenberg, W.: *Science* 214:919 (1981).
Levinger, I.M., Edery, H.: *Experientia* 27:291 (1971).
Leysen, J., Laduron, P.: *Life Sci.* 23:419 (1978).
Lindstrom, L.H.: *Acta Univ. Uppsaliensis* 136:1 (1972).
Lippert, T.H.: *Klin. Wschr.* 55:515 (1977).
Lloyd, K.G., Davidson, L.: *Science* 205:1147 (1979).
Loewi, O.: *Pfluegers Arch.* 189:239 (1921).
Logan, W.J., Snyder, S.H.: *Nature* 234:297 (1971).
Logan, W.J., Snyder, S.H.: *Brain Res.* 42:413 (1972).
Londos, C., Wolff, J.: *Proc. Natl. Acad. Sci. USA* 74:5482 (1977).
Lorden, J.F., Rickert, E.J., Dawson, R., Pelleymott, M.A.: *Brain Res.* 190:569 (1980).
Lovenberg, W., Weissbach, H., Udenfriend, S.: *J. Biol. Chem.* 237:89 (1962).
Lund-Karlsen, R., Fonnum, F.: *Brain Res.* 151:457 (1978).
Mabry, P.D., Campbell, B.A.: *Brain Res.* 49:381 (1973).
MacDonald, J.F., Barker, J.L., Paul, S.M., Marangos, P.J., Skolnick, P.: *Science* 205:715 (1979).
Malthe-Sorenssen, D., Fonnum, F.: *Biochem. J.* 127:229 (1972).
Mandell, A.J., Knapp, S., Hsu, L.L.: *Life Sci.* 14:1 (1974).
Marchand, A., Chapouthier, G., Massoulian, J.: *FEBS Lett.* 78:236 (1977).
Margules, D.L., Margules, A.: *Am. J. Physiol.* 224:1475 (1973).
Marshall, K.C., Engberg, I.: *Science* 205:422 (1979).
Martin, W.R., Sloan, J.W., Buchwald, W.F., Clements, T.H.: *Psychopharmacologia* 43:131 (1975).
Martinet, M., Fonlupt, P., Pacheco, H.: *Psychopharmacologia* 66:63 (1979).
Martinez-Hernandez, A., Bell, K.P., Norenberg, M.D.: *Science* 195:1356 (1977).
Maslinski, C.: *Agents Actions* 5:87 (1975).
Mason, S.T., Fibiger, H.C.: *Nature* 269:704 (1979).
Mason, S.T., Fibiger, H.C.: *Brain Res.* 166:341 (1979a).
Mason, S.T., Roberts, D.C.S., Fibiger, H.C.: *Pharmacol. Biochem. Behav.* 10:11 (1979).
Masserano, J.M., Takimoto, G.S., Weiner, N.: *Science* 214:662 (1981).
Massotti, M., Mazzari, S., Schmid, R., Guidotti, A., Costa, E.: *Neurochem. Res.* 6:551 (1981).
Matthies, H., Rauca, C., Liebmann, H.: *J. Neurochem.* 23:1109 (1974).
Maura, G., Versace, P., Paudice, P.: *Pharmacol. Res. Com.* 10:235 (1978).
McBurney, R.N., Crawford, A.C.: *Fed. Proc.* 38:2080 (1979).
McCaleb, M.L., Myers, R.D., Singer, G., Willis, G.: *Am. J. Physiol.* 236:R312 (1975).
McCarthy, D.: *Fed. Proc.* 25:385 (1966).
McGeer, E.G., Singh, E.A.: *Neurosci. Lett.* 17:85 (1980).
McGeer, E.G., McGeer, P.L., Singh, K.: *Brain Res.* 139:381 (1978).
McIntosh, C.H.S., Plummer, D.T.: *J. Neurochem.* 27:449 (1976).
McLennan, H., Liu, J.R.: *Can. J. Physiol. Pharmacol.* 59:239 (1981).
McLennan, H., Hoffman, R.D., Marshall, K.C.: *Nature* 219:387 (1968).
McManaman, J.L., Blosser, J.C., Appel, S.H.: *J.Neurosci.* 1:771 (1981).
McNamara, J.O.: *Exp. Neurol.* 61:582 (1978).
Meek, J.L., Neckers, L.M.: *Brain Res.* 91:336 (1975).
Messing, R.B., Lytle, L.D.: *Pain* 4:1 (1977).
Messing, R.B., Fisher, L.A., Phebus, L., Lytle, L.D.: *Life Sci.* 18:707 (1976).
Meyer, E.M., Cooper, J.R.: *J. Neurochem.* 36:467 (1981).
Michaelis, E.K., Michaelis, M.L., Boyarsky, L.L.: *Biochim. Biophys. Acta.* 367:338 (1974).
Michaelis, M.L., Michaelis, E.K., Myers, S.L.: *Life Sci.* 24:2083 (1979).

Michaelson, D., Vandlen, R., Bode, J., Moody, T., Schmidt, J., Raftery, M.A.: *Arch. Biochem. Biophys.* 165:796 (1975).
Michel, T., Hoffman, B.B., Lefkowitz, R.J.: *Nature* 288:709 (1980).
Miliaressis, E.: *Pharmacol. Biochem. Behav.* 7:177 (1977).
Misgeld, U., Wagner, A., Ohno, T.: *Exp. Brain Res.* 45:108 (1982).
Misra, C.H.: *J. Neurosci. Res.* 5:507 (1980).
Misra, C.H., Olney, J.W.: *Brain Res.* 97:117 (1975).
Misslin, R., Ropartz, P., Mandel, P.: *Pharmacol. Biochem. Behav.* 4:643 (1976).
Modigh, K.: *Psychopharmacologia* 33:1 (1973).
Mogenson, G.D., Wu, M., Jones, D.L.: *Brain Res.* 191:569 (1980).
Mohler, H.: *Trends Pharmacol. Sci.* 2:117 (1981).
Mohs, R.C., Davis, K.L., Levy, M.I.: *Life Sci.* 29:1317 (1981).
Molenaar, P.C., Polak, R.L.: *J. Neurochem.* 26:95 (1976).
Molinoff, P.B., Sporn, J.R., Wolfe, B.B., Harden, T.K.: *Adv. Cyclic Nucl. Res.* 9:465 (1978).
Moore, W.M., Brady, R.N.: *Biochim. Biophys. Acta.* 444:252 (1976).
Morley, B.J., Kemp, G.E.: *Brain Res. Rev.* 3:81 (1981).
Morrison, J.H., Molliver, M.E., Grzanna, R., Coyle, J.T.: *Neuroscience* 6:139 (1981).
Moss, D.E., Rogers, J.B., Deutsch, J.A., Salome, R.R.: *Pharmacol. Biochem. Behav.* 14:321 (1981).
Muller, J., Da Lage, C.: *J. Histochem. Cytochem.* 25:337 (1977).
Murphy, D.L.: *Biochem. Pharmacol.* 27:1889 (1978).
Murrin, L.C.: *Pharmacology* 21:132 (1980).
Musacchio, J.M.: *Biochim. Biophys. Acta.* 191:485 (1969).
Myers, R.D., McCaleb, M.L., Hughes, K.A.: *Pharmacol. Biochem. Behav.* 10:923 (1979).
Myers, R.D., Yaksh, T.L.: *J. Physiol. (London)* 202:483 (1969).
Nelson, D.L., Herbet, A., Enjalbert, A., Bockaert, J., Hamon, M.: *Biochem. Pharmacol.* 29:2445 (1980).
Nemeroff, C.B., Lipton, M.A., Kizer, J.S.: *Dev. Neurosci.* 1:102 (1978).
Newlin, S.A., Schlapfer, W.T., Barondes, S.H.: *Brain Res.* 181:89 (1980).
Newman, M., Levitzki, A.: *Biochim. Biophys. Acta* 685:129 (1982).
Nickolson, V.J.: *J. Neurochem.* 38:289 (1982).
Nomura, Y., Okuma, Y., Segawa, T., Schmidt-Glenewinkel, T., Giacobini, E.: *Neurochem. Res.* 6:391 (1981).
Nordenfelt, I.: *J. Exp. Physiol.* 49:103 (1964).
Norenberg, M.: *J. Histochem. Cytochem.* 27:756 (1979).
Norenberg, M.D., Martinez-Hernandez, A.: *Brain Res.* 161:303 (1979).
Oh, T.H., Markelonis, G.J.: *Science* 200:337 (1978).
Oke, A., Lewis, R., Adams, R.N.: *Science* 200:1411 (1978).
Oliverio, A.: *Psychopharmacologia* 11:39 (1967).
Olney, J.W.: *J. Neuropath. Exp. Neurol.* 30:75 (1971).
Olschowka, J.A., Molliver, M.E., Grzanna, R., Rice, F.L., Coyle, J.T.: *J. Histochem. Cytochem.* 29:271 (1981).
Olsen, R.W.: *J. Neurochem.* 37:1 (1981).
Olsen, R.W., Bergman, M.O., Van Ness, P.C., Lummis, S.C., Watkins, A.E., Napias, C., Greenlee, D.V.: *Mol. Pharmacol.* 19:217 (1981).
Orrego, F., Miranda, R.: *Eur. J. Pharmacol.* 44:275 (1977).
Oswald, R.E., Freeman, J.A.: *Neuroscience* 6:1 (1981).
Pace-Asciak, C.R., Nashat, M.: *J. Neurochem.* 27:551 (1976).
Pandey, G.N., Heinze, W.J., Brown, B.D., Davis, J.M.: *Nature* 280:234 (1979).
Parent, A., Descarries, L., Beaudet, A.: *Neuroscience* 6:115 (1981).

Pasantes-Morales, H., Gamboa, A.: *J. Neurochem.* 34:244 (1980).
Patel, A.J., Balazs, R., Richter, D.: *Nature* 226:1160 (1973).
Pepeu, G., Mulas, A., Mulas, M.L.: *Brain Res.* 57:153 (1973).
Peroutka, S.J., Snyder, S.H.: *Brain Res.* 208:339 (1981).
Peroutka, S.J., Lebovitz, R.M., Snyder, S.H.: *Science* 212:827 (1981).
Persinger, M.A.: *Behav. Biol.* 21:426 (1977).
Pert, A., Avis, H.H.: *Physiol. Psychol.* 2:111 (1974).
Pestronk, A., Drachman, D.B.: *Science* 199:1223 (1978).
Peterson, N.A., Ragupathy, E.: *J. Neurochem.* 19:1423 (1972).
Pettigrew, J.D., Kasamatsu, T.: *Nature* 271:761 (1978).
Philips, S.R., Rozdilsky, B., Boulton, A.A.: *Biol. Psychiat.* 13:51 (1978).
Phillipson, O.T., Emson, P.C., Horn, A.S., Jessell, T.: *Brain Res.* 136:45 (1977).
Phillis, J.W., Wu, P.H.: *Progr. Neurobiol.* 16:187 (1981).
Pilc, A., Nowak, J.Z.: *Eur. J. Pharmacol.* 55:296 (1979).
Pohorecky, L.A., Zigmond, M., Karten, H., Wurtman, D.J.: *J. Pharmacol. Exp. Ther.* 165:190 (1969).
Prado-Alcala, R.A., Signoret, L., Figueroa, M.: *Pharmacol. Biochem. Behav.* 15:633 (1981).
Psychoyos, S.: *Life Sci.* 23:2155 (1978).
Purpura, D.P., Girado, M., Smith, T.G., Callan, D.A., Grundfest, H.: *J. Neurochem.* 3:238 (1959).
Pycock, C.J., Kerwin, R.W.: *Life Sci.* 28:2679 (1981).
Ramm, P.: *Behav. Neural Biol.* 25:415 (1979).
Remold-O'Donnell, E.: *J. Biol. Chem.* 249:3615 (1974).
Reader, T.A., Masse, P., De Champlain, J.: *Brain Res.* 160:217 (1979).
Reid, J.L., Zivin, J.A., Foppen, F.H., Kopin, I.J.: *Life Sci.* 16:975 (1975).
Reisine, T.: *Neuroscience* 6:1471 (1981).
Ribak, C.E., Vaughn, J.E., Saito, K., Barber, R., Roberts, E.: *Brain Res.* 126:1 (1977).
Riccioppo Neto, F.: *Eur. J. Pharmacol.* 49:351 (1978).
Roberts, D.J., Broadley, K.J.: *Lancet* 1:1219 (1965).
Roberts, E., Hammerschlag, R.: In: *Basic Neurochemistry,* G.J. Siegel, R.W. Albers, R. Katzman, B.W. Agranoff (Eds.). Little, Brown: Boston (1976). p.218.
Robison, G.A., Butcher, R.W., Sutherland, E.W.: *Ann. Rev. Biochem.* 37:149 (1968).
Rodbell, M., Lin, M.C., Soloman, Y., Landos, C., Harwood, J.P., Moutin, B.R., Rendall, M.: *Adv. Cyclic Nucl. Res.* 5:3 (1975).
Rose, S.B.: *Pharmacology* 21:123 (1980).
Roseghini, M.: *Gen. Pharmacol.* 7:221 (1976).
Roth, R.H., Salzman, P.M., Morgenroth, V.H.: *Biochem. Pharmacol.* 23:2779 (1974).
Roufogalis, B.D., Wickson, V.M.: *Mol. Pharmacol.* 11:352 (1975).
Rumigny, J.F., Maitre, M., Cash, C., Mandel, P.: *FEBS Lett.* 117:111 (1980).
Sabelli, H.C., Borison, R.L., Diamond, B.I., Havdala, H.S., Narashimhan, N.: *Biochem. Pharmacol.* 27:1729 (1978).
Saeed, S.A., McDonald-Gibson, W.J., Cuthbert, J., Copas, J.L., Schneider, C., Gardiner, P.J., Butt, N.M., Collier, H.O.J.: *Nature* 270:32 (1977).
Saller, C.F., Chiodo, L.A.: *Science* 210:1269 (1980).
Samanin, R., Garattini, S.: *Life Sci.* 17:1201 (1975).
Schildkraut, J.J.: *Am. J. Psychiat.* 122:509 (1965).
Schmidt, D.E., Wecker, L.: *Neuropharmacology* 20:535 (1981).
Schmidt, J., Raftery, M.A.: *Biochemistry* 12:852 (1973).
Schotten, C.: *Z. Physiol. Chem.* 8:60 (1883).
Schousboe, A., Fosmark, H., Svenneby, G.: *Brain Res.* 116:158 (1976).

Schubert, P., Kreutzberg, G.W.: *Brain Res.* 76:526 (1974).
Schubert, P., Mitzdorf, U.: *Brain Res.* 172:186 (1979).
Schubert, P., Rose, G., Lee, K., Lynch, G., Kreutzberg, G.W.: *Brain Res.* 134:347 (1977).
Schultz, J.: *J. Neurochem.* 24:1237 (1975).
Schultz, J.: *Nature* 261:417 (1976).
Schurr, A.: *Life Sci.* 30:1059 (1982).
Schwabe, U., Kiffe, H., Puchstein, C., Trost, T.: *Naunyn-Schmiedeberg's Arch. Pharmacol.* 310:59 (1979).
Schwarcz, R., Coyle, J.T.: *Brain Res.* 127:235 (1977).
Schwartz, J.C.: *Life Sci.* 25:895 (1979).
Segal, M., Edelson, A.: *Brain Res. Bull.* 3:203 (1978).
Seiler, N., Wiechmann, M., Fischer, H.A., Werner, G.: *Brain Res.* 128:317 (1971).
Seligman, B., Miller, L.P., Brockman, D.E., Martin, D.L.: *J. Neurochem.* 330:371 (1978).
Seto, A., Arimatsu, Y., Amano, T.: *Neurosci. Lett.* 4:115 (1977).
Sgaragli, G., Pavan, F.: *Neuropharmacology* 11:45 (1972).
Shank, R.F., Aprison, M.H.: *Life Sci.* 28:837 (1981).
Shank, R.F., Campbell, G.L.: *Life Sci.* 28:843 (1981).
Shear, M., Insel, P.A., Melmon, K.L., Coffino, P.: *J. Biol. Chem.* 251:7572 (1976).
Shearer, G.M., Cudkowicz, G.: *Science* 190:894 (1975).
Shute, C.C.D., Lewis, P.R.: *Brain* 90:497 (1967).
Silver, A.: *The Biology of Cholinesterases*. Elsevier: New York (1974).
Simhadri, P., Devi, B.U.: *Indian J. Med. Res.* 58:96 (1970).
Simon, J.R., Kuhar, M.J.: *Nature* 255:162 (1975).
Sladek, J.R., Walker, P.: *Brain Res.* 134:359 (1977).
Snead, O.C.: *Neurology* 28:636 (1978).
Snyder, S.H.: *Trends Neurosci.* 4:242 (1981).
Snyder, S.H., Creese, I., Burt, D.R.: *Psychopharmacol. Comm.* 1:663 (1975).
Soulairac, A.: *Ann. Endocrinol.* 24(Suppl.1):98 (1963).
Spafford, D.C., Pengelley, E.T.: *Comp. Biochem. Physiol.* 38A:239 (1971).
Sperk, G., Hortnagl, H., Reither, H., Hornykiewicz, O.: *J. Neurochem.* 37:525 (1981).
Starke, K.: *Trends Pharmacol. Sci.* 1:268 (1980).
Starke, K., Endo, T.: *Gen. Pharmacol.* 7:307 (1976).
Steele, M.K., Rowland, D., Moltz, H.: *Pharmacol. Biochem. Behav.* 11:123 (1979).
Steranka, L.R., Barrett, R.J.: *Behav. Biol.* 11:205 (1974).
Stern, W.C., Morgane, P.J.: *Behav. Biol.* 11:1 (1974).
Sternberg, D.B., Gold, P.E.: *Behav. Neural Biol.* 29:289 (1980).
Sternberger, L.A., Hardy, P.H., Cuculis, J.J., Meyer, H.G.: *J. Histochem. Cytochem.* 18:315 (1970).
Stone, E.A.: *J. Neurochem.* 21:589 (1973).
Stone, T.W.: *Br. J. Pharmacol.* 66:291 (1979).
Stone, T.W.: *Neuroscience* 6:523 (1981).
Stoof, J.C., Kebabian, J.W.: *Nature* 294:366 (1981).
Storm-Mathisen, J.: *Brain Res.* 120:379 (1977).
Stratton, L.O., Petrinovich, L.: *Psychopharmacologia* 5:47 (1963).
Strittmatter, W.J., Hirata, F., Axelrod, J.: *Adv. Cycl. Nucl. Res.* 14:83 (1981).
Struyker Boudier, H.A., Gielen, W., Cools, A.R., Van Rossum, J.M.: *Arch. Internat. Pharmacodyn. Ther.* 209:324 (1974).
Sturman, J.A.: *J. Neurochem.* 36:304 (1981).
Su, J.F., Cubeddux, L., Perkins, J.P.: *J. Cycl. Nucleotide Res.* 2:257 (1976).
Subramanian, N., Mulder, A.H.: *Eur. J. Pharmacol.* 35:203 (1976).

Subramanian, N., Whitmore, W.L., Seidler, F.J., Slotkin, T.A.: *Life Sci.* 27:1315 (1980).

Sudak, H.S., Maas, J.W.: *Science* 146:418 (1964).

Suetake, K., Kojima, H., Inanaga, K., Koketsu, K.: *Brain Res.* 205:436 (1981).

Sulakhe, P.V., Phillis, J.W.: *Life Sci.* 17:551 (1975).

Sun, M.C., McIlwain, H., Pull, I.: *J. Neurobiol.* 7:109 (1977).

Sze, P.Y., Neckers, L., Towle, A.C.: *J. Neurochem.* 26:69 (1976).

Takagi, H., Shiomi, H., Kuraishi, Y., Fukui, K., Ueda, H.: *Eur. J. Pharmacol.* 54:99 (1979).

Takasaki, S.: *Toxicology* 9:293 (1978).

Takeda, M., Tanaka, R.: *Neurochem. Res.* 4:643 (1979).

Talman, W.T., Perrone, M.H., Reis, D.J.: *Science* 209:813 (1980).

Tamir, H., Gershon, M.D.: *J. Neurochem.* 33:35 (1979).

Tamir, H., Liu, K.P.: *J. Neurochem.* 38:135 (1982).

Tamir, H., Bebirian, R., Muller, F., Casper, D.: *J. Neurochem.* 35:1033 (1980).

Tappaz, M.L., Brownstein, M.J.: *Brain Res.* 132:95 (1977).

Tenen, S.S.: *Psychopharmacologia* 10:204 (1967).

Terasaki, W.L., Brooker, G., de Vellis, J., Inglish, D., Hsu, C.Y., Moylan, R.D.: *Adv. Cyclic Nucl. Res.* 9:33 (1978).

Thagnipon, W., Storm-Mathisen, J.: *Neurosci. Lett.* 23:181 (1981).

Thompson, R.W.: *Psychol. Rec.* 1:109 (1977).

Toffano, G., Guidotti, A., Costa, E.: *Proc. Natl. Acad. Sci. USA.* 75:4024 (1978).

Toffano, G., Aldinio, C., Balzano, M., Leon, A., Savoini, G.: *Brain Res.* 222:95 (1981).

Toyoshima, Y., Kinemuchi, H., Kamijo, K.: *J. Neurochem.* 32:1183 (1979).

Trams, E.G.: *Differentiation* 19:125 (1981).

Trost, T., Stock, K.: *Naunyn-Schmiedeberg's Arch. Pharmacol.* 310:59 (1977).

Tufik, S., Lindsey, C.J., Carlini, E.A.: *Pharmacology* 16:98 (1978).

Uchida, M.K.: *Gen. Pharmacol.* 9:145 (1978).

Ungerstedt, U.: In: *Neurosciences Research.* Vol. 5, S. Ehrenpreis, I.J. Kopin (Eds.). Academic Press: New York (1973). p. 73

Valdes, F., Fanelli, R.J., McNamara, J.O.: *Life Sci.* 29:1895 (1981).

Valentino, R.J., Dingledine, R.: *J. Neurosci.* 1:784 (1981).

Van Abeelen, J.H.F.: In: *The Genetics of Behaviour.* J.H.F. Van Abeelen (Ed.). Elsevier: New York (1974). p. 347.

Van Calker, D., Muller, M., Hamprecht, B.: *Nature* 276:839 (1978).

Van Der Heyden, J.A., Dekloet, E.R., Korf, J., Versteeg, D.H.: *J. Neurochem.* 33:857 (1979).

Van Der Kloot, W.G., Cohen, I.: *Science* 203:1351 (1979).

Van Gelder, N.M.: *Can. J. Physiol. Pharmacol.* 49:513 (1971).

Van Gelder, N.M., Koyama, T., Jasper, H.H.: *Epilepsia* 18:45 (1977).

Van Harreveld, A.: *J. Neurobiol.* 9:419 (1978).

Van Harreveld, A.: *J. Neurobiol.* 10:355 (1979).

Van Harreveld, A., Fifkova E.: *Brain Res.* 81:455 (1974).

Van Harreveld, A., Strumwasser, F.: *Neuroscience* 6:2495 (1981).

Vetulani, J., Stawarz, R.J., Dingell, J.V., Sulser, F.: *Naunyn-Schmiedeberg's Arch. Pharmacol.* 293:109 (1976).

Vogt, M.: *J. Physiol. (London)* 28:451 (1954).

Von Euler, U.S.: *Acta Physiol. Scand.* 12:73 (1946).

Von Hungen, K., Roberts, S., Hill, D.F.: *Brain Res.* 84:257 (1975).

Waddington, J.L., Cross, A.J.: *Nature* 276:618 (1978).

Waldmeier P.C., Feldtrauer, J-J., Maitre, L.: *J. Neurochem.* 29:785 (1977).

Walsh, T.J., Palfai, T.: *Pharmacol. Biochem. Behav.* 11:449 (1979).

Wauquier, A., Niemegeers, C.J.: *Psychopharmacologia* 27:191 (1972).

Weill, C.L., McNamee, M.G., Karlin, A.: *Biochem. Biophys. Res. Commun.* 61:997 (1974).

Weinreich, D.: *Nature* 267:854 (1977).

Welch, A.S., Welch, B.L.: *Biochem. Pharmacol.* 17:699 (1968).

Welch, B.L., Hendley, E.D., Turek, I.: *Science* 183:220 (1974).

Westerink, B.H.C.: *Eur. J. Pharmacol.* 56:313 (1979).

Wheeler, D.D.: *Pharmacology* 21:141 (1980)

White, R.D., Neal, M.L.: *Brain Res.* 111:79 (1976).

Williams, J.W., Rudy, T.A., Yaksh, T.L., Viswanathan, C.T.: *Brain Res.* 120:251 (1977).

Williams, L.T., Lefkowitz, R.J.: *Receptor Binding Studies in Adrenergic Pharmacology.* Raven Press: New York (1978).

Winkler, M.H., Nicklas, W.J., Berl, S.: *J. Neurochem.* 32:79 (1979).

Wirtz, K.W.A., Jolles, J., Westermann, J., Neys, F.: *Nature* 260:354 (1976).

Wise, R.A.: *Life Sci.* 22:535 (1978).

Wolfe, L.S.: *J. Neurochem.* 38:1 (1982).

Wolfe, L.S., Rostworowski, K., Marion, J.: *Biochem. Biophys. Res. Commun.* 70:907 (1976).

Wolfe, L.S., Pappius, H.M., Marion, J.: In: B. Samuelsson, P.W. Ramwell, R. Paoletti (Eds.), *Advances in Prostaglandin and Thromboxane Research,* Vol. 1. Raven Press: New York (1976a). p.345.

Wolff, J., Londos, C., Cooper, D.M.F.: *Adv. Cycl. Nucl. Res.* 14:199 (1981).

Wong, T.Y., Dreyfus, H., Nguyen Vu, K., Harth, S., Massarelli, R.: In: *Synaptic Constituents in Health and Disease.* M. Brzin, Sket, H. Bachelard (Eds.). Pergamon Press: Oxford (1980). p. 98.

Woodward, D.J., Moises, H.C., Waterhouse, B.D., Hoffer, B.J., Freedman, R.: *Fed. Proc.* 38:2109 (1979).

Wooley, D.W., Van der Hoeven, T.: *Int. J. Neuropsychiat.* 1:529 (1965).

Wooten, G.F.: *Brain Res.* 55:491 (1973).

Wurtzburger, R.J., Musacchio, J.M.: *J. Pharm. Exp. Ther.* 177:155 (1971).

Yaksh, T.L., Wilson, P.R.: *J. Pharm. Exp. Ther.* 208:446 (1979).

Yamamoto, C., Yamashita, H., Chujo, T.: *Nature* 262:286 (1976).

Yamauchi, T., Fujisawa, H.: *Biochem. Biophys. Res. Commun.* 90:28 (1979).

Yarowsky, P.J., Carpenter, D.O.: *Science* 192:807 (1976).

Young, A.B., Oster-Granite, M.L., Herndon, R.M., Snyder, S.H.: *Brain Res.* 73:1 (1974).

Zingsheim, H.P., Neugebauer, D.C., Barrantes, F.J., Frank, J.: *Proc. Natl. Acad. Sci. USA* 77:952 (1980).

Zumstein, A., Karduck, W., Starke, K.: *Naunyn-Schmiedeberg's Arch. Pharmacol.* 316:205 (1981).

V

THE BRAIN AS AN ENDOCRINE GLAND

Chapter 22

Endocrine and "Paracrine" Effects on Brain Activity

The brain, as any other organ of the body, is continually subject to the influence of hormones secreted by the various endocrine glands. Some of these hormones are secreted by the nervous tissue itself; some are produced simultaneously by the cells within the nervous tissue and some other organ of the body, such as the stomach or intestine. They influence a wide range of brain activities. And, while the names given to some of the peptide hormones were based upon early attributions to them of single specific functions associated with one system, further research revealed that most had several other independent actions (Kastin *et al.*, 1981). Various hypothalamic peptides, for instance, were shown to exhibit certain central behavioral effects, in addition to their previously acknowledged pituitary hormonal activities.

The evidence accumulated in recent years shows that hormones are involved in the control of instinctive behavior, vegetative and metabolic functions, and, in particular, in the fixation of the memory trace and recall of stored information (Zetler, 1978). Because this influence is so extensive, Section V is intended to provide a reasonably comprehensive examination of the various hormonal and modulatory agents that have been identified in the brain.

411

GENERAL ACTIONS OF HORMONES

Both the hormones and the nervous system serve coordinate, interlocking, regulatory functions that permit the organism to react to specific stimuli and environmental shifts in a cohesive way. Actually, the alterations in the patterns of glandular activity depend largely upon the activity of the central pathways, and the collection and storage of information within the CNS is influenced by neurohormonal agents.

Hormones generally fall into one of two classes: substances of low molecular weight, such as the amines (usually derived from amino acids) and steroids [derived chemically from cyclopentanohydrophenanthrene (Fig. 22.1)], or a class of peptides and proteins. They are produced in certain endocrine cells within various organs, or in the cells of tissues specialized as endocrine glands. After their synthesis, the hormones are stored within the cells until the arrival of a specific impulse, at which time they are released through the cell membrane into the circulation. In the blood, some hormones, such as estrogens, thyroxine and corticosteroids, are bound to particular transport proteins; others migrate by themselves. The hormones, after reaching the target organ and being bound to their receptor molecules, typically undergo a rapid inactivation. Still, their effects may continue to persist for a considerable length of time.

Within the cells, the hormones govern the rates of certain critical metabolic processes. For example, the hormones of the thyroid gland do not induce the synthesis of the enzymes of oxidative metabolism; rather, they influence the rate of their activity. They stimulate oxygen consumption by the tissue, but even in the absence of this facilitatory effect - for example, after thyroidectomy - the oxygen consumption does not drop to zero.

The principal actions of hormones are directed towards cell membranes, particular enzymes, or the system of protein synthesis. They may activate some specific genes and induce the synthesis of new messenger RNA, or they may modulate the process of protein synthesis in ribosomes and the final shaping of proteins by proteolytic, methylating, or other enzymes. All components of the cellular biochemical machinery, then, may be considered as potentially modifiable by hormones.

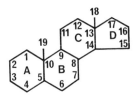

Figure 22.1 The steroid precursor, perhydrocyclopentanohydrophenanthrene.

In order to exert their particular actions, the hormones have to react with specific molecular receptors within the cells. The receptors for hormones are localized in various regions of the target cells. For example, the receptors for peptide hormones and catecholamines are positioned primarily in plasma membranes, while thyroid hormones have receptors in the cytoplasm, or on the surface of mitochondria. The receptors for steroid hormones are usually intracellular. When the steroid reaches the cell and is bound to the receptor, the hormone-receptor complex actively migrates to the cell nucleus, where it undergoes a conformational change. This process is under the control of a "receptor transforming factor" (RTF) which is actually a calcium-activated protease. The shift in conformation appears necessary for the receptor-hormone complex to subsequently activate a specific part of the genome.

The number of receptors may vary with the functional state of the cell, and it is often regulated by the presence of corresponding hormones. The number of receptor molecules generally seems to be limited, so that the cell does not become overstimulated by an excess amount of the hormone.

The actions of the hormones may be mediated by intracellular cyclic nucleotide or calcium ion second messengers, or by the polyamines. The hormones functioning through the activation of adenylate cyclase are numerous and include ACTH, TSH, and vasopressin (for review see Tixier-Vidal and Gourdji, 1981). Basically, the hormone receptors behave in a way similar to neurotransmitter receptors, and their affinity for the hormone ligand is regulated by the state of the cell. When the hormone binds to the receptor, the receptor-ligand structure likely associates with, or conformationally alters a guanine nucleotide-binding protein, which then activates adenylate cyclase or a corresponding effector. Adenylate cyclase then initiates a cellular response to the hormone. As a result, the receptor and the adenylate cyclase become temporarily desensitized. This receptor - hormone complex later uncouples from the effector enzyme and is subject to one of a number of possible fates which depend upon the hormone and tissue in question. The classic situation is that hormone is released and degraded, and the receptor is reutilized. The hormone - receptor complex may be also released from the membrane, and either be lost in the extracellular space or be internalized. The binding protein may lose its attached guanine nucleotide by the action of GTPase, thereby functionally dissociating the complex from adenylate cyclase. Within the cell, the complex may be degraded in the lysosomes, or may perform some specific trophic function. In addition, unoccupied receptors, together with the hormone - receptor complex, may also be internalized and degraded, leading to a further decrease in cell sensitivity. Later, during recovery, the receptor molecules are replenished by protein synthesis. In some cells, following an exposure to the hormone, the number of receptors increases. This is true for prolactin receptors and angiotensin II receptors in the kidney.

All of these changes in receptor sensitivity and number are accompanied by receptor movements and the formation of molecular clusters in the membrane, along with changes in receptor conformation. This clustering of receptors into surface aggregates seems to be an important prelude to the internalization of the hormone - receptor complex.

Many hormones, regardless of their tissue of origin, exert effects upon the brain that have behavioral consequences which, as a rule, are consistent with their endocrine effects. This is particularly true for the polypeptide hormones. Thus, luteinizing hormone releasing hormone (LHRH, also known as gonadotropin releasing hormone, GnRH) controls the secretion of pituitary gonadotropins and at the same time influences some aspects of sexual behavior. In addition, thyrotropin releasing hormone has behavioral effects even in species where it has no demonstrable endocrine actions.

These endocrine effects are especially important during the development of the brain. Changes in the secretory activity of the endocrine glands often cause some kind of brain dysfunction, and behavioral abnormalities caused by a hormonal imbalance during certain periods of brain development may even be permanent. In addition, the presence of several hormones, such as thyroxine, the sex hormones, and some pituitary hormones, is continuously required for the optimal functioning of the adult central nervous system.

CLASSIFICATION OF HUMORAL AGENTS IN THE BRAIN

Some humoral agents which affect the brain are well recognized hormones which satisfy all definitions of the word. They are released into the circulation and reach distant target organs via the blood flow. Some other biologically active substances, notably peptides produced by some parts of the central nervous system, influence their target cells humorally, although there is no evidence that they enter the general circulation in meaningful concentrations. These substances, examples of which are thyrotropin releasing hormone (TRH), gonadotropin releasing hormone (GnRH), and growth hormone release inhibitory hormone (GHRIH, somatostatin), are hormones, but travel only a short distance from the hypothalamus to the pituitary. In other parts of the brain, this situation is even more restrictive, in that peptides are released to serve only local roles. Since peptides acting in this manner actually do not perform as neurotransmitters or hormones in the strict sense, their effect has been termed a paracrine action. Guillemin (1977) labeled these substances cybernins to imply a local spreading of information. Some authors (e.g., Scharrer, 1978) have referred to these peptide-releasing neurons as peptidergic neurons. However, this term suggests a real synaptic neurotransmitter action for these substances, which would have to be sufficiently documented in each case.

It is sometimes difficult to distinguish between hormones, local hormones (cybernins) responsible for a paracrine action, and neurotransmitters. Generally, we may say that neurotransmitters are released by the nerve endings, react with specific receptors in the postsynaptic membranes, and are quickly degraded or transported back into the cells from which they were liberated. When there is no synapse, the response may be termed paracrinic, an example of which is the action of the hypothalamic releasing hormones in the pituitary. The classic hormones are those substances which circulate and are able to influence widespread areas of the body.

Not all substances that are considered to be neurotransmitters behave according to this convention. Norepinephrine released from the varicosities of fibers originating in the locus coeruleus and reaching masses of cells in the cerebral cortex, may diffuse through nervous tissue and interact with the receptors present in the extrasynaptic neuronal membrane. Here, the effect may actually be described as a localized paracrinic action. Some true hormones, on the other hand, may depolarize certain neurons, an action that is characteristic of a neurotransmitter.

For a long time, neurons were believed to be so specialized in structure and function that they could easily be distinguished from other cells. Some recent evidence has shown that this is not always the case, and it is now difficult to categorize some cells either as neurons or as endocrine cells. There are no specific morphological criteria for neurons. Even Nissl substance, microtubules and neurofilaments are also present in other cells. Furthermore, there is no functional characteristic that is unique to the neuron. The generation of an action potential cannot be considered to be a distinguishing feature, since both muscle and secretory cells show changes of electrical potentials which depend upon movements of ions across the cell membranes via ion-selective channels. Some secretory cells such as pancreatic β-cells and certain cells of anterior pituitary even produce voltage-dependent action potentials (Williams, 1981).

For these reasons, Fujita (1976) has proposed the term "paraneuron". Paraneurons are cells with some features in common with neurons (Fig. 22.2). They may possess neurosecretory-like or synaptic vesicle-like granules, which may produce substances identical with, or related to, neurohormones or neurotransmitters, and which may react to physical or chemical stimuli by a release of secretary substances. They need not originate from the neural crest; some are formed from epithelia *in situ*. Such paraneurons which display endocrine activity are, for instance, peptide-producing cells, pancreatic endocrine cells, or pinealocytes (Fig. 22.3). Some cells, including neurons, may even produce more than one factor, by secreting, for example, a low-molecular neurotransmitter and a peptide (Hokfelt *et al.*, 1980).

A number of these substances, particularly the peptide hormones, may function in several ways. They may have a transmitter-like action inducing a

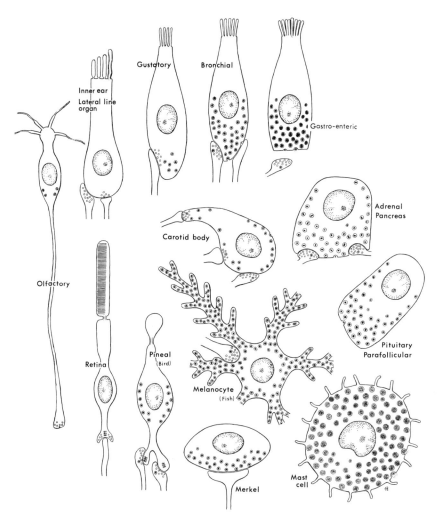

Figure 22.2 Examples of some important paraneurons [from T. Fujita, in: *Chromaffin, Enterochromaffin and Related Cells,* T. Fujita and R.E. Coupland (Eds.), p. 198 (1976); © 1976 by Elsevier Scientific Publishing Company].

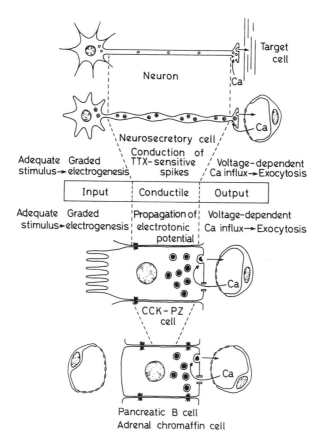

Figure 22.3 Schematic representation of three different portions of the cell membrane in a neuron, a neurosecretory cell, and paraneurons (a CCK-PZ cell, a pancreatic B cell and an adrenal chromaffin cell). The functions of the input, conductile, and output portions are explained in the center. Paraneurons may be distinguished from the neuron and the neurosecretory cell by the function of the conductile portion [from T. Kanno, *Biomed. Research* 1/suppl; 10 (1980); © 1980 by Biomedical Research Foundation, Tokyo].

rapid change in channel conductance, or they may alter the spike threshold without a corresponding electrical change in the membrane. Or, they may serve to modulate the neurotransmitter response. All of these three situations have been experimentally demonstrated in tissue cultures by Barker *et al.* (1980). The changes of the surface potential of the cell elicited by the peptides were found to alter the configuration of membrane proteins, causing subsequent modifications in neurotransmitter receptors, membrane transport, etc. (Zierler and Rogus, 1981). In this way, TRH (thyrotropin releasing hormone) can potentiate the effect of dopamine or other catecholamines on neurons. The onset of the effect of these substances is often slow, taking from seconds to minutes, but the duration of the action is long, lasting anywhere from minutes to hours. Moreover, this neuromodulatory action of peptides may be rather selective, with only some neurons being affected. One of the possibilities that could account for this extended duration relates to the existence of the aforementioned guanine nucleotide-binding regulatory component, intervening between the hormone's receptor and the metabolic machinery of the cell. Such a component, interposed in this manner, may function to prolong the stimulatory effect upon the cell's metabolism of a brief exposure to the hormone (Johnson *et al.*, 1980).

NEUROENDOCRINE SYSTEMS

One of the more prominent examples of the relationship that exists between the neural and endocrine systems is the hypothalamo-pituitary system. Originally, only the pituitary-adrenal axis was considered to function via a psychoendocrine relationship (Selye, 1936). Later, several other endocrine systems were found to be similarly responsive. Most of them are associated with the action of relatively small peptides produced by the central nervous system. Four classes of neuropeptides have been distinguished:

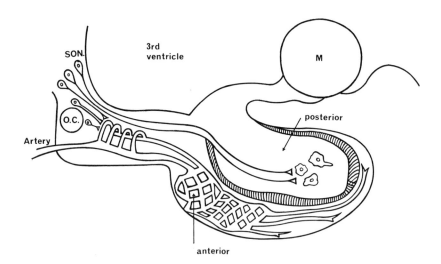

Figure 22.4 Longitudinal section through the pituitary, showing the relationships to the hypothalamus for the anterior and posterior regions. Abbreviations: SON, supraoptic nucleus; O.C., optic chiasma; M, mammillary body.

(1) the hypothalamic peptide hormones,
(2) the pituitary peptides,
(3) peripheral peptide hormones, which are also produced in places such as the gastrointestinal tract, blood plasma and skin, and
(4) peptides produced exclusively, or almost exclusively, by the brain.

Hypothalamic peptide hormones and pituitary peptides are functionally interrelated, and both of them are present in the hypothalamus and anterior pituitary, a neurohumoral system where chemical factors produced by the former are transferred by local blood flow into the latter (Fig. 22.4). There is evidence that this system is both subject to psychological influences and is able to affect directly several neural systems within the CNS (Fig. 22.5). Moreover, during various behavioral states, several hormones may be released at one time and influence the general state of the organism (e.g., Skrabanek et al., 1981).

Another neuroendocrine linkage is between the anterior hypothalamus and the posterior pituitary (see Fig. 22.4). Two hormones, vasopressin and oxytocin, are produced in the hypothalamus and transported along the axons into the posterior pituitary to be released whenever needed. At least one of these two, vasopressin, has been found capable of modifying behavior.

A multitude of other contacts and relationships exists so that no hormone can, at least for the present, be excluded from the neuroendocrine category. The hormones are subject to the influence of the central nervous system and, in turn, are able to alter nervous activity. The overall balance of hormonal effects - antagonistic, synergistic, additive, and permissive - is probably controlled by the nervous system.

The effects of hormones on nervous activity are usually direct, and are a consequence of a binding of the hormones to receptors positioned on the neuronal surface or within the cytoplasm. But, there are also indirect effects. Testosterone, for instance, can both directly affect the central nervous system and modify the sensitivity of the glans penis to tactile stimulation, thus influencing neuronal input to the brain. Similarly, the estrogens, which increase breast and nipple sensitivity in human females, may also alter other sensory thresholds, including those for hearing, smell, and taste. In this way, estrogens can precipitate a preference for sweet-tasting substances in the female rat, but not in the male.

The effect of hormones on behavior depends upon the particular animal species, the season of the year, previous experience, and upon the psychological expectancies of the subject. These psychological effects are often readily evident in humans and sometimes, when exaggerated, may even induce pathological endocrine states, such as hyperthyroidism or menstrual and reproductive disorders.

An interesting group of active agents is comprised of peptides that are produced both by cells of the gastrointestinal tract and the brain. The following are examples of those which have already been identified:

(1) Substance P, which is found in relatively high concentrations in the substantia nigra and hypothalamus and also in the enterochromaffin cells of the gastrointestinal tract.

(2) Somatostatin (GHRIH), which inhibits the secretion of growth hormone by the pituitary, in addition to suppressing the release of insulin, glucagon, and gastrin by the pancreas and gastrointestinal tract. In the stomach and pancreas, it has been found in concentrations that are as high as in the hippocampus. Somatostatin is also present in the periventricular nucleus, in nerve fibers within the posterior pituitary, and in the intestinal wall.

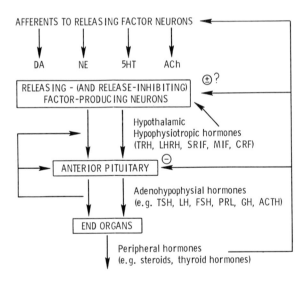

Figure 22.5 Schematic representation of relationships between brain neurotransmitter systems, hypothalamic peptidergic (releasing factor) neurons, anterior pituitary, and peripheral endocrine organs illustrating established feedback loops. Dopamine, DA; norephinephrine, NE; serotonin, 5-HT; acetylcholine, ACH; thyrotropin-releasing hormone, TRH; somatostatin, SRIF; melanocyte-stimulating hormone release-inhibiting factor, MIF; corticotropin-releasing hormone, CRF; prolactin-inhibiting factor, PIF; thyroid-stimulating hormone, TSH; luteinizing hormone, LH; follicle-stimulating hormone, FSH; prolactin, PRL; growth hormone, GH; and adrenocorticotropic hormone, ACTH [from C.B. Nemeroff and A.J. Prange, *Arch. Gen. Psychiat.* 35:999 (1978); © 1978 by American Medical Association].

(3) Gastrin, originally believed to be restricted to G cells of the pyloric antrum, has also been demonstrated in mammalian brain tissue. Some authors claim that brain gastrin exhibits a close structural relationship with that found in the gastrointestinal tract, although the two are not identical.

(4) Vasointestinal peptide (VIP), originally isolated from porcine duodenum, is additionally present throughout the entire gastrointestinal tract from the oesophagus to the rectum. Its presence in the brain has been verified, and concentrations were found to be higher in, for example, the frontal lobe and hypothalamus, than in the duodenum, ileum or colon. Structurally, this peptide appears to be identical in brain and intestine.

All of these peptides probably play an endocrine (or paracrine) role both in the brain and in the gastrointestinal tract. According to Pearse (1976), the cells secreting them are derived from a common neuroectodermal ancestor found originally in the neural crest, neural tube and neural ridges of the early embryo.

Another group of peptides includes those found both in the brain and in the amphibian skin. These skin peptides, caerulein, phyllocaerulein, physalaemin and bombesin are derived from skin cells which originate from cells adjacent to the embryonic neural plate and neural crest. Some have also been identified elsewhere in the body. Bombesin, for example, is also present in gastric mucosa and lung tissue (see Burt, 1980). A few more peptides are produced simultaneously in different parts of the body and in the brain. Such substances are the bradykinin-like peptides and angiotensin, synthesized in the blood plasma from material supplied by liver and kidney.

All of these biologically active substances, together with some others that have been recently isolated and studied, will be discussed in more detail in succeeding chapters. These peptides, which are often able to alter or even induce various mental states as anxiety, depression, pain, attention, and motivation, are often associated with learning or important behavioral adaptations to a changing environment. In the future, these and related substances may prove to have some clinical utility in the treatment of various forms of psychopathology. Conceivably, various types may also be found beneficial to patients with disorders involving cerebral blood flow or vascular permeability, sexual responsivity, and chronic pain, epilepsy or memory disturbances.

A recent impetus in the area of neuropeptide research has been the adoption of certain techniques from molecular biology. With them, it is possible to construct specific complementary DNA molecules (cDNA) that are able to detect mRNA units for the peptide hormones. Since brain cells producing the hormones also possess the mRNA molecules for them, this approach is able to detect, with precision and efficiency, the presence and localization of these various peptide hormones, endorphins, etc.

It is becoming increasingly evident that these previously unknown or neglected peptides exhibit considerable pharmacological activity within the central nervous system. If administered parenterally, most have the ability to induce changes in behavior, indicating that they are able to penetrate the blood-brain barrier with relative ease. However, their binding within synaptosomes is passive and varies considerably (Greenberg *et al.*, 1976), in addition to being unaffected by temperature or sodium ion concentration. Such findings would speak against any claims that these substances are true neurotransmitters.

These peptides do react with cell membrane receptors which have been detected in many tissues and organs, including CNS neurons. Usually, the complex of receptor and peptide is rather long-lived. The peptide receptors have typically been found to be glycoproteins, which wholly or partially span the lipid bilayer of the cellular membrane. The glycoprotein receptors are activated or inactivated by adjacent membrane phospholipids. Guanyl nucleotides also appear to influence hormone binding to the receptors (Rodbell, 1980).

The peptide molecule often has several active sites, each of which may react with a different type of receptor. In this way, the same hormone would be able to trigger a number of metabolic activities. In addition, it may possess auxilliary sites that are used for transport or species labelling (Schwyzer, 1980).

After binding to its receptor, the hormone undergoes a translocaton through the cell membrane. It is not yet certain that the hormone-surface receptor complex is maintained as the hormone penetrates the cell. But, an interesting possibility is that the receptors themselves, not the hormones, may be the biologically active structure. In this case, then, the hormones would only serve to release them from the membrane. It would also mean that this stripping away of membrane receptors causes a temporary depletion of available receptors and could function to avoid an excessive response to large amounts of hormones. The receptors, with their attached peptide hormones, would eventually be degraded by lysosomal action.

The effect of these peptides persists long after they have left the blood stream, indicating that the complex of a peptide with a receptor may induce metabolic processes within the neuron which are long-lived or possibly even permanent. These processes would include the regulation of protein synthesis, the stimulation of carbohydrate and lipid metabolism, altered membrane permeability, ion transport or secretion, and the release of target cell products. The majority of these actions are mediated by cyclic AMP and may be modulated by calcium ions. The short-term effects of the hormones usually do not operate through gene transcription, but through the phosphorylation, activation, or modification of existing gene products.

HYPOTHALAMIC PEPTIDES

Currently, the most widely known brain peptides are probably those synthesized in the hypothalamus. Anatomically, as the name would suggest, this area is positioned below the thalamus, forming the floor and part of the lateral wall of the third ventricle. The activity over its numerous afferent and efferent fiber tracts makes the hypothalamus an efficient coordination region that is able to influence the functioning of many bodily systems.

One of the main target areas of the hypothalamus, situated just below the ventral hypothalamic surface, is the hypophysis or pituitary gland (see Fig. 22.4). About one centimeter in diameter, the pituitary is a major release point for many regulatory hormones. It is composed of two distinct parts that differ both in their function and embryological origin. The anterior portion, or adenohypophysis, develops during the early embryonic period from the pharyngeal epithelium. It secretes six known hormones, each of which is synthesized by a particular group of specialized cells. Most have trophic functions, in that they promote other endocrine gland activities. They are: adrenocorticotrophic hormone (ACTH), which controls the secretory activity of the adrenal cortex; thyroid stimulating hormone (TSH), which controls the secretory activity of the thyroid gland; somatotropin (growth hormone), which stimulates tissue protein synthesis, mobilizes lipids for energy production, and decreases carbohydrate metabolism; follicle stimulating hormone (FSH), which stimulates growth of the ovarian follicles and activates the male sperm producing epithelial tissue in the testis; luteinizing hormone (LH), which is involved in ovulation and the regulation of estrogen secretion by the follicle and also stimulates androgen secretion in the male; and prolactin, which contributes to the production and release of milk by the mammary gland. These last three hormones are the main instrument by which the brain controls the reproductive functions.

In addition to these six hormones, the pituitary contains many related peptides that may be either degradation products, or larger precursor molecules (Fig. 22.6) from which hormones are split (prohormones). These may also, by themselves, have endocrine or behavioral effects.

The posterior pituitary is also termed the neurohypophysis. As this name suggests, the area embryologically arises from the brain, as an outgrowth of the hypothalamus itself. As mentioned previously, it stores two hormones: vasopressin, which has an antidiuretic action, controlling the concentration of the urine by reabsorption of water from the kidney tubules,

LARGE PRECURSORS FOR SMALL PEPTIDE HORMONES

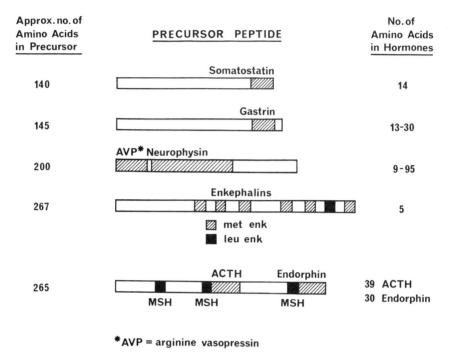

Approx. no. of Amino Acids in Precursor	PRECURSOR PEPTIDE	No. of Amino Acids in Hormones
140	Somatostatin	14
145	Gastrin	13-30
200	AVP* Neurophysin	9-95
267	Enkephalins	5
265	ACTH Endorphin	39 ACTH 30 Endorphin

met enk
leu enk

MSH   MSH   MSH

*AVP = arginine vasopressin

Figure 22.6 Examples of small neuropeptides derived from larger precursor proteins [redrawn from E. Herbert, N. Birnberg, J.C. Lissitsky, O. Civelli, M. Uhler, *Neurosci. Comment.* 1:16 (1982); © 1982 by the Society for Neuroscience].

and oxytocin, which is involved in the ejection of milk from the lactating breast and in promoting uterine contractions during parturition.

Of these two areas of the pituitary, only the neurohypophysis has direct neural connections with the hypothalamus, since that is where its embryological origins lie. Nerve fibers extending down from the hypothalamus form a part of what is known as the pituitary stalk, before they reach their neurohypophyseal termination points. But, while there is no corresponding hypothalamic-anterior pituitary nerve fiber link, there is a distinct functional association via a network of blood capillaries, appropriately termed the hypothalamic-hypophyseal portal system. Hypothalamic messages to the adenohypophysis, then, are blood-borne and humoral in nature.

Secretory neurons located in several hypothalamic areas produce specific releasing hormones. These special neurosecretory cells have axons with a comparatively low impulse conduction velocity (0.46 m/sec), and their firing rate is usually below 10 impulses per second. The releasing factors are conveyed by axoplasmic transport to nerve endings in the vicinity of the portal system capillaries, where they diffuse into the blood to be carried to the anterior pituitary. The releasing hormones are then able to stimulate the pituitary to produce its corresponding hormones for release into the general circulation.

The hypothalamus, in addition, secretes several inhibitory factors, which function to block the release of specific pituitary hormones. Schally (1978) has provided a concise and well-organized review of these regulatory substances, some of which have multiple actions and are capable of influencing the secretion of more than one pituitary hormone.

Besides the directional transport of hypothalamic factors to the adenohypophysis, pituitary hormones, in turn, are likely carried back to the brain. The original Wislocki (Wislocki and King, 1936) model of the hypothalamo-pituitary portal system proposed that the adenohypophysis receives both a small amount of arterial blood and a larger quantity of portal blood from the hypothalamus. Pituitary venous blood then returns to the systemic circulation via the cavernous sinus. The vascular bed of the pituitary is not, according to Wislocki, connected to the vascular bed of the brain. Recent data, summarized by Bergland and Page (1979), indicate that there is probably a back flow of blood from the pituitary to the brain which directly transports pituitary hormones into brain tissue. This backflow may actually occur only as short-lived, intermittent passages that depend upon local changes of pressure which temporarily reverse the circulation. As a result, peptides injected into the pituitary reach the central nervous system very rapidly in a fairly high concentration (Mezey et al., 1978). These peptides may also be transported into the brain through extracellular spaces (Mezey et al., 1979), and this could be an additional reason why pituitary hormones and their degradation products have been detected in the central nervous system.

The presence of pituitary peptides in the brain may also be attributable to a synthesis by certain neuronal groups (Krieger and Liotta, 1979). There is some evidence for such a possibility. Tissue from the amygdala grown in culture was detected to contain an increasing amount of immunoreactive growth hormone, even when the medium was completely replenished every few days (Pacold et al., 1978). Tissue cultures of the rat arcuate nucleus release ACTH and β-endorphin. These peptides have also been detected in the central nervous system long after hypophysectomy. The hormones are produced in specialized neurons and transported by axoplasmic flow into other brain areas, as the limbic system, cerebral cortex and brainstem. From nerve endings in these various regions, they are then released by exocytosis.

The releasing hormones of the hypothalamus are also found in other circumventricular organs (Fig. 22.7), where they are stored in so-called tany-cytes and in small neurons or their processes. All of these structures are localized around the brain ventricles and contain vascular plexuses which empty into the systemic circulation. The releasing hormones are probably transported from them via the cerebrospinal fluid, since the ependymal cells of the ventricles contain many neurosecretory granules (Polleri *et al.*, 1978).

The releasing hormones undergo a relatively rapid degradation in the blood plasma by at least two distinct enzymatic mechanisms, an endopepti-dase cleavage and a C-terminal cleavage. The stability of peptidyl hormones circulating in the blood is an important factor in a consideration of their clinical usefulness. Accordingly, analogs of these hormones, which are degraded less rapidly than natural hormones, would be more appropriate for any medical use.

Indirectly involved in the control of the secretion of all six established anterior pituitary hormones are systems of neurons located both within and without the boundaries of the hypothalamus (Fig. 22.8). These neurons transfer neural information from different parts of the brain to the hypothalamic hormone-secreting nerve cells that constitute the final pathway of neuroendocrine regulation. One of the major fiber tracts concerned with the neural control of hypophyseal hormone release lies within the median eminence (for review see Weiner and Ganong, 1978). The dopa-

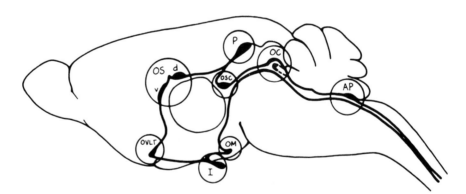

Figure 22.7 Circumventricular organs, their association with the third and fourth venticles of the brain. In these areas, cells are accumulated that show a nuclear concentration of steroid hormones. AP, area postrema; I, infundibulum; OC, organum colliculi caudalis; OM, organum mammillare; OS, organum subfornicale (d), including the nucleus triangular septi (v); OSC, organum subcommissurale; OVLT, organum recessus optici; P, organum pineale [from W.E. Stumpf and M. Sar, *Fed. Proc.* 36:1973 (1977); © 1977 by Federation of American Societies for Experimental Biology].

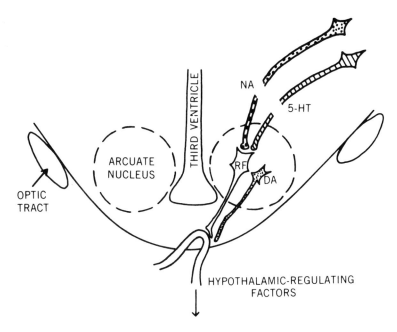

*NA=noradrenaline; 5-HT=serotonin; DA=dopamine; RF=releasing factor.

Figure 22.8 Possible sites of biogenic amine control of hypothalmic hypophysiotropic activity [from P.G. Ettigi and G.M. Brown, *Am. Psychiat.* 134:5 (1977); © 1977 by American Psychiatric Association].

mine concentration here is among the highest in the brain, and nerve endings belong to three independent dopaminergic pathways - the tuberoinfundibular, incertohypothalamic, and mesolimbic. The tuberoinfundibular dopaminergic neurons secrete dopamine into the hypothalamo-hypophyseal portal system, causing a suppression of prolactin secretion by the pituitary. Thus, dopamine is a well established prolactin inhibitory factor. Dopamine receptors subserving this action are localized in the anterior pituitary. Dopaminergic neurons are also directly involved in the regulation of growth hormone and gonadotropin secretion. The release of LHRH that is controlled by this transmitter also depends upon the presence of gonadal steroids.

Three major noradrenergic systems are also involved in hypothalamic secretion:

(1) one localized in the locus coeruleus, with fibers distributed throughout the forebrain via the dorsal noradrenergic bundle;

(2) a lateral tegmental system comprised of neurons in the lateral medulla, locus subcoeruleus, and related lateral tegmental areas

which project to the hypothalamus via the ventral noradrenergic bundle; and

(3) the dorsal tegmental system formed by neurons of the dorsal motor nucleus of the vagus nerve and nucleus tractus solitarius which also projects to the hypothalamus via the ventral noradrenergic bundle. These noradrenergic fibers have been found to be capable of inhibiting ACTH release, increasing growth hormone and TSH secretion, and playing a role in the preovulatory surge of LH. Norepinephrine is probably also involved in regulating of the release of the posterior pituitary hormones, oxytocin and vasopressin.

Epinephrine-containing fibers which reach the hypothalamus originate in the ventrolateral medulla and the dorsal medulla near the nucleus tractus solitarius. At present, their role in the release of the hypothalamic hormones is uncertain.

Serotonergic fibers originate in the raphe nuclei, and the hypothalamus is innervated by those from the nucleus raphe dorsalis and nucleus raphe centralis superior. Some cells in the medial basal hypothalamus are also capable of synthesizing serotonin. Serotonergic neurons regulate the secretion of growth hormone, and they are also involved in the suckling-induced release of prolactin. However, the role of this neurotransmitter in the control of gonadotropins and the other pituitary hormones is still uncertain.

Histamine is found in both hypothalamic neurons and mast cells. Its role there is also unknown, but it may have some contributions in common with serotonin.

Chapter 23

The Control of Sexual Behavior

It is hardly possible to discuss the control of sexual behavior exclusively from the perspective of brain chemistry. As in all other types of behavior, neurochemical phenomena take place in specific brain structures and in neurotransmitter systems where the same biochemical process may, as a consequence of its location, contribute in different ways to the observed behavior.

BRAIN AREAS CONTROLLING SEXUAL BEHAVIOR

The hypothalamus lies at the core of the neuroendocrine system controlling sexual behavior. Several of its areas are involved in the control of both sexual behavior and pituitary gonadotropic activity. Probably the most important areas in this regard are the arcuate nucleus, regulating the steady tonic secretion of male pituitary gonadotropins, and the preoptic and anterior hypothalamic areas responsible for the cyclic (phasic) secretion of gonadotropins in females. Several other diencephalic areas, the ventral premamillary nucleus and medial preoptic area, are also involved in the control of sexual behavior and the feedback control of neuroendocrine processes.

The "hypophysiotropic" area of the hypothalamus is not sufficient, in and of itself, for the maintenance of normal pituitary activity. Consequently, areas of the hypothalamus that regulate sexual behavior are unable to function appropriately without the participation of other controlling mechanisms having both excitatory and inhibitory effects. The amygdaloid complex, interventricular septum, some mesencephalic regions and perhaps the frontal neocortex are generally excitatory.   On the other hand, the hippocampus and other mesencephalic areas localized in the central gray and extending from the diencephalon to the rostral edge of the fourth ventricle, are generally inhibitory. The activity of some of these areas is at present difficult to interpret and beyond the scope of this book.

These control regions are characterized by the presence of intracellular receptors for the sex hormones, of which the high affinity saturable estradiol receptors have been most often studied. The binding and uptake of these hormones is highly selective, and independent receptors for each main sex hormone have been detected in the brains of both males and females of several animal species.

Several neurotransmitters are probably involved in the control of sexual behavior in the above areas. Serotonin has been found to be one of the neurotransmitters that may function to inhibit sexual behavior. A block in its synthesis by parachlorophenylalanine stimulates male and female sexual activity. Correspondingly, the stimulation of serotonin receptors, or an elevation in the serotonin level within the brain, suppresses male sexual behavior and female receptivity toward males.

The neuroendocrine system involved in the control of sexual behavior is subject to the influence of a number of environmental factors, including light, smell, temperature, and sound. In addition, neural impulses from the genital tract are especially significant.

LUTEINIZING HORMONE RELEASING HORMONE

The hormonal control of the endocrine activity of the sex glands is primarily attributable to a single releasing factor, luteinizing hormone releasing hormone (LHRH) (Fig. 23.1), which has also been referred to as gonadotropin-releasing hormone (GnRH, GRH, or gonadoliberin). In nanogram quantities, it induces the release of both luteinizing hormone and follicle-stimulating hormone from the pituitary. At the present time, it is the

$$\overset{1}{\text{pGlu}}\text{-His-Trp-Ser-Tyr-}\overset{5}{\text{Gly}}\text{-Leu-Arg-Pro-}\overset{10}{\text{Gly}}\text{-NH}_2$$

Figure 23.1 Luteinizing hormone releasing hormone.

only known factor generally acknowledged to regulate these two adenohypophyseal hormones, although the existence of several other hypothalamic agents, such as gonadotropin inhibitory factor, FSH-releasing hormone and luteinizing hormone inhibitory hormone, has been postulated

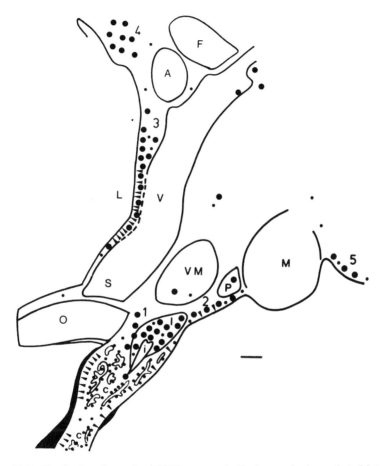

Figure 23.2 Distribution of reactive LHRH neurons in the human brain, projected into the mid-sagittal plane. Each black circle corresponds to a single perikaryon. 1, infundibular group; 2, post infundibular and premammillary groups; 3, preoptico-terminal group; 4, septal and pericommissural groups; 5, retromammillary and rostral mesencephalic groups; a, rostral commissure; c, long capillary loops; F, fornix; I, infundibular nucleus; i, infundibular recess; L, lamina terminalis; M, mammillary body; O, optic chiasm; P, premammillary nucleus; S, supraoptic recess; V, third ventricle; VM, ventromedial nucleus; black arrows, radiating collaterals of the tubero-infundibular and preoptico-terminal LHRH tracts; small black points, reactive axons. Intercalated plexus of median eminence not represented. Black bar 1 mm [from J. Barry, *Cell Tiss. Res.* 181:1 (1977); © 1977 by Springer Verlag].

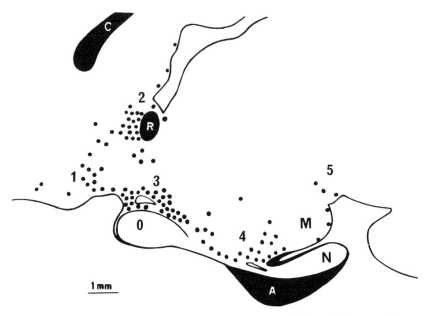

Figure 23.3 Topography of the perikarya of LHRH neurons in the rabbit. 1, parolfactory group; 2, pre- and pericommissural group; 3, supra- and retrochiasmatic groups; 4, infundibular and premammillary groups; 5, retromammillary group; A, adenohypophysis; C, corpus callosum; M, mammillary body; N, neural lobe; O, optic chiasm; R, rostral commissure [from J. Barry, *Neurosci. Lett.* 2:201 (1976); © 1976 by Elsevier/North-Holland, Amsterdam].

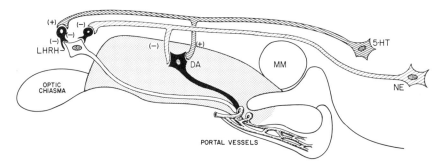

Figure 23.4 Suggested relationship of noradrenergic (NE), dopaminergic (DA), serotonergic (5-HT), and LHRH neurons. The perikaryon of the LHRH neuron is pictured as lying rostral to the hypophysis (stippled). Stimulation is coded as plus (+) and inhibition as minus (-). The small black cells synapsing with neuron are inhibitory interneurons. MM, mammillary body [from C.H. Sawyer, *Can. J. Physiol. Pharm.* 57:677 (1979); © 1979 by National Research Council of Canada].

(Cooper, 1969; Johansson *et al.*, 1975). In addition, a hypothalamic extract devoid of LHRH stimulates gonadotropin release (Yu *et al.*, 1979), but this may be a nonspecific effect.

In different mammalian species, the LHRH secretory cells are situated in various hypothalamic and extrahypothalamic areas (see Fig. 23.2 and 23.3). They are typically small and scattered over fairly large areas of nervous tissue. In primates, there are four main groups of LHRH-secreting cells, in the mediobasal hypothalamus, the septo-preoptic area, the anterior pericommissural area, and the perimamillary region. These cells, which can be visualized by immunohistochemical methods, give rise to the hypothalamo-infundibular LHRH tract, preoptico-terminal LHRH tract, and various extrahypophyseal LHRH tracts ending in the telencephalon (hippocampus, amygdala, pyriform cortex, cingulate cortex), epithalamus (median habenular nucleus) and mesencephalon (midbrain raphe) (Barry, 1976). Intrahypothalamic fibers terminate around the primary portal plexus of the median eminence, where LHRH is released into the circulation. Other fibers also reach the vascular organ of the lamina terminalis in which the axons terminate around the primary and secondary vascular plexus, and upon the ependyma of the ventricles and even the outer surface of the brain (Jennes and Stumpf, 1980). Diagrams of the localization of LHRH fibers in the brains of the guinea pig, rhesus monkey, mouse, frog *Xenopus laevis*, and rabbit have been prepared, and species differences were noted (Silverman and Zimmerman, 1978; Doerr-Schott and Dubois, 1976; Brownstein, 1977; Hoffman *et al.*, 1978).

When depolarized, the LHRH containing neurons release the hormone by a mechanism which is potassium-induced and calcium-dependent (Drouva *et al.*, 1981). Calcium is critical for the amplitude of the response. The neurons themselves are controlled by serotoninergic and dopaminergic neurons which terminate on their surfaces (Bird *et al.*, 1976; McNeill and Sladek, 1978). Acetylcholine, prostaglandins and GABA also appear to be involved in this regulation. Serotonin probably has an inhibitory effect upon LHRH secretion, as do the dopaminergic neurons. However, contradictory data concerning the character of the effects have been published, including a description of the excitatory action of dopamine upon LHRH secretion. The dopaminergic neurons are directly controlled by norepinephrinergic fibers, which are therefore able to activate LHRH release (Fig. 23.4) (for review see Sawyer, 1977). Therefore, norepinephrine and epinephrine may also induce ovulation. In this regard, the involvement of acetylcholine (Donoso and Bacha, 1975) also is likely indirect. There additionally appears to be some control exercised over the secretion of LHRH by the opiate receptors and vasointestinal peptide (Drouva *et al.*, 1981a).

The excitability of those structures regulating the release of LHRH is, in turn, affected by gonadal hormones (Robyn *et al.*, 1976). Thus, estradiol and progesterone increase the liberation of LHRH two- to three-fold. This is a positive feedback mechanism which may induce, among other things, the surge of LH secretion responsible for ovulation. Luteinizing hormone, which is high in the hypothalamus, may also participate in this control (Emanuele *et al.*, 1981).

LHRH excreted into the hypothalamo-hypophysial portal circulation is transported toward the anterior pituitary, where it is attached to the cells secreting gonadotropins and prolactin. Their surfaces, cell nuclei and cytoplasmic secretory granules contain at least two types of binding sites which differ in their affinity for the peptide (Sternberger and Petrali, 1975). The high-affinity site is competitively saturable by thyrotropin releasing hormone, while the low-affinity site is probably the physiological receptor for LHRH. After binding, LHRH is degraded by membrane-bound peptidases present in several cell components, including the synapses (Joseph-Bravo *et al.*, 1979). The interaction of LHRH with its receptor is subject to the influence of the sex steroids. Testosterone is able to effectively block it and, consequently, inhibit the release of luteinizing hormone (Spona, 1975). Estradiol appears to increase pituitary responsiveness to LHRH. The latent periods of these two reactions are quite long, extending more than 12 hours (Kamel and Krey, 1982). During the estrous cycle, the regulation of gonadotropin secretion is associated with an alteration in receptor number, not with an effect upon the affinity of the receptor for LHRH (Marian *et al.*, 1981).

LHRH not only affects the pituitary, but also acts directly on the central nervous system. The fibers containing LHRH are not very numerous, but as mentioned above, they are widespread and terminate in a number of brain areas. Acting in these areas, LHRH may directly induce mating behavior in animals without the participation of the pituitary gonadotropins, or the adrenal or sex hormones. Accordingly, the systemic administration of this releasing hormone to female rats that have been hypophysectomized, ovariectomized and estradiol-primed, induces lordosis in the presence of a male. Direct infusion of LHRH into the preoptic area, arcuate nucleus, or lateral hypothalamic area has the same effect (Moss, 1977). Other hypothalamic peptides are inactive in this respect, and TRH has been found to block the induction of lordosis by LHRH.

In intact or castrated rat males, LHRH accelerates ejaculation without having any effect upon the number of mounts or intromissions. For these reasons, LHRH has been used experimentally in humans for the treatment of delayed puberty, and it was reported to induce frequent spontaneous erections without an accompanying change in sex hormone level in two patients who were still prepubertal at 20 and 22 years of age (for review see

Hays, 1978). In normal males (Doering *et al.*, 1977), LHRH infusion in the morning caused a moderate increase in sexual arousal a few hours later. The effect of LHRH upon sexual functions, observed both in experimental animals and in humans, is typically delayed for several hours. This indicates that LHRH does not act, in the strict sense, as a neurotransmitter, but rather functions to alter the excitability of the neuronal systems on a longer-term basis (Barry *et al.*, 1974). The mechanism of this longlasting effect is still unknown. In contrast, microelectrophoresis of LHRH towards the preoptic-hypothalamic neurons and into the arcuate nucleus caused an instantaneous excitation of about 50% of the nerve cells. TRH has been typically noted to inhibit the same cells. LHRH also has a potent and immediate depressant action upon cortical, cerebellar cortical and brainstem neurons (Renaud *et al.*, 1975), and it has been reported to inhibit neurons in the vascular organ of the lamina terminalis (Felix and Phillips, 1979). LHRH additionally has a direct effect upon the ovary and inhibits the FSH-induced release of estrogen, as well as the synthesis of progesterone (Hsueh and Erickson, 1979).

LHRH and its synthetic derivatives have been recommended as a post-coital contraceptive. In rats, it may affect pregnancy (Corbin and Beattie, 1975) by disrupting the normal relationship of LH and FSH, decreasing serum prolactin and progesterone, and causing both a delay and reduction in the preimplantation surge of estradiol. It probably acts through the downregulation of the number of LH receptors (Bex and Corbin, 1979).

PITUITARY GONADOTROPIC HORMONES

The pituitary gonadotropic hormones, LH and FSH, are glycoproteins that are produced by small, ovoid, basophil cells of the δ_1 and δ_2 type. In the female, they stimulate the growth and transformation of the ovarian follicles. In the male, they serve to maintain spermatogenesis and testosterone secretion.

There are three patterns of gonadotropin secretion by the pituitary:

(1) Tonic, which is controlled by a classic negative feedback mechanism and is the only control mechanism in males. In females, it is part of the control of the sex glands.

(2) Cyclic, which requires both negative and positive feedback, and where the increment in circulating estrogens in the female initiates the synchronous release of LH and FSH.

(3) Pulsatile, which is due to intrinsic brain influences and is independent of the sex steroids.

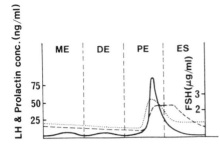

Figure 23.5   Change of the secretion of LH, FSH and prolactin in rats during the estrous cycle. LH, full line; FSH, broken line; prolactin, dotted line; ME, metaestrus; DE, distrus; PE, proestrus; ES, estrus.

At the beginning of the ovarian cycle, relatively small amounts of LH and FSH are secreted (Fig. 23.5), and one of the Graafian follicles grows. As the follicle continues to grow, it begins producing estrogens and progesterone. Positive feedback at this stage causes a burst in the secretion of LH, inducing ovulation. After having released its ovum, the ovarian follicle is transformed into the corpus luteum, which continues to secrete estrogens and progesterone under the influence of the appropriate gonadotropic hormones. Shortly thereafter, negative feedback again becomes predominant and the levels of FSH and LH decrease slightly. Finally, there occurs an involution of the corpus luteum that is caused by a sudden decrease in FSH and LH which is part of the cyclic hypothalamic activity. Estrogens and progesterone production is halted, and the mucosa of the uterus, the endometrium, loses its vitality. The result is menstruation.

The origin of the menstrual cycle lies in the hypothalamo-pituitary system, and there are at least three areas where the feedback control of gonadotropic activity by sex hormones is exercised. They are the anterior pituitary, arcuate nucleus, and suprachiasmatic-anterior hypothalamic area. The cells of these areas contain the appropriate molecular receptors that enable them to react to the sex hormones. The effect of hormones on the receptor cells is metabolic and may be blocked, for example, by an inhibitor of RNA synthesis, actinomycin D. Fluctuating levels of sex hormones therefore induce changes in protein production in the hypothalamus. The peak of protein synthesis in the area is around the time of ovulation, with increased RNA levels being present prior to this period (Foreman et al., 1977). In the pituitary, the estrogens elevate protein synthesis as well, in addition to activating thymidine kinase, an enzyme necessary for the synthesis of DNA.

The presence of both estrogens and progesterone inhibit the production of FSH and LH by the pituitary, although the effect of progesterone is relatively weak, and estrogens must be administered first to obtain an optimal response. This is a negative feedback loop which keeps the levels of FSH and LH low when estrogens and progesterone are high.   There are, however, oscillations in this system which depend upon a positive feedback mechanism localized in the hypothalamus.

Species difference exist in the positive and negative feedback control of gonadotropin secretion. In the monkey, estradiol appears to exert both positive and negative feedback effects at the hypophysial level. In the rat, inhibitory and stimulatory activity of estradiol on the pituitary are present, although additional influences upon the medial basal hypothalamus and preoptic area have been postulated (for review see Goodman and Knobil, 1981).

In the male, maintenance of both spermatogenesis and testosterone secretion depends upon LH and FSH acting synergistically. This tonic system is subject to the influence of environment and sensory activity, a relationship that is supported by many pieces of anecdotal evidence. LH is released from the pituitary during the exposure of males of various species to females (Saginor and Horton, 1968), although this effect quickly habituates (Coquelin and Bronson, 1979). Male rats can begin to secrete LH and testosterone in anticipation of sexual activity through a classical conditioning paradigm (Graham and Desjardin, 1980). Correspondingly in humans, a sexually explicit film can increase the plasma testosterone level (La Ferla *et al.*, 1978). And, in one study of a human volunteer, coitus increased plasma testosterone shortly before and after intercourse (Fox *et al.*, 1972), although this was not confirmed in a similar study (Stearns *et al.*, 1973). Newer work has even shown that there is a negative correlation between the mean level of plasma testosterone and the mean frequency of sexual activity in men (Kraemer *et al.*, 1976).

In contrast to the effect of LHRH on nervous tissue, there is little direct effect of FSH and LH on the central nervous system, at least in humans. In cats, LH and FSH alter aggressive behavior, and, in this respect, they may have a synergistic action with the gonadal steroids.

PROLACTIN

Another hormone that is involved in sexual and parenting behavior is prolactin, produced in a specific species of cells within the anterior pituitary. Prolactin controls the activity of the mammary gland during lactation, although some other effects, such as the onset of maternal behavior and an effect upon the kidney and vascular system, have also been postulated. At the cellular level, prolactin probably activates the synthesis of cyclic GMP through receptors localized in the plasma membrane (for review see Bohnet and McNeilly, 1979).

The most important specific stimulus for prolactin release is suckling, which discharges the secretory granules from their storage sites in the lactotroph cells of the pituitary. Prolonged suckling induces new hormone synthesis. The response involves a reflex action that is mediated by the hypothalamus through a complex series of pathways. Ascending stimuli from the nipple reach the midbrain and pass through the dorsal longitudinal fasciculus to the dorsal and lateral hypothalamus and finally into the lateral preoptic area. A descending pathway originates in the prefrontal cortex and activates the lateral preoptic area through the striatum, claustrum, and septal nuclei. The descending pathway reinforces prolactin release and is also involved in olfactory-mediated prolactin secretion. Stress can also induce a release, as can exercise and sleep. The prolactin is liberated in a pulse-like fashion, which is also true for other pituitary hormones (Dannies, 1980). This pulsatile release is an inherent property of the pituitary, since it is present even when the structure is transplanted into some other area of the body (Shin and Reifel, 1981).

The secretion of prolactin by the pituitary gland is controlled by two systems, one stimulatory and the other inhibitory, that are both localized in the medial basal hypothalamus (Wolinska et al., 1977). The primary action of the hypothalamus on prolactin is inhibitory. The regulatory humoral agent is prolactin inhibitory factor (PIF or prolactostatin) produced by the tuberoinfundibular neurons and transported via the portal system to the pituitary (for review see Blech, 1978). This factor is apparently identical to dopamine, which is not only able to inhibit the release, but can block prolactin synthesis as well. Other substances, such as the steroid hormones and acetylcholine, have a permissive effect upon prolactin secretion, acting indirectly through the hypothalamus.

The hypothalamic releasing factor for prolactin has not been identified with certainty, and its structure is currently unknown although there is some physiological evidence for its existence (Shin, 1980). And, while the opioid peptides, vasoactive intestinal peptide, substance P and TRH are all able to release prolactin, their actions do not appear identical with the releasing factor (Ruberg et al., 1978; Frawley and Neill, 1981).

The secretion appears to involve a serotonergic system, since destruction of the midbrain dorsal raphe nucleus decreases both brain serotonin and prolactin release (Ferrari et al., 1978). Estrogens that induce this secretion act through noradrenergic systems (Carr et al., 1977). Also, the pineal gland and its hormone melatonin have been reported to be inhibitory (Blask et al., 1977). Nicholson et al. (1980) have demonstrated an autoregulation of the secretion by prolactin itself. Prolactin released into the cerebrospinal fluid is responsible for the effect, probably through the activation of dopaminergic hypothalamic neurons (Moore et al., 1980).

Prolactin is excreted both in males and females. In boys, its level in blood plasma is unchanged from the age of eight years to adulthood, while in girls it increases two-fold during puberty, with the sharpest increase occuring at menarche. Its role in the female body during puberty is probably associated with the growth of the breasts. In adult women, it may also be somehow associated with premenstrual tension, since Halbreich *et al.* (1976) found that women with premenstrual distress had higher prolactin levels in their blood plasma than women without such difficulties.

Prolactin-sensitive neurons appear to be localized almost entirely in the hypothalamus (Clemens and Meites, 1968). After the implantation of a prolactin pellet, some neurons in the hypothalamus are activated while others are inhibited. The hypothalamic binding sites are probably the site of the feedback control of prolactin secretion by prolactin itself. Specific prolactin binding sites have also been found in the ependyma of the choroid plexus (Walsh *et al.,*1978). The hormone is not known to have any direct influence upon the firing of cortical neurons (Yamada, 1975), but it does have a direct effect on the CNS. Thus, Carter *et al.* (1978) described a favorable response to lowering prolactin levels by the use of bromocriptine in impotent males with hyperprolactinemia (and a normal concentration of plasma testosterone). Prolactin is also present in fibers and nerve terminals in many hypothalamic areas, in the anterior and posterior periventricular regions, arcuate nucleus, preoptic area, premamillary nuclei and the paraventricular nucleus (Krieger and Liotta, 1979). It is still present in these areas even a month after hypophysectomy and is probably synthesized there (Toubeau *et al.*, 1979). Fibers containing prolactin are also widely distributed in the brain stem, thalamus, septum, and central gray of the midbrain. The existence of prolactin-induced grooming in the rat (Drago *et al.*, 1981) implies that this hormone may also have some general actions within the brain which are not related to sexual functions.

HORMONES OF THE OVARY

The third factor in the hormonal control of sexual behavior is the production of sex hormones by the ovary and testis. All ovarian follicles progress through two stages of development: a primary or early growth period that is continuous and largely autonomous, and a secondary stage during which follicular growth is dependent upon the presence of gonadotropins, particularly follicle-stimulating hormone. Graafian follicles are those structures that progress into this secondary stage. During each menstrual cycle, regularly shifting hormonal conditions induce a further tertiary stage that will lead to ovulation.

At the beginning of the cycle, the maturing Graafian follicle begins producing several estrogens, the most important being estradiol, estron, and estriol (Fig. 23.6). Their primary sites of action are the secondary sexual tis-

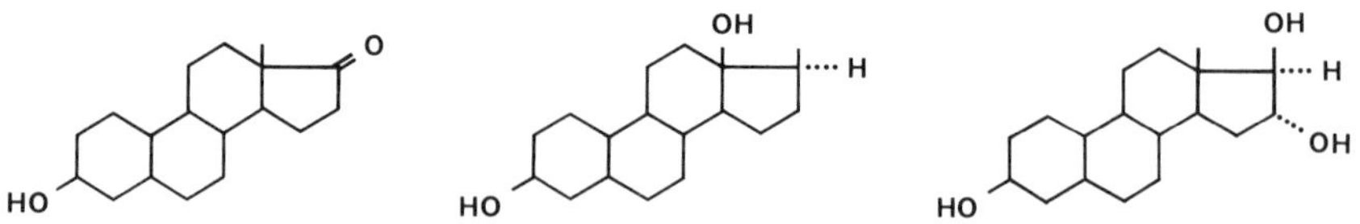

Estrone   Estradiol   Estriol

Figure 23.6 Estron, estradiol and estriol.

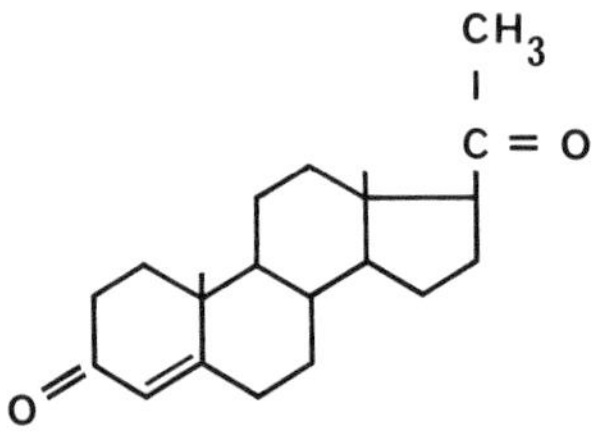

Figure 23.7 Progesterone.

sues. They are carried by the blood flow and diffuse into the target tissues, where they are transported into the cells. In the cytoplasm, the hormones are bound to protein receptors, and the resultant complex migrates into the cell nucleus, inducing an increase in RNA synthesis. In turn, this change is followed by increased protein synthesis and subsequent tissue growth. In addition, the estrogens are able to elevate cellular mitotic activity. Their hormonal influence is not only limited to the genital tissues and breasts, but also affects the skin and skin glands, osteoblastic activity, hair distribution, and the deposition of fat.

After about two weeks of follicle maturation under FSH control, the follicle receives a sudden burst of LH and ruptures, discharging the ovum. The Graafian follicle then undergoes a dramatic change, being influenced by high levels of circulating luteinizing hormone. The cells accummulate large amounts of lipids and cholesterol, among other substances, and in a few hours, the structure of the follicle is converted into a discrete endocrine body, the corpus luteum. The function of the corpus luteum is to produce the hormone progesterone (Fig. 23.7). Its secretion actually begins 1 to 2 days prior to ovulation. If fertilization and uterine implantation of the fertilized ovum do not occur, the corpus luteum will endure for about two weeks and then undergo degenerative changes, cellular atrophy and fibrous growth that convert it into the corpus albicans, which then remains in a shrunken form for long periods of time in deeper ovarian cortical tissue. However, fertilization and an ensuing pregnancy allow the corpus luteum to persist, maintained by the presence of gonadotropins secreted by the placenta.

Both estrogens and progesterone also control the levels of pituitary gonadotropins by several of the feedback mechanisms described above. They also influence the development of the female central nervous system and of adult sexual behavior. Here, the influence of sex hormones (including estrogens) resembles the actions of the neurotransmitters. There are short-term shifts in cell firing that have a very brief (milliseconds) latency and a short duration. The long-term, metabolic effects have a slow onset, up to 18-29 hours, and outlast the stimulus for many hours.

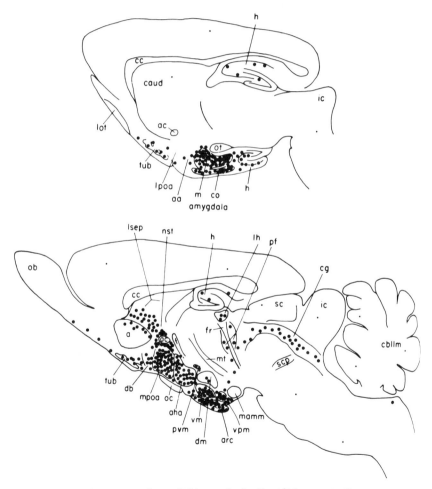

Figure 23.8 Uptake pattern of estradiol by rat brain. Estradiol-concentrating neurons represented by black dots [from D.W. Pfaff and M.Keiner, *J. Comp. Neurol.* 151:121 (1973); © 1973 by Alan R. Liss, Inc.].

In the brain and pituitary, estrogens bind to cellular receptors that are similar to those receptors in the uterus. A mapping of these receptive neurons shows that they are scattered throughout the periventricular area of the hypothalamus, in addition to being present in the amygdala, entorhinal cortex, mesencephalic central gray, ventrolateral septum, the bed nucleus of the stria terminalis and elsewhere in the limbic system (Fig. 23.8) (for review see Morrell *et al.*, 1975). Progesterone is also concentrated in the hypothalamus and several other areas. For most mammalian species, the topography of estrogen-concentrating cells is the same in both males and females.

The estrogen receptor proteins are primarily localized in the cytosol of the neurons (Fig. 23.9) (Davies *et al.*, 1975). Direct nuclear translocation is high only in the pituitary gland, preoptic anterior hypothalamic area, and the medial basal hypothalamus. Progesterone receptors are also located in the cytoplasm and are transferred to the cell nucleus when bound to progesterone. Here, they are attached to acceptor sites on the chromatin. These receptors have been isolated from the cytosol of guinea pig brains. They are specific and can mediate at least some of the behavioral effects of progesterone (Blaustein and Feder, 1979). And, it appears that estrogens are able to induce the synthesis of these receptors in estrogen sensitive cells.

In the neurons, estrogens and progestins also have several metabolic effects. One of them is the induction of enzymes inactivating the hypothalamic peptides. For example, L-cystine aminopeptidase, a proteolytic enzyme that inactivates LHRH, is stimulated by ethinyl estradiol and testosterone. This form of LHRH inactivation is one of the mechanisms that controls the entire feedback system. The estrogens and progestins are also involved in the control of neurotransmitter synthesis, release and uptake and the production and activation of transmitter receptors. Thus, estrogen binding decreases

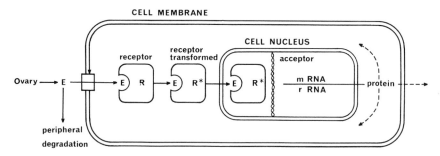

Figure 23.9 The binding of estradiol to its receptor and its effect on cellular metabolism. E, estradiol; R, protein receptor [redrawn from E.E. Baulieu, *Klin. Wschr.* 56:683 (1978); © 1978 by Springer Verlag].

glutamate decarboxylase activity in certain neurons (Wallis and Luttge, 1980) and increases muscarinic cholinergic receptor binding (Rainbow *et al.*, 1980), as well as norepinephrine activity in the brain (Wagner *et al.*, 1979). Such findings suggest that in sensitive neurons these hormones may have a role in the mechanisms of neuronal plasticity (McEwen, 1981).

The binding of sex hormones to the neurons causes an alteration in neuronal activity. Cells which respond to the estrogens by a shift in their firing pattern are localized in the hypothalamus, septum, and a few other parts of the limbic system. Most are inhibited by estrogens, but some have been observed to be activated by them (Dufy *et al.*, 1976). Estrogen-sensitive neurons are also under the influence of a number of classical neurotransmitters, either directly or indirectly. Typically, sexual behavior in female rats is inhibited by serotonin (for review see Carter and Davis, 1977). Estrogens are able to modulate the number of serotonin receptors in neurons containing estrogen receptors. This may contribute to the control of sexual behavior in females (Biegon and McEwen, 1982).

Dopamine also can influence sexual behavior. A decrease in dopamine action, caused by the administration of dopamine receptor blockers or inhibitors of dopamine synthesis, facilitates sexual behavior, including lordosis. While these relationships have been well established in the rat, they have not yet been demonstrated in other species.

Estrogens can also alter the effect of dopamine upon neurons. Arnauld *et al.* (1981) observed that an iontophoretic application of dopamine to caudate neurons in the rat caused an inhibition of about 86% of these cells. After estradiol administration, the proportion of dopamine-inhibited neurons dropped to 39%, and a majority of the inhibited cells became excited. The results indicate the existence of a strong modulatory effect of estrogens upon dopamine-mediated transmission.

Estrogens also affect several other parts of the central nervous system. They are able to improve discrimination in the visual, olfactory and auditory modalities. Estrogens can particularly influence norepinephrinergic responses in the peripheral and central nervous system. During the period of high estrogen levels in proestrus, the sensitivity of the norepinephrinergic neurons increases. But, the chronic administration of estrogens will decrease the number of β-adrenergic receptors in the cerebral cortex (Wagner *et al.*, 1979).

The effects of norepinephrine, epinephrine and acetylcholine on sexual behavior are not that predictable. Beta-adrenergic receptors may inhibit lordosis, if occupied by epinephrine or norepinephrine. A facilitatory cholinergic effect on lordosis in female rats has also been reported. It is safe to say that cholinergic systems probably interact with monoaminergic systems in the control of female sexual behavior.

The successive administration of an estrogen and a progesterone is necessary to elicit lordosis in female rats (for review see Morin, 1977). Progesterone by itself, without the estrogenic priming, commonly has an inhibitory effect on the endocrine system and sexual behavior. It reduces sex-related odor detection, terminates the period of receptivity, prevents post-estrus reinduction of receptivity, and antagonizes the uterine contractile activity. Maternal behavior that is induced by estrogens in hysterectomized-ovariectomized virgin rats is blocked by progesterone, with the unit activity in limbic structures typically being inhibited as well. A decline in serum progesterone before parturition may be an essential precondition for an estrogenic facilitation of maternal behavior (Numan, 1978). Progestins also inhibit unit activity in the mesencephalic reticular formation, hippocampus and hypothalamus and are able to induce cortical EEG synchronization.

HORMONES OF THE TESTIS

The primary male sexual endocrine gland, the testis, secretes testosterone as its main hormone (Fig. 23.10). The testis has two component functions: hormonal secretion and the production of spermatozoa. The spermatozoa are produced in the seminiferous tubules. The spaces between the tubules are occupied by connective tissue containing numerous large Leydig cells. It is these cells which secrete testosterone.

Testosterone, once released from its site of synthesis, is bound to plasma proteins and transported to its target organs, where it is attached to the cell nuclei. Here, it increases DNA and RNA synthesis, which is eventually followed by a boost in protein production. These changes, in turn, induce cell division and the consequent development of the male secondary sexual characteristics.

In the brain, testosterone feedback is necessary for the control of the LH level. The regulation of FSH is more complicated, because it is dependent upon the amount of seminiferous tubule activity. It has been assumed that the seminiferous tubules produce an FSH inhibitor which locally binds to FSH and inactivates it. The last stage of spermatogenesis is involved in this process. When spermatogenesis is impaired, the hypophysis undergoes

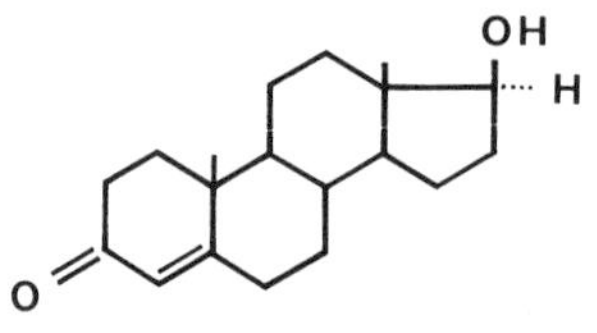

Figure 23.10 Testosterone.

morphological changes typical of castration, even if the Leydig cells function normally. This indicates the existence of a humoral connection between the seminiferous tubules and the anterior pituitary.

The presence of testosterone-receptive neurons in the brain is difficult to map because CNS testosterone is converted into estradiol and 5-α-dihydrotestosterone. They appear to predominate in the hypothalamus, amygdala, brain stem, and cerebral cortex. Neurons projecting from the corticomedial amygdala to medial preoptic-anterior hypothalamic junction are especially sensitive to the presence of testosterone. In castrated rats, the absolute refractory period of these fibers increases and can be lowered again by testosterone injection (Kendrick and Drewett, 1979). This pathway may therefore be involved in the control of sexual behavior.

The localization of brain testosterone receptors is similar in rodents, carnivores and primates. In the pituitary gland, about 10-15% of all cells are labeled by radioactive testosterone. The receptors are present in the cytoplasm of the brain cells (Attardi and Ohno, 1978), and after binding to the hormone, they migrate toward the nucleus. Before this happens, testosterone in the brain is converted into at least five metabolites, of which 5-α-dihydrotestosterone and 17-β-estradiol are the major forms. Both of them support male sexual behavior. The expression of this behavior in animals is probably exclusively due to these metabolites. Sexual behavior in castrated male rats can be maintained only by those androgens which can be aromatized and converted into 17-β-estradiol. This conversion takes place in the hypothalamus and limbic system, and the activity of the corresponding enzyme (5-α-reductase) is high in the brain. In embryonic rabbit brain, it is almost as high as the activity within an adult ovary and is greater than in any other tissue in the male embryo. Also, more 17-β-estradiol is found in the brains of male than female animals (Rezek, 1977).

The conversion of testosterone is additionally influenced by the social environment. The biosynthesis of estradiol is, for example, increased in socially deprived (isolated) male rats, although the level of plasma testosterone in these animals is substantially decreased (Lupo di Prisco *et al.*, 1978).

TESTOSTERONE AND BEHAVIOR

In the wild, males must compete with one another for the breeding rights to females. This function implies that some antagonistic behavior may be induced by testosterone. In species living in groups, levels of testosterone are often associated with aggressive behavior that is designed to lead to social dominance. Aggressivity generally decreases in castrated males, while the injection of androgens is able to reestablish it. Even in females, aggression can be evoked by an injection of testosterone. Dominance among male monkeys has been correlated with the level of plasma testosterone. The dominant males have been discovered to have up to 238% more testosterone than the average, whereas subordinant males showed an 89% decline (Rose *et al.*, 1975). Observations in different primates, including rhesus monkeys and Savannah baboons, indicate that sexual behavior is correlated with rankings in dominance hierarchies. However, genetic tests of paternity in groups of animals indicate that the correlation between dominance rankings and reproductive success is not very high. Females do not necessarily choose the highest ranking males. In Savannah baboons in Kenya, dominance rank alone could account for only 56% of the genetic variance of the offspring. Besides, some species, rhesus monkeys for example, live in matriarchial societies, and both male and female offspring inherit their relative positions from their mothers.

In humans, this question is rather controversial. Some authors (Ehrenkranz *et al.*, 1974) have claimed that aggressive prisoners have higher levels of blood testosterone. A positive correlation has also been reported between testosterone and individual aggression in psychiatric patients. However, considering the subjects, both of these situations are rather exceptional. In randomly selected populations, there is little relationship between aggressivity and the level of plasma testosterone (for review see Oades, 1979). Moreover, overall hostility bears no relationship to the level of testosterone in the blood plasma.

Testosterone is capable of influencing other types of behavior that are non-sexual in character. In young men, electroencephalographic activity is slowed after the infusion of testosterone, and simple, automated, repetitive tasks are performed better with less fatigue. Accordingly, serial subtractions are improved after injection of the hormone (Klaiber *et al.*, 1971). Androgens also have a positive effect on mood and performance and have been reported to increase extroversion and decrease neuroticism on the Eysenck Personality Inventory Scale.

EFFECTS OF SEX HORMONES ON BRAIN FUNCTIONS

As with testosterone, the behavioral effects of estrogens vary. In humans, most of our knowledge in this area has been derived from studies with postmenopausal women. During menopause, estrogen production steadily decreases, and the drop is supposedly associated with a high incidence of depression. However, this associated behavioral change has not been confirmed by many investigators, and it actually appears that mental morbidity is higher before menopause than after it. Rather, an increased incidence of depression following menopause may primarily stem from non-endocrine factors, such as family changes and the departure of the children from home. In most cases, however, estrogen therapy after menopause has been found to ameliorate depression and improve sex-related activities (for review see Herrmann and Beach, 1978).

Even before menopause, depression is much more frequently reported in women than in men. During the menstrual cycle, the mood of some women varies. In the premenstrual phase, irritability, depression, sadness, anxiety, insecurity, impatience, and tension are common. Suicide attempts, psychiatric crises, and criminal activity are also significantly higher. In the premenstrual and menstrual periods, the levels of both estrogen and progesterone are low, and this could contribute to these psychological changes in a certain percentage of women.

The sensitivity to sensory input fluctuates during the course of the menstrual cycle, with accompanying shifts in the levels of estrogen and progesterone. In normally cycling women, visual sensitivity is lowest during menstruation, but it rises until ovulation occurs and remains elevated for the remainder of the cycle. This shift in sensitivity does not appear related to the mood levels. It is, however, not yet possible to correlate such human empirical data with any definite neurophysiological or neurochemical mechanisms.

Chapter 24

The Pituitary-Adrenal Axis and Behavior

In 1922, Uno noted that rats, following a six hour period of excitement, exhibited an increase in the weight of the pituitary gland. His finding led him to conclude that the pituitary gland is involved in the responsiveness of the organism to changes in the environment. In a whole series of subsequent experiments begun in 1936, Selye explored further components of this system of responsiveness to adverse environmental shifts. He observed that numerous conditions, such as surgical injuries, chronic pain and inflammation, drug administration and immobilization, caused an enlargement of the adrenal glands with an accompanying loss of lipids from the adrenal cortex. This reaction, which he called the "stress response" or "general adaptation syndrome", requires the presence of hypothalamic centers and the pituitary gland for the release of the adrenocorticotrophic hormone (ACTH).

The above response to changes in the environment, and in particular to noxious stimuli, is actually a component of a general multiple endocrine response that involves not only the adrenal cortex, but also the production and release of catecholamines, estrogens, testosterone, thyroxine, aldosterone, insulin, and growth hormone (Mason, 1972). Such a coordinated reaction of the endocrine system to an environmental stress serves as a mechanism for the homeostatic regulation of physiological processes. The classical concept of humoral self-regulation by feedback mechanisms therefore requires some modification in order to account for these more flexible endocrine adjustments. It is possible that these two aspects of endocrine regulation are relatively independent. Correspondingly, two types of changes in the activity of the hypothalamo-pituitary-adrenal axis have been recognized: a rhythmic, circadian fluctuation of hormonal levels and those changes which depend upon a functional overloading of the system. The rhythmic, circadian secretion of ACTH and glucocorticoids is associated with the secretion of ACTH and corticoids that is dependent upon the stress response, but the connection is only partial. It is possible to abolish this rhythmic secretion by an anterior hypothalamic lesion without altering the response to stress. During the maturation of the rat central nervous system, the stress response appears prior to weaning, whereas the circadian rhythm arises later. Furthermore, the circadian rhythm is not subject to habituation, unlike the stress response (Redgate, 1976).

CORTICOTROPIN RELEASING FACTOR

In 1955, Saffran and Schally began reporting evidence that extracts from the rat hypothalamus were able to stimulate the release of ACTH from anterior pituitary tissue, suggesting that adenohypophyseal secretions might be under hypothalamic control. They believed a single chemical substance to be responsible for this effect, giving it the name corticotropin releasing factor (CRF). By 1964, Schally and Bowers had proposed several possible structures for CRF, based upon data collected on its molecular weight and amino acid composition. Although as of yet no single chemical structure has generally been accepted, Seelig and Sayers (1977) have purified a factor which induces ACTH synthesis and release from the pituitary and which has a molecular weight of about 1,000 daltons.

Interestingly, the hypothalamus also contains several other peptides which act as corticotropin-releasing factors. Oxytocin, vasopressin, several vasopressin- and melanocyte-stimulating hormone-like peptides, and a higher molecular weight substance that is a possible precursor of CRF are all found in the hypothalamus and have been reported to stimulate the secretion of ACTH (Saffran and Schally, 1977). Yasuda and Greer (1979) isolated this "large" CRF and found that it is relatively stable at $-20^{0}C$ in water. Other substances reported to participate in the secretion of ACTH are the neurotransmitters norepinephrine, histamine and acetylcholine (Ganong, 1980). Synthetic α-melanotropin induces the release of ACTH from cultures of rat anterior pituitary cell, particularly in interaction with arginine-vasopressin (Lis *et al.*, 1982). Vale *et al.* (1981) were able to isolate and characterize a peptide with a strong ACTH-releasing effect which they suggest could be the long sought-after CRF. Further investigations of its physiological activity are necessary to establish whether this is so.

The highest CRF activity is present in the medial basal hypothalamus, the median eminence, and the paraventricular, supraoptic, suprachiasmatic, and arcuate nuclei (Lang *et al.*, 1976). CRF release from the hypothalamus is regulated by acetylcholine and serotonin, which increase its content and release from the hypothalamus, and norepinephrine and glycine, which decrease the release (Buckingham and Hodges, 1977; for review see Fuller, 1981). Dopamine, GABA, epinephrine, melatonin, histamine and glutamic acid are all without effect. In a form of feedback control, corticosterone has been found to modulate CRF release (Edwardson and Bennett, 1974), as does ACTH.

The secretion of CRF fluctuates during the day-night cycle and depends upon an intact amygdalo-hypothalamic pathway. It is possible that the amygdala acts as a central sensor for the hypothalamo-hypophyseal-adrenal axis (Allen and Allen, 1975). Following adrenalectomy, the secretion of ACTH sharply increases, and this hypersecretion may be blocked by the transection of the ventral amygdalo-hypothalamic pathway.

The hypothalamus is not the only source of CRF. It has also been found in the cerebral cortex and the liver. However, since it has not been well characterized biochemically, the physiological and behavioral effects are not yet that well established.

ADRENOCORTICOTROPIC HORMONE

The second hormonal component of the hypothalamo-pituitary-adrenal system is ACTH. The classic function of this hormone is to trigger the secretion of glucocorticoids by the adrenal cortex. Here, ACTH acts upon receptors in the plasma membranes to activate adenylate cyclase. Also, ACTH has been discovered to directly influence several areas and functions of the central nervous system. For this reason, the behavioral effects of ACTH and its peptide derivatives are numerous and widespread. They are a consequence of a direct action upon the neuronal membrane and are not due to corticosterone mediation.

ACTH and ACTH-derived peptides are widely distributed throughout the central nervous system (Fig. 24.1). Immunoreactive ACTH (reacting with the midportion of the ACTH antibody) has been found in the arcuate and periarcuate nuclei of the hypothalamus, in the cerebral and cerebellar cortices, thalamus, and hippocampus (Krieger *et al.*, 1977), and in the neurons and axons of the amygdala, midbrain periaqueductal gray, and the brain-stem reticular formation (Watson *et al.*, 1978). Its localization and concentration is not changed after hypophysectomy, meaning that this immunoreactive ACTH does not arise exclusively from the pituitary gland, but is probably synthesized by some neurons (Larsson, 1978). According to Orwoll *et al.* (1979), extrapituitary immunoreactive ACTH activity is related to its rather inactive high-molecular weight precursors. The cells producing ACTH also generate endorphins, α-MSH and β-LPH from the same precursor substance (Bloch *et al.*, 1979). ACTH-like peptides have

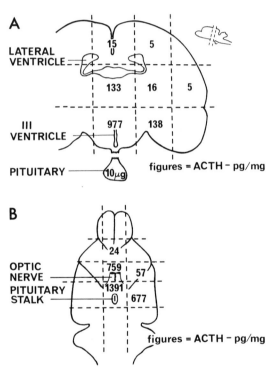

Figure 24.1 A. Distribution of ACTH in rat brain (frontal section). Concentrations of ACTH (in picograms per mg wet tissues) are representative values determined in one intact rat by the *N*-terminal antibody. The pituitary value represents total glandular ACTH content. ACTH values are highest in central hypothalamus-pituitary samples, with an apparent gradient to lower values in more peripheral areas. B. distribution of ACTH in rat brain horizontal section. In this horizontal section, ACTH values are higher near the hypothalamus, with radiation to lower values peripherally. A similar distribution is noted in A. [redrawn from E. Orwoll, J.W. Kendall, L. Lamorena, R. McGilvra, *Endocrinology* 104:1845 (1979); © 1979 by the Endocrine Society].

also been found in pancreatic endocrine cells and in cells of the stomach antrum which are known to simultaneously produce the peptidic hormone, gastrin. The function of these peptides is presently unknown.

The intermediary lobe of the pituitary contains peptides immunologically similar to ACTH that have been termed corticotropin-like intermediate lobe peptides (CLIP). They have behavioral and biochemical effects similar to ACTH. Their role in the control of adrenocortical secretion is probably negligible, but they do possess insulin-like activity. The secretion of these peptides is induced by hypothalamic extracts, but the hypothalamic factor controlling their release differs from CRF (Mialhe and Briaud, 1976). The intermediary lobe is also innervated from the hypothalamus, and serotonin appears to be involved as a neurotransmitter regulating the release.

The precursor of ACTH is a larger protein, pro-opiomelanocortin (Rubinstein et al., 1978). It has already been isolated and purified and has a molecular weight of about 30,000 daltons (Nakanishi et al., 1979). Several peptides may be cleaved from it, since its structure contains sequences for ACTH, α-MSH, β-MSH, γ-MSH, β-lipotropin, α-endorphin, β-endorphin, the enkephalins and a "signal peptide" with 26 amino acid residues. The complementary DNA sequence for pro-opiomelanocortin has been reported (Roberts and Herbert, 1977), and the corresponding mRNA has been produced in large quantities. This precursor is gradually degraded by "maturation enzymes", which are specific endopeptidases. β-LPH and ACTH appear to be formed mainly in the pituitary gland, whereas β-endorphin and α-MSH are produced primarily in the brain (Gramsch et al., 1980).

The ACTH and its related peptides are degraded in the brain by several hydrolases which are able to break them down to free amino acids. Some of these enzymes have been purified and characterized (Neidle and Reith, 1980). They are relatively non-specific and can also function to degrade other peptides, such as angiotensin, substance P, glucagon, and the A and B chains of insulin (Reith et al., 1979).

One of the principal biochemical effects of ACTH and its fragments in the brain cells is an alteration in the incorporation of amino acids into newly formed proteins (Reith et al., 1975). In a cell-free system from rat brain tissue, ACTH in low concentrations will stimulate protein synthesis, while at higher concentrations it is inhibitory. The amino acid sequence 1-24 is responsible for the stimulatory effect; the inhibition is attributable to the C-terminal segment (Schotman et al., 1980). The increase is not selective with regard to a particular protein species; the synthesis of all proteins is equally enhanced. ACTH, acting through cyclic AMP or cyclic GMP, may also activate messenger RNA synthesis. But in the brain, this effect upon RNA is rather small, if not non-existant (Gispen and Schotman, 1976).

Associated with this effect may be another function of ACTH, an increase of cerebral polyamines through the stimulation of ornithine decarboxylase (Tintner *et al.*, 1979). These polyamines are probably involved in cell growth and multiplication (see Chapter 12).

ACTH-activated receptors can influence the synthesis of cyclic AMP by adenylate cyclase. The phosphorylation of membrane proteins by cAMP modifies their functional properties, including their membrane permeability, and the process of neurotransmission. In low concentrations, ACTH can affect the phosphorylation of at least three proteins within the synaptosomal membranes (Zwiers *et al.*, 1976), and the effect is not related to an indirect activation by any other neurotransmitter. At least one protein kinase described by Zwiers *et al.* (1979) is inhibited by ACTH. This kinase catalyzes the phosphorylation of a 48,000 dalton membrane protein that has been designated by this group as "protein B-50". Both the kinase and B-50 protein have already been isolated and characterized (Zwiers *et al.*, 1980). The behavioral effects of ACTH may be related to its influence upon this kinase (Witter *et al.*, 1981). This research group has also reported that the incubation of $ACTH_{1-24}$ with synaptosomal plasma membranes triggers the release of one membrane protein with a molecular weight of 41,000 daltons (Aloyo *et al.*, 1982). The protein is distinct from both B-50 and B-50 kinase, and the effects of ACTH upon the 41,000 dalton and B-50 proteins seem only remotely related. It is, however, too early to speculate on the importance of this event to other ACTH-induced changes.

Van Duk *et al.* (1981) have described eight soluble brain phosphoproteins that are sensitive to ACTH. The ACTH effect on the phosphorylation of these proteins was primarily an inhibitory one. Moreover, this phosphorylation was very sensitive to GTP.

An influence of ACTH upon synaptic transmission, particularly neuromuscular transmission, has also been demonstrated. In the peripheral motor system, Birnberger *et al.* (1977) reported that ACTH decreased the quantum content of the end-plate potentials, while increasing the transmission failure rate and the frequency of miniature end-plate potentials. Consequently, the strength of muscle contraction decreased. A few other functions are influenced by ACTH as well, including serotonin metabolism, the turnover rates of brain dopamine and norepinephrine and the regulation of some cholinergic neurons (Botticelli and Wurtman, 1981). In the frontal cortex, $ACTH_{1-24}$ can selectively activate dopamine synthesis (Delanoy *et al.*, 1982). Synaptic transmission may also be affected by ACTH, since the hormone stimulates the synthesis of polyanionic phospholipids, particularly triphosphoinositides (Jolles *et al.*, 1981).

MELANOCYTE STIMULATING HORMONE

A molecule of human ACTH, with its 39 amino acids, is structurally very similar to melanocyte stimulating hormone (MSH) of the pituary's intermediary lobe. The two forms of MSH, α and β (containing 13 and 22 amino acids residues, respectively), have a particular heptapeptide sequence (-Met-Glu-His-Phe-Arg-Trp-Gly-) in common with ACTH (Fig. 24.2). As a matter of fact, α-MSH is identical to the first 13 amino acids in ACTH. A third MSH, a γ form, has also been recently detected. However, this molecule appears to lack any significant hormone-like, releasing, steroidogenic, or lipolytic activity (Shibasaki *et al.*, 1980).

Alpha-MSH is known to be involved in the control of pigmentation, primarily in lower vertebrates, and is also believed to play a role in the control of behavior. It has been detected not only in the intermediary lobe, but in many parts of the central nervous system, including the cerebral cortex (mostly occipital cortex), cerebellum, medulla and pons, thalamus, hypothalamus, and especially the pineal gland (Oliver *et al.*, 1974). This MSH system in the brain is distinct from MSH derived from the pituitary (O'Donohue *et al.*, 1979). In the hypothalamus, it is highest in the arcuate nucleus. A small number of nerve cell bodies in this region sends fibers containing α-MSH throughout the brain, which implies that this hormone may act as a neurotropic substance and modify the electrical activity in those areas (Eskay *et al.*, 1979). It has also been noted that hypothalamic synaptosomes can mobilize their MSH in a calcium-dependent manner in response to depolarizing concentrations of potassium (Warberg *et al.*, 1979).

MSH has several general effects upon metabolism and function. It causes a reduction in tissue respiration in the brain and, *in vivo,* reduces the blood flow toward several brain areas. Within the pons, medulla, cerebellum, hippocampus, and parietal cerebral cortex, this decrease in blood flow lasts at least 20 minutes following a single injection (Goldman *et al.*, 1976). No such changes, however, have been detected in the occipital cortex. During

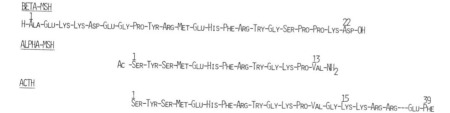

Figure 24.2 Amino acid sequences of β-MSH, α-MSH and ACTH.

the first hour after its administration in rats, MSH also decreases food intake and increases water consumption (Panksepp *et al.*, 1976).

O'Donohue and his associates (1982) have found that the *N*-acetylated form of α-MSH was more potent in its behavioral actions than the deacetylated hormone. Since both forms are present in rat and human brain, the authors suggest that the mechanism of deacetylation is an important regulatory component of the behavioral effects of MSH and related peptides.

The secretion of MSH is under the inhibitory control of the hypothalamus. Excision of the pituitary gland and its maintenance *in vitro* leads to a rapid, uninhibited release of MSH, which can be blocked by dopamine, norepinephrine, and epinephrine. Dopaminergic tubero-infundibular neurons, whose terminals have been detected in the intermediary lobe of pituitary, are primarily responsible for the inhibition.

A hypothalamic tripeptide (prolyl-leucyl-glycinamide) has also been identified as an agent blocking MSH secretion and has been appropriately termed melanostatin or MSH release-inhibiting factor (MIF-I). MIF-I has further been reported to have metabolic and behavioral effects, indicating that its actions are more widespread than merely an inhibition of MSH secretion (for review see Kastin *et al.*, 1980). In 1971, Plotnikoff *et al.* first observed that an injection of MIF is followed by behavioral activation in both normal and hypophysectomized rats. Increases in social interaction, aggressiveness, fighting, jumping, defecation, urination, salivation, and the possible appearance of ataxia are probably a result of the potentiation of dopaminergic neurotransmission by this factor (Spirtes *et al.*, 1976). However, MIF-I by itself does not have dopaminergic properties. It also weakly, but selectively inhibits the μ type of opioid receptor and may function as an endogenous inhibitor of these receptors (Dickinson and Slater, 1980). And, probably in this way it is able to affect opiate tolerance and dependence (Van Ree and de Wied, 1976).

In humans, MIF-I improves motivation, causes a brightening in mood, and substantially improves some patients with unipolar or bipolar endogenous depression (Ehrensing and Kastin, 1978). MIF has also been observed to ameliorate the symptoms of clinical parkinsonism. As is commonly the case with brain-related peptides, low doses (e.g., 75 mg/day) have been found more effective than higher ones.

BEHAVIORAL EFFECTS OF ACTH/MSH PEPTIDES

The behavioral effects of ACTH, MSH, and their peptide derivatives are almost identical. The smallest behaviorally effective peptide contains four amino acids and is labeled $ACTH_{4-7}$. It is a sequence common to both ACTH and MSH. Other active peptides that have been commonly studied are $ACTH_{1-10}$, $ACTH_{1-24}$, and $ACTH_{4-10}$. These are peptides with no adrenocorticotrophic activity; they act directly upon central neurons. Some also have melanotropic effects, causing the expansion of melanocytes in the skin.

Since the ACTH-derived peptides affect the neuronal membrane and, consequently, the firing of the neurons, their effect may also be studied electrophysiologically. Local injections of $ACTH_{1-24}$ cause hippocampal or cortical spreading depression, and $ACTH_{4-10}$ has been found to shift the occipital EEG to higher frequencies (Miller et al., 1974), an indication of desynchronization and perhaps arousal. In humans, following the injection of $ACTH_{4-9}$ analog, some components of the cortical evoked potentials have been noted to be augmented, while others (P300) were depressed (Rockstroh et al., 1981).

Specialized types of behavior are influenced by ACTH or ACTH fragments. Intracerebroventricular injection of these peptides can elicit exaggerated grooming in rats. This ACTH-induced type of grooming is a rather typical response that appears quite natural and can easily be distinguished from the stereotypical grooming which follows the intracranial injection of dopaminergic agonists and amphetamines. ACTH-induced grooming is characterized by a sequence of actions similar to those observed in normal animals. First, there is a vibration of the forelimbs which is then followed by face washing, body grooming, scratching, and, finally, licking. In normals, such behavior is tied to the periods following sleep, eating, or drinking, although it may also appear after the presentation of an unexpected stimulus as a fear-inducing event, or in conflict situations. Under experimental conditions, it has been observed as an aftereffect of electrical stimulation of the hypothalamus or brain stem and as a response to the local heating of limbic system structures. After the intracranial injection of ACTH or its fragments, this normal grooming is enhanced, unlike after hypophysectomy when it diminishes (Dunn et al., 1976). As opposed to a peripheral administration, the intracranial injection of an antiserum to ACTH reduces the grooming behavior, indicating that the behavior is truly due to the action of the hormone.

ACTH fragments are also antagonistic toward analgesia and opiate binding to the opioid receptors. The injection of morphine in mice causes behavioral excitation, running, Straub tail, and environmental oblivion, all of which are opposed by the $ACTH_{4-10}$ peptide (Katz, 1979). Furthermore, the ACTH fragment, α-MSH, stimulates sexual behavior, such as lordosis, in the female rat (Thody et al., 1981).

ACTH AND LEARNING

Considerable attention has been focused upon the effect of ACTH and ACTH fragments upon learning and upon the retention of specific learned behaviors (for review see Bohus, 1979). In hypophysectomized animals, the acquisition of avoidance tasks is impaired, but ACTH or $ACTH_{4-10}$ is able to restore a normal rate of learning. ACTH also delays the extinction of certain acquired behaviors, notably conditioned avoidance, conditioned taste aversion, the kindling effect, approach behavior, and sociosexually motivated behavior (Dunn and Gispen, 1977). It also facilitates bar-pressing for a brain stimulation award. Moreover, the hormone and its fragments can reverse the effects of several amnestic agents. Thus, ACTH injected up to four hours after electroconvulsive shock preceded by passive avoidance training reactivates the memory for the task. α-MSH and β-MSH have the same result, and α-MSH also facilitates reversal training in a complex maze. These effects resemble those of catecholaminergic agonists, and some authors (Dunn, 1980) propose that there is an interaction between the pituitary-adrenal system and catecholaminergic system in the process of acquisition and retention.

Synthetic peptides containing, for example, D-amino acid instead of L-amino acid often have an opposite influence; they facilitate extinction. Thus, a peptide having D-phenylalanine in the seventh position (D-Phe-7-$ACTH_{4-10}$) facilitates the extinction of a conditioned avoidance response, if injected into the rostral mesencephalon or caudal diencephalon (Flood et al., 1976).

Most of these peptides are maximally effective when injected into the cerebrospinal fluid of the brain ventricles or into the posterior thalamus. Brush and Fraley (1979) hypothesize that the ACTH effects are mediated by a circuit formed by the hippocampal subiculum, thalamus and hypothalamus.

All of the above influences upon behavior have also been demonstrated in adrenalectomized animals, so that it is clear that these peptides do not act through the adrenal gland. Moreover, the rate of acquisition is generally not affected in intact animals injected with ACTH peptides. And conversely, in hypophysectomized animals response acquisition still occurs, in spite of a complete absence of ACTH. This hormone, therefore, is not a factor which gives rise to avoidance learning, but one that only modifies it.

Vasopressin and its fragments have effects upon the extinction of learned behavior that are similar to ACTH. Consequently, it was thought that both vasopressin and ACTH might be acting through a common mechanism that involved an ACTH-induced activation of vasopressin release. In 1978, Bailey and Weiss found that this was not the case. Even in rats that were completely lacking in vasopressin (the Battleboro strain having a genetically transferred diabetes insipidus), ACTH and ACTH fragments influenced the extinction of a passive avoidance response.

In humans, ACTH/MSH and their fragments can also modify the activity of the visual system. MSH was found to facilitate visual-motor learning, and in volunteers injected with ACTH, there were improvements in selective visual attention and motivation (Miller *et al.*, 1980). Fragments of MSH and ACTH were also observed to enhance interpersonal and environmental awareness in mentally retarded individuals (Sandman *et al.*, 1980). Ferris *et al.* (1976) were similarly able to help cognitively impaired geriatric patients, particularly with respect to their memory retrieval (Van Riezen *et al.*, 1977). Ward *et al.* (1979), among others, attribute this improvement more to an effect upon attention than memory. In this regard, ACTH analogs, such as Organon 2766, have been reported to improve the state of alertness in subjects during long-term performance (Gaillard, 1981).

A generally acceptable explanation for these actions of ACTH in experimental animals is still not available. There has been no substantial effect reported for the acquisition of new behavior, but a detailed analysis of the behavioral state of the animals under different experimental conditions and learning paradigms implies that ACTH/MSH peptides may interfere with the attentional mechanisms involved in both the receptivity to and the selection of sensory input. Such a sensory gating-type mechanism has been stressed by Colpaert *et al.* (1978).

Brunia and Van Boxtel (1978), in their study of the effect of $ACTH_{4-10}$ on the T-reflex (Achilles tendon reflex) and H-reflex (Hoffman reflex), were able to demonstrate a central state of arousal, involving an activation of the midbrain reticular formation and the limbic circuits. The effect of ACTH injection may therefore simulate a natural situation, wherein the release of ACTH is a component of the pituitary-adrenal response to fear or stress-motivated behavior.

Miller *et al.* (1974) have postulated that the fear drive is enhanced by ACTH and ACTH-derived peptides, a possibility that is consistent with the observed reduction in social interaction. However, some authors have attempted to show that ACTH and its fragments relieve anxiety. Moreover, the effect of ACTH peptides has been related to the extinction of appetitively-motivated behavior, making it far from clear as to the possible role of ACTH as a fear-associated peptide.

Another hypothesis, the "memory hypothesis", first proposed by De Wied and Bohus (1966) is based upon the notion that ACTH/MSH peptides affect memory processes by enhancing the retrieval of information. The multiplicity of the effects of ACTH-related peptides was examined by Stewart and Channabasavaiah (1979), who compared the primary structures of various physiologically active peptides and found many similarities. Some fundamental structures are maintained with little change throughout evolution, but their roles may undergo a gradual development. Therefore, Stewart and Channabasavaiah relate ACTH-elicited sexual excitement in mammals to an original signalling role of some amino acid sequences in the regulation of reproduction.

All of these explanations are hampered by our inadequate knowledge of the relevant neurophysiological mechanisms and of the sites of memory formation, storage, and retrieval. If we say that ACTH/MSH affects the flow of information rather than the storage process per se, how shall we interpret this in terms of the passage of nerve impulses and activity on a cellular level? Most interpretations of the effects of ACTH upon memory consider the action of the peptides to be but a small component of the processes of memory storage and retrieval. Although there is no agreement as to the mechanism that is involved, the existence of a peptide with such a circumscribed action within the brain is an interesting finding, and one may envision a brain that contains plentiful amounts of similar substances with specific, local functions.

The behavioral effects of brain peptides long outlast the actual presence of the peptide in the brain, something which is particularly true during the early developmental periods. In this regard, the early treatment of neonatal rats with MSH has been found to improve their later ability to learn and respond efficiently to reinforcement in several experimental situations (Beckwith et al., 1977). However, as a result of this neonatal administration, several differences between the sexes have been noted, specifically in social behavior and choice of body contact.

According to Roche and Leshner (1979), the effect of ACTH peptides upon acquired behavior may be seen as a component of a relationship in which the hormonal response to experience is an important mediator of the effects of such experience upon subsequent behaviors. They observed that a mouse, fighting with an aggressive male mouse while being simultaneously injected with ACTH or lysine-vasopressin, became increasingly submissive for a few days afterwards. But while this experiment suggests a functional importance for increased ACTH, there is still no clue as to the neurophysiological mechanism of its effect. Interestingly, results comparable to those described above can be obtained when $ACTH_{4-10}$ is injected daily during the postnatal period. Recipient adult rats show delays in the extinction of a conditioned avoidance response, while passive avoidance learning was facilitated (Nyakas et al., 1981). This suggests that at certain periods of life, ACTH may have a long-lasting effect upon the organization of brain activity.

The actions of ACTH/MSH peptides have been studied and observed mostly in males of different species, including humans. In females, their actions are different. Thus, for example, Veith *et al.* (1978) found that in human males ACTH/MSH peptides primarily influenced visual memory, whereas in females auditory and verbal memories were facilitated. Visual memory in females is impaired by ACTH peptides. Such findings emphasize the need for prudence in any one attempt to construct a general theory of learning and memory based upon the actions of behavioral peptides on subjects of a single sex.

THE ADRENAL CORTEX AND THE BRAIN

Although some actions of ACTH are the result of a direct effect upon nervous tissue, most of its physiological actions within the body are mediated by glucocorticoids (Fig. 24.3) synthesized and released by the adrenal cortex. After their release in response to ACTH, glucocorticoids combine in the blood with the plasma proteins, transcortin and albumin, and are transported toward target organs, including the brain.

The effects of glucocorticoids are widespread, and their complexity precludes a detailed discussion within this book. Briefly, glucocorticoids promote gluconeogenesis in tissues; affect protein and fat metabolism; influence the activity of the striated muscles, gastrointestinal tract, and cardiovascular system; modify the numbers of blood cells; and cause alterations in antibody formation and immunological effectiveness. Their mechanism of action at a cellular level resembles that of the sex hormones. Glucocorticoids bind to a specific receptor in the target cell cytoplasm, and the subsequent complex of receptor plus hormone enters the cell nucleus, where it influences gene transcription. The binding of the hormone to its receptor is probably followed by a conformational change in the latter. In an inactive state, the receptor is likely bound to a small inhibitory peptide molecule which maintains it in a state that prevents an attachment to chromatin. After the reaction with the hormone, this small molecule is released, and the hormone-

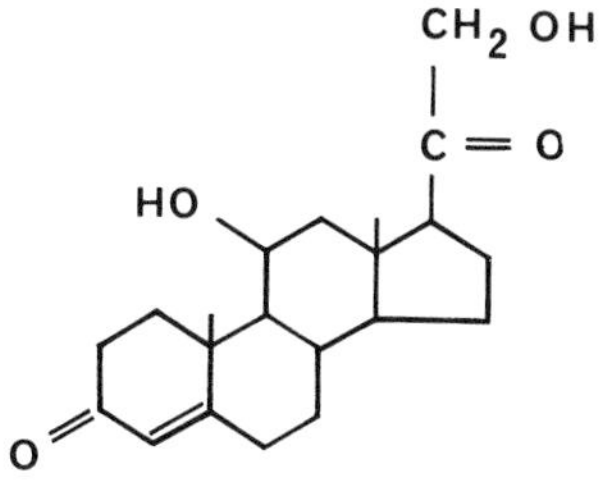

Figure 24.3 Corticosterone.

protein complex enters the cell nucleus. This complex is very unstable, being difficult to purify, and in a single glucocorticoid-binding cell there are only about 5,000 - 100,000 binding sites. The attachment of glucocorticoids to the cytosol receptors is also altered by a low-molecular "modulator", which could be pyridoxal-5′-phosphate (Litwack, 1979).

The glucocorticoids regulate protein synthesis in a variety of tissues by an activation of previously repressed genes and by a synthesis of new mRNA. This has been demonstrated for mRNA coding for growth hormone, tryptophan hydroxylase, and tyrosine aminotransferase. The stimulation of the synthesis of new growth hormone by corticosteroids has been observed even in cultured rat pituitary cells. In these cells, the effect is specific for growth hormone; no other protein synthesis is stimulated. In the brain, corticosterone elevates the synthesis of at least one soluble hippocampal cytoplasmic protein (MW 54,000), but has no observable cerebral effect (Etgen et al., 1979). This increase has been found to be receptor-mediated (Etgen et al., 1980).

After the onset of physical or neurogenic stress, the secretion of glucocorticoids, particularly cortisol, markedly increases in a matter of minutes. It is not known of what benefit the increase in cortisol is to the animal. One possibility is the increased energy supply from newly-formed glucose, or the selective increase in the synthesis of some enzymes and their products.

Glucocorticoids have some direct metabolic effects upon the central nervous system. The binding of corticosteroids to neuronal nuclei causes an increase in the activity of RNA polymerase (Stith and Weingarten, 1978). Lysosomal enzymes, glutamate dehydrogenase, glycerol phosphate dehydrogenase, and others, are influenced by them, some permanently and some only during specific developmental periods.

Corticosteroids are bound to receptive neurons in many areas of the brain, even in those which are not directly involved in pituitary-adrenocortical regulation. Radioactively labeled hormones have been found in the cytosol and cell nuclei of neurons in the interventricular septum, hypothalamus, hippocampus, amygdala, pituitary, and cerebral cortex (for review see Oades, 1979). Particular protein receptors in these areas have a high degree of specificity (including stereospecificity) for corticosterone. It seems that the hypothalamus, in particular, serves as a major target of glucocorticoids in the brain.

The binding of corticosterone in glucocorticoid-sensitive neurons varies with shifts in the environment (Valeri et al., 1978). The uptake of corticosterone in the hippocampus and septum was found to be reduced in socially-deprived and crowding-stressed mice, as compared to normally grouped controls. The magnitude of binding appeared to be related to rank in the social hierarchy, but was unrelated to the aggressiveness of the animals. It was also unaffected by adrenalectomy. Accordingly, it is possible that the selective uptake of corticosterone in the hippocampus may be one of the components of the link between behavior and the corresponding changes in the pituitary-adrenal axis (de Kloet and McEwen, 1976).

The binding of corticosteroids to neurons of the limbic system, as well as their effect upon neuronal firing in this area, indicates that these hormones can modify neuronal activity in those areas implicated in the control of the basic drives. In turn, these areas also participate in the regulation of the level of ACTH and corticosteroids in the organism. It is possible that some neurons binding the corticosteroids are identical with those neurons producing the polypeptide hormones (Stumpf and Sar, 1977). However, the evidence is still incomplete.

The immediate effect of corticosteroid binding to the neurons is a change in the electroencephalogram, sensory evoked potentials, and single cell activity. Cortisol has been shown to slow down the spontaneous electrical activity of the dorsal hippocampus, septum, hypothalamus, and pontine reticular formation.

The learning process, although more strongly influenced by ACTH/MSH-derived peptides, may also be facilitated or inhibited by corticosteroids. Corticosterone, hydrocortisone, and dexamethasone administered following training facilitate the retention of passive and active avoidance in rats (Flood *et al.*, 1978). Corticosterone could interact with the locus coeruleus norepinephrinergic system in the control of aversive learning (Archer *et al.*, 1981). Adrenalectomy, however, was not observed to alter the acquisition of the avoidance response (Bohus and Lissak, 1968). The literature in the area is rather conflicting, with several authors claiming the absence of any effect whatsoever upon acquisition, retention, and extinction of the learned tasks.

Chapter 25

Hypothalamus-Pituitary-Thyroid

The feedback system that is responsible for the regulation of thyroid activity can be divided into three components: the hypothalamus, producing thyrotropin releasing hormone (TRH); the thyrotrope cells of the anterior pituitary, secreting thyroid stimulating hormone (TSH); and the thyroid gland itself, which produces two hormones, thyroxine (T_4) and triiodothyronine (T_3). In addition, the thyroid gland has an autoregulatory control mechanism that depends upon the amount of iodine stored in the gland.

THYROTROPIN RELEASING HORMONE

The thyrotropin releasing hormone (Fig. 25.1) is a tripeptide (pGlu-His-Pro-NH$_2$) that is synthesized in hypothalamic neurons (Fig. 25.2), possibly from a macromolecular precursor (Rupnow *et al.*, 1979). The synthesis is stimulated by thyroxine, so that the entire process represents a positive form of feedback control. In contrast, a system of negative feedback control by thyroxine is localized in the pituitary.

The production and release of TRH by the hypothalamus is regulated by several types of neurons. Norepinephrine stimulates, or at least facilitates, its release. Dopamine is supposed to have an inhibitory action, but this

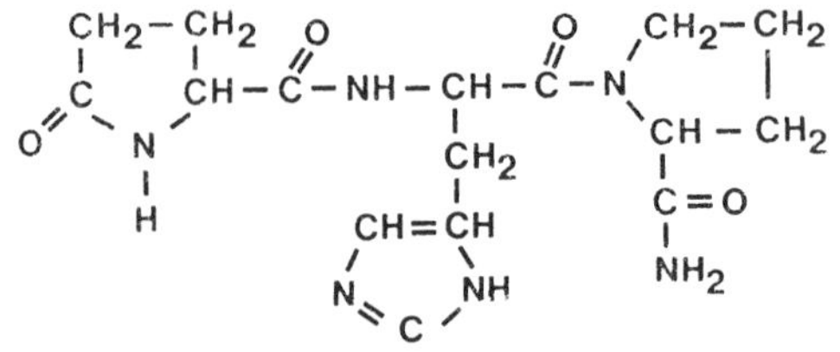

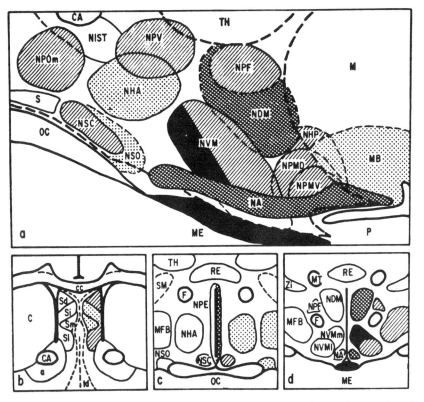

Figure 25.1 Thyrotropin releasing hormone (TRH, pyroglutamyl-histidyl-prolineamide).

Figure 25.2 Localization of TRH in the hypothalamus, septum, and preoptic area. Drawing (a) is of a parasagittal section through the rat hypothalamus and (b) to (d) are of frontal sections. Drawing (b) depicts the septal region, (c) the anterior hypothalamus, and (d) the tuberal region. Abbreviations: C, nucleus caudatus; CA, commissura anterior; CC, corpus callosum; F, fornix; M, mesencephalon; MT, tractus mammillothalamicus; NIST, nucleus interstitialis striae terminalis; OC, chiasma opticum; P, pituitary; RE, nucleus reuniens thalami; S, nucleus preopticus suprachiasmaticus; SM, stria medullaris; TH, thalamus; Zi, zona incerta; a, nucleus accumbens; td, nucleus tractus diagonalis. Key: Darker shading indicates higher concentration of TRH [from M.J. Brownstein, M. Palkovits, J.M. Saavedra, R.M. Bassiri and R.D. Utiger, *Science* 185:267 (1974); © 1974 by the American Association for the Advancement of Science].

probably depends upon the basal levels of TSH. The effects of serotonin, GABA, histamine and acetylcholine have not been that well documented (for review see Annunziato *et al.*, 1981).

TRH is released from hypothalamic synaptosomes even *in vitro*, and the release can be triggered by electrical stimulation or by potassium ions. It is liberated from nerve terminals in the median eminence of the hypothalamus into the primary plexus of the hypothalamo-hypophyseal portal system. After reaching the pituitary, it leaves the secondary plexus and binds to specific membrane receptors on thyrotroph cells to induce the secretion of TSH. It also attaches itself to the lactotrophs to release prolactin. The extent of this prolactin response is dependent upon the sex of the individual, being more pronounced in women than men. The somatotrophs, which produce growth hormone, are also able to bind TRH, but in this case the result is a reduction in the release of growth hormone (Dannies and Tashjian, 1974) and possibly the phosphorylation of some specific peptides in the target cells (Drust *et al.*, 1982). However, in some pathologic states, TRH has been found to induce the secretion of growth hormone (in anorexia nervosa) or ACTH (in Nelson's syndrome). In these conditions, TRH first causes a hyperpolarization of the pituitary cells, which is followed by the appearance of true action potentials. The hyperpolarization is due to an increase in the membrane conductance to potassium; the spikes depend mainly upon the entry of calcium into the cell. In tissue culture, spiking activity appears within one minute of TRH administration and is associated with the secretion of pituitary hormones (Dufy *et al.*, 1979). In somatotrophs, TRH has been reported to cause a rapid increase in phosphatidylinositol labeling that is probably independent of the activity of cAMP (Sutton and Martin, 1982). It is possible that this phospholipid response is involved in regulating the trans-membrane movements of calcium, which may be an early event in hormone action.

The response of the pituitary thyrotrope cells to TRH is also directly influenced by thyroxine and triiodothyronine. Both decrease the responsiveness of these cells, unlike the estrogens, which increase it. Estrogens also facilitate the release of prolactin induced by TRH, as does stress, sleep, sexual intercourse, pregnancy, and the mechanical stimulation of the breasts.

The amount of TRH present in the anterior pituitary far exceeds the amount that is capable of being bound. It is present in secretory granules of the thyrotropes, gonadotropes, and lactotropes, and Childs (Moriarty) *et al.* (1978) propose that most of this TRH is of endogenous origin, being produced within the pituitary.

In the hypothalamic area, the highest concentrations of TRH are in the median eminence and the ventromedial, periventricular, arcuate, and dorsomedial nuclei. The hypothalamus may contain only about one third of the total TRH content in the brain, with the remaining two thirds having been reported to be distributed throughout the CNS, including the retina and spinal cord (Hokfelt *et al.*, 1975). Nerve endings containing TRH are found in many cranial nerve nuclei and around the motoneurons in the spinal cord. The majority of TRH may be produced independently of the hypothalamus, since it still appears in many brain areas after the destruction of the "thyrotropic area" of the hypothalamus (Jackson and Reichlin, 1977). The source of this extrahypothalamic TRH is uncertain, and it is still not clear whether this TRH is synthesized *in situ* within those regions positive for it.

Since TRH has also been detected by immunological methods in blood plasma and even urine, in spite of a half-life of less than one minute (Nagai *et al.*, 1980), there must be a degree of caution exercised in evaluating its presence in various locations. After a profusion of papers identifying TRH in many parts of the brain, more rigorous methods have been employed to distinguish TRH from other peptides. Youngblood *et al.* (1979), using chromatographic separation of TRH-like immunoreactivity by thin layer chromatography, found true TRH in only the hypothalamus and septal-preoptic area. In other parts of the brain, the immunoreactive activity is "TRH-like". In other words, it is associated with a macromolecule containing the tripeptide segment of TRH. Even in the hypothalamus, Youngblood *et al.* reported that a portion of the activity was only "TRH-like". No TRH tripeptide was detected in the cerebral cortex, amygdala, brain stem, serum or urine.

High-affinity receptors and binding sites for TRH are reported to be distributed throughout the brain, as are the relevant degradative enzymes. Consequently, TRH fulfills some of the criteria for a putative neurotransmitter. The hormone itself does not enter synaptosomes from the hypothalamus and cerebral cortex. Only its precursor, proline, may be taken up. This indicates that after its liberation from the nerve endings, the releasing hormone may be inactivated by catabolism rather than by uptake processes (Parker *et al.*, 1977). However, no clear evidence for a transmitter function has been offered, and it is still safer to discuss TRH within the context of a paracrine action.

The hormonal role of TRH may have emerged as a relatively late evolutionary adjustment. While amphibian blood, skin and brain contain high levels of TRH, their thyroids and pituitaries are not responsive to the hormone (for review see Jackson, 1978). And, Grimm-Jorgensen *et al.* (1975) have detected the presence of immunoreactive TRH in circumoesophageal ganglia of snails, which are without a pituitary. This absence of a thyroid effect in lower vertebrates, coupled with the extensive distribution of TRH-like activity in the brain, implies that the hormone or its related peptides may have an important role in the central nervous system. A number of papers have shown that TRH administered iontophoretically has an inhibitory action upon some nerve cells and an excitatory action upon others. The application of TRH to spinal motoneurons excites them, causing an elevation of muscle tonus and the appearance of tremors and shivering- like movements. TSH, thyroxine, deamidated TRH, and individual amino acids are without effect (Cooper and Boyer, 1978). Analogs of TRH injected into the nucleus accumbens cause prolonged locomotor activity. Identical, but short-lasting, changes appear following an injection of TRH (Heal *et al.*, 1981). TRH also enhances the excitatory actions of iontophoretically applied acetylcholine on spontaneously active rat cortical neurons (Yarbrough and Singh, 1978). It may also interact perhaps indirectly, with central norepinephrinergic mechanisms (Yarbrough and Lotti, 1978). According to Renaud *et al.* (1979), it acts by depressing the glutamate excitation of cerebral cortical neurons. Also, the analeptic actions of TRH may be mediated by an inhibition of the GABA system. The variety of these effects suggests that TRH may have multiple modulatory influences upon the activity of cerebral neuronal systems, involving different neurotransmitters.

More behavioral effects have been claimed for TRH than for any other releasing factor. The first observations of its extrapituitary behavioral actions were published by Plotnikoff and his group in 1972. They found that in hypophysectomized rats TRH potentiated the behavioral activation that was triggered by a combination of L-DOPA and pargyline. Hypophysectomy does not alter this action. TRH has been suggested to function as an "endogenous analeptic substance" (Horita *et al.*, 1976), which "participates in the coordination of the hormonal, behavioral and vigilance status of the organism" (Yarbrough, 1979). It antagonizes the pharmacological actions of pentobarbital, thiopental, phenobarbital and other barbiturates, reserpine, chlorpromazine, diazepam and ethanol. And, TRH will promote a prompt emergence from ether anaesthesia in rats. On the other hand, it potentiates the anticonvulsant effects of phenobarbital and antagonizes methamphetamine-induced hyperactivity in rhesus monkeys. It has been found to protect against audiogenic seizures in rats, alter footshock- and isolation-induced fighting behavior in mice (but not in rats), and cause hypermotility, body shakes, lacrimation and tachypnea. TRH has an influence upon thermoregulation, but one that varies across animal species. In cats, it induces a profound hypothermia that is probably related to an increase in the respiratory rate. In several other species, however, it causes hyperthermia. Several of these changes have been attributed to an effect upon various brain structures. Masserano and King (1981) localized the influence of TRH upon motor activity to the hypothalamus. The effect on pentobarbital anaesthesia is localized in the septum (Kalivas and Horita,

1980). Intracerebral injections of TRH into the periaqueductal grey elicit a response that resembles some abstinence signs seen during morphine withdrawal. It also activates the EEG in several animal species and enhances photically evoked potentials in the reticular formation (Tonoue, 1977).

Some of these multiple effects can be distinguished pharmacologically. Thus, the analeptic actions are inhibited by muscarinic cholinergic antagonists. Some other actions are affected by adrenergic and serotonergic blockers, amine depletors, or depressants.

While these changes are well documented in experimental animals, the

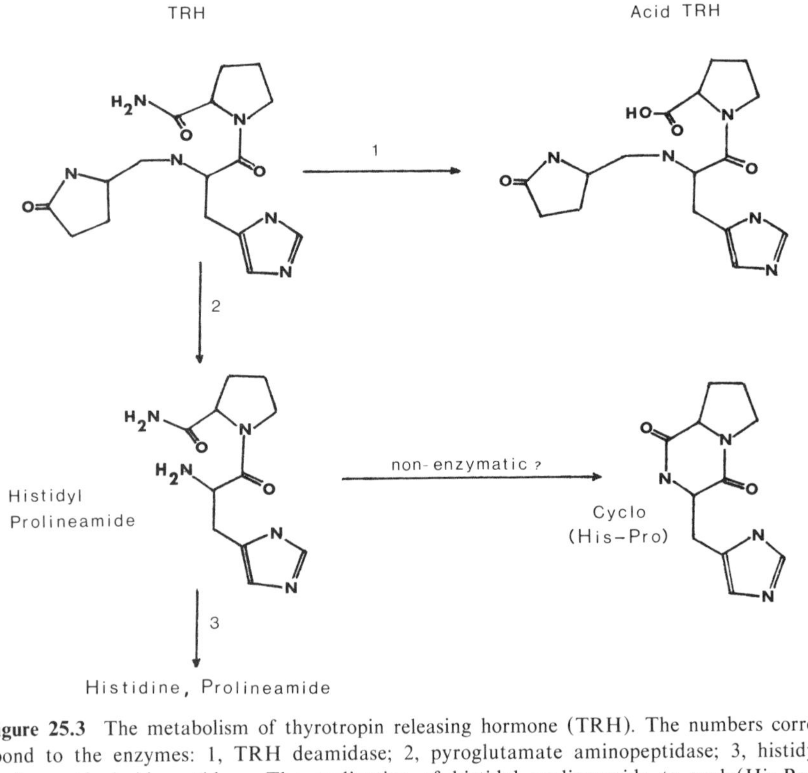

Figure 25.3 The metabolism of thyrotropin releasing hormone (TRH). The numbers correspond to the enzymes: 1, TRH deamidase; 2, pyroglutamate aminopeptidase; 3, histidyl prolineamide imidopeptidase. The cyclization of histidyl prolineamide to cyclo(His-Pro) appears to be a non-enzymatic process which is suppressed by the presence of histidyl prolineamide imidopeptidase [from A. Peterkofsky, F. Battaini, Y. Koch, Y. Takahara and P. Dannies, *Molec. Cell. Biochem.* 42:45 (1982); © by Martinus Nijhoff, Dr. W. Junk Publishers, The Hague].

behavioral effects of TRH in humans are still a matter of controversy. In normal subjects, an injection of TRH is reported to cause feelings of relaxation, mild euphoria, and a sense of increased energy (Wilson *et al.*, 1973). This was especially true in women. TRH also aroused sleeping subjects (Chihara *et al.*, 1976). Originally, it has been recommended as a treatment for endogenous depression, but its therapeutic effect, if present, was only transient, disappearing shortly after injection (Prange and Wilson, 1972). Further studies have revealed that those individuals suffering from depression exhibited an abnormal production of TSH following the TRH injection (Kastin *et al.*, 1972). As compared with a control group, the release of TSH from the pituitary after the injection is decreased in manic patients and elevated in bipolar manic-depressive patients (Extein *et al.*, 1980). However, these findings by themselves are unable to account for the depression, since no well-defined thyroid endocrine disorder in depressed women has thus far been described. Most depressed patients are considered to be euthyroid.

The metabolic degradation of TRH is associated with the activity of three enzymes: TRH deamidase, pyroglutamate aminopeptidase, and histidyl prolineamide imidopeptidase (Fig. 25.3). The deamidase converts TRH to pGlu-His-Pro, also known as acid TRH. *In vivo,* this reaction probably represents a minor pathway in TRH metabolism (Emerson *et al.*, 1980). Except for the ability to cause wet dog shakes in rats (Boschi *et al.*, 1980), acid TRH is apparently physiologically inactive.

The second pathway involves splitting off glutamate from TRH to form His-ProNH$_2$. Since this dipeptide is unstable under physiological conditions (Boschi *et al.*, 1980), there occurs either a further degradation to histidine and prolineamide or a cyclization to histidyl-proline diketopiperazine, also termed cyclo(His-Pro). The latter reaction appears to be non-enzymatic, and the cyclo(His-Pro) that is generated has been found to be biologically active and widely distributed throughout the brain (Yanagisawa *et al.*, 1980). But, the relative distributions of TRH and cyclo(His-Pro) do not always correspond (Mori *et al.*, 1982). Such discrepancies could reflect differences in the regional presence and enzymatic activity of the imidopeptidase, which has been noted to reduce the cyclization. Although the evidence is still preliminary, the results of cyclo(His-Pro) administration infer that this substance may function as a regulatory peptide in sleep, feeding, and thermoregulation (for review see Peterkofsky *et al.*, 1982).

THYROID STIMULATING HORMONE

The second component of the hypothalamo-pituitary-thyroid system is comprised of the thyrotrope cells of the anterior pituitary and their synthetic product, thyroid stimulating hormone (TSH). In the thyroid gland, TSH rapidly and firmly binds to its particular receptor in the cell membrane. The binding likely involves the membrane gangliosides and causes a hyperpolarization of the thyroid cell membrane, along with an activation of adenylate cyclase to produce cyclic AMP. The hyperpolarization is an early event that takes place before adenylate cyclase is affected. It is probable that some, but not all, of the effects of TSH are mediated by cyclic AMP.

In addition to its direct effect upon the thyroid gland, TSH also affects some other tissues. It can directly stimulate fat-mobilizing activity, and a part of its molecule, the exophthalmogenic fragment, influences the retroorbital tissues to cause exophthalmus in thyrotoxicosis. Unlike the direct effects upon nervous tissue or nervous activity described for hormones such as ACTH, there is presently no evidence attributing analogous responses to TSH. Still, TSH has been detected in extracts of rat amygdaloid nucleus, in a concentration of about 100 nanograms/mg of tissue. After hypophysectomy, this amount quadruples. TSH can also be found in the thalamus, midbrain, pons, medulla, and the preoptic area of the hypothalamus.

The level of TSH is controlled by TRH, but with contributions by thyroxine and triiodothyronine, somatostatin, cortisol, and possibly the gonadal steroids. And, TSH release can be stimulated by an acute exposure to cold, while it can be depressed by other types of stress, serial bleeding, exposure to ether, or physical restraint.

The activity of the pituitary-thyroid system is very much under the influence of the emotional state. As early as 1927, Bram had noticed that 85% of patients with exophthalmic goiter had a history of previous psychic trauma, involving impending surgery, periods of worry, grief or disappointment, or an exposure to a life-threatening crisis such as fire, earthquake, shipwreck, or combat experience. Plasma iodine would increase even in response to hypnotically-induced emotional disturbances. Further investigations of the emotional effects showed that these changes are not easily detectable, and

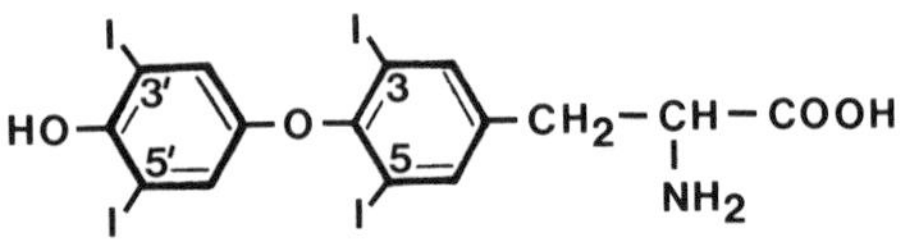

Figure 25.4 Thyroxine.

emotionally triggered fluctuations in plasma iodine, for example, may be beyond the sensitivity of the methods employed.

THE THYROID AND THE BRAIN

The principal thyroid hormones, thyroxine and triiodothyronine, are synthesized by the thyroid gland, using the amino acid tyrosine as the starting material. Both are iodine-containing amino acids that differ from one another by the number of iodine atoms positioned on two linked phenolic rings. Thyroxine contains four such atoms (Fig. 25.4), while triiodothyronine has three (Fig. 25.5). Both hormones are stored in the colloid of the thyroid follicles and are released under the control of TSH. Qualitatively, they serve the same functions, but differ in their physiological effectiveness. Although present in much smaller quantities than thyroxine, triiodothyronine is the more potent form. It appears that in the tissues thyroxine is first converted to this triiodo structure by a monodeiodinating enzyme, and it is in this form that the hormones influence metabolic activity. The hormones are transported from the thyroid gland toward the tissues by several plasma proteins, the primary one being thyroxine binding protein, a glycoprotein with one highly specific binding site for thyroxine in each molecule.

The actions of thyroid hormones depend upon the presence of specific receptors in the cell nuclei. Unlike the mechanism of action of the sex hormones, a preliminary interaction of triiodothyronine with cytosolic receptor sites is not required for the penetration of the hormone-receptor complex into the nucleus (for review see Oppenheimer, 1979). The receptor is associated with a transcriptionally active portion of the nuclear chromatin (Jump and Oppenheimer, 1980). It has been extracted and characterized as an acidic chromosomal protein with a molecular weight of about 50,000-70,000 daltons (Baxter *et al.*, 1979). Its affinity for the thyroid hormone may be altered during development, fasting, or changes in the hormonal status, and this is associated with the activities of other chromosomal proteins (De Nayer and Dozin-van Roye, 1981). The occupation of nuclear receptors is

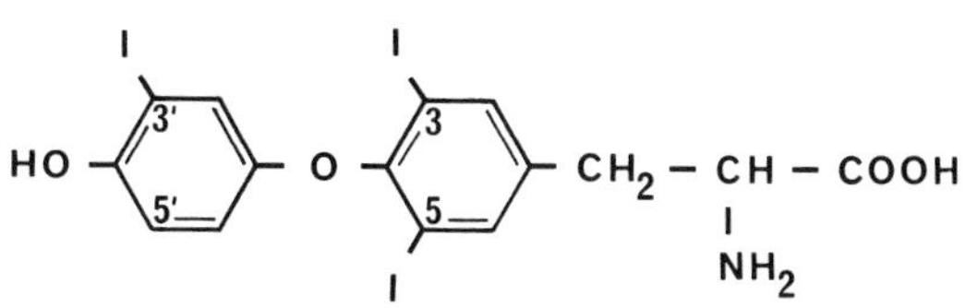

Figure 25.5 Triiodothyronine.

followed by a many-fold increase in the production of those types of mRNA necessary for synthesis of proteins induced by thyroxine. There are also thyroxine-related cytosolic binding proteins in the brain, but their function is uncertain. Cell-surface receptors for thyroid hormones probably only permit the entry of the hormone into the cell (Maxfield *et al.*, 1981).

Each tissue responds to the thyroid hormones in a characteristic fashion. In most tissues, they increase oxygen comsumption, heat production and the synthesis of new proteins. In the pituitary, they inhibit the synthesis of TSH, but selectively stimulate the synthesis of growth hormone by affecting the transcription of the corresponding mRNA (Augustine and Hymer, 1978).

It has long been acknowledged that there exists an important relationship between the thyroid gland and brain development. The available evidence presents a brain that, during a limited developmental period, is uniquely dependent upon the thyroid hormones for the full functional expression of its potential. These hormonal effects probably depend upon the binding of the hormone to its brain receptors. With increasing age, the binding capacity of the neuronal receptors for the thyroid hormones decreases, as does the density of the receptors in brain cell nuclei (Valcana and Timiras, 1978).

In recent years, studies have shown that the neurological and psychological symptoms of the adult hyper- and hypothyroid states may be mediated through the activation of peripheral and central adrenergic systems. Some manifestations of the altered thyroid state resemble those physiological changes that accompany shifts in adrenergic activity. Accordingly, thyroxine administration causes tachycardia, elevated blood pressure, sweating, hyperthermia, and signs of increased adrenergic activity. On the other hand, hypothyroid individuals show evidence of decreased peripheral adrenergic function. In the central nervous system, this effect is mediated by β-adrenergic receptors associated with the synthesis of cAMP. Hypothyroidism in rats blocks the developmental increase in the number of β-adrenergic receptors in the forebrain and cerebellum (Smith *et al.*, 1980). Consequently, the neurons are less sensitive to norepinephrine (Marwaha and Prasad, 1981).

An interaction of thyroid hormones with the adrenergic system may also be responsible for their effect upon learning and memory. Very low levels of the hormones have been observed to increase the rate of memory decay (Cassane and Molinengo, 1981). Central dopaminergic receptors also appear to be affected (Benakis, 1979).

Chapter 26

Growth Hormone and Its Secretion

In humans, the sixth pituitary hormone, somatotropin or growth hormone, consists of 190 amino acids and two disulfide bridges linked to form a single chain (Fig. 26.1). By enhancing the growth of the organism after birth, it has widespread actions throughout most body tissues. More properly, it increases protein synthesis, decreases carbohydrate utilization, and causes the mobilization of fat and other reserves. The brain has been found to serve as a target organ for growth hormone, particularly during the early stages of its development.

Growth hormone is produced by the somatotroph cells (in humans termed A cells) of the anterior pituitary. Its synthesis and secretion are controlled by two hypothalamic factors, growth hormone releasing factor (GHRF) and growth hormone release inhibiting factor (GHRIF, somatostatin).

GROWTH HORMONE RELEASING AND RELEASE INHIBITING FACTORS

The biochemistry and structure of the GHRF has not as yet been clearly defined. It is probably synthesized in the ventromedial nucleus of the hypothalamus and subsequently stored in the median eminence. Its release is

Figure 26.1 The amino acid sequence of the human growth hormone molecule.

stimulated by serotonin and inhibited by the presence of melatonin. Fasting, exercise, anesthesia, and general cooling have all been found to promote GHRF secretion. In the pathological condition acromegaly, the responsiveness of the somatotroph cells is abnormal, allowing both TRH and LHRH, in addition to GHRH, to increase growth hormone release.

The growth hormone release inhibiting factor, also called somatostatin or somatotropin release inhibiting factor (SRIF), is a cyclic tetradecapeptide of hypothalamic origin which inhibits the secretions of growth hormone by the somatotroph cells. Structurally, it has a ring of amino acids bound together by a disulfide bridge between amino acids 3 and 14 (Fig. 26.2). A hydrophobic end region is formed by neutral amino acids, while an ionized amino and carboxyl group comprise a hydrophilic terminus.

After its production in the hypothalamus, somatostatin is transported into the median eminence, where cholinergic and dopaminergic terminals regulate its release into the portal circulation. Regional assays of hypothala-

ALA-GLY-CYS-LYS-ASN-PHE-PHE-TRP-LYS-THR-PHE-THR-SER-CYS   **Figure 26.2** Somatostatin (GH-RIH).

mic tissue have shown that a large population of neurons containing somatostatin lies in the periventricular areas of hypothalamus and preoptic area. Hoffman and Hayes (1979) report other such neurons in the paraventricular nucleus, arcuate nucleus and tuberal area. Their axons project to the median eminence, third ventricle, neurohypophysis, vascular organ of the lamina terminalis, and the interstitial nucleus of the stria terminalis (Fig. 26.3).

Somatostatin directly affects the somatotroph cells of the pituitary, interfering with the release of secretory granules. It inhibits the release of growth hormone induced by insulin, hypoglycemia and such stimuli as arginine, L-DOPA, chlorpromazine, morphine, electroconvulsive shock, pentobarbital, neurotensin, substance P, catecholamines, sleep, muscle work, and suckling. The effect is dependent upon the presence of receptors for

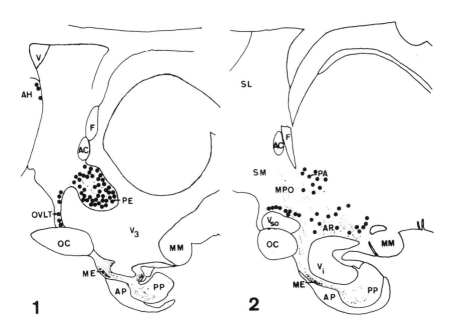

Figure 26.3 Distribution of somatostatin cells (large filled circles) and fibers (dots) as seen in sagittal sections of the dog diencephalon, (1) 20 mm from the midline; (2) 24 mm from the midline. Abbreviations: AC, anterior commissure; AH, anterior hippocampus; AP, anterior pituitary; AR, arcuate nucleus; F, fornix; ME, median eminence; MM, medial mammillary nucleus; MPO, medial preoptic area; OC, optic tectum; OVLT, organum vasculosum of the lamina terminalis; PA, paraventricular nucleus; PE, periventricular nucleus; PP, posterior pituitary; SL, lateral septal area; SM, medial septal area; V, ventricle; V_3, third ventricle; Vi, infundibular recess of the third ventricle; Vso, supraoptic recess of the third ventricle [from G.E. Hoffman and T.A. Hayes, *J. Comp. Neurol.* 186:371 (1979); © 1979 by Allan R. Liss, Inc.].

somatostatin (Watkins, 1980) and calcium ions. In the pituitary, aside from inhibiting the release of growth hormone from the somatotroph cells, somatostatin also blocks the release of prolactin, ACTH, FSH, LH, and TSH, and stimulates the release of arginine vasopressin from the posterior pituitary (Gerich et al., 1975).

Beyond its presence in the central nervous system, somatostatin has also been detected in abundant quantities in the D cells of the pancreatic islets of Langerhans, where it participates in the endocrine activity of the pancreas, blocking both insulin and glucagon secretion. The concentration of somatostatin in the pyloric region of the stomach is comparable to that in the cerebral cortex. Here, it blocks the release of the gastrointestinal hormones, gastrin and secretin (Vale et al., 1977; for review see Efendic et al., 1978). It is also found in the thyroid gland and in nerve cells and plexuses of the colon. In the blood of the portal vein, the concentrations of somatostatin are high, but its level decreases during the passage of blood through the liver. After a meal, the somatostatin-like immunoreactivity in the portal vein and the arterial blood rapidly increases (Schusdziarra et al., 1980). In most animal species, somatostatin abolishes gastric contractions and decreases movements of the gastrointestinal tract. It is also present in the urinary bladder, epithelium and renal tubules and in parts of the urinary system which are also sensitive to antidiuretic hormone (Bolaffi et al., 1980).

Substantial amounts of somatostatin have been discovered in non-hypothalamic parts of the brain, primarily within the synaptosomal tissue fraction (Epelbaum et al., 1977). It is present in both interneurons and projection neurons and has been identified in the cerebral cortex, brain stem, olfactory lobe, cerebellum, spinal cord, amygdala, septal region, hippocampus, thalamus, claustrum, mesencephalic central gray, circumventricular organs and even the pineal gland, retina and cerebrospinal fluid. It may be released from the synaptosomes in these areas, an effect which is calcium dependent and enhanced by potassium ions. After the release, somatostatin is short-lived and quickly degraded by a neutral endopeptidase (Marks and Stern, 1975). This action of this endopeptidase, as well as that of an acid proteinase present in the hypothalamus (Akopyan et al., 1978), may be a limiting factor in the activity of somatostatin in the brain.

Brain somatostatin does not appear to arise from the hypothalamus and is likely produced elsewhere possibly from larger precursor molecules (Ensinck et al., 1978). It may also be that the radioimmunoassay and immunocytochemical methods used for somatostatin detection are sensitive not only to the hormone, but also to these larger precursor molecules. In 1979, Lauber et al. reported the presence in hypothalamic extracts of a probable somatostatin precursor with a molecular weight of 15,000 daltons. Later, the same research group (Morel et al., 1981) demonstrated the existence of an associated protease (or proteases) in these extracts which could selectively convert this prosomatostatin molecule to somatostatin. The release of somatostatin from this physiologically inactive precursor may be an important mechanism for controlling the functional activity of somatostatinergic cells (Zingg and Patel, 1982).

In the spinal ganglia, a number of small neurons contain somatostatin (Hokfelt *et al.*, 1976). The somatostatinergic system in the spinal cord is rather extensive, and in addition to nerve endings originating from the primary afferent neurons and terminating in the substantia gelatinosa, there is also a network surrounding the central canal and extending into other cord zones (Forssman, 1978).

In the brain, somatostatin has several direct effects that are independent of the secretion of growth hormone (reviewed by Blech, 1978). In low

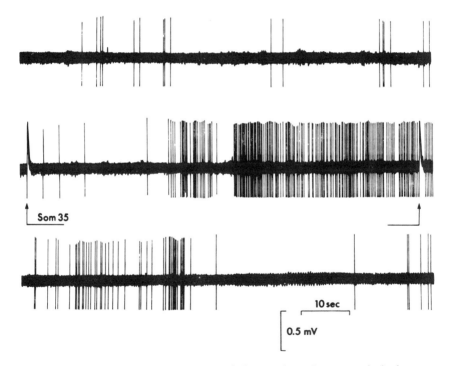

Figure 26.4 Excitatory effect of SRIF on a cortical neuron in awake, unanaesthetized, unparalyzed habituated rabbit. Upper panel: background activity seen before application of SRIF; middle panel: SRIF 35 nA applied continuously between arrows. Lower panel: neuronal activity after termination of SRIF ejections. The bottom of all traces has been cut off by the screen of the oscilloscope [from S. Ioffe, V. Havlicek, H. Friesen, V. Chernick, *Brain Res.* 153:414 (1978); © 1978 by Elsevier/ North-Holland Biomedical Press].

doses, injected intraventricularly or supracortically or into the hippocampus, it has a general arousal effect and reduces slow-wave activity. In larger doses, it causes irritation, hyperkinesia, stereotypic motor behavior, muscle tremors, rigidity, catatonia, and eventually tonic and clonic seizures.

In anesthetized rats, the iontophoretic application of somatostatin to neurons causes a decrease in neuronal excitability, while in conscious animals (Ioffe et al., 1978) it increases neuronal firing and is even capable of inducing firing in silent neurons (Fig. 26.4). Microiontophoretic introductions of somatostatin increase the firing of 74% of the neurons in frontal cortex and 66% of those in the hippocampus (Olpe et al., 1980). In the brain, it inhibits cAMP accummulation, but enhances guanylate cyclase activity (Vesely, 1981). It also selectively inhibits norepinepherine release from hypothalamic neurons (Goethert, 1980), while augmenting a similar release from electrically stimulated cerebral cortex (Tsujimoto and Tanaka, 1981).

The mechanism of the somatostatin actions is not clear, but it is possible that its influence upon neuronal excitability is a consequence of alterations in calcium transport (Tan et al., 1977). All of the antisecretory activity of somatostatin, the inhibitory effects upon the secretion of growth hormone, thyroid stimulating hormone, insulin and glucagon, may be due to its interference with the passage of calcium across the membranes that is essential for normal secretory processes (Bicknell and Schofield, 1981).

GROWTH HORMONE

Growth hormone (GH) is localized in the somatotroph cells of the anterior pituitary. Its importance in development is underscored by its presence in the fetal pituitary as early as the sixth week of gestation and in the umbilical cord blood as early as the tenth week. After birth, it remains high in the circulating blood for about two weeks before it begins to drop to lower levels that are characteristic for the older child and adult. Growth hormone is also distributed in significant amounts within the neurons of various areas of the central nervous system and is present even in hypophysectomized animals. This growth hormone is immunologically and chromatographically identical with growth hormone isolated from the pituitary. At the present time, its function in the adult brain is not clear.

Both catecholaminergic and serotonergic neurons in the hypothalamus participate in the regulation of growth hormone secretion (Vijayan et al., 1978). A blockage of the β-adrenergic receptors by propranolol elevates its synthesis, and α-adrenergic stimulation enhances its release. However, the actual role of central noradrenergic neurons in growth hormone secretion has not as yet been resolved. This is also true for the involvement of the neurotransmitters dopamine and serotonin, which have been found to alter the levels of the hormone. Dopamine injected intraventricularly inhibits the secretion, while serotonin elevates the growth hormone concentration in rat blood serum, an effect that is blocked by the serotonin antagonist cyproheptadin (Smythe *et al.*, 1975). It is possible that these physiological mechanisms depend upon several independent neural pathways. There are some pharmacological data that suggest this to be true (Mendelson *et al.*, 1979).

In humans and non-human primates, many stressful stimuli trigger the release of growth hormone. The time course is similar to that of ACTH secretion, although the secretion of both hormones is independent and a dissociation of both responses is possible. Estrogens and androgens increase GH secretion, with the response being suppressed by progesterone. Insulin has also been found to reduce its secretion. Similarly, pentobarbital anesthesia has a stimulatory effect which is antagonized by TRH.

Growth hormone concentration fluctuates with meals, fasting, physical activity and exercise, age, emotions, surgical stress, hypoglycemia, diabetes mellitus, and the infusion of arginine (for review see Brown and Reichlin, 1972). Data on the effect of starvation upon growth hormone secretion, however, are inconsistent. All of the values that have been reported in the literature need to be correlated with an endogenous rhythm of growth hormone secretion that has a cycle of approximately 3.3 hours (Terry *et al.*, 1976). When tied to this rhythm, growth hormone levels are shown to be depressed by food deprivation. The rhythm itself is depressed as well (Tannenbaum *et al.*, 1979). There is a positive correlation between the rate at which the body temperature rises during exercise and the rate of growth hormone increase. Correspondingly, bathing in warm water and exposure to warm air elevate the level of GH.

During sleep, particularly during its early stages, serum levels of growth hormone rise. This has been shown to correlate with the four phases of slow-wave sleep. On the other hand, during the REM stage there is a decrement. This episodic nature of growth hormone release over the sleep/wakefulness cycle is dependent upon the activity of the medial basal hypothalamus. The physiological significance of the nocturnal release of growth hormone, especially in adults, is not clear. An injection of GH in cats causes a selective elevation in the relative proportion of REM sleep that becomes evident about three hours after administration. It could be that the elevated level of the hormone that coincides with slow-wave sleep plays a role in the onset of the REM phase (Stern *et al.*, 1975).

Several psychiatric and psychogenic disorders are accompanied by disturbances in the pattern of growth hormone secretion. However, these findings may relate more to disruptions in the normal sleep pattern than to an involvement in the pathogenesis of the conditions.

Discrete peaks of growth hormone secretion during the early episodes of human sleep may be theoretically correlated with the fixation of long-term memory and the extinction of inconsequential memories. Although this relationship has long been denied (e.g., Gold and Van Buskirk, 1976), some data do suggest an inhibitory effect upon memory. Ekstrand *et al.* (1977) found a proactive inhibitory effect in humans, which has since been substantiated by Hoddes (1979) in mice. Memory has been suppressed when growth hormone was administered shortly before or shortly after an acquisition session. In contrast, however, a retroactive enhancement was reported by Stern and Morgane (1977).

During the early stages of development, growth hormone has a selective effect upon fetal brain growth, particularly when experimentally administered to starving pregnant female animals. Such injections increase the number of cells within the brains of the offspring and result in the incorporation of a larger amount of thymidine label into their brain DNA. Nevertheless, these experiments, performed mainly in rats, were unable to determine whether, under physiological conditions, the hormone is necessary for brain growth. Growth hormone deficits in children do not lead to any intellectual impairments, and even its long-lasting administration does not alter their EEG or measures of intelligence. These observations contradict some rat data, which indicate that prenatal or early postnatal administration of the hormone causes precocious behavioral development and an improvement in adult learning ability (Clendinnen and Eayrs, 1961). The actions of the prenatal and early postnatal GH administration appear thus far to be restricted to a therapeutic effect under conditions of malnutrition.

Many of the effects of growth hormone upon tissues, cartilages, erythropoiesis and even the brain probably require the involvement of polypeptides, summarily called somatomedins (for review see Van Wyk and Underwood, 1975). These substances have a relatively low molecular weight (around 9900), and their synthesis and presence in the blood plasma and body tissues are dependent upon growth hormone. The factors designated somatomedins A, B and C, "multiplication stimulating activity" (MSA), and "non-suppressible insulin-like activity" (NSILA) are all categorized as somatomedins. They circulate in the plasma bound to larger proteins, a linkage which is probably due to the presence of growth hormone (Moses *et al.*, 1976). This binding extends their functional life-span, which would otherwise be rather short, not more than 10 to 30 minutes. The plasma protein - somatomedin complex prolongs their half-life to about 3-4 hours. Berelowitz *et al.* (1981) have singled out somatomedin C as being particularly important in the brain, suggesting that it mediates the actions of growth hormone upon neural tissue.

The somatomedins are produced in the liver and function, for example, to stimulate the incorporation of thymidine into DNA, uridine into RNA, leucine into collagen protein, and inorganic sulfate into cartilaginous chondroitin sulfate. Somatomedin C competes with insulin for binding sites on the cell membranes, although some sites appear highly specific for somatomedin C alone. In every tissue thus far studied, it is able to mimic the effects of insulin. The effect of growth hormone upon brain development may require a mediation by another somatomedin, "brain trophin", a heat-stable, non-dialyzable factor which stimulates the uptake of tritiated thymidine into fetal brain DNA (Sara et al., 1976). It has also been termed BGA or Brain Growth Promoting Activity (Westall et al., 1978). Since growth hormone does not cross the placenta, it is possible that the regulation of brain growth during the fetal period is at least partly attributable to the influence of BGA (Sara and Hall, 1979).

Genetic defects in the somatomedins have recently been discovered. As a result of their functional ties with growth hormone, it is not unexpected that such defects are associated with retardations in body growth or with dwarfism (Laton dwarfism). This appears to be the case in African pygmies, whose tissues have been found insensitive to somatomedin.

Chapter 27

Neurochemistry of Thirst and Hunger

Discussions of the control of food and water intake have typically focused upon the associated physiological mechanisms or the complexity of pertinent neurotransmitter activity. Without intending to disregard the importance of such forms of control, the present chapter will consider the contributions to the generation and inhibition of these basic drive states by a number of biologically active peptides, some of which are produced by cells of the gastrointestinal tract or kidney and are carried into the brain by the blood or are generated in brain tissue itself.

CONTROL OF WATER METABOLISM

The feeling of thirst is basically a response to one or both of two types of changes in the tissue water content:

(1) Intracellular - due to a loss of cellular water because of an increase in the osmotic pressure of the extracellular fluid.

(2) Extracellular - due to a bulk loss of extracellular fluid without an accompanying change in the general osmolarity of the intracellular compartment volume.

485

Although they are regulated by somewhat different mechanisms, both employ a common final efferent pathway to generate the relevant behavior. The principal area of the brain that regulates water metabolism and its corresponding biological drive, thirst, is the hypothalamus, although several other areas, notably the globus pallidus, amygdala, septal area, ventral thalamus, preoptic region, hippocampus, and cingulate region, influence and modulate this hypothalamic activity.

At least two peptides are associated with water metabolism. One is angiotensin II, and the other is vasopressin. It had been originally believed that both were very specialized substances that served to control a single physiological function, water balance in the organism. However, over the past fifteen years evidence has been accumulating which indicates that these peptides also have behavioral and physiological effects unrelated to water metabolism. In fairness and before going any further, it should also be mentioned that as of yet there exists no compelling evidence that the renin-angiotensin system does play a direct, immediate role in normal physiological thirst.

THE RENIN-ANGIOTENSIN SYSTEM

The renin-angiotensin system depends upon the degradation of a plasma protein, angiotensinogen, by the proteolytic enzyme renin. The resulting product is angiotensin I, a decapeptide which is further degraded by a converting enzyme to an octapeptide, angiotensin II (Fig. 27.1). It is in this form that the molecule is biologically active.

The enzyme component of this system, renin, is synthesized, stored and secreted mainly by the kidneys, but it has also been found in the uterus, placenta, fetal membranes, adrenal gland, and brain. It is likely released from the kidney in the form of a prorenin precursor (for review see Inagami and Murakami, 1980). Both renin and prorenin have molecular weights higher than 40,000 daltons.

The specific stimulus for renin release from the kidney is a decrease in the arterial pulse pressure that triggers activity in the renal sympathetic nerves. More specifically, renin is secreted when the renal vascular receptors respond to changes in the wall tension within the renal afferent arterioles, or when the macula densa, the sodium and chloride sensor in the vicinity of the renal glomeruli, detects a change in the ionic composition of the renal blood. However, little is actually known about the way in which the macula densa receptor actually does work.

The effects of angiotensin II upon various bodily systems is mediated by the angiotensin receptors. Regoli (1979) described two types of these recep-

Angiotensinogen
Asp-Arg-Val-Tyr-Ile-His-Pro-Phe-His-Leu-Leu-Val-Tyr-Ser
⬆
Renin
Angiotensin I
Asp-Arg-Val-Tyr-Ile-His-Pro-Phe-His-Leu
⬆
Converting enzyme

Angiotensin II
Asp-Arg-Val-Tyr-Ile-His-Pro-Phe
⬆
Aminopeptidase

Angiotensin III
Arg-Val-Tyr-Ile-His-Pro-Phe
⬆
Aminopeptidase
Inactive fragment
Val-Tyr-Ile-His-Pro-Phe

Figure 27.1 Gradual degradation of angiotensinogen to angiotensin I,II and III.

tors: one in the intestinal and vascular smooth muscle cells of the heart and vas deferens, and another which mediates the release of catecholamines from the adrenal medulla. Receptors in other parts of the body have not yet been classified.

The octapeptide, angiotensin II, regulates the circulatory volume and pressures. Beside having a direct peripheral action, this pressor response is also induced by the activation of several brain areas, including the area postrema and some areas around the third cerebral ventricle (Fig. 27.2) and in the vicinity of the superior colliculus.

An injection of angiotensin into the brain elicits thirst and drinking behavior (Severs *et al.*, 1980). Under physiological conditions, this peptide enters the brain only in those structures which lack an association with the blood-brain barrier. Three of the circumventricular organs, the area postrema, the subfornical organ, and the organum vasculosum, have all been suggested to be sites of its action (for review see Simpson, 1981).

At least four areas of the CNS have been implicated in angiotensin-induced thirst: the preoptic region, the subfornical organ, the area proximal to the optic recess of the third ventricle, and the vascular organ of the lamina terminalis. The area most responsive to the presence of angiotensin is located at the caudal border of the medial preoptic region and the rostral border of the anterior hypothalamus. The neural pathway from this area extends along the medial forebrain bundle through the midlateral hypothalamus to the paramedial area of the midbrain tegmentum, and to an area ventrolateral to the mescencephalic central gray. Lesions of this pathway attenuate drinking which has been induced by microinjections of angiotensin II into the preoptic

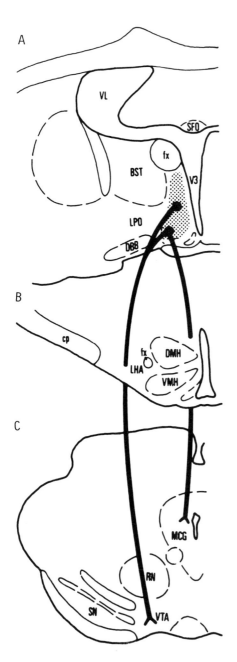

Figure 27.2 A region in the caudal part of the medial preoptic area and rostral tip of the anterior hypothalamic area (stippled region in section A) which is sensitive to the dipsogenic effects of angiotensin II is shown. (A) Microinfusions of [^{3}H]-amino acids were made into this region and autoradiographically labeled pathways to the midbrain were demonstrated (see sections B and C). Note the pathway passing through the medial aspect of the lateral hypothalamus and terminating in the ventral tegmental area (VTA). Projections to the central gray (MCG) were also observed [from L.W. Swanson, J. Kucharczyk and G.J. Mogenson, *J. Comp. Neurol.* 178:645 (1978); © 1978 by Alan R. Liss, Inc.].

area. There are, however, no comparable lesion effects upon water intake as a result of the administration of angiotensin II into the subfornical organ, leading Mogenson and Kucharczyk (1978) to conclude that intracellular thirst signals, induced by a stimulation of the preoptic area, and extracellular thirst, which is more dependent upon the subfornical organ, are subserved by two separate neural pathways. These pathways probably rely on the β-adrenergic neurotransmitter system, since isoproterenol, a β-adrenergic agonist, causes copious drinking with a simultaneous inhibition of water diuresis. The drinking response, then, seems to be elicited by β-adrenergic stimulation of the renin-angiotensin system, either within the brain or in the periphery (Ramsay, 1978). But, while β-adrenergic neurons facilitate thirst, α-adrenergic fibers seem to inhibit it. The effect of angiotensin upon drinking is quite specific, and the dipsogenic response can be selectively blocked by the administration of an angiotensin antiserum.

Angiotensin II acts through molecular receptors in the neuronal membranes, and the highest specific binding has been detected in those areas where its injection induces drinking - the lateral septum, midbrain, thalamus, hypothalamus, preoptic region, vascular organ of the lamina terminalis, and tissue proximal to the optic recess of the third ventricle (for review see Phillips, 1978). Very low binding levels have been detected in the cerebral cortex, hippocampus, and corpus striatum. Of all the tissues examined, the greatest binding occurs in the lateral septum, while within the medulla oblongata, the area postrema has been found to contain the largest amount.

Although the receptors are localized in the neuronal membrane, the angiotensin-receptor complex is eventually released from it and enters the neuron. These receptors are glycoproteins, and the sialic acids in their polysaccharide moiety have been implicated in the formation of the angiotensin-receptor complex. Their affinity for angiotensin II may be temporarily altered by calcium ions, or other divalent ions. On the whole, the number of receptors is inversely related to the level of renin and angiotensin in the body. Thus, bilateral nephrectomy causes an increase of angiotensin receptors in several organs and tissues.

In the nervous tissues, angiotensin receptors are localized in and around the synapses both in the presynaptic and postsynaptic membranes. In norepinephrine-containing neurons, the presynaptic angiotensin receptors facilitate the release of the neurotransmitter from the nerve endings and depress its reuptake. In doing so, angiotensin enhances norepinephrine synthesis. It also liberates serotonin from the nerve endings and accelerates its synthesis through the activation of tryptophan hydroxylase. Low doses, on the other hand, inhibit the synthesis.

Nerve fibers containing angiotensin II, or angiotensin-like material, are scattered all throughout the brain and spinal cord, with the exception of large parts of the neocortex and cerebellar cortex. They are concentrated in the substantia gelatinosa of the spinal cord, the median eminence, and in some brain stem nuclei. Problems with the localization methods, however, have caused discrepancies in its distribution mapping.

In most neurons that possess the receptors, angiotensin II induces an increase in neuronal firing. This is true for those cells within the lateral hypothalamus, zona incerta, dentate gyrus and thalamus (Wayner et al., 1973). The neurons are not only responsive to the complete octapeptide, but also to its fragments, an angiotensin II (2-8) heptapeptide and an angiotensin II (5-8) tetrapeptide. A dramatic increase in firing is present in cells of the supraoptic nucleus, which produce and release vasopressin, a second peptide involved in water metabolism.

The effects of angiotensin have also been observed in the subfornical organ, a small, highly vascularized area formed mainly by accumulated ependyma cells. It is localized in the wall of the third ventricle, protruding into the ventricular space near the interventricular foramen. The subfornical organ lies outside of the blood brain barrier, so that substances from the blood may enter it relatively freely. It is one of the "seven windows of the brain", as Knigge (1975) termed the circumventricular organs. Since angiotensin II cannot pass the blood-brain barrier, these organs are probably the sites of the angiotensin II effects. Lesions introduced in this structure reduce the drinking elicited by the intravenous injection of angiotensin II (Abdelaal et al., 1974) or by an injection into the vascular organ, another sensitive circumventricular area. As little as 50 femtograms of angiotensin II injected into this organ are able to induce drinking and a blood pressure response.

The reaction of the brain to body dehydration is only partially dependent upon angiotensin taken up from the circulating blood. Some amount of the peptide is also presumably produced and degraded by the nervous tissue itself. The angiotensin-generating activity of the brain was suggested in 1971 by Fischer-Ferraro et al. They found that an angiotensin I-like substance persisted in the brain after nephrectomy. Also, Ganten et al. (1971) was able to identify the renin substrate angiotensinogen in the CNS. This globulin is too large a molecule to cross the blood-brain barrier, and it is therefore likely that it is synthesized within the brain.

At present, there appears to be more evidence for existence of an endogenous brain renin-angiotensin system than against it. A specific inhibitor of angiotensin activity, saralasin, administered to the brain influences thirst and drinking behavior (Brooks and Malvin, 1979). Angiotensin-sensitive receptors can be found in the brain, and the peptide is present in cultured cells from fetal rat brain (Weyhenmeyer et al., 1980).

Tissue cultures of hybrid neuroblastoma X glioma cells (Fishman et al., 1981) contain all components of the renin-angiotensin system, including angiotensinogen, angiotensin I and II, the converting enzyme, and the angiotensinogen-cleaving enzyme, renin.

Recent methodological advances have permitted a distinction between true renin in the brain and other proteolytic enzymes (Hirose et al., 1980). Brain renin has a molecular weight and a pH-dependence that is identical with the renin in plasma and kidney. It is synthesized in the brain and can be found in areas such as the cerebellum, medulla, hypothalamus and amygdala. The highest levels are present in the pineal gland, adenohypophysis and choroid plexus. And, it appears to be present in brain synaptosomal fractions (Husain et al., 1981). Slater et al. (1980) actually found immuno-reactive renin in most neurons throughout the brain, suggesting that it may have some general metabolic role in the CNS.

The level of renin in the brain is affected by factors related to water metabolism and ionic homeostasis. For example, the intravenous injection of 10% saline causes an increase in its activity in the cerebral cortex, brain stem, and hypothalamus. In contrast, aldosterone, an adrenocortical hormone controlling the sodium level in body fluids, decreases this activity.

Peptidyl carboxypeptidase, the angiotensin-converting enzyme necessary for the operation of the renin-angiotensin system, is also present in the brain. It converts angiotensin I into angiotensin II by cleaving the dipeptide Leu-His from the carboxyl end of the decapeptide angiotensin I. It is widely distributed throughout the brain, and its level is higher there than in any other tissue, with the exception of the lungs. Its greatest activity is found in the pituitary gland (Benuck and Marks, 1979). The same enzyme also inactivates enkephalins and the nonapeptide vasodepressor bradykinin. It can also act upon the β-chain of insulin, and consequently is a rather nonspecific enzyme.

The central angiotensin system affects cAMP metabolism in many areas of the brain, including the cerebral cortex and hippocampus (Schmid et al., 1982). Endogenous angiotensin is likely responsible for the stimulation of cells in the preoptic area, where plasma angiotensin is unable to pass the blood-brain barrier. Applications of the substance appear to affect almost 50% of the neurons in the medial preoptic area, some of which increase their firing, while others decrease it (Simonnet et al., 1980). Other sensitive regions are the septal region and mesencephalic gray. In the anterior hypothalamus, the angiotensin stimulates the release of vasopressin (Wayner et al., 1976) and oxytocin (Lang et al., 1981). The level of sodium ions in this area is also important for vasopressin release, probably more so than the general osmolarity which was earlier believed to be the main factor in its secretion.

Angiotensin II has also been found to have other biological actions. Higher doses activate neurons in the cerebral cortex and thalamus. It inhibits some neurons in the septum and also depolarizes spinal motoneurons, possibly in an indirect manner through an effect upon interneurons. It also appears to play some role in the central control of the cardiovascular system (Buckley, 1981).

Electrophysiological changes in the brain following the intracerebroventricular injection of angiotensin show that not only single neurons, but also the activity of the cerebral cortex and other brain areas as a whole may be affected. Visual evoked potentials increase in amplitude, and the electrical activity of the hippocampus becomes synchronized (Martin et al., 1976). Even behavioral effects have been reported. Its introduction into the dorsal neostriatum disrupts the retention of a passive avoidance task when tested 24 hours later. An injection of renin is effective as well (Koller et al., 1979). Similar injections into the ventral striatum or thalamus are without influence. The results suggest that angiotensin II may be involved within that particular area in the acquisition of the task, in a way that is quite unassociated with water metabolism (Morgan and Routtenberg, 1977).

The emerging data on the diverse effects of and responsiveness to angiotensin in the brain, including its influence upon norepinephrine synthesis and release, could reflect a functional involvement of the peptide in the modulation of noradrenergic activity that is unassociated with salt and water metabolism. This effect may, however, be indirect and dependent upon a primary change in other neurotransmitter systems.

VASOPRESSIN AND OXYTOCIN

The posterior pituitary is a distal component of a neurosecretory system that includes the supraoptic and paraventricular nuclei of the hypothalamus (Fig. 27.3). Particular cells in these hypothalamic nuclei produce one of two neurohormones, vasopressin or oxytocin. Although both hormones are synthesized in these two areas, vasopressin production [in two forms, arginine-vasopressin and lysine-vasopressin (Fig. 27.4)] is more concentrated in the supraoptic nucleus. Here, vasopressin neurons outnumber oxytocin neurons by a ratio of 5 to 1. In the paraventricular nucleus, the more medially positioned cells synthesize the oxytocin.

The cells that generate the hormones are large and have relatively thick axons. They can fire continuously or in bursts and have been found to shift quickly from one type of activity to another or to complete silence. The axons of these cells travel within at least three pathways (Zimmerman and Robinson, 1976): a major, supraoptico-hypophyseal tract to the posterior

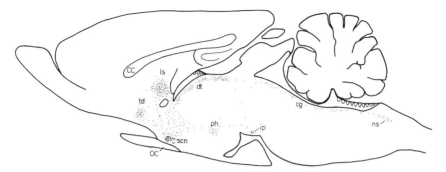

Figure 27.3 Drawing of a sagittally sectioned rat brain, diagrammatically depicting the various efferent fiber pathways arising from the vasopressin and neurophysin-producing parvocellular neurons of the suprachiasmatic nucleus, as determined by immunohistochemistry. The drawing includes several sagittal planes, since no single plane contains all the depicted structures. Abbreviations: CC, corpus callosum; ls, lateral septum; td, nucleus of the diagonal tract; dt, dorsal thalamus; scn, suprachiasmatic nucleus; ph, posterior hypothalamus; ip, interpeduncular nucleus; OC, optic chiasma; cg, central grey; ns, nucleus of the solitary tract [from M.V. Sofroniew and A. Weindl, *Am. J. Anat.* 153:391 (1978); © 1978 by Alan R. Liss, Inc.].

pituitary, a pathway extending to the external zone of the median eminence for secretion into the hypophyseal portal blood, and a fiber tract running toward the third ventricle for secretion into the cerebrospinal fluid. All of these transport the neurohormones by axoplasmic flow.

The oxytocin- and vasopressin-containing neurons and fibers are spread from the hypothalamus to the septum, amygdala, hippocampus, diencephalon, mesencephalon, brain stem and spinal cord (Buijs *et al.*, 1978). Oxytocin-containing fibers have also been found to reach the medulla oblongata (Sofroniew and Schrell, 1981). By radioimmunoassay, vasopressin has been detected in several nuclei of the medulla oblongata (Morris *et al.*, 1980). A number of hypothalamic nuclei, notably the arcuate, dorsomedial, ventromedial, and suprachiasmatic nuclei, probably produce vasopressin for these brain areas. Thus, Sofroniew and Weindl (1978) found that fine caliber fibers from the suprachiasmatic nucleus contain vasopressin and could easily be distinguished from the large caliber fibers coming from the supraoptic nucleus, which also contain vasopressin. These fine fibers pass rostrodorsally to the lateral septum and dorsally to the medial dorsal thalamus and lateral habenula, and from the thalamus to the central gray of the mesencephalon and into the area containing the nucleus of the solitary tract.

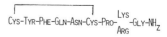

Figure 27.4 Lysine- and arginine-vasopressin.

Travelling in a dorsocaudal direction, they reach the posterior hypothalamus and interpeduncular nuclei. Large caliber fibers project to the amygdala, mesencephalic central gray, the nucleus of the solitary tract, dorsal motor nucleus of the vagus, lateral reticular nucleus, and portions of the spinal cord (Sofroniew and Weindl, 1981). The choroid plexus is also a target tissue for vasopressin, and tracts from the paraventricular field of the hypothalamus reach the choroid plexus of the lateral ventricle.

Vasopressin and oxytocin are transported along the axon bound to carrier proteins called neurophysins. Thus far, three neurophysins have been isolated from the hypothalamus and posterior pituitary of the albino rat and other animal species, two of them appearing in a much greater concentration than the third (Rauch et al., 1969). Neurophysins are also present in axons and in the neurosecretory granules within the posterior lobe, and they are an essential component for the formation of these granules. They have been detected in the kidney, uterus, and mammary gland, but appear to be absent in the liver, spleen, and skeletal muscle. And, neurophysins are secreted into the blood stream, where they are present in a relative excess, when compared with the level of vasopressin. This is because they have a longer half-life (for review see Seif and Robinson, 1978).

According to Brownstein et al. (1980), a vasopressin precursor, propressophysin, is synthesized in the neuronal cell body on the rough endoplasmic reticulum. It is then packaged into secretory granules by the Golgi apparatus and cleaved. One part of the precursor molecule then becomes vasopressin, another neurophysin. The residual part has characteristics of a glycopeptide. In contrast, pro-oxyphysin, the precursor of oxytocin, is not a glycoprotein.

A complementary molecule of DNA for the vasopressin precursor has been prepared by Land et al. (1982). It has shown that the precursor contains 166 amino acids, with a signal peptide of 19 residues followed directly by arginine-vasopressin connected to neurophysin II by a Gly-Lys-Arg sequence. A glycopeptide forms the end of the molecule.

Neurophysins may have additional, independent functions within the body. They may serve a lipolytic role, or may possibly be a natriuretic factor, since there is an increase in plasma neurophysin in response to hypertonic saline. Plasma neurophysin is also found in higher quantities in pregnant women or in women taking oral contraceptives. This is an estrogenic effect to which the term "estrogen-stimulated neurophysin" (ESN) is often applied.

The pituicytes are cells similar to glia which form the mass of the posterior lobe. At the present time, their function is unknown, although it has been suspected that they store vasopressin and oxytocin. They also contain acetylcholine, acetylcholinesterase and a concentrating mechanism for

Thirst and Hunger

triiodothyronine, but their composition reveals little that can be attributed to any particular function.

In addition to vasopressin, the posterior pituitary also contains a number of other active small peptides, including a vasopressin that is devoid of glycine (desglycinamide vasopressin), arginine-vasotocin, $ACTH_{1-8}$, and several unrelated peptides. Vasopressin is also present in the adenohypophysis, where it is probably involved in the control of ACTH secretion. After adrenalectomy, its level in the anterior pituitary increases (Chateau *et al.*, 1979), and it is able to stimulate ACTH secretion both *in vivo* (after microinjection into the pituitary) and *in vitro*. It is not, however, functionally identical to corticotropin releasing factor.

The complex of neurophysin bound to vasopressin or oxytocin is secreted from the nerve endings in the posterior pituitary. The neurosecretory granule membranes containing this complex are activated by cyclic AMP to initiate the extrusion of the contents (Baker and Hope, 1976). This mechanism appears to be calcium-dependent. Nervous activity in the magnocellular system promotes the release of the secretory granules. The vasopressin-containing cells increase their firing rate during dehydration, when they shift from a slow irregular rate to a phasic firing pattern. At this time, the oxytocin cells are also activated (Wakerley *et al.*, 1978). Consequently, after an oral administration of hypertonic saline, both vasopressin and oxytocin are depleted from both the hypothalamic nuclei and the posterior pituitary. As was mentioned previously, the magnocellular system is also responsive to angiotensin II, and vagal and carotid sinus afferents are similarly capable of stimulating it. Stimulation of the cingulate gyrus, posterior hypothalamus, medial and lateral mamillary nuclei, mamillary peduncle, midbrain central gray, amygdala, hippocampus, olfactory tubercle, piriform cortex, septum, medial lemniscus, subthalamus, and several other areas also triggers the activity of the system with a corresponding secretion of vasopressin and oxytocin (Fig. 27.5).

The level of vasopressin in the external zone of the median eminence is greatly increased by the absence of adrenal cortical steroids, implying that this hormone may also play a role in the activity of the hypothalamo-pituitary-adrenal system (McCann, 1957). This increase was prevented by dexamethasone (Silverman *et al.*, 1981).

The paraventricular nucleus possesses neurons containing both estradiol and neurophysin-associated oxytocin. This indicates that estrogen could well be a stimulus for the release of oxytocin (Rhodes *et al.*, 1981).

In the body, vasopressin has several effects. It elevates the vascular muscle tonus and, as a result, increases blood pressure. Its primary function is enhancing the permeability to water of the urinary tract epithelia in the kidney's collecting tubules and loop of Henle. This effect is mediated by

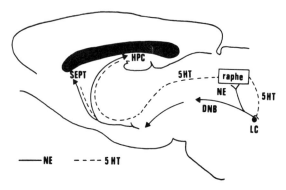

Figure 27.5 Schematic illustration of neurotransmitter pathways involved in the action of vasopressin. Abbreviations: HPC, hippocampus; sept, septum; LC, locus coeruleus; DNB, dorsal noradrenergic bundle; NE, norepinephrine; 5HT, serotonin [from G.L. Kovacs, B. Bohus and D.H.G. Versteeg, *Brain Res.* 172: (1979); © 1979 by Elsevier/North-Holland Biomedical Press].

cyclic AMP, which induces structural changes by the rearrangement of intramembranous particles in the liminal membrane of the urinary tract epithelial cells (Kachadorian *et al.*, 1975). Vasopressin is also possibly involved in the production of hyperglycemia and hyperlipemia. It regulates the permeability of the blood-brain barrier to water and in doing so controls the hydration of cerebral tissue (Raichle and Grubb, 1978). It is also antipyretic, blocking a fever response when perfused through the septal area.

Vasopressin has a very significant influence upon nervous activity. The route of transport of vasopressin to its sites of action within the brain (principally within the limbic system) is not clear, but may take place by direct blood flow from the pituitary (Oliver *et al.*, 1977). The transport via peripheral blood circulation is probably not important, because vasopressin levels in peripheral blood are not sufficiently elevated or depressed by behaviors that are specifically influenced by vasopressin, such as the acquisition and retention of a passive avoidance task. However, after their peripheral injection, both vasopressin and oxytocin can cross the blood-brain barrier in small amounts to cause changes in neuronal firing which persist long after the peptides have left the blood stream (Landgraf *et al.*, 1979).

Invertebrates, such as *Aplysia,* provide a useful model system to study the direct effects of vasopressin and oxytocin upon neurons, since many of their nerve cells have been individually identified. The administration of vertebrate peptides causes an increase in both cAMP and cGMP levels in these cells and modifies their endogenous electrical rhythms. A change in cAMP alone, if present, causes hyperpolarization of these neurons, while alterations in both cyclic nucleotides lead to an increase in neuronal activity.

Even in peripheral nerves of other species, vasopressin causes an increase in excitability. Such effects are all caused by changes in sodium and potassium membrane conductance (Barker and Smith, 1976).

An intracerebroventricular injection of arginine-vasopressin increases the nerve impulse flow in norepinephrinergic neurons within the mammalian hypothalamus, thalamus, and medulla oblongata. This effect, however, is probably restricted only to a small number of sites. Catecholamine metabolism is most prominently affected by vasopressin in the substantia nigra and caudate nucleus. Arginine-vasopressin accelerates the catabolism of norepinephrine. The exception to this effect is in the supraoptic nucleus, where instead of an increase in breakdown, there is a retardation. Vasopressin also influences the activity of larger areas of the brain, altering the pattern of the EEG in a manner that resembles the electroencephalographic records following the administration of nicotine. The EEG is observed to slow down, and hypersynchrony is clearly expressed.

The Brattleboro rat has come to serve as an important animal subject for studies in this area, since this strain exhibits a genetic defect in the synthesis of vasopressin. Homozygotes suffer from inborn diabetes insipidus, an inability to form concentrated urine in the kidney, along with other endocrine defects, such as a reduced hormonal response to mild stressors and an elevated release of oxytocin into the circulation (Bailey and Weiss, 1981). In addition, they display deficiencies in hearing and in the sensory processes. Their brain levels of serotonin, GABA and norepinephrine are significantly higher than in their heterozygote littermates (Leonard et al., 1976). Most of these changes are in direct contrast to the pharmacological effects of vasopressin in normal rats.

Several behaviors have been thus far reported that may be related to the effect of vasopressin upon neurotransmitter metabolism or may be a direct consequence of its presence or absence within the brain. The above-mentioned Brattleboro rats exhibit disturbances in paradoxical sleep, and there are hippocampal theta rhythm abnormalities that occur during this phase (De Wied et al., 1975). On the other hand, the administration of desglycinamide-vasopressin has been observed to increase the high frequency components of this hippocampal rhythm. Such effects may possibly prove important to an appraisal of the roles of vasopressin and paradoxical sleep in the consolidation of the memory trace.

An injection of arginine vasopressin or lysine vasopressin into the cerebral ventricles of the rat in doses of less than 100 micrograms per animal causes hyperactivity and an enhancement in grooming. In larger amounts (somewhat less than 1 mg per animal), excessive scratching, foraging (a combination of burrowing and manipulations of bedding material), and squealing have been observed (Delanoy et al., 1978). Similar doses of

	EXTINCTION ACTIVE AVOIDANCE BEHAVIOR	PASSIVE AVOIDANCE BEHAVIOR (INTRAVENTRICULAR)	PREVENTION AMNESIA	MORPHINE TOLERANCE	HEROIN SELF-ADMINISTRATION
DG-AVP/DG-LVP	+ + +	+ + +	+ + +	+	− − −
OXT	+ +	− −	o	+ + +	+
PA	+	+ + +	o	o	− −
TA	o	−/+	o	o	o
PAG	o	+	+	+	−
PLG	o	o	+ +	+ + +	+ + +

facilitation + + +100 + +50 +20 o<10   inhibition − − −100 − −50 − 20 o<10

AVP H- Cys - Tyr - Phe - Gln - Asn - Cys - Pro - Arg - Gly - NH$_2$ OXT H- Cys - Tyr - Ile - Gln - Asn - Cys - Pro - Leu - Gly - NH$_2$
        PA   PAG   TA   PLG

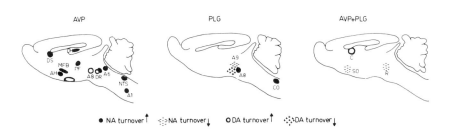

● NA turnover↑   ⦂⦂NA turnover↓   ○ DA turnover↑   ⦂⦂DA turnover↓

Figure 27.6 Summary of the effects of neurohypophyseal principles on various memory tests and on catecholamine metabolism in restricted brain areas. The effectiveness of the peptides is expressed as approximate potency relative to the most effective peptide in all particular assay. Abbreviations: A1, A6, A8, A9 refer to catecholaminergic cell body regions; AH, anterior hypothalamic nucleus; C, caudate nucleus; CO, nucleus commissuralis; DA, dopamine; DH, dorsal hippocampal nuclei; DS, dorsal septal nucleus; DR, dorsal raphe nucleus; EM, median eminence; NA, noradrenaline; NTS, nucleus tractus solitarii; MFB, medial forebrain bundle; PF, parafascicular nucleus; R, nucleus ruber; S, supraoptic nucleus [from J.M. van Ree, B. Bohus, D.H. G. Versteeg, D. de Wied, *Biochem. Pharmacol.* 27:1793 (1978); © 1978 by Pergamon Press].

arginine-vasopressin in rats and mice induce "barrel-rotation", a rotation of the animal about the longitudinal axis of the body (Kruse *et al.*, 1977).

Although it is without any detectable effect upon brain protein synthesis, vasopressin appears to participate in a consolidation of memory for several behavioral tasks. In 1966, de Wied and Bohus found that rats without a posterior pituitary showed less resistance to the extinction of a shuttlebox avoidance response than sham-operated controls. Acquisition of the response was unaffected. An injection of lysine vasopressin restored the resistance, with the effect lasting for several weeks, much longer than the presence of the neurohormone in the body.

In intact animals, vasopressin increases the resistance to extinction of a shuttlebox avoidance response, step-through passive avoidance, and pole-climbing active avoidance. Desglycinamide-lysine-vasopressin, which is lacking in the classical endocrine activities of the whole lysine vasopressin molecule, has the same effect. These data indicate that vasopressin facilitates the consolidation of some memories, particularly aversibly motivated ones (Fig. 27.6). Injected intracerebroventricularly, it is effective in a dose of 25 pg, which is actually within the physiological range (Van Wimersma Greidanus *et al.*, 1981). Reward performance, such as sexually motivated behavior, is also improved (Bohus, 1977). Some other kinds of behavior, primarily those which depend upon an approach response for food, are not changed. A comparable study in humans has shown that an analog of vasopressin, 1-desamino-8-D-arginine-vasopressin, is also capable of improving the effectiveness of learning, particularly in the treatment of progressive dementia (Weingartner *et al.*, 1981, 1981a).

Experiments with Brattleboro rats also suggest that this hormone participates in the acquisition of learned behaviors. The rats have difficulty in establishing escape and avoidance responses, which are then extinguished more rapidly than in normal controls or Brattleboro heterozygotes. These differences may be eradicated by arginine-vasopressin or desglycinamide-lysine-vasopressin (Bohus *et al.*, 1975). An analysis of the behavior of Brattleboro rats during the learning of several other tasks has demonstrated that these animals have fairly intact working-memory processes, but are deficient in reference-memory mechanisms and have an altered adaptability (Brito *et al.*, 1981).

The administration of serum that has been immunologically established against vasopressin facilitates the extinction of avoidance tasks. But, since the effect of vasopressin is central, this antivasopressin serum is effective only if injected into the central nervous system.

Amnesia caused by puromycin, pentobarbital or carbon dioxide, as described in Chapter 14, is antagonized by vasopressin or its desglycinamide-lysine analog. Injections shortly after an active avoidance training session (or prior to a test of retention 24 hours later) are ineffective. The hormone is therefore able to overcome the effect of puromycin-related peptides on the consolidation and retrieval processes.

An analysis of the effect of vasopressin analogs and degradation products indicates that the C-terminal portion of the vasopressin molecule is important, and a replacement of one C-terminal amino acid by another decreases the potency of the peptide. The ring structure is particularly important for the effect upon consolidation of the active avoidance behavior. Phenylalanine in the third position and asparagine in the fifth position are most critical in this respect. The linear parts of the molecule may have a greater influence upon the retrieval of the information (de Wied and Versteeg, 1979).

The facilitation of some types of learning involves the ascending dorsal noradrenergic bundle. Its destruction prior to learning interferes with the effects caused by the administration of arginine-vasopressin (Kovacs et al., 1979). Destruction following learning has no effect. Vasopressin would therefore appear to influence memory processes through a modulation of the catecholaminergic system, particularly in the limbic midbrain terminals of the dorsal noradrenergic bundle.

It has been speculated that the events involved in learning and memory may be analogous to the development of a tolerance to morphine. In mice, lysine-vasopressin has been shown to facilitate the development of resistance to the analgesic action of morphine. In Brattleboro rats, the development of tolerance is delayed, but may be restored by arginine-vasopressin or desglycinamide-lysine-vasopressin, an effect requiring the integrity of the C-terminal of the molecule.

Oxytocin, the second neurohypophyseal peptide (Fig. 27.7), has several physiological effects, the foremost of which is its action on the smooth muscle-like myoepithelial cells lining the ducts of the breast. By causing these cells to contract in the lactating breast, milk is expressed from the alveoli and out of the nipple. This milk-ejection reflex is also under the control of the hypothalamic magnocellular system, and can be elicited by stimulation of the nucleus accumbens, hippocampal rudiment, midbrain central gray, subthalamus, and posterior hypothalamus. Oxytocin is similarly released following the stimulation of some areas of the limbic cortex. Functionally, the hormone also induces the contraction of the uterine smooth muscles during parturition and could participate in the induction of labor.

$$
\overset{\overline{\rule{2.5cm}{0.4pt}}}{\text{Cys-Tyr-Ile-Gln-Asn-Cys-Pro-Leu-Gly-NH}_2}
$$ **Figure 27.7** Oxytocin.

Centrally injected oxytocin has behavioral effects that are in contrast to those of vasopressin. It facilitates the extinction of passive avoidance, while its antiserum increases retention. In fact, Bohus *et al.* (1978) believe that oxytocin may be a naturally occurring amnestic neuropeptide. This conclusion is further supported by a study using human volunteers (Ferrier *et al.*, 1980). Vasopressin did not affect the learning of a paired associate word task or a picture matching task, but later recall was impaired.

The "tail" of the oxytocin molecule, formed by the amino acids proline, leucine and glycine, can also cause biochemical and behavioral changes. Proline-leucine-glycinamide (PLG) is produced by a   hydrolysis of the oxytocin molecule, a process that normally takes place in the pituitary and hypothalamus. PLG is alternatively known as melanostatin inhibitory factor I (MIF-I), and its behavioral actions were discussed in Chapter 24. This biochemical relationship between oxytocin and MIF-I implies that there also exists a functional link in their behavioral effects.

NEUROTENSIN

In an attempt to obtain substance P from bovine hypothalamic extracts, Carraway and Leeman in 1973 isolated instead a tridecapeptide with the amino acid sequence pGlu-Leu-Tyr-Glu-Asn-Lys-Pro-Arg-Arg-Pro-Tyr-Ile-Leu-COOH. Commonly referred to as neurotensin, this peptide has been demonstrated to have potent pharmacological effects both *in vivo* and *in vitro.* Outside of the brain, it causes hypotension, vasodilation, cyanosis, and an increase in vascular permeability. After parenteral administration, it produces hyperglycemia (Carraway *et al.*, 1976) and the sensation of pain. This hyperglycemic response may involve glycogen degradation and a release of glucose. In this respect, neurotensin is thirty times more active than glucagon. An increased uptake of glucose from the intestine and *de novo* glucose production from available precursors may also contribute to this change (Wolfe *et al.*, 1978). Its role in the periphery, then, may be to modulate the secretion of insulin and glucagon (Brown and Vale, 1976). It may also be involved in the inflammatory response of the tissues, either directly or through the stimulation of corticosterone secretion.

Endocrine cells producing neurotensin, termed N-cells by Polak *et al.* (1978), are scattered throughout the jejuno-ileum and gastric antrum. Here, these cells are intermingled with numerous somatostatin- and gastrin-producing cells. And, while it has been determined (at least in the rat) that 95% of the total amount of body neurotensin is contained within the gut (Carraway and Leeman, 1976), it does not appear that this endogenous gastrointestinal or intravenously administered neurotensin is able to cross the blood-brain barrier.

Although widely distributed, the neurotensin present in the central nervous system displays an uneven regional pattern. It is high in the hypothalamus, thalamus, median eminence, pituitary, amygdala, and central gray of midbrain, much higher than in the cerebral cortex or cerebellum (Uhl *et al.*, 1977a). The lowest levels have been found in the spinal cord. As revealed by immunofluorescence, neurotensin is associated with neuronal cell bodies and processes, and its presence has been reported in synaptosomal subcellular fractions (Uhl and Snyder, 1976). It has a high affinity for synaptic membranes, where it is bound in a specific, saturable and reversible manner (Uhl *et al.*, 1977).

Palacios and Kuhar (1981) have reported a high concentration of neurotensin binding sites on dopaminergic cell bodies. A large depletion of these sites in the substantia nigra occurs following a local injection of 6-hydroxydopamine. The findings suggest the existence of a direct form of interaction between neurotensin and dopaminergic systems. Neurotensin actually lowers the level of dopamine in corpus striatum by inhibiting dopamine synthesis. The finding suggests that it functions as a modulator of dopamine action (Haubrich *et al.*, 1982).

The administration of neurotensin has been observed to cause a rise in secretions of FSH and LH (Caraway and Leeman, 1975). It is also able to increase the plasma concentrations of glucagon, insulin, growth hormone, and prolactin (Brown and Vale, 1976; Rivier *et al.*, 1977). The effects on pituitary hormone secretion may be due to an influence upon the hypothalamus rather than the pituitary itself (Rivier *et al.*, 1977; Martin *et al.*, 1980). The possibility has also been raised that TRH either acts as a specific antagonist of neurotensin or induces opposing behavioral activity (as reviewed by Nemeroff, 1980).

Neurotensin also potentiates the hypothermic and sedative effect of an intracranial injection of pentobarbital (Nemeroff *et al.*, 1976) by reducing the rate of pentobarbital degradation (Mason *et al.*, 1980). An intracisternal injection has been reported to cause an anti-nociceptive effect in rats and mice (Clineschmidt *et al.*, 1979). On a molecular basis, this effect is less potent than β-endorphin, but more so than methionine enkephalin or leucine enkephalin.

PEPTIDES PRESENT IN THE BRAIN AND GUT

There are several hormones that are produced by cells localized in different parts of the gastrointestinal tract and its associated glands. They are able to influence some specialized functions of the central nervous system, and at least some are produced in the brain as well (for review see Fuxe *et al.*, 1979).

1 5 10
Lʏs-Aʟᴀ-Pʀᴏ-Sᴇʀ-Gʟʏ-Aʀɢ-Vᴀʟ-Sᴇʀ-Mᴇᴛ-Iʟᴇ-

11 15 20
Lʏs-Asɴ-Lᴇᴜ-Gʟɴ-Sᴇʀ-Lᴇᴜ-Asᴘ-Pʀᴏ-Sᴇʀ-His-

21 25 30
Aʀɢ-Iʟᴇ-Sᴇʀ-Asᴘ-Aʀɢ-Asᴘ-Tʏʀ-Mᴇᴛ-Gʟʏ-Tʀᴘ-
SO₃

31
Mᴇᴛ-Asᴘ-Pʜᴇ-CONH₂

Figure 27.8 Cholecystokinin.

One of these hormones, cholecystokinin (CCK), is secreted by cells located in the duodenum, jejunum and ileum. Its secretory activity has been found to be most intense in the rostral areas of the small intestine and responds to the products of fat and protein digestion. In the body, cholecystokinin exists in two forms, one containing 33 amino acid residues (Fig. 27.8) and other containing 39 (Lamers *et al.*, 1980). The functionally effective part of the molecule has been identified as an octapeptide (CCK-8) that contains the COOH-terminal portion. It has a behavioral potency that is approximately eight fold greater than the complete molecule (CCK-33). This COOH-terminal fragment may be further split into two tetrapeptides (CCK-4), which have also been found in both the brain and gut.

The release of cholecystokinin from the intestinal sites of synthesis is stimulated by components of the food chyme, hydrogen ions, amino acids, proteins, fats, and magnesium and calcium ions. Classically, upon its release, cholecystokinin is known to increase the motility of the gallbladder and the secretion of the pancreatic enzymes. In addition, it causes a release of bicarbonate and insulin from the pancreas, stimulates intestinal motility, induces the contraction of the quiescent stomach and pyloric sphincter, and augments blood flow in the superior mesenteric artery.

Besides its direct physiological actions, cholecystokinin administered by peripheral injection inhibits food intake even in hungry experimental animals. This effect has been demonstrated in rats and monkeys, although in humans the data are inconsistent. It appears then to act as a short-term satiety factor that can regulate meal size and the between meal interval. In addition, injections of the peptide have been observed to produce sedation and analgesia (Zetler, 1980), as well as mild hypothermia and hyperglycemia. The effect upon satiety does not depend upon previous food deprivation. It is dose-related and mediated by the nigro-neostriatal neuronal system (Mueller and Hsiao, 1979; Nemeroff *et al.*, 1980). A peripheral mechanism of cholecystokinin action is also active, because vagotomy abolishes its anti-appetitive action (Lorenz and Goldman, 1978). The feeding - inhibiting system is much more complex (Morley *et al.*, 1980), involving the added influences of other peptides (such as TRH, endogenous opiates and bombesin) and neurotransmitters (including dopamine, GABA and serotonin). Norepinephrine infused into the hypothalamus of satiated rats induces spontaneous feeding. Cholecystokinin is able to attenuate this effect and shows that norepinephrine has a functional role in this system (McCaleb and Myers, 1980). It also modulates catecholamine metabolism in the brain (Fekete *et al.*, 1981), and it may coexist with the catecholamines within a single neuron (Skirboll *et al.*, 1981).

Cholecystokinin is present in the brain, predominantly in the cortex and mostly in the form of the octapeptide, although larger and smaller forms have been found. Following an injection of labeled methionine, there appears a large component with more than 39 amino acids, along with CCK 39, CCK 33, CCK 8, and CCK 4 fragments. The cortex also contains two enzymes that are able to reduce the larger molecules into smaller fragments (Malesci *et al.*, 1980). Immunochemical observations show that cholecystokinin is located in neuronal cell bodies throughout the cortical gray matter. These neurons are also numerous in the hippocampus, mesencephalic central gray, medulla oblongata, and magnocellular hypothalamic system.

The nerve fibers containing cholecystokinin are widely distributed throughout the brain. They are particularly dense in the hippocampus, caudate nucleus, interpeduncular nucleus, the dorsal part of the medulla and in the dorsal horns of the spinal cord (Loren *et al.*, 1979). Cholecystokinin and its COOH-terminal fragments have also been detected in synaptosomes and are released from them by high levels of potassium and calcium ions in the medium (Pinget *et al.*, 1979). The peptide has been speculated to be a transmitter of the pathway linking the cortex and olfactory system to the caudoputamen (Meyer *et al.*, 1982).

The receptors for cholecystokinin are especially enriched within synaptosomal membrane fractions prepared from areas which contain the peptide (Hays *et al.*, 1980). The binding is reversible, saturable, and inhibited by CCK analogs (Saito *et al.*, 1980, 1981). During fasting in the mouse, their number in hypothalamus and olfactory bulb increases (Saito *et al.*, 1981b). The effect has not been observed in other brain areas.

A deficiency of cholecystokinin synthesis is probably present in genetically obese mice (*ob/ob*). Their brains contain only 0.05 micrograms of CCK-8, while their non-obese littermates contain 0.15 micrograms. Mixed controls have about 0.20 micrograms. In the *ob/ob* mice, there is also an increase in the binding of CCK to its receptors in the cerebral cortex that Saito *et al.* (1981a) attribute to an elevation in the number of receptor sites. This effect was specific for the cortex and not present in other brain areas,

$$\overset{1}{\underset{}{\text{GLX}}}\text{-Leu-Gly-Pro-}\overset{5}{\underset{}{\text{Gln}}}\text{-Gly-His-Pro-Ser-}\overset{10}{\underset{}{\text{Leu-}}}$$

$$\overset{11}{\underset{}{\text{Val}}}\text{-Ala-Asp-Pro-}\overset{15}{\underset{}{\text{Ser}}}\text{-Lys-Lys-Gln-Gly-}\overset{20}{\underset{}{\text{Pro-}}}$$

$$\overset{21}{\underset{}{\text{Trp}}}\text{-Leu-Glu-Glu-}\overset{25}{\underset{}{\text{Glu}}}\text{-Glu-Glu-Ala-Tyr-}\overset{30}{\underset{}{\text{Gly-}}}$$

$$\overset{}{\underset{}{\text{SO}_3}}$$

Figure 27.9 Gastrin (GLX indicates the presence of either glutamine or glutamic acid which has not been distinguished).

$$\overset{31}{\underset{}{\text{Trp}}}\text{-Met-Asp-Phe-CONH}_2$$

including the hypothalamus. It could be, then, that in *ob/ob* mice normal appetite restraints are deficient (Straus and Yalow, 1978) due to inherited alterations in CCK metabolism.

Another peptide found in the brain and the gastrointestinal tract is gastrin (Fig. 27.9) (Vanderhaegen *et al.*, 1975). Both it and cholecystokinin have a common COOH terminus. Gastrin-like immunoreactivity is found in relatively high concentrations in brain tissue and in the cerebrospinal fluid. However, true gastrin is probably present only in the hypothalamus, infundibulum, pituitary and lower part of medulla (Rehfeld *et al.*, 1979). It has been localized in the pituitary cells producing ACTH and MSH, as well as in the nerve fibers of the pituitary stalk and posterior lobe (Larsson and Rehfeld, 1981).

A third peptide isolated from the gastrointestinal tract and subsequently from the brain is vasoactive intestinal peptide (VIP). It is a 27-residue structure that is chemically related to secretin and glucagon. In the CNS, its highest levels are present in the striatum, hippocampus, and cerebral cortex, while the cerebellum and brain stem seem to contain very little of this peptide (Besson *et al.*, 1979). It has also been detected in the hypophyseal portal blood, where it could be associated with pituitary endocrine functions (Said and Porter, 1979). This possibility has been supported by findings that centrally applied VIP stimulates the release of prolactin, growth hormone and luteinizing hormone (Kato *et al.*, 1978; Vijayan *et al.*, 1979).

VIP-containing nerve fibers form a network in several nuclei within the hypothalamus, choroid plexus and the walls of the cerebral blood vessels. VIP-like immunoreactivity is also present in the amygdala, frontal cortex, olfactory tubercle, striatum, and hippocampus. And, it appears in sympathetic ganglia and in nerve fibers within the gastrointestinal and female genito-urinary tracts. In those areas of the brain in which it is present, VIP is primarily localized in synaptosomes (Emson *et al.*, 1978) and can be released from them by potassium ions in a high-calcium incubation medium (Giachetti *et al.*, 1977). VIP receptors in the synaptic membranes bind this peptide rapidly and reversibly (Robberecht *et al.*, 1978). They are specific for VIP, but do have some cross-reaction with another gastrointestinal peptide, secretin. High binding levels have been found in the cerebral cortex, hippocampus, striatum and thalamus. The hypothalamus, on the other hand, has a comparatively low level of binding (Taylor and Pert, 1979).

The application of VIP to the surface of the cerebral cortex elicits a firing of individual neurons (Phillis *et al.*, 1978). The peptide is also able to activate adenylate cyclase (Deschodt-Lanckmann *et al.*, 1977; Borghi *et al.*, 1979), an effect which is modulated by dopamine (Onali *et al.*, 1981) and most pronounced within the hippocampus and cerebral cortex. The extent of its activity appears to be at least partly associated with the function of the adrenal steroids, since adrenalectomy decreases VIP concentration in the hippocampus (Rotsztejn *et al.*, 1980). Through its effect upon cAMP, VIP triggers an enzymatic breakdown of neuronal glycogen. Magistretti *et al.* (1981) propose that this effect is a component of the local regulation of energy metabolism.

Bombesin, a tetradecapeptide first isolated from frog skin, has been detected in a variety of mammalian tissues, including lung, gastric mucosa and brain (Brown *et al.*, 1978). It appears to be a member of a family of other frog skin peptides, which includes litorin, ranatensin, and alytesin (Erspamer and Melchiorri, 1973). Along with bombesin, these substances share a common -Gln-Trp-Ala-Val-Gly-His- sequence. The highest levels of bombesin in the brain are found in the hippocampus, striatum, cerebral cortex and hypothalamus, while the cerebellum, medulla and pons contain only small amounts (Moody *et al.*, 1978, 1981). There seem to be some structural differences between the bombesin in the CNS and that in the gut, notably involving an extension of the peptide chain at the N-terminus (Villarreal and Brown, 1978).

Injections of this substance have been observed to alter gastric motility, reduce feeding, cause hyperglycemia (Morley and Levine, 1981), and increase the secretion of gastrin, cholecystokinin, insulin, glucagon and pancreatic amylase (Brown and Vale, 1979; Erspamer and Melchiorri, 1975). It is also capable of producing poikilothermia in rats, disrupting the ability of the animals to regulate their body temperatures in warm or cold environments. Furthermore, there appears to be an interaction between bombesin and active neural peptides as TRH (Brown *et al.*, 1978a), somatostatin (Brown and Vale, 1979), growth hormone, and prolactin (Rivier *et al.*, 1978), suggesting that it may serve as a neuromodulator of their actions and/or their release.

Another peptide, caerulein, has also been extracted from amphibian skin and contains amino acid sequences that are analogous to those in cholecystokinin. It is similarly effective in reducing food intake, as is a synthetic caerulein. There is some evidence that tyrosine in the seventh position on its chain is an essential component for its biological activity.

All of these peptides that have been discovered to exist both in the CNS and gastro-intestinal tract may function in the brain as hormones, neuromodulators or neurotransmitters within circumscribed regions. Those presented here are really only representative examples on a list of peptides detectable in a variety of tissues, including the brain. The list continues to expand yearly, providing us with further confirmations of the complexity of interactions within the nervous system.

INSULIN

The central nervous system has not been considered to be an insulin-dependent tissue. Early tracer studies using an insulin molecule labeled with radioactive iodine showed little, if any, accumulation in the brain (Elgee *et al.*, 1954). Consequently, it was believed that all of the effects of insulin, those upon glucose, fat metabolism, and protein synthesis, were absent in the brain. Szabo and Szabo (1975), however, detected specific receptors in the brain which, when occupied by insulin, triggered a decrease of plasma glucose independent of peripheral insulin effects. In the rat, binding sites have been detected in nerve terminals throughout the brain, including the median eminence and arcuate nucleus (van Houten *et al.*, 1980). This binding of insulin to its receptor facilitates the transport of glucose into the neurons (Debons *et al.*, 1968), alters their electrical activity and stimulates the release of norepinephrine (McCaleb *et al.*, 1979). Furthermore, when implanted into the ventromedial area, it produced a short-term decrease in food consumption (Panksepp and Nance, 1972). Cerebral blood vessels have also been found to be capable of specifically binding plasma insulin (van Houten and Posner, 1979). In the brain, the highest levels of insulin are in the hypothalamus, followed in decreasing order by the olfactory bulb, cerebellum, cerebral cortex, and brain stem.

Insulin is able to cross the blood-brain barrier in significant quantities, and the CNS form is either identical or extremely similar to that in the plasma. Its level in the brain actually exceeds the level in the blood plasma by 25 fold, and Havrankova *et al.* (1978) have postulated that it may be synthesized there. When implanted into the ventromedial area of the hypothalamus, insulin produces a short-term decrease in food consumption (Panksepp and Nance, 1972). In addition, it is released from the brain following the ingestion of sweet foods, a response that Bernstein and Woods (1980) have indicated is probably learned. However, the level of brain insulin appears to a be relatively resistant to short-term plasma fluctuations. Functionally, the widespread distribution of receptors and their localization within synaptosomes would seem to suggest some form of activating or inactivating role in neurotransmission or neuromodulation.

Chapter 28

Neurochemistry of Pain

Somatic sensory information has been acknowledged to reach the cerebral cortex by one or more of three afferent pathways. Upon entering the spinal cord, dorsal root fibers may ascend as part of the lemniscal system, the spinothalamic tract or the spino-reticulothalamic system. Different somatic sensations are experienced, in part, due to the selective sensitivity of the skin receptors and also because the impulses generated by the stimulation of these receptors are channeled along the above pathways to various areas of the cortex.

Along with touch and temperature, pain has long been regarded as a distinct cutaneous sense. However, the extent to and ease with which pain can be altered by attentional and attitudinal variables sets it apart from the other two categories. This modifiability has prompted a substantial research effort directed at practical means of clinically attenuating pain and at clarifying the underlying mechanisms involved in its generation.

The morphology and physiological characteristics of pain receptors in the periphery are still only partially known. Free nerve endings in the skin and other tissues are most often associated with the sensation of pain. Their threshold for natural stimuli is high, but after the initial activation by a strong stimulus, they become sensitized and subsequently respond to a much less intensive stimulus.

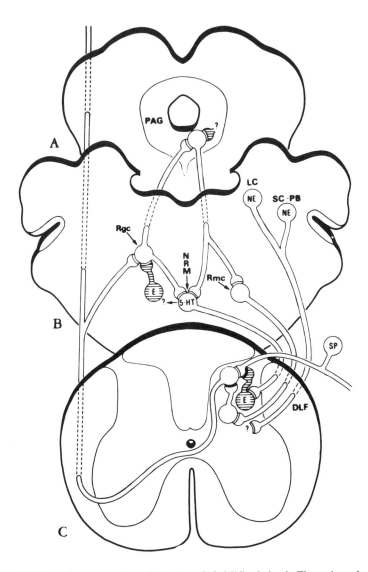

Figure 28.1 The endogenous pain control system. (A) Midbrain level. The periaqueductal gray (PAG), an important locus for stimulation-produced analgesia, is rich in enkephalins (E) and opiate receptor, though the anatomical details of the enkephalinergic connections are not known. Microinjection of small amounts of opiates into PAG also produces analgesia. (B) Medullary level. Serotonin (5TH)-containing cells of the nucleus raphe magnus (NRM) and the adjacent nucleus reticularis magnocellularis (Rmc) receive excitory input from PAG and, in turn, send efferent fibers to the spinal cord. (C) Spinal level. Efferent fibers from the NRM and Rmc travel in the dorsolateral funiculus (DLF) to terminate among pain-transmission cells concentrated in lamina I and V of the dorsal horn. The NRM and Rmc exert an inhibitory

The particular afferent pathways for pain belong to neurons with nerve cell bodies lying in the dorsal root ganglia and with axons that terminate in the dorsal horns (see Fig. 28.1). These dorsal horns of the spinal cord are formed by six layers of cells that differ not so much by their morphological appearance, as by their functional identity. This becomes meaningful when one considers that the correlation between the anatomical and functional distribution of those cells transmitting pain information is not very high, although a large proportion of them are located in the lamina externa.

In the spinal cord, the ascending tracts that carry the pain impulses are not all that well defined. Originally, it was believed that the spinothalamic tract was almost exclusively responsible for the transmission of this information. But alternative routes for pain transmission have also been discovered, including those within the spino-reticulothalamic pathway, the dorsal columns, the proprio-spinal system, and, in some animal species, the spino-cervical tract. Fibers in these tracts, upon reaching the brain stem, terminate mostly in the midbrain (periaqueductal gray), medulla and pons (medullary reticular nuclei and nucleus raphe magnus), and in the thalamus (intralaminar nuclei and the posterior nuclear complex).

An interesting feature of the whole system is a feedback loop that originates in the periaqueductal gray and reaches the medulla. From here, at least three pathways reach the spinal cord, all of which have been determined to have an inhibitory function. One originates from the dorsal nucleus reticularis gigantocellularis, another from the raphe nuclei, and the third from an area adjacent to the raphe nuclei (the juxta-raphe region in the ventromedial medulla). All are able to inhibit neurons in the dorsal horns. They are responsible for so-called "stimulus-produced analgesia". The feeling of pain in response to damage in the various organs is an important life-preserving mechanism, but the capacity to suppress awareness of the pain could contribute to subsequent survival by preventing incapacitation as a result of the intensive influx of nerve impulses during such a life-threatening situation. This function is primarily associated with the periaqueductal gray. Thus, Reynolds in 1969 found that electrical stimulation of this area,

---

effect specifically on pain-transmission neurons. The pain-transmission neurons, which are activated by substance P (SP) containing small-diameter primary afferents, project to supraspinal sites and indirectly via the nucleus reticularis gigantocellularis (gc), contact the cells of the descending analgesia system in the PAG and NRM, thus establishing a negative-feedback loop. Catecholamine-containing neurons of the locus coeruleus (LC) in rat and subcoeruleus-parabrachialis (SC-PB) in cat may also contribute to pain-modulating systems in the DLF. (NE,norepinephrine). [from A.I. Basbaum and H.L. Fields, *Ann. Neurol.* 4:451 (1978); © 1978 by A.I. Basbaum].

particularly of its ventromedial aspects, and of some periventricular thalamic sites reduced the behavioral responses to noxious stimuli in both the visceral and somatic areas. Stimulation of the nucleus raphe magnus has the same effect. Stimulus-produced analgesia appears to be functionally related to the analgesia caused by morphine, and a cross-tolerance may even develop between them. Stimulation of some other brain areas has a corresponding, though less pronounced effect. However, these areas - the lateral hypothalamus, medial forebrain bundle, caudate nucleus, septum, cerebellum and ventrobasal thalamic nucleus - have been less extensively studied.

The neurons in the periaqueductal gray may act as a "gate" which regulates the transmission of pain impulses to higher centers. But, it might be more appropriate to talk about a feedback mechanism rather than a blockage (Fields and Basbaum, 1978). The neurons in the periaqueductal gray influence those in the nucleus raphe magnus, which in turn inhibit the pain-transmitting neurons in the dorsal horns of the spinal cord. Transection of those fibers leading from the medulla to the dorsal horns that descend mainly in the dorsolateral funiculus of the spinal white matter (see Fig. 28.1) is able to block the analgesia produced by either morphine or the stimulation of the dorsal gray.

The principal antinociceptive action of the natural endogenous opioid peptides, the endorphins, and narcotic analgesics of the morphine type, depends upon the functional integrity of the raphe system. The raphe nuclei (dorsalis, medialis, and magnus) receive projections from the ventrolateral periaqueductal gray matter, which is the primary supraspinal site where morphine and the opioid peptides act to produce antinociception. The system appears to have a serotonergic component, since the depletion of serotonin from it antagonizes the analgesia. This effect of serotonin, however, is only facilitatory and cannot be regarded as the sole essential factor for the opioid effect.

Stimulation of the periaqueductal gray has been used as a technique for the treatment of intractable pain in cancer, the phantom-limb phenomenon, or in states following some types of brain damage. In human patients, this type of analgesia is often accompanied by nausea and dizziness. Acupuncture, a method of analgesia employed by the Chinese for more than 2000 years, also activates the periaqueductal gray. The development of analgesia after acupuncture is rather slow, requiring 20-30 minutes to develop. As in the analgesic effect elicited by direct stimulation of the periaqueductal gray, it triggers the release and activity of a group of related peptides having a morphine- or opioid-like pharmacologic action. Opioid-containing or enkephalinergic interneurons are also localized in the dorsal horns of the spinal cord, particularly in the substantia gelatinosa, and are probably involved in stimulus-inhibited pain.

PRECURSORS OF OPIOID PEPTIDES

Endogenous brain opioids are related to a group of peptides, originally isolated from the pituitary gland, which are able to mobilize lipids from fat deposits (Birk and Li, 1964). In 1936, Best and Campbell had already recognized such a substance, which was termed lipotropic hormone (LPH). Of the three known lipotropic hormones, which differ in their amino acid structure, the opioid peptides most resemble β-lipotropin. Li *et al.* in 1965 reported β-lipotropin to have 91 amino acid residues. Their sequence in certain sections of the molecule resembles the peptide hormones ACTH, growth hormone, and secretin. In fact, part of the β-LPH molecule (amino acids 41-58) is identical with the melanocyte-stimulating hormone (Fig. 28.2). These hormones are formed in the pituitary from a common precursor (Mains *et al.*, 1977), now termed pro-opiocortin or pro-opiomelanocortin (Rubinstein *et al.*, 1978). This molecule has a molecular weight of about 30,000 daltons (Nakanishi *et al.*, 1979).

One of the important questions that arises concerns just how the compo-

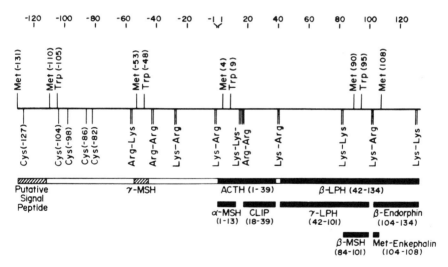

Figure 28.2 Schematic representation of the structure of bovine ACTH-β-LPH precursor. Characteristic amino acid residues are shown, and the positions of the methionine, tryptophan and cysteine residues are given in parentheses. The location of known component peptides are shown by closed bars; the amino acid numbers are given in parentheses. The location of MSH and the putative signal peptide are indicated by shaded bars [from S. Nakanishi, A. Inoue, T. Kita, M. Nakamura, A.C.Y. Chang, S.N. Cohen, S. Numa, *Nature* 278:423 (1979); © 1979 by Macmillan Co. Ltd.].

nent hormones and opioids are segmented from this parent protein. Childers (1980) has proposed that the points of cleavage on the precursor might be at certain pairs of basic amino acids which are especially vulnerable to various trypsin-like enzymes. These paired amino acids (i.e., Arg-Lys, Arg-Arg, Lys-Lys) appear to bracket the segments of the molecule that comprise the different hormones and opioids. Childers goes on to further suggest that the hydrolytic process could be controlled by post-translational modifications of the pro-opiocortin precursor, particularly glycosylation, which seems to protect it from non-specific hydrolysis (Loh and Gainer, 1978).

Orlowski and Wilk (1981) have recently reported the existence of an intriguing 700K protease complex in rabbit pituitary and brain which is able to generate the two major enkephalins (see below) from precursor sequences. In solution, the enzyme behaves as a single protein, but was discovered to have three distinct activities that are likely attributable to separate catalytic units on the complex:

(1) a chymotrypsin-like activity, splitting bonds between hydrophobic and small neutral amino acids,

(2) a trypsin-like activity toward bonds in which a carboxyl group is provided by an arginine residue, and

(3) an activity that hydrolyzes bonds on the carboxyl side of glutamyl residues.

The enkephalins that are formed are resistant to further degradation by this enzyme complex, which incidently is inhibited by low concentrations of sodium and potassium ions.

The β-lipotropin contained within the precursor is an important intermediary in the biosynthetic pathway of the endorphins and enkephalins. It is glycosylated, which again may protect it from premature intracellular degradation (Loh and Gainer, 1978a). While β-lipotropin has a very weak opioid action, it also exhibits melanocyte-stimulating and adrenocortical-stimulating activity.

Beta-lipotropin is distributed uniformly throughout all cells of the pars intermedia of the pituitary. It is also found in some hypothalamic neurons and in several other brain areas (Bugnon et al., 1981). In general, its presence in the brain has been found to parallel the distribution of endorphins (to be discussed below). While it has been identified in the circulating blood, lipotropin is also formed in the CNS rather than transported there, since its level in the brain is unaltered by hypophysectomy.

Beta-lipotropin itself has several biological functions. As mentioned previously, it mobilizes the lipids from fat depots. It also causes hyperglycemia through its insulinotropic and glucagonotropic effect. Moreover, it can stimulate the blood coagulation system and, in some tissues, activate adenylate cyclase.

ENDORPHINS

The 91 amino acids of β-lipotropin include sequences that comprise two biologically distinct segments (see Fig. 28.2). The amino-terminal (β-LPH$_{1-57}$) contains MSH, and the carboxyl terminal segment represents one of opioid peptides, β-endorphin (β-LPH$_{61-91}$). There are two other similar endorphins: the α form, having 16 amino acids (61-76), and the γ, with 17 amino acids (61-77). The cleavage of β-lipotropin is catalyzed by several rather specific enzymes that were mentioned previously, the endopeptidases. The enzymes convert β-lipotropin into the endorphins by a selective splitting of the peptide chain at certain defined points. The pituitary gland contains considerable amounts of these enzymes (Bradbury et al., 1976). The newly detached endorphins are stored in the cells either in their active form, or inactivated by acetylation. The inactivation renders them unable to bind to their receptors and without analgesic properties (Smyth et al., 1979).

The main degradation product of β-lipotropin and the one with the highest analgesic activity is the C-terminal segment of 31 amino acids, β-LPH$_{61-91}$ or β-endorphin. Within it are contained the sequences for α- and γ-endorphins, which by themselves have only a weak, transient opioid action. This short duration is attributable to a rapid degradation of endorphins by inactivating enzymes (see below), which may be non-specific aminopeptidases or a more specific type of dipeptidase (Malfroy et al., 1978).

Endorphins are distributed in many areas of the brain, but the localization of the individual species, β-endorphin, Met-enkephalin and Leu-enkephalin, differs. Some neurons contain more than one peptide. Bugnon et al. (1979), for example, found neurons in the arcuate nucleus of the hypothalamus that contained β-lipotropin, α- and β-endorphin, and even ACTH and α- and β-MSH. On the surface, this would not be entirely unexpected, considering the nature of the precursor, and suggests the interesting possibility that these peptides act in concert within certain areas to modulate neuronal functioning. Generally, however, the anatomical distribution of β-endorphin is much more restricted than that for β-LTH (Bloom et al., 1978; Watson et al., 1978), and it is likely that the opioid peptides comprise separate systems with their own physiological effects.

The nerve endings and fibers containing and/or reacting to the opioid peptides are also widely dispersed throughout the CNS. Applications of β-endorphin will cause an inhibition of most neurons in the brain, with at least 65% of tested cortical neurons being slowed (Palmer et al., 1978). On the other hand, spinal cord Renshaw cells and hippocampal pyramidal cells are excited by it. This action is caused by the binding of endorphin to brain opiate receptors. In some experiments, this binding has been reversed by a morphine antagonist, naloxone, indicating that β-endorphin is able to act as a morphine agonist.

It appears that more than one type of opiate receptor exists in the brain. Differences in opiate and opioid binding have been reported (Lord *et al.*, 1977; Chang and Cuatrecasas, 1979) that suggest this to be the case. The existance of two receptors, designated μ and δ, has been substantiated by a number of biochemical and pharmacological approaches. There is still some uncertainty, however, as to the nature of the endogenous ligand for each. The term μ refers to a low affinity site that preferentially interacts with morphine-like opiates. The high affinity site, δ, displays a preference for peptide structures. Fournie-Zaluski *et al.* (1981) have shown that the μ type tends to interact more strongly with hydrophilic compounds having compact structures. This is in contrast to the δ receptors, which bind larger peptides that can be more hydrophilic. But, Goodman *et al.* (1980) have suggested that the endogenous ligand for the μ receptor is Met-enkephalin. Leu-enkephalin would serve as the δ ligand. β-endorphin appears to react equally well with both receptors.

While both μ and δ receptors co-exist on the same (peripheral) neuron (Egan and North, 1981), Goodman *et al.* (1980) observed anatomical differences in their distribution. The μ type tended to predominate in thalamus, hypothalamus, corpus striatum, and in the hippocampal pyramidal cell layer, while the pontine nuclei, nucleus accumbens and amygdala contained relatively high levels of the δ form. Both receptors are distributed throughout the cerebral cortex, but their appearance there seems to conform to a general pattern. In the frontal cortex, where the sharpest distinctions are found, the μ receptors are more concentrated in layers I and IV, while the δ type is more focused in layers II, III, and V. Layer VI contains comparable concentrations of each.

Larger numbers of μ receptors are located in areas associated with the sensation of pain or stimulus-produced analgesia (such as the substantia gelatinosa, periaqueductal gray, median raphe, dorsomedial thalamus and cortical layer IV). This observation and the finding that μ-selective drugs are stronger analgesics than δ-selective drugs (Herz *et al.*, 1978) suggested to Chang and Cuatrecasas (1981) that the μ receptors may be involved in the mediation of opiate-induced analgesia. In contrast, many areas with higher numbers of δ receptors are limbic structures concerned with emotionality and reward behavior. It is conceivable, then, that these receptors function in the euphoric and affective components of opiate action.

Other receptors have been reported, but the evidence for them is much less compelling. A number of pharmacological studies have disclosed the presence of binding sites that may represent distinct κ and σ opioid receptors

(Kosterlitz and Paterson, 1980; Zukin and Zukin, 1981a; for review see Zukin and Zukin, 1981).

Endorphin-binding receptors are localized both in the presynaptic and postsynaptic membranes. Beta-endorphin attachment at the presynaptic sites is able to suppress the release of at least some neurotransmitters (Loh et al., 1976; Arbilla and Langer, 1978). There is also a substantial amount of evidence that endorphins can interfere with postsynaptic neurotransmitter actions. It is not clear at the moment which of these effects is functionally more important.

The opioid receptors have been successfully extracted from the brain and purified (Simon et al., 1975; Bidlack et al., 1981). They are lipoproteins that are closely bound to phospholipids. The receptor itself had been considered to be lipid-like or lipid-associated (Dunlap et al., 1979). One of its important components may be cerebroside sulfate, since cerebroside sulfatase, an enzyme cleaving cerebroside sulfate, interferes with the binding of opioids to synaptic membranes (Law et al., 1979), and antibodies to this glycolipid inhibit the effects of β-endorphin (Craves et al., 1980). Cerebroside sulfate itself has an affinity for opioids that correlates with the analgesic potencies of tested drugs (Loh et al., 1974). But, McLawhon et al. (1981) have reported evidence that the opioid receptors are not identical with this lipid. It may just be that negatively charged lipids, and not cerebroside sulfate in particular, are involved in opioid binding, since gangliosides and phosphatidylserine also have an affinity for the opiates (Abood et al., 1980).

The regional opioid receptor localization within the brain varies among animal species. In monkeys and humans, the highest concentrations of receptors are found in the limbic structures, while in other mammalian species, they are primarily within the striatum. In most animals, the concentration within the cerebral cortex tends to be low, and the receptors appear to be absent from white matter. Their number is very low in the cerebellum, but high in amygdala, hypothalamus, thalamus, and parts of lateral midbrain, including the lateral ventricular nucleus, substantia nigra and red nucleus. The presence of opioid receptors tends to overlap with that of the opioid peptides, although their concentration does not often correspond that well. Thus, in most species, the most effective site of injection is the periaqueductal and periventricular gray.

The binding of morphine and morphine agonists to the receptor depends upon the presence of sodium ions. In vitro, these ions cause a dose-dependent decrease in the agonist binding and an increase in the binding of antagonists. The effect is specific for sodium, which probably acts as an allosteric effector which changes the configuration of the opioid receptor and, therefore, its affinity for agonists or antagonists (Simon et al., 1975).

The reaction of the opioid peptides with the receptor triggers a series of actions within the cells, which may involve the presence of cyclic nucleotides. Beta-endorphin typically inhibits adenylate cyclase (Klee and Nirenberg, 1976; Goldstein *et al.*, 1977), although some other peptides are known to stimulate it. It also blocks the phosphorylation of specific membrane proteins, for example, within the rat neostriatum (Ehrlich *et al.*, 1980), but can stimulate the calcium-dependent phosphorylation of other membrane proteins. Methionine-enkephalin has been reported to activate adenylate cyclase in the rat brain stem, while inhibiting it within the cortex (Wollemann *et al.*, 1979). It has also been noted to enhance the phosphorylation of a 50K protein in synaptic membranes from the rat hippocampus (Baer *et al.*, 1980). Evidently, then, the relationships between the systems of second messengers and the opioids do not readily lend themselves to a general interpretation. O'Callaghan *et al.* (1982) feel that at least some of these effects may be linked to differences in the calcium/calmodulin requirements of the pertinent protein kinases.

Chronic treatment with opiates or opioid peptides induces the development of tolerance, but there is no evidence that increased tolerance to opioids causes either a quantitative or a qualitative change in the receptors. Lahti and Collins (1978), however, found that the administration of the morphine antagonist naloxone increased the number of opioid receptors and resulted in a supersensitivity to the analgesic action of morphine.

Repeated injections of β-endorphin can cause both the development of a morphine-like tolerance to subsequent doses of the opioid and the appearance of a cross-tolerance to morphine. But, the pain-reducing systems in the brain are protected against the development of such tolerance to their own opioid peptides. This seems to be due to the presence in the brain of substances which antagonize this development (Jacquet *et al.*, 1977). Rothman and Westfall (1979) subsequently demonstrated the existance of such an inhibitor in the high speed supernatant of brain homogenates.

The main consequence of the administration of β-endorphin is the development of deep analgesia, involving a marked catatonic state that lasts for hours. The most powerful effect has been observed after its injection into the periaqueductal gray. On the other hand, the stimulation of the periaqueductal gray by electrical impulses increases the release of β-endorphin from this area into the cerebrospinal fluid.

Figure 28.3 Met-enkephalin.   TYR–GLY–GLY–PHE–MET

ENKEPHALINS

The enkephalins, the smallest opioid peptides in the brain, contain five amino acids (β-LPH$_{61-65}$). The sequence of methionine-enkephalin (Fig. 28.3) is contained within the amino acids of β-endorphin, whereas leucine-enkephalin (Fig. 28.4) is part of the sequence of another opioid peptide, dynorphin (Goldstein *et al.*, 1979). However, it does not appear that the enkephalins are generated from these peptides (for review see Rossier, 1981). Lewis *et al.* (1980) found a 50,000 dalton protein in the adrenal medulla which contains, within its sequence, several copies of Met-enkephalin and one copy of Leu-enkephalin. This molecule is apparently the actual precursor of both enkephalins. Their biosynthesis from this protein is probably gradual, since at least two polypeptides have been isolated from the adrenal medulla which contain within them smaller numbers of the enkephalins (Stern *et al.*, 1981).

The primary structure of the Met- and Leu- enkephalin precursor and its mRNA has been established from cDNA by Comb *et al.* (1982) and Guble *et al.* (1982). It has 267 amino acids and is composed of 6 interspersed Met-enkephalin sequences and one sequence of Leu-enkephalin. It does not contain segments for dynorphin or endorphins.

Fibers and neurons containing Met-enkephalin and Leu-enkephalin are present in many brain areas, including the limbic system, hypothalamus, median eminence, thalamus, subthalamus, globus pallidus, caudate nucleus, and substantia nigra. In the hippocampus, enkephalins have been reported in short interneuronal axons (Hong and Schmid, 1981), and a functional strio-pallidal enkephalin-containing pathway has been described by Bayon *et al.* (1981). Additional circuits include a projection to the spinal cord from the parolivary cells of the medulla (Bloom and McGinty, 1981) and an innervation of the bed nucleus of the stria terminalis from cell bodies in the central amygdaloid nucleus. Immunologically detected "enkephalinergic" fibers are additionally present in the midbrain nucleus interpeduncularis, central gray, reticular formation, and within the hindbrain in the locus coeruleus, raphe and cochlear nuclei and the motor nuclei of several cranial nerves. These opioids also coexist with oxytocin and vasopressin in nerve terminals of the

Figure 28.4 Leu-enkephalin.   TYR-GLY-GLY-PHE-LEU

posterior pituitary (Martin and Voigt, 1981). Enkephalin-containing interneurons and fibers have been further identified in the spinal cord (Jessell and Iverson, 1977), striato-nigral pathway (Cuello *et al.*, 1981), and peripheral nerves. In all of these areas, the enkephalins are sparsely distributed in neurons, nerve fibers, and terminals (Sar *et al.*, 1978).

A stimulation of the sciatic nerve, which excites Aα, Aδ and C fibers, causes an increase in the release of Met-enkephalin from cerebroventricular and spinal perfusates. The results hint at the existence of an intrinsic opioid system which can be activated by somatic stimulation (Yaksh and Elde, 1981).

DYNORPHIN

The opioid peptide dynorphin contains seventeen amino acids and has been identified in the posterior lobe of the pituitary, as well as in several other parts of the brain, where its regional distribution is distinct from any of the other opioid peptides. Immunoreactive dynorphin is also present in the ventral and dorsal aspects of the spinal cord and in dorsal root ganglia (Botticelli *et al.*, 1981). The dynorphin amino acid sequence has already been established (Goldstein *et al.*, 1981), and its physiological actions are associated with the first thirteen residues (Fig. 28.5). It binds to its own receptor, which may be identical to the κ opioid receptor (Chavkin *et al.*, 1982). The presence of arginine in the seventh position and lysine in the eleventh and thirteenth positions seem to be important for its attachment (Chavkin and Goldstein, 1981).

An additional opioid peptide has been recently reported. Named kyotorphin, it is a dipeptide (Tyr-Arg) whose analgesic properties have been determined to be about four-fold greater than those of Met-enkephalin (Shiomi *et al.*, 1981). It is reported to be present exclusively in synaptosomes (Ueda *et al.*, 1982), but does not appear to bind to specific opiate receptors (Manvalan and Momany, 1982). The analgesic properties of kyotorphin likely derive from its ability to trigger the release of endorphins. A heptapeptide, Met-enkephalin-Arg^6-Phe^7, is also found in the brain. It acts as an opioid agonist, but is probably a precursor of Met-enkephalin (Rossier *et al.*, 1980).

TYR-GLY-GLY-PHE-LEU-ARG-ARG-ILE-ARG-PRO-LYS-LEU-LYS

Figure 28.5 First 13 amino acids of dynorphin.

CELLULAR EFFECTS OF OPIOID PEPTIDES

Met-enkephalin and Leu-enkephalin are able to bind to the brain opiate receptors to cause a short-lived analgesic action. As with the endorphins, their effect is greatest when injected into the periaqueductal gray (Malick and Goldstein, 1977). Some authors, however, have disputed the claim that Met-enkephalin has analgesic properties, and Leybin et al. (1976) even contend that its intraventricular injection lowered the pain threshold. According to them, Met-enkephalin is also able to induce behavior that is typical of opiate withdrawal.

Much of the disagreement over the effects of the naturally-occurring enkephalins may be due to their rapid degradation in the brain (Hambrook et al., 1976; Wei et al., 1977). Longer-lived analogs, such as FK-33-824 (Tyr-D-Ala^2-Gly-MePhe-Met(0)-ol, Sandoz) and Ly 127623 (D-Ala^2-N(Me)Met^5-enkephalin, Lilly), are more resistant to proteolytic destruction and much more effective than either the Met or Leu forms in inducing analgesia (Roemer et al., 1977; Frederickson et al., 1980).

Met-enkephalin also has epileptogenic properties when introduced into the periaqueductal gray (Urca et al., 1977). Such an effect is consistent with the finding that the quantities of both enkephalins are elevated in the rat brain following sessions of amygdaloid kindling (Vindrola et al., 1981). The results indicate that there may be a direct involvement of these opioids in the seizure process. In addition, intraventricular injections in the cat have been reported to induce hyperthermia. However, the involvement of these peptides in temperature regulation would appear to be rather complex, with some dosages even causing hypothermia (Clark and Ponder, 1980).

Their widespread distribution suggests that enkephalins are not only endogenous analgesic agents, but that they may also have some other functions within the central nervous system. Since 85% of these enkephalins have been detected in the synaptosomal fraction of the brain homogenate, it is possible that they not only modulate the effects of "classical" neurotransmitters, but that they themselves act as neurotransmitters. Their rate of release from tissue slices of the striatum, for example, increases 7-10 fold in response to a depolarization by potassium ions, a finding which would be consistent with a neurotransmitter action.

There is evidence that an opioid binding to its receptor is associated with a change in the activity of adenylate cyclase. Collier and Roy (1974) noted that morphine suppressed the stimulation of this enzyme by prostaglandin E_1 in rat brain homogenates. Moreover, morphine abstinence resulted in an increase in levels of cAMP in the brain (Collier and Francis, 1975). Enkephalins have corresponding inhibitory effects upon adenylate cyclase activity in a hybrid cell line (Klee and Nirenberg, 1976), but are much more potent than morphine.

Iontophoresis of Met-enkephalin toward the cells in the dorsal horns of spinal cord depresses about one third of all units. A few are excited, while the rest are unaffected. The change begins slowly, after about 20 seconds, and reaches a maximum at 30-60 seconds. Naloxone antagonizes this effect. The change does not influence the membrane potential or membrane resistance of these cells (Zieglgansberger and Fry, 1976), but the membrane depolarization induced transynaptically or by glutamate is blocked.

While the actions of opioid peptides are mostly associated with an inhibition of single unit discharges (for review see Zieglgansberger and Fry, 1978), there are some exceptions. A naloxone-reversible excitatory response in hippocampal pyramidal cells has been observed (Hill et al., 1977), which involves an increase in the duration and size of the EPSP (Dingledine, 1981). However, this effect may be indirect and actually result from an inhibition of the neighboring inhibitory interneurons (Zieglgansberger et al., 1979).

Inasmuch as enkephalins change the quantal content of the excitatory postsynaptic potential and naloxone is able to reverse this action, it is possible that their action is also indirect and presynaptic, affecting transmitter release rather than postsynaptic responsiveness. In this way, acting as neuromodulators, opioid peptides would interfere with the excitatory and inhibitory putative neurotransmitters. Some effects may also be postsynaptic, mediated by postsynaptic opioid receptors.

The individual opioid peptides, β-endorphin and the enkephalins, are not identical in their actions and localization. Methionine-enkephalin, for instance, does not appear to be present in the hypothalamus. Watson et al. (1980) proposed that in the brain there are two separate opioid peptide systems. One is an enkephalin system, while the other is a β-endorphin system. If this is so, although their precise functions are presently unclear, both may contribute in a different manner to the organization of behavior.

The nature of the opioid effect and the affinity of these molecules for their receptors indicates that an efficient mechanism should be present in the synapses to inactivate the opioid signal. These peptides are capable of being degraded by several enzymes belonging to the aminopeptidase and endopeptidase groups. A spontaneous, non-enzymatic degradation also appears possible which involves a conversion of the tyrosine residue to an indole derivative (Vogel et al., 1978). Malfroy et al. (1978) have identified a carboxypeptidase in mouse brain particulate fractions which cleaves the enkephalin molecule at the Gly_3-Phe_4 bond. This enzyme, enkephalin-dipeptidyl-carboxypeptidase (or enkephalinase) has a regional specificity that parallels that of the enkephalins (Malfroy et al., 1979) and appears to be localized in neuronal membranes (De La Baume et al., 1981). These findings suggest that it serves as the normal means of enkephalin inactivation, unlike the various other enzymes (Lane *et al.*, 1977; Gorenstein and Snyder, 1979; Malfroy *et al.*, 1979; Schwartz *et al.*, 1981), which are also able to cleave the opioid but lack its particular regional and subcellular specificities.

POSSIBLE FUNCTIONS OF OPIOID PEPTIDES

As discussed previously, enkephalin and endorphin analogs, if injected in large doses, have an analgesic effect, for which an acute or long-lasting tolerance may develop. It is possible that the tolerance is caused by a compensatory increase in adenylate cyclase activity in the neurons. New molecules of the enzyme may also be generated (Sharma *et al.*, 1977). The development may be accompanied by the production of another type of peptide reported to be able to induce tolerance in a non-tolerant animal. First reported by Ungar in 1965, it was not isolated and characterized by him until 1977. This peptide was identified as a hexapeptide, Arg-Tyr-Gly-Gly-Phe-Met, and was observed to antagonize opiate activity, reducing its effect in mice.

When evaluating the effects of opioid peptides upon analgesia and behavior, one should bear in mind that some of their effects may be indirect and mediated by other brain peptides, including those related to the pituitary hormones. β-endorphin, for instance, is also present in the anterior pituitary and is secreted in response to acute stress or following adrenalectomy. This may be related to stress-induced analgesia, which is further associated with the elevation of corticosteroids (Mousa *et al.*, 1981). A synthetic glucocorticoid, dexamethasone, inhibits the secretion of both ACTH and β-endorphin (Guillemin *et al.*, 1977). Since the co-existence of ACTH and the opioids is likely regulated by related synthetic and secretory control mechanisms, acute stress, then, causes an increase in the release of the opioid peptides, with a subsequent decrease in their concentrations in the hypothalamus and pituitary. Thus, it is possible that endorphins are involved not only in pain, but also in other types of stress-related behavioral change.

The relationship of ACTH to the opioid peptides has one more important aspect. An injection of ACTH or its fragments into the periaqueductal gray induces, even in non-tolerant experimental animals, a complex of behavioral symptoms, including fearful reactivity and explosive motor behavior, that is otherwise characteristic for the opiate abstinence syndrome. The *N*-terminal ACTH fragments have been found to antagonize the opioid binding to specific receptor sites. Endorphin injected into the same area has an opposite effect, causing sedation, analgesia or even catatonia. ACTH and endorphin may, therefore, be a part of an integrated system which modulates emotionally-induced behavior. The system would be subject to modification by narcotic analgesics, and the opioid abstinence syndrome may be an expression of an imbalance of two antagonistic actions within this system, one dependent upon ACTH and the other upon the opioid peptides (Jacquet et al., 1978).

Descriptions of the subjective feelings of human volunteers following endorphin injections have shown that the effect is not true analgesia, but a reduction of the affective component of pain perception. The pain simply does not bother the individual any more. The complex of data, including the relationship of the endorphins to stress and the type of subjective response to their injection, together with the further behavioral effects of the endorphins, indicates that an interpretation of opioid peptides simply as "endogenous brain analgesics" is too confined and ultimately misleading.

The influence of the endorphins upon the release of other pituitary hormones was briefly touched upon previously. The secretion of growth hormone, ACTH, prolactin, oxytocin and vasopressin is stimulated, while the release of LH, FSH and TSH is inhibited. The opioids also participate in the regulation of LHRH and somatostatin secretion (Drouva et al., 1980). It is apparently β-endorphin and dynorphin which are able to regulate LH secretion in the arcuate nucleus of the mediobasal hypothalamus (Schulz et al., 1981). These peptides may even be involved in events leading to puberty and sexual maturation (Blank et al., 1979). The effect upon oxytocin and vasopressin appears to be attributable to an opioid disinhibition of a dopaminergic mechanism controlling the secretion of the neurohypophyseal hormones (Vizi and Volbekas, 1980).

There is an interaction of the opioid peptides with catecholaminergic systems, so that for the full expression of enkephalin-induced activity, intact catecholaminergic transmission is necessary. Furthermore, the locus coeruleus is one site of action of β-endorphin, which has been shown to inhibit many of the neurons there (Strahlendorf et al., 1980; Watson et al., 1980). It has also been observed that opioids increase the excitability of neural elements within the medial forebrain bundle and, by doing so, lower the positive reinforcement thresholds for electrical stimulation (or self-stimulation) within that structure. No development of tolerance has been demonstrated to this facilitation. The effect upon self-stimulation implies that opioids can increase the sensitivity of neuronal pathways subserving the brain reward system that participates in the learning process (Esposito and Kornetsky, 1978). Consequently, the opioid peptides may also be involved in the acquisition and recall of learned responses.

The amygdaloid nuclei, which participate in memory formation, particularly for aversive experiences, are rich in both opioid peptides and opioid receptors. When levorphanol, an opiate agonist, is injected into the rat amygdala following passive avoidance conditioning, a dose-and time-dependent decrease in retention is produced which can be antagonized by naloxone (Gallagher and Kapp, 1978). Also, the subcutaneous administration of β-endorphin delays the extinction of a pole-jumping avoidance behavior in rats (Koob et al., 1981). The immediate post-learning injection of Met-enkephalin facilitates the long-term retention of passive avoidance. On the other hand, β-LPH and the enkephalins attenuate carbon dioxide-induced amnesia for passive avoidance. In this situation, the enkephalins have to be administered prior to the memory retrieval test.

Izquierdo et al. (1980, 1981) have proposed that β-endorphin can act as a physiological amnestic agent, since its injection immediately after training causes retrograde amnesia for the learned task. Leu-enkephalin and Met-enkephalin have a similar effect. This, however, may be an undue generalization. Pharmacological studies have shown that the dose-response curve has an inverted U-shape, since very high and very low doses are ineffective (Kastin et al., 1980). Also, only some learned behaviors are influenced, e.g. avoidance responses, but not escape swimming (Rigter et al., 1980), which may perhaps explain some of the contradictory results.

Since the opioid receptors are also present in the caudate nucleus, it is possible that endorphins and enkephalins are additionally involved in the control of the extrapyramidal system. This system of neurons possesses pre- and postsynaptic opioid receptors and modulates nigro-striatal function (Diamond and Borison, 1978) by suppressing dopamine release from the striatum. At the same time, the opioid peptides induce immobility, loss of the righting response, and a generalized muscular rigidity.

Endorphins have also been implicated in the control of feeding behavior. In rats, food intake can be increased by β-endorphin and decreased by naloxone (Baile et al., 1981). Dynorphin is also able to induce feeding in satiated rats (Morley and Levine, 1981). There is a clear dose-dependent effect here that peaks at 200 ng/rat (McKay et al., 1981).

The endorphin system appears to have some effect upon social relationships, since during acute social isolation, infants of several species produce a distress call that is prevented by opiates. The brain opioid system may therefore reduce a negative affective state arising from social isolation, something which has been reported for domestic chicks and guinea pigs. Panksepp et al. (1978) speculate from these data that social bonds are sustained by opiate-sensitive systems.

SUBSTANCE P

Endorphins and enkephalins are not the only brain peptides associated with pain and analgesia. Substance P (Fig. 28.6), a peptide with eleven amino acids (undecapeptide), also likely acts as either a neurotransmitter or a neuromodulator associated with the pain pathways (Stern et al., 1974; Hokfelt et al., 1975). It was first detected in 1931 by Von Euler and Gaddum in alcoholic extracts of brain and intestine. For many years, it remained an enigmatic substance. It was only in 1968 that Lembeck and Starke discovered that sialogen, a substance extracted from the brain which stimulated salivary secretion, was identical to substance P.

Functionally, this substance belongs to a group of tachykinins, peptides characterized by their potent action upon vascular and extravascular smooth muscles and upon the exocrine glands. It is also produced by endocrine cells of the gut, and its secretion into the blood takes place in episodic secretory bursts, primarily at night. Until recently, substance P was regarded as the only tachykinin in the vertebrate CNS. But, physalaemin, a peptide originally extracted from amphibians, may addtionally be present.

In the brain, neurons containing substance P are located in the medial and central nuclei of the amygdala and in the short projections between these two nuclei. The highest levels are found in the substantia nigra. It is present, selectively, in nerve endings and nerve fibers, particularly in the striato-nigral, pallido-nigral, and habenulo-interpeduncular pathways. It has also been identified in hypothalamus, thalamus, spinal cord, and in the spinal root ganglia and sensory afferent fibers (for review see Leeman and Gamse, 1981). Most of the neocortex and cerebellar cortex have no substance P-positive elements (Mayer et al., 1980).

Substance P has a strong, slow, prolonged excitatory action upon spinal neurons (Henry et al., 1975; Konishi and Otsuka, 1974), depolarizing about 50% of all neurons in the lumbar spinal cord. Its application to the amygdala (Le Gal LaSalle and Ben-Ari, 1977), substantia nigra (Davies and Dray, 1976) and cerebral cortex (Phillis, 1977) also caused excitation, although some evidence of depression was recorded from the latter two areas. It is released from nerve endings upon depolarization, but is probably not taken up back into the nerve terminals and glial cells after its action is completed.

Substance P is specifically bound to synaptic membranes throughout the brain (Nakata, 1980), on protein receptors that may be associated with lipids, particularly phosphatidylserine. It has also been observed to bind to synaptic vesicle membranes (Mayer et al., 1980a), but this is considered to be related more to substance P storage than an attachment to a receptor

ARG–PRO–LYS–PRO–GLN–GLY–PHE–PHE–GLY–LEU–MET–NH$_2$ **Figure 28.6** Substance P.

Figure 28.7 Schematic representation of a possible mechanism for opiate-induced suppression of Substance P (SP) release. SP is shown localized within the terminal of a small diameter afferent fibre which forms an excitatory axodendritic synapse with the process of a spinal cord neurons originating in lamina IV or V and projecting rostrally. A local enkephalin-containing inhibitory interneuron (ENK), confined to laminae II and III, forms a presynaptic contact on the terminal of the primary afferent. Opiate receptor sites are depicted presynaptically on the primary efferent terminal. Numbers on the right refer to the laminae of Rexed [from T.M. Jessell and L.L. Iversen, *Nature* 268:549 (1977); © 1977 by Macmillan Journals Ltd.].

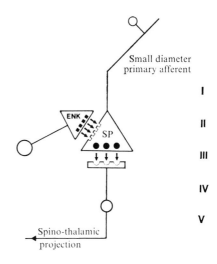

recognition site (Mayer *et al.*, 1979). In 1976, Henry discovered that substance P excited only those units in the spinal cord which were similarly affected by noxious radiant heat applied to the skin. The findings implied that this peptide was a component of the system transmitting nociceptive information. Its action in the spinal cord lowers the pain threshold. Jessell and Iverson (1977) have suggested that its activity is controlled by presynaptic opioid receptors which reduce the amount of liberated substance P (see Fig. 28.7). The net effect is a retardation in the transmission of nociceptive stimulation. The mechanism appears to involve a reduction of the calcium influx into the nerve endings containing substance P (Mudge *et al.*, 1979). Following intensive pain stimulation, substance P may be depleted and this serves to increase the pain thresholds, at least to some noxious stimuli (Yaksh *et al.*, 1979).

An analgesic effect of substance P injected into the periaqueductal gray has also been reported. It lasts at least 30-60 minutes, and on a molar basis, substance P is 25 times more potent than morphine. This effect may possibly be artifactual and appear when doses of substance P elevate concentrations beyond physiological levels (Oehme *et al.*, 1980). In contrast, Frederickson *et al.* (1978) noted that only small quantities produced analgesia in mice. Larger doses did not. His interpretation was that the small doses of substance P likely triggered the release of opioids, while larger amounts directly excited neurons within pathways associated with the perception of pain. Such a relationship between substance P and Met-enkephalin has been demonstrated by Naranjo *et al.* (1982).

The peptide also has several other effects upon CNS functions. It facilitates transmission in the monosynaptic spinal arc (Krivoy *et al.*, 1980), indicating that it is involved in the control of motor functions within the spinal cord (Piercey *et al.*, 1981). In addition, substance P decreases body temperature and lowers the blood pressure (Uyeno *et al.*, 1979). It has also been found to suppress aggressive responses in rats and mice and can elicit drinking behavior when injected into those areas sensitive to the influence of angiotensin. Furthermore, substance P is able to stimulate the release of antidiuretic hormone, suggesting that it may also play some role in water balance (Gullner *et al.*, 1979).

It is possible that the typical influence of substance P upon neurons is indirect, modulating the actions of other neurotransmitters. Renshaw cells in the spinal cord are normally excited by acetylcholine, but substance P selectively blocks this action by affecting the cholinergic nicotinic receptors (Ryall and Belcher, 1977). It enhances cholinergic receptor desensitization, but this depends on the simultaneous action of a cholinergic agonist (Stallcup and Patrick, 1980).

The principal effect of substance P upon the substantia nigra is activation, followed by an increase in spontaneous activity. In larger doses, rotatory behavior appears in a direction contralateral to the side of injection. This effect has been found to be mediated by dopaminergic fibers. In contrast, another consequence of the administration of substance P into the substantia nigra, grooming, probably does not depend upon dopamine.

The effect upon learning is interesting. An injection of substance P into the lateral hypothalamus enhances the retention of a step-down passive avoidance task. Similarly, an introduction into the medial septal nucleus facilitates passive avoidance learning (Huston and Staubli, 1981). On the other hand, its injection into the substantia nigra or amygdala causes retrograde amnesia for passive avoidance. In this way, it mimics the effect of electrical stimulation of the substantia nigra or amygdala, which is also able to block passive avoidance performance (Huston and Staubli, 1978; Staubli and Huston, 1979).

BRADYKININ

Bradykinin is a peptide originally isolated from several peripheral tissues that has recently been detected in the brain and implicated in pain receptor action. It has nine amino acids and, as a result, is often called kinin-9. Graeff (1971) believes it to be a neurotransmitter that is endogenous to the brain. This view is buttressed by the presence in the brain of a bradykinin-synthesizing enzyme, kallikin, as well as by the presence of the bradykinin-inactivating enzymes, prolylendopeptidase, cation-sensitive neutral endopeptidase and other similar peptidases. This endogenous production appears to be the source of most of the detectable brain bradykinin, since only small amounts of it may penetrate the brain from the blood plasma.

Injected into the brain tissue or cerebral ventricles, bradykinin has several physiological and neurochemical effects. It decreases the levels of norepinephrine and dopamine and elevates serotonin and 5-hydroxyindoleacetic acid (Moniuszko-Jakoniuk and Wisniewski, 1976). The largest changes have been detected in the corpus striatum and hypothalamus.

Bradykinin causes the excitation of most neurons in the cerebral cortex, although a few are depressed. Spinal neurons are also depolarized, but this effect may be attributable more to the activation of interneurons than to any direct effect of the peptide. All of these excitatory changes could possibly be indirect and dependent upon the modulation of central cholinergic and adrenergic synapses. Also, bradykinin is a potent hypotensive agent when injected systematically. Its intraventricular injection, on the other hand, induces hypertension. The site of this action seems to be the lateral septal area, where it influences the α-adrenergic systems.

Chapter 29

Some Other Notable Brain Peptides

In addition to those peptides previously discussed, a number of others have been isolated from the central nervous system and found to have a distinct effect upon behavior or upon the regulation of metabolic and vegetative functions. While the list of identified CNS peptides has been rapidly growing, there is an accompanying uncertainty about their functional importance within the brain. Some appear to have a very specialized action in the brain, in addition to a general endocrine-like effect beyond the confines of the CNS.

CALCITONIN

Calcitonin, a 32-amino-acid peptide produced in mammals by the thyroid gland, was considered to be exclusively a hormone that controlled plasma calcium. In reducing the blood concentration of calcium ions, it has effects opposite to those of parathormone, the parathyroid hormone. Perfusion of the thyroid gland with blood containing a slightly elevated concentration of calcium causes a rapid increase in calcitonin secretion. It is synthesized from a large precursor molecule, wherein its sequence is flanked on either side by peptide extensions (Jacobs *et al.*, 1981). The findings have since been confirmed using cDNA (Amara *et al.*, 1982).

Calcitonin has been detected in the cells of the pituitary intermediate lobe and in the CNS (Becker *et al.*, 1979). Calcitonin binding sites are present in the brain, particularly within the hypothalamus and brain stem. The binding is very firm, and following the attachment of labeled calcitonin, even six hours of incubation with unlabeled hormone failed to displace it (Fischer *et al.*, 1981). The lowest binding is in the cerebral cortex and cerebellum (Rizzo and Goltzman, 1981). Its function in the brain is not known, although labeled calcitonin is apparently able to inhibit, rather than stimulate, the basal activity of adenylate cyclase. Cortical evoked potentials to painful stimuli are inhibited by its presence (Yamamoto *et al.*, 1981). And, an intracerebroventricular injection of calcitonin causes analgesia in conscious rabbits, which reaches a maximum about 90 minutes after the administration. The effect is not reversible by naloxone, and no cross-tolerance with morphine develops. Thus, centrally induced calcitonin analgesia is opiate-independent (Pecile *et al.*, 1975; Braga *et al.*, 1978). Calcitonin has also been found to inhibit prolactin (Olgiati *et al.*, 1981) and gastric secretions (Morley *et al.*, 1981) following intracerebroventricular injections.

SLEEP-RELATED PEPTIDES

Interest in the study of humoral changes during sleep has a fairly extended history. A review by Kleitman in 1939 lists some sixteen proposed "hypnotoxins". Recent emphasis on the role of biogenic amines in the regulation of sleep, in addition to the emergence of sophisticated biochemical techniques and experimental procedures involving cross-circulation, have revived and maintained an interest in these humoral theories. Sleep is associated with an increase in brain protein synthesis, as well as with an elevation in the secretion of anabolic hormones, such as growth hormone. In addition, the secretory pattern of trophic hormones, such as prolactin and TSH, is circadian in nature and dependent upon the sleep/wake cycle. These hormones may, moreover, contribute to some of the observed behavioral and biochemical changes that accompany sleep.

The brain produces at least one, and possibly more, sleep-dependent peptides. Kornmueller *et al.* provided the first demonstration of the existance of such a peptide in 1961. This substance, delta sleep-inducing peptide (DSIP), is a nonapeptide obtained by dialysis from the blood of animals in which sleep was induced by electrical stimulation of the thalamus. Its amino acid composition was determined by Monnier *et al.* (1977) to be Trp-Ala-Gly-Gly-Asp-Ala-Ser-Gly-Glu. Radioimmunoassays of DSIP have shown that it is present mainly in thalamus, but since there are many proteins in the brain which share up to a five amino acid sequence with DSIP, immunoreactivity has been detected throughout the brain (Kastin *et al.*, 1979).

DSIP administered by intravenous or intraventricular injection causes the appearance in recipient animals of slow wave sleep, with prominent sleep spindles and δ waves (Monnier *et al.*, 1977). With the exception of mild bradycardia, it has no other known physiological effects. DSIP is effective only in small doses, about 30 nmol per kg (in the cat). Larger doses are without effect.

The actual physiological role of DSIP is not clear. It is released from the brain in moderate quantities only during electrical stimulation of hypnogenic zones of the thalamus, not during natural sleep. Also, in calves with two brains (diplocephaly), or in parabiotic mice, there is no significant coincidence of their sleep periods. Studies of Siamese twins with circulatory connections have also indicated that their sleep patterns are independent, with their periods of sleep often differing. All of these findings indicate that DSIP, if produced during natural sleep, does not leave the brain in quantities sufficient to induce sleep in another individual (Webb, 1978). Furthermore, a few researchers contend that its role goes beyond sleep and that it is able to exert a complex programming effect upon all circadian activities (Graf *et al.*, 1981).

Fencl *et al.* (1971) isolated a natural sleep-promoting substance from the cerebrospinal fluid of goats previously deprived of sleep. It was neither identical to DSIP, nor a DSIP breakdown product. An injection into the rat of 0.1 ml of cerebrospinal fluid from these sleep-deprived goats induces sleep that can last upto several hours. It is a smaller molecule than DSIP, having a molecular weight of about 500 daltons, as compared to the 849 dalton DSIP. Partially purified and concentrated, it also elicits a slow-wave cortical EEG pattern resembling slow-wave sleep. A similar substance isolated by Krueger *et al.* in 1978, causes a gradual enhancement of slow-wave sleep. Arginine-vasotocin also has a sleep-inducing effect in the cat, even in a low dose of 600 molecules (Pavel *et al.*, 1977).

Spanis *et al.* (1976) obtained two proteins by perfusion of the midbrain reticular formation during REM sleep, one with a molecular weight of 73,000 daltons and the other with a weight of 45,000. They are not present in perfusates, CSF, or the serum of waking animals, and it is possible that both could participate in the regulation of sleep.

Nagasaki *et al.* (1975) extracted a sleep-promoting substance from the rat brain which is able to increase the total daily sleep time by 50-70%. It had a dose-dependent effect and was capable of inducing spontaneous discharges in crayfish abdominal ganglia. Brain extracts from hibernating ground squirrels contain a factor, termed antabalone, which, when injected into waking rats, causes a mean decrease in oxygen consumption by 35% and a 5^0C decline in body temperature. These effects lasted from 75 minutes to 30 hours (Swan and Schatte, 1977). The chemical nature of this factor is not clear, but it could very well be associated with the humoral induction of mammalian hibernation (Kalter and Folk, 1979).

All of these findings are no doubt interesting and may be of value in eventually resolving many of the long-standing questions regarding the normal initiation, maintenance and termination of sleep. However, the influence that these peptides have upon sleep should not necessarily be assumed as their only or even primary effect. From what is already known about the dose-effect relationships of many peptides, it is possible that other actions of these substances typically exist which are quite dissociated from sleep. On the other hand, considering the integrative complexity of sleep, involving as it does multiple neurotransmitters, brain areas and functional systems, such disparate actions, if they exist, could ultimately be integrated to generate the characteristic patterns of activity seen in sleep.

ADDITIONAL BRAIN PEPTIDES

The freshwater coelenterate *Hydra* contains an undecapeptide with the sequence, pGlu-Pro-Pro-Gly-Gly-Ser-Lys-Val-Ile-Leu-Phe. This peptide has been identified as the head activator substance (controlling head specific growth and differentiation) and is produced by the *Hydra's* nerve cells. Schaller (1975) detected a similar peptide in the brains of rats, cows and pigs that was mostly concentrated in the hypothalamus. It has subsequently been detected in the human brain and intestine, but its role is presently unknown. Similarly, a complex peptide system that is distributed throughout the brain, spinal cord, and posterior pituitary contains an amino acid sequence for the molluscan cardioexcitatory peptide, Phe-Met-Arg-Phe-NH_2 (Weber *et al.*, 1981), which is able to modify potassium currents in the neuron (Cottrell, 1982). Such a homology across the phylogenetic scale suggests that this evolutionary conservation may extend from the simplest to the most complex nervous systems. The findings also hint that some of these peptides have a common ancestry and may conceivably serve in comparable functional processes (Bodenmuller and Schaller, 1981).

A potentially important substance has an endogenous digitalis-like action which may control the activity of membrane Na^+, K^+-dependent adenosinetriphosphatase. It was detected in the mammalian brain by Fishman (1979) and found to block ATPase in a manner similar to the action of ouabain or other digitalis glycosides. It seems potentially capable of regulating ionic fluxes and the concentration gradients of ions across the cell membrane. Details of its distribution, activities and chemical structure are not yet available. The TRH metabolite, histidyl-proline diketopiperazine, has a comparable effect, although it does not influence the binding site for ouabain (Battaini and Peterkofsky, 1980).

A number of other potentially important peptides have been discovered, including an inhibitory tripeptide that was extracted from the cat spinal cord (Lote *et al.*, 1976), a peptide with an antistrychnine potency (Kawaguchi *et al.*, 1968), a peptide inhibiting cocaine binding in the brain (Reith *et al.*, 1980) and a substance termed nerveside that was detected by Toh in 1967. And, Chang *et al.* (1980) reports that at least ten peptides have been extracted from porcine hypothalamus. Thus far, there is little information available concerning their physiological and pharmacological activities.

BRAIN DIPEPTIDES

Several dipeptides have been isolated from nervous tissue and found to be present there in considerable quantities. Nevertheless, their functions are largely unknown. A number of glutamyl dipeptides were obtained by Kakimoto *et al.* (1964) from extracts of bovine brain. The most abundant are γ-glutamylglutamic acid and γ-glutamylglutamine. Their concentrations are higher in the brain than in any other tissue, and in humans appear to be evenly distributed throughout. Ophthalmic acid and norophthalmic acid, two other glutamyldipeptides, have been isolated from the retina. They have no detectable physiological effect upon the brain after their injection, and their physiological significance is unknown. In the retina, they could conceivably function to alter postsynaptic discharges, although this would be utter speculation at this point.

The pathway of γ-glutamyl dipeptide formation is probably via a γ-glutamyl transpeptidation, which is the reversible transfer of a glutamyl residue from glutathione to acceptor amino acids or peptides. This reaction is freely reversible.

Another group of dipeptides abundant in the brain are those containing γ-aminobutyric acid and β-alanine. Four peptides of this group have been isolated from nervous tissue. All contain either histidine or 1-methylhistidine. Carnosine is β-alanyl-L-histidine; anserine is β-alanylmethylhistidine (Fig. 29.1); homocarnosine is γ-aminobutyryl-L-histidine; and homoanserine is γ-aminobutyryl-L-methyl histidine. They are all synthesized by carnosine

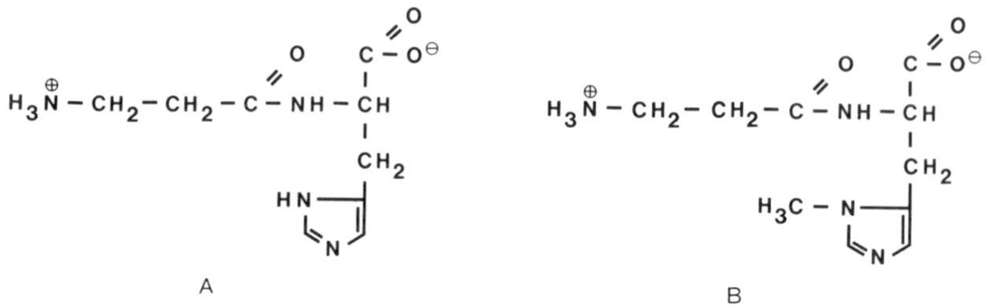

Figure 29.1 Carnosine (A) and anserine (B).

synthetase, an ATP-requiring enzyme that is fairly nonspecific and could catalyze the synthesis of many related dipeptides. These γ-aminobutyryl dipeptides are present in the brain as a consequence of the unique localization of γ-aminobutyric acid there. They may have a certain clinical significance. Bessman and Baldwin (1962), for example, have found an increased urinary excretion of carnosine and anserine in juvenile amaurotic idiocy. These substances have also been found in the urine of patients with other progressive neuronal degenerations.

Carnosine is high in the primary olfactory pathway, leading Margolis *et al.* (1974) to propose that it may be a neurotransmitter in this system. It is produced by the chemoreceptor neurons in the olfactory mucosa and in the olfactory bulb. There are also specific receptors for carnosine in these two regions (Brown *et al.*, 1977). Carnosine binding is saturable, reversible, of high affinity, stereo-specific and seems restricted to the olfactory system (Margolis, 1978).

BEHAVIORAL PEPTIDES

It is evident from the literature, some of which has been reviewed in the preceding chapters of this section, that a number of peptides have well-defined behavioral effects. However, studies done by several groups of workers over the last 20 years have indicated that some brain peptides may have rather specialized actions upon behavior, in that they are able to promote the acquisition of particular types of learned behavior. The term "memory transfer", originally used in a large number of older studies, was regretfully misleading, although it has been used for almost two decades to categorize those experiments concerned with the use of different brain extracts for the modification of behavior in untrained recipient animals.

In 1962, McConnell published a report on experiments with Planaria trained in a simple conditioning situation, in which light was the conditioning stimulus and a weak electrical shock served as an unconditioned stimulus. When the training was completed, the Planaria were killed and fed to naive, untrained worms. After a short incubation period, the recipients were then exposed to the same situation as were their cannibalized predecessors. They were found to exhibit a considerable savings in the number of trials necessary to reach a predetermined level of competence. At the time, the results were attributed to RNA molecules transferred from one worm to another that served as a biochemical substrate of memory.

A search of the literature by Corning (1971) revealed that the first published account of this phenomenon was by Plavilshchikov in 1928. Plavilshchikov classically conditioned the colonial ciliate *Carchesium lachmanni*, before transplanting part of the trained population to an untrained, naive recipient colony. The recipient colony was subsequently observed to behave as if it had been trained.

One of the first questions that emerged from these experiments was whether the learning in these primitive species was similar or identical to that learning displayed by vertebrates. This was the question that prompted at least four groups of experimenters to extend these "memory transfer" experiments to rodents. Reinis (1965), using a classical conditioning paradigm, with sound as a conditioning stimulus associated with a food reward, showed that intraperitonal injections of brain homogenates from trained subjects increased the rate of learning in untrained recipients. Several other reports appeared at approximately the same time, employing a variety of training procedures (Ungar and Oceguerra-Navarro, 1965; Fjerdingstad *et al.*, 1965; Jacobson *et al.*, 1965). All of these experiments have since been frequently replicated and expanded to include other animal species and training situations. They have generated both positive and negative results and, in the process, considerable controversy.

In addition to the well-known and often employed tasks, such as active or passive avoidance or alimentary conditioning, induced audiogenic seizure sensitivity was found to be "transferable" (Fjerdingstad 1973; Corwin and Stanford, 1973; Schreiber and Santos, 1976). And, Maldonado and Tablante (1976) described a "transfer" of learning behavior using a praying mantis trained not to attack a moving black star.

One of the initial questions associated with "memory transfer" concerned the specificity of the effective substances. Were these substances merely stimulants which lacked any direct influence upon the content of learning, or was their activity related to the sensory and behavioral components of the learning process? Early experiments by Fjerdingstad *et al.* (1965) provided some relevant information. The authors trained albino rat donors in a Y maze and found that the recipients of the brain extracts preferred the arm of the maze to which the donors were trained. The data suggested that the phenomenon had something to do not only with the process of learning as such, but also with the specificity of the learned task.

Another piece of evidence concerning the specificity of the behavioral modification came from Zippel and Domagk (1971). As a conditioning stimulus, they trained goldfish to feed on *Tubifex* worms only during the activation of a green light. A red light was a discriminatory, non-reinforcing stimulus. This differentiation was transferred to recipients who readily indicated a preference for the green as compared with the red light. The similar training of a taste preference was performed later. Their experiments completed since 1972 have been interpreted to denote the existence of independently synthesized substances for taste and color preference.

Establishing the chemical identity of the substances that underlie this behavioral modification was another problem. Early papers in this area claimed that the effective substance was ribonucleic acid. However, there were difficulties with the interpretation of the effect because a macromolecular substance like RNA could not easily penetrate the blood-brain barrier. Moreover, subsequent improvements in the extraction techniques demonstrated that the effective material was not RNA. Interestingly enough, most of the early papers which were unable to give credence to the transfer phenomenon employed an RNA extraction procedure. Ungar and Fjerdingstad (1969) suggested that those experimental successes using extracted RNA could be explained by presence of RNA-bound peptides in the donor extract.

There are a few peptides which have been isolated, characterized, and associated with behavioral modifications. Probably the best known is scotophobin (Fig. 29.2). First reported by Ungar in 1970, it was purported to cause a fear of darkness in naive recipient animals. Ungar and Burzynski (1973) also isolated a hexapeptide that they believed to be responsible for a habituation to sound. They named this substance ameletin (Fig. 29.3). "Blue-avoiding" and "green-avoiding" peptides (Fig. 29.4, 29.5) extracted from the brains of trained goldfish have also been reported (Tate *et al.*, 1976). The blue-avoiding peptide (chromodiopsin B - G) has thirteen amino acids, as does the green avoiding peptide (chromodiopsin G - B).

Up until now, the debate over the existence of brain peptides that are tied to specific behavioral events has been primarily focused on scotophobin.

H-Ser-Glu-Gly-Lys-Ser-Ala-Gln-Gln-Gly-Gly-Tyr-NH$_2$ **Figure 29.2** Proposed formula of scotophobin.

pGlu-Ala-Gly-Tyr-Ser-Lys-OH   **Figure 29.3** Ameletin.

Figure 29.4 Chromodiopsin B-G.   pGLU-ILE-GLY-ALA-VAL-PHE-PRO-LEU-LYS-TYR-GLY-SER-OH

Figure 29.5 Chromodiopsin G-B.   NAc-LYS-GLY-GLN-ILE-ALA-VAL-PHE-PRO-LEU-LYS-TYR-GLY-SER-OH

Methodologically, the extraction and synthesis of scotophobin have been described several times (e.g., Ungar, 1970, 1971). However, the method of extraction, the peptide structure, and its biological effects have all been cause for extensive criticism (Ali *et al.*, 1971; Stewart, 1972; Goldstein, 1973). Of the total number of samples of scotophobin, only a few were actually found to be as effective as described by Ungar *et al.* in 1972 (Misslin *et al.*, 1978). The peptide has also been observed to have several general behavioral effects in the recipient animals, including an increase in motor activity (Wojcik and Niemierko, 1978). The training paradigm employed by Ungar has been attacked as being too stressful (Goldstein, 1973), suggesting that scotophobin might be produced in the brain under the effect of stress and not as a correlate of the learning process.

Featherstone and Reinis (1978), however, showed that a more stressful situation, inescapable foot shock, is not transferred in the same way as is the learned behavior. Mice were trained in a "jump-out" apparatus, where the animals were expected to leave a pit with an electrified floor within five seconds of the appearance of a stimulus. The recipient animals were doing so substantially earlier than the untrained animals. When the donors were not allowed to leave the electrified area, then their recipients differed behaviorally from both the recipients of extracts from fully trained animals and from the recipients of naive brain extracts.

Behavioral modification by brain preparations has been accepted with reservations by some researchers, since it did not appear to fit into accepted interpretations of the learning phenomena. Concepts of closed circuits of neurons with strictly fixed schedules of firing and memory stores within individual cells, small groups of cells, or individual synapses have been used in the past to interpret the process of learning and memory storage. Behavioral modification by learning-dependent substances indicated, to the contrary, that the process of learning is accompanied by the synthesis of significant quantities of biochemicals which were capable of modifying brain activity in untrained recipients. However, "non-neurological" hypotheses of learning, in which the coded molecules act independently of any recognized pathway, clearly violated what had been known about the functioning of the central nervous systems. Such a non-traditional view could potentially and profoundly alter our conceptions concerning the adaptive activities of the brain.

Researchers in this area agree that learning-dependent substances do not transfer a real memory trace to another organism. There are a few hypotheses which have attempted to define the nature of this behavioral modification. Rosenblatt and Miller (1967) proposed that these substances modify the passage of nerve impulses across certain synapses, probably by binding to intrasynaptic fibers and joining the pre- and postsynaptic membranes firmly together. This idea of synaptic connectivity was substantially altered by Ungar (1969), who postulated that during learning new pathways are assembled in the brain by a mechanism corresponding to the "chemospecificity of pathways" first proposed by Sperry (1945). During learning, markers of new connections, which he called "metacircuits" are produced, which facilitate a mutual recognition of neurons and their synaptic connections. A logical consequence of this view would be that information is stored in small circuits which are newly formed in response to this incoming information. These circuits are assembled under the control of peptides whose composition depends upon the quality of the informational influx. In 1974, Ungar presented a "one-peptide-one behavior" hypothesis. He contended that enough variability in peptide structure was theoretically possible to allow each bit of information to be encoded in individual peptides. Using a 15 amino acid chain as an example, Ungar (1980) noted that the 20 common amino acids could be built into 20^{15} (or 3×10^{19}) differenct sequences. And, since von Neumann (1958) had estimated that a lifetime of accumulated information was in the area of 10^{15} bits, there would be more than enough different peptides to code for the total.

However, several objections can be raised against such a view. First, the peptides that are produced by the brain are not assembled de novo from individual amino acid precursors by some non-ribosomal process. They are cleaved from larger parent molecules. This mechanism substantially lowers the number of possible peptides (although it still remains incredibly high). Second, no peptide conforming to a "one peptide-one behavior" definition has ever been isolated. Even scotophobin has other actions which do not directly relate to the "fear of darkness" that is purportedly transferred. Third, any learned behavior is a concerted function of millions of neurons within many brain areas that act in either a simultaneous or sequential manner. Some are inhibited; others are facilitated or otherwise transformed. It would seem inconceivable that all of these alterations could be induced by a single peptide modulator.

Consequently, one must begin to look for alternative possibilities regarding the actions of these behavioral peptides and the other brain peptides previously mentioned. In the process, one must also be cognizant of certain considerations which may be applicable to many of these substances (Kastin et al., 1980a).

(1) Many known peptides, when injected into recipient animals, have a bell-shaped dose-response curve. This may explain the lack of success reported in numerous replications of the original transfer experiments. A high dose is often less effective than a low one. On frequent occasions, there was observed a "negative transfer" or a sustaining of a response opposite to the one which had been anticipated. This may also be attributable to these atypical dose-response relationships.

(2) A central effect can often be elicited by a peripheral route of peptide administration. Such has often been the case in memory transfer experiments. Intracerebroventricular, as well as intraperitoneal injections, have both been found to be effective.

(3) Many peptides seem to penetrate the blood-brain barrier in essentially intact form. This was true for scotophobin, although no other data on "memory peptides" are presently available.

(4) The effect has a delayed and prolonged time course, which has been observed in peptide studies as well as in the transfer work. The onset of the effect appears hours following administration and persists long after the peptide has disappeared from the brain.

One explanation for the phenomenon of "memory transfer" is that it is an effect of peptides whose actions are comparable to those of the dozens of other peptides thus far isolated from nervous tissue. These substances may serve as modulators or even transmitters in certain areas and pathways within the CNS. They have a long-lasting influence upon neuronal metabolism that is similar to the effects of some other peptides, even though they may only be present in the brain during an acquisition stage of learning (Reinis, 1971). It was found that learning-dependent peptides could be extracted from the brains of trained animals only until that time at which the learning was completed. Later, when the memory trace was fixed, "memory transfer" was not possible. This suggests that these substances are associated with the process of learning and not with the permanent storage of information. Injections of actinomycin D, puromycin, and other memory-blocking drugs do not interfere with "memory transfer" when given to the donors. In the recipients, these drugs block the appearance of the behavioral modification, indicating that the learning-dependent substances induce biochemical changes (protein synthesis) subject to antibiotic inhibition. In this way, the action of these peptides resembles the effect of ACTH, ACTH fragments and other peptides on specific aspects of learning and brain protein metabolism.

The origin, actual mechanism of synthesis, and degradation of these substances, as well as their distribution throughout the brain, is presently unclear. An important issue in this field of research concerns whether these substances are in fact continuously present in the brain and whether their synthesis (probably by a proteolytic release from their precursors) is activated by the process of learning or simply by an increase in the use of a certain pathway. There is evidence in the literature that the synthesis of brain peptides is constantly being adjusted to the functional needs of the brain. For example, Christie and Chesher (1982) required mice to swim daily in warm water. The accompanying stress likely induced the production of increased amounts of opioid peptides, leading to the appearance of a naloxone-precipitated withdrawal reaction which approximated that observed in mice after chronic morphine administration.

There are considerable difficulties associated with the replication of transfer experiments using pure peptides, such as scotophobin. De Wied *et al.* (1973) found that the scotophobin he tested had only 2% of the natural activity. It also caused other, unexpected effects, such as a delay in the extinction of a pole-jumping avoidance response and an increase in motor activity. This may suggest the necessity for a novel, more complex approach to the problem. The experiments with crude homogenates or extracts were generally more successful and reproducible. One possible explanation is that in the crude extracts, there is actually a mixture of various peptides which may modulate the sensory input, motor output and motivational state of the recipient. Such a mixture could influence behavior in a seemingly "specific" way, although each of the components may actually have either a more general or more circumscribed effect upon brain function. This possibility would not violate known principles of the organization of the brain function. More recent, precise examinations of the transfer phenomena, as presented by Tozzi *et al.* (1980), indicate the need for improvements in the behavioral paradigms, in addition to the use of updated methods of biochemical analysis.

SUMMARY AND SPECULATIONS

The central nervous system produces various groups of peptides that are structurally and physiologically distinct. Within and across animal species, some peptides contain homologous structures which indicate that certain amino acid sequences have remained unchanged over long periods of evolutionary history. A number of peptides (including peptide hormones) that serve as chemical messengers in lower organisms also perform comparable functions in higher animals, or may be used for some other roles within more complex nervous systems.

The importance of the roles that these various peptides play in the brain is underscored by the presence of the relevant synthetic and degradative mechanisms, as well as by the existence of specific receptors in the neuronal membrane. The brain peptides are apparently synthesized from larger precursors by the actions of particular proteinases and peptidases that are able to recognize and cleave specific points on the amino acid chain.

Although specific functions have been found for some peptides, all of them have other, sometimes rather remote, effects upon brain functioning. The multiple actions of individual brain peptides may be essentially independent of one another. An injection into one site within the brain may elicit a particular behavioral response that is in direct contrast to the effect caused by an identical injection into a second site.

While these peptides may act as CNS transmitters, it is equally likely that they function as modulators of synaptic activity. They may facilitate or inhibit traffic across synapses which is otherwise dependent upon the more "classical" neurotransmitters. In this way, they could affect the functional plasticity of neurons in specific pathways and systems, and participate in the formation, maintenance, and retrieval of the memory trace. Reports of a number of "behavioral peptides" could suggest such a role.

The mechanism of the synaptic modulation is unknown. Some peptides could conceivably bind to membrane lipids, such as the cerebrosides, gangliosides or phospholipids, and alter their configuration and that of adjoining proteins, affecting ionic relationships, ionic channels, and the functional characteristics of neurotransmitter receptors and other membrane components.

The binding of peptides to the neuronal membrane also induces a number of intracellular biochemical changes, including the synthesis of proteins and cyclic AMP. Thus, the peptide influence upon neuronal functioning may be quite long-lasting or even permanent. It is also interesting that applications of these substances are most effective in a particular concentration. This inverted U-shaped dose/effect curve means that too great or too little quantities can be without observable effects. It additionally suggests a defined role for these peptides in the brain.

At least some of the peptides are produced by neurons which concurrently give rise to a classic neurotransmitter. It is possible that this occurs as a general rule and that particular peptides are released from the nerve ending along with the neurotransmitter. The transmitter might then be predominantly responsible for short-lived synaptic phenomena (the excitatory and inhibitory postsynaptic potentials), while the peptide triggers more persistant changes, lasting minutes, hours, or days, that modulate the responsiveness of the target neurons.

Neurotransmitters are regionally rather nonspecific, in that the same neurotransmitter is typically distributed throughout many brain areas. The peptide, in a sense, is a more specific substance that may be associated with particular states, such as hunger, thirst, general stress, the sex drive, pain, slow-wave sleep, or even a more explicit situation that relates to an organism's response to environmental events. If this should be the case, then one could expect many additional discoveries of such peptides over the coming years.

The difficulty in explaining the behavioral effects of these peptides in terms of the involved pathways and physiology is a reflection of the sizable gaps in our understanding of complex brain functions. The emerging evidence does indicate that they are important to the overall activity of the nervous system. It is quite likely that once we do grasp the specific nature of their contributions to behavior, we will have taken a large step toward a comprehensive understanding of the brain in general.

RECOMMENDED READINGS

Annunziato, L., Di Renzo, G., Quattrone, A., Schettini, G., Preziosi, P.: Brain neurotransmitters regulating TRH producing neurons. *Pharmacol. Res. Commun.* 13:1-10 (1981).

Bohnet, H.G., McNeilly, A.S.: Prolactin-assessment of its role in the human female. *Horm. Metab. Res.* 11:533 (1979).

Bohus, B.: Effects of ACTH-like neuropeptides on animal behavior and man. *Pharmacology* 18:113-122 (1979).

Brown, G.M., Reichlin, S.: Psychologic and neural regulation of growth hormone secretion. *Psychosom. Med.* 34:45-72 (1972).

Carter, C.S., Davis, J.M.: Biogenic amines, reproductive hormones and female sexual behavior: A review. *Biobehav. Rev.* 1:213-224 (1977).

Efendic, S., Hokfelt, T., Luft, R.: Somatostatin. *Adv. Metab. Disord.* 9:367-424 (1978).

Fields, H.L., Basbaum, A.I.: Brainstem control of spinal pain-transmission neurons. *Ann. Rev. Physiol.* 40:217-248 (1978).

Fujita, T.: Paraneuron, its current implications. In: T. Kanno (Ed.), *Paraneurons, Their Features and Functions.* Excerpta Medica: Amsterdam (1981). pp. 3-9.

Fuller, R.W.: Serotonergic stimulation of pituitary-adrenocortical function in rats. *Neuroendocrinology* 32:118-127 (1981).

Fuxe, K., Andersson, K., Hokfelt, T., Mutt, V., Ferland, L., Agnati, L.F., Ganten, D., Said, S., Eneroth, P., Gustafsson, J.A.: The localization and possible function of peptidergic neurons and their interactions with ventral catecholamine neurons, and the central action of gut hormones. *Fed. Proc.* 38:2333-2340 (1979).

Ganong, W.F.: Neurotransmitters and pituitary function: Regulation of ACTH secretion. *Fed.Proc.* 39:2923-2930 (1980).

Goodman, R.L., Knobil, E.: The sites of action of ovarian steroids in the regulation of LH secretion. *Neuroendocrinology* 32:57-63 (1981).

Hays, S.E.: Strategies for psycho-endocrine studies of puberty. *Psychoneuroendocrinology* 3:1 (1978).

Hebert, E.: Discovery of pro-opiomelanocortin - A cellular polyprotein. *Trends Biochem. Sci.* 6:184-188 (1981).

Herrmann, W.M., Beach, R.C.: Psychotropic properties of estrogens. *Pharmacopsychiatry* 11:164-176 (1978).

Jackson, I.M.D.: Phylogenetic distribution and function of hypophysiotropic hormones of hypothalamus. *Amer. Zool.* 18:385-399 (1978).

Kastin, A.J., Schally, A.V., Kostrzewa, R.M.: Possible aminergic mediation of MSH release and of the CNS effects of MSH and MIF- I. *Fed. Proc.* 39:2931-2936 (1980).

Krieger, D.T., Liotta, A.S.: Pituitary hormones in brain - Where, how, and why. *Science* 205:366-372 (1979).

Leeman, S.E., Gamse, R.: Substance P in sensory neurons. *Trends Pharmacol. Sci.* 2:119-121 (1981).

Margolis, F.L.: Carnosine. *Trends Neurosci.* 1:42-44 (1978).

McEwen, B.S.: Neural gonadal steroid actions. *Science* 211:1303-1311 (1981).

Morin, L.P.: Progesterone inhibition of rodent sexual behavior. *Physiol. Behav.* 18:701-715 (1977).

Morley, J.E.: The neuro-endocrine control of appetite - the role of the endogenous opiates, cholecystokinin, TRH, gamma-aminobutyric acid and the diazepam receptor. *Life Sci.* 27:355-368 (1980).

Morrell, J.I., Kelley, D.B., Pfaff, D.W.: Sex steroid binding in the brains of vertebrates: Studies with light microscopic autoradiography. In: K.M. Knigge, D.E. Scott, H.

Kobayashi (Eds.), *Brain - Endocrine Interaction* Vol.2. Karger: Basel (1975). pp.230-256.

Nemeroff, C.B.: Neurotensin: Perchance an endogenous neuroleptic? *Biol. Psychiat.* 15:283-302 (1980).

North, R.A.: Opiates, opioid peptides and single neurons. *Life Sci.* 24:1527-1546 (1979).

Oades, R.D.: Search and attention: Interactions of the hippocampal-septal axis, adrenocortical and gonadal hormones. *Neurosci. Biobehav. Rev.* 3:31-48 (1979).

Oppenheimer, J.H.: Thyroid hormone. Action at the cellular level. *Science* 203:971-979 (1979)

O'Shea, M.: Peptide neurobiology: An identified neurone approach with special reference to Proctolin. *Trends Neurosci.* 5:69-75 (1982).

Phillips, M.I.: Angiotensin in brain. *Neuroendocrinology* 25:354-377 (1978).

Regoli, D.: Receptors for angiotensin: A critical analysis. *Can. J. Physiol. Pharmacol.* 57:129-139 (1979).

Saffran, M., Schally, A.V.: The status of the corticotropin releasing factor. *Neuroendocrinology* 24:359-375 (1977).

Sara, V.R., Hall, K.: Growth hormone, growth factors and the brain. *Trends Neurosci.* 2:263 (1979).

Sawyer, C.H.: Brain catecholamines and pituitary-ovarian function. *Acta Biol. Acad. Sci. Hung.* 28:11-23 (1977).

Seif, S.M., Robinson, A.G.: Localization and release of neurophysins. *Ann. Rev. Physiol.* 40:345-376 (1978).

Vale, W., Rivier, C., Brown, M.: Physiology and pharmacology of hypothalamic regulatory peptides. In: *Handbook of the Hypothalamus.* Vol. 2. *Physiology of the Hypothalamus.* P.J. Morgane, J. Panksepp (Eds.). Marcel Dekker: New York (1980). pp. 165-252.

Van Wyk, J.J., Underwood, L.E.: Relation between growth hormone and somatomedin. *Ann. Rev. Med.* 26:427 (1975).

Weiner, R.I., Ganong, W.F.: Role of brain monoamines and histamine in regulation of anterior pituitary secretion. *Physiol. Rev.* 58:905-976 (1978).

Witter, A., de Wied, D. Hypothalamic-pituitary oligopeptides and behavior. In: *Handbook of the Hypothalamus.* Vol. 2. *Physiology of the Hypothalamus.* P.J. Morgane, J. Panksepp (Eds.). Marcel Dekker: New York (1980). pp. 307-451.

Yarbrough, G.G.: On the neuropharmacology of thyrotropin releasing hormone (TRH). *Progr. Neurobiol.* 12:291-312 (1979).

Zimmerman, E.A., Robinson, A.G.: Hypothalamic neurons secreting vasopressin and neurophysin. *Kidney Internat.* 10:12-24 (1976).

REFERENCES

Abdelaal, A.E., Assaf, S.Y., Kucharczyk, J., Mogenson, G.J.: *Can. J. Physiol. Pharmacol.* 52:1217 (1974).

Abood, L.G., Butler, M., Reynolds, D.: *Mol. Pharmacol.* 17:290 (1980).

Akopyan, T.N., Arutunyan, A.A., Lajtha, A., Galoyan, A.A.: *Neurochem. Res.* 3:89 (1978).

Ali, A., Faesel, J.H.R., Sarantakis, D., Stevenson, D., Weinstein, B.: *Experientia* 27:1138 (1971).

Allen, J.P., Allen, C.F.: *Neuroendocrinology* 19:115 (1975).

Aloyo, V.J., Zwiers, H., Gispen, W.H.: *J. Neurochem.* 38:871 (1982).

Amara, S.G., Jonas, V., O'Neil, J.A., Vale, W., Rivier, J., Roos, B.A., Evans, R.M., Rosenfeld, M.G.: *J. Biol. Chem.* 257:2129 (1982).

Annunziato, L., Di Renzo, G., Quattrone, A., Schettini, G., Preziosi, P.: *Pharmacol. Res. Commun.* 13:1 (1981).

Arbilla, S., Langer, S.Z.: *Nature* 271:559 (1978).

Archer, T., Ogren, S.O., Fuxe, K., Agnati, L.E., Eneroth, P.: *Neurosci. Lett.* 27:341 (1981).

Arnauld, E., Dufy, B., Pestre, M., Vincent, J.D.: *Neurosci. Lett.* 21:325 (1981).

Attardi, B., Ohno, S.: *Endocrinology* 103:760 (1978).

Augustine, E.C., Hymer, W.C.: *Mol. Cell Endocrinol.* 10:225 (1978).

Baer, P., Schotman, P., Gispen, W.H.: *Eur. J. Pharmacol.* 65:165 (1980).

Baile, C.A., Keim, D.A., Dell-Fera, M.A., McLaughlin, C.L.: *Physiol. Behav.* 26:1019 (1981).

Bailey, W.H., Weiss, J.M.: *Horm. Behav.* 10:22 (1978).

Bailey, W.H., Weiss, J.M.: In: J.L. Martinez Jr., R.A. Jensen, B. Messing, H. Rigter, J.L. McGaugh (Eds.), *Endogenous Peptides and Learning and Memory Processes.* Academic Press: New York (1981). p. 371.

Baker, R.V., Hope, D.B.: *J. Neurochem.* 27:197 (1976).

Barker, J.L., Gruol, D.L., Huang, L.Y.M., MacDonald, J.F., Smith, T.J. Jr.: *Neuropeptides* 1:63 (1980).

Barker, J.L., Smith, T.G.: *Brain Res.* 103:167 (1976).

Barry, J.: *Neurosci. Lett.* 2:201 (1976).

Barry, J., Dubois, M.P., Carette, B.: *Endocrinology* 95:1416 (1974).

Battaini, F., Peterkofsky, A.: *Biochem. Biophys. Res. Commun.* 94:240 (1980).

Baxter, J.D., Eberhardt, N.L., Apriletti, J.W., Johnson, L.K., Ivarie, R.D., Schachter, B.S., Morris, J.A., Seeburg, P.H., Goodman, H.M.: *Recent Progr. Horm. Res.* 35:97 (1979).

Bayon, A., Shoemaker, W.J., Lugo, L., Azad, R., Ling, N., Drucker-Colin, R.R., Bloom, F.E.: *Neurosci. Lett.* 24:65 (1981).

Becker, K.L., Snider, R.H., Moore, C.F., Monaghan, K.G., Silva, O.L.: *Acta Endocrinol. (Kbh).* 92:746 (1979).

Beckwith, B.E., Sandman, C.A., Hothersall, D., Kastin, A.J.: *Physiol. Behav.* 18:63 (1977).

Benakis, A.: *Arch. Toxicol. Suppl.* 2:105 (1979).

Benuck, M., Marks, N.: *Biochem. Biophys. Res. Commun.* 88:215 (1979).

Berelowitz, M., Szabo, M., Frohman, L.A., Firestone, S., Chu, L., Hintz, R.L.: *Science* 212:1279 (1981).

Bergland, R.M., Page, R.B.: *Science* 204:18 (1979).

Bernstein, I.L., Woods, S.C.: *Physiol. Behav.* 24:529 (1980).

Bessman, S.P., Baldwin, R.: *Science* 135:789 (1962).

Besson, J., Rotsztehn, W., Laburthe, M., Epelbaum, J., Beaudet, A., Kordon, K., Rosselin, G.: *Brain Res.* 165:79 (1979).

Best, C.H., Campbell, J.: *J. Physiol. (London).* 86:190 (1936).

Bex, F.J., Corbin, A.: *Endocrinology* 105:139 (1979).

Bidlack, J.M., Abood, L.G., Osei-Gyimah, P., Archer, S.: *Proc. Natl. Acad. Sci. USA.* 78:636 (1981).

Bicknell, R.J., Schofield, J.G.: *J. Physiol.* 316:85 (1981).

Biegon, A., McEwen, B.S.: *J. Neurosci.* 2:199 (1982).

Bird, E.D., Chiappa, S.A., Fink, G.: *Nature* 260:536 (1976).

Birnberger, K.L., Rudel, R., Struppler, A.: *Ann. Neurol.* 1:270 (1977).

Birk, Y., Li, C.H.: *J. Biol. Chem.* 239:1084 (1964).

Blank, M.S., Panerai, A.E., Friesen, H.G.: *Science* 203:1129 (1979).

Blask, D.E., Reiter, R.J., Johnson, L.Y.: *J. Neurosci. Res.* 3:127 (1977).

Blaustein, J.D., Feder, H.H.: *Brain Res.* 177:489 (1979).

Blech, W.: *Endokrinologie* 71:325 (1978).

Blech, W.: *Endokrinologie* 72:77 (1978a).

Bloch, B., Bugnon, C., Fellmann, D., Lenys, D., Gouget, A.: *Cell Tissue Res.* 204:1 (1979).

Bloom, F., Battenberg, E., Rossier, J., Ling, J., Guillemin, R.: *Proc. Natl. Acad. Sci. USA* 75:1591 (1978).

Bloom, F.E., McGinty, J.F.: In: J.L. Martinez Jr., R.A. Jensen, B. Messing, H. Rigter, J.L. McGaugh (Eds.), *Endogenous Peptides and Learning and Memory Processes.* Academic Press: New York (1981). p. 199.

Bodenmuller, H., Schaller, H.C.: *Nature* 293:579 (1981).

Bohnet, H.G., McNeilly, A.S.: *Horm. Metab. Res.* 11:533 (1979).

Bohus, B.: *Horm. Behav.* 8:52 (1977).

Bohus, B.: *Pharmacology* 18:113 (1979).

Bohus, B., Lissak, K.: *Int. J. Neuropharmacol.* 7:301 (1968).

Bohus, B., Urban, I., Van Wimersma-Greidanus, T.B., DeWied, D.: *Neuropharmacology* 17:239 (1978).

Bohus, B., Van Wimersma Greidanus, T.B., De Weid, D.: *Physiol. Behav.* 14:609 (1975).

Bolaffi, J.L., Reichlin, S., Goodman, D.B.P., Forrest, J.N. Jr.: *Science* 210:644 (1980).

Borghi, C., Nicosia, S., Grachetti, A., Said, S.I.: *Life Sci.* 24:65 (1979).

Boschi, G., Launay, N., Rips, R.: *Neurosci. Lett.* 16:209 (1980).

Botticelli, L.J., Wurtman, R.J.: *Nature* 289:75 (1981).

Botticelli, L.J., Cox, B.M., Goldstein, A.: *Proc. Natl. Acad. Sci. USA* 78:7783 (1981).

Bradbury, A.F., Smyth, D.G., Snell, C.R.: *Biochem. Biophys. Res. Commun.* 69:950 (1976).

Braga, P., Ferri, S., Santagostino, A., Olgiati, V.R., Pecile, A.: *Life Sci.* 22:971 (1978).

Bram, I.: *Endocrinology* 11:106 (1927).

Brito, G.N.O., Thomas, G.J., Gingold, S.I., Gash, D.M.: *Brain Res. Bull.* 6:71 (1981).

Brooks, V.L., Malvin, R.L.: *Fed. Proc.* 38:2272 (1979).

Brown, G.M., Reichlin, S.: *Psychosom. Med.* 34:45 (1972).

Brown, C.E., Margolis, F.L., Williams, T.H., Pitcher, R.G., Elgar, G.: *Neurochem. Res.* 2:555 (1977).

Brown, M., Vale, W.: *Endocrinology* 98:819 (1976).

Brown, M., Vale, W.: *Trends Neurosci.* 2:95 (1979).

Brown, M., Allen, R., Villarreal, J., Rivier, J., Vale, W.: *Life Sci.* 23:2721 (1978a).

Brown, M., Rivier, J., Kobayashi, R., Vale, W.; In: *Gut Hormones.* S.R. Bloom (Ed.), Churchill Livingstone: Edinburgh (1978b). p.550.

Brownstein, M.: *Fed. Proc.* 36:1960 (1977).

Brownstein, M.J., Russell, J.T., Gainer, H.: *Science* 207:373 (1980).

Brunia, C.H.M., Van Boxtel, A.: *Pharmacol. Biochem. Behav.* 9:615 (1978).

Brush, F.R., Fraley, S.M.: *Acta Neurobiol. Exper.* 39:433 (1979).

Buckingham, J.C., Hodges, J.R.: *J. Physiol. (London)* 272:469 (1977).

Buckley, J.P.: *Trends Pharmacol. Sci.* 2:161 (1981).

Bugnon, C., Bloch, B., Lenys, D.: *Neuroscience* 6:1299 (1981).

Bugnon, C., Bloch, B., Lenys, D., Gouget, A., Fellmann, D.: *Neurosci. Lett.* 14:43 (1979).

Buijs, R.M., Swaab, D.F., Dogterom, J., Van Leeuwen, F.W.: *Cell Tissue Res.* 186:423 (1978).

Burt, D.R.: In: *Neurotransmitter Receptors* Part 1 (Receptors and Recognition, Series B, Vol.9), S.J. Enna, H.I. Yamamura (Eds.). Chapman & Hall: London (1980). p.149.

Carr, L.A., Conway, P.M., Voogt, J.L.: *Brain Res.* 133:305 (1977).

Carraway, R., Leeman, S.E.: *J. Biol. Chem.* 248:6854 (1973).

Carraway, R., Leeman, S.E.: *J. Biol. Chem.* 250:1907 (1975).

Carraway, R., Leeman, S.E.: *J. Biol. Chem.* 251:7045 (1976).

Carraway, R.E., Demers, L.M., Leeman, S.E.: *Endocrinology* 99:1452 (1976).

Carter, C.S., Davis, J.M.: *Biobehav. Rev.* 1:213 (1977).

Carter, J.N., Tyson, J.E., Tolis, G., Van Vliet, S., Faiman, C., Friesen, H.G.: *N. Engl. J. Med.* 299:847 (1978).

Cassone, M.C., Molinengo, L.: *Life Sci.* 29:1983 (1981).

Chang, K.-J., Cuatrecasas, P.: *J. Biol. Chem.* 254:2610 (1979).

Chang, K.-J., Cuatrecasas, P.: *Fed. Proc.* 40:2729 (1981).

Chang, R.C.C., Huang, W.Y., Redding, T.W., Arimura, A., Coy, D.H., Schally, A.V.: *Biochim. Biophys. Acta* 625:266 (1980).

Chateau, M., Marchetti, J., Burlet, A., Boulange, M.: *Neuroendocrinology* 28:25 (1979).

Chavkin, C., Goldstein, A.: *Proc. Natl. Acad. Sci. USA* 78:6543 (1981).

Chavkin, C., James, I.F., Goldstein, A.: *Science* 215:413 (1982).

Chihara, K., Kato, Y., Ohgo, S., Iwasaki, Y., Maeda, K., Miyamoto, Y.: *Endocrinology* 98:1396 (1976).

Childers, S.R.: In: *Neurotransmitter Receptors,* Part 1 (Receptors and Recognition, Series B, Vol.9), S.J. Enna, H.I. Yamamura (Eds.). Chapman & Hall, London (1980). p.105.

Childs (Moriarty), G.V., Cole, D.E., Kubek, M., Tobin, R.B., Wilber, J.F.: *J. Histochem. Cytochem.* 26:901 (1978).

Christie, M.J., Chesher, G.B.: *Life Sci.* 30:1173 (1982).

Clark, W.G., Ponder, S.W.: *Brain Res. Bull.* 5:415 (1980).

Clemens, J.A., Meites, J.: *Endocrinology* 82:878 (1968).

Clendinnen, B., Eayrs, J.T.: *J. Endocrinol.* 22:183 (1961).

Clineschmidt, B.V., McGuffin, J.C., Bunting, P.B.: *Eur. J. Pharmacol.* 54:129 (1979).

Collier, H.O.J., Francis, D.L.: *Nature* 255:159 (1975).

Collier, H.O.J., Roy, A.C.: *Nature* 248:24 (1974).

Colpaert, F.C., Niemegeers, C.J.E., Janssen, P.A.J., Van Ree, J.M., De Wied, D.: *Psychoneuroendocrinology* 3:203 (1978).

Comb, M., Seeburg, P.H., Adelman, J., Eiden, L., Herbert, E.: *Nature* 295:663 (1982).

Cooper, T.: *Can. J. Physiol. Pharmacol.* 47:739 (1969).

Cooper, B.R., Boyer, C.E.: *Neuropharmacology* 17:153 (1978).

Coquelin, A., Bronson, F.H.: *Science* 206:1099 (1979).

Corbin, A., Beattie, C.W.: *Endocrin. Res. Commun.* 2:445 (1975).

Corning, W.C.: *J. Biol. Psychol.* 13:39 (1971).

Corwin, T.M., Stanford, A.L.: *Physiol. Psychol.* 1:324 (1973).

Cottrell, G.A.: *Nature* 296:87 (1982).

Craves, F.B., Zalc, B., Leybin, L., Baumann, N., Loh, H.H.: *Science* 207:75 (1980).

Crawley, J.N., Hays, S.E., Paul, S.M., Goodwin, F.K.: *Physiol. Behav.* 27:407 (1981).

Cuello, A.C., Del Fiacco, M., Paxinos, G., Somogyi, P., Priestley, J.V.: *J. Neural Transm.* 51:83 (1981).

Daniel, P.M., Love, E.R., Moorhouse, S.R., Pratt, O.E.: *J. Physiol.* 312:551 (1981).

Dannies, P.S.: *Trends Pharmacol. Sci.* 1:206 (1980).

Dannies, P.S., Tashjian, A.H.: *Israel J. Med. Sci.* 10:1294 (1974).

Davies, J., Dray, A.: *Nature* 262:606 (1976).

Davies, J., Naftolin, F., Ryan, K.J., Siu, J.: *J. Clin. Endocrinol.* 40:909 (1975).

Debons, A.F., Krimsky, I., Likuski, H.J., From, A., Cloutier, R.J.: *Am. J. Physiol.* 214:652 (1968).

De Kloet, E.R., McEwen, B.S.: *Biochim. Biophys. Acta* 421:115 (1976).

De La Baume, S., Patey, G., Schwartz, J.C.: *Neuroscience* 6:315 (1981).

Delanoy, R.L., Dunn, A.J., Tintner, R.: *Horm. Behav.* 11:348 (1978).

Delanoy, R.L., Kramarcy, N.R., Dunn, A.J.: *Brain Res.* 231:117 (1982).

Del Fiacco, M., Paxinos, G., Cuello, A.C.: *Brain Res.* 231:1 (1982).

De Nayer, P., Dozin-Van Roye, B.: *Biochem. Biophys. Res. Commun.* 98:1 (1981).

Deschodt-Lanckmann, M., Robberecht, P., Christopher, J.: *FEBS Lett.* 83:76 (1977).

De Wied, D., Bohus, B.: *Nature* 212:1484 (1966).

De Wied, D., Versteeg, D.H.G.: *Fed. Proc.* 38:2348 (1979).

De Wied, D., Bohus, B., Van Wimersma Greidanus, T.B.: *Brain Res.* 85:152 (1975).

De Wied, D., Sarantakis, D., Weinstein, B.: *Neuropharmacology* 12:1109 (1973).

Diamond, B.I., Borison, R.L.: *Neurology* 28:1085 (1978).

Dickinson, S.L., Slater, P.: *Peptides* 1:293 (1980).

Dingledine, R.: *J. Neurosci.* 1:1022 (1981).

Doering, C.H., McAdoo, B.C., Kraemer, H.C., Brodie, H.K.H., Dessert, N.J., Hamburg, D.A.: In: *Neuroregulators and Psychiatric Disorders*, E. Usdin, D.A. Hamburg, J.D. Bardias, (Eds.). Oxford University Press: New York (1977). p.267.

Doerr-Schott, J., Dubois, M.P.: *Cell Tissue Res.* 172:477 (1976).

Donoso, A.O., Bacha, J.C.: *J. Neural Transm.* 37:155 (1975).

Drago, F., Bohus, B., Canonico, P.L., Scapagnini, U.: *Pharmacol. Biochem. Behav.* 15:61 (1981).

Drouva, S., Epelbaum, J., Tapia-Arancibia, L., Laplante, E., Kordon, C.: *Eur. J. Pharmacol.* 61:411 (1980).

Drouva, S.V., Epelbaum, J., Hery, M., Tapia-Arancibia, L., Laplante, E., Kordon, C.: *Neuroendocrinology* 32:155 (1981).

Drouva, S.V., Epelbaum, J., Tapia-Arancibia, L., Laplante, E., Kordon, C.: *Neuroendocrinology* 32:163 (1981a).

Drust, D.S., Sutton, C.A., Martin, T.F.J.: *J. Biol. Chem.* 257:3306 (1982).

Dufy, B., Partouche, C., Poulain, D., Dufy-Barbe, L., Vincent, J.D.: *Neuroendocrinology* 22:38 (1976).

Dufy, B., Vincent, J.D., Fleury, H., Du Pasquier, P., Gourdji, D., Tixier-Vidal, A.: *Science* 204:509 (1979).

Dunlap, C.E., Leslie, F.M., Rado, M., Cox, B.M.: *Mol. Pharmacol.* 16:105 (1979).

Dunn, A.: *Ann. Rev. Psychol.* 31:343 (1980).

Dunn, A.J., Gispen, W.H.: *Biobehav. Rev.* 1:15 (1977).

Dunn, A.J., Iuvone, P.M., Rees, H.D.: *Pharmacol. Biochem. Behav.* 5(Suppl.1):139 (1976).

Edwardson, J.A., Bennett, G.W.: *Nature* 251:425 (1974).

Efendic, S., Hokfelt, T., Luft, R.: *Adv. Metab. Disord.* 9:367 (1978).

Egan, T.M., North, R.A.: *Science* 214:923 (1981).

Ehrensing, R.H., Kastin, A.J.: *Am. J. Psychiat.* 135:562 (1978).

Ehrenkranz, J., Bliss, E., Sheard, M.H.: *Psychosom. Med.* 36:469 (1974).

Ehrlich, Y.H., Davis, L.G., Keen, P.I., Brunngraber, E.G.: *Life Sci.* 26:1765 (1980).

Ekstrand, B.R., Barrett, T.R., West, J.N., Maier, W.G.: In: *Neurobiology of Sleep and Memory*, R.R. Drucker-Colin, J. McGaugh (Eds.). Acad. Press: New York (1977). p.419.

Elgee, N.J., Williams, R.H., Lee, N.D.: *J. Clin. Invest.* 33:1252 (1954).

Emanuele, N., Oslapa, R., Connick, E., Kirsteins, L., Lawrence, A.M.: *Neuroendocrinology* 33:12 (1981).

Emerson, C.H., Vogel, W., Currie, B.L.: *Endocrinology* 107:443 (1980).

Emson, P.C., Fahrenkrug, J., Schaffalitzky de Muckadell, O.B., Jessel, T.M., Iverson, L.L.: *Brain Res.* 143:174 (1978).

Ensinck, J.W., Laschansky, E.C., Kanter, R.A., Fujimoto, W.Y., Koerker, D.J., Goodner, C.J.: *Metabolism* 27 (Suppl.1):1207 (1978).

Epelbaum, J., Brazeau, P., Tsang, D., Brawer, D., Martin, J.B.: *Brain Res.* 126:309 (1977).

Erspamer, V., Melchiorri, P.: *Pure Appl. Chem.* 35:463 (1973).

Erspamer, V., Melchiorri, P.: In: *Gastrointestinal Hormones*, J.C. Thompson (Ed.). Univ. Texas Press: Austin (1975). p.575.

Eskay, R.L., Giraud, P., Oliver, C., Brownstein, M.J.: *Brain Res.* 178:55 (1979).

Esposito, R.U., Kornetsky, C.: *Neurosci. Biobehav. Rev.* 2:115 (1978).

Etgen, A.M., Lee, K.S., Lynch, G: *Brain Res.* 165:37 (1979).

Etgen, A.M., Martin, M., Gilbert, R., Lynch, G.: *J. Neurochem.* 35:598 (1980).

Extein, I. Pottash, A.L.C., Gold, M.S., Cadet, J., Sweeney, D.R., Davies, R.K., Martin, D.M.: *Psychiat. Res.* 2:199 (1980).

Featherstone, J.W., Reinis, S.: *Experientia* 34:854 (1978).

Fekete, M., Kadar, T., Penke, B., Kovacs, K., Telegdy, G.: *J. Neural Transm.* 50:81 (1981).

Felix, D., Phillips, M.I.: *Brain Res.* 169:204 (1979).

Fencl, V., Koski, G., Pappenheim, J.R.: *J. Physiol. (London)* 216:565 (1971).

Ferrari, C., Caldara, R., Rampini, P., Telloli, P., Romussi, M., Bertazzo, A., Polloni, G., Mattei, A., Crossignani, P.G.: *Metabolism* 27:1499 (1978).

Ferrier, B.M., Kennett, D.J., Devlin, M.C.: *Life Sci.* 27:2311 (1980).

Ferris, S.H., Sathananthan, G., Gershon, S., Clark, C., Moshinsky, J.: *Pharmacol. Biochem. Behav.* 5:23 (1976).

Fields, H.L., Basbaum, A.I.: *Ann. Rev. Physiol.* 40:217 (1978).

Fischer, J.A., Sagar, S.M., Martin, J.B.: *Life Sci.* 29:663 (1981).

Fishman, M.C., Zimmerman, E.A., Slater, E.E.: *Science* 214:921 (1981).

Fischer-Ferraro, C., Nahmod, V.E., Goldstein, D.J., Finkielman, S.: *J. Exp. Med.* 133:353 (1971).

Fishman, M.C.: *Proc. Natl. Acad. Sci. USA* 76:4661 (1979).

Fjerdingstad, E.J.: In: *Current Biochemical Approaches to Learning and Memory,* W.B. Essman, S. Nakajima, (Eds.). Spectrum: New York (1973). p.73.

Fjerdingstad, E.J., Nissen, T., Roigaard-Petersen, H.H.: *Scand. J. Psychol.* 6:1 (1965).

Flood, J.F., Jarvik, M.E., Bennett, E.L., Orme, A.E.: *Pharmacol. Biochem. Behav.* 5(Suppl.1):41 (1976).

Flood, J.F., Vidal, D., Bennett, E.L., Orme, A.E., Vasquez, S., Jarvik, M.E.: *Pharmacol. Biochem. Behav.* 8:81 (1978).

Foreman, M.M., Wickersham, E.W., Anthony, A.: *Brain Res.* 119:471 (1977).

Forssman, W.G.: *Neurosci. Lett.* 10:293 (1978).

Fournie-Zaluski, M.-C., Gacel, G., Maigret, B., Premilat, S., Roques, B.P.: *Molec. Pharmacol.* 20:484 (1981).

Fox, C.A., Ismail, A.A.A., Love, D.N., Kirkham, K.E., Loraine, J.A.: *J. Endocrinol.* 52:51 (1972).

Frawley, L.S., Neill, J.D.: *Neuroendocrinology* 33:79 (1981).

Frederickson, R.C.A., Burgis, V., Harrell, C.E., Edwards, J.D.: *Science* 199:1359 (1978).

Frederickson, R.C.A., Smithwick, E.L., Henry, D.P.: In: *Neuropeptides and Neural Transmission,* C. Ajmone Marsan, W.Z. Traczyk (Eds.). Raven Press: New York (1980). p.227.

Fujita, T.: In: R.E. Coupland, T. Fujita (Eds.), *Chromaffin, Enterochromaffin and Related Cells.* Elsevier: Amsterdam (1976). p. 191.

Fuller, R.W.: *Neuroendocrinology* 32:118 (1981).

Fuxe, K., Andersson, K., Hokfelt, T., Mutt, V., Ferland, L., Agnati, L.F., Ganten, D., Said, S., Eneroth, P., Gustafsson, J.A.: *Fed. Proc.* 38:2333 (1979).

Gaillard, A.W.K.: In: J.L. Martinez Jr., R.A. Jensen, B. Messing, H. Rigter, J.L. McGaugh (Eds.), *Endogenous Peptides and Learning and Memory.* Academic Press: New York (1981). p. 181.

Gallagher, M., Kapp, B.S., *Life Sci.* 23:1973 (1978).

Ganong, W.F.: *Fed. Proc.* 39:2923 (1980).

Ganten, D., Minnich, J.L., Granger, I.P., Hayduk, K., Brecht, H.M., Barbeau, A., Boucher, R., Genest, J.: *Science* 173:64 (1971).

Gerich, J.E., Lovinger, R., Grodsky, G.M.: *Endocrinology* 96:749 (1975).

Giachetti, A., Said, S.I., Reynolds, R.C., Koniges, F.C.: *Proc. Natl. Acad. Sci. USA* 74:3424 (1977).

Gispen, W.H., Schotman, P.: *Neuroendocrinology* 21:97 (1976).

Goethert, M.: *Nature* 287:86 (1980).

Gold, P.E., Van Buskirk, R.: *Horm. Behav.* 7:509 (1976).

Goldman, H., Skelley, C.A., Sandman, C.A., Kastin, A.j., Murphy, S.: *Pharmacol. Biochem. Behav.* 5(Suppl.1):15 (1976).

Goldstein, A.: *Nature* 242:60 (1973).

Goldstein, A., Cox, B.M., Klee, S.W., Nirenberg, M.: *Nature* 265:362 (1977).

Goldstein, A., Fischli, W., Lowney, L.I., Hunkapiller, M., Hood, L.: *Proc. Natl. Acad. Sci. USA* 78:7219 (1981).

Goodman, R.L., Knobil, E.: *Neuroendocrinology* 32:57 (1981).

Goodman, R., Snyder, S.H., Kuhar, M.J., Young, W.S.III: *Proc. Natl. Acad. Sci. USA* 77:6239 (1980).

Gorenstein, C., Snyder, S.H.: *Life Sci.* 25:2065 (1979).

Graeff, F.G.: *Cien. Cultra* 23:465 (1971).

Graf, M., Christen, H., Tobler, H.J., Maier, P.F., Schoenenberger, G.A.: *Pharmacol. Biochem. Behav.* 15:717 (1981).

Graham, J.M., Desjardin, C.: *Science* 210:1039 (1980).

Gramsch, C., Kleber, G., Hollt, V., Pasi, A., Mehraein, P., Herz, A.: *Brain Res.* 192:109 (1980).

Greenberg, I., Whalley, C.E., Jourdikian, F., Mendelson, I.S, Walter, R.: *Pharmacol. Biochem. Behav.* 5(Suppl.1):151 (1976).

Grimm-Jorgensen, Y., McKelvy, J.F., Jackson, I.M.D.: *Nature* 254:620 (1975).

Guble, R.U., Seeburg, P., Hoffman, B.J., Gage, L.P., Udenfriend, S.: *Nature* 295:206 (1982).

Guillemin, R., Vargo, T., Rossier, J., Minick, S., Ling, N., Rivier, C., Vale, W., Bloom, F.: *Science* 197:1367 (1977).

Gullner, H.G., Campbell, W.B., Pettinger, W.A.: *Life Sci.* 24:2351 (1979).

Halbreich, V., Assael, M., Bendavid, M., Borenstein, R., Lancet, M.: *Israel J. Med. Sci.* 12:1336 (1976).

Hambrook, J.M., Morgan, B.A., Rance, M.J., Smith, C.F.C.: *Nature* 262:782 (1976).

Haubrich, D.R., Martin, G.E., Pflueger, A.B., Williams, M.: *Brain Res.* 231:216 (1982).

Havrankova, J., Roth, J.: *Nature* 272:827 (1978).

Hays, S.E.: *Psychoneuroendocrinology* 3:1 (1978).

Hays, S.E., Beinfeld, M.C., Jensen, R.T., Goodwin, F.K., Paul, S.M.: *Neuropeptides* 1:53 (1980).

Heal, D.J., Sabbagh, A., Youdim, M.B.H., Green, A.R.: *Neuropharmacology* 20:947 (1981).

Henry, J.L.: *Brain Res.* 114:439 (1976).

Henry, J.L., Krnjevic, K., Morris, M.E.: *Can. J. Physiol. Pharmacol.* 53:423 (1975).

Herrmann, W.M., Beach, R.C.: *Pharmacopsychiatry* 11:164 (1978).

Herz, A., Blasig, J., Emrich, H.M., Cording, C., Piree, S., Kolling, A., Zerssen, D.V.: *Adv. Biochem. Psychopharmacol.* 18:333 (1978).

Hill, R.G., Mitchell, J.F., Pepper, C.M.: *J. Physiol.* 272:50P (1977).

Hirose, S., Yokosawa, H., Inagami, T., Workman, R.J.: *Brain Res.* 191:489 (1980).

Hoddes, E.S.: *Sleep* 1:287 (1979).

Hoffman, G.E., Knigge, K.M., Moynihan, J.A., Melnyk, V., Arimura, A.: *Neuroscience* 3:219 (1978).

Hoffman, G.E., Hayes, T.A.: *J. Comp. Neurol.* 186:371 (1979).

Hokfelt, T., Fuxe, K., Johansson, O., Jeffcoate, S., White, N.: *Eur. J. Pharmacol.* 34:389 (1975).

Hokfelt, T., Kellerth, J.O., Nilsson, G., Pernow, B.: *Brain Res.* 100:235 (1975).

Hokfelt, T., Elde, R., Johansson, O., Luft, R., Nilsson, G., Arimura, A.: *Neuroscience* 1:131 (1976).

Hokfelt, T., Lundberg, J.M., Schultzberg, M., Johansson, O., Ljungdahl, A., Rehfeld, J.: In: *Neural Peptides and Neuronal Communication,* E. Costa, M. Trabucchi (Eds.). Raven Press: New York (1980). p.1.

Hong, J.S., Schmid, R.: *Brain Res.* 205:415 (1981).

Horita, A., Carino, M.A., Smith, J.R.: *Pharmacol. Biochem. Behav.* 5:(Suppl.1):111 (1976).

Hsueh, A.J.W., Erickson, G.F.: *Science* 204:854 (1979).

Husain, A., Smeby, R.S., Krontiris-Litowitz, J., Speth, R.C.: *Brain Res.* 222:182 (1981).

Huston, J.P., Staubli, V.: *Brain Res.* 159:468 (1978).

Huston, J.P., Staubli, V.: In: J.L. Martinez Jr., R.A. Jensen, B. Messing, H. Rigter, J.L. McGaugh (Eds.), *Endogenous Peptides and Learning and Memory Processes.* Academic Press: New York (1981). p. 521.

Inagami, T., Murakami, K.: *Biomed. Res.* 1:456 (1980).

Ioffe, S., Havlicek, V., Friesen, H., Chernick, V.: *Brain Res.* 153:414 (1978).

Izquierdo, I., Souza, D.O., Carrasco, M.A., Dias, R.D., Perry, M.L., Eisinger, S., Elisabetsky, E., Vendite, D.A.: *Psychopharmacologia* 70:173 (1980).

Izquierdo, I., Perry, M.L., Dias, R.D., Souza, D.O., Elisabetsky, E., Carrasco, M.A., Orsingher, O.A., Netto, C.A.: In: J.L. Martinez Jr., R.A. Jensen, B. Messing, H. Rigter, J.L. McGaugh (Eds.), *Endogenous Pepides and Learning and Memory Processes.* Academic Press: New York (1981). p. 269.

Jackson, I.M.D.: *Amer. Zool.* 18:385 (1978).

Jackson, I.M.D., Reichlin, S.: *Nature* 267:853 (1977).

Jacobs, J.W., Goodman, R.H., Chin, W.W., Dee, P.C., Habener, J.F.: *Science* 213:457 (1981).

Jacobson, A.L., Babich, F.R., Bubash, S., Jacobson, A.: *Science* 150:636 (1965).

Jacquet, Y.F., Klee, W.A., Rice, K.C., Iijima, I., Minamikawa, J.: *Science* 198;842 (1977).

Jacquet, Y.F., Klee, W.A., Smyth, D.G.: *Brain Res.* 156:396 (1978).

Jennes, L., Stumpf, W.E.: *Neuroendocrinol. Lett.* 2:241 (1980).

Jessell, T.N., Iverson, L.L.: *Nature* 268:549 (1977).

Johansson, K.N.G., Greibrokk, T., Carrie, B.L., Hanson, J., Folkers, K.: *Biochem. Biophys. Res. Commun.* 63:62 (1975).

Jolles, J., Bar, P.R., Gispen, W.H.: *Brain Res.* 224:315 (1981).

Joseph-Bravo, P., Loudes, C., Charli, J.L., Kordon, C.: *Brain Res.* 166:321 (1979).

Jump, D.B., Oppenheimer, J.H.: *Science* 209:811 (1980).

Kachadorian, W.A., Wade, J.B., Di Scala, V.A.: *Science* 190:67 (1975).

Kakimoto, Y., Nakajima, T., Kakesada, M., Sano, I.: *Biochim. Biophys. Acta* 93:333 (1964).

Kalivas, P.W., Horita, A.: *J. Pharmacol. Exp. Ther.* 212:202 (1980).

Kalter, V.G., Folk, G.E.: *Comp. Biochem. Physiol. A.* 63:7 (1979).

Kamel, F., Krey, L.C.: *Mol. Cell. Endocrinol.* 26:151 (1982).

Kastin, A.J., Ehrensing, R.H., Schalch, D.S., Anderson, M.S.: *Lancet* II:740 (1972).

Kastin, A.J., Coy, D.H., Jacquet, Y., Schally, A.V., Plotnikoff, N.P.: *Metabolism* 27(Suppl.1):1247 (1978).

Kastin, A.J., Olson, R.D., Schally, A.V., Coy, D.H.: *Life Sci.* 25:401 (1979).

Kastin, A.J., Olson, G.A., Schally, A.V., Coy, D.H.: *Trends Neurosci.* 3:163 (1980).

Kastin, A.J., Mauk, M.D., Schally, A.V., Coy, D.H.: *Physiol. Behav.* 25:959 (1980a).

Kastin, A.J., Olson, R.D., Sandman, C.A., Coy, D.H.: In: J.L. Martinez Jr., R.A. Jensen, B. Messing, H. Rigter, J.L. McGaugh (Eds.), *Endogenous Peptides and Learning and Memory Processes.* Academic Press: New York (1981). p. 563.

Kato, Y., Iwasaki, Y., Iwasaki, J., Abe, H., Yanaihara, N., Imura, H.: *Endocrinology* 103:554 (1978).

Katz, R.J.: *Eur. J. Pharmacol.* 53:383 (1979).

Kawaguchi, S., Imaizumi, M., Shio, H., Kataoka, K.: *Naunyn-Schmiedeberg's Arch. Pharmakol.* 260:284 (1968).

Kendrick, K.M., Drewett, R.F.: *Science* 204:877 (1979).

Klaiber, E.L., Brovermann, D.M., Vogel, W., Abraham, G.E., Cone, F.L.: *J. Clin. Endocrinol.* 32:341 (1971).

Klee, W.A., Nirenberg, M.: *Nature* 263:609 (1976).

Kleitman, N.: *Sleep and Wakefulness as Alternating Phases in the Cycle of Existence.* Univ. of Chicago Press: Chicago (1939).

Knigge, K.M.: In: *Brain-Endocrine Interactions II,* K.M. Knigge, D.E. Scott, H. Kobayashi (Eds.). Karger: Basel (1975). p.1.

Koller, M., Krause, H.P., Hoffmeister, F., Ganten, D.: *Neurosci. Lett.* 14:71 (1979).

Konishi, S., Otsuka, M.: *Nature* 252:734 (1974).

Koob, G.F., Lemoal, M., Bloom, F.E.: In: J.L. Martinez Jr., R.A. Jensen, B. Messing, H. Rigter, J.L. McGaugh (Eds.), *Endogenous Peptides and Learning and Memory Processes.* Academic Press: New York (1981). p. 249.

Kornmueller, A., Lux, H.D., Winkel, K., Klee, M.: *Naturwissenschaften* 48:503 (1961).

Kosterlitz, H.W., Paterson, W.: *Proc. Roy. Soc. (London)* 210:113 (1980).

Kovacs, G.L., Bohus, B., Versteeg, D.H.G.: *Neurosciences* 4:1529 (1979).

Kraemer, G.W., Mueller, R., Breese, G.R., Prange, A.J., Lewis, J.K., Morrison, H., McKinney, W.T.: *Pharmacol. Biochem. Behav.* 4:709 (1976).

Krieger, D.T., Liotta, A.: *Science* 205:366 (1979).

Krieger, D.T., Liotta, A., Brownstein, M.J.: *Proc. Natl. Acad. Sci. USA* 74:648 (1977).

Krivoy, W.A., Couch, J.R., Stewart, J.M., Zimmermann, E.: *Brain Res.* 202:365 (1980).

Krueger, J.M., Pappenheim, J.R., Karnovsky, M.L.: *Proc. Natl. Acad. Sci. USA* 75:5235 (1978).

Kruse, H., Van Wimersma-Greidanus, T.B., De Wied, D.: *Pharmacol. Biochem. Behav.* 7:311 (1977).

La Ferla, J.J., Anderson, D.L., Schalch, D.S.: *Psychosom. Med.* 40:166 (1978).

Lahti, R.A., Collins, R.J.: *Eur. J. Pharmacol.* 51:185 (1978).

Lamers, C.B., Morley, J.E., Poitras, P., Sharp, B., Carlson, H.E., Hershman, J.M., Walsh, J.H.: *Am. J. Physiol.* 239:E232 (1980).

Landgraf, R., Ermisch, A., Hess, J.: *Endocrinology* 73:77 (1979).

Land, H., Schutz, G., Schmale, H., Richter, D.: *Nature* 295:299 (1982).

Lane, A.C., Rance, M.J., Walter, D.S.: *Nature* 269:75 (1977).

Lang, R.E., Voigt, K.H., Fehm, H.L., Pfeiffer, E.F.: *Neurosci. Lett.* 2:19 (1976).

Lang, R.E., Rascher, W., Heil, J., Unger, T., Wiedemann, G., Ganten, D.: *Life Sci.* 29:1425 (1981).

Larsson, L.-I.: *Histochemistry* 55:225 (1978).

Larsson, L.-I., Rehfeld, J.F.: *Science* 213:768 (1981).

Lauber, M., Camier, M., Cohen, P.: *Proc. Natl. Acad. Sci. USA* 76:6004 (1979).

Law, P.-Y., Fischer, G., Loh, H.H., Herz, A.: *Biochem. Pharmacol.* 28:2557 (1979).

Leeman, S.E., Gamse, R.: *Trends Pharmacol. Sci.* 2:119 (1981).

Le Gal LaSalle, G., Ben-Ari, Y.: *Brain Res.* 135:174 (1977).

Lembeck, F., Starke, K.: *Naunyn-Schmiedeberg's Arch. Pharmakol.* 259:375 (1968).

Leonard, B.F., Kafoe, W.F., Thody, A.J., Shuster, S.: *J. Neurosci. Res.* 2:39 (1976).

Lewis, R.V., Stern, A.S., Kimura, S., Rossier, J., Stein, S., Udenfriend, S.: *Science* 208:1459 (1980).

Leybin, L., Pinsky, C., LaBella, F.S., Havlicek, V., Rezek, M.: *Nature* 264:458 (1976).

Li, C.H., Barnafi, L., Chretien, M., Chung, D.: *Nature* 208:1093 (1965).

Lis, M., Julesz, J., Gutkowska, J., Genest, J.: *Science* 215:675 (1982).

Litwack, G.: *Trends Biochem. Sci.* 4:217 (1979).

Loh, H.H., Brase, D.A., Sampath-Khanna, S., Mar, J.B., Way, E.L.: *Nature* 264:567 (1976).

Loh, H.H., Cho, T.M., Wu, Y.C., Way, E.L.: *Life Sci.* 14:2231 (1974).

Loh, Y.P., Gainer, H.: *Endocrinology* 105:474 (1978).

Loh, Y.P., Gainer, H.: *FEBS Lett.* 96:269 (1978a).

Loh, Y.P., Gainer, H.: *Proc. Natl. Acad. Sci. USA* 79:108 (1982).

Lord, J.A.H., Waterfield, A.A., Hughes, J., Kosterlitz, H.W.: *Nature* 267:495 (1977).

Loren, I., Alumets, J., Hakanson, R., Sundler, F.: *Histochemistry* 59:249 (1979).

Lorenz, D.N., Goldman, S.A.: *Neurosci. Abstr.* 4:178 (1978).

Lote, C.J., Gent, J.P, Wolsten-Croft, J.H., Szelke, M.: *Nature* 264:188 (1976).

Lupo Di Prisco, C., Lucarini, N., Dessifulvio, F.: *Physiol. Behav.* 20:345 (1978).

Magistretti, P.J., Morrison, J.H., Shoemaker, W.J., Sapin, V., Bloom, F.E.: *Proc. Natl. Acad. Sci. USA* 78:6535 (1981).

Mains, R.E., Eipper, B.A., Ling, N.: *Proc. Natl. Acad. Sci. USA* 74:3014 (1977).

Maldonado, H., Tablante, A.: *Physiol. Behav.* 16:617 (1976).

Malesci, S., Straus, E., Yalow, R.S.: *Proc. Natl. Acad. Sci. USA* 77:597 (1980).

Malfroy, B., Swerts, J.P., Guyon, A., Roques, B.P., Schwartz, J.C.: *Nature* 276:523 (1978).

Malfroy, B., Swerts, J.C., Llorens, G., Schwartz, J.C.: *Neurosci. Lett* 11:329 (1979).

Malick, J.B., Goldstein, J.M.: *Life Sci.* 20:827 (1977).

Manaka, S., Sano, K.: *Neurosci. Lett.* 8:255 (1978).

Manvalan, P., Momany, F.A.: *Biochem. Biophys. Res. Commun.* 105:847 (1982).

Margolis, F.L.: *Trends Neurosci.* 1:42 (1978).

Margolis, F.L., Roberts, N., Ferriero, D., Feldman, J.: *Brain Res.* 81:469 (1974).

Marian, J., Cooper, R.L., Conn, P.M.: *Mol. Pharmacol.* 19:399 (1981).

Marks, N., Stern, F.: *FEBS Lett.* 55:220 (1975).

Martin, G., Baumann, H., Grieger, F.: *Acta Biol. Med. Germ.* 35:995 (1976).

Martin, G.E., Bacino, C.B., Papp, N.L.: *Peptides* 1:333 (1980).

Martin, R., Voigt, K.H.: *Nature* 289:502 (1981).

Marwaha, J., Prasad, K.N.: *Science* 214:675 (1981).

Mason, G.A., Nemeroff, C.B., Luttinger, D., Hatley, O.L., Prange, A.J. Jr.: *Regulatory Peptides* 1:53 (1980).

Mason, J.W.: In: *Handbook of Psychophysiology*, N.S. Greenfield, R.A. Sternbach (Eds.). Holt, Rinehart and Winston: New York (1972). p.3.

Masserano, J.M., King, C.: *Eur. J. Pharmacol.* 69:217 (1981).

Maxfield, F.R., Willingham, M.C., Pastan, I., Dragsten, P., Cheng, S.Y.: *Science* 211:63 (1981).

Mayer, N., Lembeck, F., Saria, A., Gamse, R.: *Naunyn-Schmiedeberg's Arch. Pharmacol.* 306:45 (1979).

Mayer, N., Gamse, R., Lembeck, F.: *J. Neurochem.* (1980).

Mayer, N., Saria, A., Lembeck, F.: In: *Neuropeptides and Neural Transmission*, C. Ajmone Marsan, W.Z. Traczyk (Eds). Raven Press: New York (1980a). p.19.

McCaleb, M.L., Myers, R.D.: *Peptides* 1:47 (1980).

McCaleb, M.L., Myers, R.D., Singer, G., Willis, G.: *Am. J. Physiol.* 236:R312 (1979).

McCann, S.M.: *Endocrinology* 60:664 (1957).

McConnell, J.V.: *J. Neuropsychiat.* 3:(Suppl.1):42 (1962).

McEwen, B.S.: *Science* 211:1303 (1981).

McKay, L.D., Kenney, N.J., Edens, N.K., Williams, R.H., Wood, S.C.: *Life Sci.* 29:1429 (1981).

McLawhon, R.W., Schoon, G.S., Dawson, G.: *Eur. J. Cell Biol.* 25:353 (1981).

McNeill, T.H., Sladek, J.R. Jr.: *Science* 200:72 (1978).

Meidan, R., Aroya, N.B., Koch, Y.: *Life Sci.* 30:535 (1982).

Mendelson, J.H., Ellingbo, J., Keuhnle, J.C., Mello, N.K.: *Psychoneuroendocrinology* 4:341 (1979).

Meyer, D.K., Beinfeld, M.C., Oertel, W.H., Brownstein, M.J.: *Science* 215:187 (1982).

Mezey, E., Palkovits, M., De Kloet, E.R., Verhoef, J., De Wied, D.: *Life Sci.* 22:831 (1978).

Mezey, E., Kivovics, P., Palkovits, M.: *Trends Neurosci.* 2:57 (1979).

Mialhe, C., Briaud, B.: *J. Physiol. (Paris)* 72:261 (1976).

Miller, L.H., Kastin, A.J., Sandman, C.A., Fink, M., Van Veen, W.J.: *Pharmacol. Biochem. Behav.* 2:663 (1974).

Miller, L.H., Groves, G.A., Bopp, M.J., Kastin, A.J.: *Peptides* 1:55 (1980).

Miller, R.E., Caul, W.F.: *Physiol. Behav.* 10:141 (1973).

Misslin, R., Ropartz, P., Ungerer, A., Mandel, P.: *Behav. Processes* 3:45 (1978).

Mogenson, G.J., Kucharczyk, J.: *Fed. Proc.* 37:2683 (1978).

Moniuszko-Jakoniuk, J., Wisniewski, K.: *Pol. J. Pharmacol. Pharm.* 28:655 (1976).

Monnier, M., Dudler, L., Gachter, R., Schoenenberger, G.A.: *Neurosci. Lett.* 6:9 (1977).

Moody, T.W., Pert, C.B., Rivier, J., Brown, M.R.: *Proc. Natl. Acad. Sci. USA* 75:5372 (1978).

Moody, T.W., O'Donohue, T.L., Jacobowitz, D.M.: *Peptides* 2:75 (1981).

Moore, K.E., Demarest, K.T., Johnston, C.A.: *Fed. Proc.* 39:2912 (1980).

Morel, A., Lauber, M., Cohen, P.: *FEBS Lett.* 136:316 (1981).

Morgan, J.M., Routtenberg, A.: *Science* 196:87 (1977).

Mori, M., Prasad, C., Wilber, J.F.: *Brain Res.* 231:451 (1982).

Morin, L.P.: *Physiol. Behav.* 18:701 (1977).

Morley, J.E.: *Life Sci.* 27:355 (1980).

Morley, J.E.: *Life Sci.* 30:479 (1982).

Morley, J.E., Levine, A.S.: *Pharmacol. Biochem. Behav.* 14:149 (1981).

Morley, J.E., Levine, A.S.: *Life Sci.* 29:1901 (1981a).

Morley, J.E., Levine, A.S., Silvis, S.E.: *Science* 214:671 (1981).

Morrell, J.I., Kelley, D.B., Pfaff, D.W.: In: *Brain-Endocrine Interaction.* Vol. 2. Karger: Basel (1975). p. 230.

Morris, R., Salt, T.E., Sofroniew, M.V., Hill, R.G.: *Neurosci. Lett.* 18:163 (1980).

Moses, A.C., Nissley, S.P., Cohen, K.L., Rechler, M.M.: *Nature* 263:137 (1976).

Moss, R.L.: *Fed. Proc.* 36:1978 (1977).

Mousa, S., Miller, C.H.Jr., Couri, D.: *Neuroendocrinology* 33:317 (1981).

Mudge, A.W., Leeman, S.E., Fischbach, G.D.: *Proc. Natl. Acad. Sci. USA* 76:526 (1979).

Mueller, K., Hsiao, S.: *Physiol. Behav.* 22:809 (1979).

Nagai, Y., Yokohama, S., Nagawa, Y., Hirooka, Y., Nihei, N.: *J. Pharmacodyn.* 3:500 (1980).

Nagasaki, H., Kitahama, K., Valatx, J.L., Jouvet, M.: *Brain Res.* 192:276 (1975).

Nakanishi, S., Inoue, A., Kita, T., Nakamura, M., Chang, A.C.Y., Cohen, S.N., Numa, S.: *Nature* 278:423 (1979).

Nakata, Y., Kusaka, Y., Yajima, H., Kitagawa, K., Segawa, T.: *Naunyn-Schmiedeberg's Arch. Pharmacol.* 316:211 (1980).

Naranjo, J.R., Sanchez-Franco, F., Garzon, J., Del Rio, J.: *Life Sci.* 30:441 (1982).

Neidle, A., Reith, M.E.A.: *Arch. Biochem. Biophys.* 203:288 (1980).

Nemeroff, C.B.: *Biol. Psychiat.* 15:283 (1980).

Nemeroff, C.B., Prange, A.J.: *Arch. Gen. Psychiat.* 35:999 (1978).

Nemeroff, C.B., Bissett, G., Prange, A.J. Jr., Loosen, P.T., Lipton, M.A.: *Endocrinology* 98:312 (1976).

Nemeroff, C.B., Mason, G.A., Hatley, O.L., Jahnke, G., Prange, A.J.: *Brain Res.* 184:529 (1980).

Nicholson, G., Greeley, G.H. Jr., Humm, J., Youngblood, W.W., Kizer, J.S.: *Brain Res.* 190:447 (1980).

North, R.A.: *Life Sci.* 24:1527 (1979).

Numan, M.: *Horm. Behav.* 11:209 (1978).

Nyakas, C., Levay, G., Viltsek, J., Endroczi, E.: *Dev. Neurosci.* 4:225 (1981).

Oades, R.D.: *Neurosci. Biobehav. Rev.* 3:31 (1979).

O'Callaghan, J.P., Juskevich, J.C., Lovenberg, W.: *J. Pharmacol. Exp. Ther.* 220:696 (1982).

O'Donohue, T.L., Holmquist, G.E., Jacobowitz, D.M.: *Neurosci. Lett.* 14:271 (1979).

O'Donohue, T.L., Handelmann, G.E., Miller, R.L., Jacobowitz, D.M.: *Science* 215:1125 (1982).

Oehme, P., Hecht, K., Presche, L., Hilse, H., Morgenstern, E., Poppei, M.: In: *Neuropeptides and Neural Transmission,* C. Ajmone Marsan, W.Z. Traczyk (Eds.). Raven Press: New York (1980). p.73.

Olgiati, V.R., Guidobono, F., Luisetto, G., Netti, C., Bianchi, C., Pecile, A.: *Life Sci.* 29:585 (1981).

Oliver, C., Eskay, R.L., Ben-Jonathan, N., Porter, J.C.: *Neuroendocrinology* 95:540 (1974).

Oliver, C., Mical, R.S., Porter, J.C.: *Endocrinology* 101:598 (1977).

Olpe, H.R., Balcar, V.J., Bittiger, H., Rink, H., Sieber, P.: *Eur. J. Pharmacol.* 63:127 (1980).

Olson, G.A., Olson, R.D., Kastin, A.J., Coy, D.H.: *Neurosci. Biobehav. Rev.* 3:285 (1979).

Onali, P., Schwartz, J.P., Costa, E.: *Proc. Natl. Acad. Sci. USA* 78:6531 (1981).

Oppenheimer, J.H.: *Science* 203:971 (1979).

Orlowski, M., Wilk, S.: *Biochem. Biophys. Res. Commun.* 101:814 (1981).

Orwoll, E., Kendall, J.W., Lamorena, L., McGilvra, R.: *Endocrinology* 104:1845 (1979).

Pacold, S.T., Kirstein, L., Hojvat, S., Lawrence, A.M., Hagen, T.C.: *Science* 199:804 (1978).

Palacios, J.M., Kuhar, M.J.:→ *Nature* 294:587 (1981).

Palmer, M.R., Morris, D.H., Taylor, D.A., Stewart, J.M., Hoffer, B.J.: *Life Sci.* 23:851 (1978).

Panksepp, J., Nance, D.M.: *Physiol. Behav.* 9:447 (1972).

Panksepp, J., Reilly, P., Bishop, P., Meeker, R.B., Vilberg, T.R.: *Pharmacol. Biochem. Behav.* 5(Suppl.1):59 (1976).

Panksepp, J., Herman, B.H., Vilberg, T., Bishop, P., De Eskinazi, F.G.: *Neurosci. Biobehav. Rev.* 4:473 (1978).

Parker, C.R. Jr., Neaves, W.B., Barnea, A., Porter, J.C.: *Endocrinology* 101:66 (1977).

Pavel, S., Psatta, D., Goldstein, R.: *Brain Res. Bull.* 2:251 (1977).

Pearse, A.G.E.: *Nature* 262:92 (1976).

Pecile, A., Ferri, S., Braga, P.C., Olgiati, V.R.: *Experientia* 31:332 (1975).

Peterkofsky, A., Battaini, F., Koch, Y., Takahara, Y., Dannies, P.: *Molec. Cell. Biochem.* 42:45 (1982).

Phillips, M.I.: *Neuroendocrinology* 25:354 (1978).

Phillis, J.W.: *Soc. Neurosci. Symp.* 2:241 (1977).

Phillis, J.W., Kirkpatrick, J.R., Said, S.I.: *Can. J. Physiol. Pharmacol.* 56:337 (1978).

Piercey, M.F., Schroeder, L.A., Folkers, K., Xu, J.C., Horig, J.: *Science* 214:1361 (1981).

Pinget, M., Straus, E., Yalow, R.S.: *Life Sci.* 25:339 (1979).

Plavilshchikov, N.N.: *Archives Russe de Protistologie* 7:1 (1928).

Plotnikoff, N.P., Kastin, A.J., Anderson, M.S., Schally, A.V.: *Life Sci.* 10:1279 (1971).

Plotnikoff, N.P., Prange, A.J., Breese, G.R., Anderson, M.S., Wilson, I.C.: *Science* 178:417 (1972).

Polak, J.M., Buchan, A.M.J., Czykowska, W., Solcia, E., Brown, S.R., Pearse, A.G.E.: In: *Gut Hormones,* S.R. Bloom (Ed.). Churchill Livingstone: Edinburgh (1978). p.541.

Polleri, A., Perrotte, E., Audibert, A.: *Neuropsychobiology* 4:26 (1978).

Prange, A.J., Wilson, I.C.: *Psychopharmacologia* 26:Suppl.82 (1972).

Raichle, M.E., Grubb, R.L.: *Brain Res.* 143:191 (1978).
Rainbow, T.C., Davis, P.G., McEwen, B.S.: *Brain Res.* 194:548 (1980).
Ramsay, D.J.: *Fed. Proc.* 37:2689 (1978).
Rauch, R., Hollenberg, M.D., Hope, D.B.: *Biochem. J.* 115:473 (1969).
Redgate, E.S.: *Life Sci.* 19:137 (1976).
Regoli, D.: *Can. J. Physiol. Pharmacol.* 57:129 (1979).
Rehfeld, J.F., Goltermann, N., Larsson, L.I., Emson, P.M., Lee, C.M.: *Fed. Proc.* 38:2325 (1979).
Reinis, S.: *Activ. Nerv. Super.* 7:167 (1965).
Reinis, S.: In: *Chemical Transfer of Learned Information,* E.J. Fjerdingstad (Ed.). North Holland: Amsterdam (1971). p.109.
Reith, M.E.A., Schotman, P., Gispen, W.H.: *Neurobiology* 5:355 (1975).
Reith, M.E.A., Neidle, A., Lajtha, A.: *Arch. Biochem. Biophys.* 195:478 (1979).
Reith, M.E.A., Sershen, H., Lajtha, A.: *Neurochem. Res.* 5:1291 (1980).
Renaud, L.P., Martin, J.B., Brazeau, P.: *Nature* 255:233 (1975).
Renaud, L.P., Blume, H.W., Pittman, Q.J., Lamour, Y., Tan, A.T.: *Science* 205:1275 (1979).
Reynolds, D.V.: *Science* 164:444 (1969).
Rezek, M.: *Psychoneuroendocrinology* 2:173 (1977).
Rhodes, C.H., Morrell, J.I., Pfaff, D.W.: *Neuroendocrinology* 33:18 (1981).
Rigter, H., Jensen, R.A., Martinez, J.L. Jr., Messing, R.B., Vasquez, B.J., Liang, K.C., McGaugh, J.L.: *Proc. Natl. Acad. Sci. USA* 77:3729 (1980).
Rivier, C., Vale, W., Ling, N., Brown, M., Guillemin, R.: *Endocrinology* 100:238 (1977).
Rivier, C., Brown, M., Vale, W.: *Endocrinology* 102:519 (1978).
Rizzo, A.J., Goltzman, D.: *Endocrinology* 108:1672 (1981).
Robberecht, P., Deneef, P., Lammens, M., Deschoot, M., Christopher, J.P.: *Eur. J. Biochem.* 90:147 (1978).
Roberts, J.L., Herbert, E.: *Proc. Natl. Acad. Sci. USA* 74:5300 (1977).
Robyn, C., Lhermite, M., Leclercq, R., Copinsch, G.: *Acta Endocrinol.* 83:692 (1976).
Roche, K.E., Leshner, A.I.: *Science* 204:1343 (1979).
Rockstroh, B., Elbert, T., Lutzenberger, W., Birbaumer, N., Fehm, H.L., Voigt, K.H.: *Psychoneuroendocrinology* 6:301 (1981).
Rodbell, M.: *Nature* 284:17 (1980).
Roemer, D., Buescher, H.H., Hill, R.C., Pless, J., Bauer, W., Cardinaux, F., Closse, A., Hauser, D., Huguenin, R.: *Nature* 268:547 (1977).
Rose, R.M.: *Psychosom. Med.* 37:50 (1975).
Rosenblatt, F., Miller, R.G.: *Proc. Natl. Acad. Sci. USA* 56:1423 (1967).
Rossier, J.: *Trends Neurosci.* 4:94 (1981).
Rossier, J., Audigier, Y., Ling, N., Cros, J., Udenfriend, S.: *Nature* 288:88 (1980).
Rothman, R.B., Westfall, T.C.: *J. Neurochem.* 33:191 (1979).
Rotsztejn, W.H., Besson, J., Briaud, B., Gagnant, L., Rosselin, G., Kordon, C.: *Neuroendocrinology* 31:287 (1980).
Ruberg, M., Rotsztejn, W.H., Arancibi, S., Besson, J., Enjalberg, A.: *Eur. J. Pharmacol.* 51:319 (1978).
Rubinstein, M., Stein, S., Udenfriend, S.: *Proc. Natl. Acad. Sci. USA* 75:669 (1978).
Rupnow, J.H., Hinkle, P.M., Dixon, J.E.: *Biochem. Biophys. Res. Commun.* 89:721 (1979).
Ryall, R.W., Belcher, G.: *Brain Res.* 137:376 (1977).
Saffran, M., Schally, A.V.: *Can. J. Biochem. Physiol.* 33:408 (1955).
Saffran, M., Schally, A.V.: *Neuroendocrinology* 24:359 (1977).
Saginor, M., Horton, R.: *Endocrinology* 82:627 (1968).
Said, S.I., Porter, J.C.: *Life Sci.* 24:227 (1979).

Saito, A., Sankaran, H., Goldfine, I.D., Williams, J.A.: *Science* 208:1155 (1980).

Saito, A., Goldfine, I.D., Williams, J.A.: *J. Neurochem.* 37:483 (1981).

Saito, A., Williams, J.A., Goldfine, I.D.: *Endocrinology* 109:984 (1981a).

Saito, A., Williams, J.A., Goldfine, I.D.: *Nature* 289:599 (1981b).

Sandman, C.A., Beckwith, B.E., Kastin, A.J.: *Peptides* 1:109 (1980).

Sar, M., Stumpf, W.E., Miller, R.J., Chang, K.J., Cuatrecasas, P.: *J. Comp. Neurol.* 182:17 (1978).

Sara, V.R., Hall, K.: *Trends Neurosci.* 2:263 (1979).

Sara, V.R., King, T.L., Stuart, M.C., Lazarus, L.: *Endocrinology* 99:1512 (1976).

Sawyer, C.H.: *Acta Biol. Acad. Sci. Hung.* 28:11 (1977).

Schaller, H.C.: *J. Neurochem.* 25:187 (1975).

Schally, A.V.: *Science* 202:18 (1978).

Schally, A.V., Bowers, C.Y.: *Metabolism* 13:1190 (1964).

Scharrer, B.: In: *Reproductive Behaviour and Evolution,* J.S. Rosenblatt, B.R. Komisaruk (Eds.). Plenum Press: New York (1978). p.111.

Schmid, G., Palkovits, M., Muller, I., Heidland, A.: *Neuropharmacology* 21:3 (1982).

Schotman, P., Von Heuven-Nolsen, D., Gispen, W.H.: *J. Neurochem.* 34:1661 (1980).

Schreiber, R.A., Santos, N.N.: *Pharmacol. Biochem. Behav.* 6:603 (1976).

Schudziarra, V., Zyznar, E., Rouiller, D.: *Science* 207:530 (1980).

Schulz, R., Wilhelm, A., Pirke, K.M., Gramsch, C., Herz, A.: *Nature* 294:757 (1981).

Schwartz, J.C., Malfroy, B., De La Baume, S.: *Life Sci.* 29:1715 (1981).

Schwyzer, R.: *Trends Pharmacol. Sci.* 1:327 (1980).

Seelig, S., Sayers, G.: *Fed. Proc.* 36:2100 (1977).

Seif, S.M., Robinson, A.G.: *Ann. Rev. Physiol.* 40:345 (1978).

Selye, H.: *Nature* 138:32 (1936).

Selye, H.: *The Stress of Life,* McGraw-Hill: New York (1976).

Severs, W.B., Summy-Long, J., Taylor, J.S., Connor, J.D.: *J. Pharmacol. Exp. Ther.* 174:27 (1970).

Sharma, S.K., Klee, W.A., Nirenberg, N.: *Proc. Natl. Acad. Sci. USA* 74:3365 (1977).

Shibasaki, T., Ling, N., Guillemin, R.: *Nature* 285:416 (1980).

Shin, S.H.: *Neuroendocrinology* 31:375 (1980).

Shin, S.H., Reifel, C.W.: *Neuroendocrinology* 32:139 (1981).

Shiomi, H., Ueda, H., Takagi, H.: *Neuropharmacology* 20:633 (1981).

Silverman, A.J., Zimmerman, E.A.: In: *Brain-Endocrine Interactions,* Vol.3, D.E. Scott, G.P. Kozlowski, A. Weindl (Eds.). Karger: Basel (1978). p.83.

Silverman, A.J., Hoffman, D., Gadde, C.A., Krey, L.C., Zimmerman, E.A.: *Neuroendocrinology* 32:129 (1981).

Simon, E.J., Hiller, J.M., Edelman, I.: *Science* 190:389 (1975).

Simonnet, G., Bioulac, B., Rodriguez, F., Vincent, J.D.: *Pharmacol. Biochem. Behav.* 13:359 (1980).

Simpson, J.B.: *Neuroendocrinology* 32:248 (1981).

Skirboll, L.R., Grace, A.A., Hommer, D.W., Rehfeld, J., Goldstein, M., Hokfelt, T., Bunney, B.S.: *Neuroscience* 6:2111 (1981).

Skrabanek, P., Balfe, A., Webb, M., Maguire, J., Powell, D.: *Psychoneuroendocrinology* 6:261 (1981).

Slater, E.E., Defendini, R., Zimmerman, E.A.: *Proc. Natl. Acad. Sci. USA* 77:5458 (1980).

Smith, R.M., Patel, A.J., Kingsbury, A.E., Hunt, A., Balazs, R.: *Brain Res.* 198:375 (1980).

Smyth, D.G., Massey, D.E., Zakarian, S.: *Nature* 279:252 (1979).

Smythe, G.A., Brandstater, J.F., Lazarus, L.: *Neuroendocrinology* 17:245 (1975).

Sofroniew, M.V., Schrell, U.: *Neurosci. Lett.* 22:211 (1981).

Sofroniew, M.V., Weindl, A.: *Am. J. Anat.* 153:391 (1978).

Sofroniew, M.V., Weindl, A.: In: J.L. Martinez Jr., R.A. Jensen, B. Messing, H. Rigter, J.L. McGaugh (Eds.), *Endogenous Peptides and Learning and Memory Processes.* Academic Press: New York (1981). p.327.

Spanis, C.W., Delcarme, M., Drucker-Colin, R.R.: *Pharmacol. Biochem. Behav.* 5:165 (1976).

Sperry, R.W.: *Quart. Rev. Biol.* 20:311 (1945).

Spirtes, M.A., Plotnikoff, N.P., Kostrzewa, R.M., Harston, C.T., Kastin, A.J., Christensen, C.W.: *Pharmacol. Biochem. Behav.* 5:(Suppl.1):121 (1976).

Spona, J.: *Endocrin. Exper.* 9:125 (1975).

Stallcup, W.B., Patrick, J.: *Proc. Natl. Acad. Sci. USA* 77:634 (1980).

Staubli, U., Huston, J.P.: *Pharmacol. Biochem. Behav.* 10:783 (1979).

Stearns, E.L., Winter, J.S.D., Faiman, C.: *J. Clin. Endocrinol.* 37:687 (1973).

Stern, A.S., Jones, B.N., Shively, J.E., Stein, S., Udenfriend, S.: *Proc. Natl. Acad. Sci. USA* 78:1962 (1981).

Stern, P., Catovic, S., Stern, M.: *Naunyn-Schmiedeberg's Arch. Pharmacol.* 281:233 (1974).

Stern, W.C., Morgane, P.J.: In: *Neurobiology of Sleep and Memory,* R.R. Drucker-Colin, J. McGaugh (Eds.). Academic Press: New York (1977). p.373.

Stern, W.C., Jalowiec, J.E., Shabshelowitz, H., Morgane, P.J.: *Horm. Behav.* 6:189 (1975).

Sternberger, L.A., Petrali, J.P.: *Cell Tissue Res.* 162:141 (1975).

Stewart, J.M., Channabasavaiah, K.: *Fed. Proc.* 38:2302 (1979).

Stewart, W.W.: *Nature* 238:202 (1972).

Stith, R.D., Weingarten, D.: *Neuroendocrinology* 26:129 (1978).

Strahlendorf, H.K., Strahlendorf, J.C., Barnes, C.D.: *Brain Res.* 191:284 (1980).

Straus, E., Yalow, R.S.: *Fed. Proc.* 38:2320 (1978).

Stumpf, W.E., Sar, M.: *Fed. Proc.* 36:1973 (1977).

Sutton, C.A., Martin, T.F.J.: *Endocrinology* 110:1273 (1982).

Swaab, B.F., Achterberg, P.W., Boer, G.J., Dogterom, J., Van Leeuwen, F.W.: In: J.L. Martinez Jr., R.A. Jensen, B. Messing, H. Rigter, J.L. McGaugh (Eds.), *Endogenous Peptides and Learning and Memory Processes.* Academic Press: New York (1981). p. 7.

Swan, H., Schatte, C.: *Science* 195:84 (1977).

Szabo, O., Szabo, A.J.: *J. Physiol. (London)* 253:121 (1975).

Tan, A.T., Tsang, D., Renaud, L.P., Martin, J.B.: *Brain Res.* 123:193 (1977).

Tannenbaum, M., Panerai, A.E., Friesen, H.G.: *Life Sci.* 25:1983 (1979).

Tate, D.F., Galvan, L., Ungar, G.: *Pharmacol. Biochem. Behav.* 5:441 (1976).

Taylor, D.P., Pert, C.B.: *Proc. Natl. Acad. Sci. USA* 76:660 (1979).

Terry, L.C., Willoughby, J.O., Brazeau, P., Martin, J.B., Patel, Y.: *Science* 192:565 (1976).

Thody, A.J., Wilson, C.A., Everard, D.: *Psychopharmacology* 74:153 (1981).

Tintner, R., Dunn, A.J., Iuvone, M., Shukla, J.B., Rennert, O.M.: *J. Neurochem.* 33:1067 (1979).

Tixier-Vidal, A., Gourdji, D.: *Physiol. Rev.* 61:974 (1981).

Toh, C.C.: *J. Physiol. (London)* 188:451 (1967).

Tonoue, T.: *Endocrin. Japon.* 24:271 (1977).

Toubeau, G., Desclin, J., Parmentier, M., Pasteels, J.L.: *Neuroendocrinology* 29:374 (1979).

Tozzi, W., Sale, P., Angelucci, L.: *Pharmacol. Biochem. Behav.* 12:7 (1980).

Tsujimoto, A., Tanaka, S.: *Life Sci.* 28:903 (1981).

Ueda, H., Tatsumi, K., Shiomi, H., Takagi, H.: *Brain Res.* 231:222 (1982).

Uhl, G.R., Snyder, S.H.: *Life Sci.* 19:1827 (1976).

Uhl, G.R., Bennett, J.P., Jr., Snyder, S.H.: *Brain Res.* 130:299 (1977).

Uhl, G.R., Kuhar, M.J., Snyder, S.H.: *Proc. Natl. Acad. Sci. USA* 74:4059 (1977a).

Ungar, G.: *Fed. Proc.* 28:647 (1969).

Ungar, G.: *Agents Actions* 1:155 (1970).

Ungar, G.: In: *Methods in Pharmacology.* Vol. 1, A. Schwartz (Ed). Appleton-Century-Crofts: New York (1971). p. 744.

Ungar, G.: *Life Sci.* 14:595 (1974).

Ungar, G.: In: *Biochemistry of Brain,* S. Kumar (Ed.). Pergamon Press: Oxford (1980). p.383.

Ungar, G., Burzynski, S.R.: *Fed. Proc.* 32:362 (1973).

Ungar, G., Cohen, M.: *Int. J. Neuropharmacol.* 5:183 (1966).

Ungar, G., Desiderio, D.M., Parr, W.: *Nature* 238:198 (1972).

Ungar, G., Fjerdingstad, E.J.: *Mol. Neurobiol. Bull.* 2:9 (1969).

Ungar, G., Oceguerra-Navarro, C.: *Nature* 207:301 (1965).

Ungar, G., Ungar, A.L.: *Fed. Proc.* 35:309 (1966).

Ungar, G., Ungar, A.L., Malin, D.H., Sarantakis, D.: *Psychoneuroendocrinology* 2:1 (1977).

Uno, T.: *Am. J. Physiol.* 61:203 (1922).

Urca, G., Frenk, H., Liebeskind, J.C., Taylor, A.N.: *Science* 197:83 (1977).

Uyeno, E.T., Chang, D., Folkers, K.: *Biochim. Biophys. Res. Commun.* 86:837 (1979).

Valcana, T., Timiras, P.S.: *Mol. Cell Endocrinol.* 11:31 (1978).

Vale, W., Rivier, C., Brown, M.: *Ann. Rev. Physiol.* 39:479 (1977).

Valeri, P., Angelucci, L., Palmery, M.: *Neurosci. Lett.* 9:249 (1978).

Vanderhaegen, J.J., Signeau, J.C., Gepts, W.: *Nature* 257:604 (1975).

Van Duk, A.M.A., King, G.B., Schotman, P., Gispen, W.H.: *Neurochem. Res.* 6:847 (1981).

Van Houten, J., Posner, B.I.: *Nature* 282:623 (1979).

Van Houten, M., Posner, B.I., Kopriwa, B.M., Brawer, J.R.: *Science* 207:1081 (1980).

Van Ree, J.M., De Wied, D.: *Life Sci.* 19:1331 (1976).

Van Riezen, H., Rigter, H., De Wied, D.: *Behav. Biol.* 20:311 (1977).

Van Wimersma Greidanus, Tj.B., Bohus, B., De Wied, D.: In: J.L. Martinez Jr., R.A. Jensen, B. Messing, H. Rigter, J.L. McGaugh (Eds.), *Endogenous Peptides and Learning and Memory Processes.* Academic Press: New York (1981). p. 413.

Van Wyk, J.J., Underwood, L.E.: *Ann. Rev. Med.* 26:427 (1975).

Veith, J.L., Sandman, C.A., Walker, D.H.C., Kastin, A.J.: *Physiol. Behav.* 20:43 (1978).

Vesely, D.J.: *Am. J. Physiol.* 240:E79 (1981).

Vijayan, E., Krulich, L., McCann, S.M.: *Neuroendocrinology* 26:174 (1978).

Vijayan, E., Samson, W.K., Said, S.I., McCann, S.M.: *Endocrinology* 104:53 (1979).

Villarreal, J.A., Brown, M.R.: *Life Sci.* 23:2729 (1978).

Vindrola, O., Briones, R., Asai, M., Fernandez-Guardiola, A.: *Neurosci. Lett.* 21:39 (1981).

Vizi, E.S., Volbekas, V.: In: *Neuropeptides and Neural Transmission,* C. Ajmone Marsan, W.Z. Traczyk (Eds.). Raven Press: New York (1980). p.257.

Vogel, Z., Miron, T., Altstein, M., Wilchek, M.: *Biochem. Biophys. Res. Commun.* 85:226 (1978).

Von Euler, U.S., Gaddum, J.H.: *J. Physiol.* 72:74 (1931).

Von Neumann, G.: *The Computer and the Brain.* Yale Univ. Press, New Haven (1958).

Wagner, H.R., Crutcher, K.A., Davis, J.N.: *Brain Res.* 171:147 (1979).

Wakerley, J.B., Poulain, D.A., Brown, D.: *Brain Res.* 148:425 (1978).

Wallis, C.J., Luttge, W.G.: *J. Neurochem.* 34:609 (1980).

Walsh, R.J., Posner, B.I., Kopriwa, B.M., Brawer, J.R.: *Science* 201:1041 (1978).

Warberg, J., Oliver, C., Barnea, A., Parker, C.R., Porter, J.C.: *Brain Res.* 175:247 (1979).

Ward, M.M., Sandman, C.A., George, J.M., Shulman, H.: *Physiol. Behav.* 22:669 (1979).

Watkins, W.B.: *Neurosci. Lett.* 17:329 (1980).

Watson, S.J., Akil, H., Richard, C.W., Barchas, J.D.: *Nature* 275:226 (1978).

Watson, S.J., Richard, C.W., Barchas, J.D.: *Science* 200:1180 (1978).

Watson, S.J., Richard, C.W. III., Ciaranello, R.D., Barchas, J.D.: *Peptides* 1:23 (1980).

Wayner, M.J.: *Pharmacol. Biochem. Behav.* 5:(Suppl.1):103 (1976).
Wayner, M.J., Ono, T., Nolley, D.: *Pharmacol. Biochem. Behav.* 1:679 (1973).
Webb, W.B.: *Sleep* 1:205 (1978).
Weber, E., Evans, C.J., Samuelsson, S.J., Barchas, J.D.: *Science* 214:1248 (1981).
Wei, E.T., Tseng, L.F., Loh, H.H., Li, C.H.: *Life Sci.* 21:321 (1977).
Weiner, R.I., Ganong, W.F.: *Physiol. Rev.* 58:905 (1978).
Weingartner, H., Gold, P., Ballenger, J.C., Smallberg, S.A., Summers, R., Rubinow, D.R., Post, R.M., Goodwin, F.K.: *Science* 211:601 (1981).
Weingartner, H., Kaye, W., Gold, P., Smallberg, S., Peterson, R., Gillin, J.C., Ebert, M.: *Life Sci.* 29:2721 (1981a).
Weinstein, B., Bartschock, R.M., Cook, R.M., Tam, P.S., Gutman, H.N.: *Experientia* 31:754 (1975).
Westall, F.C., Lennon, V.A., Gospodarowicz, D.: *Proc. Natl. Acad. Sci. USA* 75:4675 (1978).
Weyhenmeyer, J.A., Raizada, M.K., Phillips, M.I., Fellows, R.E.: *Neurosci. Lett.* 16:41 (1980).
Williams, J.A.: *Fed. Proc.* 40:128 (1981).
Wilson, I.C., Prange, A.J. Jr., Lara, P.P., Alltop, L.B., Stikeleather, R.A., Lipton, M.A.: *Arch. Gen. Psychiat.* 29:15 (1973).
Wislocki, G.B., King, L.S.: *Am. J. Anat.* 58:421 (1936).
Witter, A., Gispen, W.H., De Wied, D.: In: J.L. Martinez Jr., R.A. Jensen, B. Messing, H. Rigter, J.L. McGaugh (Eds.), *Endogenous Peptides and Learning and Memory Processes.* Academic Press: New York (1981). p. 37.
Wojcik, M., Niemierko, S.: *Acta Neurobiol. Exp.* 38:25 (1978).
Wolfe, R.R., Allsop, J.R., Burke, J.F.: *Life Sci.* 22:1043 (1978).
Wolinska, E., Polkowski, J., Domanski, E.: *J. Endocrinol.* 73:21 (1977).
Wollemann, M., Szebeni, A., Bajusz, S.S., Graf, L.: *Neurochem. Res.* 4:627 (1979).
Wolozin, B.L., Pasternak, G.W.: *Proc. Natl. Acad. Sci. USA* 78:6181 (1981).
Yaksh, T.L., Elde, R.P.: *J. Neurophysiol.* 46:1056 (1981).
Yaksh, T.L., Farb, D.H., Leeman, S.E., Jessell, T.M.: *Science* 206:481 (1979).
Yamada, Y.: *Neuroendocrinology* 18:263 (1975).
Yamamoto, M., Tachikawa, S., Maeno, H.: *Neuropharmacology* 20:83 (1981).
Yanagisawa, T., Prasad, C., Peterkofsky, A.: *J. Biol. Chem.* 255:10290 (1980).
Yarbrough, G.G.: *Progr. Neurobiol.* 12:291 (1979).
Yarbrough, G.G., Lotti, V.J.: *Pharmacology* 20:207 (1978).
Yarbrough, G.G., Singh, D.K.: *Experientia* 34:390 (1978).
Yasuda, N., Greer, M.A.: *Life Sci.* 24:549 (1979).
Youngblood, W.W., Humm, J., Kizer, J.S.: *Brain Res.* 163:101 (1979).
Yu, J.Y.L., Namiki, H., Gorban, A.: *Neuroendocrinology* 29:54 (1979).
Zetler, G.: *Adv. Biochem. Psychopharmacol.* 18:1 (1978).
Zetler, G.: *Neuropharmacology* 19:415 (1980).
Zieglgansberger, W., Fry, J.P.: In: H.W. Kosterlitz (Ed.), *Opiates and Endogenous Opioid Peptides.* Elsevier/North Holland: Amsterdam (1976). p. 213.
Zieglgansberger, W., Fry, J.P.: In: A. Herz (Ed.), *Development in Opiate Research.* Marcel Dekker: New York (1978).
Zieglgansberger, W., French, E.D., Siggins, G.R., Bloom, F.E.: *Science* 205:415 (1979).
Zierler, K., Rogus, E.M.: *Fed. Proc.* 40:121 (1981).
Zimmerman, E.A., Robinson, A.G.: *Kidney Internat.* 10:12 (1976).
Zingg, H.H., Patel, Y.C.: *Life Sci.* 30:525 (1982).
Zippel, H.P., Domagk, G.F.: *Pflueger's Arch.* 323:258 (1971).
Zukin, R.S., Zukin, S.R.: *Life Sci.* 29:2681 (1981).
Zukin, R.S., Zukin, S.R.: *Mol. Pharmacol.* 20:246 (1981a).

Zwiers, H., Veldhuis, D., Schotman, P., Gispen, W.H.: *Neurochem. Res.* 1:669 (1976).
Zwiers, H., Tonnaer, J., Wiegant, V.M., Schotman, P., Gispen, W.H.: *J. Neurochem.* 33:247 (1979).
Zwiers, H., Schotman, P., Gispen, W.H.: *J. Neurochem.* 34:1689 (1980).

VI

A MODEL OF NEURONAL
PLASTICITY AND SOME
SPECULATIONS ON ITS
RELATIONSHIP TO
LEARNING AND MEMORY

The issues pertaining to the continued adaptation of the brain's functional activity to a changing environment comprise one of the major unresolved problems in contemporary neurobiology. A particularly contentious area no doubt has been the nature of the biochemical changes underlying learning and memory. Since those impetuous days in the '60s and early '70s when this work began to occupy a prominent position within biopsychology, an enormous amount and variety of biochemical data have entered the literature. When assembled in a logical way, these findings can provide a rather comprehensive picture of events taking place within the brain and its individual neurons during learning.

It is quite evident that we have to go beyond postulations that memory is stored in chemical form as ribonucleic acids, peptides, or proteins. This is also true for the short-lived fascinations with a learning-induced restructuring of genes or with a memory process that is the exclusive domain of one or another neurotransmitter system. If we want to evaluate meaningfully the vast amount of available information within the context of memory, there are three questions with which we must contend.

Question 1: What are the chemical changes within an individual neuron which define an engram?

Question 2: Where is the engram localized?

Question 3: How is an engram formed; how is it retrieved; and how are the pieces of information coordinated?

Question 1

WHAT ARE THE CHEMICAL CHANGES WHICH DEFINE
AN ENGRAM?

The problem of the functional adaptability of the brain needs to be viewed at two levels. The first involves the brain as a whole. As a unit, it is continuously modifying its function, subject to both environmental and genetic influences. Moreover, it can respond to the presence of drugs with temporary changes or the development of long-term tolerance and dependence. The brain is affected by various types of chemical, thermal and mechanical insult, whose effects can differ in degree and duration, in addition to the extent of recovery from the damage. It is also capable of recording events, consolidating experience as memory traces and then recombining or reanalyzing the experiences to generate new information.

The effectiveness with which the brain handles incoming information is influenced by a continuing series of modifications in neuronal and synaptic excitability which constitute the functional state of the brain at any given time. Such states can actually be viewed as overall modulators of processing strategies and are determined by an interaction of the following factors:

(1) the genetic composition,
(2) stage of neural development, the plastic capacity of the brain and its neurons during development,
(3) motivational state,
(4) availability of stored information and related processing strategies,
(5) significant environmental influences,
(6) metabolic and hormonal conditions, and
(7) dysfunctional states.

By continually modifying the functional state of the brain, such factors serve to shape the process of learning and the storage of information in memory.

The functional adjustments of the neurons themselves underlie all of the above changes and constitute the second, lower level. The neuron itself is actually able to perform only a few functions. It is able to integrate the postsynaptic potentials, to become depolarized or hyperpolarized, and finally, to produce a single or series of nerve impulses.

Variations in the number of impulses have an informational importance to the neuron. The rate and pattern of impulses reaching the neuron through its synapses determine the level of its excitation and consequently the rate and pattern of its own impulse production. But, the same quantity or patterning of stimulation may have an entirely different content of information, depending upon the pathways or brain areas which are involved. Thus, for example, firing in one part of the primary auditory cortex may represent a signal for a frequency of 2 kHz. However, in another part, the identical firing pattern may indicate that the incoming frequency is 15 kHz. The same would be true for most systems in the brain.

An individual neuron, then, does not "recognize" the nature of the information as such - a specific color, sound, a painful stimulus, or information to be stored or retrieved. The cells typically respond to excitation from other neurons, and this is their only specific stimulus. The neuron does not distinguish whether the pattern of impulses reaching its surface has been altered by brain damage, drugs, or a learning event.

An important point is that any biochemical process that functions to establish and maintain neuronal plasticity, as it relates to the content of learning, must be responsive to stimulation. But at the same time, due to the topographic organization of the informational coding (somatotopic, retinotopic, tonotopic, etc.), it has to be sufficiently general in character to permit the same process in different neurons or neuronal systems to code for a diverse content of information. It must further be variable enough in degree and direction in order to allow for graded changes in excitability which would be necessary for the adequate functioning of neuronal networks under shifting environmental conditions. But, by itself, the process must be independent of the interpreted content of the incoming information.

These considerations make it difficult to conceptualize the mode of action of some "memory-specific substance" which could uniformly influence neurons within one functional system to generate a particular type of behavior. It would therefore be inappropriate to expect that all of the neurons within a given brain region could produce or be affected by some uniform "memory-linked" RNA or protein. While memory-specific biochemical events have been postulated, the importance of each to the process of learning and memory has been a contentious issue. It would appear that the answer to the problem does not reside in the existence of some molecular memory-specific event, but most likely in adjustments of the functioning of masses of neurons, each component of which would have its own pattern of activity.

Over the past 20 years, there have been theories of memory that have stressed the importance of one chemical change or another. The actual situation, however, would appear to be more complex. Each neuron is a metabolic unit, whose activity is the expression of a host of interrelated biochemical events. Alterations in one biochemical system or one topographical region of the cell invariably influence other systems. Consequently, any exploration of the various forms of neuronal plasticity must realistically consider more than just one or two intracellular phenomena. All components of the neurons and glia interact and are mutually dependent upon one another, relationships which were continually emphasized throughout the previous five sections.

In our assessment of the literature concerning the molecular mechanisms of learning and memory, we were unable to single out any decisive event which by itself can control functional plasticity. Most, if not all components of the cell's metabolic machinery are likely of comparable importance in producing the alterations in neuronal excitability. Consequently, we felt it important systematically to present and interrelate all aspects of nerve cell metabolism in order to assemble a working model of neuronal plasticity.

The possibility that individual nerve cells have their own particular excitability and firing pattern that adapts to the functional demands placed upon them raises a question concerning the quality of underlying biochemical changes responsible for the adaptation.

As presented in the preceding chapters, the alteration in neuronal excitability has three essential components:

(1) the receptor function of the neuron, involving several species of protein receptors present in the cell membrane, cytoplasm, cell nucleus or elsewhere. Their activation triggers a number of immediate, proximate changes in the membrane, the most prominent of which is a shift in membrane permeability.

(2) a system of second messengers which responds to receptor stimulation and conveys the message to various metabolic systems within the cell, and

(3) a biochemical adaptation of the cell as a functional entity, involving pre-and post-translational protein alterations and the metabolism of various cell components.

In order for the nervous system to function, its neurons must interact with one another. This interaction of single units is what underlies any brain activity and ultimately behavior. The communication between neurons may occur in at least nine different ways, all of which are probably involved in functional plasticity within the brain.

(1) Classical neurotransmission using the putative transmitters, namely acetylcholine, the catecholamines, indoleamines, the excitatory and inhibitory amino acids, histamine and perhaps a few others released from the presynaptic area.

(2) A diffusion of neurotransmitters from the nerve endings into the brain's extracellular space where they can react with extrasynaptic receptors on neighboring neurons. Although there is little information available on the importance of this mechanism, all components of this form of communication are present in nervous tissue and should be taken into consideration.

(3) Neurotransmitters, peptides, adenosine, prostaglandins and other substances which modify the release of classical neurotransmitters and the responses of the target cells. Their action would be typically neuromodulatory in nature.

(4) Hormones that are synthesized in tissues elsewhere in the body, such as the steroids and thyroid hormones, bind to those neurons which possess specific receptors for them and alter the functional state of those cells.

(5) Transneuronally transported proteins carried from one cell to another either in an orthograde or a retrograde fashion.

(6) The ionic environment of the neurons affected by the firing of neighboring neurons.

(7) Ephaptic transmission, a direct electrotonic transfer of excitation from one unit to another.

(8) A spread of small electromagnetic fields generated by active neurons.

(9) An excitation of neurons by their own metabolic processes which are able to induce periodic neuronal discharges. These cells are the "pacemaker" neurons.

The synapse has long been considered as a prime site for the alterations in neuronal plasticity. As a point of interneuronal communication, the synapse would appear to provide numerous possibilities for the functional modulation of the target neuron. However, this does not mean to imply that the region is the sole domain of plasticity. Other membranous regions could well be involved, including the axon hillock, initial segment and the remainder of the axonal fiber. The presence of large numbers of neurotransmitter receptors distributed all over the extrasynaptic neuronal surface indicates that these areas are more than just a passive conveyor of excitation.

Intracellular neuronal recordings in various species and brain regions have shown that repeated stimulation of the synapse alters the amplitude of the postsynaptic potential. In the spinal cord, this post-tetanic potentiation is a relatively short-lived phenomenon. But in the hippocampus (and possibly elsewhere), even a brief stimulation, perhaps lasting as little as 100 msec, causes a long-term potentiation that persists days, weeks or even longer.

The sequence of events leading to a modification in neuronal excitability begins with the arrival of a nerve impulse at the synapse. An entry of calcium into the synaptic knob triggers the release of the neurotransmitter in a quantity that is probably dependent upon such things as the amount of calcium present in the vicinity of the synapse, the extent of calcium binding to various macromolecules, and the status of calcium channel permeability. The availability of calcium itself is further regulated by the mitochondria (which are able both to accumulate and release it) and the number of electrically negative charges over the surface of the cell membrane. These charges are primarily associated with the sialic acid components of the polysaccharide chains of membrane gangliosides and glycoprotein. In an excitatory synapse, the amplitude and duration of the local depolarization of the postsynaptic membrane appears, at least initially, to be related to the quantity of the liberated transmitter. From this perspective, calcium ions are one of the factors able to control the excitability of the synapse.

The quantity of transmitter produced by the neuron is also governed by its rate of release. The larger is the amount liberated, the larger is the amount synthesized. However, the production of the neurotransmitter is not an isolated phenomenon. The process requires increases in the precursor and energy supplies and the activity of the relevant synthetic enzymes. The augmentation of these metabolic systems is at least partly attributable to a system of second messengers that includes cAMP and the calcium ions.

The most critical of the control processes are those which normally limit the rate of a reaction, but which are responsive to changes in the demands upon that reaction and its products. For example, in the synthesis of acetylcholine, the production of acetylcoenzyme A precursors and the transport of choline into the nerve endings influence the amount of transmitter that is produced. The acetyl-CoA is provided by glycolysis, and its supply increases in response to the rising needs for acetylcholine. There is some evidence that it is this availability of acetyl-CoA that is the rate-limiting step in acetylcholine synthesis. If this is true, it would stress the importance of the regulation of the pyruvate dehydrogenase enzyme complex in the functioning and functional alteration of the cholinergic synapse. The control is based upon a cycle of enzymatic phosphorylation and dephosphorylation of this complex. These processes (and consequently acetylcholine production) are further associated with the presence of pyruvate, adenosine diphosphate, and calcium and magnesium ions.

The uptake of the choline precursor is under the influence of extracellular potassium, chloride and calcium ions and is known to be coupled to the impulse flow. This relationship between metabolism and the traffic across the synapse is also known to hold for the long-term activation of choline acetyltransferase, the enzyme catalyzing the transfer of the acetyl group from acetyl-CoA to choline to form acetylcholine.

The same complex relationships also exist for the catecholamines and other putative neurotransmitters. For the catecholamines, the first synthetic enzyme of the pathway is tyrosine hydroxylase (TH), which is under the control of a number of regulatory factors. TH activity has been linked to a phosphorylation of the enzyme by a cyclic adenosine monophosphate-dependent protein kinase. This in turn is affected by the impulse rate and consequent depletion of the terminal stores of catecholamines. Although the influence is temporary, a long-lived increase in TH activity can also occur which is mainly associated with an increase in protein synthesis.

In addition, the synthesis of dopamine by DOPA-decarboxylase is enhanced by the flow of impulses through the synapse. The increase depends upon the presence of presynaptic dopamine receptors, whose binding to the neurotransmitter stimulates the activity of adenylate cyclase.

The production of norepinephrine from dopamine by dopamine-β-hydroxylase requires the presence of molecular oxygen and ascorbic acid as cofactors. The reaction is also stimulated by adenosine triphosphate (ATP), potassium ions and acetylcholine and can be controlled by various endogenous inhibitor proteins. On the other hand, the post-stimulatory increase in norepinephrine synthesis is blocked by puromycin and cycloheximide, antibiotics that inhibit protein synthesis. The effect may indicate that such an increase depends upon an induced synthesis of the relevant enzymes.

The presynaptic release of the neurotransmitter typically involves a preferential liberation of the more recently produced molecules. They diffuse toward the postsynaptic membrane where they react with their specific receptors. Although there initially exists a straightforward relationship between the extent of receptor binding and the magnitude of the postsynaptic potential, an acute increase in transmitter level soon causes a sharp fall in the sensitivity of the receptor. Conversely, a marked drop or absence of the transmitter results in a receptor hypersensitivity. However, it would seem that if the synaptic efficacy is to be continuously maintained at a higher level, there would not only exist an augmentation in neurotransmitter synthesis, but some additional mechanism to stabilize the postsynaptic receptors against this drop in sensitivity. The long-term potentiation of synaptic activity (such as in the hippocampus) suggests that cellular events may occur that are quite distinct from those related to the more transient forms of synaptic facilitation or depression.

In spite of the known data on the alterations of receptor sensitivity there is at present little evidence as to how such mechanisms function in this capacity. It has been proposed, for example, that the actions of receptors are altered by their dissociation from ionic channels. There is also a possibility that, due to an excess of neurotransmitter at the synapse, the sensitivity of the receptor permanently decreases, and this induces a sprouting of axons and the formation of new terminals.

From what we know about receptor-neurotransmitter interactions, the stabilization of the increase in synaptic efficacy is likely a complex process necessitating the coordination of various components of the postsynaptic membrane. One important factor in the control of receptor binding capacity is the lipid and protein membrane environment. For instance, the removal of phospholipids from the membrane decreases the affinity of the receptor for acetylcholine by two-fold. A subsequent reprovision of lipids, such as phosphatidylinositol or phosphatidylcholine, is able to restore the high affinity state. Membrane lipids are also required to maintain long-lived incremental adjustments in the responsiveness of the postsynaptic second messengers systems.

The alterations of the membrane phospholipids that might normally underlie the shifts in receptor excitability have been linked to the action of methylating enzymes and such things as phospholipid exchange protein that has been found to be present in the synaptosomal plasma membrane fraction. These shifts can be activated, for example, by acetylcholine. The findings support the possibility that the postsynaptic receptors can exist in physiologically heterogeneous forms which may differ in such characteristics as saturability and binding capacity.

There is evidence that the catecholaminergic receptors are affected in a comparable way, and various functional states may even alter their numbers, a response which would in turn influence the excitability of the neuron. These types of changes under discussion may also relate to serotonergic, histaminergic, glutaminergic, and GABAergic synapses and can take either direction, depending upon the nature of the receptor-transmitter complex, ionic movements, and postsynaptic potentials. The activities of enzymes and receptors may either gradually increase or decrease, creating a spectrum of neurons with varying sensitivities.

The reaction of the neurotransmitter with its receptor represents only the beginning of a cascade of events which involve the various metabolic systems of the cell. This activity is mediated by second messenger systems which include cyclic adenosine monophosphate (cAMP) and cyclic guanosine monophosphate (cGMP). There is evidence that most putative transmitters, many neuromodulatory substances and various ions are able to activate adenylate or guanylate cyclase, both of which are functionally and structurally closely associated with the transmitter receptors. Functionally interposed among these postsynaptic events is the operation of another second messenger system that is composed of calcium and a number of calcium-related binding proteins, the most prominent of which is calmodulin. In general, these systems serve to regulate various cellular metabolic processes in response to particular types of external stimulation. Calcium and calmodulin have been shown to be necessary for the activity of certain types of adenylate cyclase, cAMP degradative phosphodiesterase, and synaptosomal adenosine triphosphase, along with phospholipase A_2 and a phosphorylase kinase.

The principal, and possibly the only, action of adenylate cyclase-generated cAMP is the activation of the protein kinases. These enzymes transfer the γ phospho group of ATP to protein substrates, a process which affects the tertiary and quaternary structure of these proteins. In doing so, it can change the functional properties of the membrane in several ways, including altering the ionic permeability or neurotransmitter sensitivity. Accordingly, a relatively simple molecule of cAMP is capable of promoting a variety of biological responses whose specificity resides in the recognition between neurotransmitter (or hormone) and receptor and in the nature of the kinases and substrate proteins in the cell. In this manner, the cyclic nucleotides are able to regulate and coordinate various intracellular activities.

One of the processes with which the second messengers are involved is the activation of the genome. Gene transcription in the cell nucleus is stimulated, at least in part, by phosphorylation of nonhistone chromosomal proteins. These phosphorylated proteins determine the availability of genetic sequences for transcription, modulate the activity of RNA polymerases and regulate the interaction of DNA with these polymerases. While cAMP-activated protein kinases may be involved in a number of these events, cyclic AMP may also mediate other cellular mechanisms by inhibiting some of these enzymes. Additional kinases, moreover, are not influenced at all. Such cyclic nucleotide-mediated activation of the genome is very possibly an important component of the biochemical processes necessary for the enduring changes in neuronal functioning.

Protein phosphorylation has also been implicated in such widespread phenomena as membrane permeability, intracellular transport, cell adhesion, growth and differentiation, and the mobilization of energy resources. In the brain, the highest protein kinase activity, some of which is Ca^{2+}- dependent, is found in the synaptic membranes, where it has been linked to synaptic transmission. Some specific proteins, especially within the hippocampus, are phosphorylated during the initial phases of memory formation. Of the synaptic proteins, one or more have been found to be responsive to behavioral change. Other similarly responsive proteins have been found to undergo other types of post-translational modification, such as methylation or glycosylation.

A role in memory formation for the second messenger-mediated activation of the genome relates to the synthesis of new molecules of RNA. Although considerable evidence exists for the involvement of RNA in memory, most probably exclusively as an intermediate of the protein synthetic system, there are some indications that alterations in DNA synthesis might be necessary as well.

The production of RNA in the nerve cell depends upon supplies of purine and pyrimidine bases from the salvage and *de novo* pathways and ribose sugars from the pentose phosphate cycle. The process also needs energy, which is one of the reasons why hypoxia is able to interfere with memory formation. Consequently, all of these processes are associated in one way or another with the mechanisms of a neuronal response to a change in function.

Ribosomal protein synthesis similarly requires adequate provisions of energy in the form of ATP and GTP and supplies of amino acids. The amino acids are partly produced in the brain and partly transported there by active mechanisms present in the capillary endothelia. Interference with this transport during the process of learning results in amnesia for an acquired task.

New proteins synthesized during the process of neuronal alteration are used for a variety of functions. Some are enzymes involved in the production and modification of neurotransmitters, membrane lipids and other cell components. Others are receptors, additional cell surface glycoproteins, or parts of the membrane ionic channels. All may also serve a structural role in the building of new dendrites, axon collaterals and synapses. For this reason, a classification of proteins as either "memory-dependent" or "constitutional" may not be that fruitful an exercise. Functional alterations may very well be capable of affecting any neuronal protein.

A model of neuronal plasticity in general or learning and memory in particular must further consider the existence of a variety of hormones and other biologically-active substances. A list would include various steroid hormones, pituitary peptide hormones, peptides produced by the brain and gastrointestinal tract, adenosine and prostaglandins. Several dozen brain peptides have already been isolated that are capable of influencing the activity of those neurons which possess the appropriate receptors for them. A few have been found to coexist within a single neuron. The most frequently mentioned are the opioids, vasopressin, oxytocin, substance P, the hypothalamic releasing factors, ACTH, and other adenohypophyseal hormones or their fragments. The possible functional importance of these peptides is underscored by their widespread distribution and receptor specificity, as well as by the presence of the relevant synthetic and degradative pathways in the brain. In most cases, they appear to be generated from larger precursor molecules by the actions of particular proteinases and peptidases that are able to recognize and cleave specific sites on an amino acid chain.

It is possible that these peptides act either as neurotransmitters within "peptidergic" neurons, or as modulators of synaptic activity that are released from neurons along with the more "classic" transmitters. In this latter situation, they would facilitate or inhibit traffic across the synapses which is otherwise dependent upon the neurotransmitters. Moreover, they could serve to induce more complex intracellular metabolic changes that may also affect the functional plasticity of neurons within particular pathways and systems.

The mechanism of synaptic modulation by the peptides is not known.

Some could conceivably attach to such membrane lipids as the gangliosides and phospholipids and alter their configuration and that of the adjoining proteins. This might affect the ionic channels and the functional characteristics of the neurotransmitter receptors or other membrane proteins in a relatively long-lasting manner.

Interestingly, the dose-response curve for many of these peptides is bell-shaped or irregular, meaning that they are most effective in a particular concentration. Too large or too small an amount can be without an effect. This finding may be particularly pertinent to the controversy surrounding the reports of memory transfer by injections of peptides from trained donor animals into naive recipients. These "memory transfer" substances may merely be a class of brain peptides that facilitate behavioral acquisition through a neuromodulatory effect upon a specific set of neurons.

All of these considerations do appear to complicate an explanation of the brain's acquisition of information. However, in another sense, they could contribute to a simplification of our understanding of various aspects of brain plasticity. If we suppose that the neuron alters its excitability solely under the effect of neurotransmitter and neuromodulators, then in any situation involving a particular change in neuronal stimulation, a particular neuron will react in the same manner. There would be, therefore, no significant differences among the responses of a single neuron to such effects as those of a simple sensory message, a learning situation, toxic, hypoxic, surgical, radiation-induced, or any other form of brain damage, the acute administration of drugs or the development of drug dependence and tolerance, or the effects of environment and the mutual neuronal influences during development. Each of these situations would modify the rate and pattern of neuronal firing and consequently alter the metabolic characteristics of the cell.

One important characteristic of this view is that the shifts in neuronal excitability depend upon the simultaneous functioning of several cellular metabolic systems. This further implies that a change in excitability is not an all-or-nothing process whereby the cell either becomes "highly excitable" or merely "excitable". The excitability may gradually increase up to a level where the cell responds with long bursts of nerve impulses, or can gradually decrease down to complete silence.

These changes in neuronal activity dispersed over large areas of the brain would result in individual alterations in neuronal functioning, a multiplicity of incremental or decremental sensitivities to the neurotransmitters. Each incoming bit of information, if retained, would alter the excitability of a number of neurons, and this would be superimposed on the excitability changes occurring over the lifetime of the individual.

This graded alteration in excitability should be an important consideration in the construction of any theoretical model of brain functioning. Some previous models of brain plasticity have characterized the neuron as being either in an "on" or "off" state. Rather, the neuron can be viewed as being "on" and responsively generating a nerve impulse somewhere within a wide range of input. The variability of the input necessary for the full excitation of the neuron is a measure of neuronal plasticity and is a function of the multiplicity of biochemical changes within the cell.

The discussions of the alterations in neuronal excitability and synaptic efficacy have primarily focused upon metabolic changes associated with previously established intercellular connections. The acquisition of information may also involve shifts in synaptic morphology or connectivity which could be triggered by an increase in the flow of impulses over a pathway. Such a new coupling or synaptic recasting could create additional intercellular connections or reaffirm existing ones. These synapses would still, nevertheless, be subject to the same metabolic shifts discussed above and would provide an additional dimension to the possibilities for functional plasticity.

The events underlying metabolic plasticity within a functioning neuron are probably more complex than the foregoing interrelationships have been able to convey. Within nervous tissue, at least 10,000 or possibly 20,000 genes may code for as many species of proteins. This means that the biochemical activities presented throughout this book may involve the actions of a large number of different and heretofore unknown activators and inhibitors, additional enzymes an receptor components. There is probably no easy solution to the problem of functional plasticity, and attempts to uncover a simple "memory substrate" will not likely become the window on the cognitive processes that many had hoped. Research into learning and memory should not be organized as a search for a needle in a haystack. It really requires a mapping of the haystack, an accumulation of relevant data and an inventory of the activities of the constantly expanding list of known substances. It seems that only then will we begin to truly understand the neuronal processes subserving cognition.

This model of neuronal plasticity is based upon the interaction of a multitude of proteins and other substances which themselves have a relatively short lifespan. In such a system in flux, why then would memory storage be an enduring process? We can speculate that plastic adjustments of neurons, once they occur, are capable of being maintained for long periods or even indefinitely. Segments of the genome may be activated, and this would be sustained by feedback activity from components of the adjustive mechanisms. Consequently, the overall process itself would endure, although individual molecules are continuously being synthesized and degraded.

Question 2

WHERE IS THE ENGRAM?

Biochemical examinations of the brain following the fixation of memory of a learned task have repeatedly indicated that these chemical changes, whatever they may be, involve large areas of the brain. Studies of RNA and protein synthesis, along with alterations in lipids, phosphoproteins and glycoproteins, have shown that these substances are produced and modified in various brain regions in quantities far exceeding their content in a small number of synapses or confined neuronal circuits. Oxygen consumption, blood flow, lesion studies and electrophysiological data have indicated the same thing. Shifts in cortical evoked potentials during the process of learning also emphasize the participation of masses of nerve cells.

The involvement of widespread areas of the brain in the memory process does not mean to imply, however, that nervous tissue should be considered as an aggregation of uniform neural units which all act in an identical manner. A cursory examination of appropriate histological sections reveals that the brain is comprised of neurons which vary tremendously in their size, shape, details of dendritic branching, number and direction of axonal collaterals, as well as in their inner structure (distribution of the mitochondria and Nissl substance, nuclear size and position, chromatin dispensation, etc.). And, since each neuron is synaptically connected to other neurons, it receives information in the form of EPSPs and IPSPs from different sources and dispatches its own impulses to various targets.

This morphological diversity is accompanied by differences in function. As mentioned above, a neuron produces its own rate and pattern of nerve impulses. There are neurons which are silent most of the time. Others respond to a small number of excitatory postsynaptic potentials with a long series of impulses. Some respond immediately and stop, while the responses of still others are delayed before entering into a period of prolonged firing. Differences have also been observed in the overall duration and amplitude of the postsynaptic potentials.

Individual neurons exhibit unique biochemical characteristics. Histochemical studies have revealed a variability of enzyme levels and neurotransmitter and peptide synthesis even in neighboring neurons.

The uniqueness of each neuron is further enhanced by the individual history of that cell. Throughout its life span, the metabolic systems of the neuron are continuously challenged by impulses from other neurons. Within the cell, there occurs, at the very least, a short-term redistribution of ions between the cellular interior and exterior. Some changes may persist for longer periods of time and become firmly embedded within the metabolic systems.

In a consideration, then, of changes taking place within large masses of neurons, it should be understood that the activity and responsiveness of each neuron will be unique. Due to the number of excitatory and inhibitory synapses which may be simultaneously activated and modified, each neuron may exist in one of an innumerable number of functional states, ranging from complete inhibition to long-lasting depolarization. Consequently, during periods of learning, recall or any other brain activity individual nerve cells will function within a particular state of excitation. And, these states would be subject to continual change.

The registration, integration and recall of each memory trace, even a relatively simple one, therefore involve millions of neurons widely distributed throughout the brain. Biochemical and histochemical studies, recordings of unit activity and the evaluation of evoked potentials have shown that modifiable neurons are located throughout the cerebral cortex, component areas of the limbic system, basal ganglia (including the caudate, putamen, pallidum and amygdala), hypothalamus, brain stem reticular formation, superior and inferior colliculi, mesencephalic central gray and tectum, median raphe, cerebellum, and even the spinal cord. Perhaps, these regions are involved in the handling and storage of different attributes of the learned information and vary with each individual task or recalled situation. Maps of areas essential for the retention of individual learned tasks have been constructed, e.g. by Thompson (1978). However, a critical examination of the literature on the role of various brain areas in learning is beyond the scope of this book.

One issue which has not been raised until now concerns the frequently used dichotomization of informational storage into short- and long-term memory. Lewis (1979) has summarized the arguments against such a distinction, and for a comprehensive presentation of this position, the reader is referred to his paper. In the present context of plasticity, particularly with regard to those aspects associated with ionic movements, second messenger systems, and post-translational modifications of synaptic proteins, we have contended that immediately following the arrival of an impulse and the release and receptor-binding of the neurotransmitter, there is initiated within the cell a complex of metabolic events which eventually leads to a functional adjustment. There exists a continuity over the individual phases of this process, such that it would be difficult to impose a boundary between temporary (short-term) and enduring (long-term) cellular metabolic changes. Rather, there is a direct transition among early ionic, receptor-dependent, pre-translational and post-translational events. No specific biochemical event appears exclusively related to short-term memory.

The early changes (before the synthesis of new proteins and their incorporation into the nerve cell structure) may be more fragile, more easily disrupted by ongoing neuronal activity than the later changes which become embedded within the metabolic machinery of the cell. A shift in the firing pattern reaching the neuron during or shortly after the initial learning situation may disrupt the alteration of synaptic or neuronal excitability and/or connectivity because of the vulnerability of the initial metabolic processes. New metabolic changes may then be imposed upon old ones. The dissimilarities between the labile and stable phases of memory may therefore be purely quantitative, being attributable to a lack of sufficient progress in the adjustment of neuronal excitability. Such a possibility is suggested by the antibiotic-induced prolongation of the labile phase of memory.

The differences between the two categories of memory may also be associated with neuronal topography and the brain area involved. Short-term memory may hypothetically depend upon the activity of rapidly changing nerve cells in the hippocampus or elsewhere, in which a single impulse or a short sequence of impulses may quickly induce a phosphorylation and/or a dephosphorylation of various synaptic proteins otherwise characterized by their relatively fast rate of turnover. These neurons would be subject to rapid functional alterations upon the arrival of new information. The participation of those units involved in long-term memory storage could come somewhat later, as part of the deposition of the enduring trace.

Short-term memory has a storage capacity which is restricted to a few items at a time. Its temporary contents are fragile and decay rapidly. This suggests that it is handled by one or more areas or systems whose ability to store information is correspondingly limited. In contrast, long-term storage systems seem to have no such limitations. These two possibilities are not actually contradictory. A labile phase of memory may be localized in a limited number of neuronal networks, from which it is transferred, perhaps through the hippocampus or under hippocampal control, into those neuronal assemblies subserving long-term storage (see Isaacson and Pribram, 1975). It may depend upon protein alterations which do not lead to the establishment of long-lasting metabolic changes. The neurons within the hippocampus could possibly be metabolically tuned to these rapid changes.

Question 3

HOW IS THE ENGRAM ORGANIZED, STORED AND RETRIEVED?

Regardless of the extent to which we are able to provide answers to Questions 1 and 2 (the what and where of memory), there still remains the inevitable confrontation with how the trace is organized, stored, and retrieved. Over the years, there have been a number of serious attempts to deal with this problem neurophysiologically, ranging from the cell assemblies of Hebb (1949) to John's (1972) continuously changing hyperneuron and Bindra's (1979) pexgos and gnostic assemblies. But, any evaluations of these models have been hindered by the paucity of adequately documented information. Even data on the cooperation of two nerve cells within a single column of cerebral cortex are minimal.

Although at present, it is not possible to relate causally the firing of a single cell to the performance of a learned behavior, the point has frequently been made that the morphological and biochemical changes in the large numbers of neurons are the basis for both altering the functional linkages among the nerve cells and modifying the flow of information over the pathways of which these cells are integral parts. Repetition of the input would enhance these events and serve to strengthen the associated information.

Those who have observed the firing pattern of single neurons on an oscilloscope, composed of frequently irregular starts, stops and bursts of activity, often cannot help but wonder about the nature of the cell's message and its route of travel to and from that cell. Sometimes, activity which is seemingly without any definite input is termed "noise" or "spontaneous activity", as opposed to a "signal" associated with a controlled experimental stimulus. However, such activity is not noise and is usually not spontaneous. In this situation, one is faced with a problem that has an analog in the game of chess. Imagine trying to understand the rules of the game by concentrating solely on the activity of one piece. Although the type of movements of which that piece is capable could be readily discerned, its repositionings would almost seem haphazard at times, often coming in flurries and interspaced with periods of relative inactivity. In and of themselves, the movements would appear to have no consistent pattern or logic. The game only begins to make sense when seen as a whole, by understanding the capabilities of each chesspiece and how the activities of these pieces relate to one another. The overall pattern of movements reflects complex strategies which, during the course of the game, may undergo modifications that are based upon the changing relationships on the board.

Since the brain has been estimated to contain ten billion neurons, a large percentage of which are each capable of establishing contacts with about ten thousand other neurons, we are confronted with a "game" that is immensely more complex. Large numbers of its pieces or units "move" simultaneously, often in response to intricate shifting strategies. These shifts or modifications in the strategies of the brain are the coordinate neuronal events which comprise the phenomenon of functional brain plasticity.

In spite of the uncertainties regarding the functional relationships between neurons, we can use the known data to speculate on a few general rules. Whenever a sense organ is stimulated, a set of nerve impulses enters the CNS and reaches a group of neurons associated with the particular modality and quality of the sensation. These neurons and many others linked to them through synaptic connections react in a specific manner by a particular level of excitation or inhibition and by a certain pattern of firing.

As a result of this activity, metabolic adjustments are made in many, or perhaps all, of the affected neurons. However, the extent and duration of these changes may vary from cell to cell. These adjustments may also be associated with modifications in synaptic, dendritic and axonal morphology, which would further contribute to the establishment of a functional linkage over groups of neurons.

The information entering the brain is therefore stored in sets of nerve cells which can be scattered throughout one or more cerebral areas. Individual neurons become metabolically altered and can undergo graded shifts in excitability. These cells form a functional ensemble and, as a result, together serve to retain a meaningful trace of past experience. The ensembles would retain the ability to reproduce the basic elements of a time-coherent pattern of activity in spite of ongoing readjustments of individual neurons responding to the continual flow of information.

The process is an ever-continuing one. The pathways are constantly carrying information and storing some of it in a multi-dimensional network of modified neurons. The pattern of prior neuronal adjustments, then, serves as a framework for the assessment and storage of new information.

An influx of information requires some degree of interpretation, some clarification of its content. This process involves a retrieval of relevant memories from storage, so that there occurs a linkage between present and prior information. Such an association could entail the establishment of a new neuronal ensemble with parts in common with the old. This might also affect relationships within the existing set and possibly between other related assemblies. Consequently, the framework represented by these sets of modified neurons is a continuously molded one.

This internal translation of perceived events, guided by past memories, also serves to control movement, and similar neuronal sets may be activated in the motor system. With each repetition of the same movement pattern, the particular neuronal assembly undergoes a developmental adjustment, organizing and refining the motoric sequences.

The importance of a recorded event and the ease with which it is retrieved are often a function of the motivational state at the time of storage and/or recall. As mentioned previously, motivational state is but one of a number of factors which are able to modulate neuronal excitability and consequently affect the processes of learning and memory. Included here are also genetic factors that provide the system with its basic structural features, which themselves impose controls upon movement, perception and the drive states.

Many of the relationships we have described are obviously still anchored in the realm of speculation. In a complex vertebrate brain, no single behavior has yet been characterized according to the activation or inactivation of all of its associated neurons. However, with time we collectively will improve our ability to interrelate structural, functional and biochemical changes within the CNS and be able to specify the biological correlates of a wide variety of behavioral events. We have come a long way in our search for the physical nature of the engram. But clearly, the journey for this Holy Grail of psychology is still far from complete.

REFERENCES

Bindra, D.: *A Theory of Intelligent Behavior.* John Wiley & Sons: New York (1979).

Hebb, D.O.: *The Organization of Behavior. A Neuropsychological Theory.* John Wiley & Sons: New York (1949).

Isaacson, R.L., Pribram, K.H. (Eds.): *The Hippocampus,* Vols. 1 and 2. Plenum Press: New York (1975).

John, E.R.: *Science* 177:850 (1972).

Lewis, D.J.: *Psychol. Bull.* 86:1054 (1979).

Thompson, R.: *A Behavioral Atlas of the Rat Brain.* Oxford University Press: New York (1978).

Index